ASSORTED FOXTROT

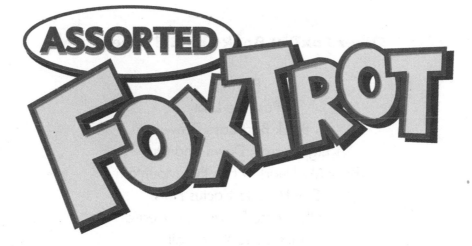

Other FoxTrot Books by Bill Amend

FoxTrot
Pass the Loot
Black Bart Says Draw
Eight Yards, Down and Out
Bury My Heart at Fun-Fun Mountain
Say Hello to Cactus Flats
May the Force Be with Us, Please
Take Us to Your Mall
The Return of the Lone Iguana
At Least This Place Sells T-shirts
Come Closer, Roger, There's a Mosquito on Your Nose
Welcome to Jasorassic Park
I'm Flying, Jack . . . I Mean, Roger
Think iFruity

Anthologies

FoxTrot: The Works
FoxTrot *en masse*
Enormously FoxTrot
Wildly FoxTrot
FoxTrot Beyond a Doubt
Camp FoxTrot

Assorted FoxTrot

by Bill Amend

**Andrews McMeel
Publishing**

Kansas City

FoxTrot is distributed internationally by Universal Press Syndicate.

00 01 02 03 04 BAM 10 9 8 7 6 5 4 3 2 1

ISBN: 0-7407-0532-6

Library of Congress Catalog Card Number: 00-103472

Visit **FoxTrot** on the World Wide Web at www.foxtrot.com

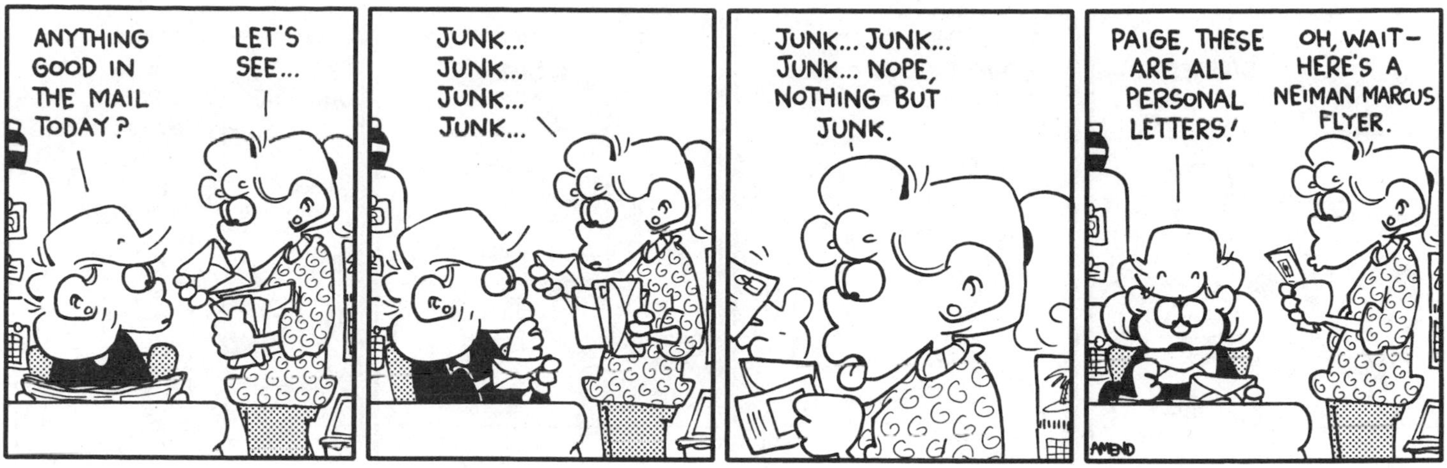
ANYTHING GOOD IN THE MAIL TODAY?
LET'S SEE...
JUNK... JUNK... JUNK... JUNK...
JUNK... JUNK... JUNK... NOPE, NOTHING BUT JUNK.
PAIGE, THESE ARE ALL PERSONAL LETTERS!
OH, WAIT— HERE'S A NEIMAN MARCUS FLYER.
AMEND

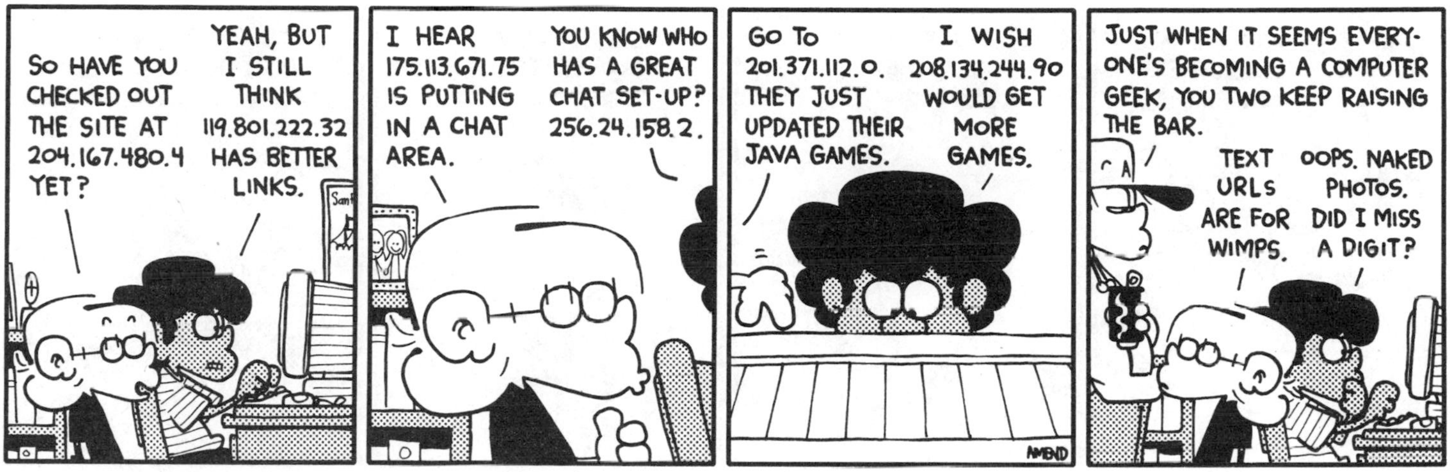
SO HAVE YOU CHECKED OUT THE SITE AT 204.167.480.4 YET?
YEAH, BUT I STILL THINK 119.801.222.32 HAS BETTER LINKS.
I HEAR 175.113.671.75 IS PUTTING IN A CHAT AREA.
YOU KNOW WHO HAS A GREAT CHAT SET-UP? 256.24.158.2.
GO TO 201.371.112.0. THEY JUST UPDATED THEIR JAVA GAMES.
I WISH 208.134.244.90 WOULD GET MORE GAMES.
AMEND
JUST WHEN IT SEEMS EVERYONE'S BECOMING A COMPUTER GEEK, YOU TWO KEEP RAISING THE BAR.
TEXT URLS ARE FOR WIMPS.
OOPS. NAKED PHOTOS. DID I MISS A DIGIT?

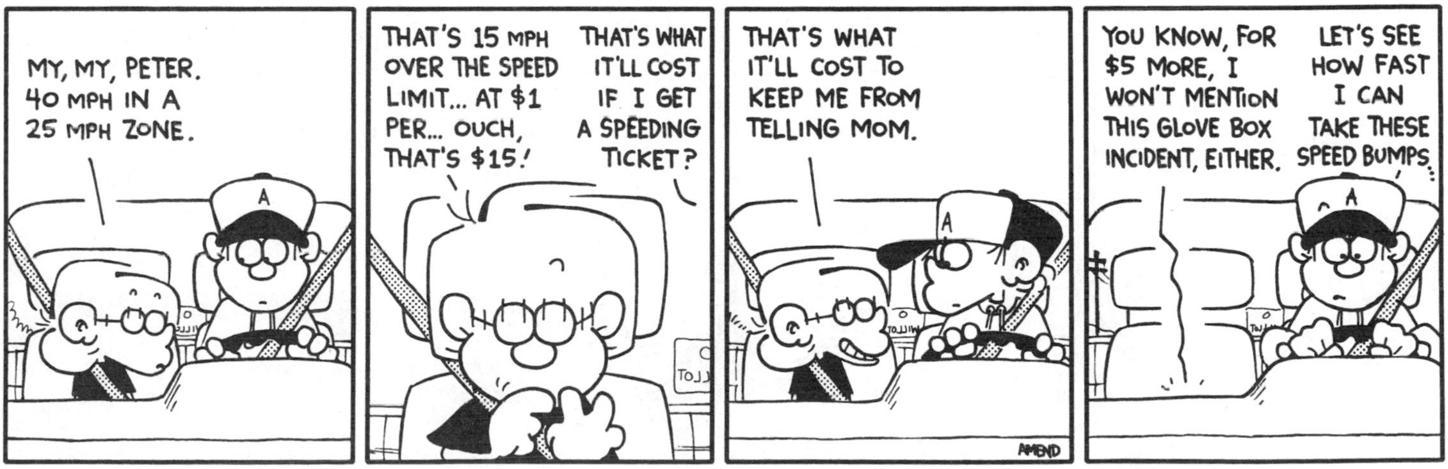
MY, MY, PETER. 40 MPH IN A 25 MPH ZONE.
THAT'S 15 MPH OVER THE SPEED LIMIT... AT $1 PER... OUCH, THAT'S $15!
THAT'S WHAT IT'LL COST IF I GET A SPEEDING TICKET?
THAT'S WHAT IT'LL COST TO KEEP ME FROM TELLING MOM.
AMEND
YOU KNOW, FOR $5 MORE, I WON'T MENTION THIS GLOVE BOX INCIDENT, EITHER.
LET'S SEE HOW FAST I CAN TAKE THESE SPEED BUMPS.

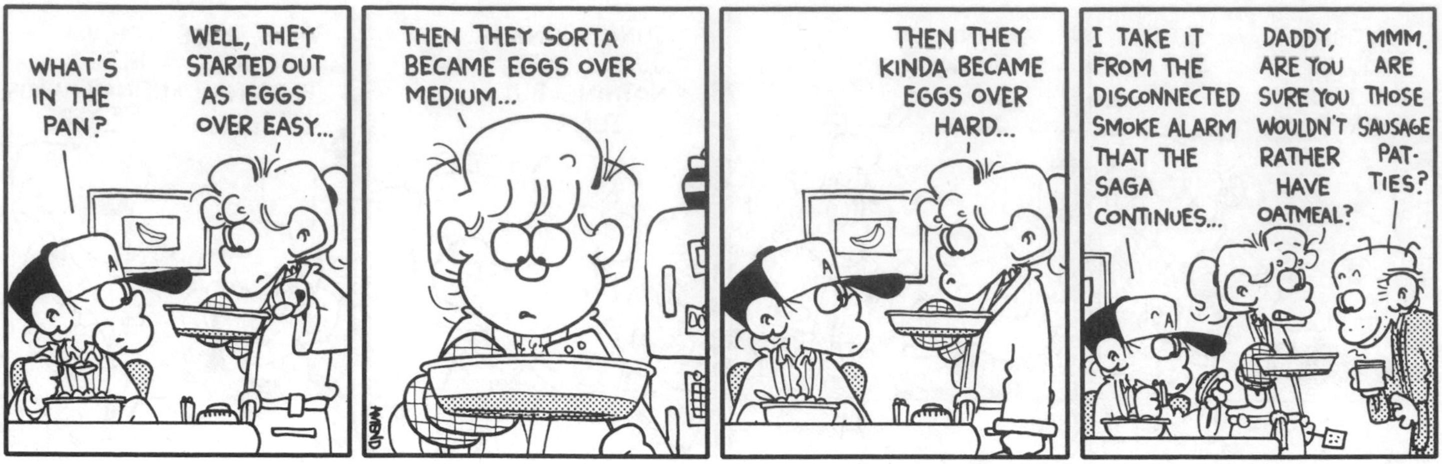
WHAT'S IN THE PAN?
WELL, THEY STARTED OUT AS EGGS OVER EASY...
THEN THEY SORTA BECAME EGGS OVER MEDIUM...
AMEND
THEN THEY KINDA BECAME EGGS OVER HARD...
I TAKE IT FROM THE DISCONNECTED SMOKE ALARM THAT THE SAGA CONTINUES...
DADDY, ARE YOU SURE YOU WOULDN'T RATHER HAVE OATMEAL?
MMM. ARE THOSE SAUSAGE PAT-TIES?

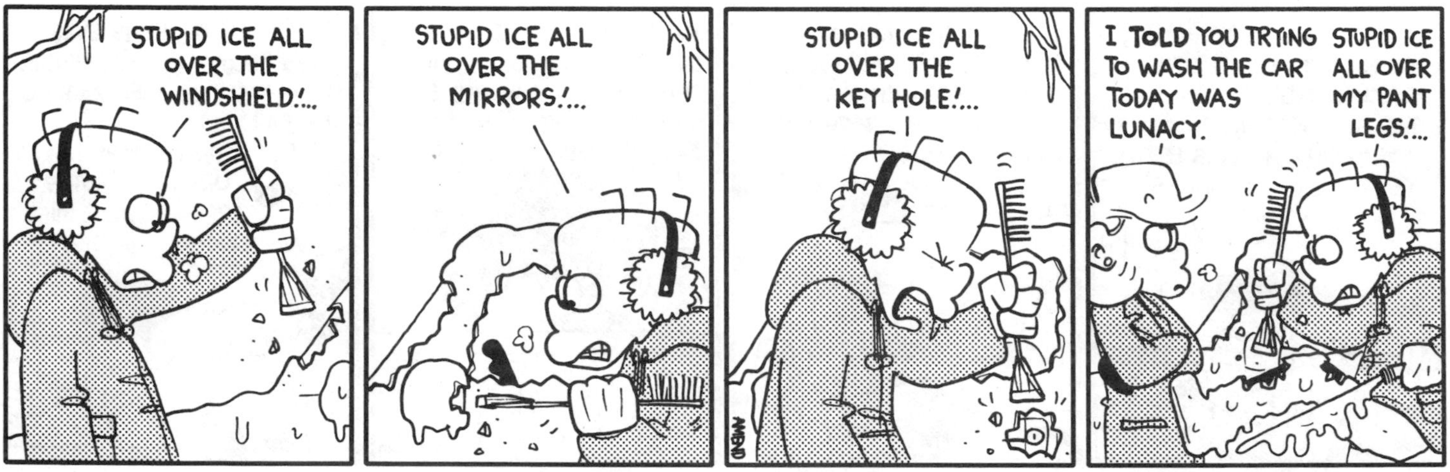
STUPID ICE ALL OVER THE WINDSHIELD!...
STUPID ICE ALL OVER THE MIRRORS!...
STUPID ICE ALL OVER THE KEY HOLE!...
AMEND
I TOLD YOU TRYING TO WASH THE CAR TODAY WAS LUNACY.
STUPID ICE ALL OVER MY PANT LEGS!...

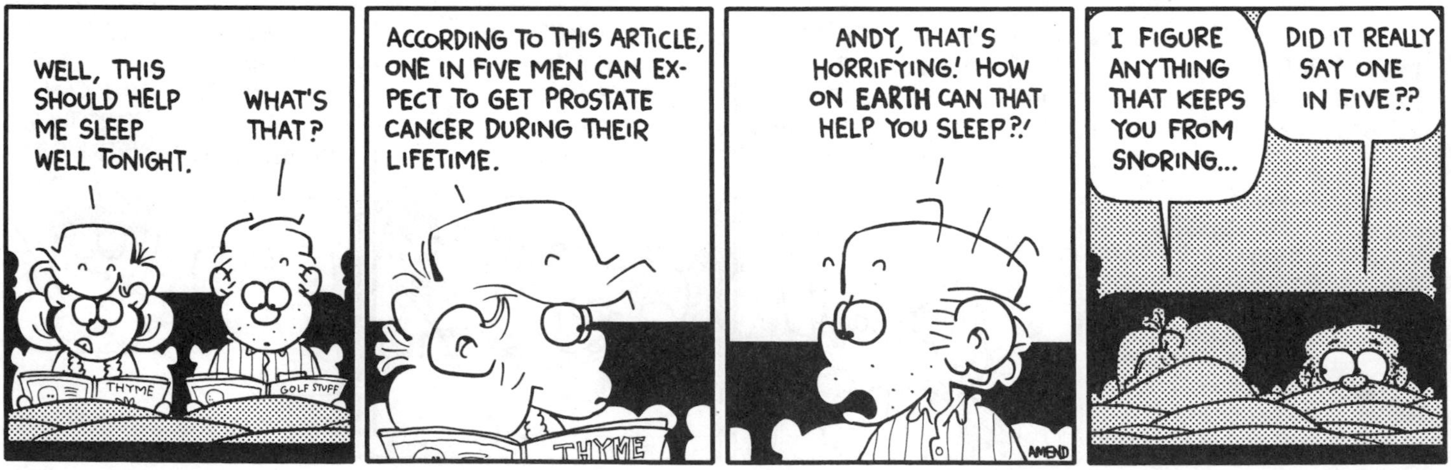
WELL, THIS SHOULD HELP ME SLEEP WELL TONIGHT.
WHAT'S THAT?
THYME
GOLF STUFF
ACCORDING TO THIS ARTICLE, ONE IN FIVE MEN CAN EX-PECT TO GET PROSTATE CANCER DURING THEIR LIFETIME.
THYME
ANDY, THAT'S HORRIFYING! HOW ON EARTH CAN THAT HELP YOU SLEEP?!
AMEND
I FIGURE ANYTHING THAT KEEPS YOU FROM SNORING...
DID IT REALLY SAY ONE IN FIVE??

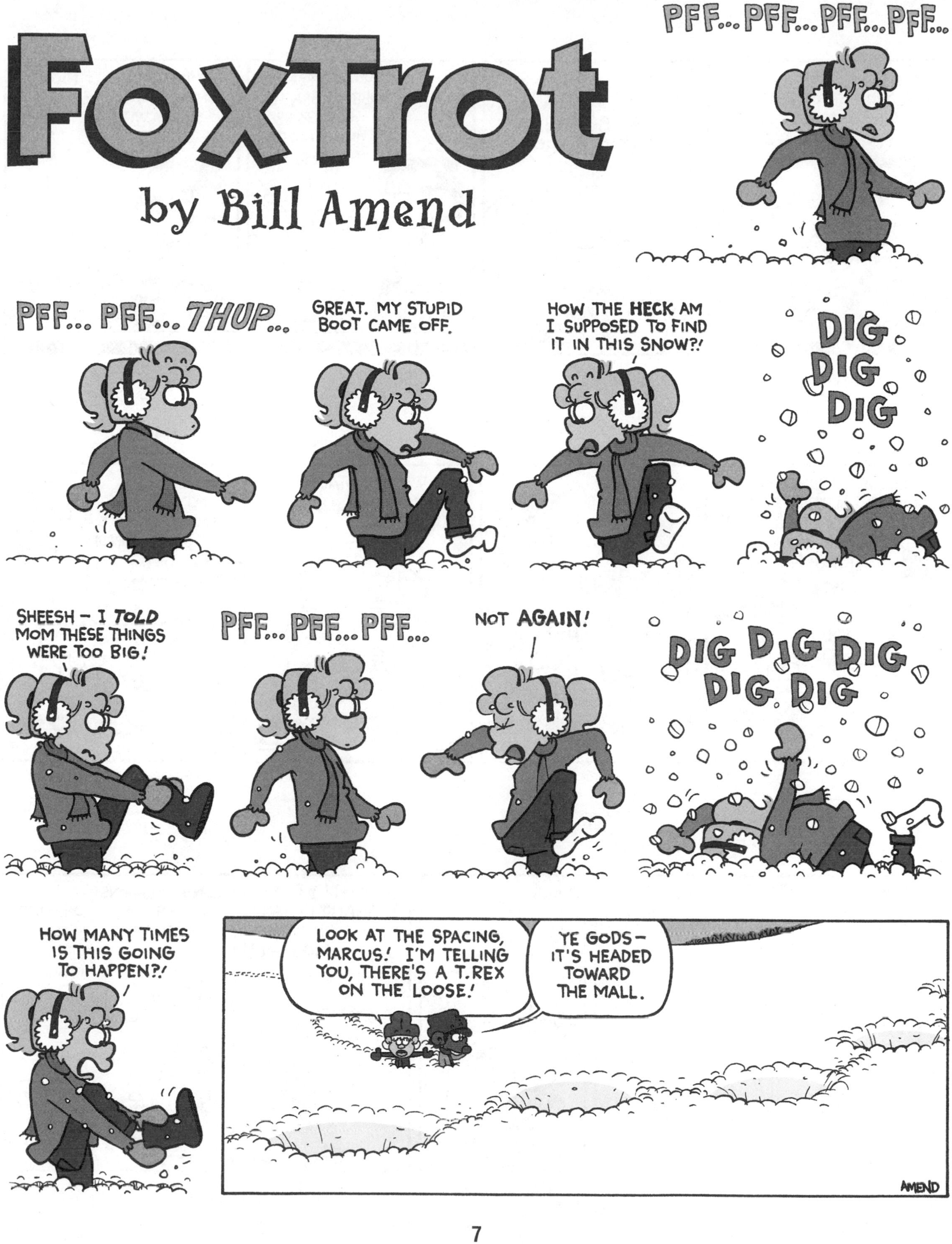
FoxTrot
by Bill Amend
PFF... PFF... PFF... PFF...
PFF... PFF... THUP...
GREAT. MY STUPID BOOT CAME OFF.
HOW THE HECK AM I SUPPOSED TO FIND IT IN THIS SNOW?!
DIG DIG DIG
SHEESH – I TOLD MOM THESE THINGS WERE TOO BIG!
PFF... PFF... PFF...
NOT AGAIN!
DIG DIG DIG DIG DIG
HOW MANY TIMES IS THIS GOING TO HAPPEN?!
LOOK AT THE SPACING, MARCUS! I'M TELLING YOU, THERE'S A T. REX ON THE LOOSE!
YE GODS – IT'S HEADED TOWARD THE MALL.
AMEND

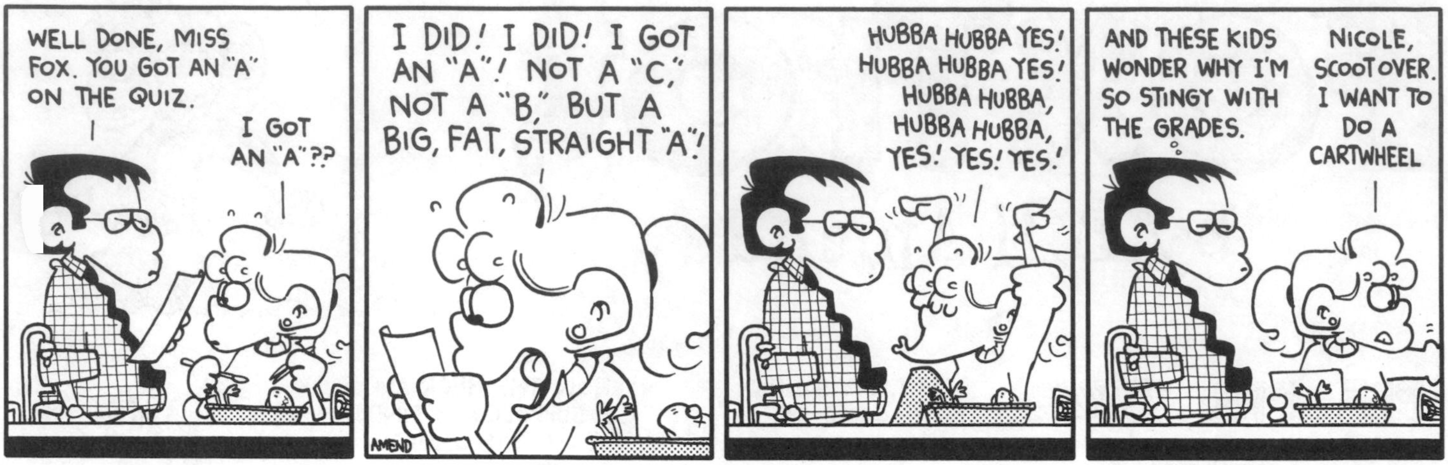
WELL DONE, MISS FOX. YOU GOT AN "A" ON THE QUIZ.
I GOT AN "A"??
I DID! I DID! I GOT AN "A"! NOT A "C," NOT A "B," BUT A BIG, FAT, STRAIGHT "A"!
AMEND
HUBBA HUBBA YES! HUBBA HUBBA YES! HUBBA HUBBA, HUBBA HUBBA, YES! YES! YES!
AND THESE KIDS WONDER WHY I'M SO STINGY WITH THE GRADES.
NICOLE, SCOOT OVER. I WANT TO DO A CARTWHEEL

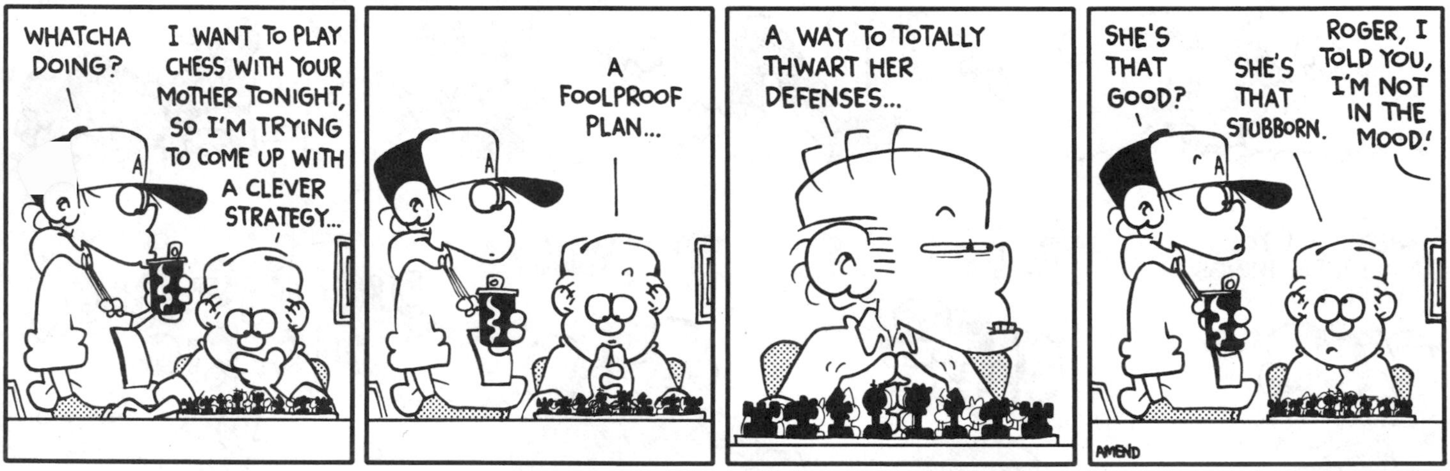
WHATCHA DOING?
I WANT TO PLAY CHESS WITH YOUR MOTHER TONIGHT, SO I'M TRYING TO COME UP WITH A CLEVER STRATEGY...
A FOOLPROOF PLAN...
A WAY TO TOTALLY THWART HER DEFENSES...
SHE'S THAT GOOD?
SHE'S THAT STUBBORN.
ROGER, I TOLD YOU, I'M NOT IN THE MOOD!
AMEND

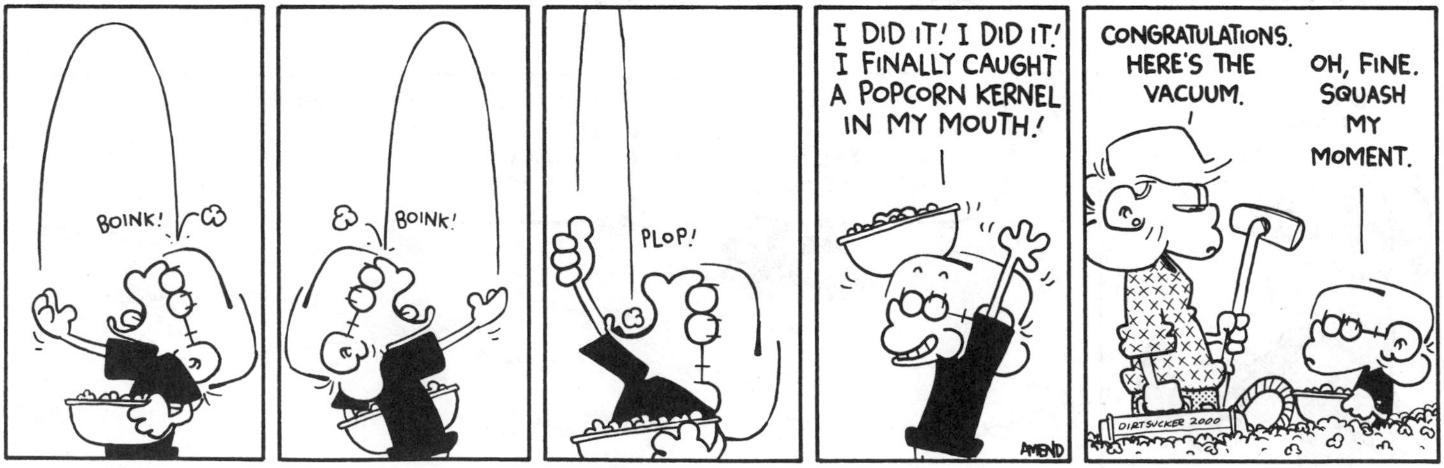
BOINK!
BOINK!
PLOP!
I DID IT! I DID IT! I FINALLY CAUGHT A POPCORN KERNEL IN MY MOUTH!
AMEND
CONGRATULATIONS. HERE'S THE VACUUM.
OH, FINE. SQUASH MY MOMENT.
DIRTSUCKER 2000

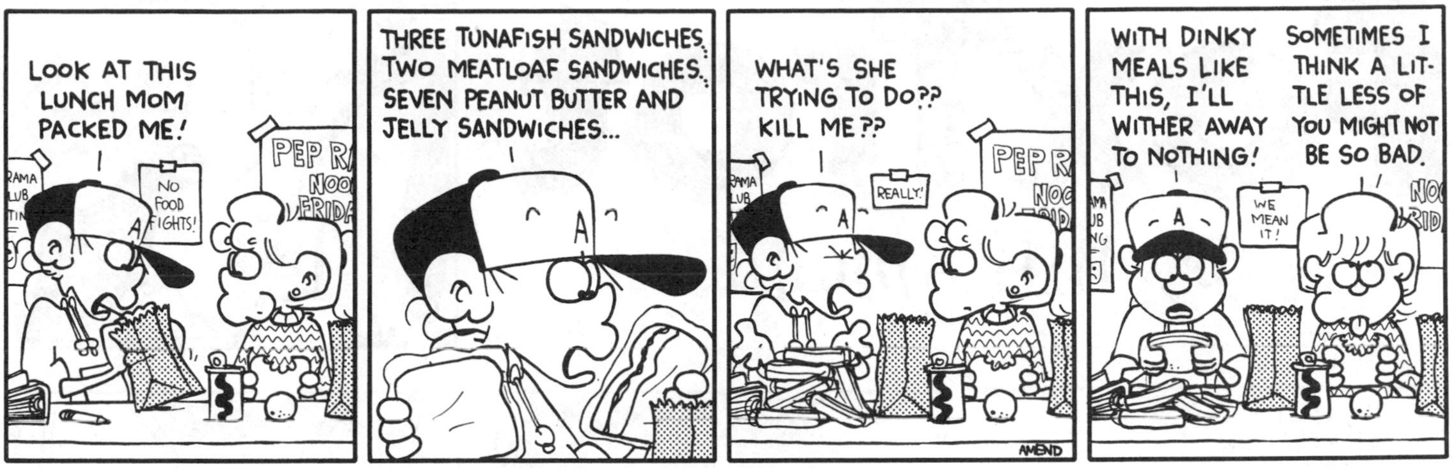
LOOK AT THIS LUNCH MOM PACKED ME!
NO FOOD FIGHTS!
THREE TUNAFISH SANDWICHES... TWO MEATLOAF SANDWICHES... SEVEN PEANUT BUTTER AND JELLY SANDWICHES...
WHAT'S SHE TRYING TO DO?? KILL ME??
REALLY!
WITH DINKY MEALS LIKE THIS, I'LL WITHER AWAY TO NOTHING!
WE MEAN IT!
SOMETIMES I THINK A LITTLE LESS OF YOU MIGHT NOT BE SO BAD.
AMEND

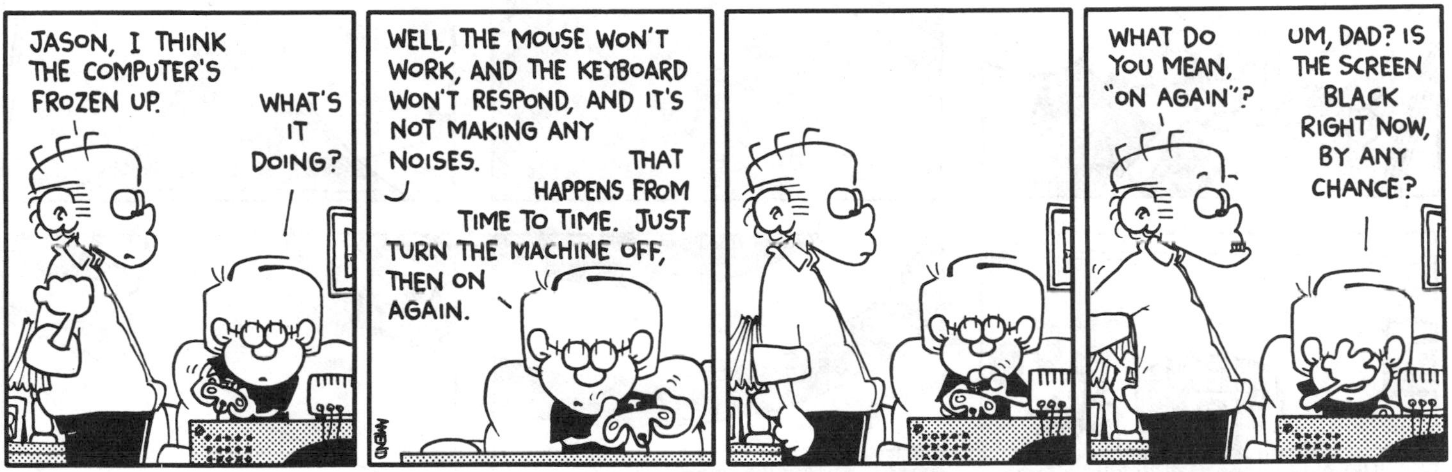
JASON, I THINK THE COMPUTER'S FROZEN UP.
WHAT'S IT DOING?
WELL, THE MOUSE WON'T WORK, AND THE KEYBOARD WON'T RESPOND, AND IT'S NOT MAKING ANY NOISES.
THAT HAPPENS FROM TIME TO TIME. JUST TURN THE MACHINE OFF, THEN ON AGAIN.
WHAT DO YOU MEAN, "ON AGAIN"?
UM, DAD? IS THE SCREEN BLACK RIGHT NOW, BY ANY CHANCE?

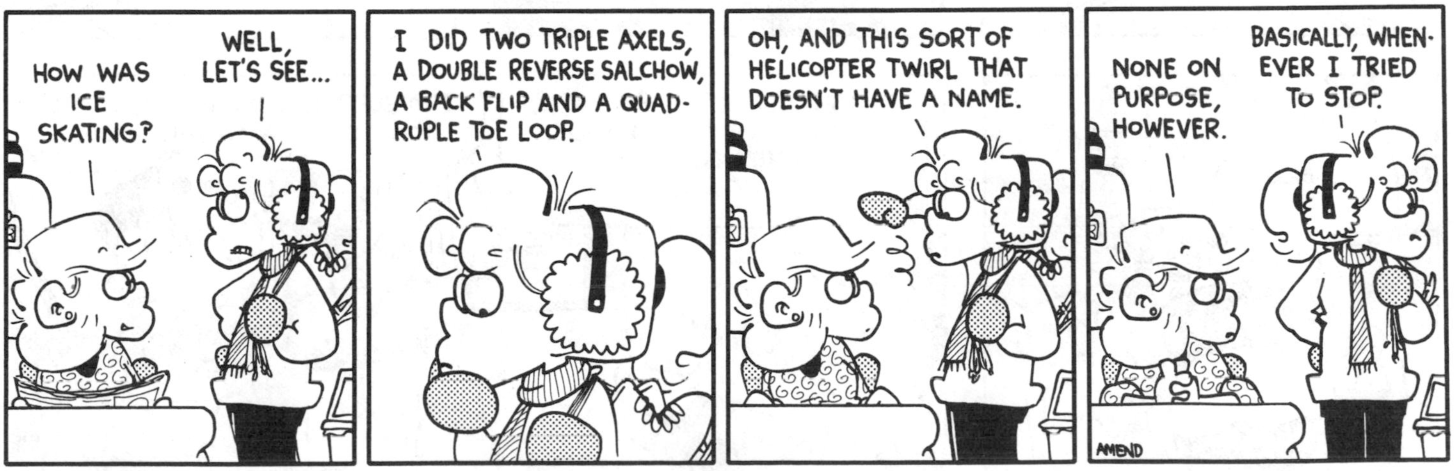
HOW WAS ICE SKATING?
WELL, LET'S SEE...
I DID TWO TRIPLE AXELS, A DOUBLE REVERSE SALCHOW, A BACK FLIP AND A QUADRUPLE TOE LOOP.
OH, AND THIS SORT OF HELICOPTER TWIRL THAT DOESN'T HAVE A NAME.
NONE ON PURPOSE, HOWEVER.
BASICALLY, WHENEVER I TRIED TO STOP.
AMEND

FoxTrot

by Bill Amend

HERE WE GO...
OH, WAIT – I FORGOT YOUR DRAMAMINE.
TV LISTINGS
IN RETROSPECT, I PROBABLY SHOULDN'T HAVE USED SUCH A BOUNCY CHAIR FOR A TARGET.
I'M SURPRISED YOUR LITTLE CARS DON'T COME WITH AIR BAGS.
AMEND

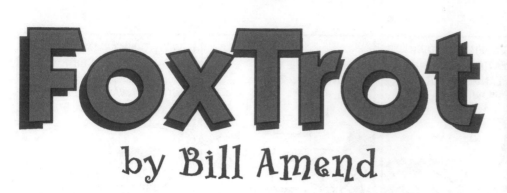

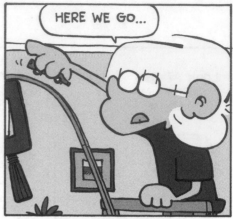

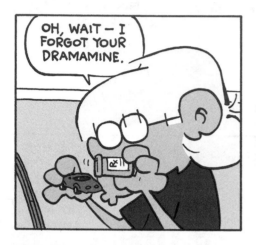

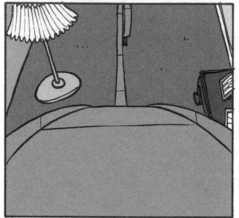

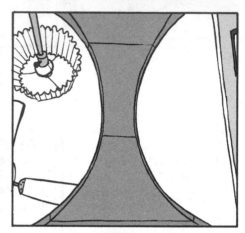

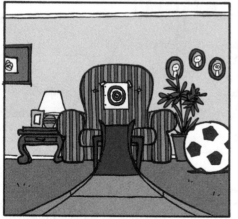

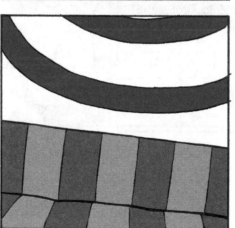

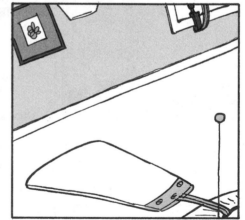

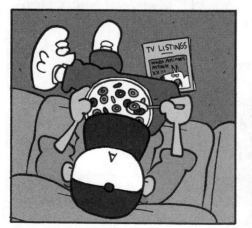

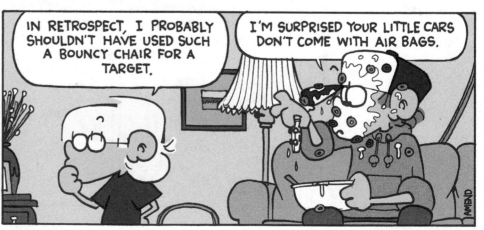

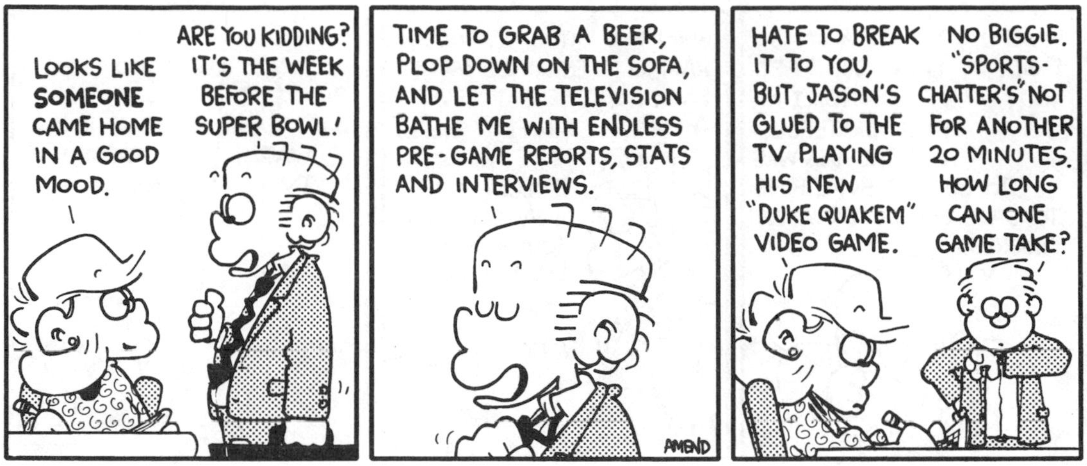
LOOKS LIKE **SOMEONE** CAME HOME IN A GOOD MOOD.
ARE YOU KIDDING? IT'S THE WEEK BEFORE THE SUPER BOWL!
TIME TO GRAB A BEER, PLOP DOWN ON THE SOFA, AND LET THE TELEVISION BATHE ME WITH ENDLESS PRE-GAME REPORTS, STATS AND INTERVIEWS.
AMEND
HATE TO BREAK IT TO YOU, BUT JASON'S GLUED TO THE TV PLAYING HIS NEW "DUKE QUAKEM" VIDEO GAME.
NO BIGGIE. "SPORTS-CHATTER'S" NOT FOR ANOTHER 20 MINUTES. HOW LONG CAN ONE GAME TAKE?
LEVEL 5 COMPLETED. TIME: 3.8 HOURS.
HOO BABY! ONLY 661 LEVELS TO GO!

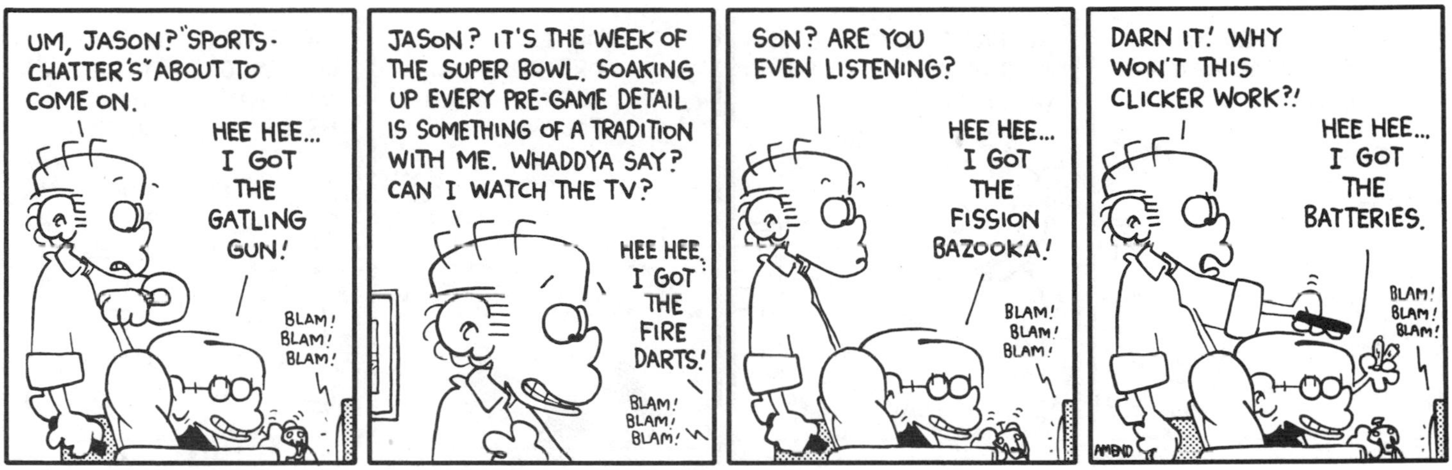
UM, JASON? "SPORTS-CHATTER'S" ABOUT TO COME ON.
HEE HEE... I GOT THE GATLING GUN!
BLAM! BLAM! BLAM!
JASON? IT'S THE WEEK OF THE SUPER BOWL. SOAKING UP EVERY PRE-GAME DETAIL IS SOMETHING OF A TRADITION WITH ME. WHADDYA SAY? CAN I WATCH THE TV?
HEE HEE. I GOT THE FIRE DARTS!
BLAM! BLAM! BLAM!
SON? ARE YOU EVEN LISTENING?
HEE HEE... I GOT THE FISSION BAZOOKA!
BLAM! BLAM! BLAM!
DARN IT! WHY WON'T THIS CLICKER WORK?!
HEE HEE... I GOT THE BATTERIES.
BLAM! BLAM! BLAM!
AMEND

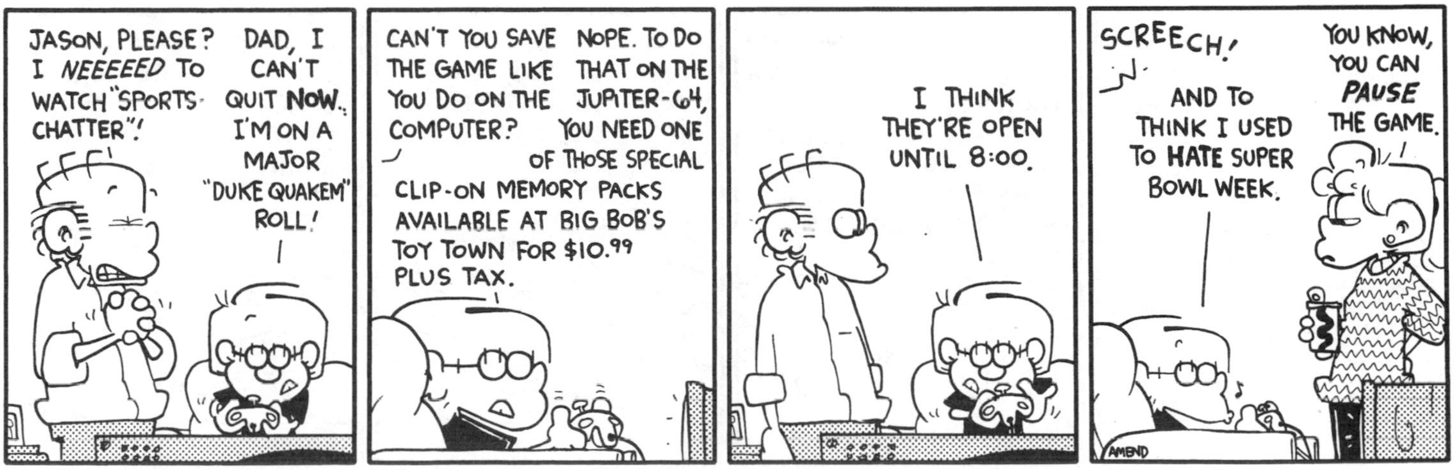
JASON, PLEASE? I *NEEEEED* TO WATCH "SPORTS-CHATTER"!
DAD, I CAN'T QUIT **NOW**. I'M ON A MAJOR "DUKE QUAKEM" ROLL!
CAN'T YOU SAVE THE GAME LIKE YOU DO ON THE COMPUTER?
NOPE. TO DO THAT ON THE JUPITER-64, YOU NEED ONE OF THOSE SPECIAL CLIP-ON MEMORY PACKS AVAILABLE AT BIG BOB'S TOY TOWN FOR $10.99 PLUS TAX.
I THINK THEY'RE OPEN UNTIL 8:00.
SCREECH!
AND TO THINK I USED TO **HATE** SUPER BOWL WEEK.
YOU KNOW, YOU CAN ***PAUSE*** THE GAME.
AMEND

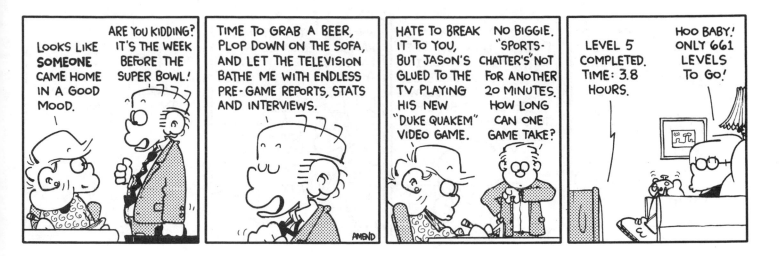

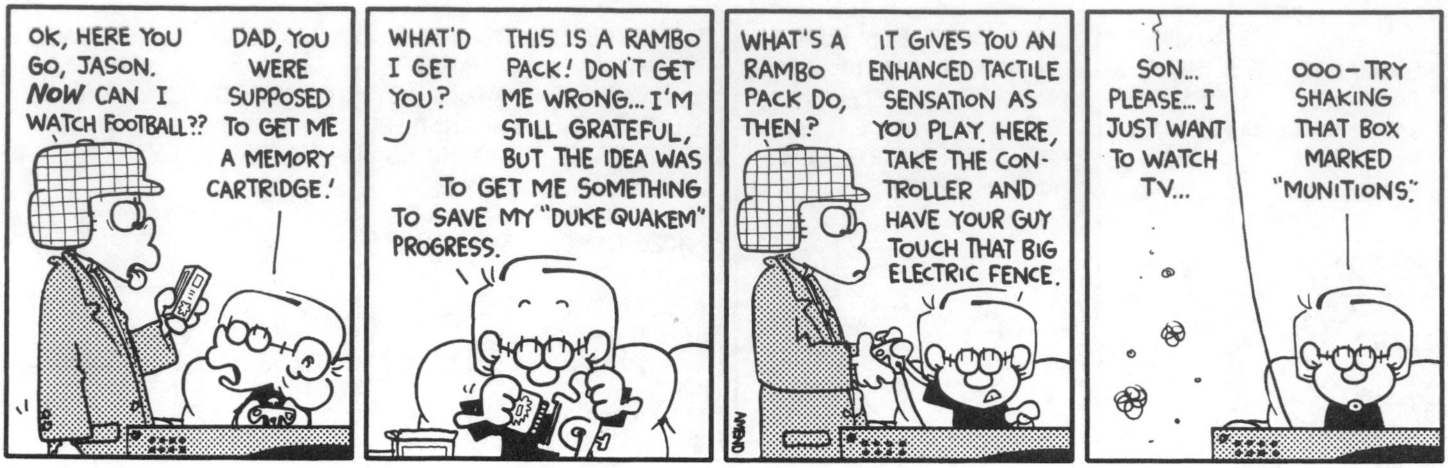
OK, HERE YOU GO, JASON. **NOW** CAN I WATCH FOOTBALL??
DAD, YOU WERE SUPPOSED TO GET ME A MEMORY CARTRIDGE!
WHAT'D I GET YOU?
THIS IS A RAMBO PACK! DON'T GET ME WRONG... I'M STILL GRATEFUL, BUT THE IDEA WAS TO GET ME SOMETHING TO SAVE MY "DUKE QUAKEM" PROGRESS.
WHAT'S A RAMBO PACK DO, THEN?
IT GIVES YOU AN ENHANCED TACTILE SENSATION AS YOU PLAY. HERE, TAKE THE CONTROLLER AND HAVE YOUR GUY TOUCH THAT BIG ELECTRIC FENCE.
SON... PLEASE... I JUST WANT TO WATCH TV...
OOO – TRY SHAKING THAT BOX MARKED "MUNITIONS."
AMEND

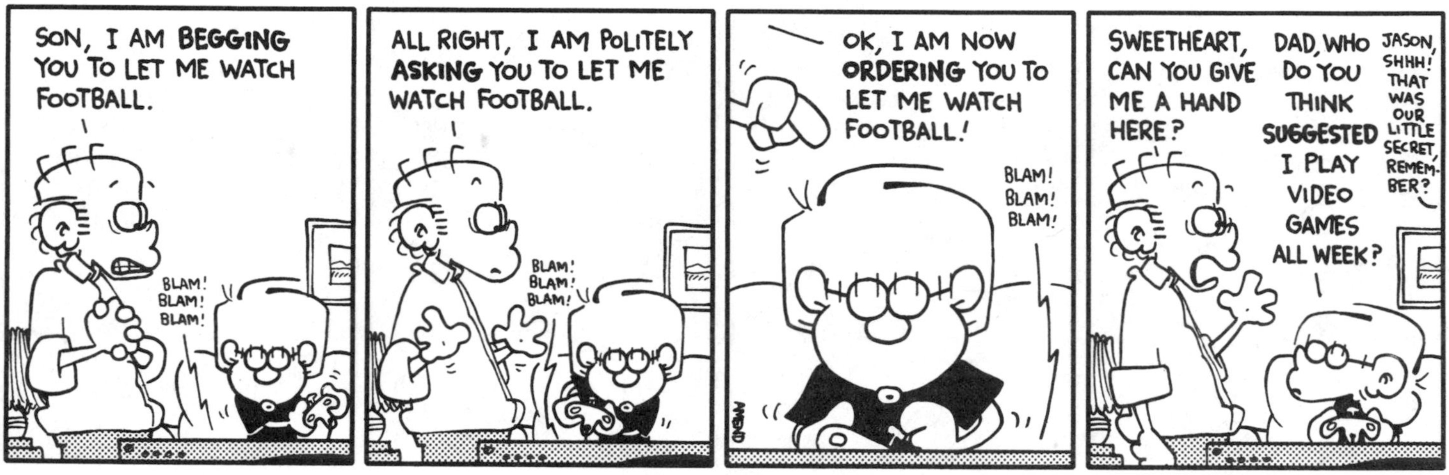
SON, I AM **BEGGING** YOU TO LET ME WATCH FOOTBALL.
BLAM! BLAM! BLAM!
ALL RIGHT, I AM POLITELY **ASKING** YOU TO LET ME WATCH FOOTBALL.
BLAM! BLAM! BLAM!
OK, I AM NOW **ORDERING** YOU TO LET ME WATCH FOOTBALL!
BLAM! BLAM! BLAM!
SWEETHEART, CAN YOU GIVE ME A HAND HERE?
DAD, WHO DO YOU THINK **SUGGESTED** I PLAY VIDEO GAMES ALL WEEK?
JASON, SHHH! THAT WAS OUR LITTLE SECRET, REMEMBER?
AMEND

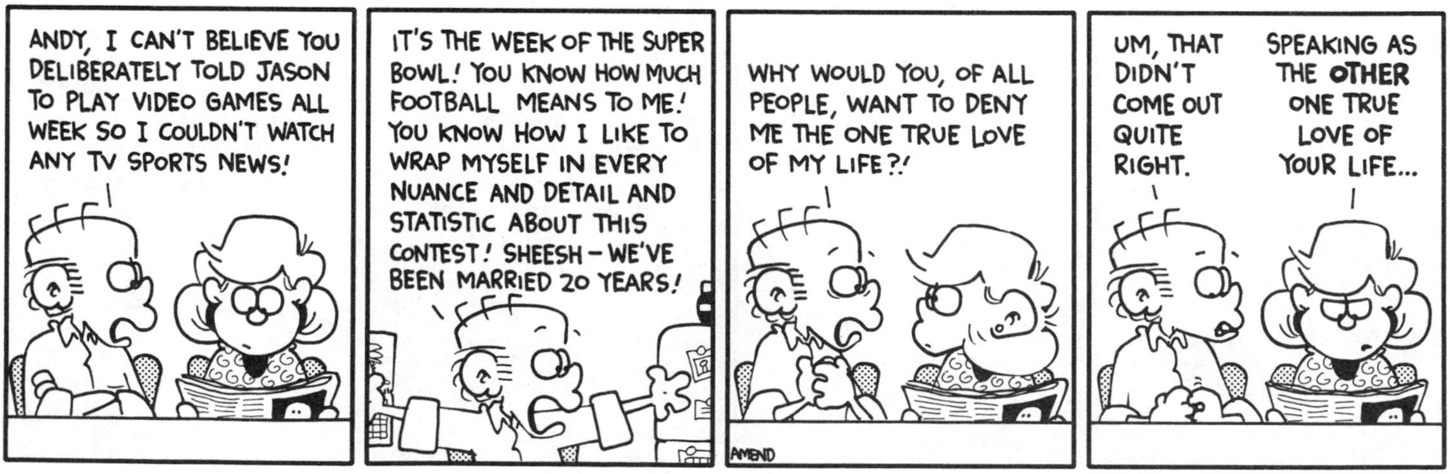
ANDY, I CAN'T BELIEVE YOU DELIBERATELY TOLD JASON TO PLAY VIDEO GAMES ALL WEEK SO I COULDN'T WATCH ANY TV SPORTS NEWS!
IT'S THE WEEK OF THE SUPER BOWL! YOU KNOW HOW MUCH FOOTBALL MEANS TO ME! YOU KNOW HOW I LIKE TO WRAP MYSELF IN EVERY NUANCE AND DETAIL AND STATISTIC ABOUT THIS CONTEST! SHEESH – WE'VE BEEN MARRIED 20 YEARS!
WHY WOULD YOU, OF ALL PEOPLE, WANT TO DENY ME THE ONE TRUE LOVE OF MY LIFE?!
UM, THAT DIDN'T COME OUT QUITE RIGHT.
SPEAKING AS THE **OTHER** ONE TRUE LOVE OF YOUR LIFE...
AMEND

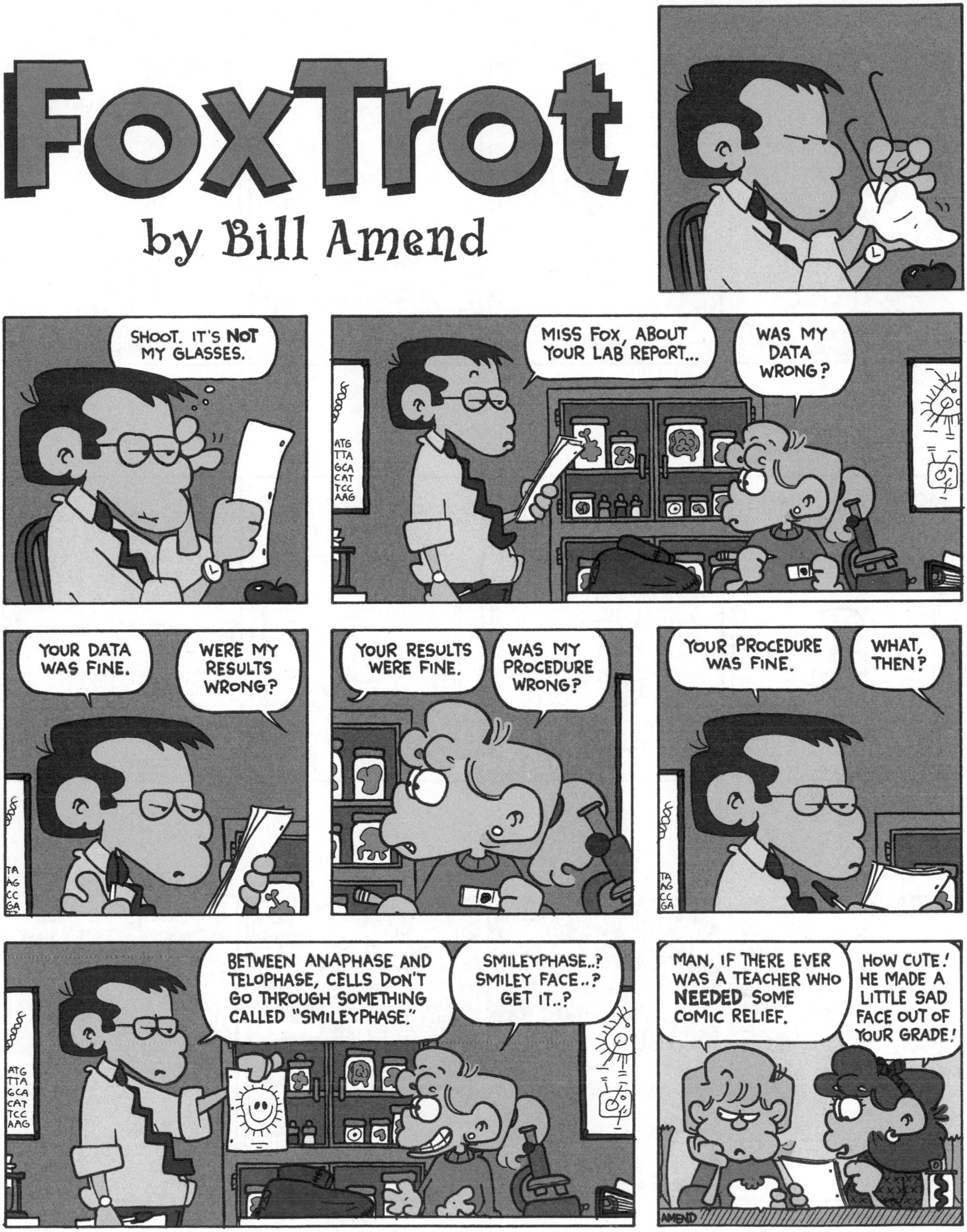
FoxTrot
by Bill Amend
SHOOT. IT'S **NOT** MY GLASSES.
MISS FOX, ABOUT YOUR LAB REPORT...
WAS MY DATA WRONG?
YOUR DATA WAS FINE.
WERE MY RESULTS WRONG?
YOUR RESULTS WERE FINE.
WAS MY PROCEDURE WRONG?
YOUR PROCEDURE WAS FINE.
WHAT, THEN?
BETWEEN ANAPHASE AND TELOPHASE, CELLS DON'T GO THROUGH SOMETHING CALLED "SMILEYPHASE."
SMILEYPHASE..? SMILEY FACE..? GET IT..?
MAN, IF THERE EVER WAS A TEACHER WHO **NEEDED** SOME COMIC RELIEF.
HOW CUTE! HE MADE A LITTLE SAD FACE OUT OF YOUR GRADE!
AMEND

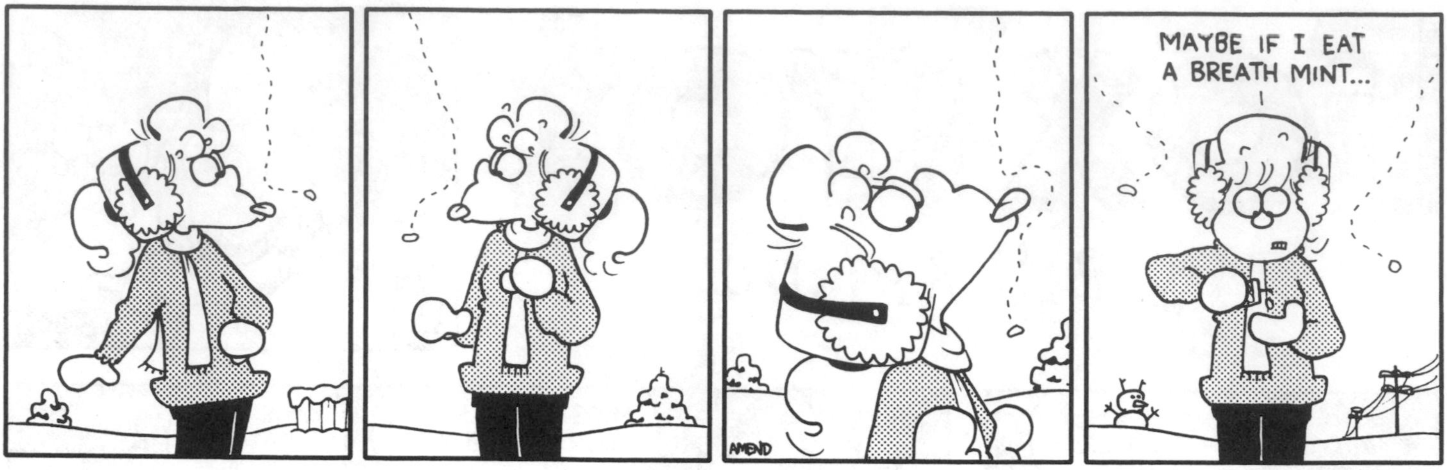
MAYBE IF I EAT A BREATH MINT...
AMEND

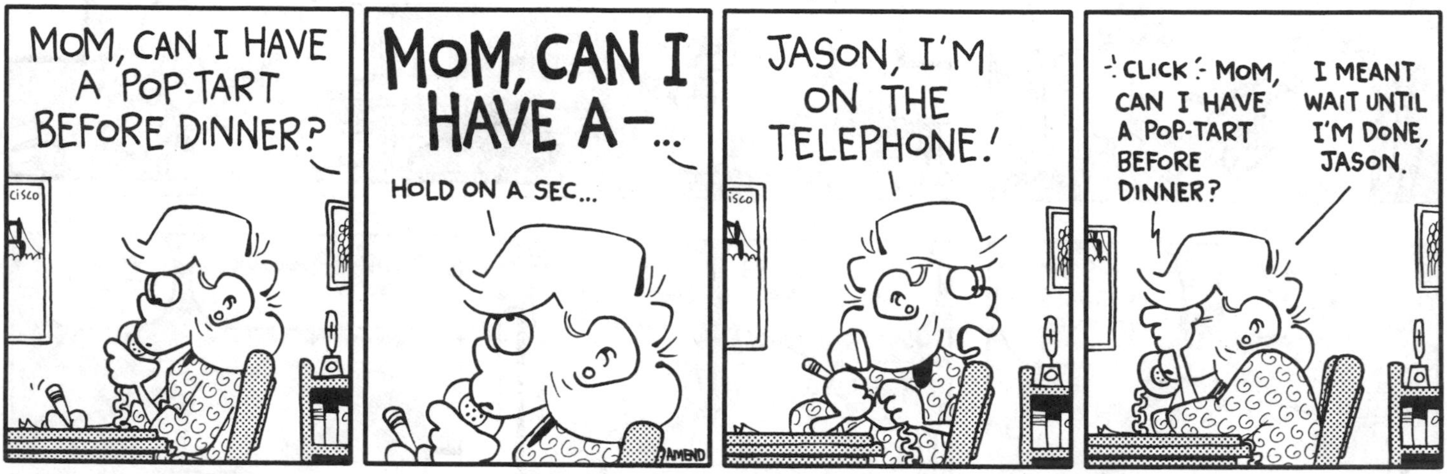
MOM, CAN I HAVE A POP-TART BEFORE DINNER?
MOM, CAN I HAVE A-...
HOLD ON A SEC...
JASON, I'M ON THE TELEPHONE!
-CLICK- MOM, CAN I HAVE A POP-TART BEFORE DINNER?
I MEANT WAIT UNTIL I'M DONE, JASON.
AMEND

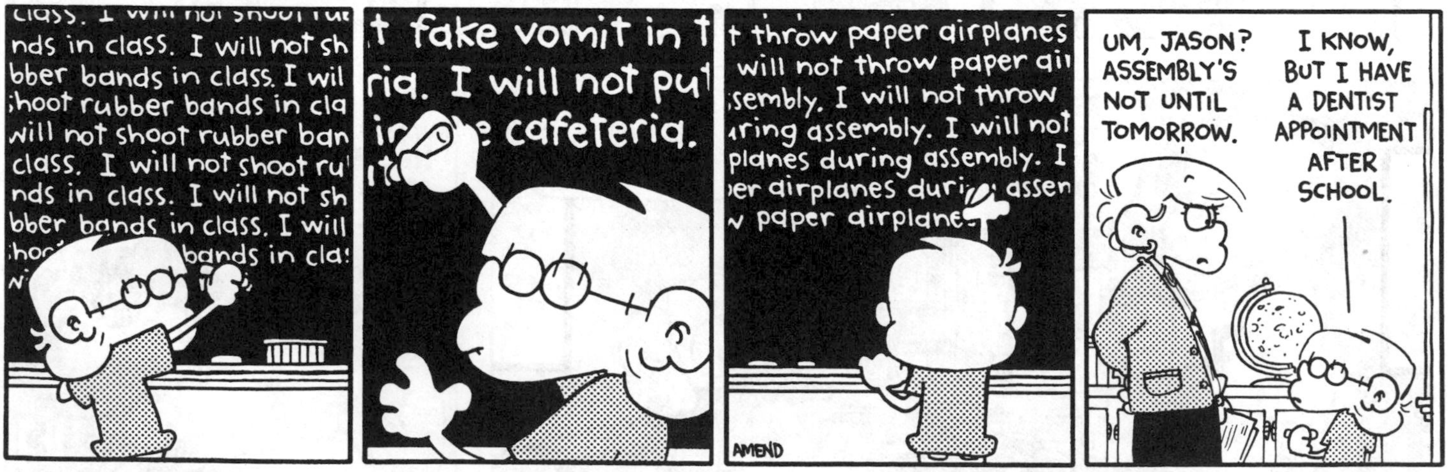
nds in class. I will not sh
bber bands in class. I wil
will not shoot rubber ban
class. I will not shoot ru
nds in class. I will not sh
bber bands in class. I will
t fake vomit in t
ria. I will not pu
cafeteria.
t throw paper airplanes
will not throw paper ai
sembly. I will not throw
uring assembly. I will not
planes during assembly. I
per airplanes duri
v paper airplane
AMEND
UM, JASON? ASSEMBLY'S NOT UNTIL TOMORROW.
I KNOW, BUT I HAVE A DENTIST APPOINTMENT AFTER SCHOOL.

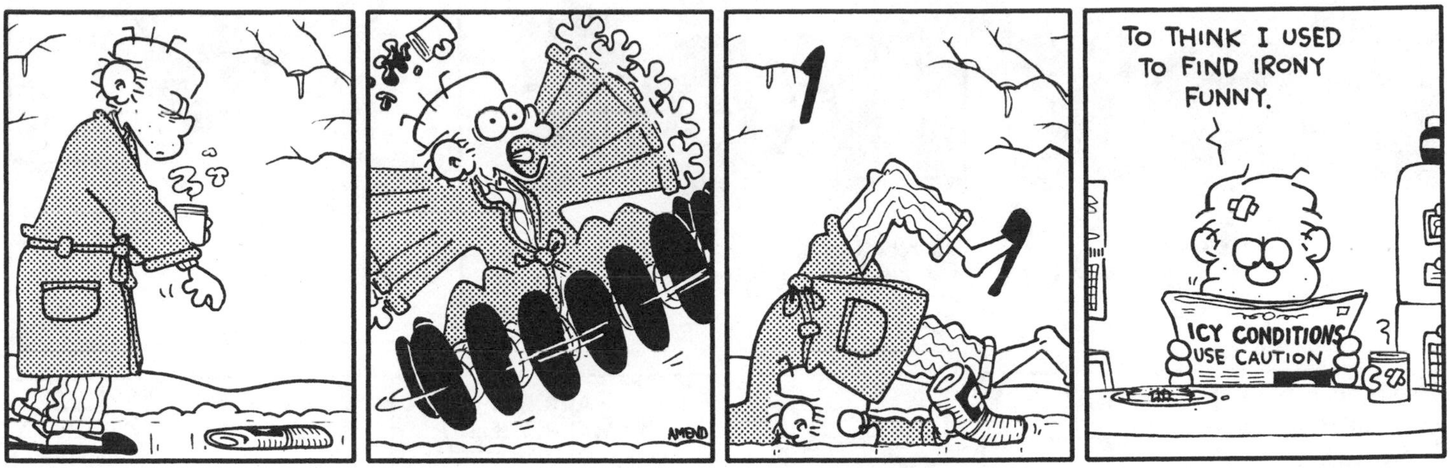
ICY CONDITIONS
USE CAUTION
TO THINK I USED TO FIND IRONY FUNNY.

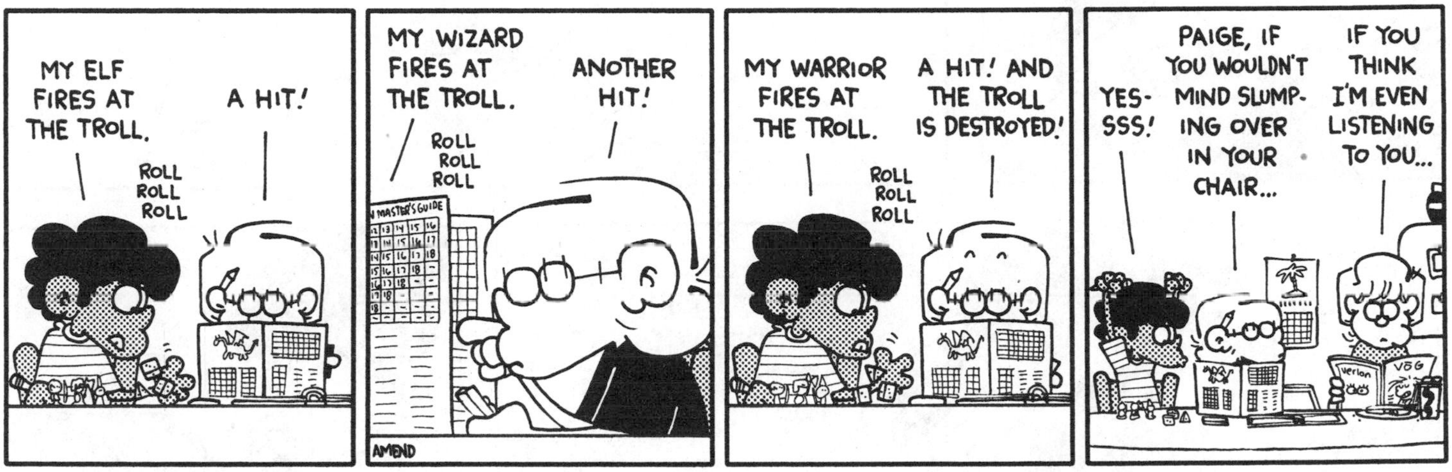
MY ELF FIRES AT THE TROLL.
ROLL ROLL ROLL
A HIT!
MY WIZARD FIRES AT THE TROLL.
ROLL ROLL ROLL
ANOTHER HIT!
MY WARRIOR FIRES AT THE TROLL.
ROLL ROLL ROLL
A HIT! AND THE TROLL IS DESTROYED!
YES-SSS!
PAIGE, IF YOU WOULDN'T MIND SLUMP-ING OVER IN YOUR CHAIR...
IF YOU THINK I'M EVEN LISTENING TO YOU...

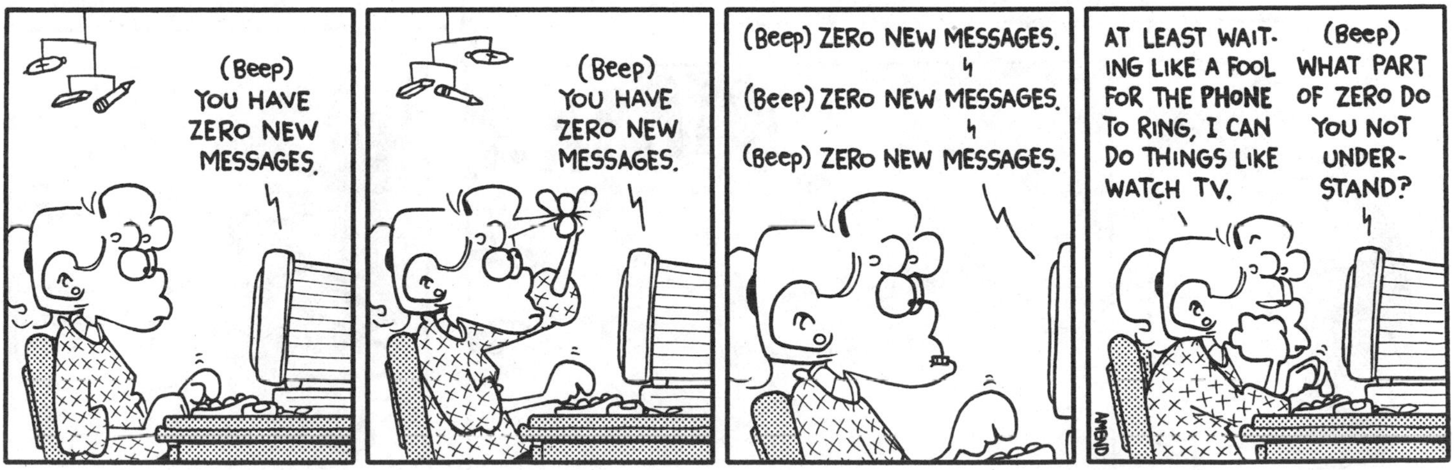
(Beep) YOU HAVE ZERO NEW MESSAGES.
(Beep) YOU HAVE ZERO NEW MESSAGES.
(Beep) ZERO NEW MESSAGES.
(Beep) ZERO NEW MESSAGES.
(Beep) ZERO NEW MESSAGES.
AT LEAST WAIT-ING LIKE A FOOL FOR THE PHONE TO RING, I CAN DO THINGS LIKE WATCH TV.
(Beep) WHAT PART OF ZERO DO YOU NOT UNDER-STAND?

FoxTrot

by Bill Amend

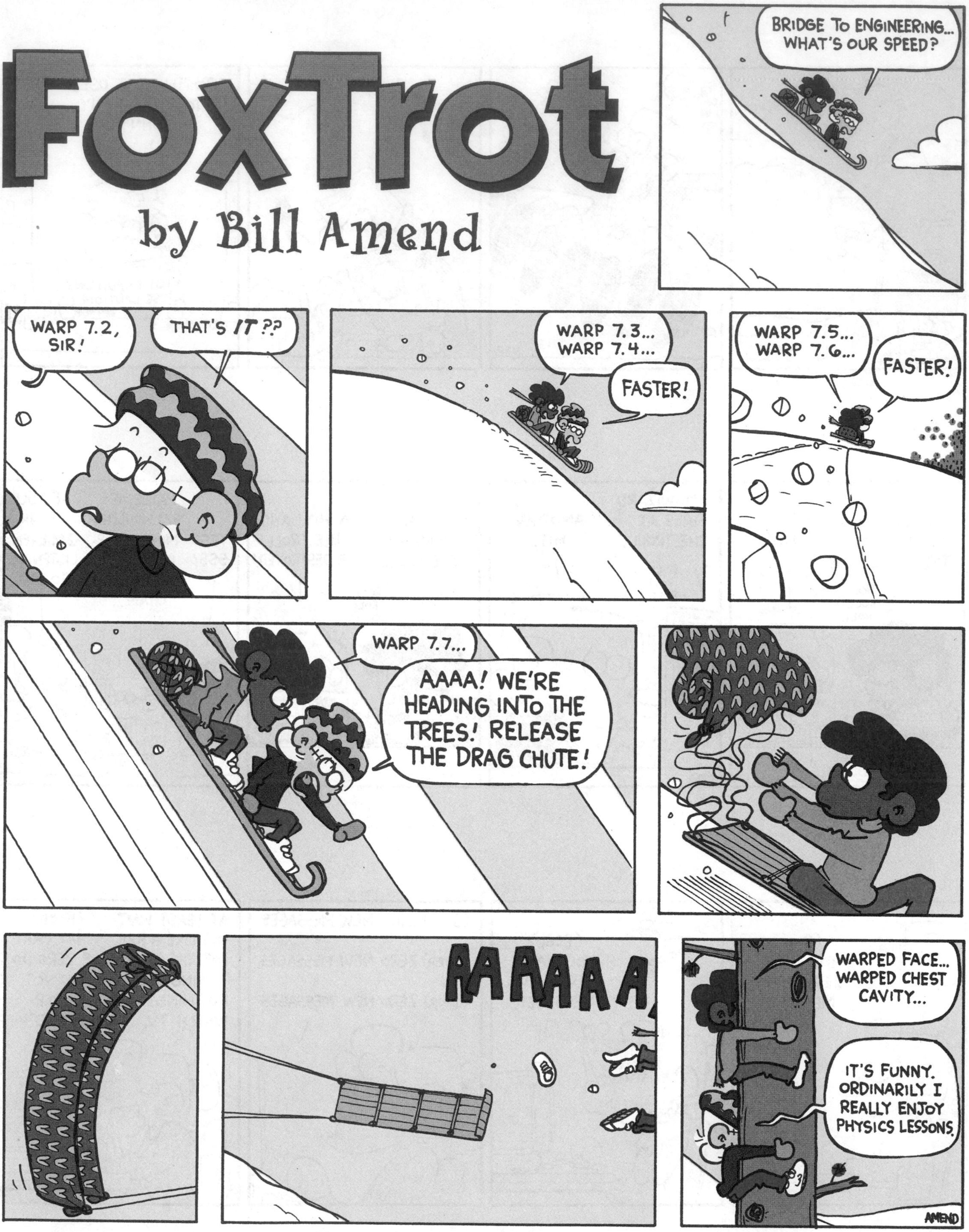
BRIDGE TO ENGINEERING... WHAT'S OUR SPEED?
WARP 7.2, SIR!
THAT'S IT??
WARP 7.3... WARP 7.4...
FASTER!
WARP 7.5... WARP 7.6...
FASTER!
WARP 7.7...
AAAA! WE'RE HEADING INTO THE TREES! RELEASE THE DRAG CHUTE!
AAAAAA
WARPED FACE... WARPED CHEST CAVITY...
IT'S FUNNY. ORDINARILY I REALLY ENJOY PHYSICS LESSONS.
AMEND

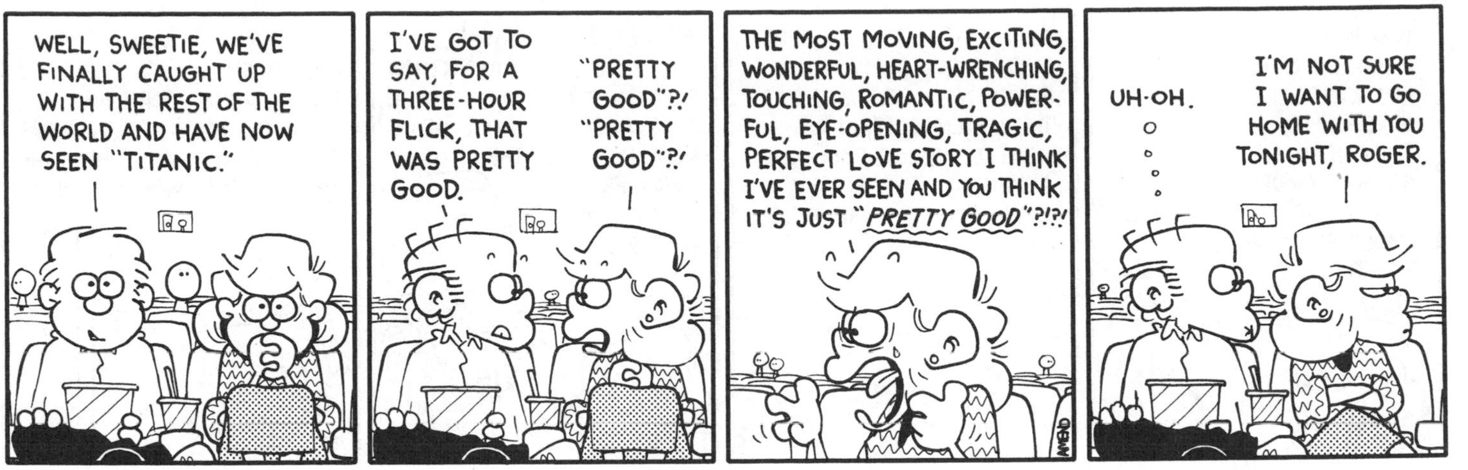
WELL, SWEETIE, WE'VE FINALLY CAUGHT UP WITH THE REST OF THE WORLD AND HAVE NOW SEEN "TITANIC."
I'VE GOT TO SAY, FOR A THREE-HOUR FLICK, THAT WAS PRETTY GOOD.
"PRETTY GOOD"?! "PRETTY GOOD"?!
THE MOST MOVING, EXCITING, WONDERFUL, HEART-WRENCHING, TOUCHING, ROMANTIC, POWERFUL, EYE-OPENING, TRAGIC, PERFECT LOVE STORY I THINK I'VE EVER SEEN AND YOU THINK IT'S JUST "PRETTY GOOD"?!?!
AMEND
UH-OH.
I'M NOT SURE I WANT TO GO HOME WITH YOU TONIGHT, ROGER.

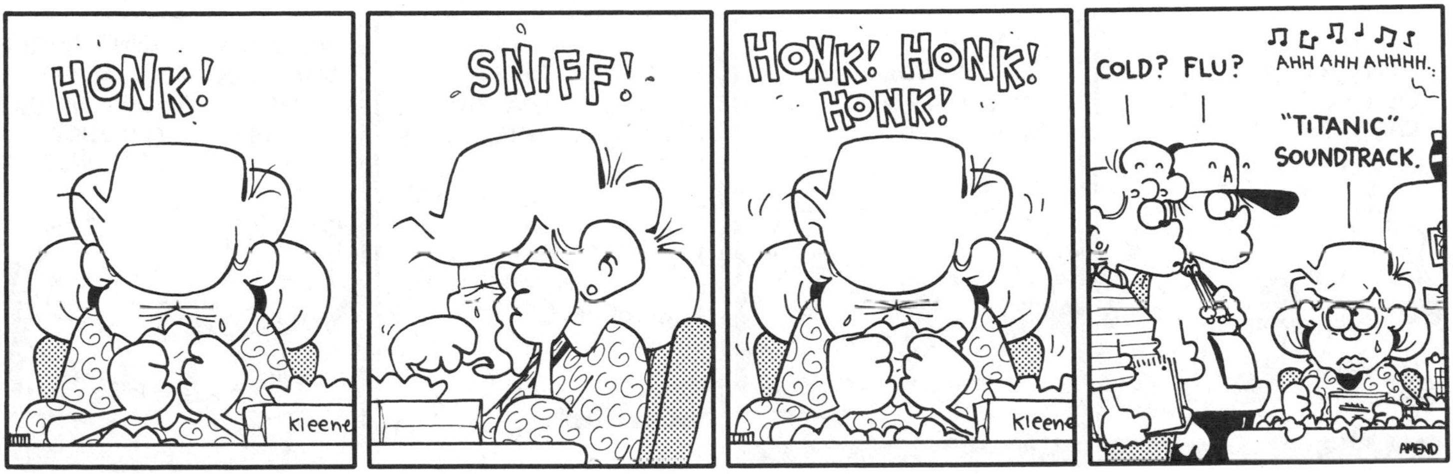
HONK!
SNIFF!
HONK! HONK! HONK!
COLD? FLU?
AHH AHH AHHHH..
"TITANIC" SOUNDTRACK.
AMEND

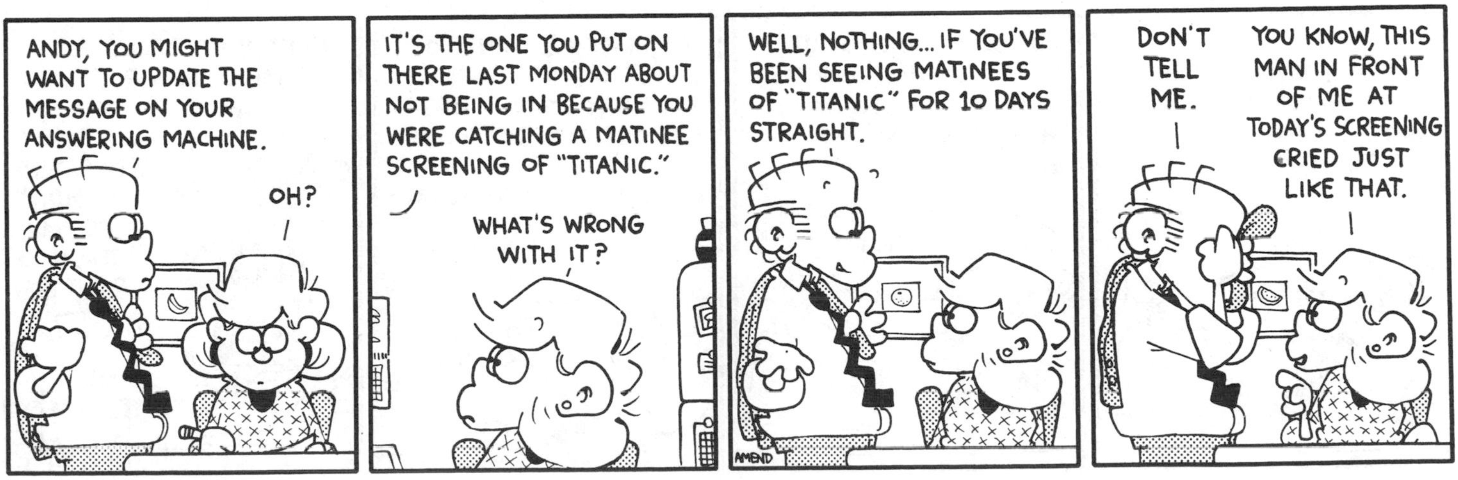
ANDY, YOU MIGHT WANT TO UPDATE THE MESSAGE ON YOUR ANSWERING MACHINE.
OH?
IT'S THE ONE YOU PUT ON THERE LAST MONDAY ABOUT NOT BEING IN BECAUSE YOU WERE CATCHING A MATINEE SCREENING OF "TITANIC."
WHAT'S WRONG WITH IT?
WELL, NOTHING... IF YOU'VE BEEN SEEING MATINEES OF "TITANIC" FOR 10 DAYS STRAIGHT.
AMEND
DON'T TELL ME.
YOU KNOW, THIS MAN IN FRONT OF ME AT TODAY'S SCREENING CRIED JUST LIKE THAT.

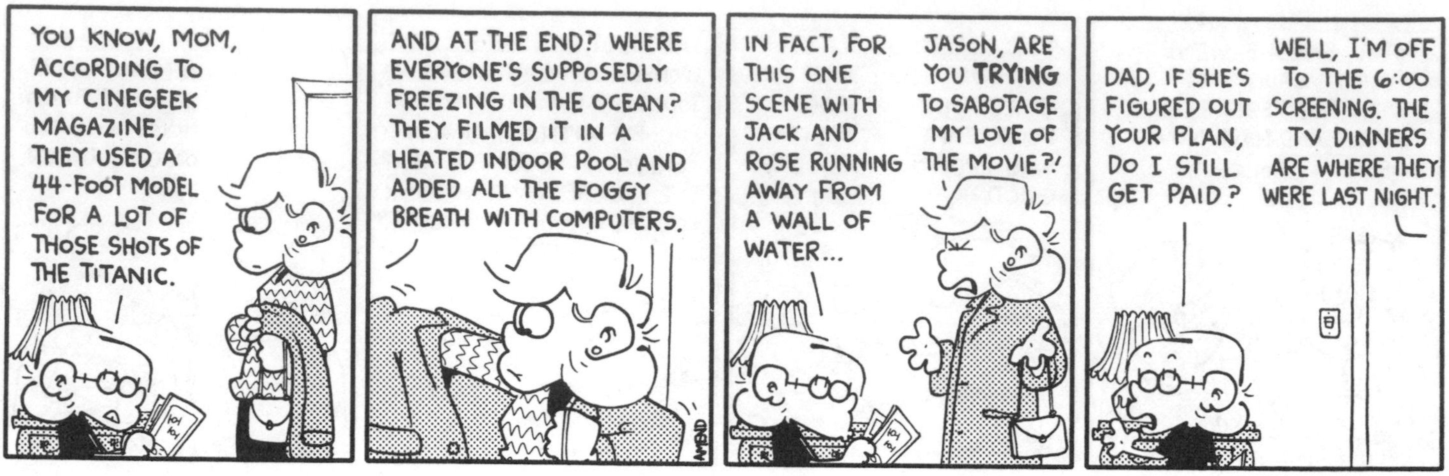
YOU KNOW, MOM, ACCORDING TO MY CINEGEEK MAGAZINE, THEY USED A 44-FOOT MODEL FOR A LOT OF THOSE SHOTS OF THE TITANIC.
AND AT THE END? WHERE EVERYONE'S SUPPOSEDLY FREEZING IN THE OCEAN? THEY FILMED IT IN A HEATED INDOOR POOL AND ADDED ALL THE FOGGY BREATH WITH COMPUTERS.
AMEND
IN FACT, FOR THIS ONE SCENE WITH JACK AND ROSE RUNNING AWAY FROM A WALL OF WATER...
JASON, ARE YOU **TRYING** TO SABOTAGE MY LOVE OF THE MOVIE?!
DAD, IF SHE'S FIGURED OUT YOUR PLAN, DO I STILL GET PAID?
WELL, I'M OFF TO THE 6:00 SCREENING. THE TV DINNERS ARE WHERE THEY WERE LAST NIGHT.

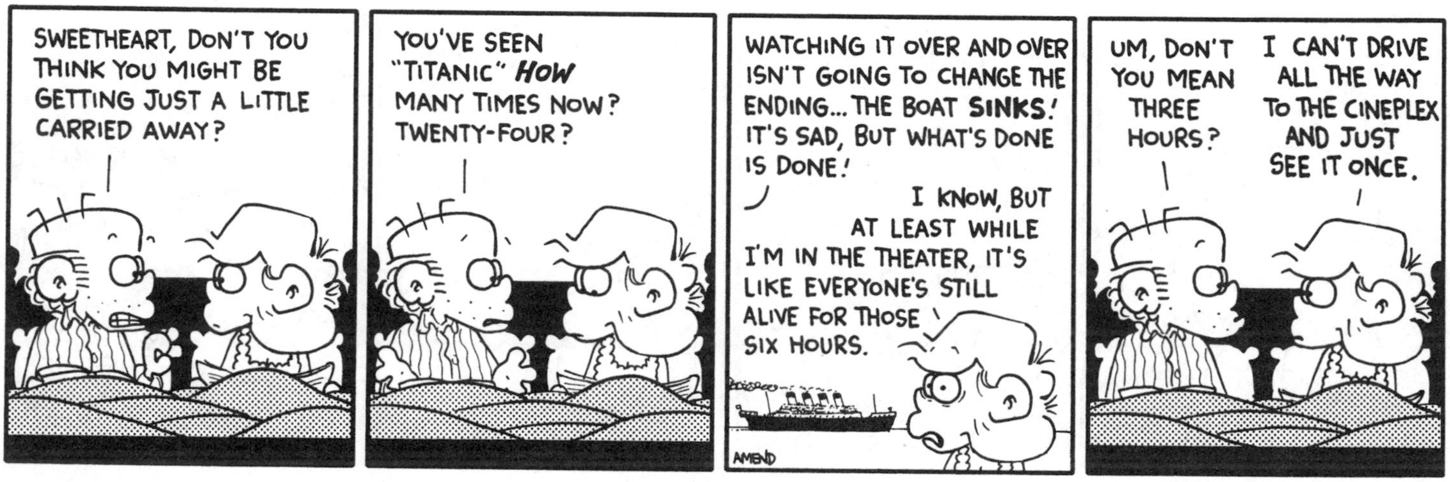
SWEETHEART, DON'T YOU THINK YOU MIGHT BE GETTING JUST A LITTLE CARRIED AWAY?
YOU'VE SEEN "TITANIC" ***HOW*** MANY TIMES NOW? TWENTY-FOUR?
WATCHING IT OVER AND OVER ISN'T GOING TO CHANGE THE ENDING... THE BOAT **SINKS**! IT'S SAD, BUT WHAT'S DONE IS DONE!
I KNOW, BUT AT LEAST WHILE I'M IN THE THEATER, IT'S LIKE EVERYONE'S STILL ALIVE FOR THOSE SIX HOURS.
AMEND
UM, DON'T YOU MEAN THREE HOURS?
I CAN'T DRIVE ALL THE WAY TO THE CINEPLEX AND JUST SEE IT ONCE.

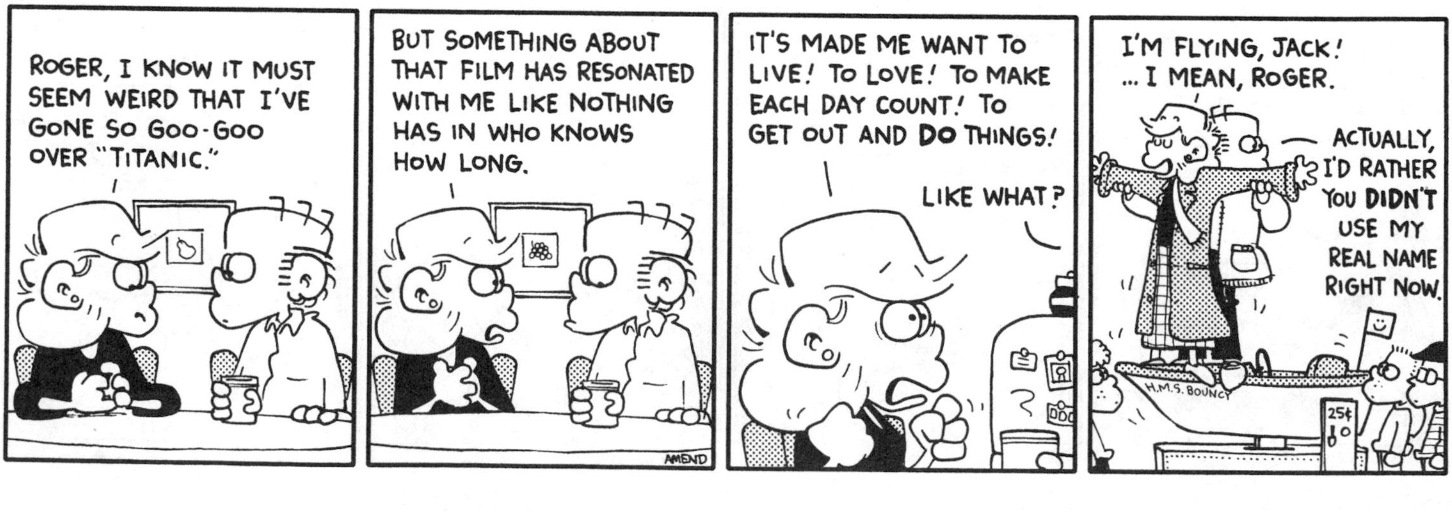
ROGER, I KNOW IT MUST SEEM WEIRD THAT I'VE GONE SO GOO-GOO OVER "TITANIC."
BUT SOMETHING ABOUT THAT FILM HAS RESONATED WITH ME LIKE NOTHING HAS IN WHO KNOWS HOW LONG.
AMEND
IT'S MADE ME WANT TO LIVE! TO LOVE! TO MAKE EACH DAY COUNT! TO GET OUT AND **DO** THINGS!
LIKE WHAT?
I'M FLYING, JACK! ... I MEAN, ROGER.
ACTUALLY, I'D RATHER YOU **DIDN'T** USE MY REAL NAME RIGHT NOW.
H.M.S. BOUNCY
25¢

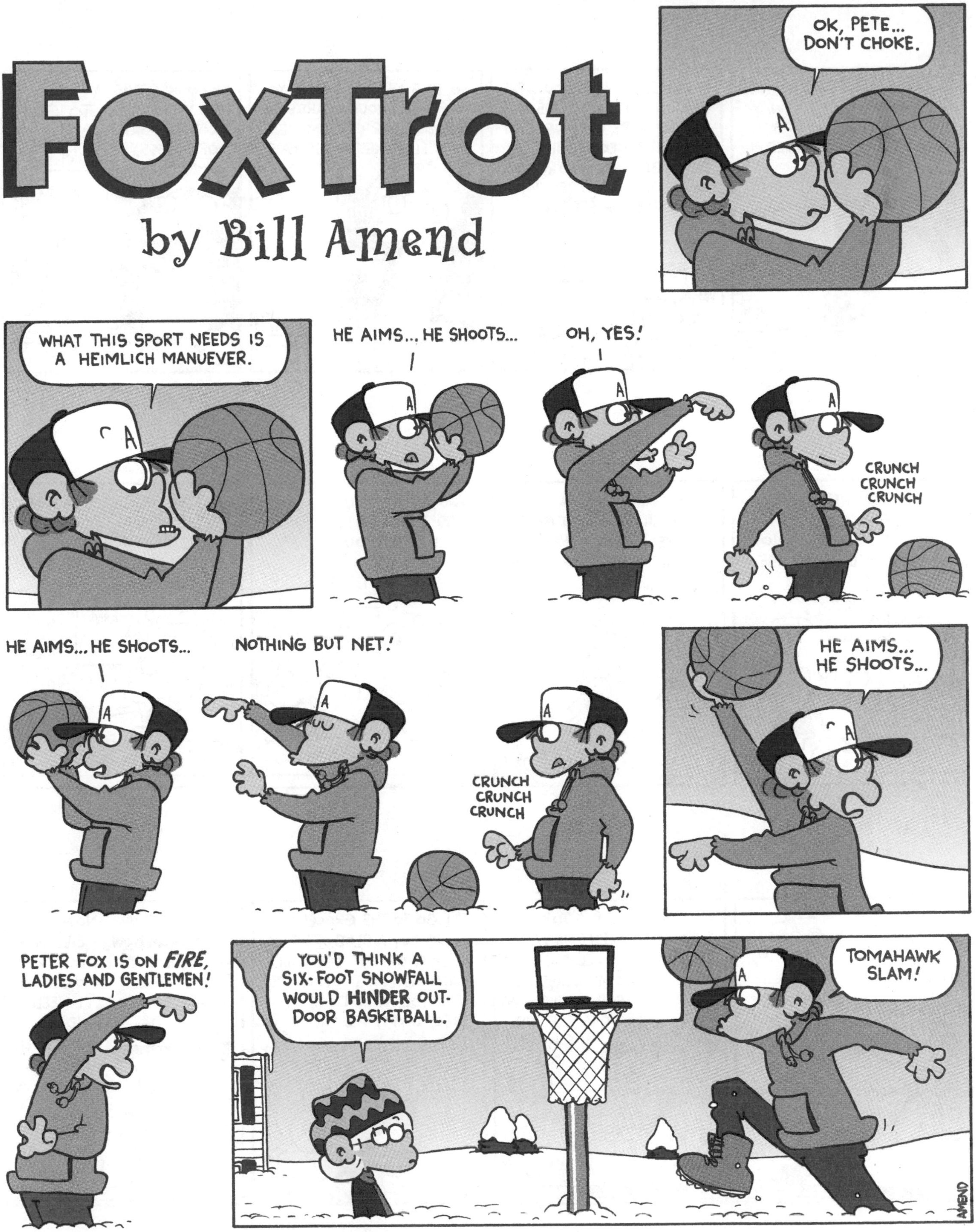
FoxTrot
by Bill Amend
OK, PETE... DON'T CHOKE.
WHAT THIS SPORT NEEDS IS A HEIMLICH MANUEVER.
HE AIMS... HE SHOOTS...
OH, YES!
CRUNCH CRUNCH CRUNCH
HE AIMS... HE SHOOTS...
NOTHING BUT NET!
CRUNCH CRUNCH CRUNCH
HE AIMS... HE SHOOTS...
PETER FOX IS ON *FIRE*, LADIES AND GENTLEMEN!
YOU'D THINK A SIX-FOOT SNOWFALL WOULD **HINDER** OUT-DOOR BASKETBALL.
TOMAHAWK SLAM!
AMEND

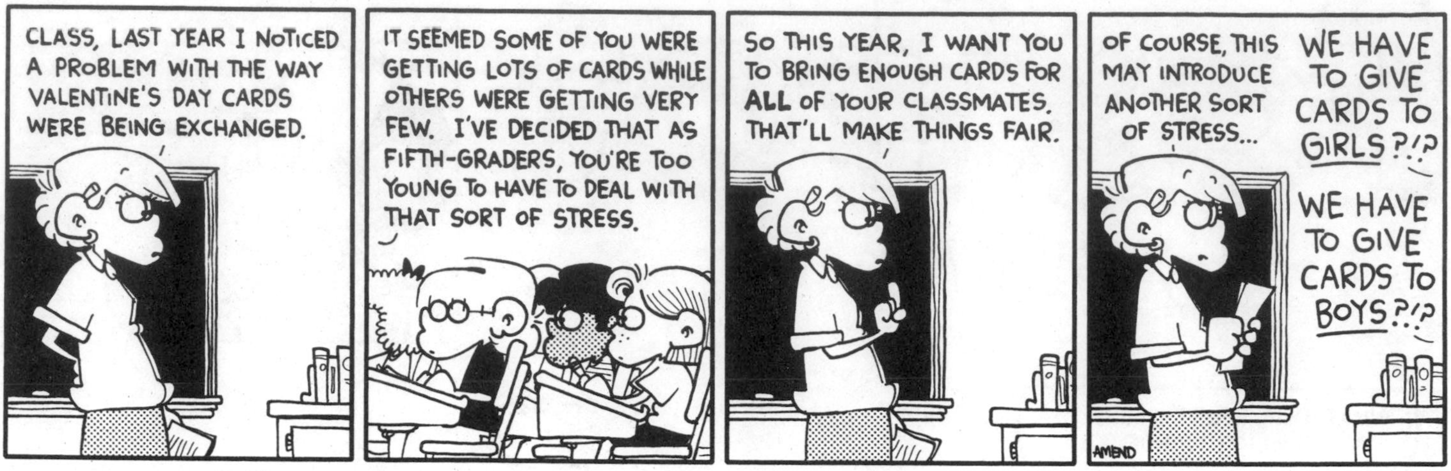
CLASS, LAST YEAR I NOTICED A PROBLEM WITH THE WAY VALENTINE'S DAY CARDS WERE BEING EXCHANGED.
IT SEEMED SOME OF YOU WERE GETTING LOTS OF CARDS WHILE OTHERS WERE GETTING VERY FEW. I'VE DECIDED THAT AS FIFTH-GRADERS, YOU'RE TOO YOUNG TO HAVE TO DEAL WITH THAT SORT OF STRESS.
SO THIS YEAR, I WANT YOU TO BRING ENOUGH CARDS FOR ALL OF YOUR CLASSMATES. THAT'LL MAKE THINGS FAIR.
OF COURSE, THIS MAY INTRODUCE ANOTHER SORT OF STRESS...
WE HAVE TO GIVE CARDS TO GIRLS?!?
WE HAVE TO GIVE CARDS TO BOYS?!?
AMEND

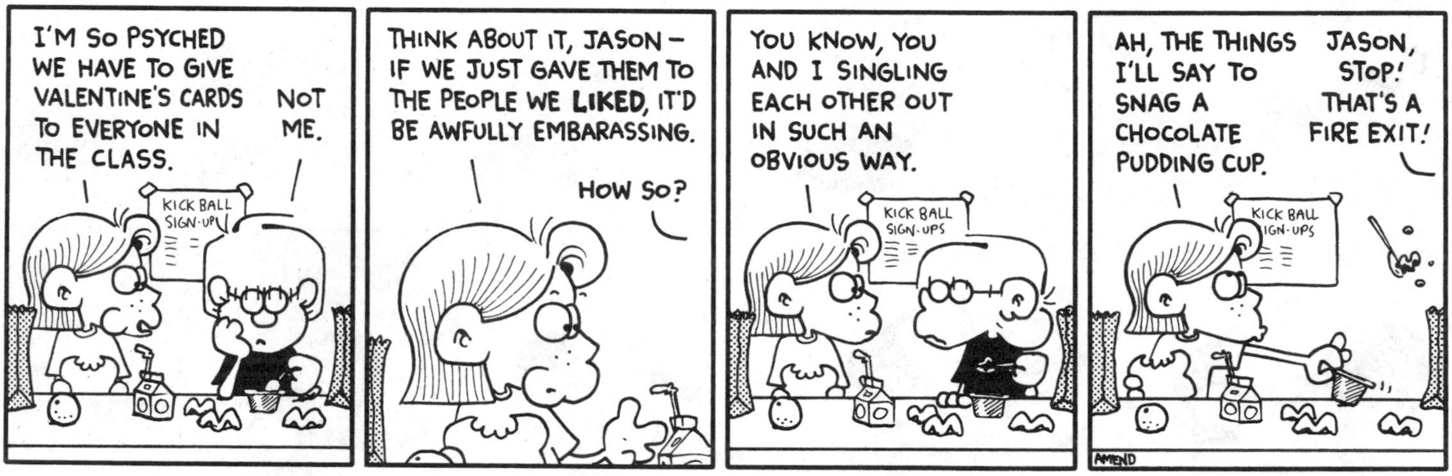
I'M SO PSYCHED WE HAVE TO GIVE VALENTINE'S CARDS TO EVERYONE IN THE CLASS.
NOT ME.
KICK BALL SIGN-UP
THINK ABOUT IT, JASON – IF WE JUST GAVE THEM TO THE PEOPLE WE LIKED, IT'D BE AWFULLY EMBARASSING.
HOW SO?
YOU KNOW, YOU AND I SINGLING EACH OTHER OUT IN SUCH AN OBVIOUS WAY.
KICK BALL SIGN-UPS
AH, THE THINGS I'LL SAY TO SNAG A CHOCOLATE PUDDING CUP.
JASON, STOP! THAT'S A FIRE EXIT!
AMEND

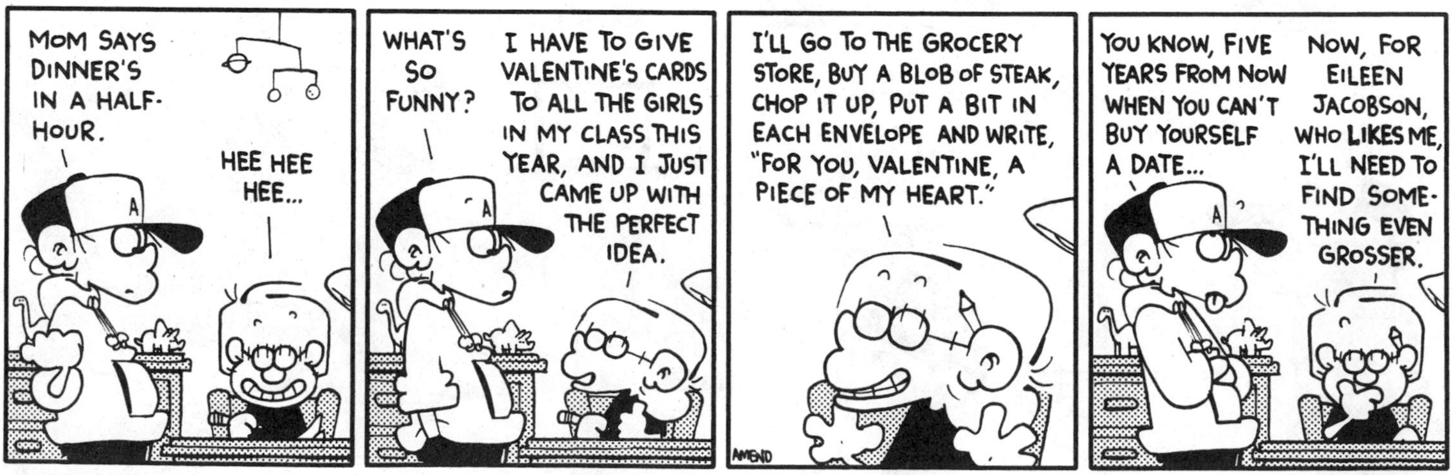
MOM SAYS DINNER'S IN A HALF-HOUR.
HEE HEE HEE...
WHAT'S SO FUNNY?
I HAVE TO GIVE VALENTINE'S CARDS TO ALL THE GIRLS IN MY CLASS THIS YEAR, AND I JUST CAME UP WITH THE PERFECT IDEA.
I'LL GO TO THE GROCERY STORE, BUY A BLOB OF STEAK, CHOP IT UP, PUT A BIT IN EACH ENVELOPE AND WRITE, "FOR YOU, VALENTINE, A PIECE OF MY HEART."
AMEND
YOU KNOW, FIVE YEARS FROM NOW WHEN YOU CAN'T BUY YOURSELF A DATE...
NOW, FOR EILEEN JACOBSON, WHO LIKES ME, I'LL NEED TO FIND SOMETHING EVEN GROSSER.

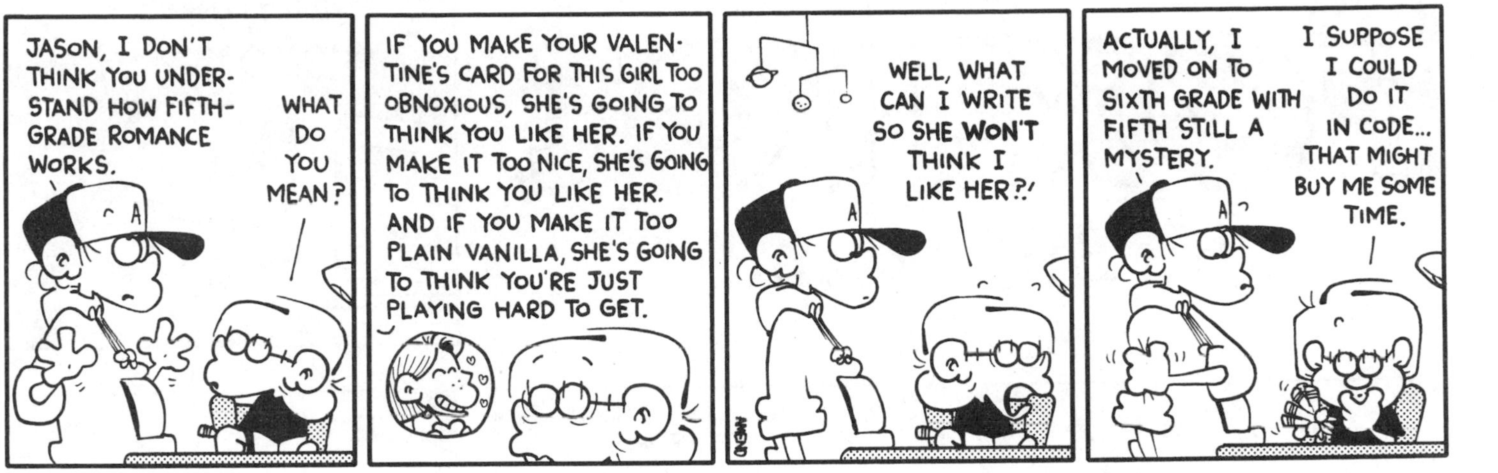
JASON, I DON'T THINK YOU UNDERSTAND HOW FIFTH-GRADE ROMANCE WORKS.
WHAT DO YOU MEAN?
IF YOU MAKE YOUR VALENTINE'S CARD FOR THIS GIRL TOO OBNOXIOUS, SHE'S GOING TO THINK YOU LIKE HER. IF YOU MAKE IT TOO NICE, SHE'S GOING TO THINK YOU LIKE HER. AND IF YOU MAKE IT TOO PLAIN VANILLA, SHE'S GOING TO THINK YOU'RE JUST PLAYING HARD TO GET.
WELL, WHAT CAN I WRITE SO SHE **WON'T** THINK I LIKE HER?!
ACTUALLY, I MOVED ON TO SIXTH GRADE WITH FIFTH STILL A MYSTERY.
I SUPPOSE I COULD DO IT IN CODE... THAT MIGHT BUY ME SOME TIME.

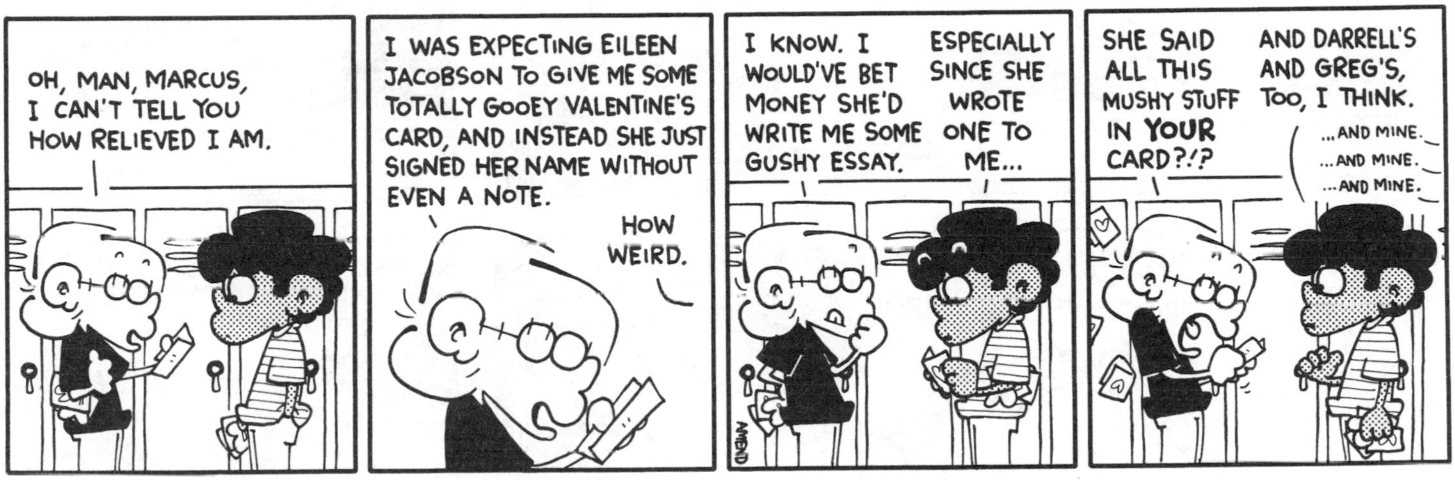
OH, MAN, MARCUS, I CAN'T TELL YOU HOW RELIEVED I AM.
I WAS EXPECTING EILEEN JACOBSON TO GIVE ME SOME TOTALLY GOOEY VALENTINE'S CARD, AND INSTEAD SHE JUST SIGNED HER NAME WITHOUT EVEN A NOTE.
HOW WEIRD.
I KNOW. I WOULD'VE BET MONEY SHE'D WRITE ME SOME GUSHY ESSAY.
ESPECIALLY SINCE SHE WROTE ONE TO ME...
SHE SAID ALL THIS MUSHY STUFF IN **YOUR** CARD?!?
AND DARRELL'S AND GREG'S, TOO, I THINK.
...AND MINE.
...AND MINE.
...AND MINE.

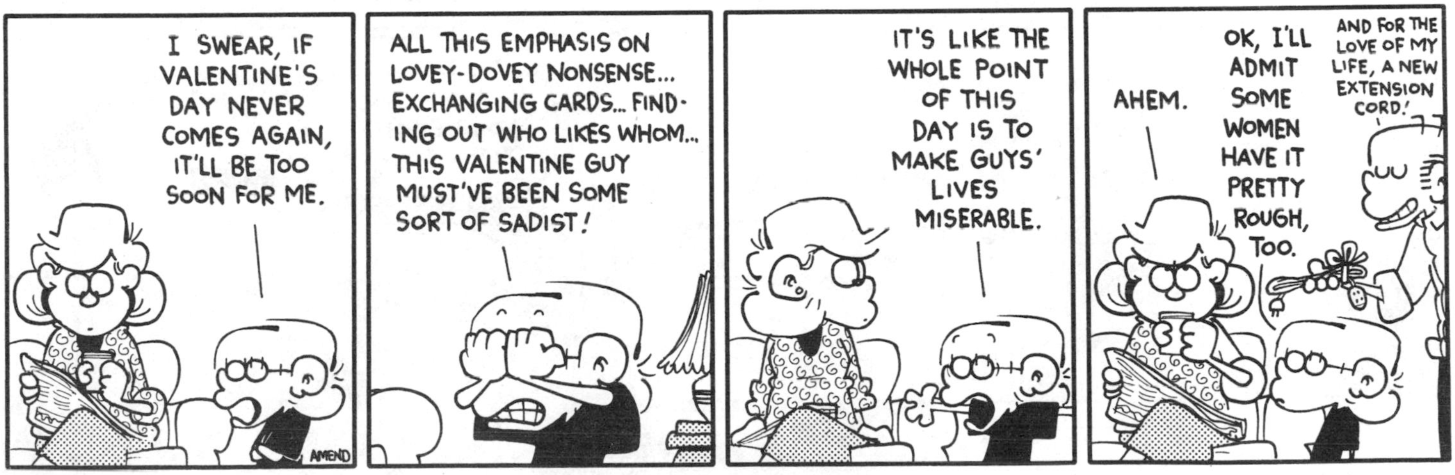
I SWEAR, IF VALENTINE'S DAY NEVER COMES AGAIN, IT'LL BE TOO SOON FOR ME.
ALL THIS EMPHASIS ON LOVEY-DOVEY NONSENSE... EXCHANGING CARDS... FINDING OUT WHO LIKES WHOM... THIS VALENTINE GUY MUST'VE BEEN SOME SORT OF SADIST!
IT'S LIKE THE WHOLE POINT OF THIS DAY IS TO MAKE GUYS' LIVES MISERABLE.
AHEM.
OK, I'LL ADMIT SOME WOMEN HAVE IT PRETTY ROUGH, TOO.
AND FOR THE LOVE OF MY LIFE, A NEW EXTENSION CORD!

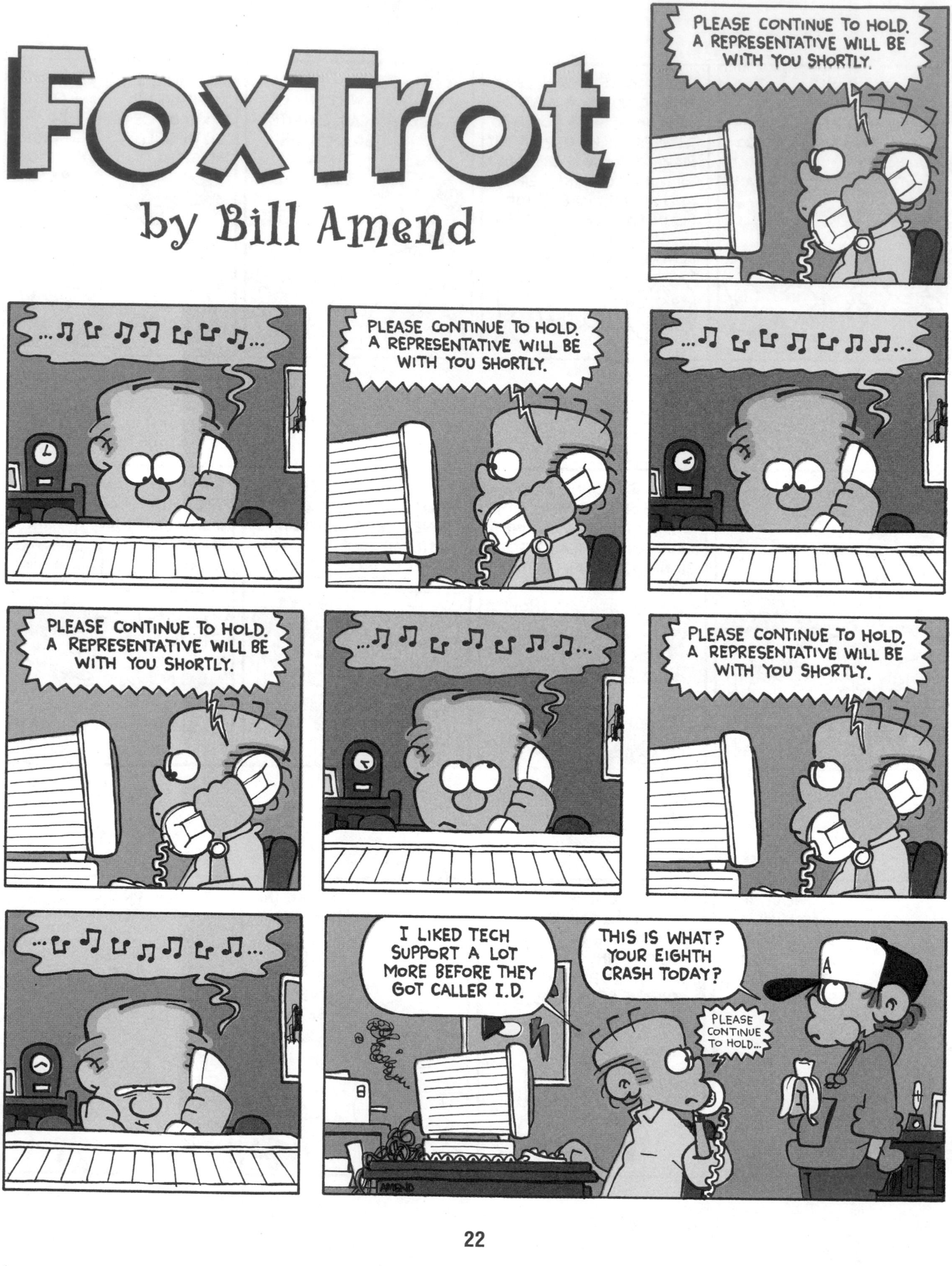
FoxTrot
by Bill Amend
PLEASE CONTINUE TO HOLD. A REPRESENTATIVE WILL BE WITH YOU SHORTLY.
PLEASE CONTINUE TO HOLD. A REPRESENTATIVE WILL BE WITH YOU SHORTLY.
PLEASE CONTINUE TO HOLD. A REPRESENTATIVE WILL BE WITH YOU SHORTLY.
PLEASE CONTINUE TO HOLD. A REPRESENTATIVE WILL BE WITH YOU SHORTLY.
THIS IS WHAT? YOUR EIGHTH CRASH TODAY?
I LIKED TECH SUPPORT A LOT MORE BEFORE THEY GOT CALLER I.D.
PLEASE CONTINUE TO HOLD...
AMEND

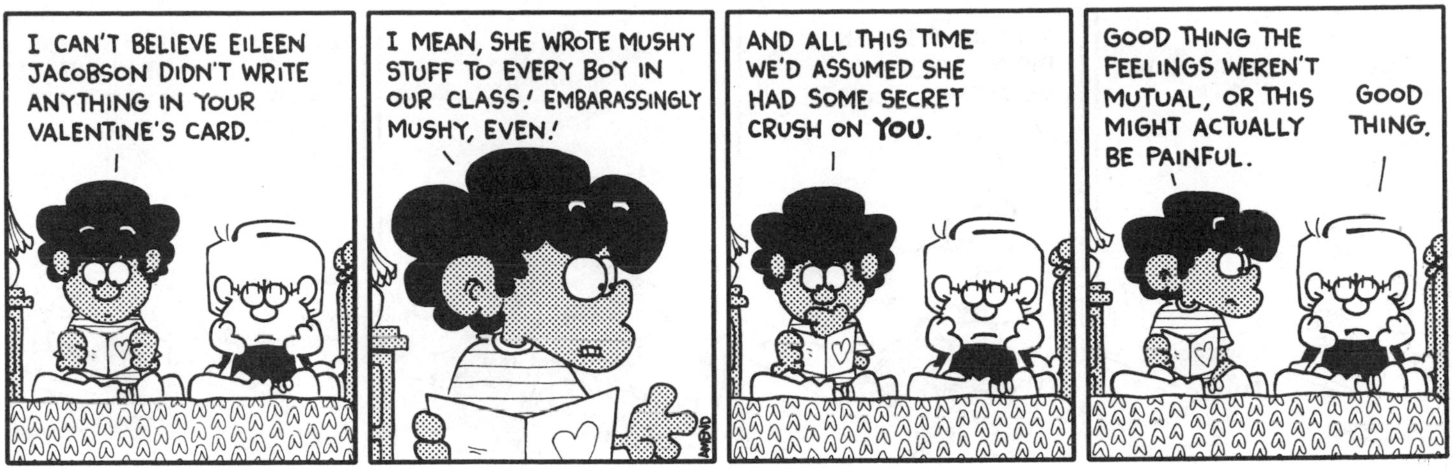
I CAN'T BELIEVE EILEEN JACOBSON DIDN'T WRITE ANYTHING IN YOUR VALENTINE'S CARD.
I MEAN, SHE WROTE MUSHY STUFF TO EVERY BOY IN OUR CLASS! EMBARASSINGLY MUSHY, EVEN!
AMEND
AND ALL THIS TIME WE'D ASSUMED SHE HAD SOME SECRET CRUSH ON **YOU**.
GOOD THING THE FEELINGS WEREN'T MUTUAL, OR THIS MIGHT ACTUALLY BE PAINFUL.
GOOD THING.

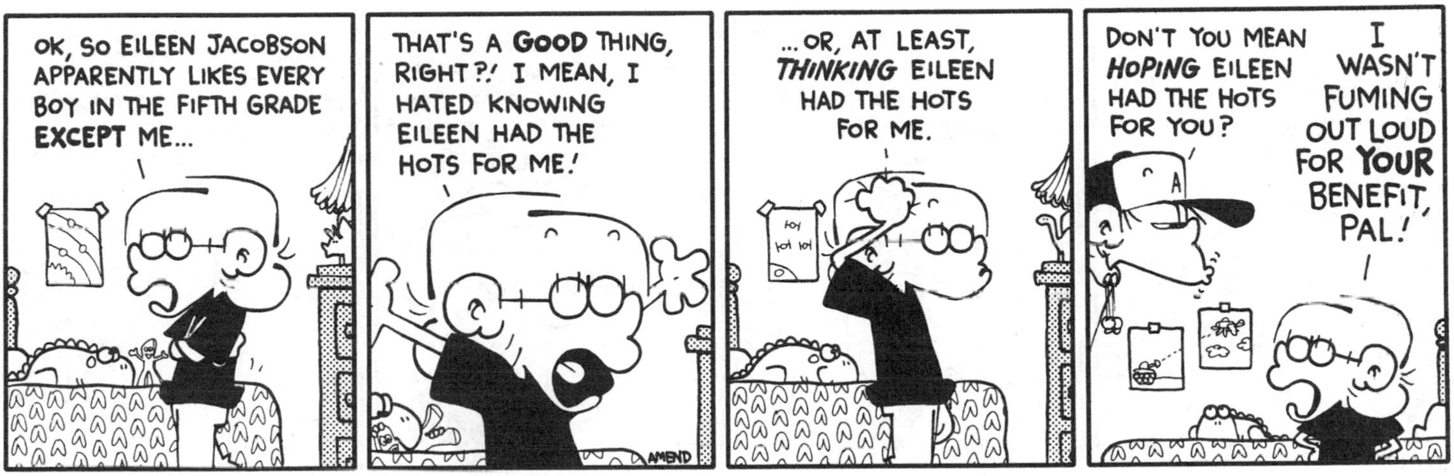
OK, SO EILEEN JACOBSON APPARENTLY LIKES EVERY BOY IN THE FIFTH GRADE **EXCEPT** ME...
THAT'S A **GOOD** THING, RIGHT?! I MEAN, I HATED KNOWING EILEEN HAD THE HOTS FOR ME!
AMEND
...OR, AT LEAST, ***THINKING*** EILEEN HAD THE HOTS FOR ME.
DON'T YOU MEAN ***HOPING*** EILEEN HAD THE HOTS FOR YOU?
I WASN'T FUMING OUT LOUD FOR **YOUR** BENEFIT, PAL!

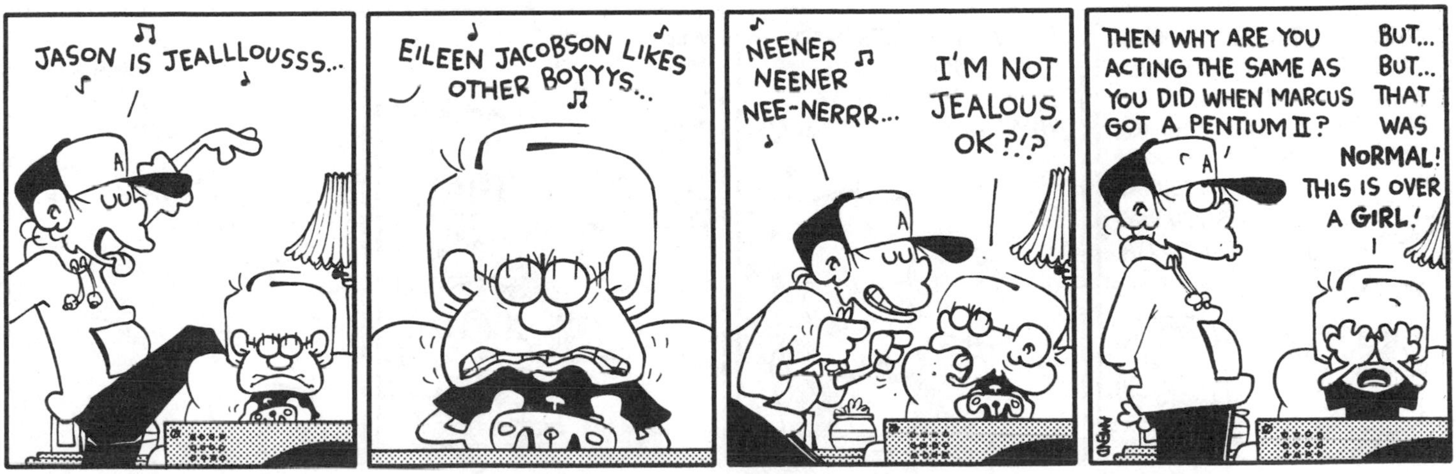
JASON IS JEALLLOUSSS...
EILEEN JACOBSON LIKES OTHER BOYYYS...
NEENER NEENER NEE-NERRR...
I'M NOT JEALOUS, OK?!?
THEN WHY ARE YOU ACTING THE SAME AS YOU DID WHEN MARCUS GOT A PENTIUM II?
BUT... BUT... THAT WAS **NORMAL**! THIS IS OVER A **GIRL**!
AMEND

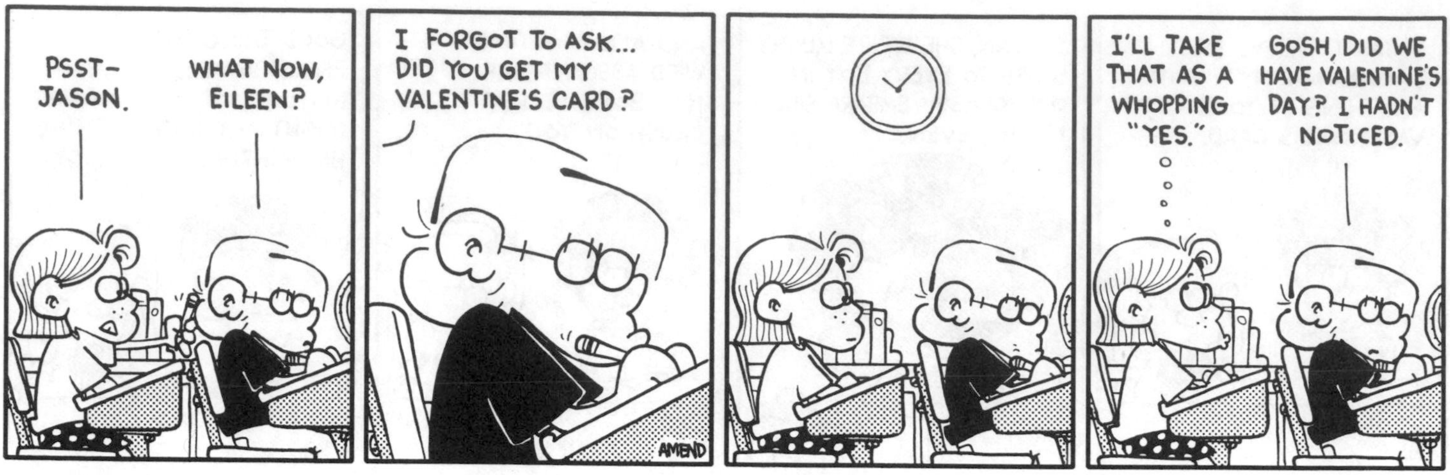
PSST– JASON.
WHAT NOW, EILEEN?
I FORGOT TO ASK... DID YOU GET MY VALENTINE'S CARD?
I'LL TAKE THAT AS A WHOPPING "YES."
GOSH, DID WE HAVE VALENTINE'S DAY? I HADN'T NOTICED.
AMEND

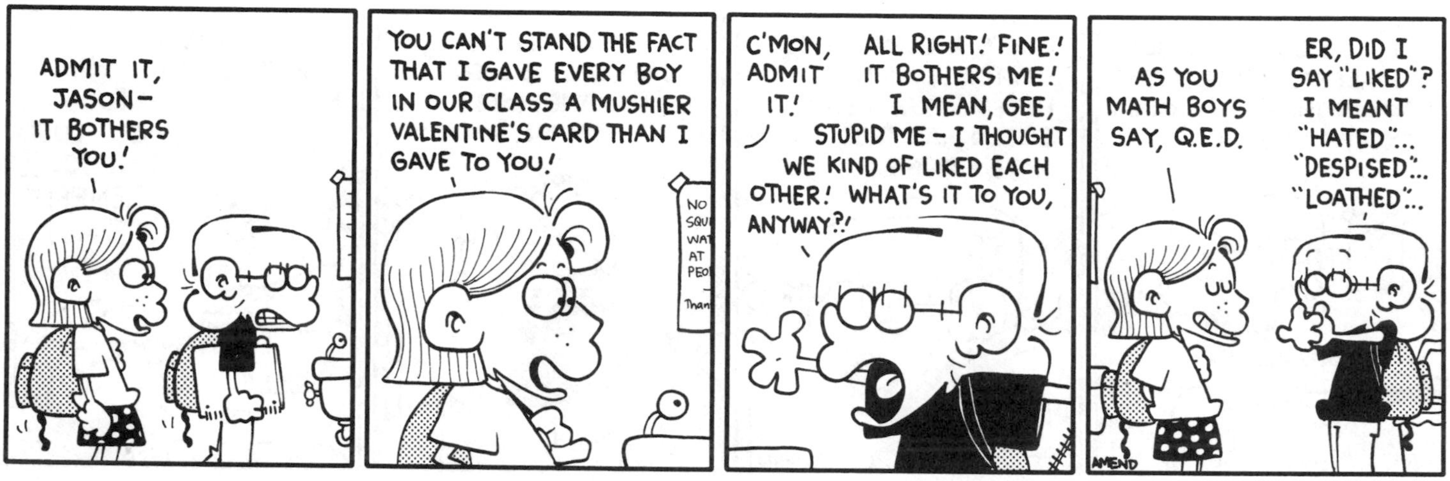
ADMIT IT, JASON– IT BOTHERS YOU!
YOU CAN'T STAND THE FACT THAT I GAVE EVERY BOY IN OUR CLASS A MUSHIER VALENTINE'S CARD THAN I GAVE TO YOU!
C'MON, ADMIT IT!
ALL RIGHT! FINE! IT BOTHERS ME! I MEAN, GEE, STUPID ME – I THOUGHT WE KIND OF LIKED EACH OTHER! WHAT'S IT TO YOU, ANYWAY?!
AS YOU MATH BOYS SAY, Q.E.D.
ER, DID I SAY "LIKED"? I MEANT "HATED"... "DESPISED"... "LOATHED"...
AMEND

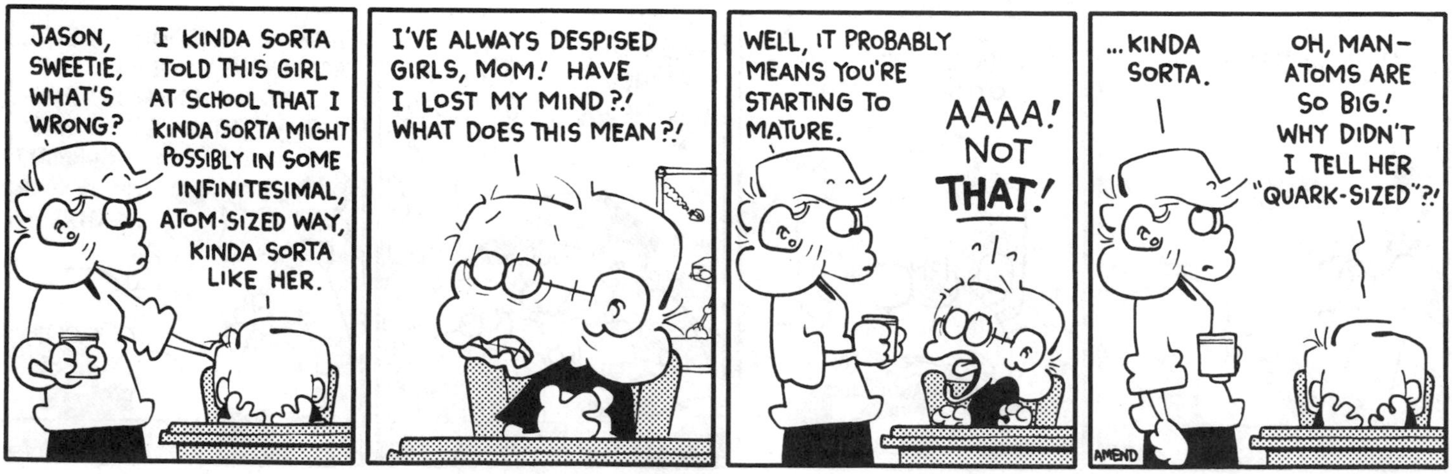
JASON, SWEETIE, WHAT'S WRONG?
I KINDA SORTA TOLD THIS GIRL AT SCHOOL THAT I KINDA SORTA MIGHT POSSIBLY IN SOME INFINITESIMAL, ATOM-SIZED WAY, KINDA SORTA LIKE HER.
I'VE ALWAYS DESPISED GIRLS, MOM! HAVE I LOST MY MIND?! WHAT DOES THIS MEAN?!
WELL, IT PROBABLY MEANS YOU'RE STARTING TO MATURE.
AAAA! NOT THAT!
...KINDA SORTA.
OH, MAN– ATOMS ARE SO BIG! WHY DIDN'T I TELL HER "QUARK-SIZED"?!
AMEND

FoxTrot

by Bill Amend

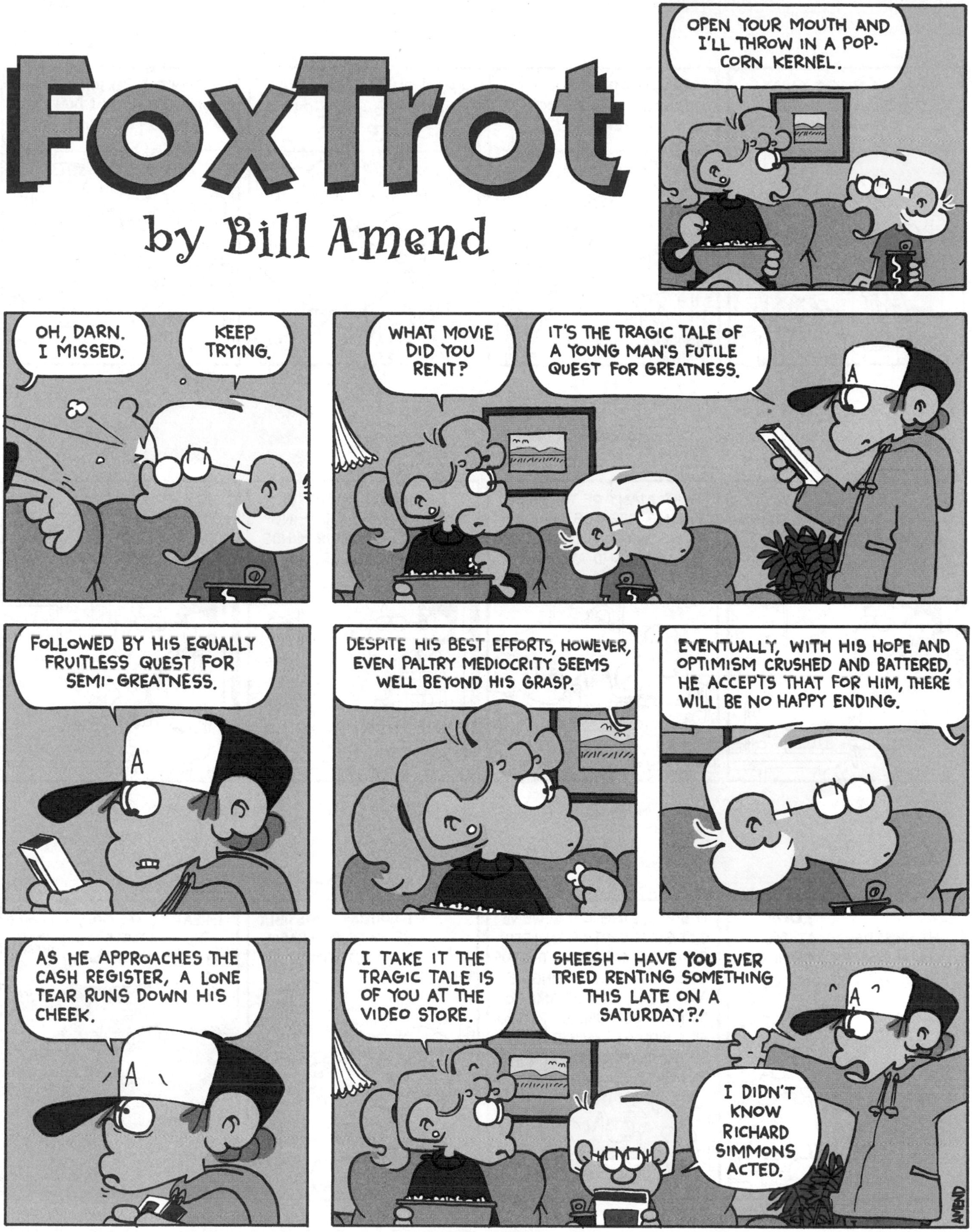

OPEN YOUR MOUTH AND I'LL THROW IN A POP-CORN KERNEL.
OH, DARN. I MISSED.
KEEP TRYING.
WHAT MOVIE DID YOU RENT?
IT'S THE TRAGIC TALE OF A YOUNG MAN'S FUTILE QUEST FOR GREATNESS.
FOLLOWED BY HIS EQUALLY FRUITLESS QUEST FOR SEMI-GREATNESS.
DESPITE HIS BEST EFFORTS, HOWEVER, EVEN PALTRY MEDIOCRITY SEEMS WELL BEYOND HIS GRASP.
EVENTUALLY, WITH HIS HOPE AND OPTIMISM CRUSHED AND BATTERED, HE ACCEPTS THAT FOR HIM, THERE WILL BE NO HAPPY ENDING.
AS HE APPROACHES THE CASH REGISTER, A LONE TEAR RUNS DOWN HIS CHEEK.
I TAKE IT THE TRAGIC TALE IS OF YOU AT THE VIDEO STORE.
SHEESH — HAVE YOU EVER TRIED RENTING SOMETHING THIS LATE ON A SATURDAY?!
I DIDN'T KNOW RICHARD SIMMONS ACTED.
AMEND

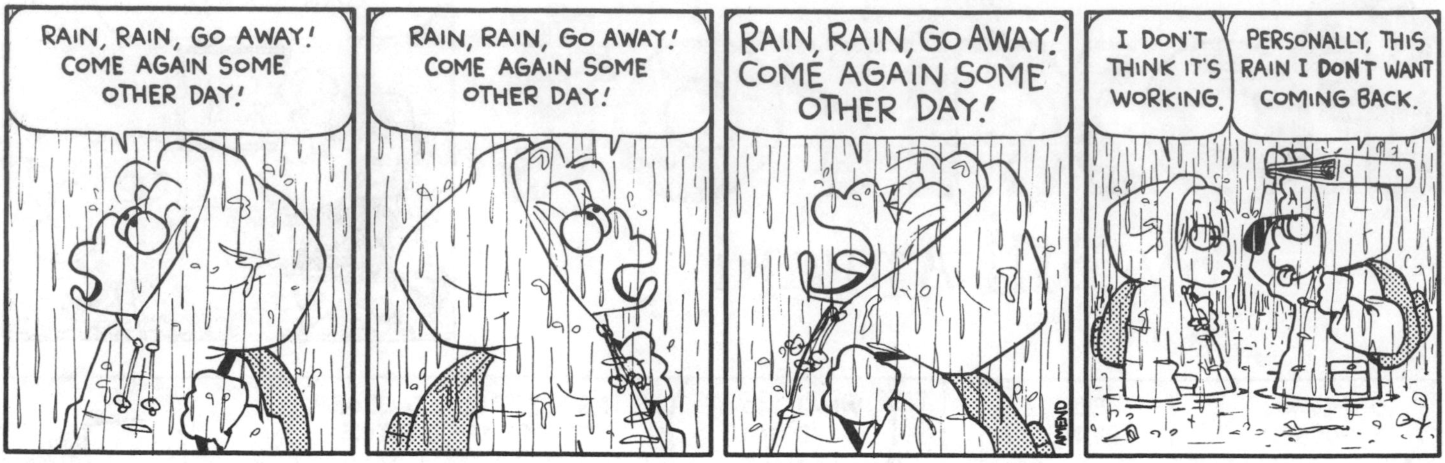
RAIN, RAIN, GO AWAY! COME AGAIN SOME OTHER DAY!
RAIN, RAIN, GO AWAY! COME AGAIN SOME OTHER DAY!
RAIN, RAIN, GO AWAY! COME AGAIN SOME OTHER DAY!
AMEND
I DON'T THINK IT'S WORKING.
PERSONALLY, THIS RAIN I DON'T WANT COMING BACK.

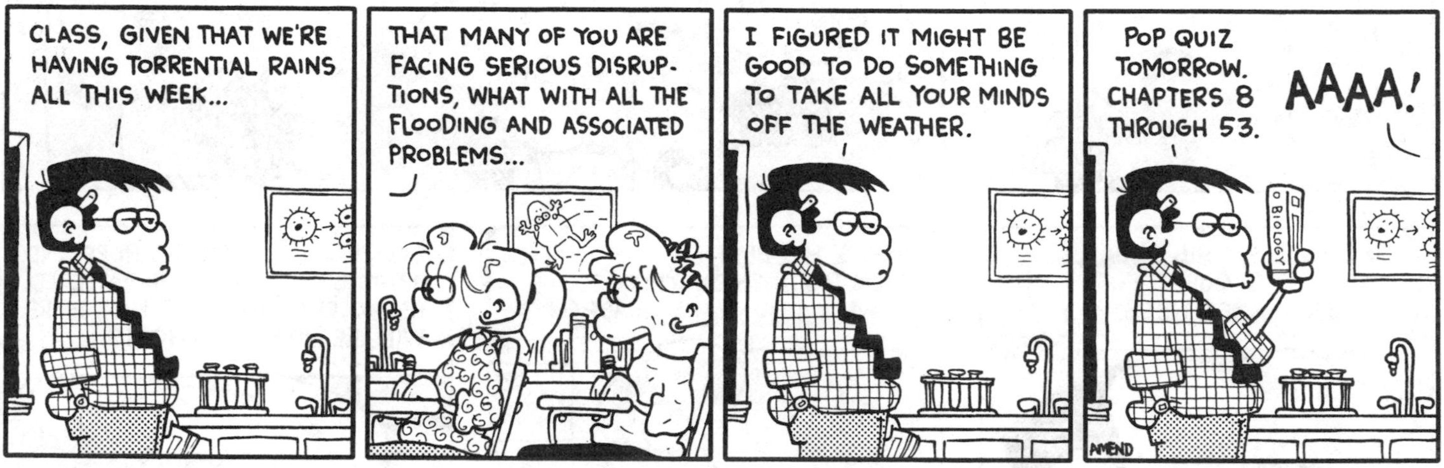
CLASS, GIVEN THAT WE'RE HAVING TORRENTIAL RAINS ALL THIS WEEK...
THAT MANY OF YOU ARE FACING SERIOUS DISRUPTIONS, WHAT WITH ALL THE FLOODING AND ASSOCIATED PROBLEMS...
I FIGURED IT MIGHT BE GOOD TO DO SOMETHING TO TAKE ALL YOUR MINDS OFF THE WEATHER.
POP QUIZ TOMORROW. CHAPTERS 8 THROUGH 53.
AAAA!
BIOLOGY
AMEND

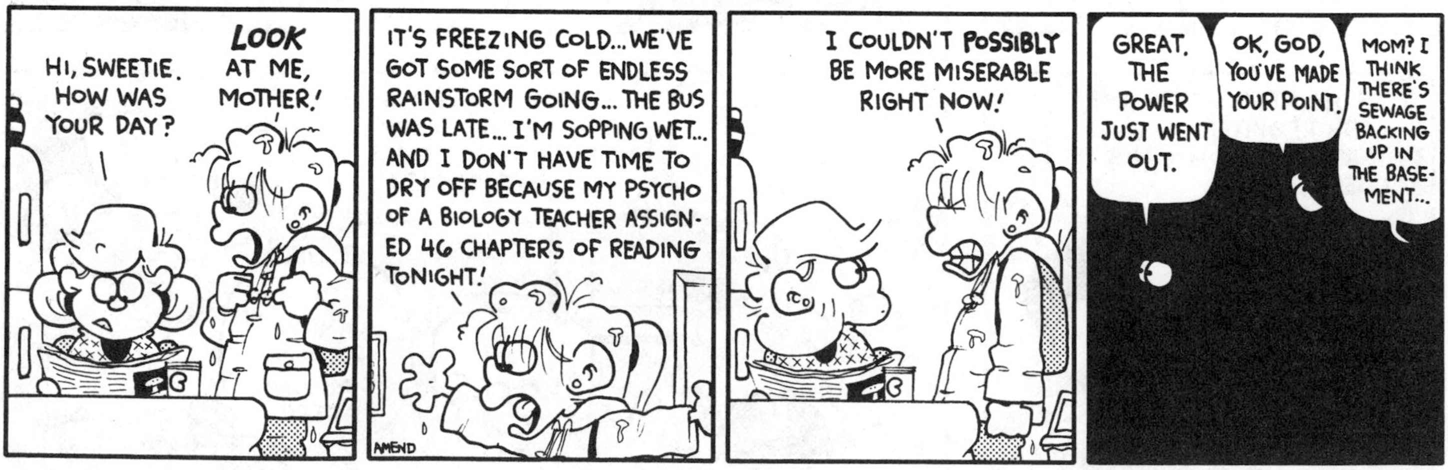
HI, SWEETIE. HOW WAS YOUR DAY?
LOOK AT ME, MOTHER!
IT'S FREEZING COLD... WE'VE GOT SOME SORT OF ENDLESS RAINSTORM GOING... THE BUS WAS LATE... I'M SOPPING WET... AND I DON'T HAVE TIME TO DRY OFF BECAUSE MY PSYCHO OF A BIOLOGY TEACHER ASSIGNED 46 CHAPTERS OF READING TONIGHT!
AMEND
I COULDN'T POSSIBLY BE MORE MISERABLE RIGHT NOW!
GREAT. THE POWER JUST WENT OUT.
OK, GOD, YOU'VE MADE YOUR POINT.
MOM? I THINK THERE'S SEWAGE BACKING UP IN THE BASEMENT...

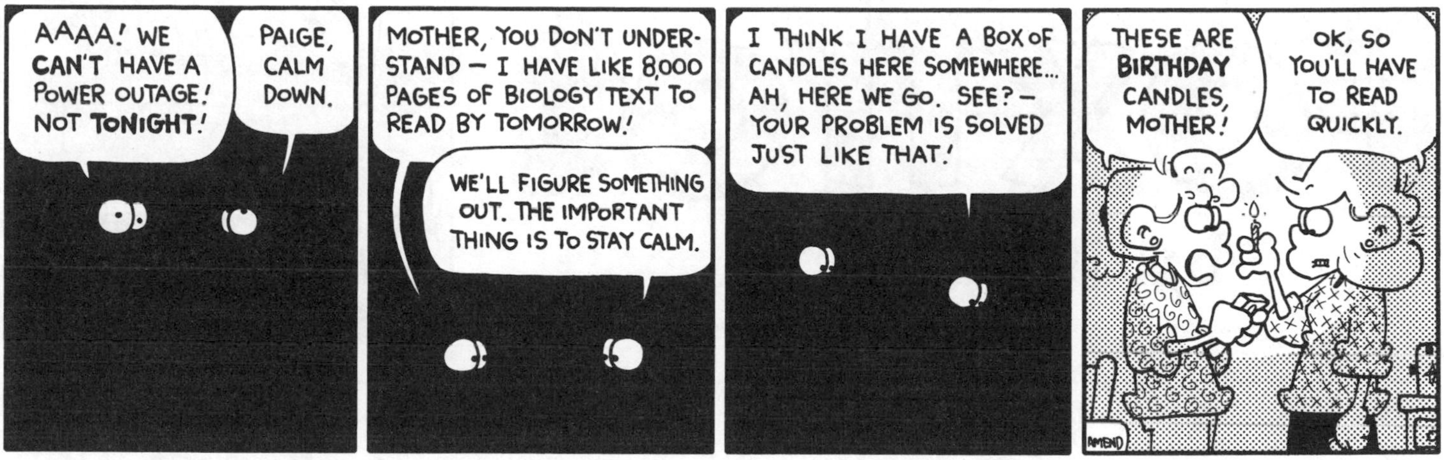
AAAA! WE CAN'T HAVE A POWER OUTAGE! NOT TONIGHT!
PAIGE, CALM DOWN.
MOTHER, YOU DON'T UNDERSTAND — I HAVE LIKE 8,000 PAGES OF BIOLOGY TEXT TO READ BY TOMORROW!
WE'LL FIGURE SOMETHING OUT. THE IMPORTANT THING IS TO STAY CALM.
I THINK I HAVE A BOX OF CANDLES HERE SOMEWHERE... AH, HERE WE GO. SEE? — YOUR PROBLEM IS SOLVED JUST LIKE THAT!
THESE ARE BIRTHDAY CANDLES, MOTHER!
OK, SO YOU'LL HAVE TO READ QUICKLY.
AMEND

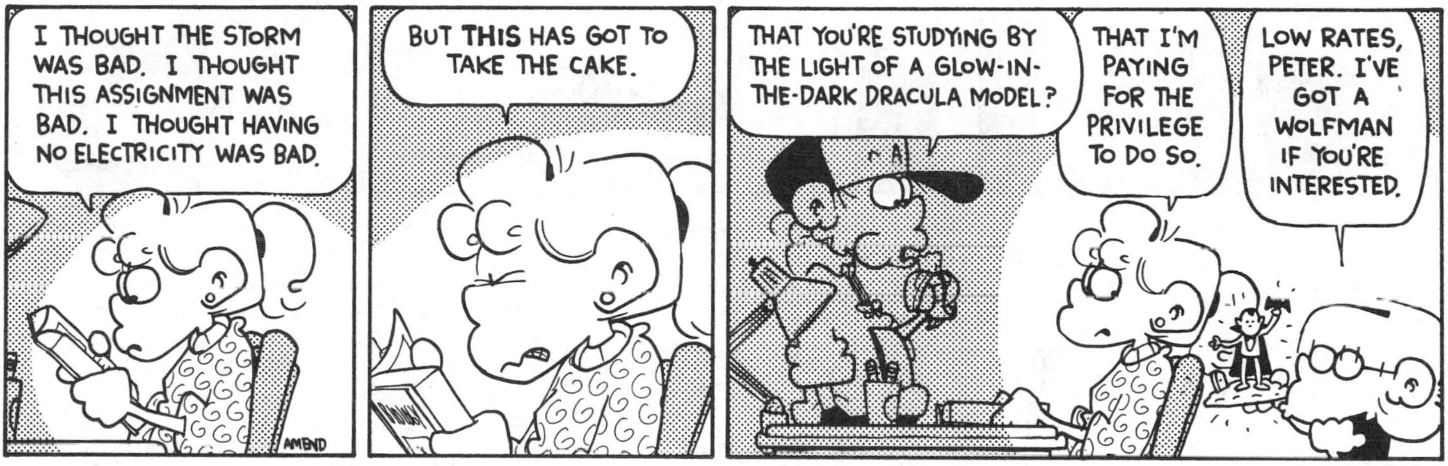
I THOUGHT THE STORM WAS BAD. I THOUGHT THIS ASSIGNMENT WAS BAD. I THOUGHT HAVING NO ELECTRICITY WAS BAD.
AMEND
BUT THIS HAS GOT TO TAKE THE CAKE.
THAT YOU'RE STUDYING BY THE LIGHT OF A GLOW-IN-THE-DARK DRACULA MODEL?
THAT I'M PAYING FOR THE PRIVILEGE TO DO SO.
LOW RATES, PETER. I'VE GOT A WOLFMAN IF YOU'RE INTERESTED.

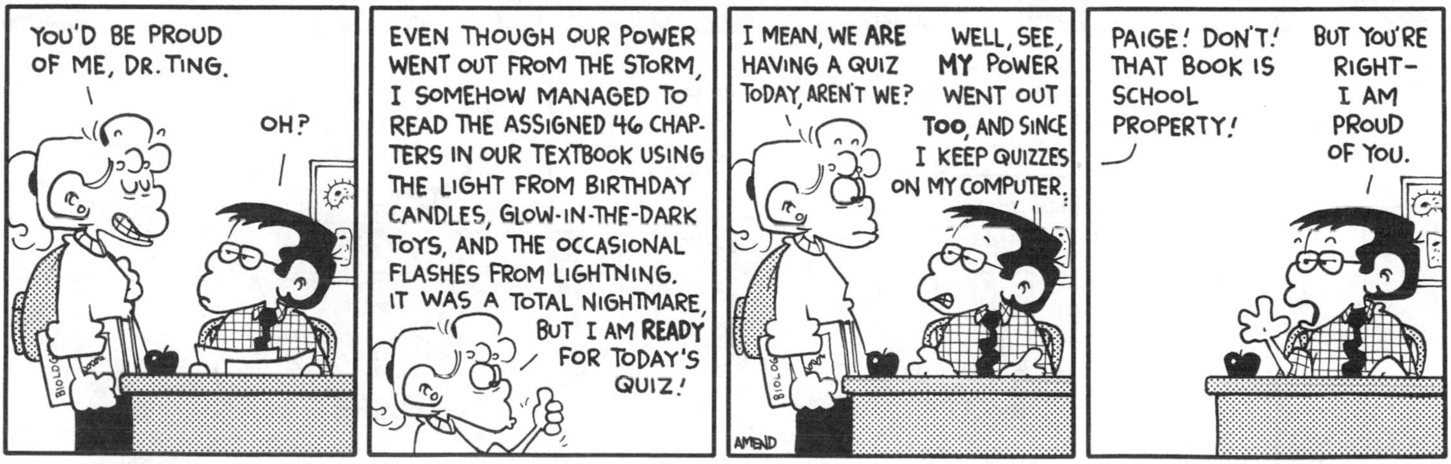
YOU'D BE PROUD OF ME, DR. TING.
OH?
EVEN THOUGH OUR POWER WENT OUT FROM THE STORM, I SOMEHOW MANAGED TO READ THE ASSIGNED 46 CHAPTERS IN OUR TEXTBOOK USING THE LIGHT FROM BIRTHDAY CANDLES, GLOW-IN-THE-DARK TOYS, AND THE OCCASIONAL FLASHES FROM LIGHTNING. IT WAS A TOTAL NIGHTMARE, BUT I AM READY FOR TODAY'S QUIZ!
I MEAN, WE ARE HAVING A QUIZ TODAY, AREN'T WE?
WELL, SEE, MY POWER WENT OUT TOO, AND SINCE I KEEP QUIZZES ON MY COMPUTER...
AMEND
PAIGE! DON'T! THAT BOOK IS SCHOOL PROPERTY!
BUT YOU'RE RIGHT— I AM PROUD OF YOU.

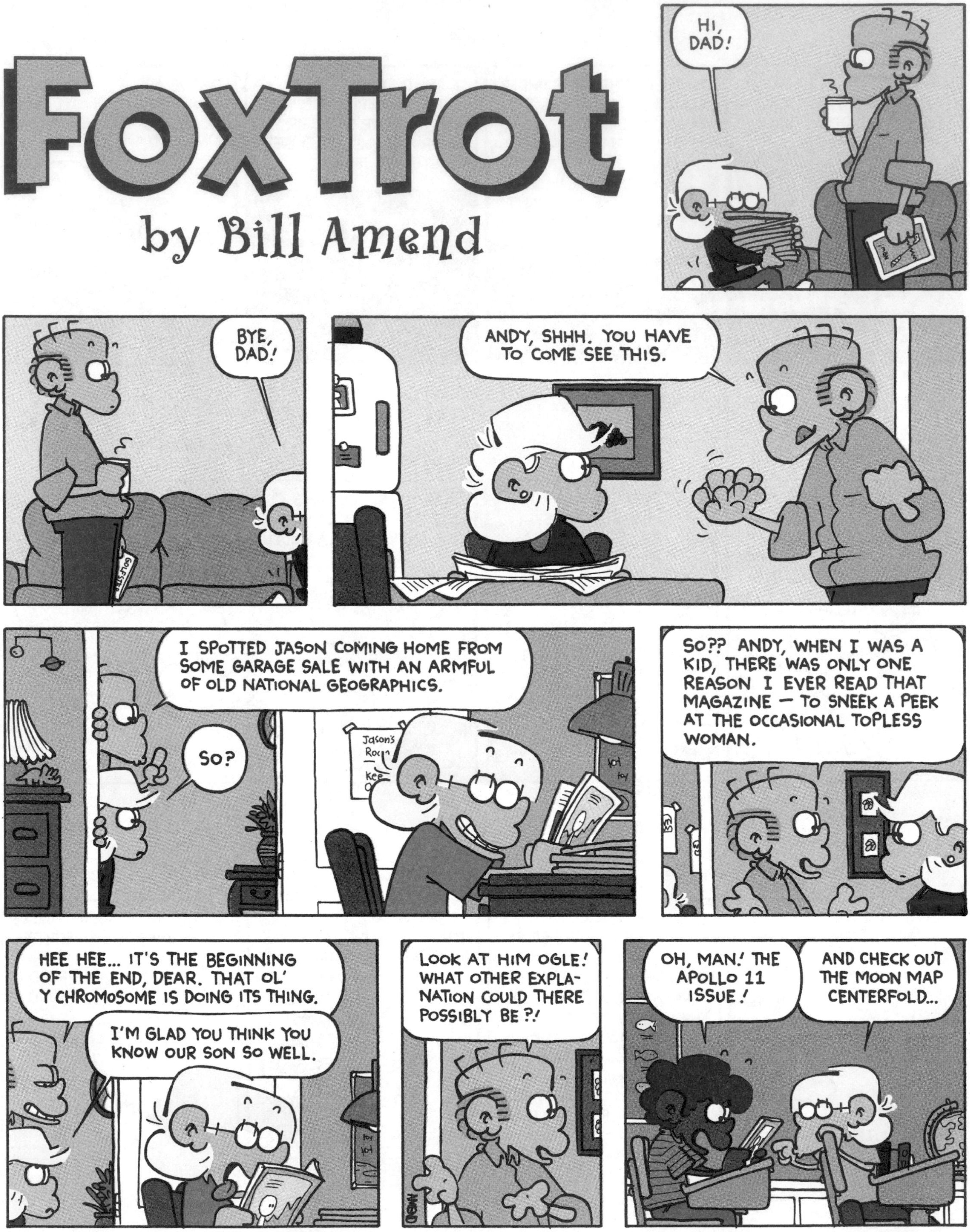
FoxTrot
by Bill Amend
HI, DAD!
BYE, DAD!
ANDY, SHHH. YOU HAVE TO COME SEE THIS.
I SPOTTED JASON COMING HOME FROM SOME GARAGE SALE WITH AN ARMFUL OF OLD NATIONAL GEOGRAPHICS.
SO?
SO?? ANDY, WHEN I WAS A KID, THERE WAS ONLY ONE REASON I EVER READ THAT MAGAZINE — TO SNEEK A PEEK AT THE OCCASIONAL TOPLESS WOMAN.
HEE HEE... IT'S THE BEGINNING OF THE END, DEAR. THAT OL' Y CHROMOSOME IS DOING ITS THING.
I'M GLAD YOU THINK YOU KNOW OUR SON SO WELL.
LOOK AT HIM OGLE! WHAT OTHER EXPLANATION COULD THERE POSSIBLY BE?!
OH, MAN! THE APOLLO 11 ISSUE!
AND CHECK OUT THE MOON MAP CENTERFOLD...

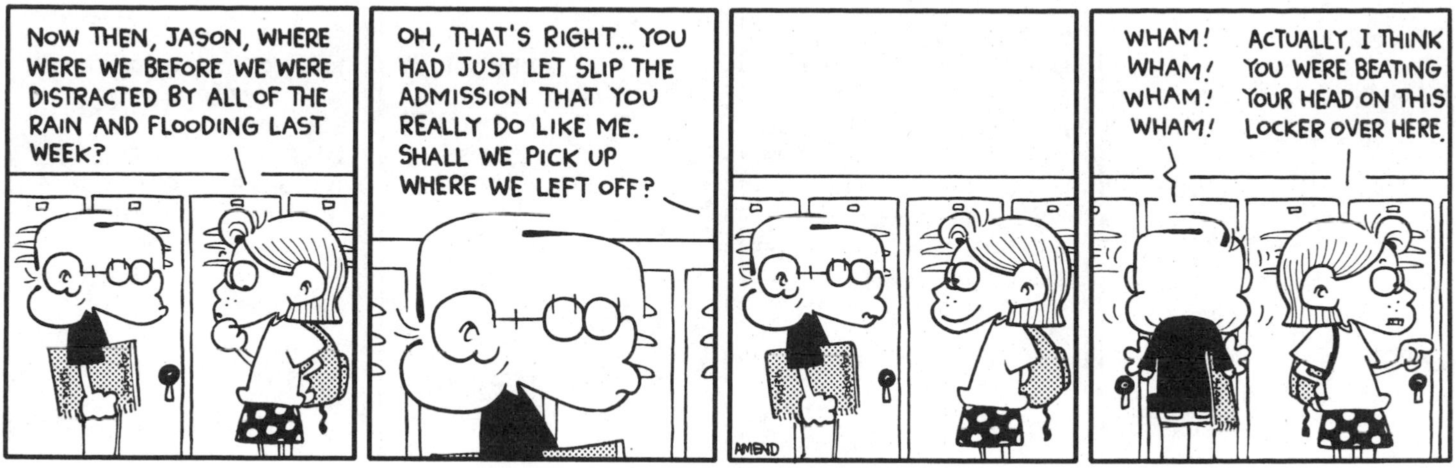
NOW THEN, JASON, WHERE WERE WE BEFORE WE WERE DISTRACTED BY ALL OF THE RAIN AND FLOODING LAST WEEK?
OH, THAT'S RIGHT... YOU HAD JUST LET SLIP THE ADMISSION THAT YOU REALLY DO LIKE ME. SHALL WE PICK UP WHERE WE LEFT OFF?
AMEND
WHAM! WHAM! WHAM! WHAM!
ACTUALLY, I THINK YOU WERE BEATING YOUR HEAD ON THIS LOCKER OVER HERE.

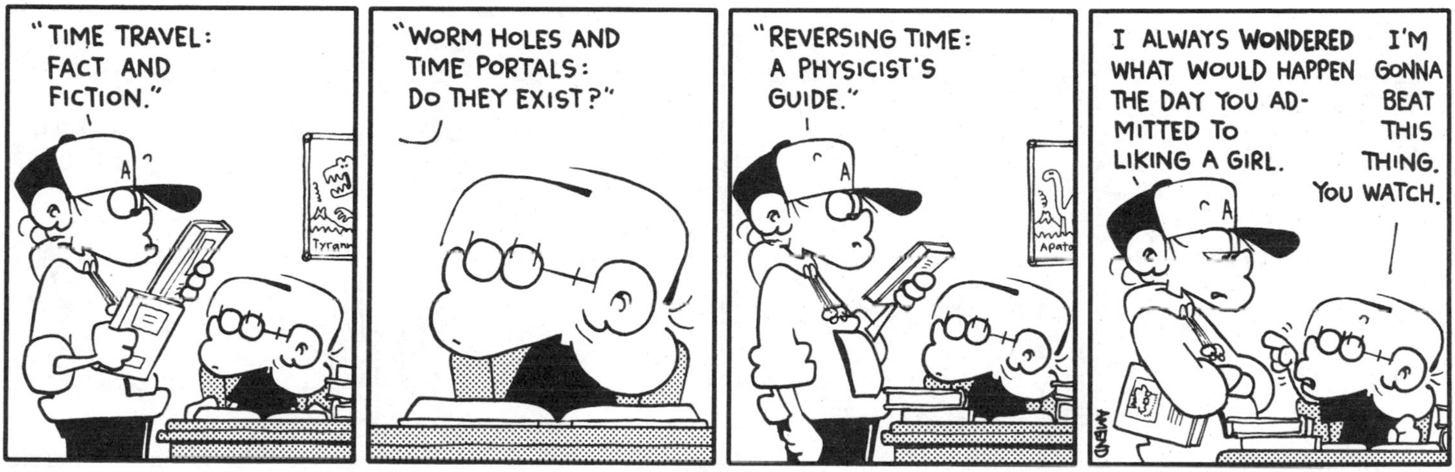
"TIME TRAVEL: FACT AND FICTION."
"WORM HOLES AND TIME PORTALS: DO THEY EXIST?"
"REVERSING TIME: A PHYSICIST'S GUIDE."
I ALWAYS WONDERED WHAT WOULD HAPPEN THE DAY YOU ADMITTED TO LIKING A GIRL.
I'M GONNA BEAT THIS THING. YOU WATCH.
AMEND

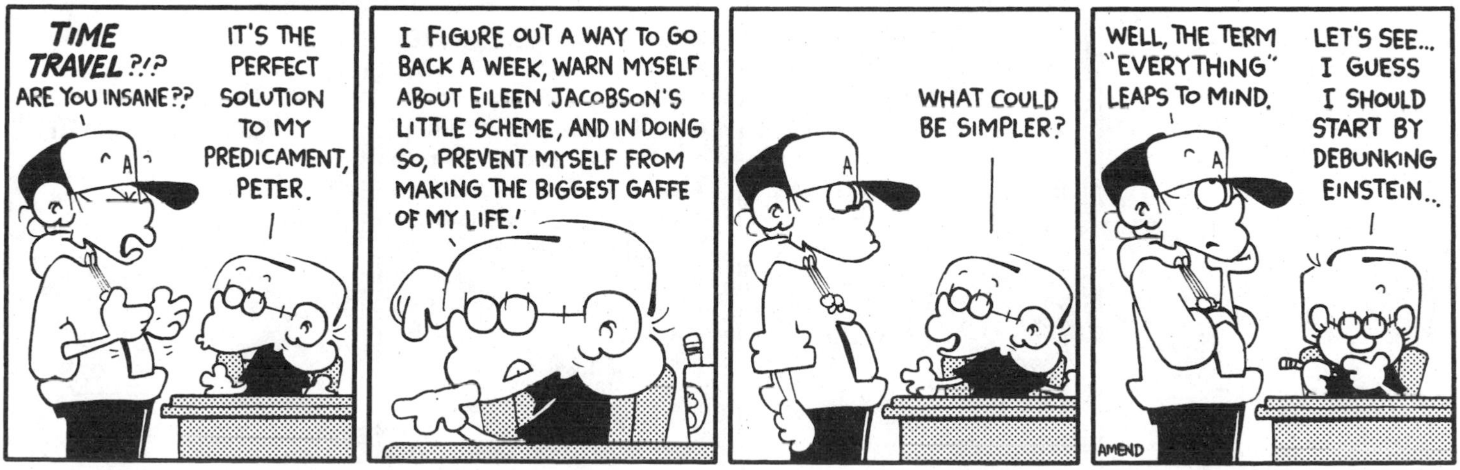
TIME TRAVEL?!? ARE YOU INSANE??
IT'S THE PERFECT SOLUTION TO MY PREDICAMENT, PETER.
I FIGURE OUT A WAY TO GO BACK A WEEK, WARN MYSELF ABOUT EILEEN JACOBSON'S LITTLE SCHEME, AND IN DOING SO, PREVENT MYSELF FROM MAKING THE BIGGEST GAFFE OF MY LIFE!
WHAT COULD BE SIMPLER?
WELL, THE TERM "EVERYTHING" LEAPS TO MIND.
LET'S SEE... I GUESS I SHOULD START BY DEBUNKING EINSTEIN...
AMEND

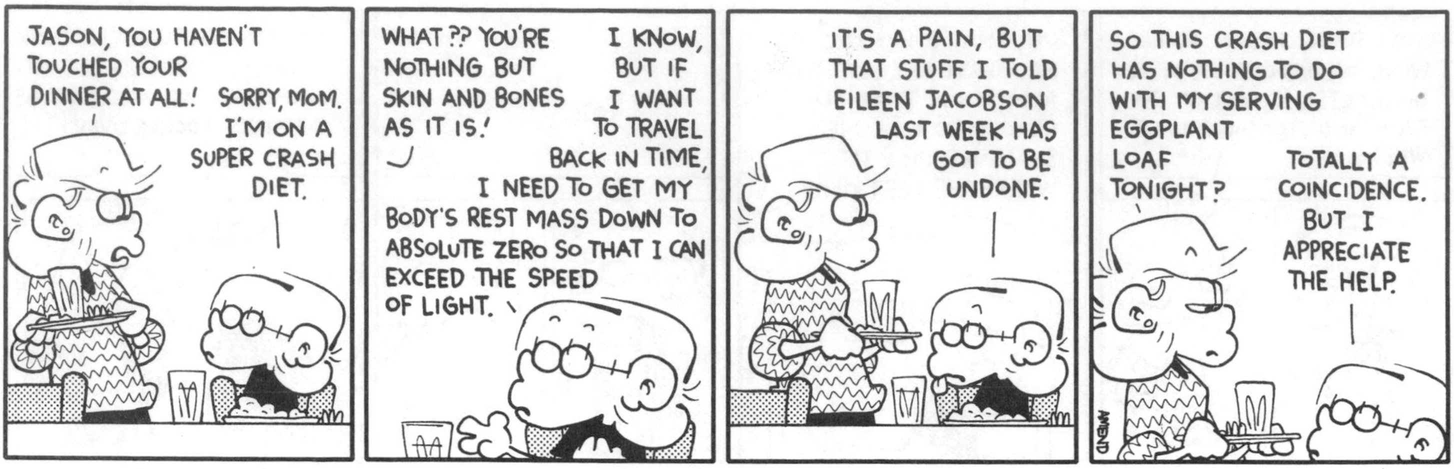
JASON, YOU HAVEN'T TOUCHED YOUR DINNER AT ALL!
SORRY, MOM. I'M ON A SUPER CRASH DIET.
WHAT?? YOU'RE NOTHING BUT SKIN AND BONES AS IT IS!
I KNOW, BUT IF I WANT TO TRAVEL BACK IN TIME, I NEED TO GET MY BODY'S REST MASS DOWN TO ABSOLUTE ZERO SO THAT I CAN EXCEED THE SPEED OF LIGHT.
IT'S A PAIN, BUT THAT STUFF I TOLD EILEEN JACOBSON LAST WEEK HAS GOT TO BE UNDONE.
SO THIS CRASH DIET HAS NOTHING TO DO WITH MY SERVING EGGPLANT LOAF TONIGHT?
TOTALLY A COINCIDENCE. BUT I APPRECIATE THE HELP.

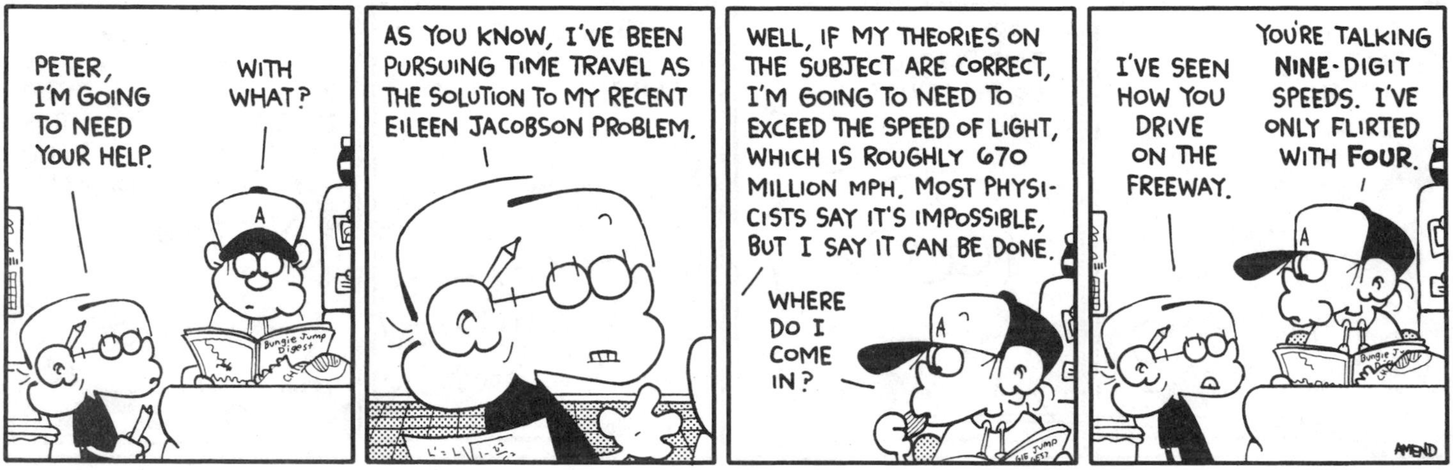
PETER, I'M GOING TO NEED YOUR HELP.
WITH WHAT?
AS YOU KNOW, I'VE BEEN PURSUING TIME TRAVEL AS THE SOLUTION TO MY RECENT EILEEN JACOBSON PROBLEM.
WELL, IF MY THEORIES ON THE SUBJECT ARE CORRECT, I'M GOING TO NEED TO EXCEED THE SPEED OF LIGHT, WHICH IS ROUGHLY 670 MILLION MPH. MOST PHYSICISTS SAY IT'S IMPOSSIBLE, BUT I SAY IT CAN BE DONE.
WHERE DO I COME IN?
I'VE SEEN HOW YOU DRIVE ON THE FREEWAY.
YOU'RE TALKING NINE-DIGIT SPEEDS. I'VE ONLY FLIRTED WITH FOUR.

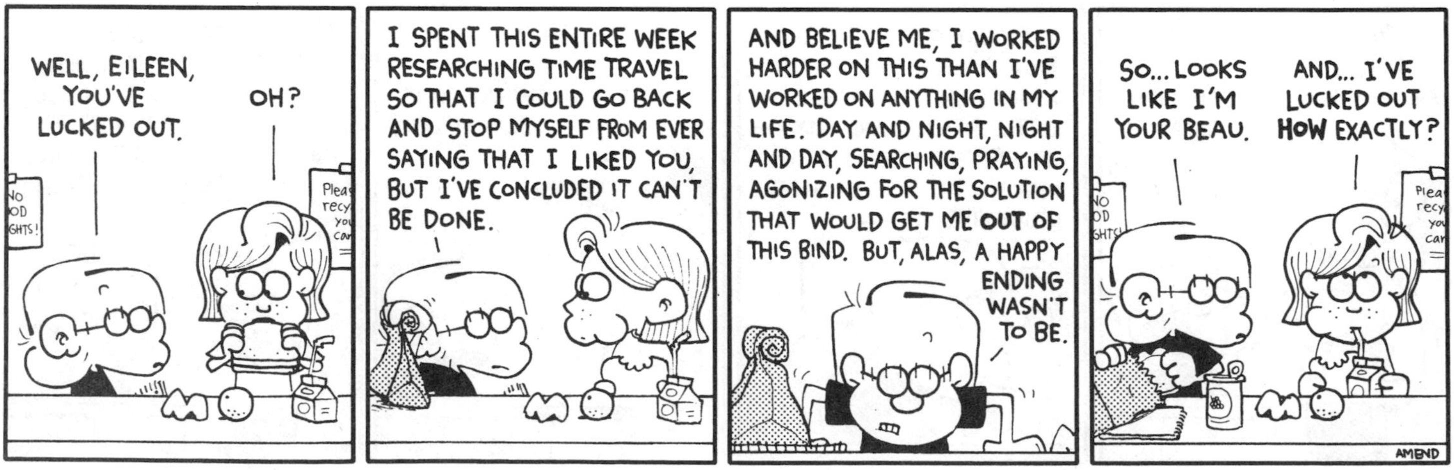
WELL, EILEEN, YOU'VE LUCKED OUT.
OH?
I SPENT THIS ENTIRE WEEK RESEARCHING TIME TRAVEL SO THAT I COULD GO BACK AND STOP MYSELF FROM EVER SAYING THAT I LIKED YOU, BUT I'VE CONCLUDED IT CAN'T BE DONE.
AND BELIEVE ME, I WORKED HARDER ON THIS THAN I'VE WORKED ON ANYTHING IN MY LIFE. DAY AND NIGHT, NIGHT AND DAY, SEARCHING, PRAYING, AGONIZING FOR THE SOLUTION THAT WOULD GET ME OUT OF THIS BIND. BUT, ALAS, A HAPPY ENDING WASN'T TO BE.
SO... LOOKS LIKE I'M YOUR BEAU.
AND... I'VE LUCKED OUT HOW EXACTLY?

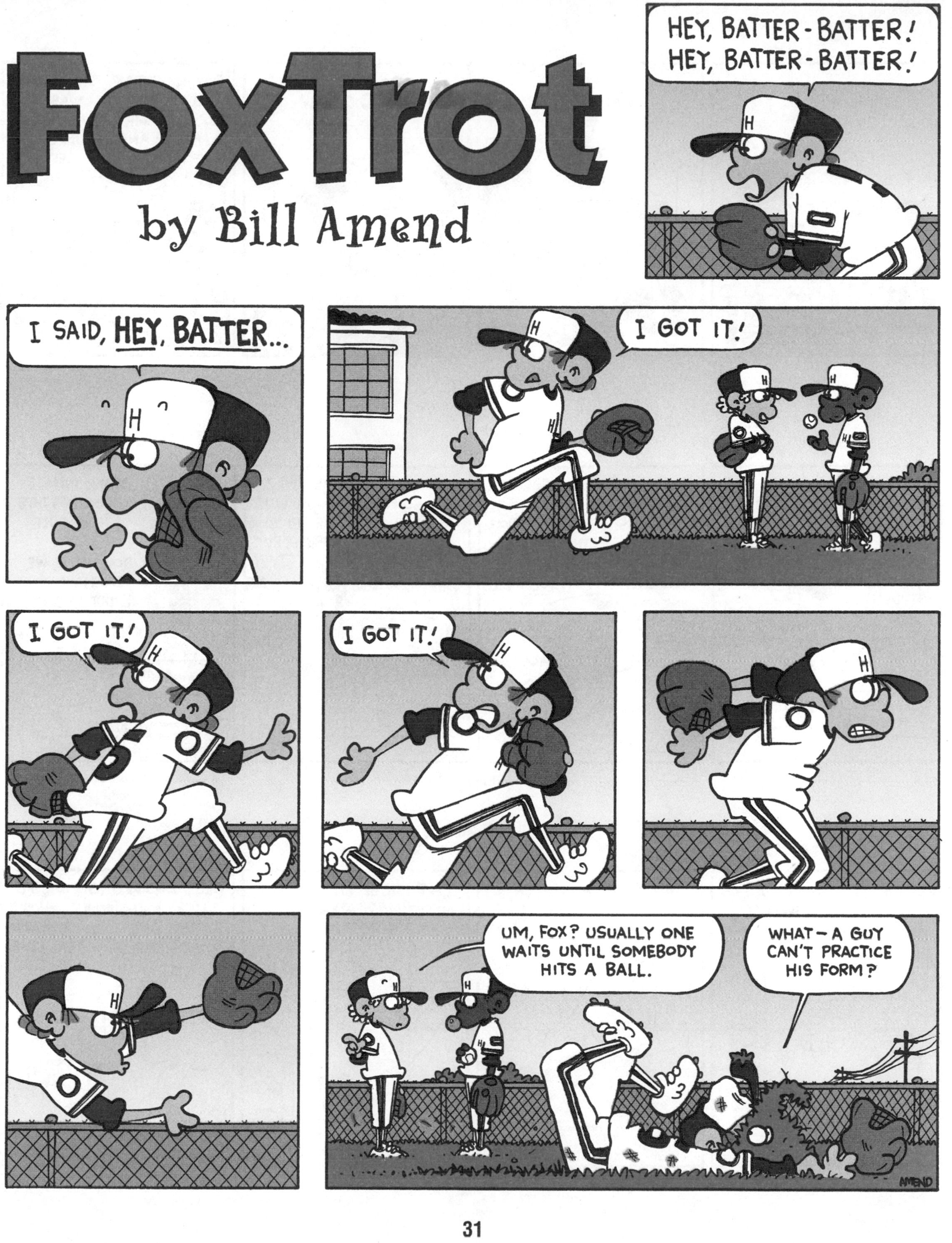
FoxTrot
by Bill Amend
HEY, BATTER-BATTER! HEY, BATTER-BATTER!
I SAID, HEY, BATTER...
I GOT IT!
I GOT IT!
I GOT IT!
UM, FOX? USUALLY ONE WAITS UNTIL SOMEBODY HITS A BALL.
WHAT—A GUY CAN'T PRACTICE HIS FORM?
AMEND

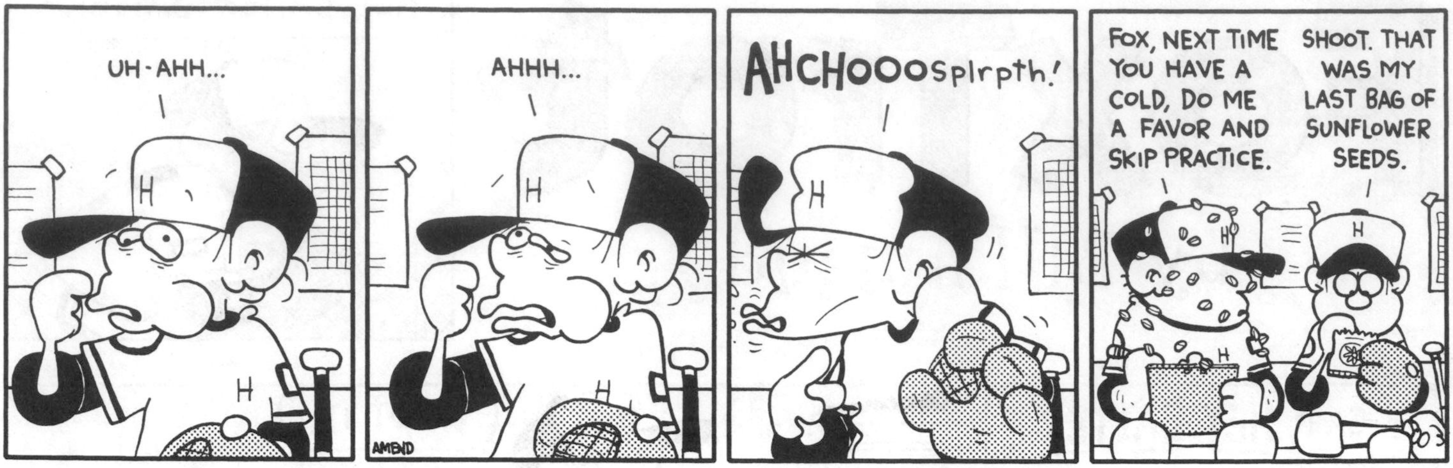
UH-AHH...
AHHH...
AHCHOOOsplrpth!
AMEND
FOX, NEXT TIME YOU HAVE A COLD, DO ME A FAVOR AND SKIP PRACTICE.
SHOOT. THAT WAS MY LAST BAG OF SUNFLOWER SEEDS.

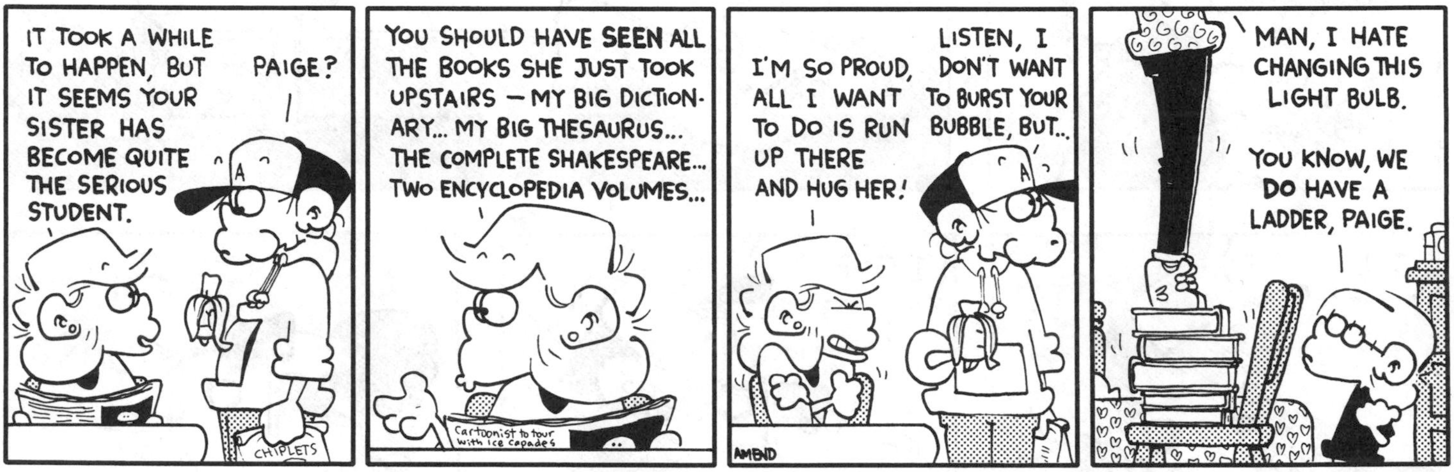
IT TOOK A WHILE TO HAPPEN, BUT IT SEEMS YOUR SISTER HAS BECOME QUITE THE SERIOUS STUDENT.
PAIGE?
CHIPLETS
YOU SHOULD HAVE SEEN ALL THE BOOKS SHE JUST TOOK UPSTAIRS — MY BIG DICTIONARY... MY BIG THESAURUS... THE COMPLETE SHAKESPEARE... TWO ENCYCLOPEDIA VOLUMES...
Cartoonist to tour with Ice Capades
I'M SO PROUD, ALL I WANT TO DO IS RUN UP THERE AND HUG HER!
LISTEN, I DON'T WANT TO BURST YOUR BUBBLE, BUT...
AMEND
MAN, I HATE CHANGING THIS LIGHT BULB.
YOU KNOW, WE DO HAVE A LADDER, PAIGE.

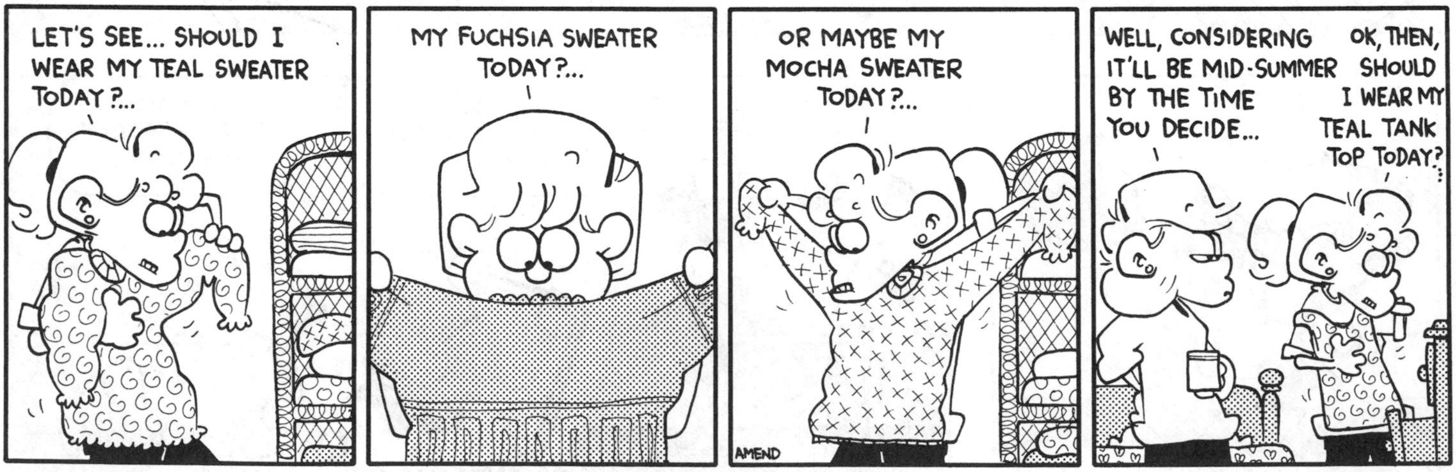
LET'S SEE... SHOULD I WEAR MY TEAL SWEATER TODAY?...
MY FUCHSIA SWEATER TODAY?...
OR MAYBE MY MOCHA SWEATER TODAY?...
AMEND
WELL, CONSIDERING IT'LL BE MID-SUMMER BY THE TIME YOU DECIDE...
OK, THEN, SHOULD I WEAR MY TEAL TANK TOP TODAY?

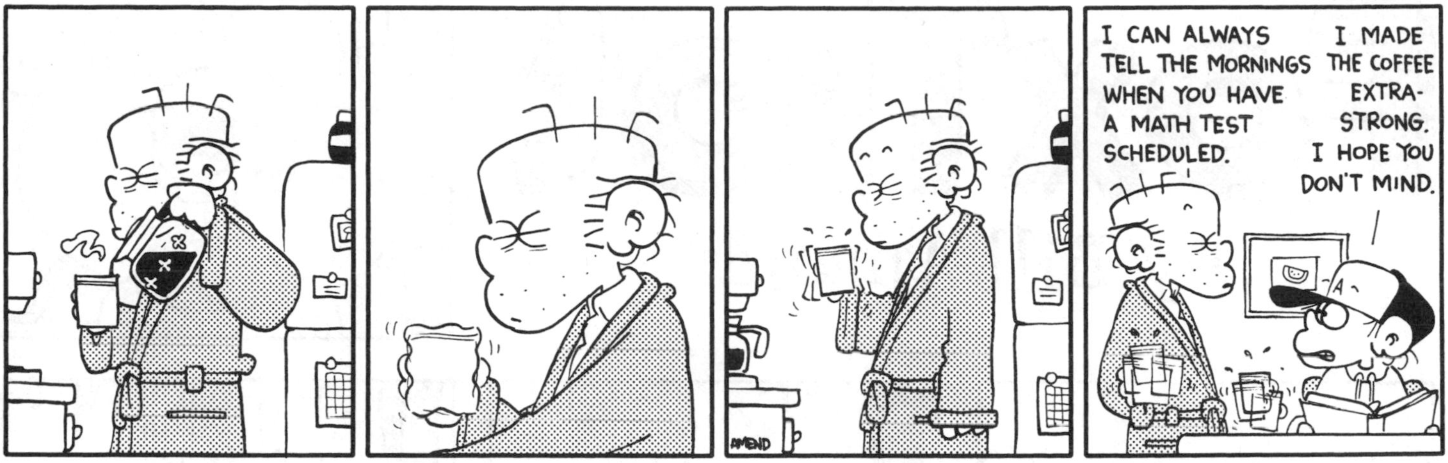
AMEND
I CAN ALWAYS TELL THE MORNINGS WHEN YOU HAVE A MATH TEST SCHEDULED.
I MADE THE COFFEE EXTRA-STRONG. I HOPE YOU DON'T MIND.

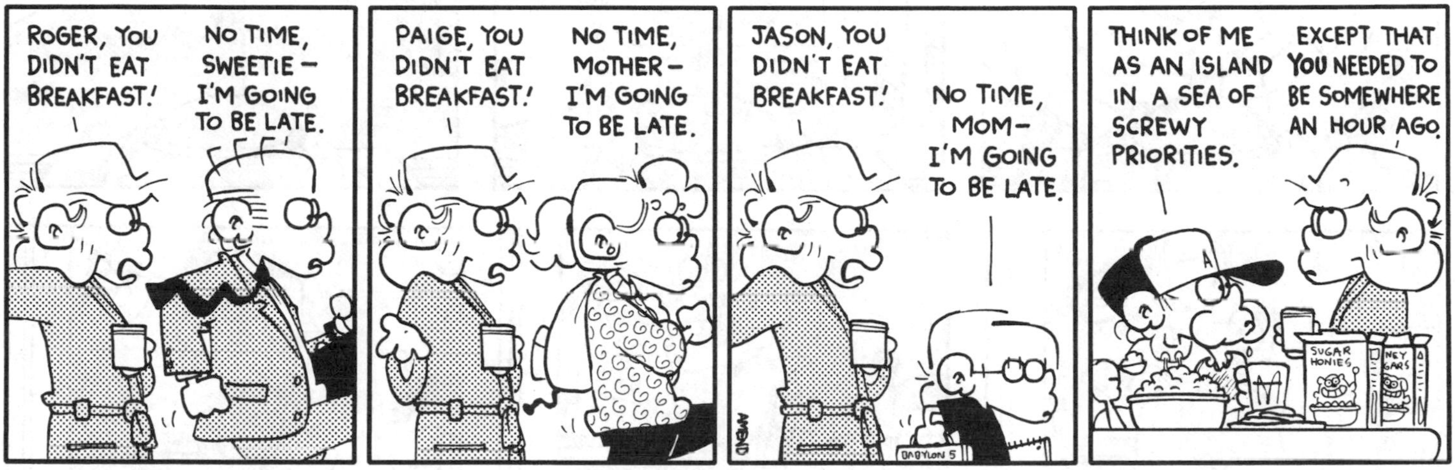
ROGER, YOU DIDN'T EAT BREAKFAST!
NO TIME, SWEETIE— I'M GOING TO BE LATE.
PAIGE, YOU DIDN'T EAT BREAKFAST!
NO TIME, MOTHER— I'M GOING TO BE LATE.
AMEND
JASON, YOU DIDN'T EAT BREAKFAST!
NO TIME, MOM— I'M GOING TO BE LATE.
BABYLON 5
THINK OF ME AS AN ISLAND IN A SEA OF SCREWY PRIORITIES.
EXCEPT THAT YOU NEEDED TO BE SOMEWHERE AN HOUR AGO.
SUGAR HONIES

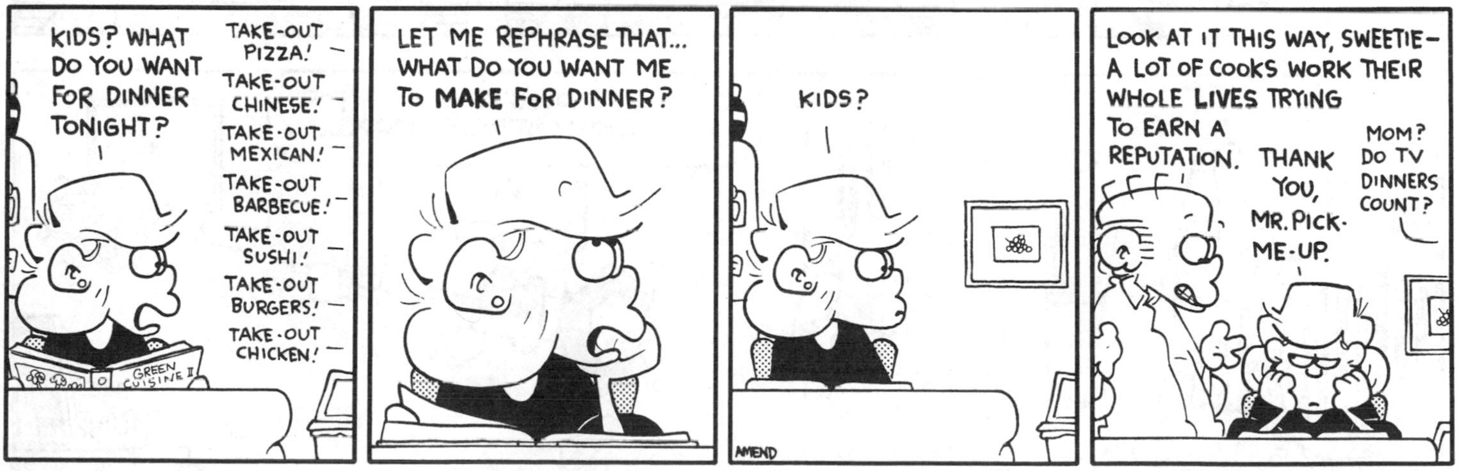
KIDS? WHAT DO YOU WANT FOR DINNER TONIGHT?
TAKE-OUT PIZZA!
TAKE-OUT CHINESE!
TAKE-OUT MEXICAN!
TAKE-OUT BARBECUE!
TAKE-OUT SUSHI!
TAKE-OUT BURGERS!
TAKE-OUT CHICKEN!
GREEN CUISINE II
LET ME REPHRASE THAT... WHAT DO YOU WANT ME TO MAKE FOR DINNER?
KIDS?
AMEND
LOOK AT IT THIS WAY, SWEETIE— A LOT OF COOKS WORK THEIR WHOLE LIVES TRYING TO EARN A REPUTATION.
THANK YOU, MR. PICK-ME-UP.
MOM? DO TV DINNERS COUNT?

FoxTrot
by Bill Amend

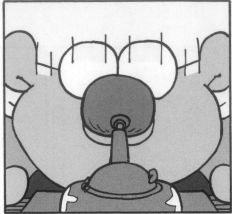

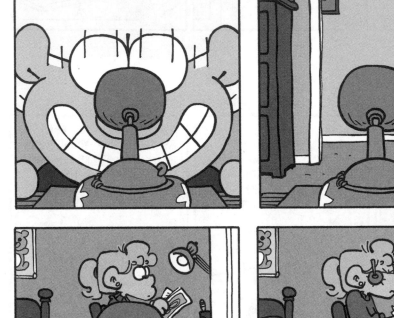

I REALLY SHOULD'VE SPRUNG FOR THE RADIO-CONTROLLED MODEL.

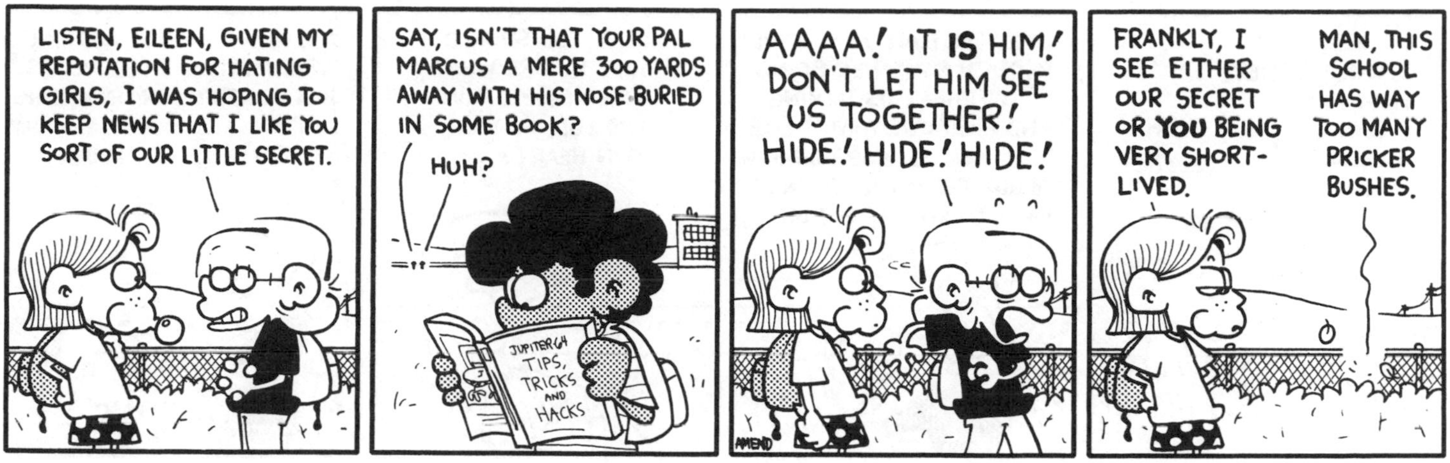
LISTEN, EILEEN, GIVEN MY REPUTATION FOR HATING GIRLS, I WAS HOPING TO KEEP NEWS THAT I LIKE YOU SORT OF OUR LITTLE SECRET.
SAY, ISN'T THAT YOUR PAL MARCUS A MERE 300 YARDS AWAY WITH HIS NOSE BURIED IN SOME BOOK?
HUH?
JUPITER 64 TIPS, TRICKS AND HACKS
AAAA! IT **IS** HIM! DON'T LET HIM SEE US TOGETHER! HIDE! HIDE! HIDE!
AMEND
FRANKLY, I SEE EITHER OUR SECRET OR **YOU** BEING VERY SHORT-LIVED.
MAN, THIS SCHOOL HAS WAY TOO MANY PRICKER BUSHES.

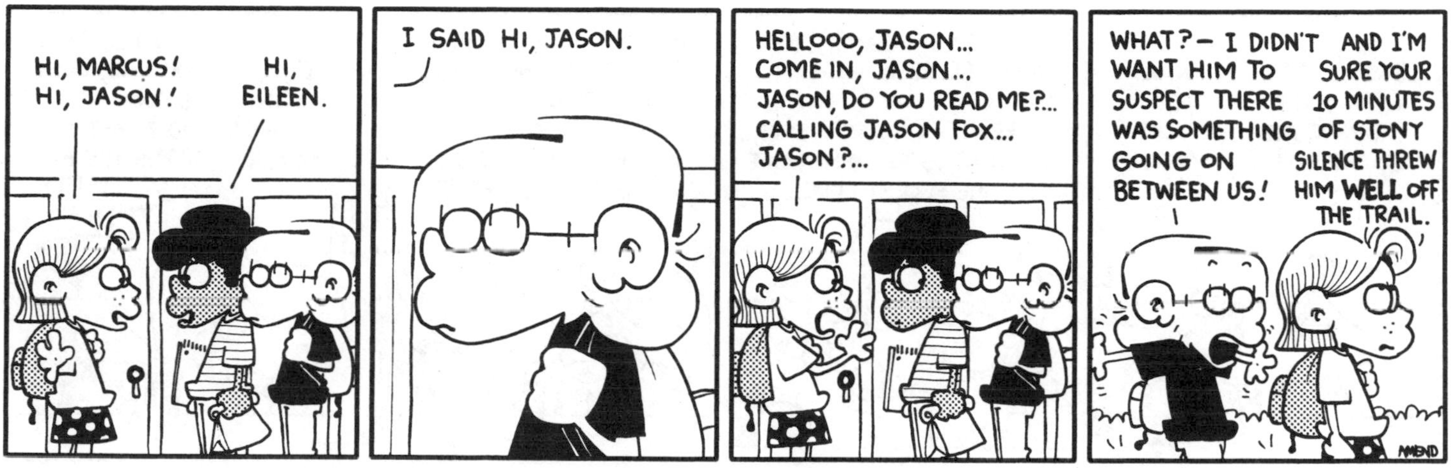
HI, MARCUS! HI, JASON!
HI, EILEEN.
I SAID HI, JASON.
HELLOOO, JASON... COME IN, JASON... JASON, DO YOU READ ME?... CALLING JASON FOX... JASON?...
WHAT?– I DIDN'T WANT HIM TO SUSPECT THERE WAS SOMETHING GOING ON BETWEEN US!
AND I'M SURE YOUR 10 MINUTES OF STONY SILENCE THREW HIM **WELL** OFF THE TRAIL.
AMEND

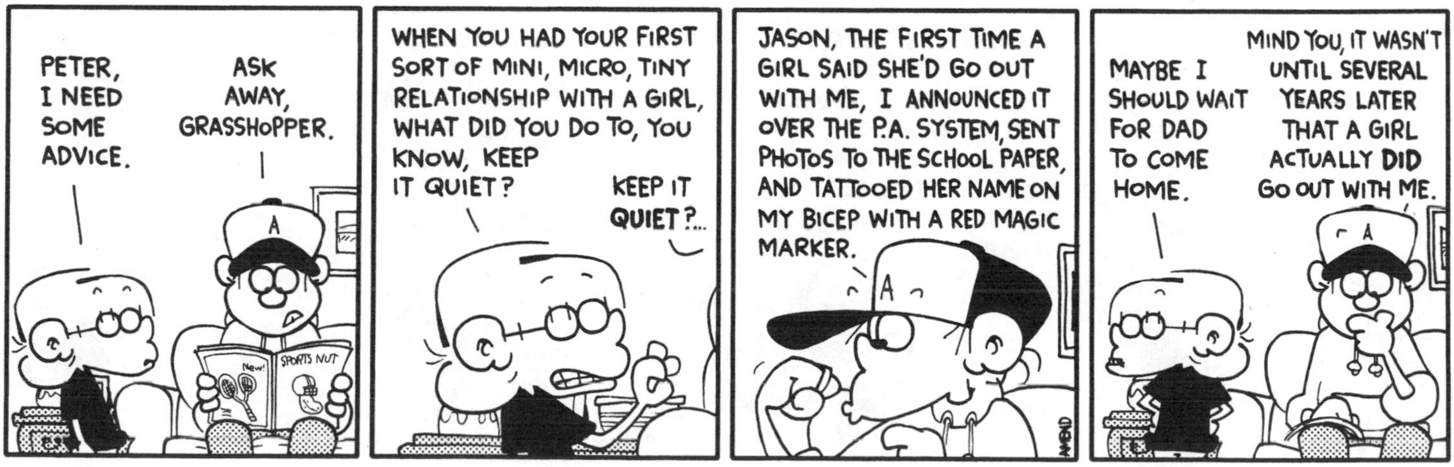
PETER, I NEED SOME ADVICE.
ASK AWAY, GRASSHOPPER.
SPORTS NUT
WHEN YOU HAD YOUR FIRST SORT OF MINI, MICRO, TINY RELATIONSHIP WITH A GIRL, WHAT DID YOU DO TO, YOU KNOW, KEEP IT QUIET?
KEEP IT **QUIET**?...
JASON, THE FIRST TIME A GIRL SAID SHE'D GO OUT WITH ME, I ANNOUNCED IT OVER THE P.A. SYSTEM, SENT PHOTOS TO THE SCHOOL PAPER, AND TATTOOED HER NAME ON MY BICEP WITH A RED MAGIC MARKER.
AMEND
MAYBE I SHOULD WAIT FOR DAD TO COME HOME.
MIND YOU, IT WASN'T UNTIL SEVERAL YEARS LATER THAT A GIRL ACTUALLY **DID** GO OUT WITH ME.

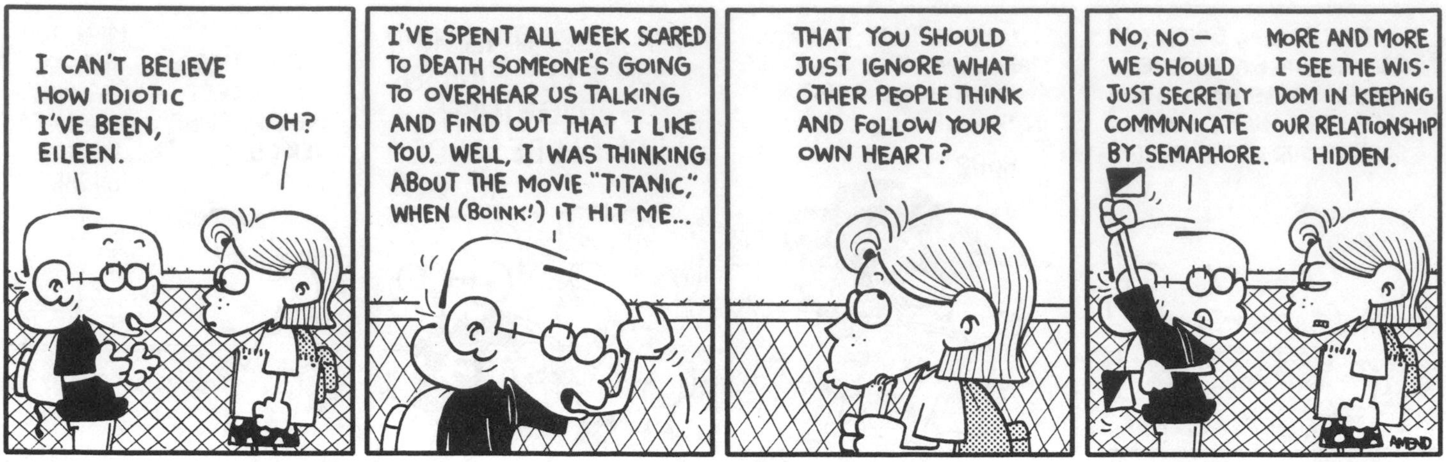
I CAN'T BELIEVE HOW IDIOTIC I'VE BEEN, EILEEN.
OH?
I'VE SPENT ALL WEEK SCARED TO DEATH SOMEONE'S GOING TO OVERHEAR US TALKING AND FIND OUT THAT I LIKE YOU. WELL, I WAS THINKING ABOUT THE MOVIE "TITANIC," WHEN (BOINK!) IT HIT ME...
THAT YOU SHOULD JUST IGNORE WHAT OTHER PEOPLE THINK AND FOLLOW YOUR OWN HEART?
NO, NO – WE SHOULD JUST SECRETLY COMMUNICATE BY SEMAPHORE.
MORE AND MORE I SEE THE WISDOM IN KEEPING OUR RELATIONSHIP HIDDEN.
AMEND

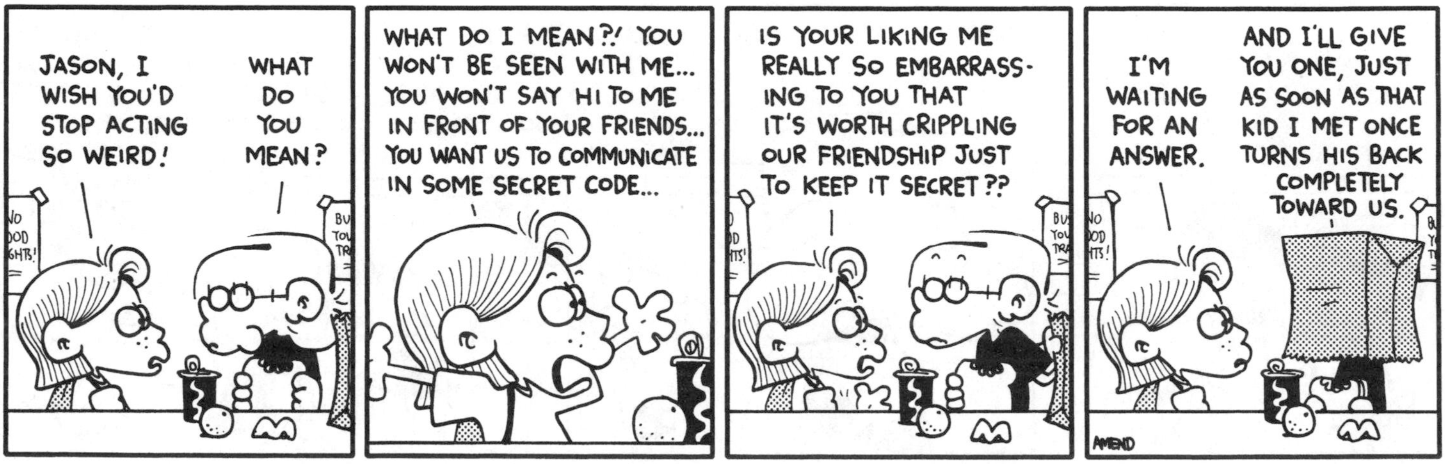
JASON, I WISH YOU'D STOP ACTING SO WEIRD!
WHAT DO YOU MEAN?
WHAT DO I MEAN?!! YOU WON'T BE SEEN WITH ME... YOU WON'T SAY HI TO ME IN FRONT OF YOUR FRIENDS... YOU WANT US TO COMMUNICATE IN SOME SECRET CODE...
IS YOUR LIKING ME REALLY SO EMBARRASSING TO YOU THAT IT'S WORTH CRIPPLING OUR FRIENDSHIP JUST TO KEEP IT SECRET??
I'M WAITING FOR AN ANSWER.
AND I'LL GIVE YOU ONE, JUST AS SOON AS THAT KID I MET ONCE TURNS HIS BACK COMPLETELY TOWARD US.
AMEND

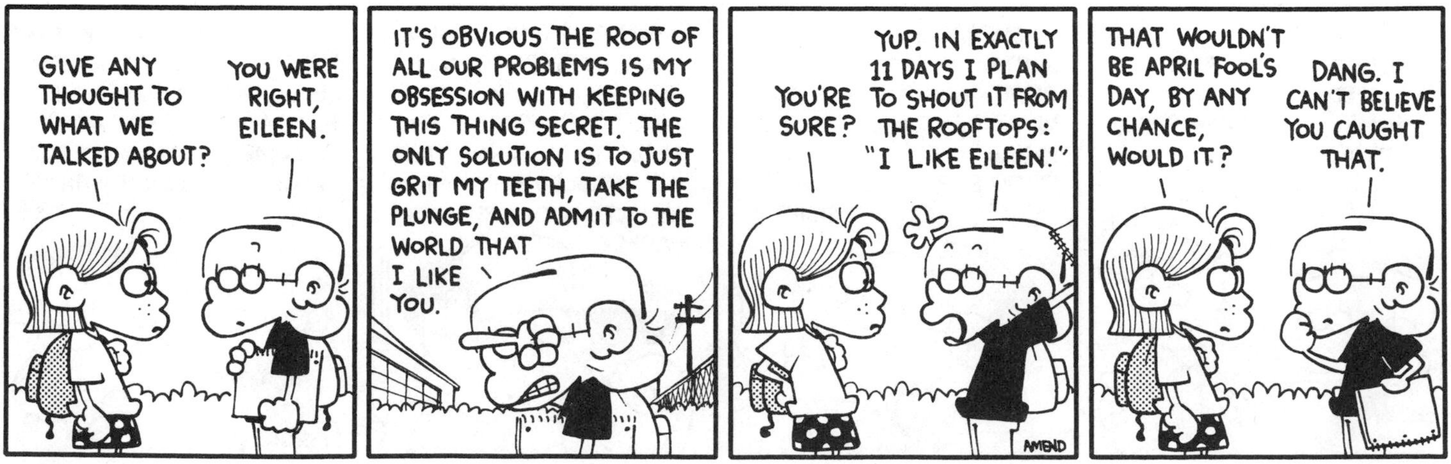
GIVE ANY THOUGHT TO WHAT WE TALKED ABOUT?
YOU WERE RIGHT, EILEEN.
IT'S OBVIOUS THE ROOT OF ALL OUR PROBLEMS IS MY OBSESSION WITH KEEPING THIS THING SECRET. THE ONLY SOLUTION IS TO JUST GRIT MY TEETH, TAKE THE PLUNGE, AND ADMIT TO THE WORLD THAT I LIKE YOU.
YOU'RE SURE?
YUP. IN EXACTLY 11 DAYS I PLAN TO SHOUT IT FROM THE ROOFTOPS: "I LIKE EILEEN!"
AMEND
THAT WOULDN'T BE APRIL FOOL'S DAY, BY ANY CHANCE, WOULD IT?
DANG. I CAN'T BELIEVE YOU CAUGHT THAT.

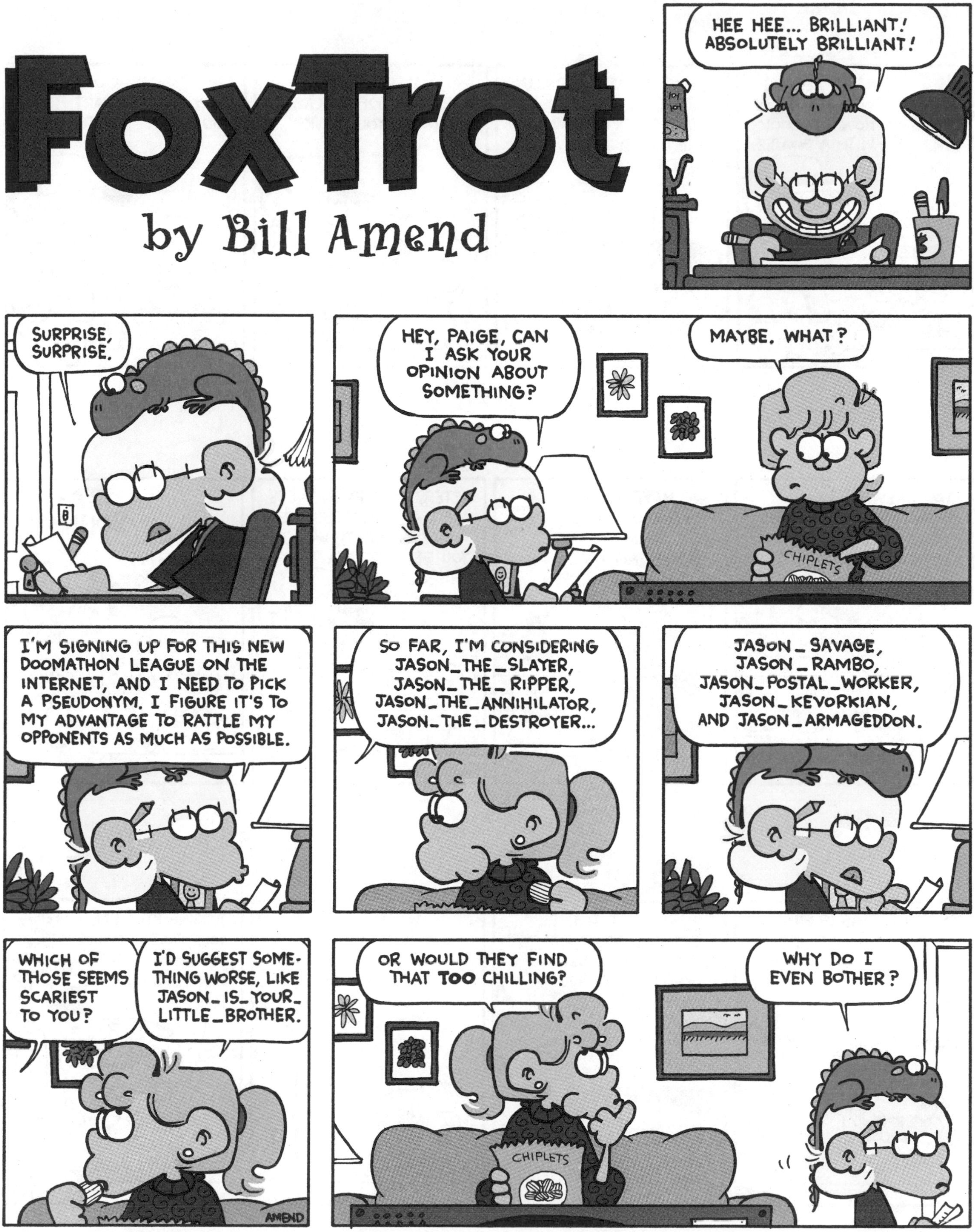
FoxTrot
by Bill Amend
HEE HEE... BRILLIANT! ABSOLUTELY BRILLIANT!
SURPRISE, SURPRISE.
HEY, PAIGE, CAN I ASK YOUR OPINION ABOUT SOMETHING?
MAYBE. WHAT?
CHIPLETS
I'M SIGNING UP FOR THIS NEW DOOMATHON LEAGUE ON THE INTERNET, AND I NEED TO PICK A PSEUDONYM. I FIGURE IT'S TO MY ADVANTAGE TO RATTLE MY OPPONENTS AS MUCH AS POSSIBLE.
SO FAR, I'M CONSIDERING JASON_THE_SLAYER, JASON_THE_RIPPER, JASON_THE_ANNIHILATOR, JASON_THE_DESTROYER...
JASON_SAVAGE, JASON_RAMBO, JASON_POSTAL_WORKER, JASON_KEVORKIAN, AND JASON_ARMAGEDDON.
WHICH OF THOSE SEEMS SCARIEST TO YOU?
I'D SUGGEST SOMETHING WORSE, LIKE JASON_IS_YOUR_LITTLE_BROTHER.
AMEND
OR WOULD THEY FIND THAT **TOO** CHILLING?
WHY DO I EVEN BOTHER?
CHIPLETS

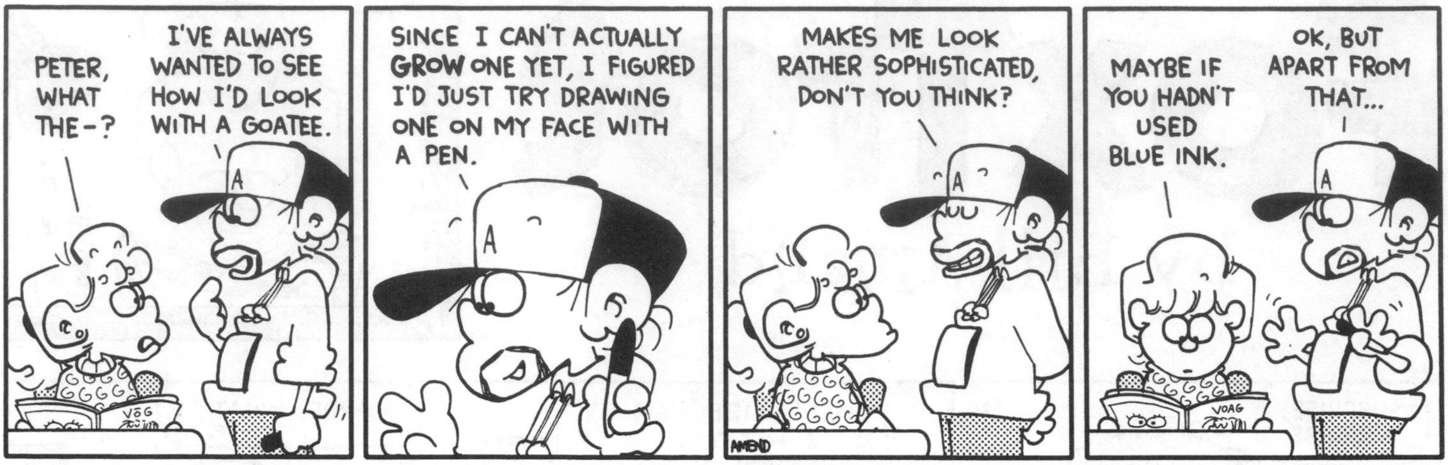
PETER, WHAT THE-?
I'VE ALWAYS WANTED TO SEE HOW I'D LOOK WITH A GOATEE.
SINCE I CAN'T ACTUALLY GROW ONE YET, I FIGURED I'D JUST TRY DRAWING ONE ON MY FACE WITH A PEN.
MAKES ME LOOK RATHER SOPHISTICATED, DON'T YOU THINK?
MAYBE IF YOU HADN'T USED BLUE INK.
OK, BUT APART FROM THAT...
AMEND

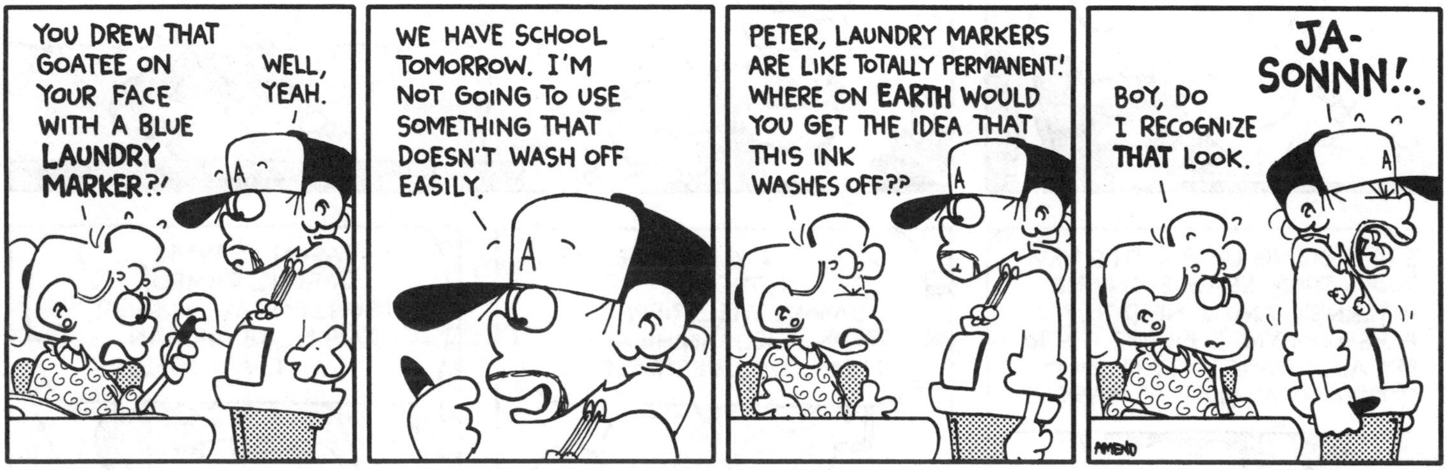
YOU DREW THAT GOATEE ON YOUR FACE WITH A BLUE LAUNDRY MARKER?!
WELL, YEAH.
WE HAVE SCHOOL TOMORROW. I'M NOT GOING TO USE SOMETHING THAT DOESN'T WASH OFF EASILY.
PETER, LAUNDRY MARKERS ARE LIKE TOTALLY PERMANENT! WHERE ON EARTH WOULD YOU GET THE IDEA THAT THIS INK WASHES OFF??
BOY, DO I RECOGNIZE THAT LOOK.
JA-SONNN!..
AMEND

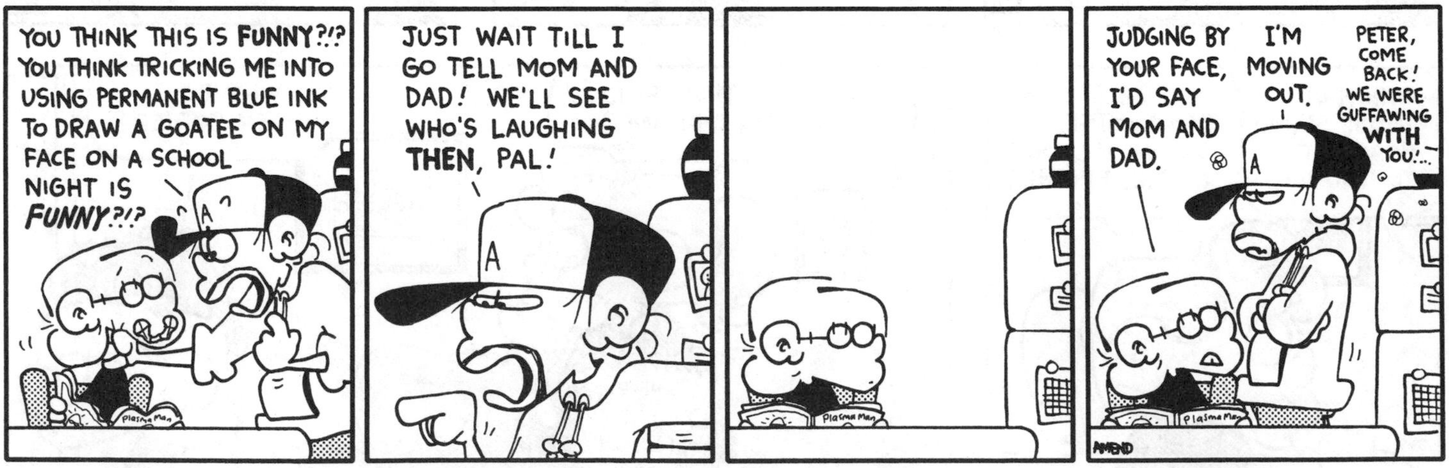
YOU THINK THIS IS FUNNY?!? YOU THINK TRICKING ME INTO USING PERMANENT BLUE INK TO DRAW A GOATEE ON MY FACE ON A SCHOOL NIGHT IS FUNNY?!?
JUST WAIT TILL I GO TELL MOM AND DAD! WE'LL SEE WHO'S LAUGHING THEN, PAL!
JUDGING BY YOUR FACE, I'D SAY MOM AND DAD.
I'M MOVING OUT.
PETER, COME BACK! WE WERE GUFFAWING WITH YOU!..
AMEND

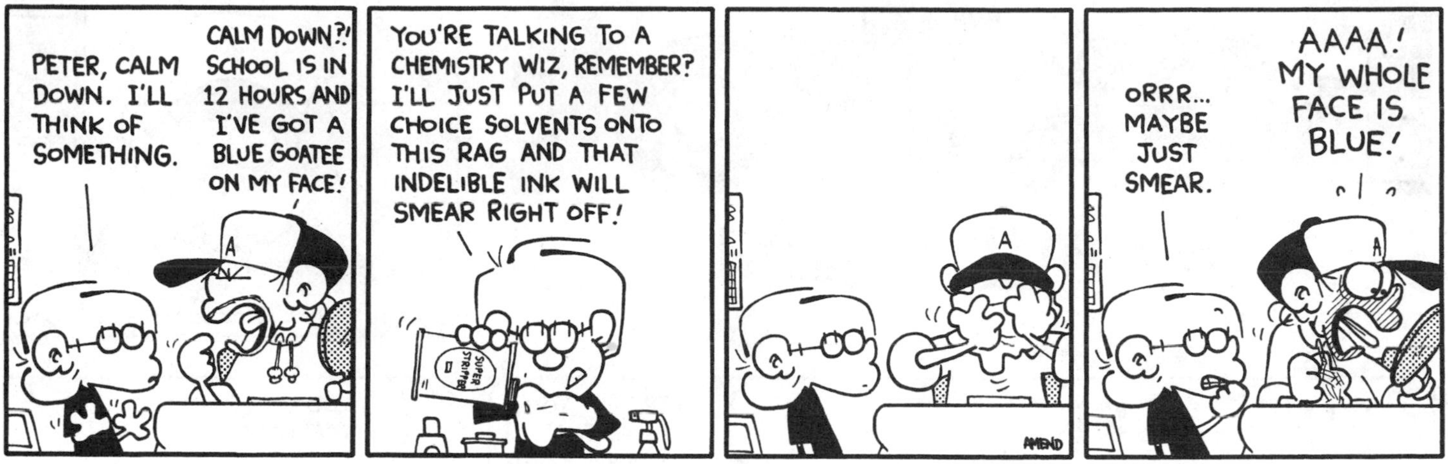
PETER, CALM DOWN. I'LL THINK OF SOMETHING.
CALM DOWN?! SCHOOL IS IN 12 HOURS AND I'VE GOT A BLUE GOATEE ON MY FACE!
YOU'RE TALKING TO A CHEMISTRY WIZ, REMEMBER? I'LL JUST PUT A FEW CHOICE SOLVENTS ONTO THIS RAG AND THAT INDELIBLE INK WILL SMEAR RIGHT OFF!
SUPER STRIPPER
ORRR... MAYBE JUST SMEAR.
AAAA! MY WHOLE FACE IS BLUE!
AMEND

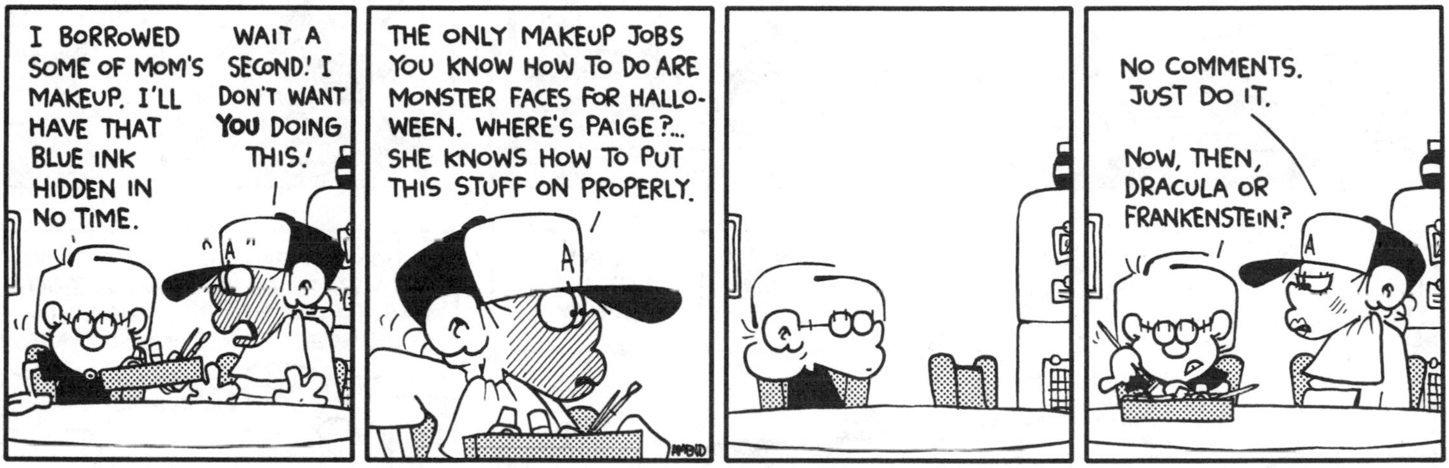
I BORROWED SOME OF MOM'S MAKEUP. I'LL HAVE THAT BLUE INK HIDDEN IN NO TIME.
WAIT A SECOND! I DON'T WANT **YOU** DOING THIS!
THE ONLY MAKEUP JOBS YOU KNOW HOW TO DO ARE MONSTER FACES FOR HALLOWEEN. WHERE'S PAIGE?... SHE KNOWS HOW TO PUT THIS STUFF ON PROPERLY.
AMEND
NO COMMENTS. JUST DO IT.
NOW, THEN, DRACULA OR FRANKENSTEIN?

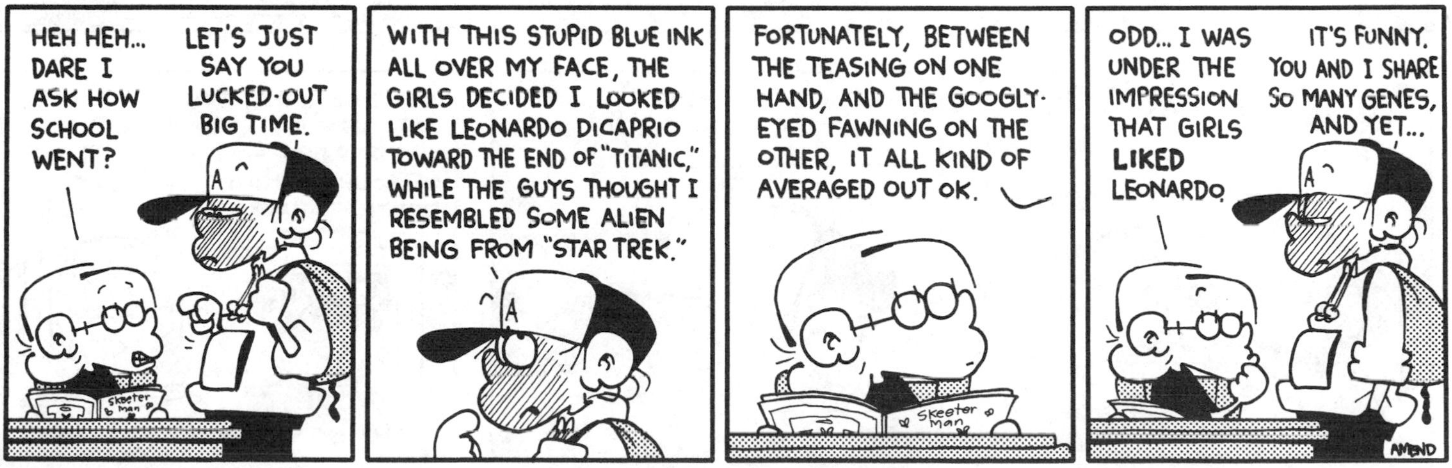
HEH HEH... DARE I ASK HOW SCHOOL WENT?
LET'S JUST SAY YOU LUCKED-OUT BIG TIME.
WITH THIS STUPID BLUE INK ALL OVER MY FACE, THE GIRLS DECIDED I LOOKED LIKE LEONARDO DICAPRIO TOWARD THE END OF "TITANIC," WHILE THE GUYS THOUGHT I RESEMBLED SOME ALIEN BEING FROM "STAR TREK."
FORTUNATELY, BETWEEN THE TEASING ON ONE HAND, AND THE GOOGLY-EYED FAWNING ON THE OTHER, IT ALL KIND OF AVERAGED OUT OK.
Skeeter Man
ODD... I WAS UNDER THE IMPRESSION THAT GIRLS **LIKED** LEONARDO.
IT'S FUNNY. YOU AND I SHARE SO MANY GENES, AND YET...
AMEND

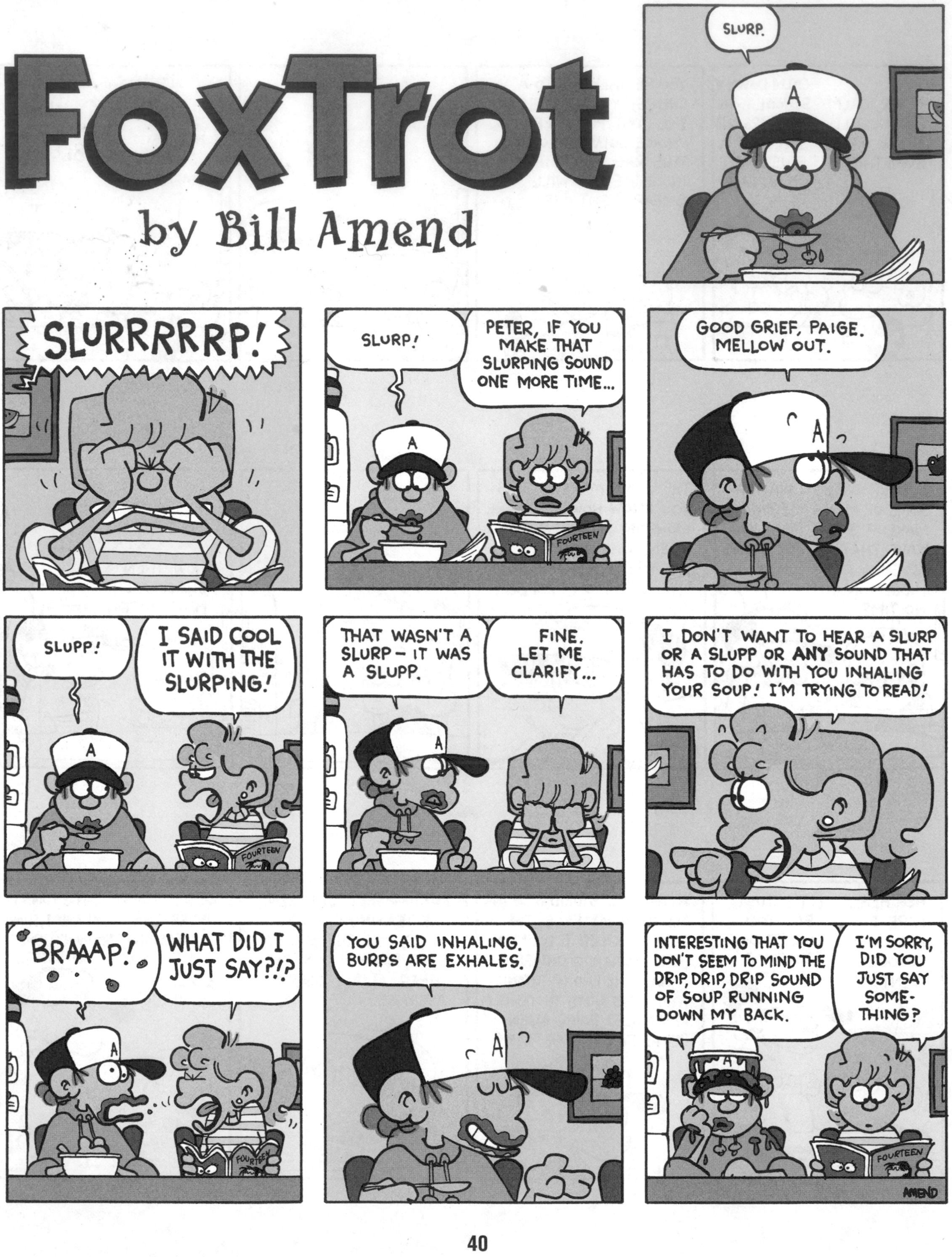
FoxTrot
by Bill Amend
SLURP.
SLURRRRRP!
SLURP!
PETER, IF YOU MAKE THAT SLURPING SOUND ONE MORE TIME...
GOOD GRIEF, PAIGE. MELLOW OUT.
SLUPP!
I SAID COOL IT WITH THE SLURPING!
THAT WASN'T A SLURP – IT WAS A SLUPP.
FINE. LET ME CLARIFY...
I DON'T WANT TO HEAR A SLURP OR A SLUPP OR ANY SOUND THAT HAS TO DO WITH YOU INHALING YOUR SOUP! I'M TRYING TO READ!
BRAAAP!
WHAT DID I JUST SAY?!?
YOU SAID INHALING. BURPS ARE EXHALES.
INTERESTING THAT YOU DON'T SEEM TO MIND THE DRIP, DRIP, DRIP SOUND OF SOUP RUNNING DOWN MY BACK.
I'M SORRY, DID YOU JUST SAY SOME-THING?
AMEND

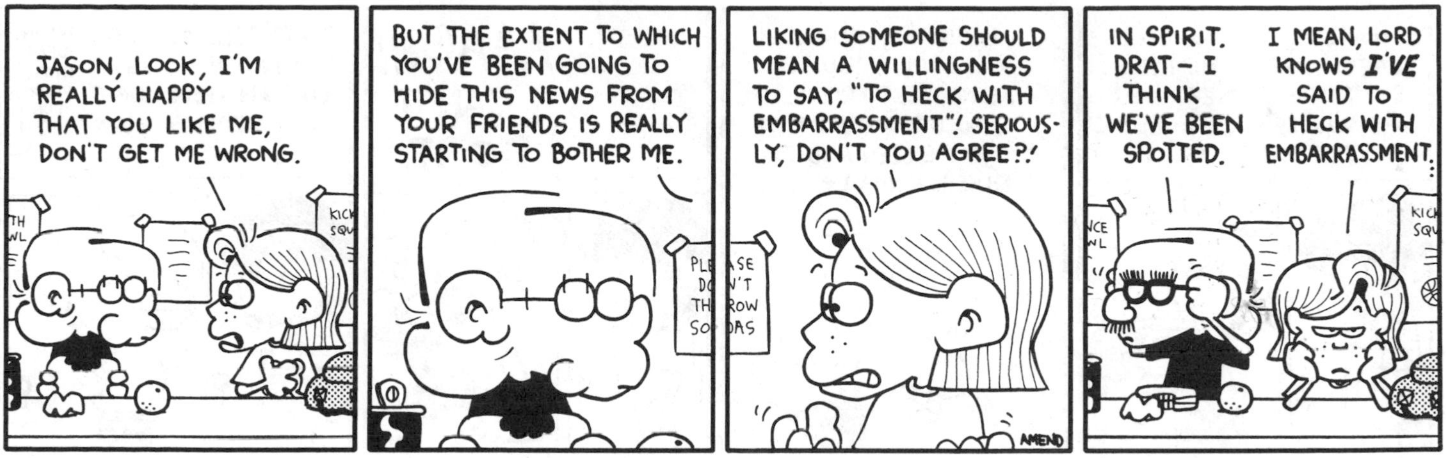
JASON, LOOK, I'M REALLY HAPPY THAT YOU LIKE ME, DON'T GET ME WRONG.
BUT THE EXTENT TO WHICH YOU'VE BEEN GOING TO HIDE THIS NEWS FROM YOUR FRIENDS IS REALLY STARTING TO BOTHER ME.
PLEASE DON'T THROW SODAS
LIKING SOMEONE SHOULD MEAN A WILLINGNESS TO SAY, "TO HECK WITH EMBARRASSMENT"! SERIOUSLY, DON'T YOU AGREE?!
AMEND
IN SPIRIT. DRAT – I THINK WE'VE BEEN SPOTTED.
I MEAN, LORD KNOWS *I'VE* SAID TO HECK WITH EMBARRASSMENT...

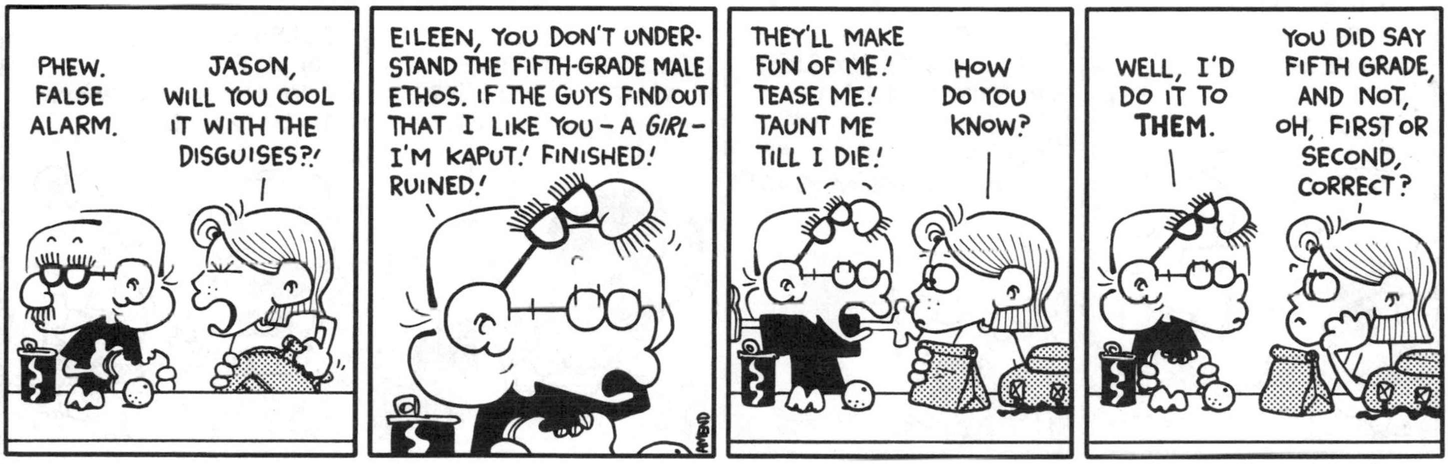
PHEW. FALSE ALARM.
JASON, WILL YOU COOL IT WITH THE DISGUISES?!
EILEEN, YOU DON'T UNDERSTAND THE FIFTH-GRADE MALE ETHOS. IF THE GUYS FIND OUT THAT I LIKE YOU – A *GIRL* – I'M KAPUT! FINISHED! RUINED!
AMEND
THEY'LL MAKE FUN OF ME! TEASE ME! TAUNT ME TILL I DIE!
HOW DO YOU KNOW?
WELL, I'D DO IT TO **THEM**.
YOU DID SAY FIFTH GRADE, AND NOT, OH, FIRST OR SECOND, CORRECT?

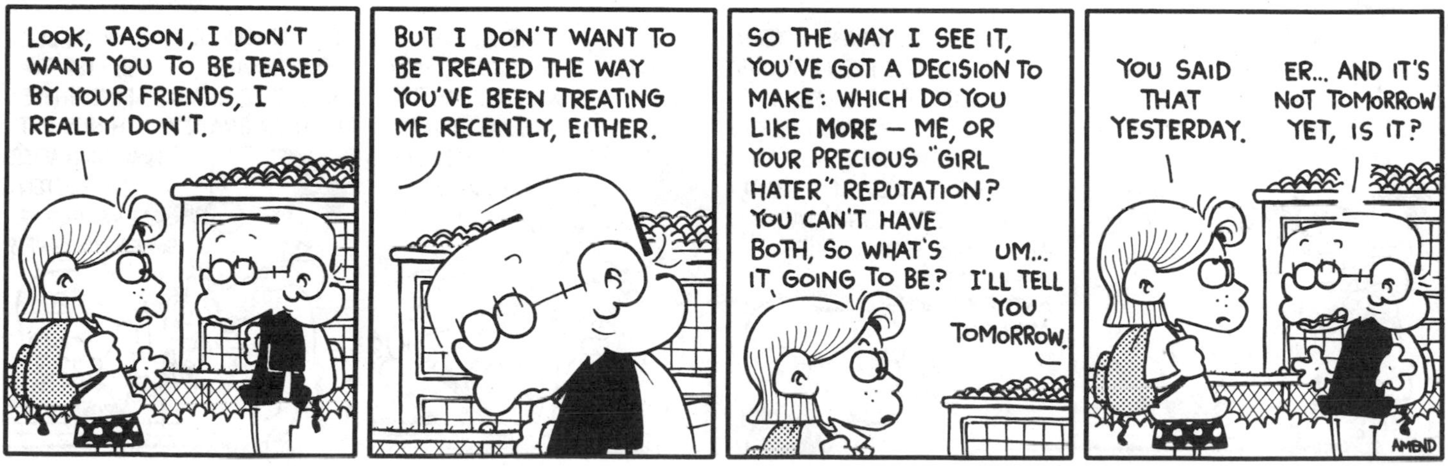
LOOK, JASON, I DON'T WANT YOU TO BE TEASED BY YOUR FRIENDS, I REALLY DON'T.
BUT I DON'T WANT TO BE TREATED THE WAY YOU'VE BEEN TREATING ME RECENTLY, EITHER.
SO THE WAY I SEE IT, YOU'VE GOT A DECISION TO MAKE: WHICH DO YOU LIKE **MORE** – ME, OR YOUR PRECIOUS "GIRL HATER" REPUTATION? YOU CAN'T HAVE BOTH, SO WHAT'S IT GOING TO BE?
UM... I'LL TELL YOU TOMORROW.
YOU SAID THAT YESTERDAY.
ER... AND IT'S NOT TOMORROW YET, IS IT?
AMEND

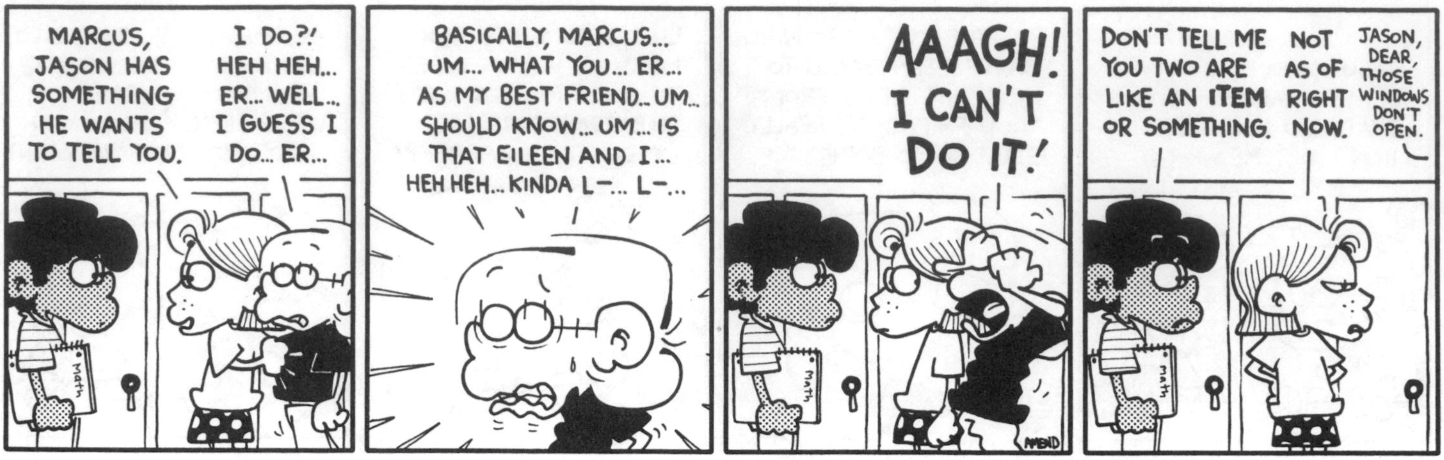

MARCUS, JASON HAS SOMETHING HE WANTS TO TELL YOU.
I DO?! HEH HEH... ER... WELL... I GUESS I DO... ER...
BASICALLY, MARCUS... UM... WHAT YOU... ER... AS MY BEST FRIEND.. UM.. SHOULD KNOW... UM... IS THAT EILEEN AND I... HEH HEH... KINDA L-... L-...
AAAGH! I CAN'T DO IT!
DON'T TELL ME YOU TWO ARE LIKE AN **ITEM** OR SOMETHING.
NOT AS OF RIGHT NOW.
JASON, DEAR, THOSE WINDOWS DON'T OPEN.

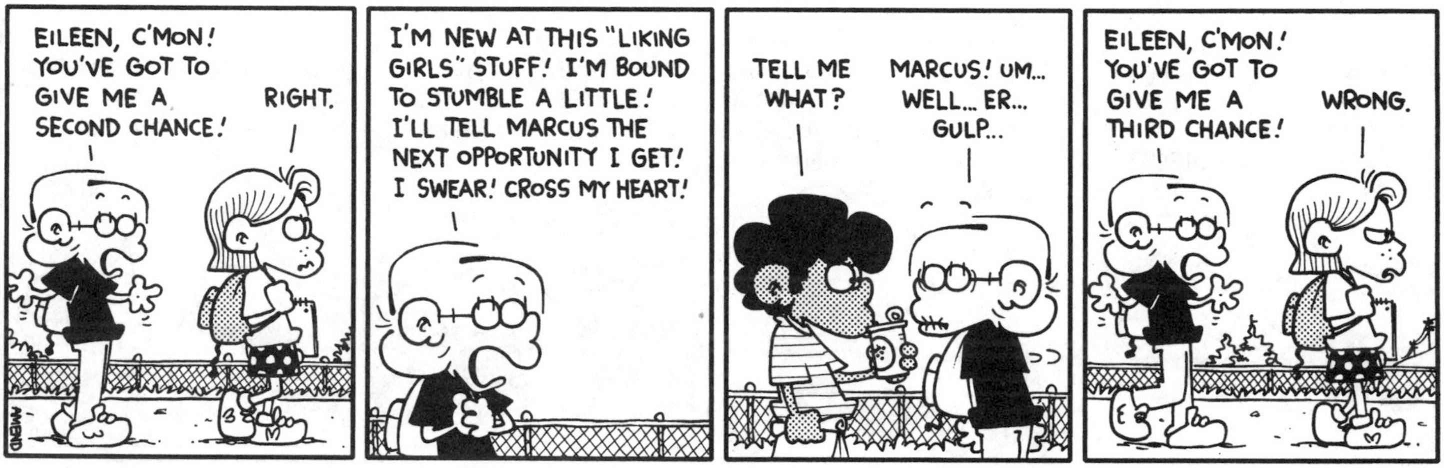

EILEEN, C'MON! YOU'VE GOT TO GIVE ME A SECOND CHANCE!
RIGHT.
I'M NEW AT THIS "LIKING GIRLS" STUFF! I'M BOUND TO STUMBLE A LITTLE! I'LL TELL MARCUS THE NEXT OPPORTUNITY I GET! I SWEAR! CROSS MY HEART!
TELL ME WHAT?
MARCUS! UM... WELL... ER... GULP...
EILEEN, C'MON! YOU'VE GOT TO GIVE ME A THIRD CHANCE!
WRONG.

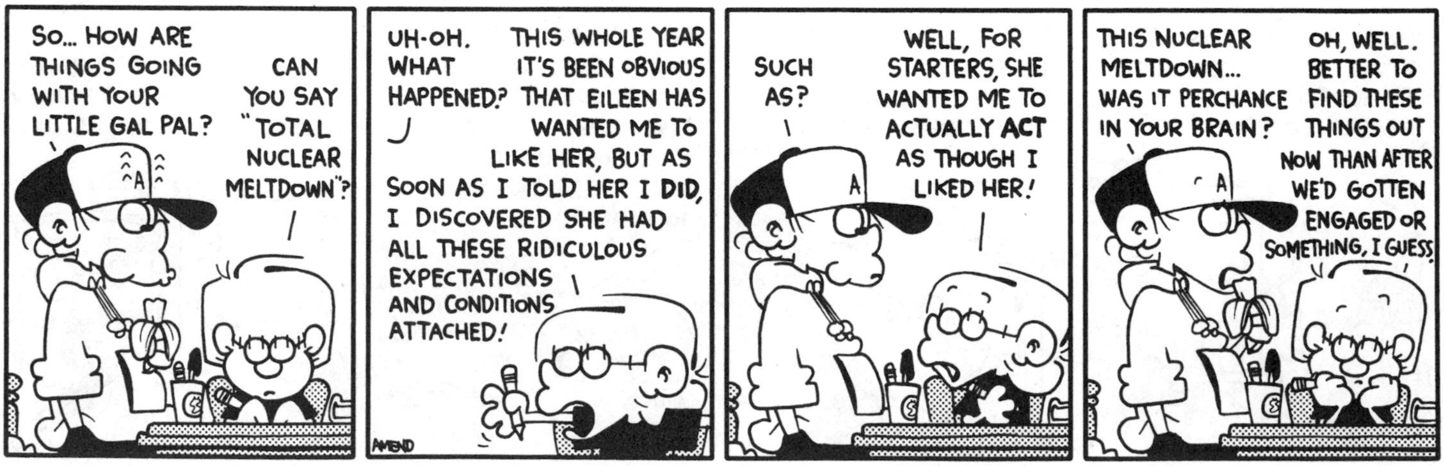

SO... HOW ARE THINGS GOING WITH YOUR LITTLE GAL PAL?
CAN YOU SAY "TOTAL NUCLEAR MELTDOWN"?
UH-OH. WHAT HAPPENED?
THIS WHOLE YEAR IT'S BEEN OBVIOUS THAT EILEEN HAS WANTED ME TO LIKE HER, BUT AS SOON AS I TOLD HER I **DID**, I DISCOVERED SHE HAD ALL THESE RIDICULOUS EXPECTATIONS AND CONDITIONS ATTACHED!
SUCH AS?
WELL, FOR STARTERS, SHE WANTED ME TO ACTUALLY **ACT** AS THOUGH I LIKED HER!
THIS NUCLEAR MELTDOWN... WAS IT PERCHANCE IN YOUR BRAIN?
OH, WELL. BETTER TO FIND THESE THINGS OUT NOW THAN AFTER WE'D GOTTEN ENGAGED OR SOMETHING, I GUESS.

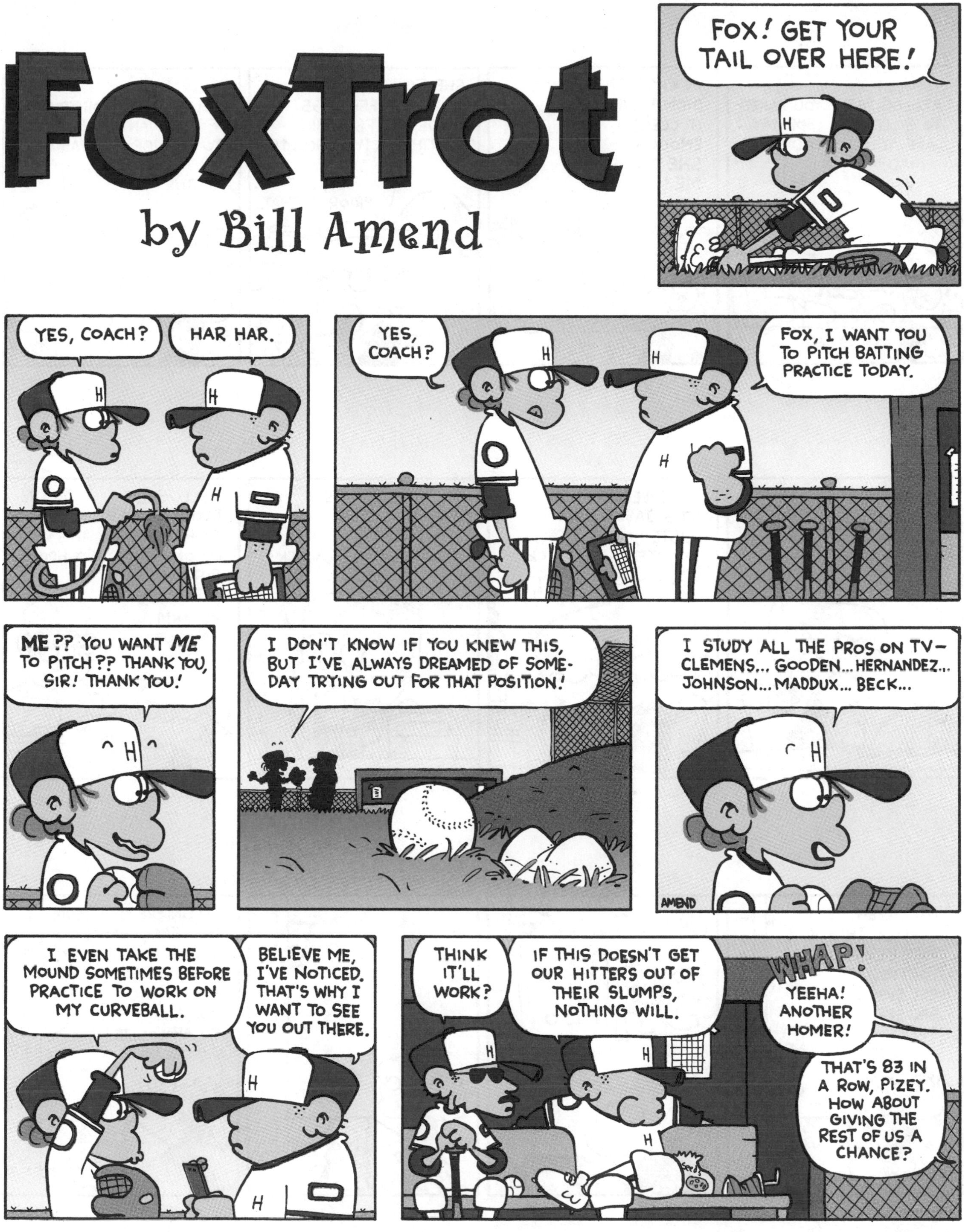

FoxTrot
by Bill Amend
FOX! GET YOUR TAIL OVER HERE!
YES, COACH?
HAR HAR.
YES, COACH?
FOX, I WANT YOU TO PITCH BATTING PRACTICE TODAY.
ME?? YOU WANT ME TO PITCH?? THANK YOU, SIR! THANK YOU!
I DON'T KNOW IF YOU KNEW THIS, BUT I'VE ALWAYS DREAMED OF SOME-DAY TRYING OUT FOR THAT POSITION!
I STUDY ALL THE PROS ON TV— CLEMENS... GOODEN... HERNANDEZ... JOHNSON... MADDUX... BECK...
AMEND
I EVEN TAKE THE MOUND SOMETIMES BEFORE PRACTICE TO WORK ON MY CURVEBALL.
BELIEVE ME, I'VE NOTICED. THAT'S WHY I WANT TO SEE YOU OUT THERE.
THINK IT'LL WORK?
IF THIS DOESN'T GET OUR HITTERS OUT OF THEIR SLUMPS, NOTHING WILL.
WHAP!
YEEHA! ANOTHER HOMER!
THAT'S 83 IN A ROW, PIZEY. HOW ABOUT GIVING THE REST OF US A CHANCE?

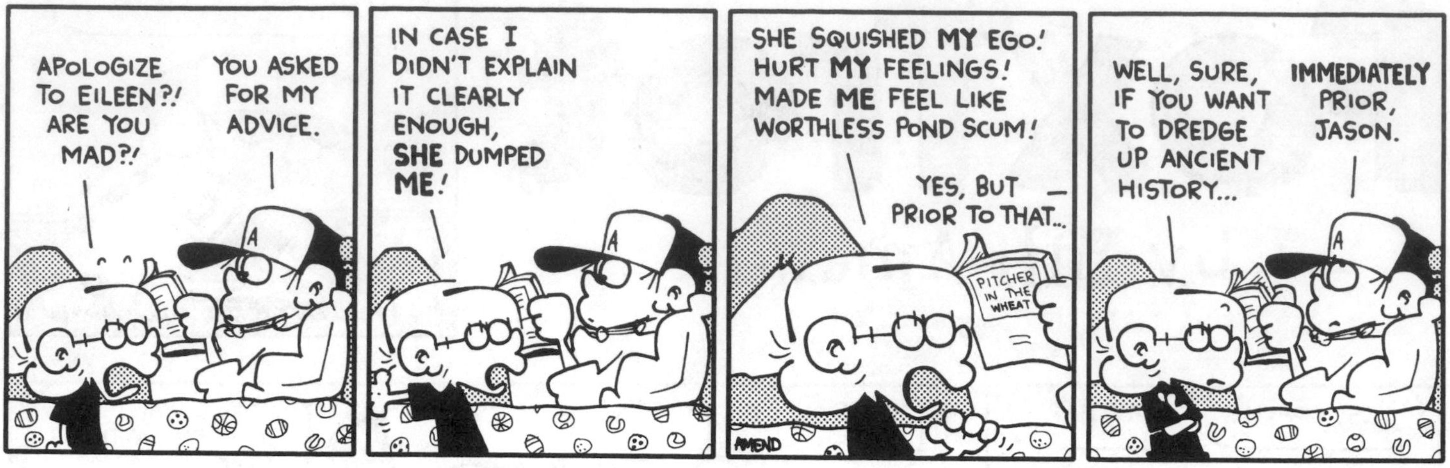
APOLOGIZE TO EILEEN?! ARE YOU MAD?!
YOU ASKED FOR MY ADVICE.
IN CASE I DIDN'T EXPLAIN IT CLEARLY ENOUGH, SHE DUMPED ME!
SHE SQUISHED MY EGO! HURT MY FEELINGS! MADE ME FEEL LIKE WORTHLESS POND SCUM!
YES, BUT — PRIOR TO THAT...
PITCHER IN THE WHEAT
WELL, SURE, IF YOU WANT TO DREDGE UP ANCIENT HISTORY...
IMMEDIATELY PRIOR, JASON.
AMEND

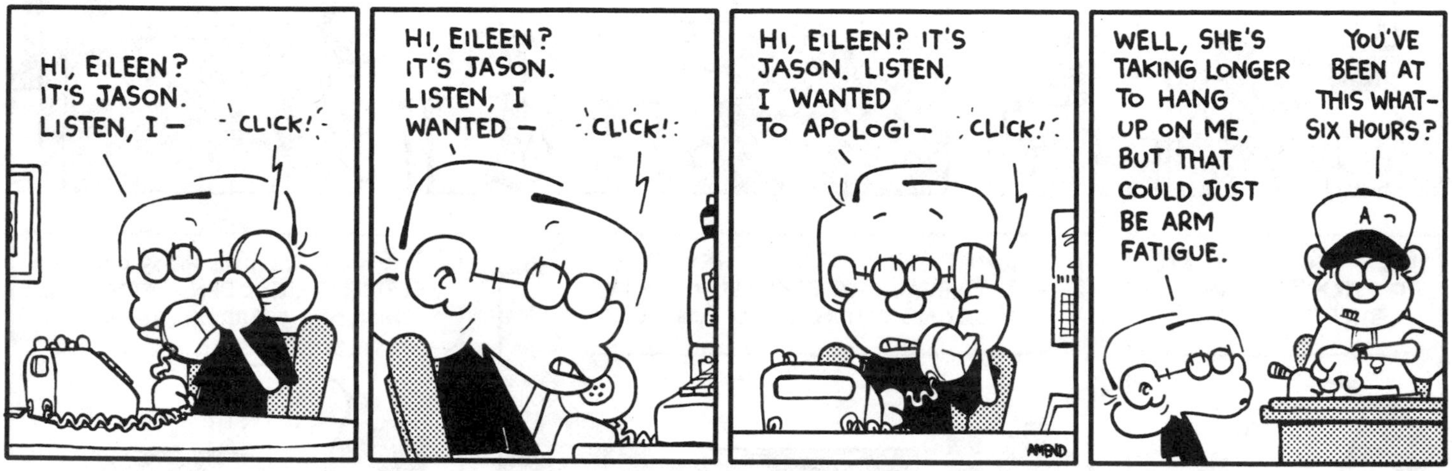
HI, EILEEN? IT'S JASON. LISTEN, I —
CLICK!
HI, EILEEN? IT'S JASON. LISTEN, I WANTED —
CLICK!
HI, EILEEN? IT'S JASON. LISTEN, I WANTED TO APOLOGI—
CLICK!
WELL, SHE'S TAKING LONGER TO HANG UP ON ME, BUT THAT COULD JUST BE ARM FATIGUE.
YOU'VE BEEN AT THIS WHAT—SIX HOURS?
AMEND

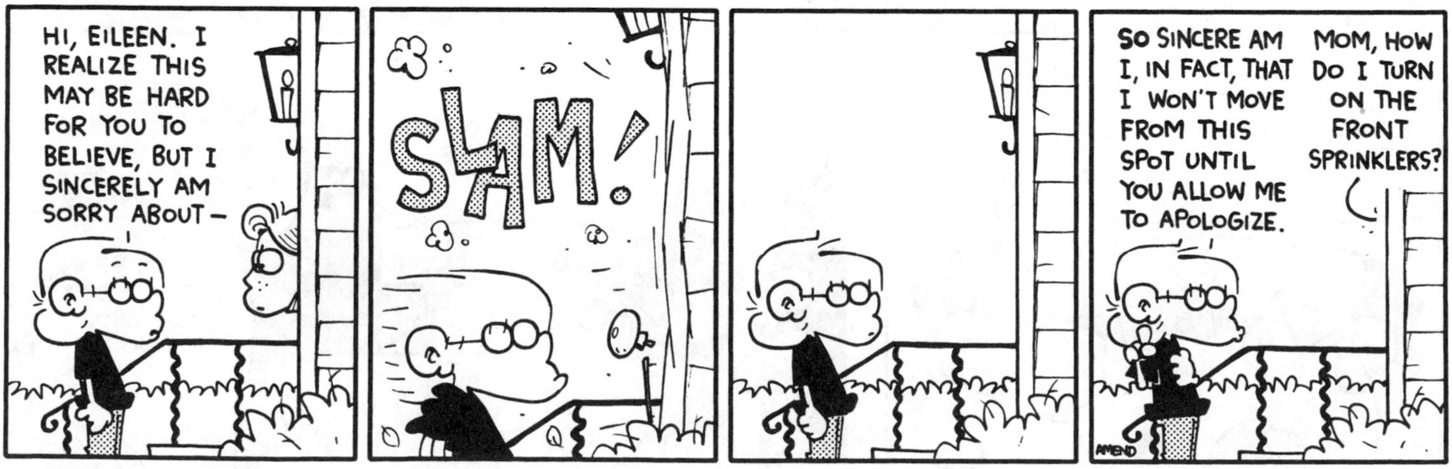
HI, EILEEN. I REALIZE THIS MAY BE HARD FOR YOU TO BELIEVE, BUT I SINCERELY AM SORRY ABOUT —
SLAM!
SO SINCERE AM I, IN FACT, THAT I WON'T MOVE FROM THIS SPOT UNTIL YOU ALLOW ME TO APOLOGIZE.
MOM, HOW DO I TURN ON THE FRONT SPRINKLERS?
AMEND

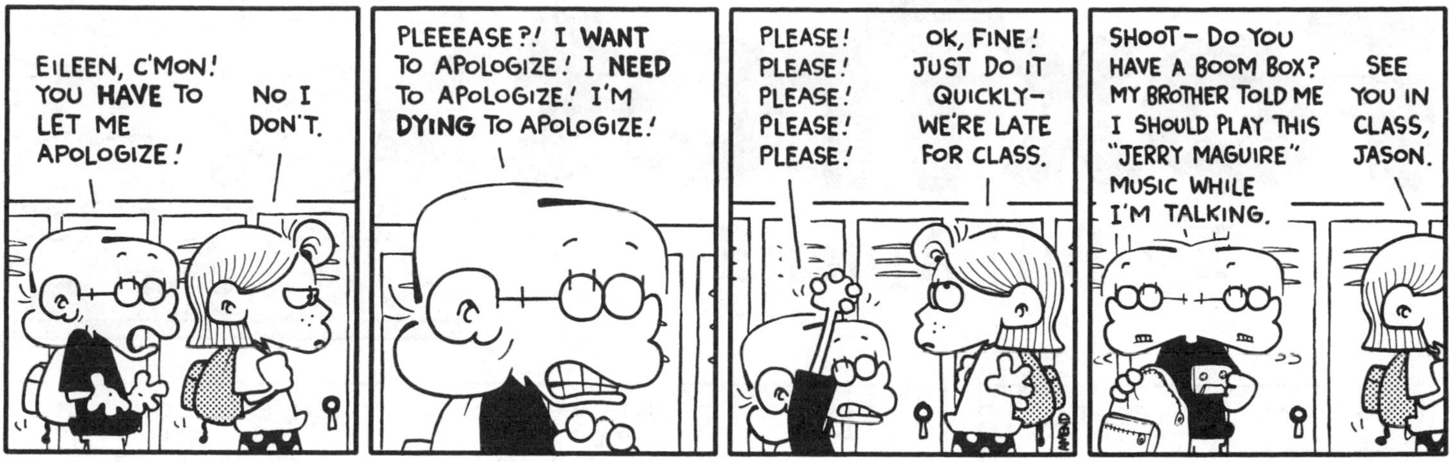
EILEEN, C'MON! YOU **HAVE** TO LET ME APOLOGIZE!
NO I DON'T.
PLEEEASE?! I **WANT** TO APOLOGIZE! I **NEED** TO APOLOGIZE! I'M **DYING** TO APOLOGIZE!
PLEASE! PLEASE! PLEASE! PLEASE! PLEASE!
OK, FINE! JUST DO IT QUICKLY– WE'RE LATE FOR CLASS.
SHOOT– DO YOU HAVE A BOOM BOX? MY BROTHER TOLD ME I SHOULD PLAY THIS "JERRY MAGUIRE" MUSIC WHILE I'M TALKING.
SEE YOU IN CLASS, JASON.
AMEND

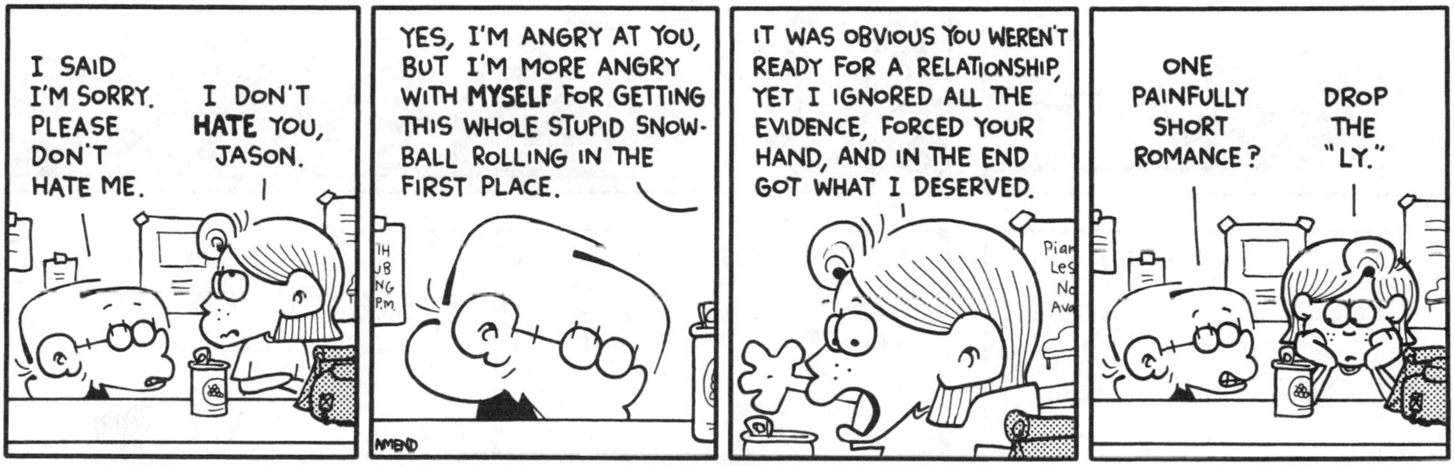
I SAID I'M SORRY. PLEASE DON'T HATE ME.
I DON'T **HATE** YOU, JASON.
YES, I'M ANGRY AT YOU, BUT I'M MORE ANGRY WITH **MYSELF** FOR GETTING THIS WHOLE STUPID SNOW-BALL ROLLING IN THE FIRST PLACE.
AMEND
IT WAS OBVIOUS YOU WEREN'T READY FOR A RELATIONSHIP, YET I IGNORED ALL THE EVIDENCE, FORCED YOUR HAND, AND IN THE END GOT WHAT I DESERVED.
ONE PAINFULLY SHORT ROMANCE?
DROP THE "LY."

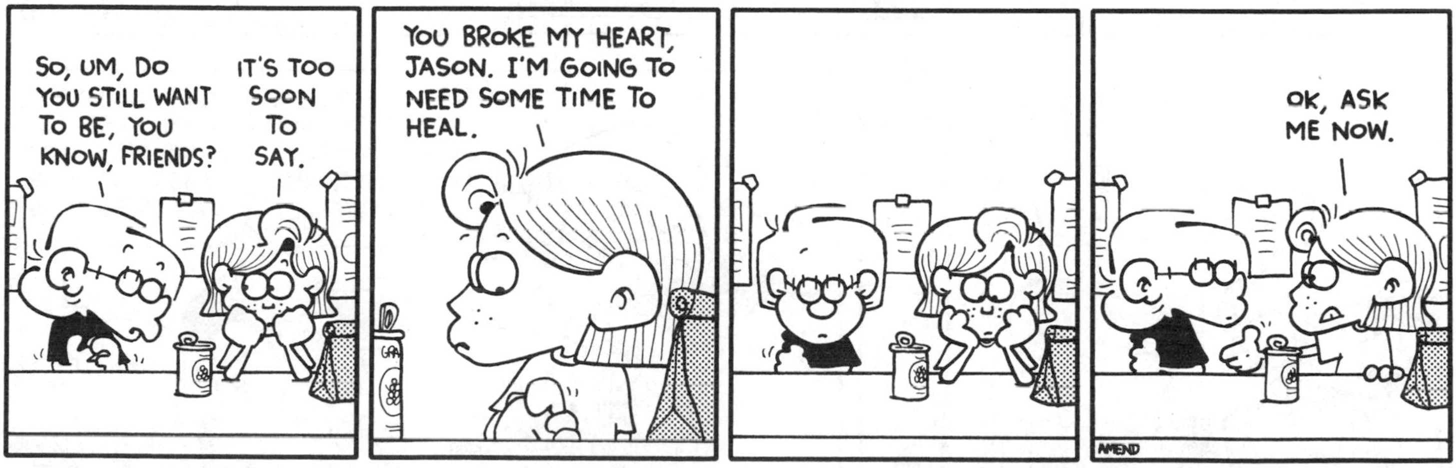
SO, UM, DO YOU STILL WANT TO BE, YOU KNOW, FRIENDS?
IT'S TOO SOON TO SAY.
YOU BROKE MY HEART, JASON. I'M GOING TO NEED SOME TIME TO HEAL.
OK, ASK ME NOW.
AMEND

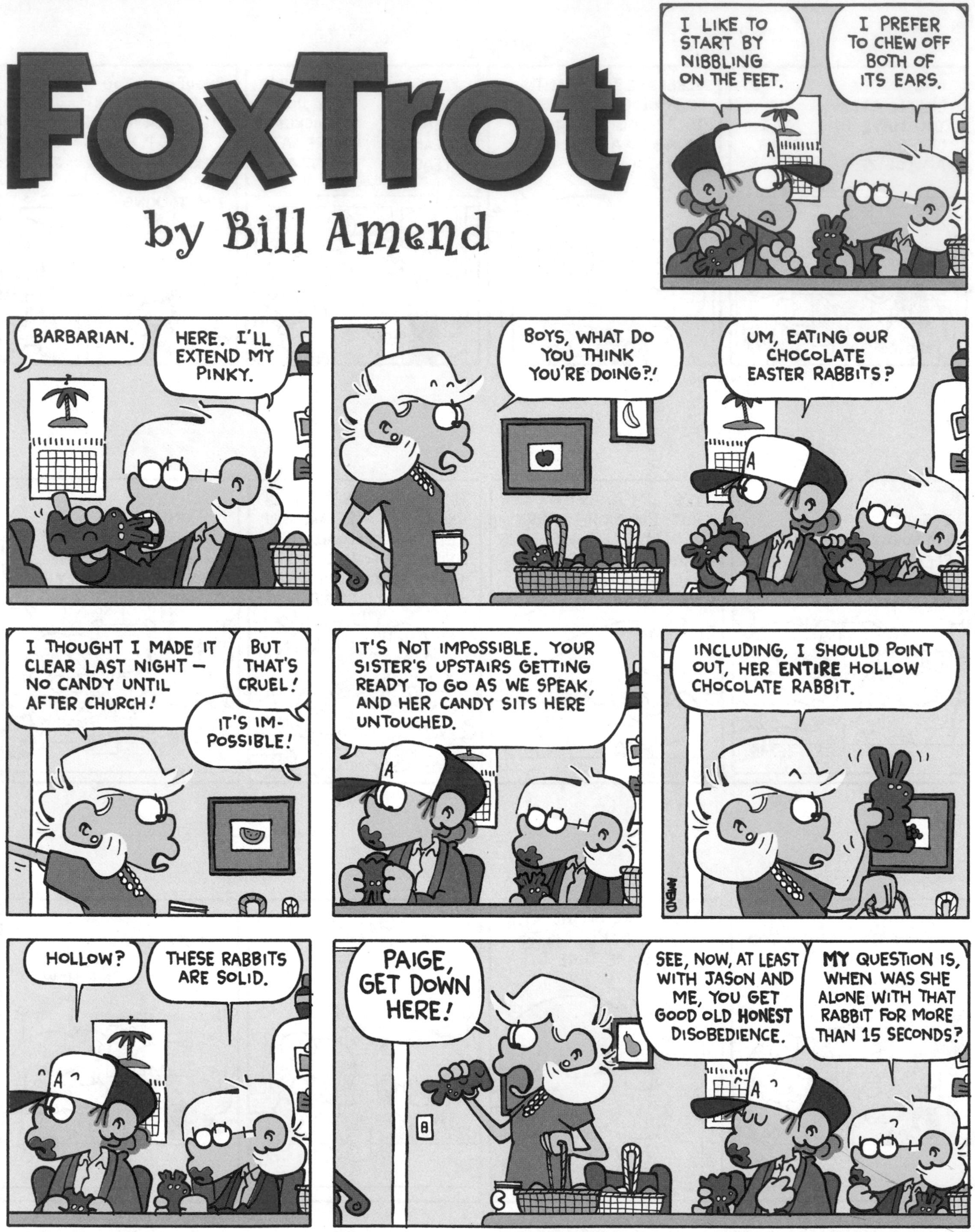
FoxTrot
by Bill Amend
I LIKE TO START BY NIBBLING ON THE FEET.
I PREFER TO CHEW OFF BOTH OF ITS EARS.
BARBARIAN.
HERE. I'LL EXTEND MY PINKY.
BOYS, WHAT DO YOU THINK YOU'RE DOING?!
UM, EATING OUR CHOCOLATE EASTER RABBITS?
I THOUGHT I MADE IT CLEAR LAST NIGHT — NO CANDY UNTIL AFTER CHURCH!
BUT THAT'S CRUEL!
IT'S IMPOSSIBLE!
IT'S NOT IMPOSSIBLE. YOUR SISTER'S UPSTAIRS GETTING READY TO GO AS WE SPEAK, AND HER CANDY SITS HERE UNTOUCHED.
INCLUDING, I SHOULD POINT OUT, HER ENTIRE HOLLOW CHOCOLATE RABBIT.
AMEND
HOLLOW?
THESE RABBITS ARE SOLID.
PAIGE, GET DOWN HERE!
SEE, NOW, AT LEAST WITH JASON AND ME, YOU GET GOOD OLD HONEST DISOBEDIENCE.
MY QUESTION IS, WHEN WAS SHE ALONE WITH THAT RABBIT FOR MORE THAN 15 SECONDS?

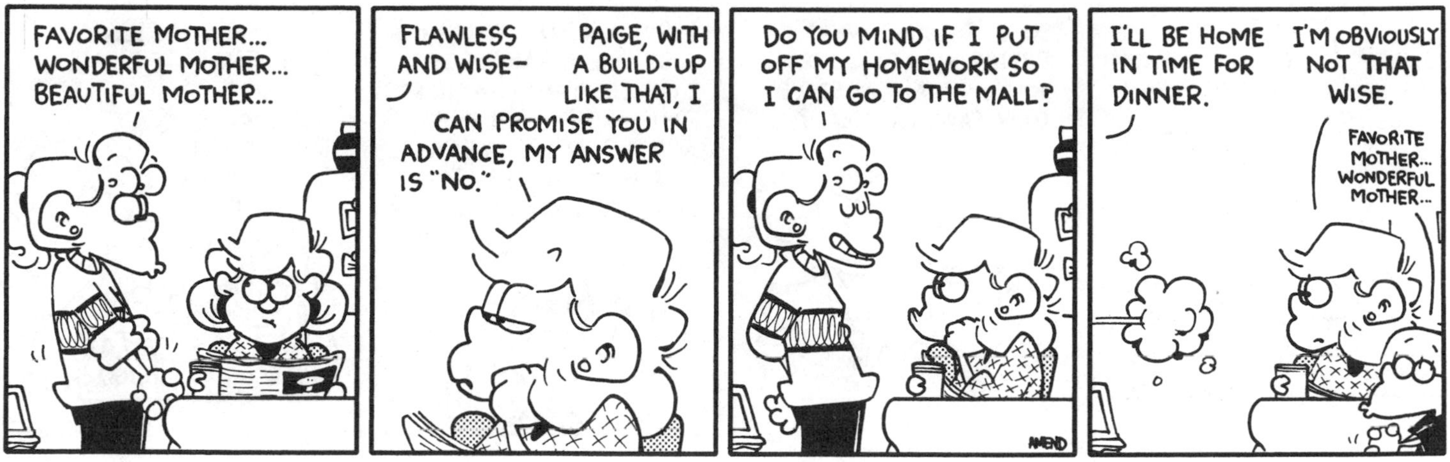
FAVORITE MOTHER... WONDERFUL MOTHER... BEAUTIFUL MOTHER...
FLAWLESS AND WISE-
PAIGE, WITH A BUILD-UP LIKE THAT, I CAN PROMISE YOU IN ADVANCE, MY ANSWER IS "NO."
DO YOU MIND IF I PUT OFF MY HOMEWORK SO I CAN GO TO THE MALL?
I'LL BE HOME IN TIME FOR DINNER.
I'M OBVIOUSLY NOT THAT WISE.
FAVORITE MOTHER... WONDERFUL MOTHER...
AMEND

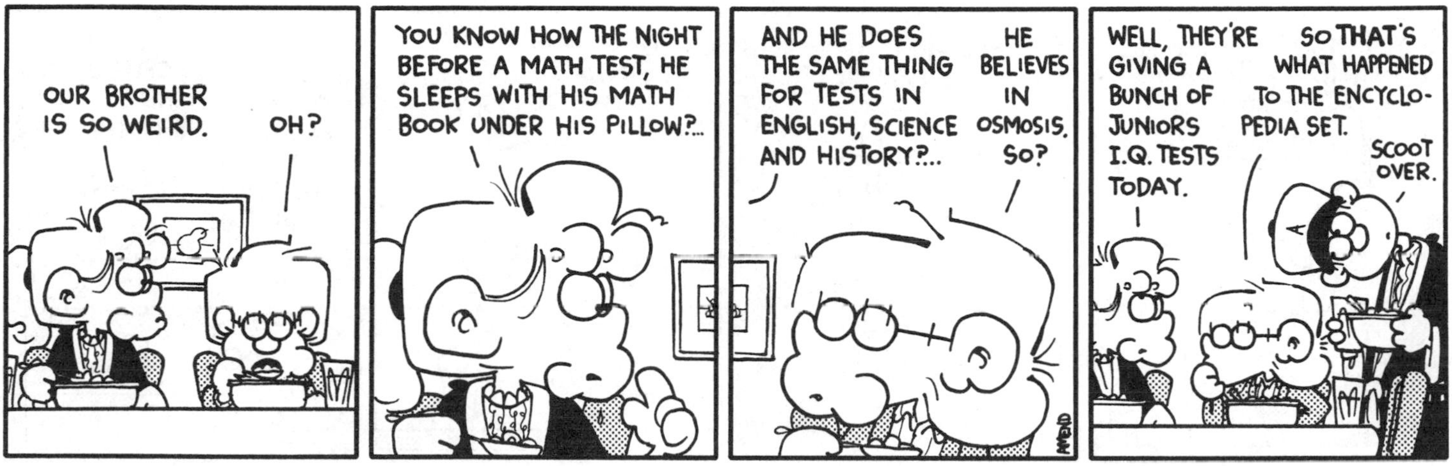
OUR BROTHER IS SO WEIRD.
OH?
YOU KNOW HOW THE NIGHT BEFORE A MATH TEST, HE SLEEPS WITH HIS MATH BOOK UNDER HIS PILLOW?...
AND HE DOES THE SAME THING FOR TESTS IN ENGLISH, SCIENCE AND HISTORY?...
HE BELIEVES IN OSMOSIS. SO?
AMEND
WELL, THEY'RE GIVING A BUNCH OF JUNIORS I.Q. TESTS TODAY.
SO THAT'S WHAT HAPPENED TO THE ENCYCLOPEDIA SET.
SCOOT OVER.

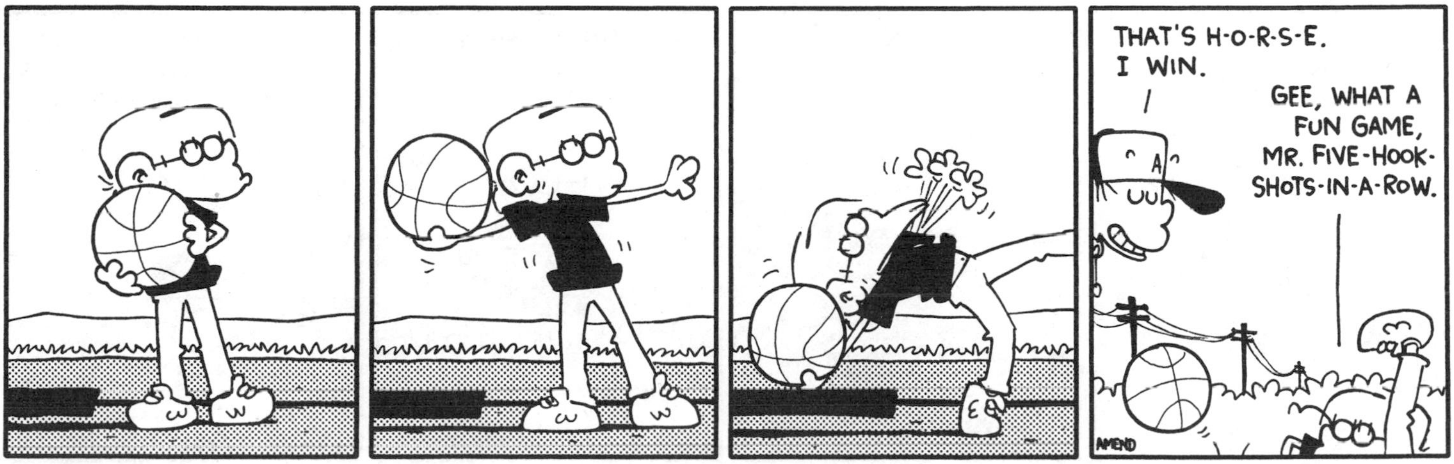
THAT'S H-O-R-S-E. I WIN.
GEE, WHAT A FUN GAME, MR. FIVE-HOOK-SHOTS-IN-A-ROW.
AMEND

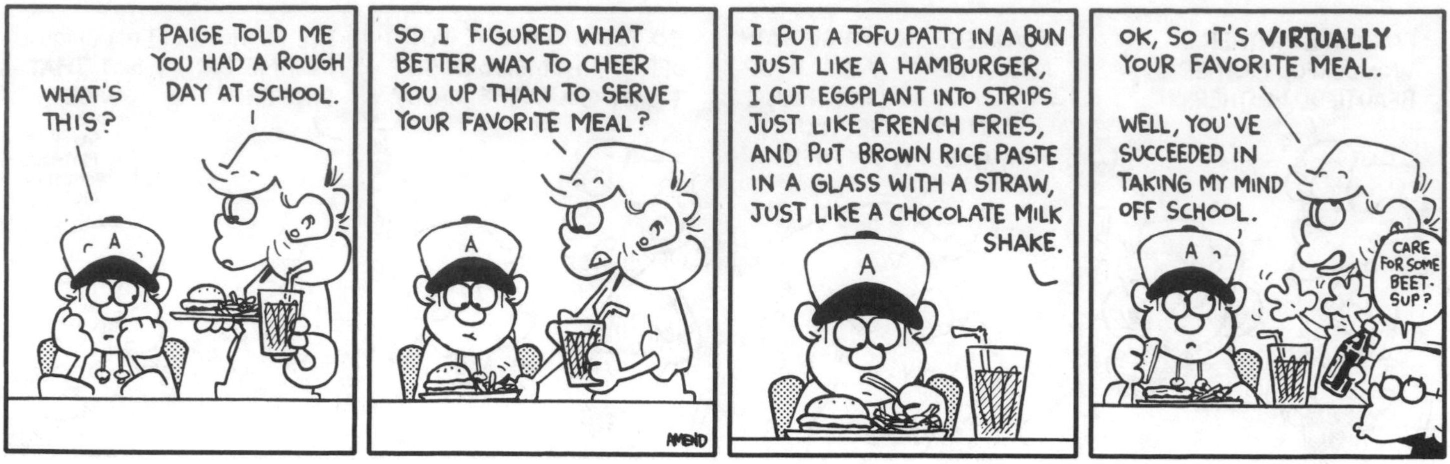
PAIGE TOLD ME YOU HAD A ROUGH DAY AT SCHOOL.
WHAT'S THIS?
SO I FIGURED WHAT BETTER WAY TO CHEER YOU UP THAN TO SERVE YOUR FAVORITE MEAL?
I PUT A TOFU PATTY IN A BUN JUST LIKE A HAMBURGER, I CUT EGGPLANT INTO STRIPS JUST LIKE FRENCH FRIES, AND PUT BROWN RICE PASTE IN A GLASS WITH A STRAW, JUST LIKE A CHOCOLATE MILK SHAKE.
OK, SO IT'S **VIRTUALLY** YOUR FAVORITE MEAL.
WELL, YOU'VE SUCCEEDED IN TAKING MY MIND OFF SCHOOL.
CARE FOR SOME BEET-SUP?

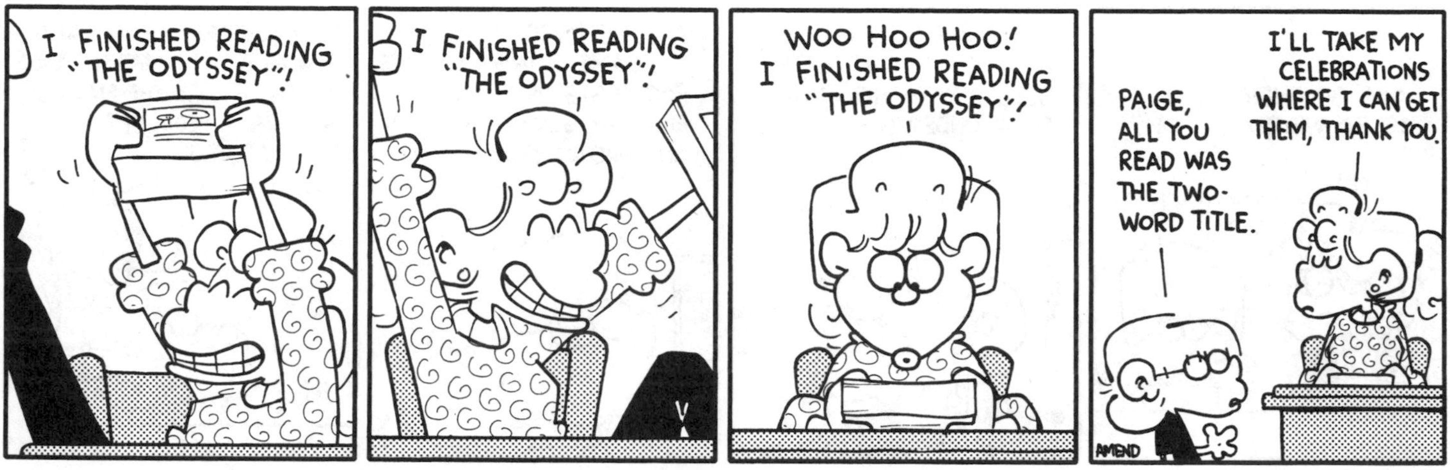
I FINISHED READING "THE ODYSSEY"!
I FINISHED READING "THE ODYSSEY"!
WOO HOO HOO! I FINISHED READING "THE ODYSSEY"!
PAIGE, ALL YOU READ WAS THE TWO-WORD TITLE.
I'LL TAKE MY CELEBRATIONS WHERE I CAN GET THEM, THANK YOU.

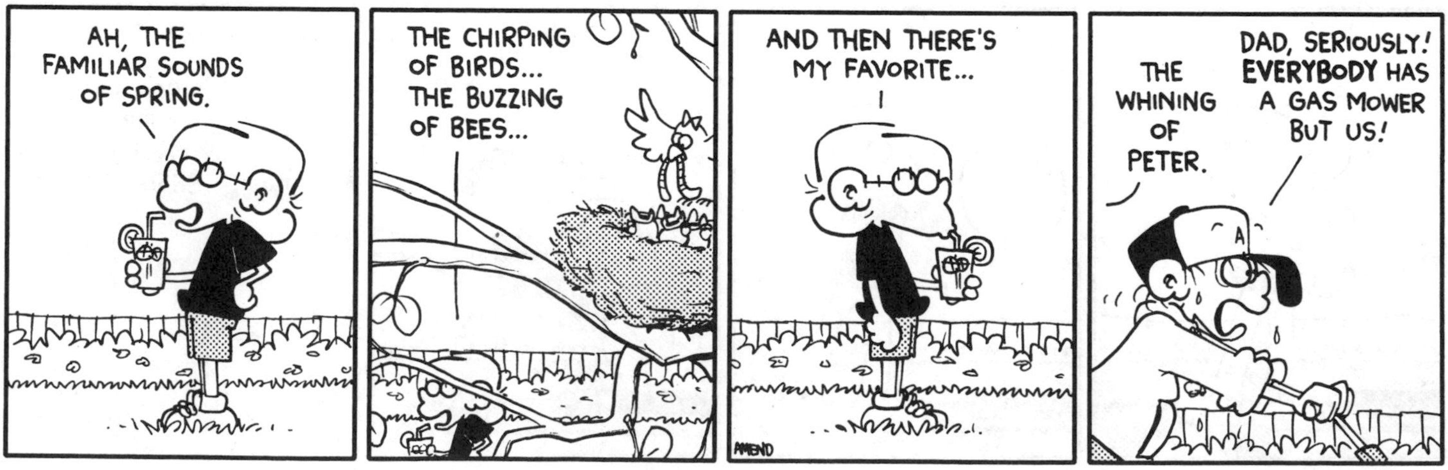
AH, THE FAMILIAR SOUNDS OF SPRING.
THE CHIRPING OF BIRDS... THE BUZZING OF BEES...
AND THEN THERE'S MY FAVORITE...
THE WHINING OF PETER.
DAD, SERIOUSLY! **EVERYBODY** HAS A GAS MOWER BUT US!

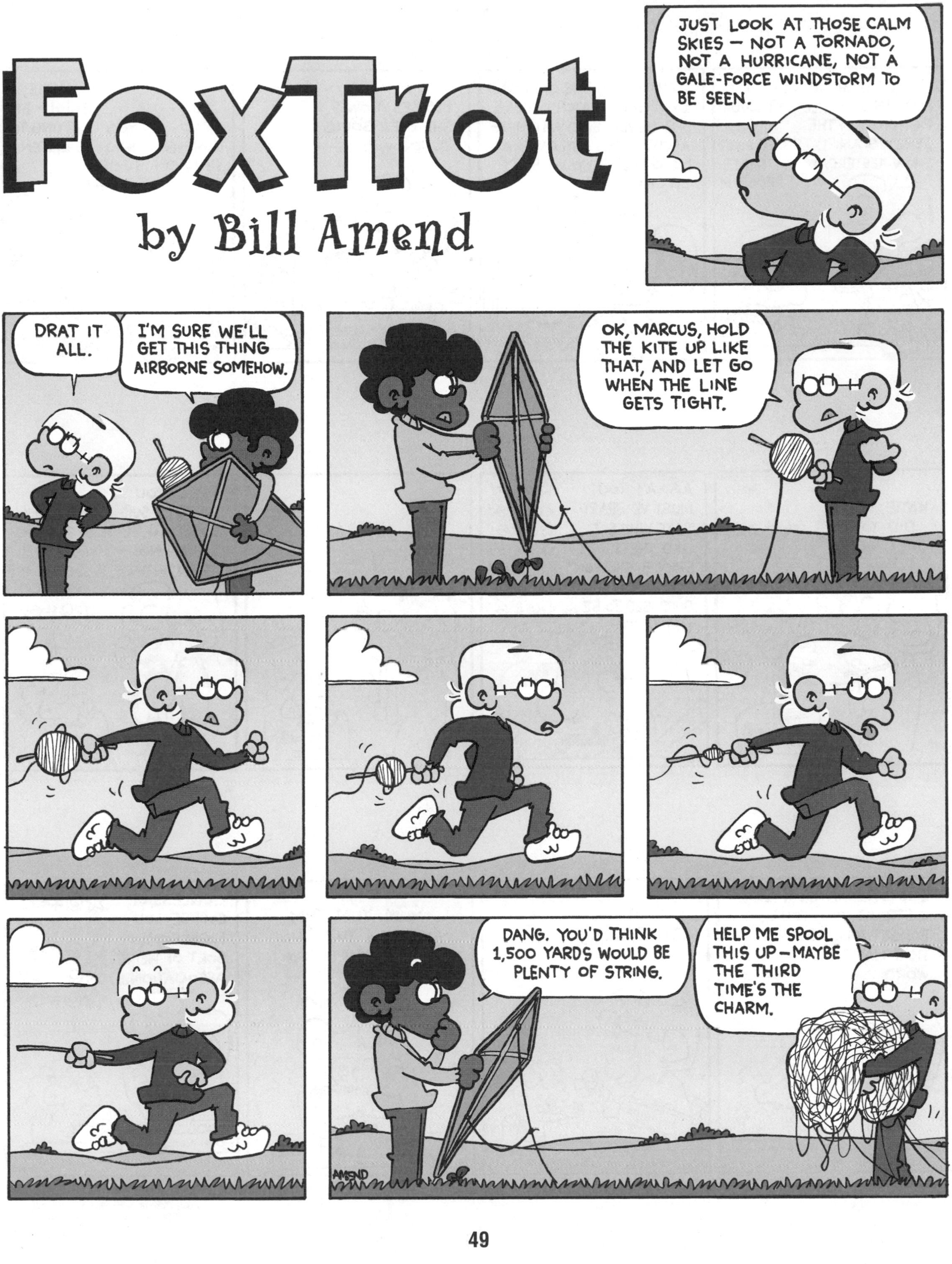
FoxTrot
by Bill Amend
JUST LOOK AT THOSE CALM SKIES — NOT A TORNADO, NOT A HURRICANE, NOT A GALE-FORCE WINDSTORM TO BE SEEN.
DRAT IT ALL.
I'M SURE WE'LL GET THIS THING AIRBORNE SOMEHOW.
OK, MARCUS, HOLD THE KITE UP LIKE THAT, AND LET GO WHEN THE LINE GETS TIGHT.
DANG. YOU'D THINK 1,500 YARDS WOULD BE PLENTY OF STRING.
HELP ME SPOOL THIS UP—MAYBE THE THIRD TIME'S THE CHARM.
AMEND

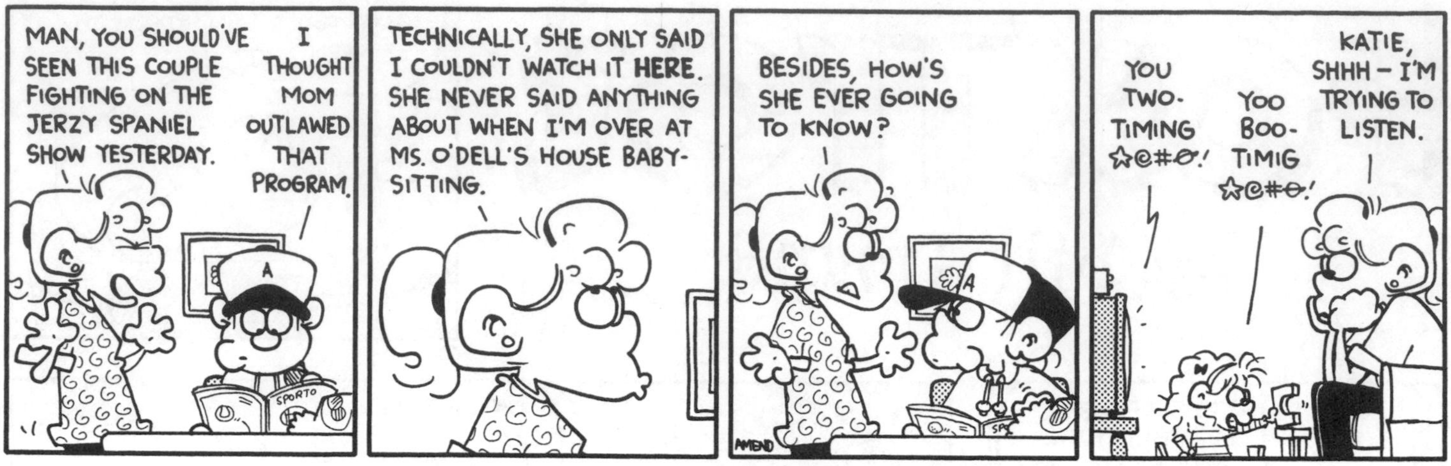
MAN, YOU SHOULD'VE SEEN THIS COUPLE FIGHTING ON THE JERZY SPANIEL SHOW YESTERDAY.
I THOUGHT MOM OUTLAWED THAT PROGRAM.
SPORTO
TECHNICALLY, SHE ONLY SAID I COULDN'T WATCH IT HERE. SHE NEVER SAID ANYTHING ABOUT WHEN I'M OVER AT MS. O'DELL'S HOUSE BABY-SITTING.
BESIDES, HOW'S SHE EVER GOING TO KNOW?
YOU TWO-TIMING ☆@#⊖!
YOO BOO-TIMIG ☆@#⊖!
KATIE, SHHH – I'M TRYING TO LISTEN.

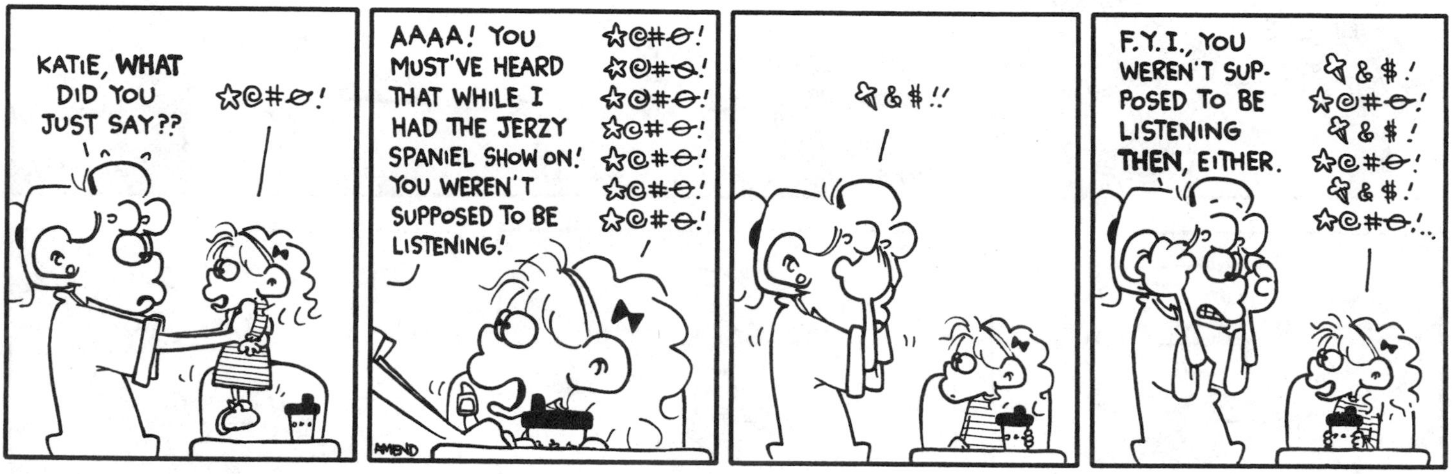
KATIE, WHAT DID YOU JUST SAY??
☆@#⊖!
AAAA! YOU MUST'VE HEARD THAT WHILE I HAD THE JERZY SPANIEL SHOW ON! YOU WEREN'T SUPPOSED TO BE LISTENING!
☆@#⊖! ☆@#⊖! ☆@#⊖! ☆@#⊖! ☆@#⊖! ☆@#⊖! ☆@#⊖!
& $!!
F.Y.I., YOU WEREN'T SUPPOSED TO BE LISTENING THEN, EITHER.
& $! ☆@#⊖! & $! ☆@#⊖! & $! ☆@#⊖!...

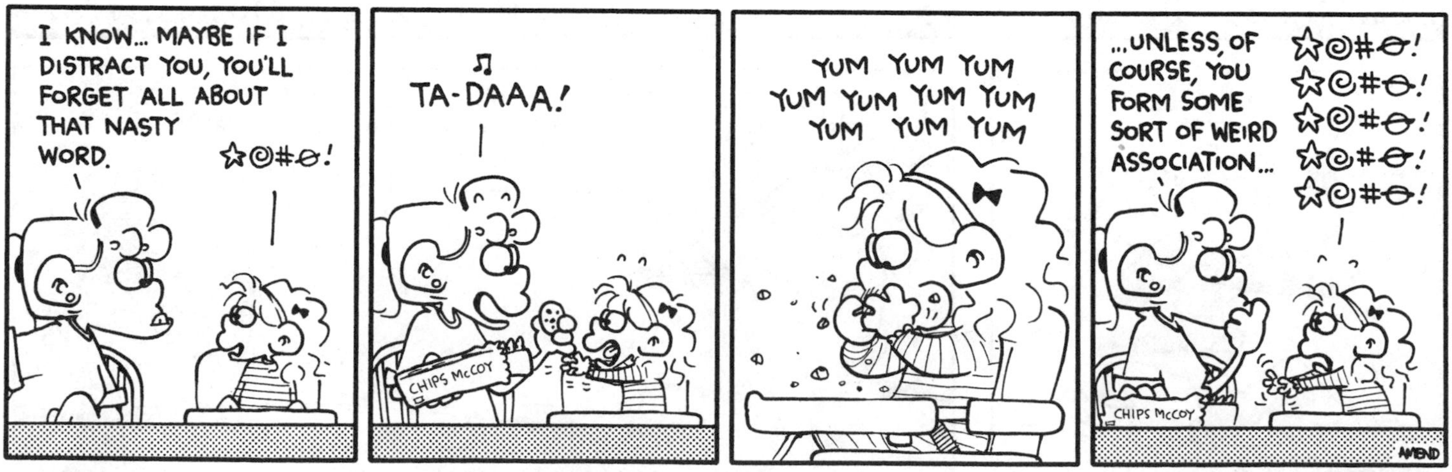
I KNOW... MAYBE IF I DISTRACT YOU, YOU'LL FORGET ALL ABOUT THAT NASTY WORD.
☆@#⊖!
♫ TA-DAAA!
CHIPS McCOY
YUM YUM YUM YUM YUM YUM YUM YUM YUM YUM
...UNLESS, OF COURSE, YOU FORM SOME SORT OF WEIRD ASSOCIATION...
☆@#⊖! ☆@#⊖! ☆@#⊖! ☆@#⊖! ☆@#⊖!
CHIPS McCOY

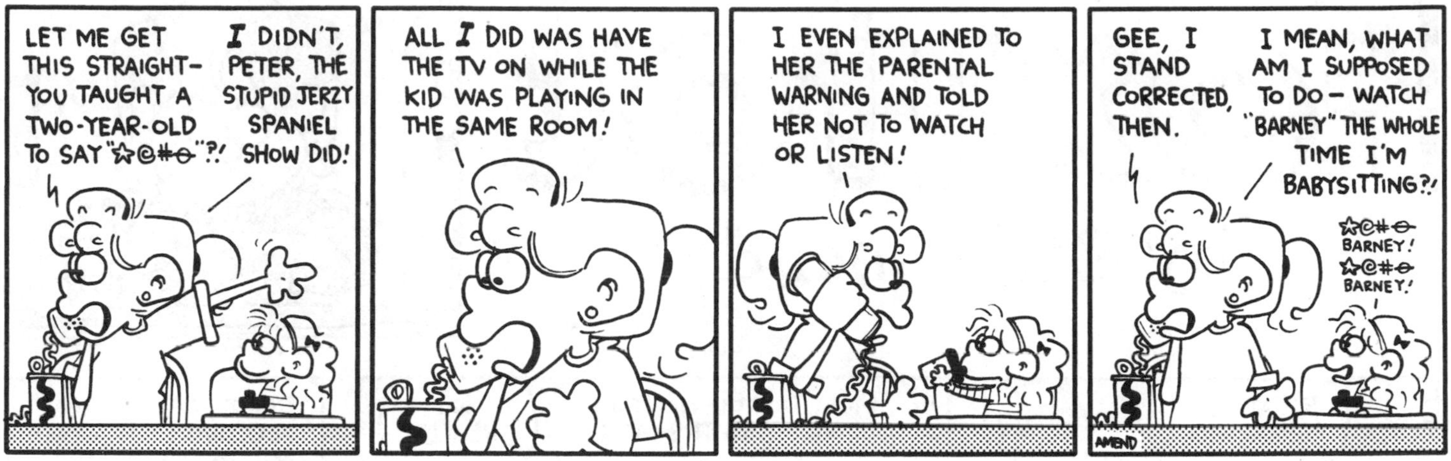
LET ME GET THIS STRAIGHT– YOU TAUGHT A TWO-YEAR-OLD TO SAY "☆@#⊖"?!
I DIDN'T, PETER, THE STUPID JERZY SPANIEL SHOW DID!
ALL I DID WAS HAVE THE TV ON WHILE THE KID WAS PLAYING IN THE SAME ROOM!
I EVEN EXPLAINED TO HER THE PARENTAL WARNING AND TOLD HER NOT TO WATCH OR LISTEN!
GEE, I STAND CORRECTED, THEN.
I MEAN, WHAT AM I SUPPOSED TO DO – WATCH "BARNEY" THE WHOLE TIME I'M BABYSITTING?!
☆@#⊖ BARNEY! ☆@#⊖ BARNEY!
AMEND

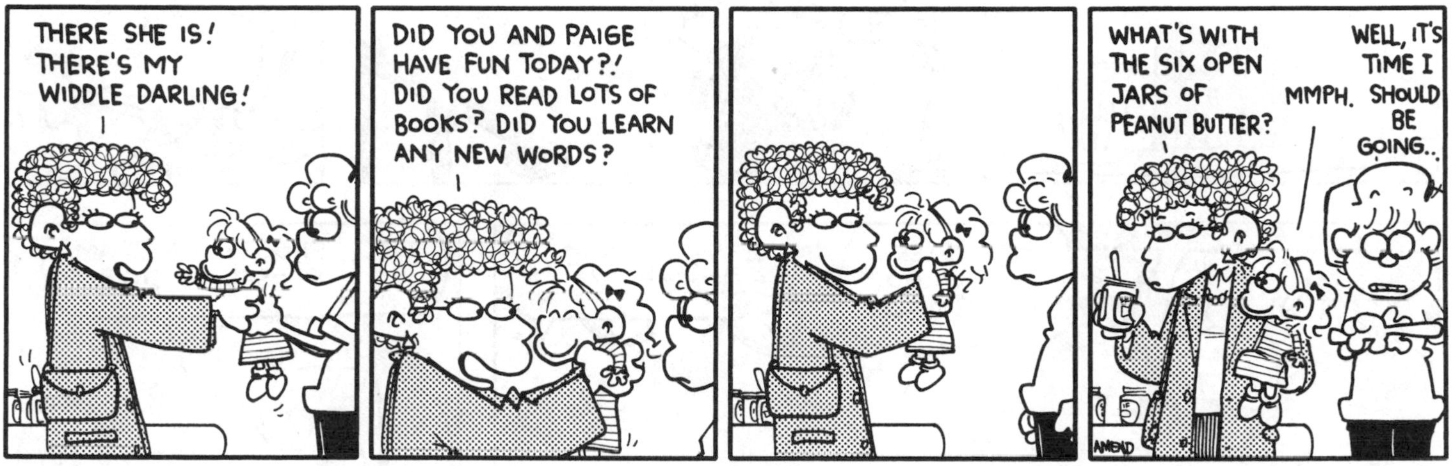
THERE SHE IS! THERE'S MY WIDDLE DARLING!
DID YOU AND PAIGE HAVE FUN TODAY?! DID YOU READ LOTS OF BOOKS? DID YOU LEARN ANY NEW WORDS?
WHAT'S WITH THE SIX OPEN JARS OF PEANUT BUTTER?
MMPH.
WELL, IT'S TIME I SHOULD BE GOING...
AMEND

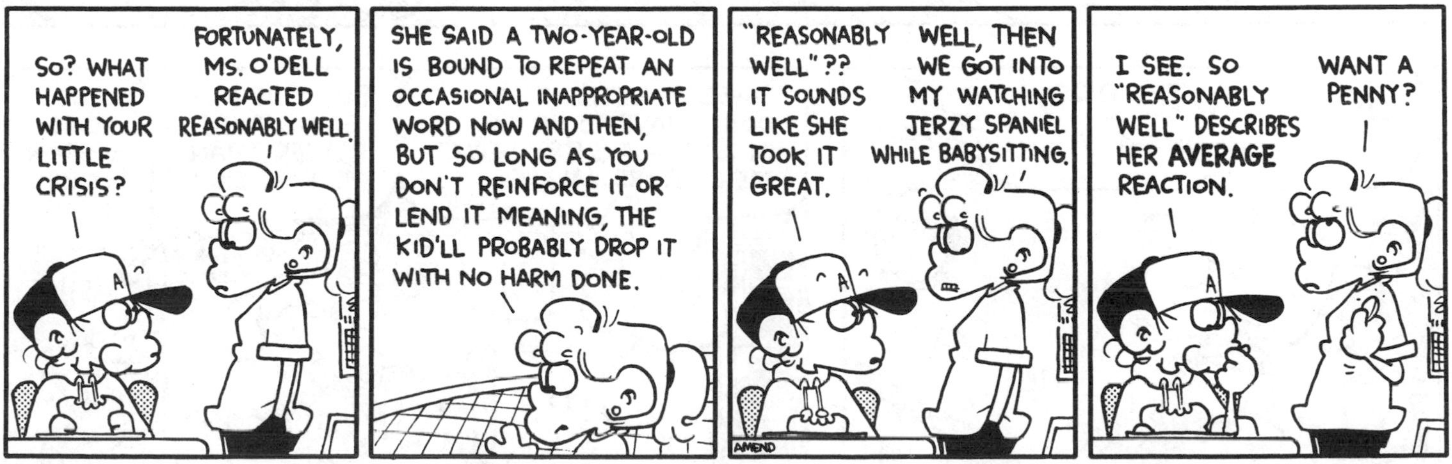
SO? WHAT HAPPENED WITH YOUR LITTLE CRISIS?
FORTUNATELY, MS. O'DELL REACTED REASONABLY WELL.
SHE SAID A TWO-YEAR-OLD IS BOUND TO REPEAT AN OCCASIONAL INAPPROPRIATE WORD NOW AND THEN, BUT SO LONG AS YOU DON'T REINFORCE IT OR LEND IT MEANING, THE KID'LL PROBABLY DROP IT WITH NO HARM DONE.
"REASONABLY WELL"?? IT SOUNDS LIKE SHE TOOK IT GREAT.
WELL, THEN WE GOT INTO MY WATCHING JERZY SPANIEL WHILE BABYSITTING.
I SEE. SO "REASONABLY WELL" DESCRIBES HER AVERAGE REACTION.
WANT A PENNY?
AMEND

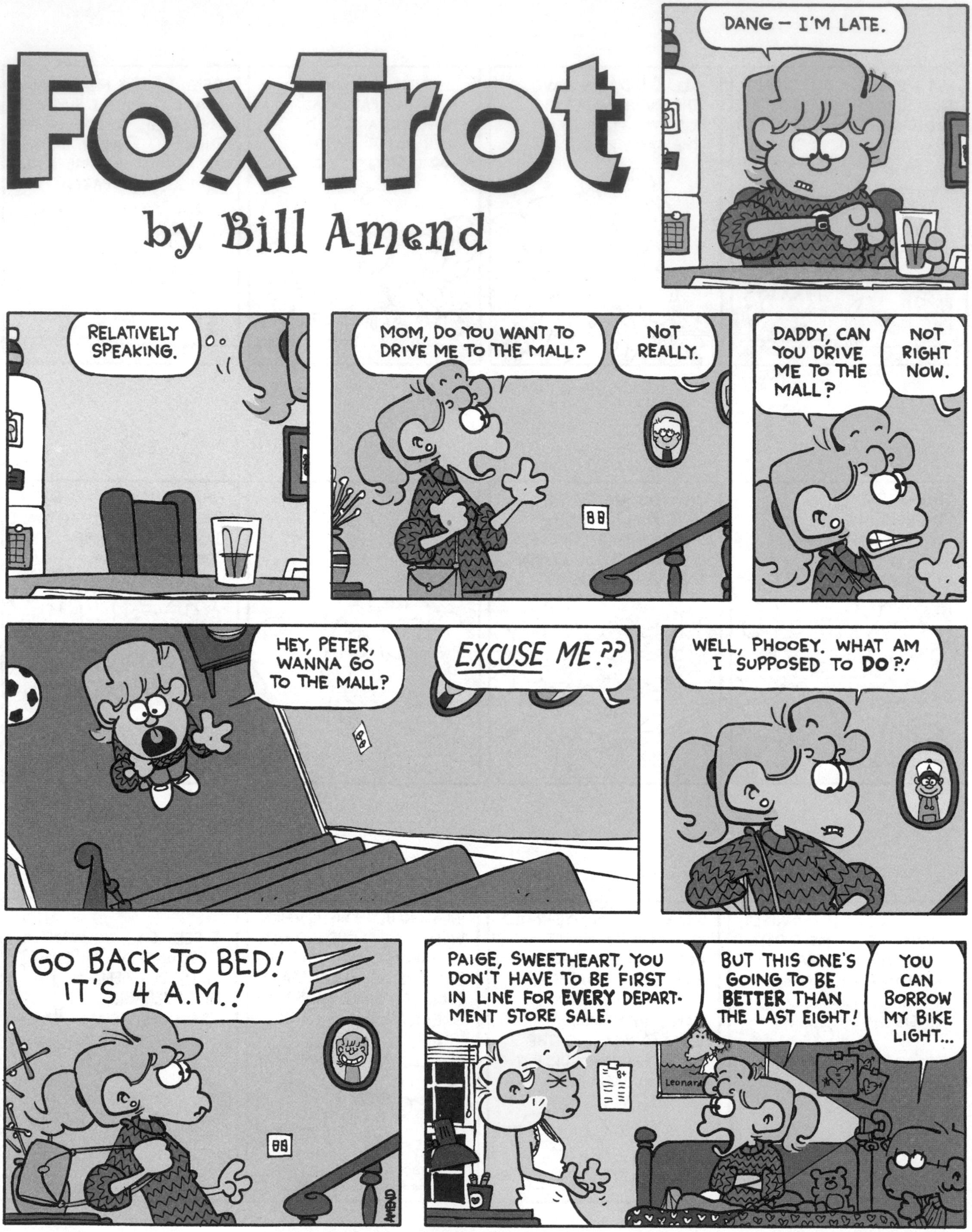

FoxTrot
by Bill Amend
DANG – I'M LATE.
RELATIVELY SPEAKING.
MOM, DO YOU WANT TO DRIVE ME TO THE MALL?
NOT REALLY.
DADDY, CAN YOU DRIVE ME TO THE MALL?
NOT RIGHT NOW.
HEY, PETER, WANNA GO TO THE MALL?
EXCUSE ME??
WELL, PHOOEY. WHAT AM I SUPPOSED TO DO?!
GO BACK TO BED! IT'S 4 A.M.!
PAIGE, SWEETHEART, YOU DON'T HAVE TO BE FIRST IN LINE FOR EVERY DEPARTMENT STORE SALE.
BUT THIS ONE'S GOING TO BE BETTER THAN THE LAST EIGHT!
YOU CAN BORROW MY BIKE LIGHT...
AMEND

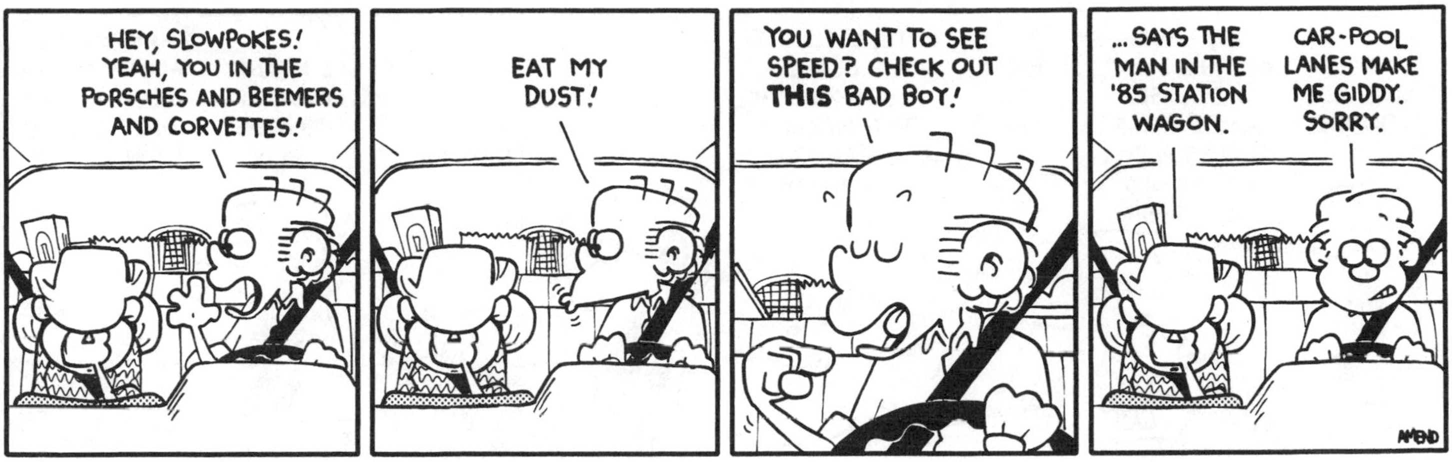
HEY, SLOWPOKES! YEAH, YOU IN THE PORSCHES AND BEEMERS AND CORVETTES!
EAT MY DUST!
YOU WANT TO SEE SPEED? CHECK OUT **THIS** BAD BOY!
...SAYS THE MAN IN THE '85 STATION WAGON.
CAR-POOL LANES MAKE ME GIDDY. SORRY.
AMEND

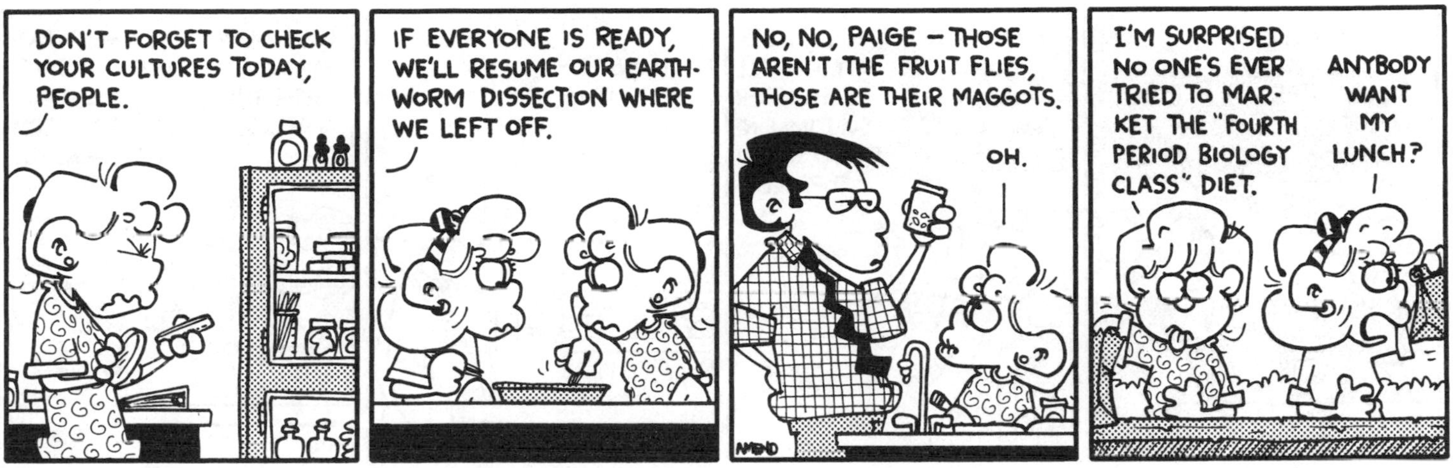
DON'T FORGET TO CHECK YOUR CULTURES TODAY, PEOPLE.
IF EVERYONE IS READY, WE'LL RESUME OUR EARTHWORM DISSECTION WHERE WE LEFT OFF.
NO, NO, PAIGE – THOSE AREN'T THE FRUIT FLIES, THOSE ARE THEIR MAGGOTS.
OH.
AMEND
I'M SURPRISED NO ONE'S EVER TRIED TO MARKET THE "FOURTH PERIOD BIOLOGY CLASS" DIET.
ANYBODY WANT MY LUNCH?

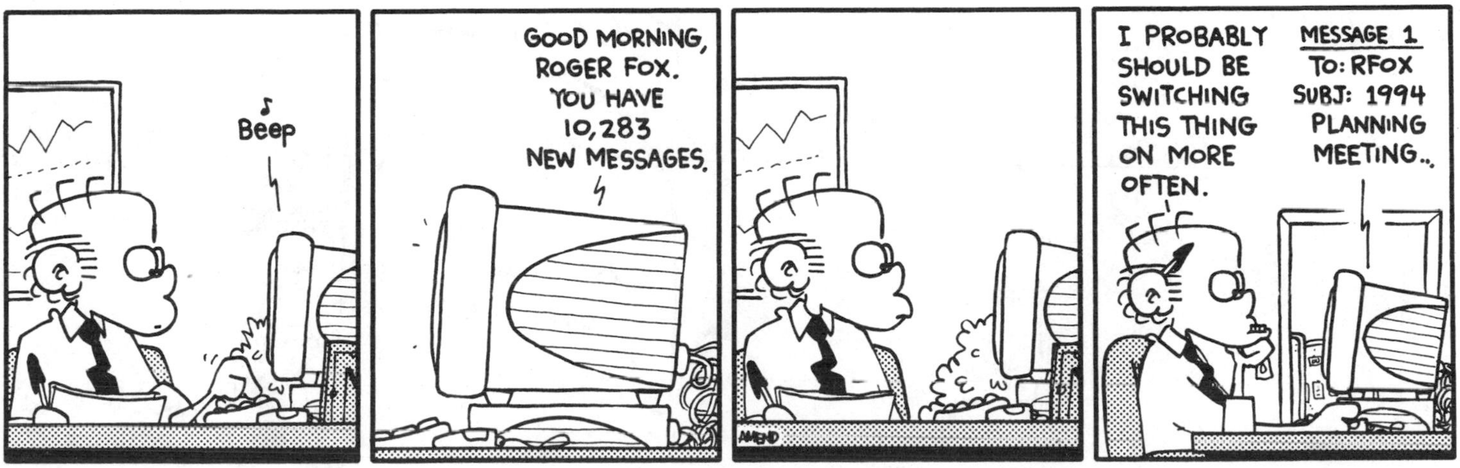
Beep
GOOD MORNING, ROGER FOX. YOU HAVE 10,283 NEW MESSAGES.
AMEND
I PROBABLY SHOULD BE SWITCHING THIS THING ON MORE OFTEN.
MESSAGE 1
TO: RFOX
SUBJ: 1994 PLANNING MEETING...

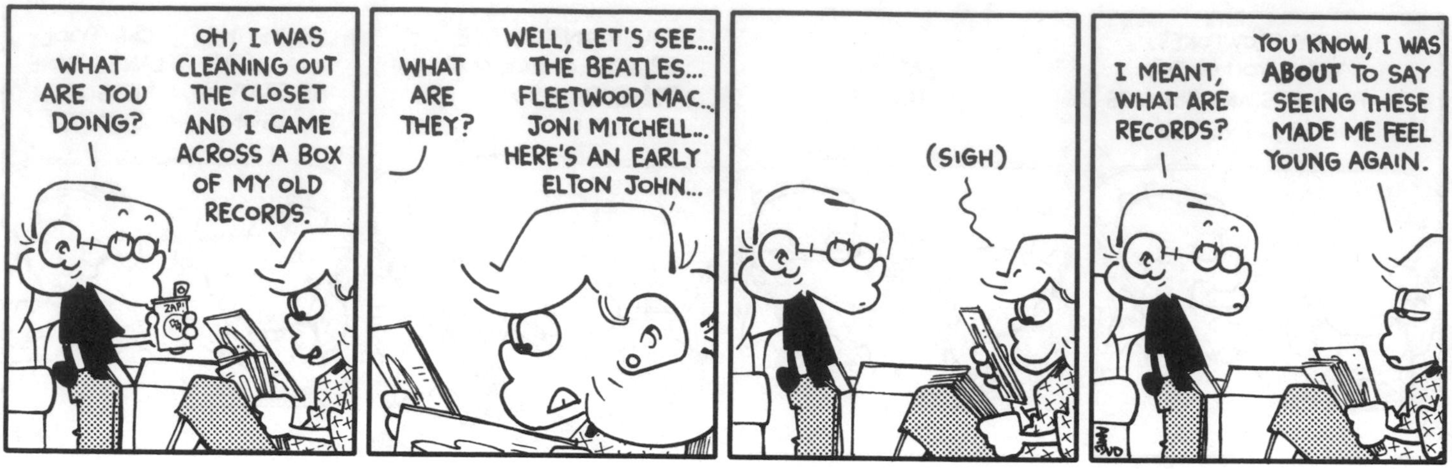
WHAT ARE YOU DOING?
OH, I WAS CLEANING OUT THE CLOSET AND I CAME ACROSS A BOX OF MY OLD RECORDS.
ZAP!
WHAT ARE THEY?
WELL, LET'S SEE... THE BEATLES... FLEETWOOD MAC... JONI MITCHELL... HERE'S AN EARLY ELTON JOHN...
(SIGH)
I MEANT, WHAT ARE RECORDS?
YOU KNOW, I WAS **ABOUT** TO SAY SEEING THESE MADE ME FEEL YOUNG AGAIN.
AMEND

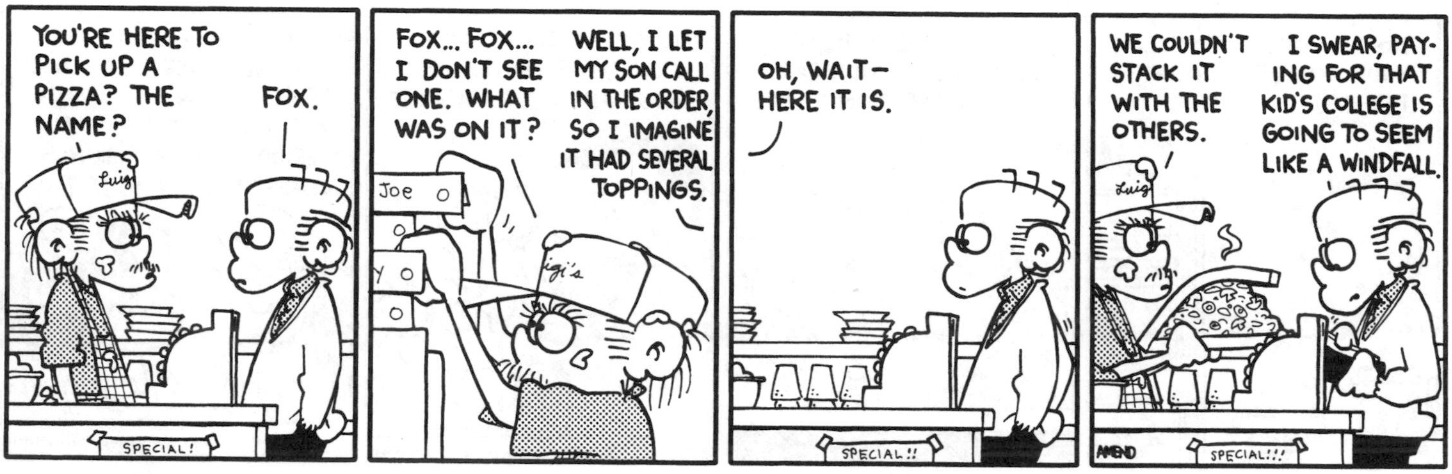
YOU'RE HERE TO PICK UP A PIZZA? THE NAME?
FOX.
SPECIAL!
FOX... FOX... I DON'T SEE ONE. WHAT WAS ON IT?
WELL, I LET MY SON CALL IN THE ORDER, SO I IMAGINE IT HAD SEVERAL TOPPINGS.
Joe
OH, WAIT— HERE IT IS.
SPECIAL!!
WE COULDN'T STACK IT WITH THE OTHERS.
I SWEAR, PAYING FOR THAT KID'S COLLEGE IS GOING TO SEEM LIKE A WINDFALL.
AMEND
SPECIAL!!!

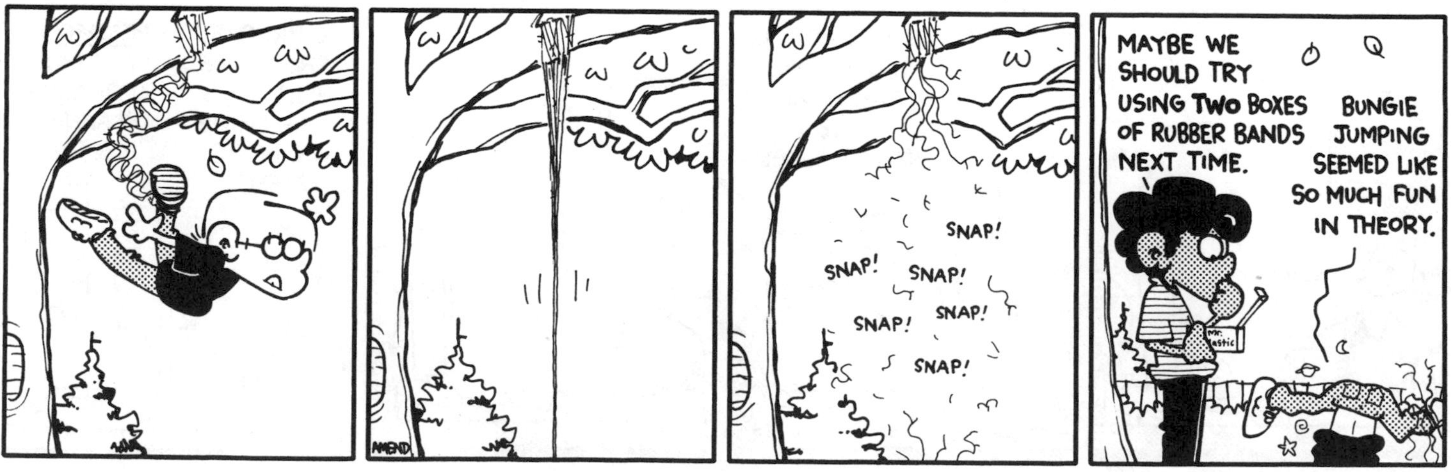
AMEND
SNAP!
SNAP!
SNAP!
SNAP!
SNAP!
SNAP!
MAYBE WE SHOULD TRY USING **TWO** BOXES OF RUBBER BANDS NEXT TIME.
BUNGIE JUMPING SEEMED LIKE SO MUCH FUN IN THEORY.

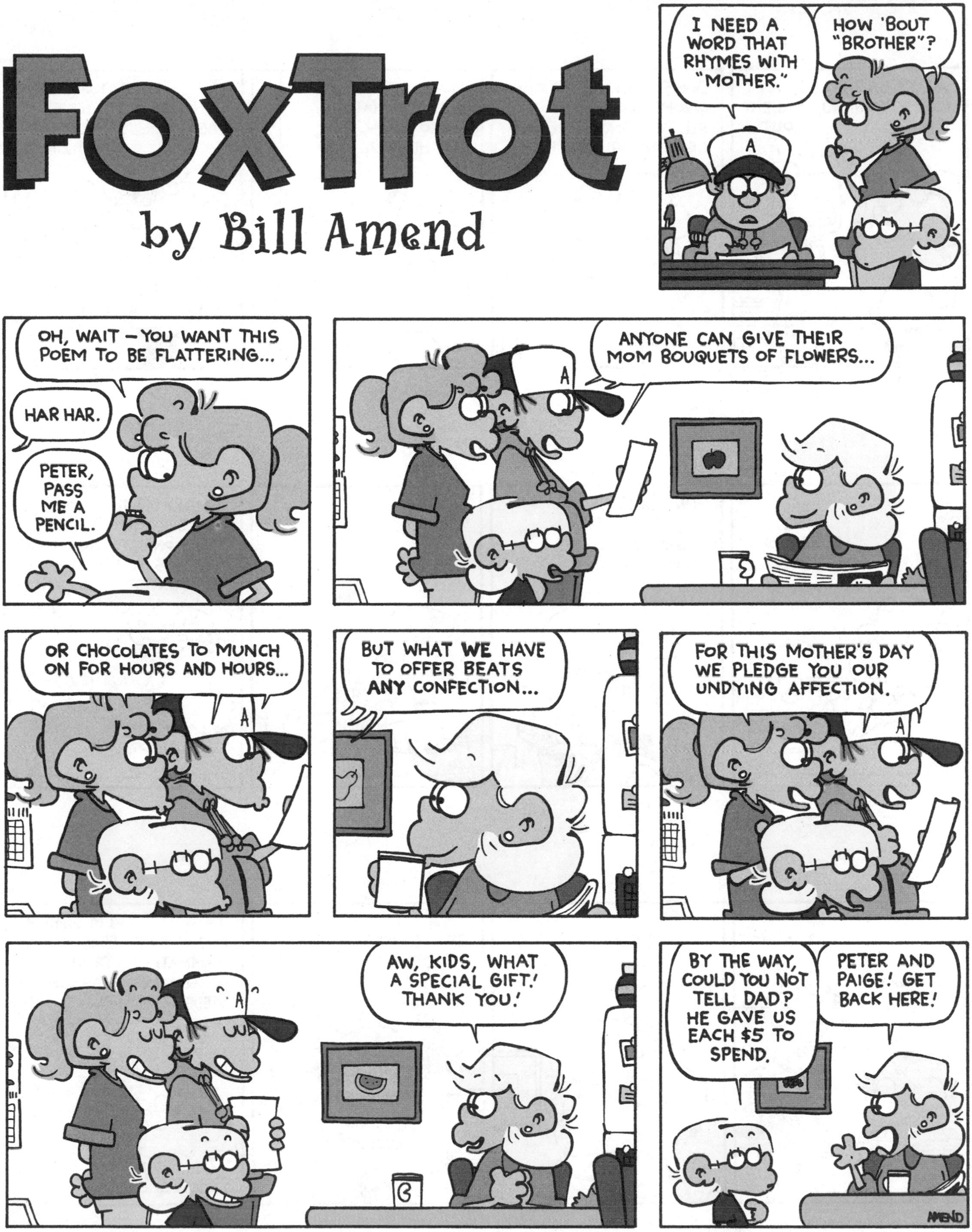
FoxTrot
by Bill Amend
I NEED A WORD THAT RHYMES WITH "MOTHER."
HOW 'BOUT "BROTHER"?
OH, WAIT – YOU WANT THIS POEM TO BE FLATTERING...
HAR HAR.
PETER, PASS ME A PENCIL.
ANYONE CAN GIVE THEIR MOM BOUQUETS OF FLOWERS...
OR CHOCOLATES TO MUNCH ON FOR HOURS AND HOURS...
BUT WHAT WE HAVE TO OFFER BEATS ANY CONFECTION...
FOR THIS MOTHER'S DAY WE PLEDGE YOU OUR UNDYING AFFECTION.
AW, KIDS, WHAT A SPECIAL GIFT! THANK YOU!
BY THE WAY, COULD YOU NOT TELL DAD? HE GAVE US EACH $5 TO SPEND.
PETER AND PAIGE! GET BACK HERE!
AMEND

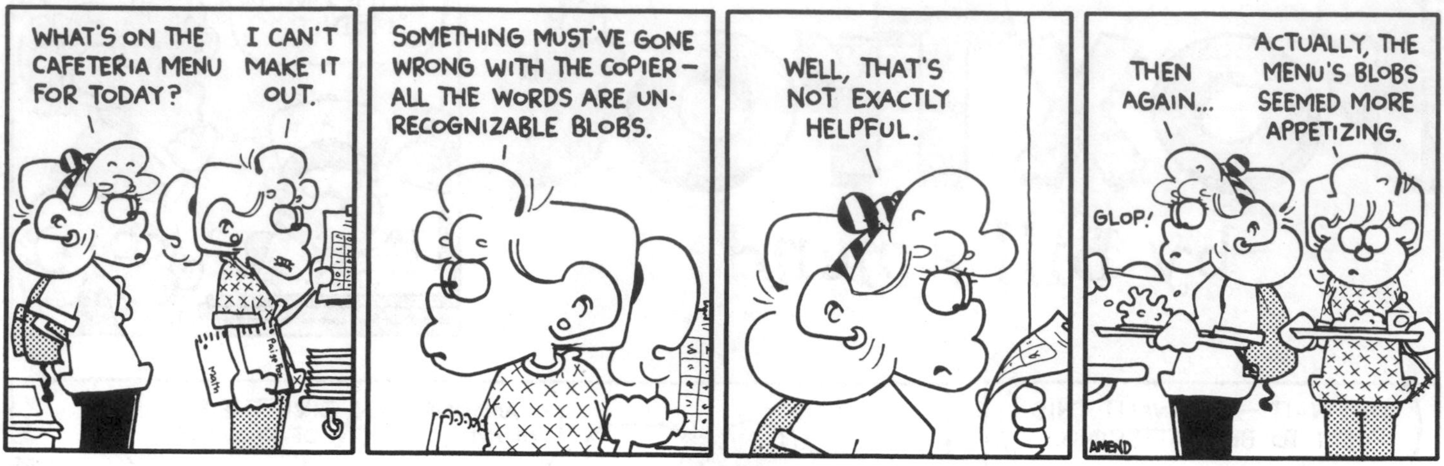

WHAT'S ON THE CAFETERIA MENU FOR TODAY?
I CAN'T MAKE IT OUT.
SOMETHING MUST'VE GONE WRONG WITH THE COPIER—ALL THE WORDS ARE UNRECOGNIZABLE BLOBS.
WELL, THAT'S NOT EXACTLY HELPFUL.
GLOP!
THEN AGAIN...
ACTUALLY, THE MENU'S BLOBS SEEMED MORE APPETIZING.
AMEND

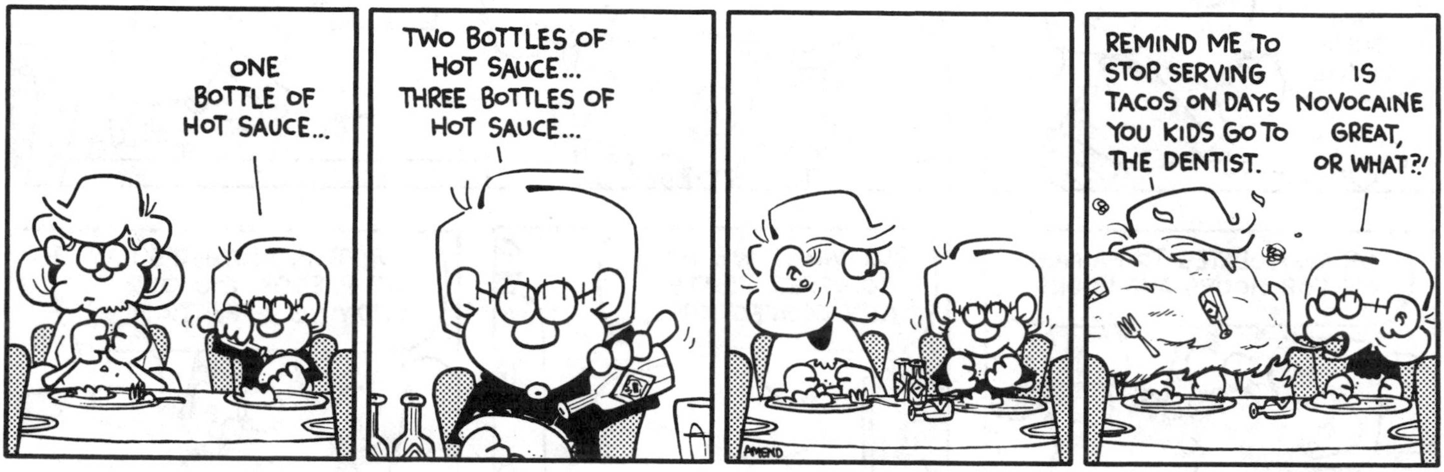

ONE BOTTLE OF HOT SAUCE...
TWO BOTTLES OF HOT SAUCE... THREE BOTTLES OF HOT SAUCE...
AMEND
REMIND ME TO STOP SERVING TACOS ON DAYS YOU KIDS GO TO THE DENTIST.
IS NOVOCAINE GREAT, OR WHAT?!

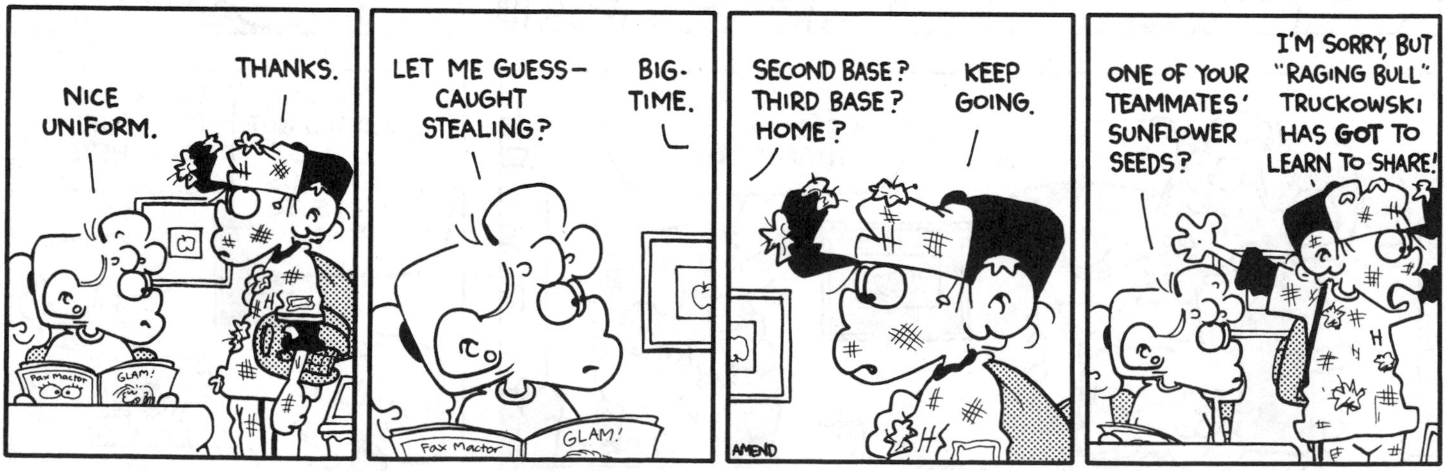

NICE UNIFORM.
THANKS.
Fax Mactor
GLAM!
LET ME GUESS—CAUGHT STEALING?
BIG-TIME.
SECOND BASE? THIRD BASE? HOME?
KEEP GOING.
AMEND
ONE OF YOUR TEAMMATES' SUNFLOWER SEEDS?
I'M SORRY, BUT "RAGING BULL" TRUCKOWSKI HAS GOT TO LEARN TO SHARE!

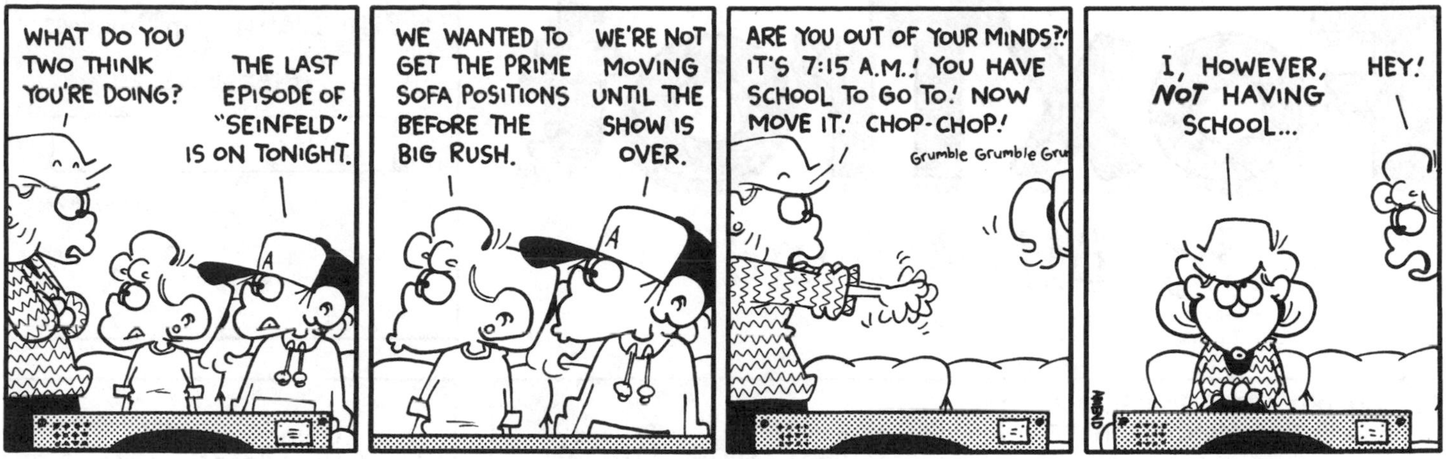
WHAT DO YOU TWO THINK YOU'RE DOING?
THE LAST EPISODE OF "SEINFELD" IS ON TONIGHT.
WE WANTED TO GET THE PRIME SOFA POSITIONS BEFORE THE BIG RUSH.
WE'RE NOT MOVING UNTIL THE SHOW IS OVER.
ARE YOU OUT OF YOUR MINDS?! IT'S 7:15 A.M.! YOU HAVE SCHOOL TO GO TO! NOW MOVE IT! CHOP-CHOP!
Grumble Grumble Gru
I, HOWEVER, NOT HAVING SCHOOL...
HEY!

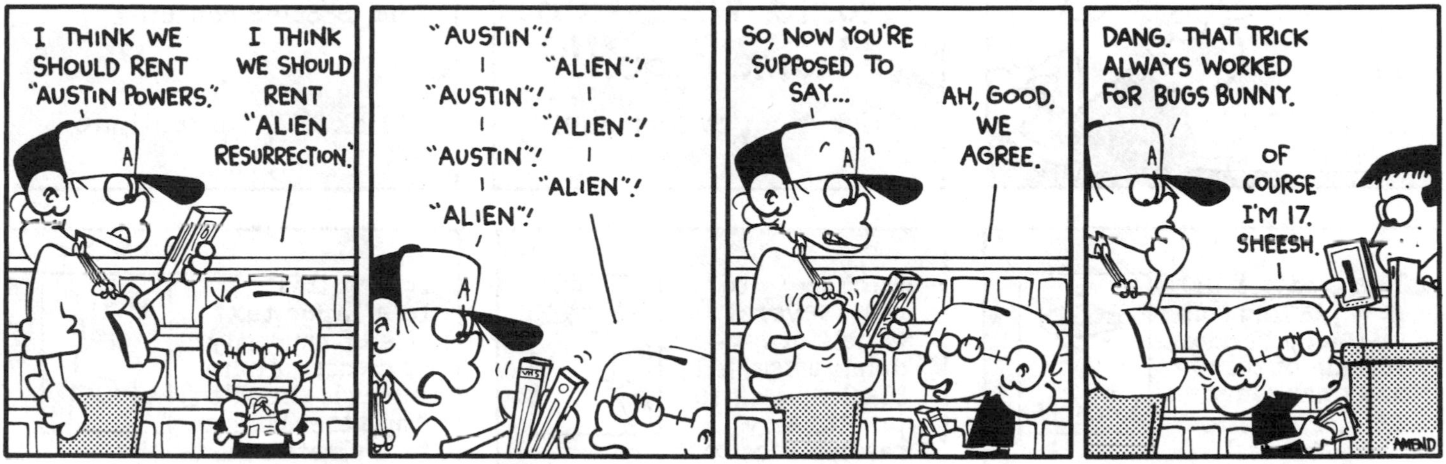
I THINK WE SHOULD RENT "AUSTIN POWERS."
I THINK WE SHOULD RENT "ALIEN RESURRECTION."
"AUSTIN"!
"ALIEN"!
"AUSTIN"!
"ALIEN"!
"AUSTIN"!
"ALIEN"!
"ALIEN"!
SO, NOW YOU'RE SUPPOSED TO SAY...
AH, GOOD. WE AGREE.
DANG. THAT TRICK ALWAYS WORKED FOR BUGS BUNNY.
OF COURSE I'M 17. SHEESH.
AMEND

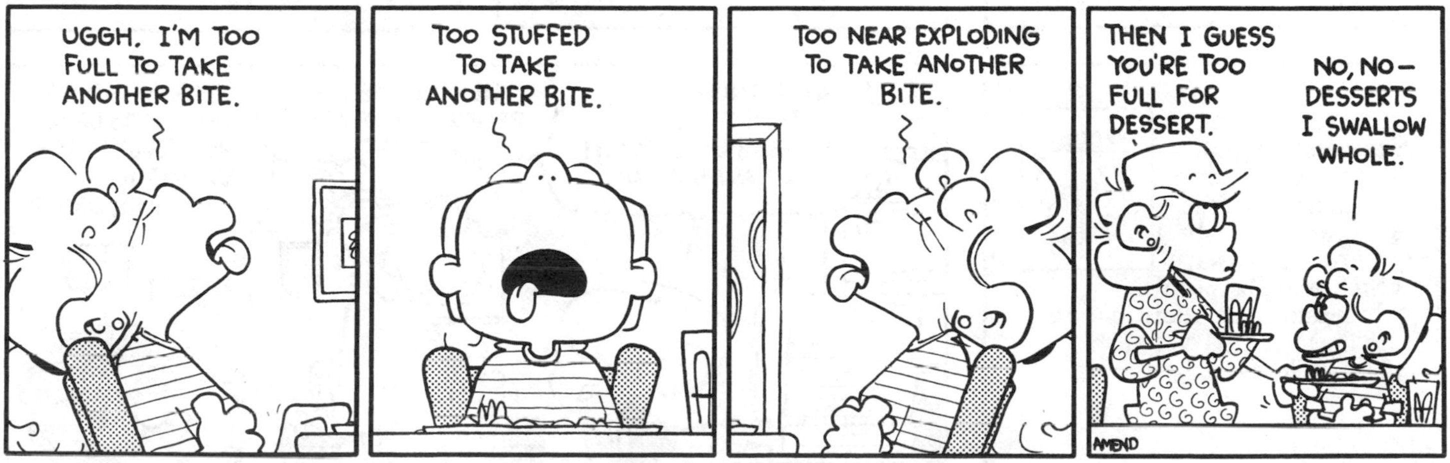
UGGH. I'M TOO FULL TO TAKE ANOTHER BITE.
TOO STUFFED TO TAKE ANOTHER BITE.
TOO NEAR EXPLODING TO TAKE ANOTHER BITE.
THEN I GUESS YOU'RE TOO FULL FOR DESSERT.
NO, NO— DESSERTS I SWALLOW WHOLE.
AMEND

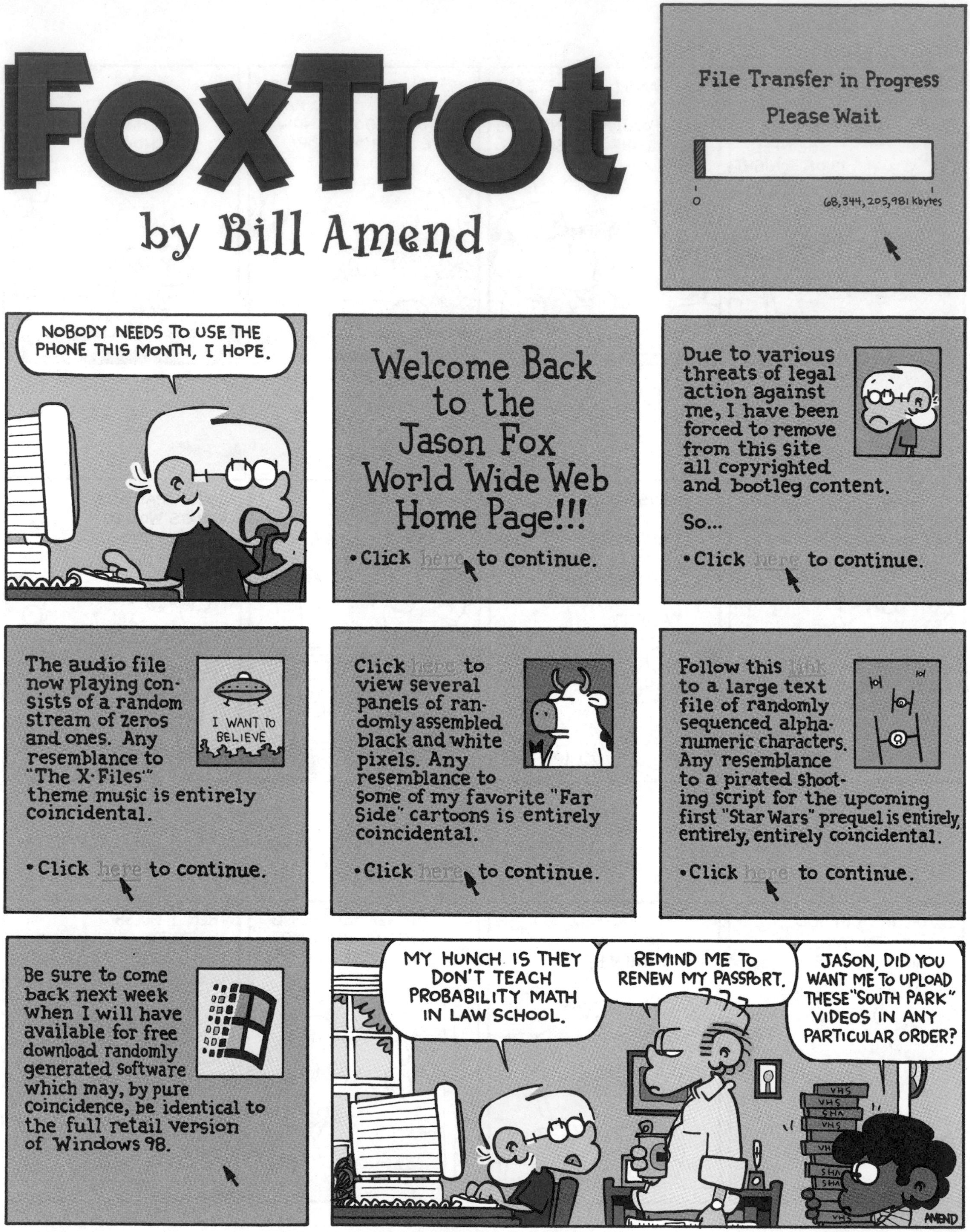
FoxTrot
by Bill Amend
File Transfer in Progress
Please Wait
0
68,344,205,981 Kbytes
NOBODY NEEDS TO USE THE PHONE THIS MONTH, I HOPE.
Welcome Back to the Jason Fox World Wide Web Home Page!!!
• Click here to continue.
Due to various threats of legal action against me, I have been forced to remove from this site all copyrighted and bootleg content.
So...
• Click here to continue.
The audio file now playing consists of a random stream of zeros and ones. Any resemblance to "The X-Files" theme music is entirely coincidental.
I WANT TO BELIEVE
• Click here to continue.
Click here to view several panels of randomly assembled black and white pixels. Any resemblance to some of my favorite "Far Side" cartoons is entirely coincidental.
• Click here to continue.
Follow this link to a large text file of randomly sequenced alphanumeric characters. Any resemblance to a pirated shooting script for the upcoming first "Star Wars" prequel is entirely, entirely, entirely coincidental.
• Click here to continue.
Be sure to come back next week when I will have available for free download randomly generated software which may, by pure coincidence, be identical to the full retail version of Windows 98.
MY HUNCH IS THEY DON'T TEACH PROBABILITY MATH IN LAW SCHOOL.
REMIND ME TO RENEW MY PASSPORT.
JASON, DID YOU WANT ME TO UPLOAD THESE "SOUTH PARK" VIDEOS IN ANY PARTICULAR ORDER?
VHS
AMEND

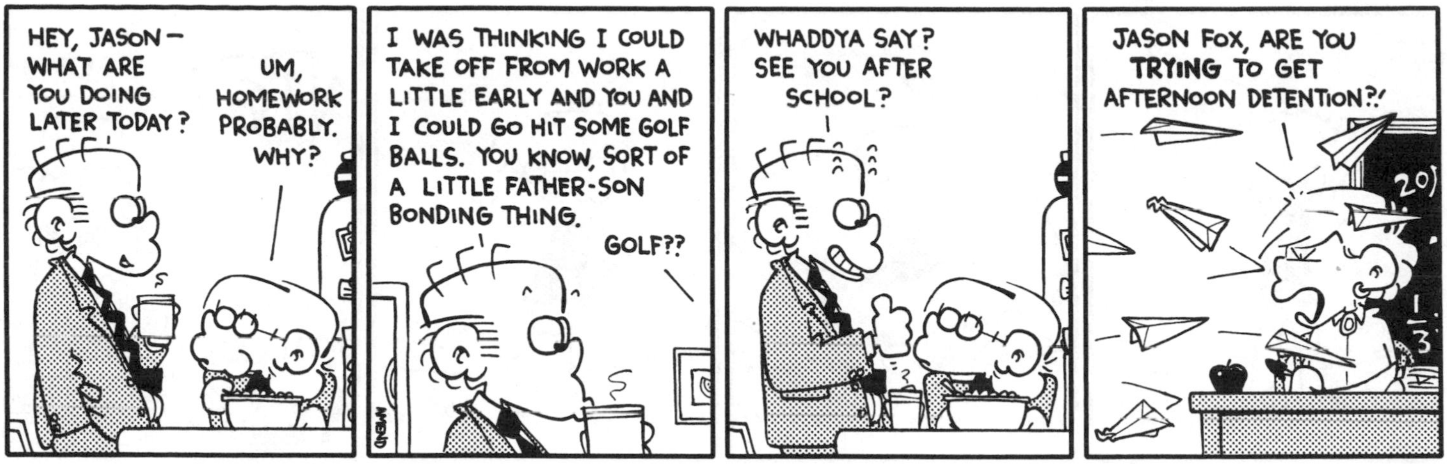
HEY, JASON— WHAT ARE YOU DOING LATER TODAY?
UM, HOMEWORK PROBABLY. WHY?
I WAS THINKING I COULD TAKE OFF FROM WORK A LITTLE EARLY AND YOU AND I COULD GO HIT SOME GOLF BALLS. YOU KNOW, SORT OF A LITTLE FATHER-SON BONDING THING.
GOLF??
AMEND
WHADDYA SAY? SEE YOU AFTER SCHOOL?
JASON FOX, ARE YOU **TRYING** TO GET AFTERNOON DETENTION?!
20)
1/3

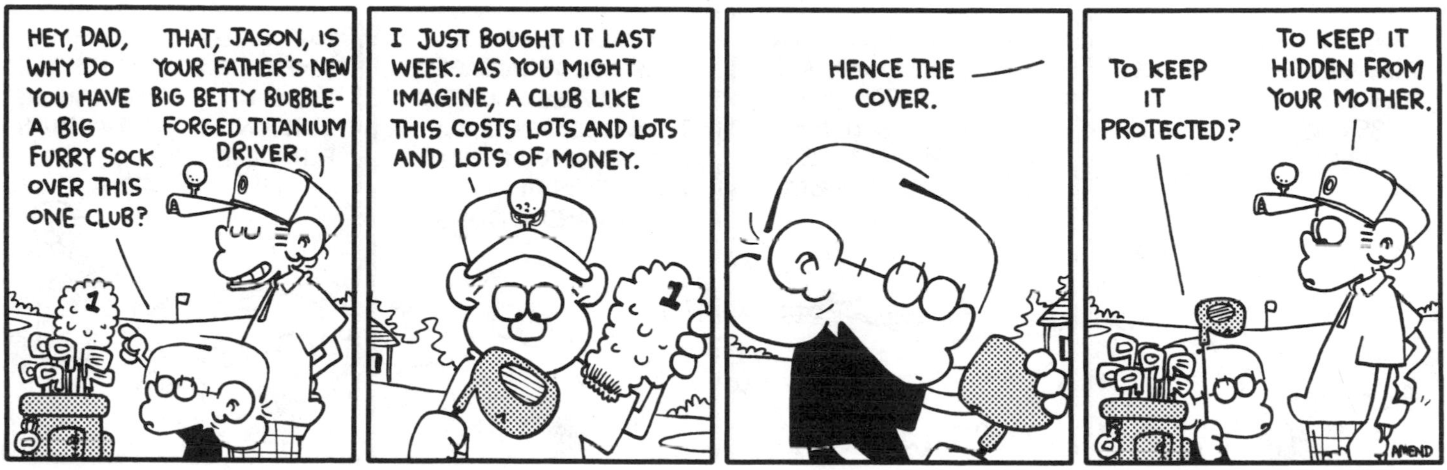
HEY, DAD, WHY DO YOU HAVE A BIG FURRY SOCK OVER THIS ONE CLUB?
THAT, JASON, IS YOUR FATHER'S NEW BIG BETTY BUBBLE-FORGED TITANIUM DRIVER.
1
I JUST BOUGHT IT LAST WEEK. AS YOU MIGHT IMAGINE, A CLUB LIKE THIS COSTS LOTS AND LOTS AND LOTS OF MONEY.
1
HENCE THE COVER.
TO KEEP IT PROTECTED?
TO KEEP IT HIDDEN FROM YOUR MOTHER.
AMEND

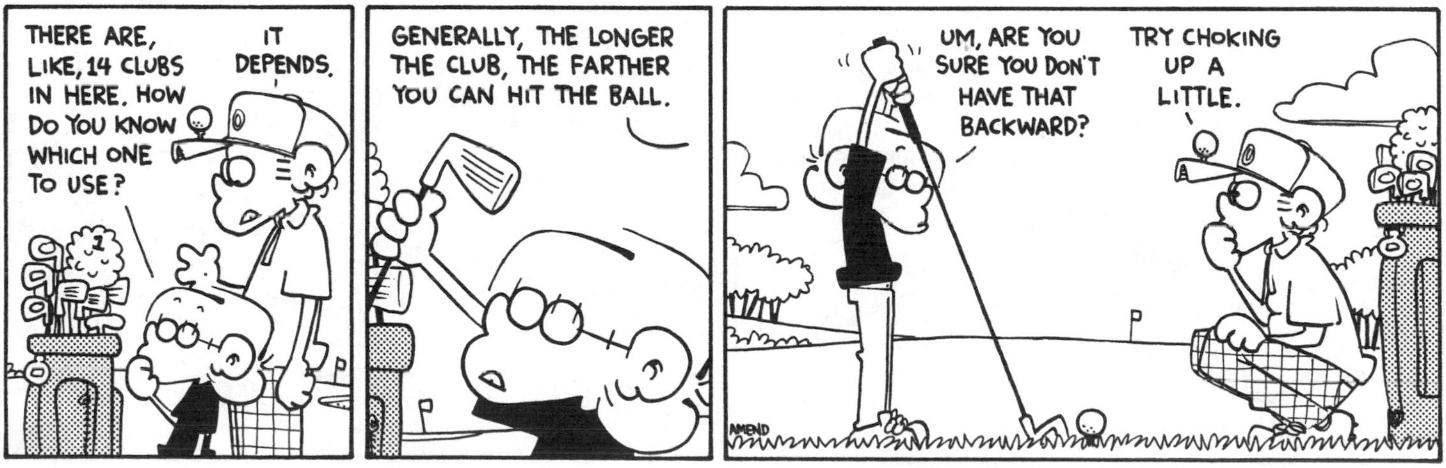
THERE ARE, LIKE, 14 CLUBS IN HERE. HOW DO YOU KNOW WHICH ONE TO USE?
IT DEPENDS.
1
GENERALLY, THE LONGER THE CLUB, THE FARTHER YOU CAN HIT THE BALL.
UM, ARE YOU SURE YOU DON'T HAVE THAT BACKWARD?
TRY CHOKING UP A LITTLE.
AMEND

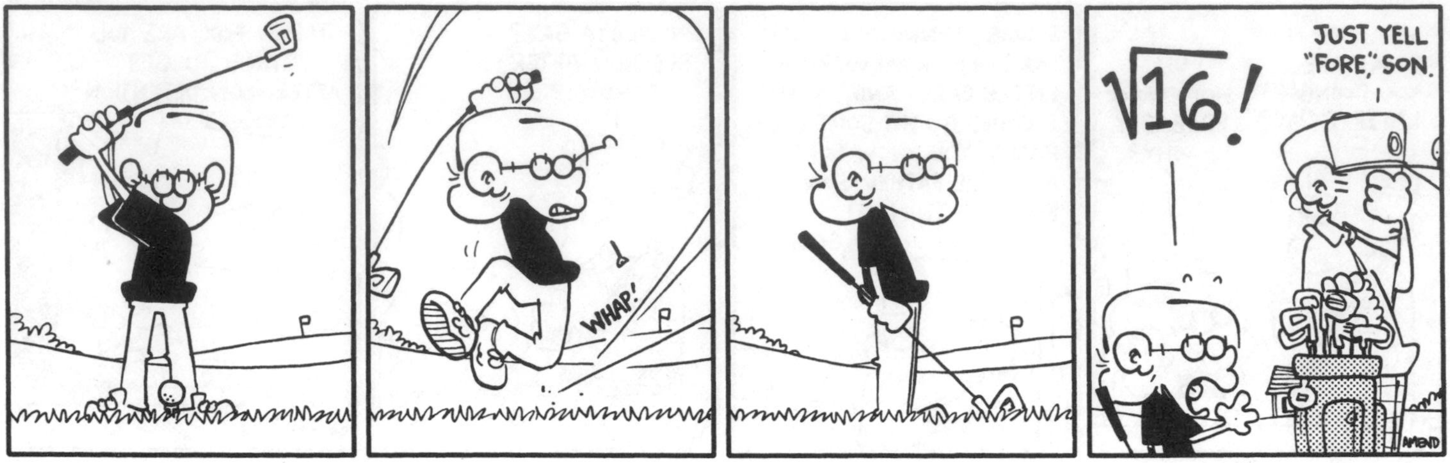
WHAP!
√16!
JUST YELL "FORE," SON.

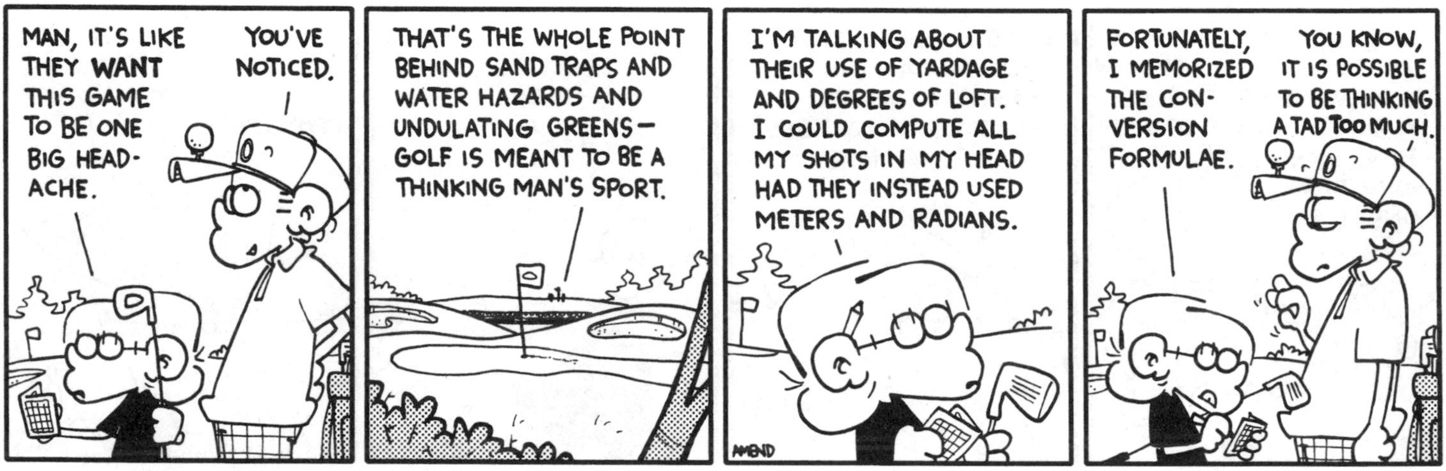
MAN, IT'S LIKE THEY WANT THIS GAME TO BE ONE BIG HEADACHE.
YOU'VE NOTICED.
THAT'S THE WHOLE POINT BEHIND SAND TRAPS AND WATER HAZARDS AND UNDULATING GREENS— GOLF IS MEANT TO BE A THINKING MAN'S SPORT.
I'M TALKING ABOUT THEIR USE OF YARDAGE AND DEGREES OF LOFT. I COULD COMPUTE ALL MY SHOTS IN MY HEAD HAD THEY INSTEAD USED METERS AND RADIANS.
FORTUNATELY, I MEMORIZED THE CONVERSION FORMULAE.
YOU KNOW, IT IS POSSIBLE TO BE THINKING A TAD TOO MUCH.
AMEND

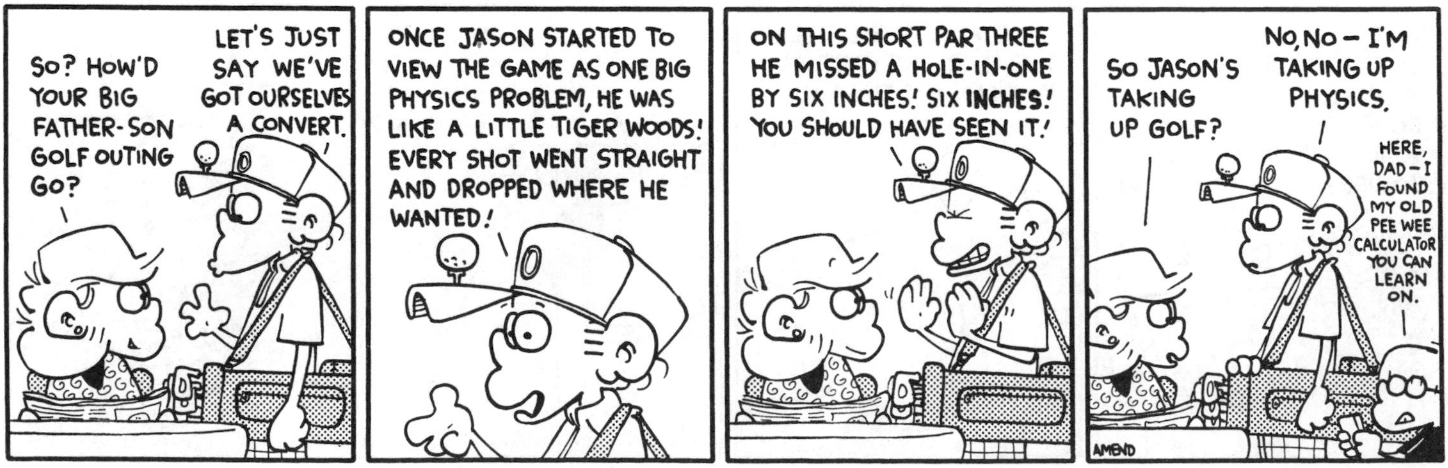
SO? HOW'D YOUR BIG FATHER-SON GOLF OUTING GO?
LET'S JUST SAY WE'VE GOT OURSELVES A CONVERT.
ONCE JASON STARTED TO VIEW THE GAME AS ONE BIG PHYSICS PROBLEM, HE WAS LIKE A LITTLE TIGER WOODS! EVERY SHOT WENT STRAIGHT AND DROPPED WHERE HE WANTED!
ON THIS SHORT PAR THREE HE MISSED A HOLE-IN-ONE BY SIX INCHES! SIX INCHES! YOU SHOULD HAVE SEEN IT!
SO JASON'S TAKING UP GOLF?
NO, NO — I'M TAKING UP PHYSICS.
HERE, DAD — I FOUND MY OLD PEE WEE CALCULATOR YOU CAN LEARN ON.
AMEND

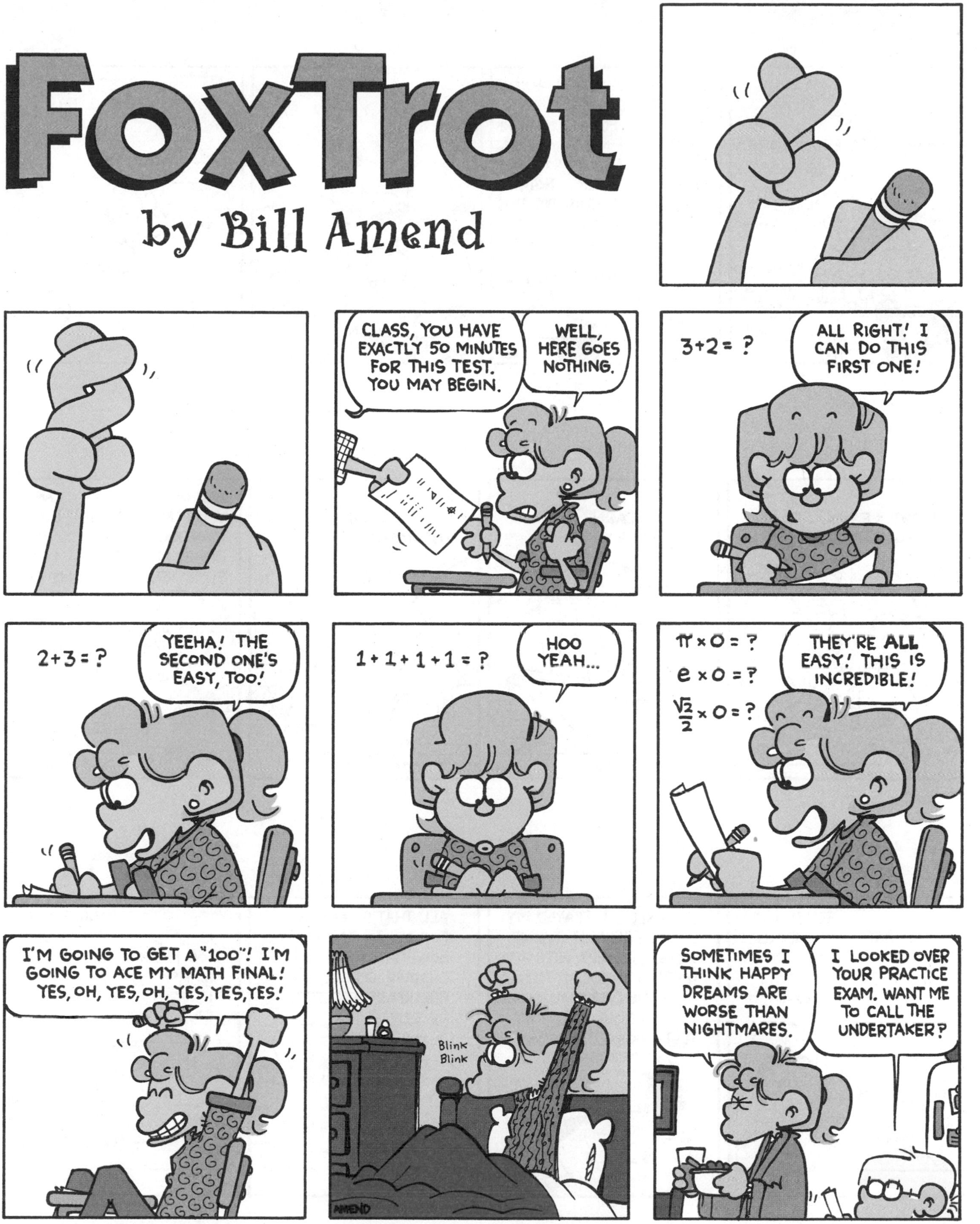
FoxTrot
by Bill Amend
CLASS, YOU HAVE EXACTLY 50 MINUTES FOR THIS TEST. YOU MAY BEGIN.
WELL, HERE GOES NOTHING.
3+2 = ?
ALL RIGHT! I CAN DO THIS FIRST ONE!
2+3 = ?
YEEHA! THE SECOND ONE'S EASY, TOO!
1+1+1+1 = ?
HOO YEAH...
$\pi \times 0 = ?$
$e \times 0 = ?$
$\frac{\sqrt{2}}{2} \times 0 = ?$
THEY'RE **ALL** EASY! THIS IS INCREDIBLE!
I'M GOING TO GET A "100"! I'M GOING TO ACE MY MATH FINAL! YES, OH, YES, OH, YES, YES, YES!
Blink Blink
AMEND
SOMETIMES I THINK HAPPY DREAMS ARE WORSE THAN NIGHTMARES.
I LOOKED OVER YOUR PRACTICE EXAM. WANT ME TO CALL THE UNDERTAKER?

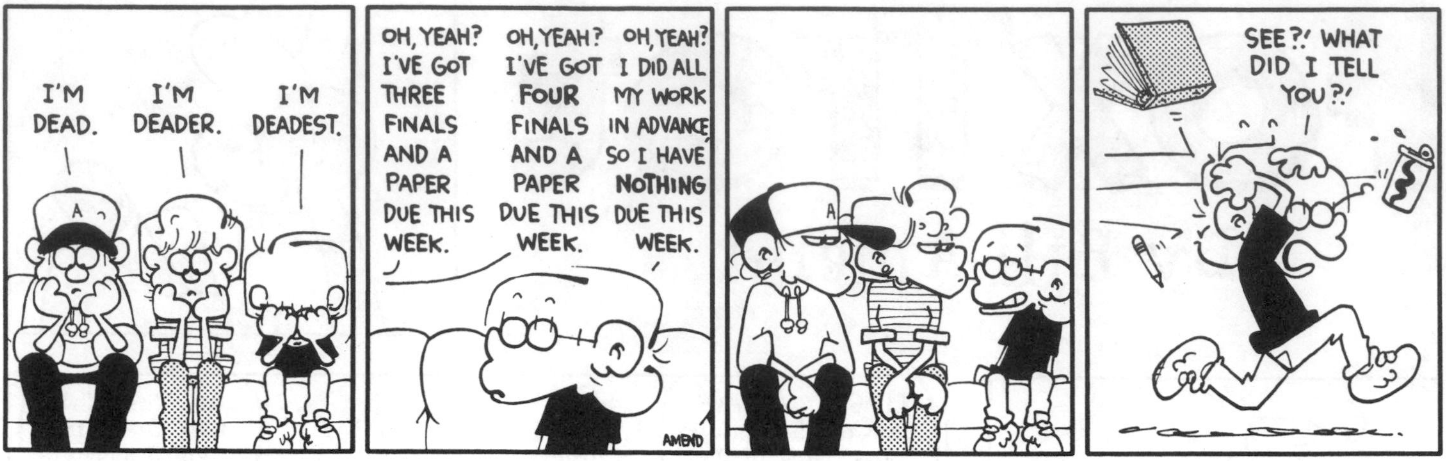
I'M DEAD.
I'M DEADER.
I'M DEADEST.
OH, YEAH? I'VE GOT THREE FINALS AND A PAPER DUE THIS WEEK.
OH, YEAH? I'VE GOT FOUR FINALS AND A PAPER DUE THIS WEEK.
OH, YEAH? I DID ALL MY WORK IN ADVANCE, SO I HAVE NOTHING DUE THIS WEEK.
AMEND
SEE?! WHAT DID I TELL YOU?!

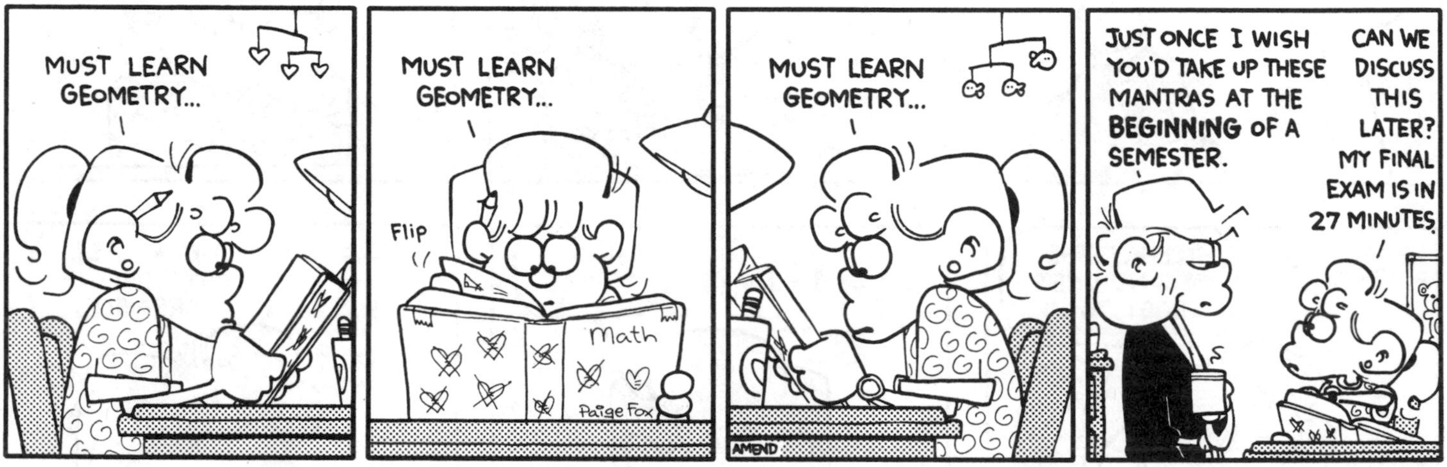
MUST LEARN GEOMETRY...
MUST LEARN GEOMETRY...
Flip
Math
Paige Fox
MUST LEARN GEOMETRY...
AMEND
JUST ONCE I WISH YOU'D TAKE UP THESE MANTRAS AT THE BEGINNING OF A SEMESTER.
CAN WE DISCUSS THIS LATER? MY FINAL EXAM IS IN 27 MINUTES.

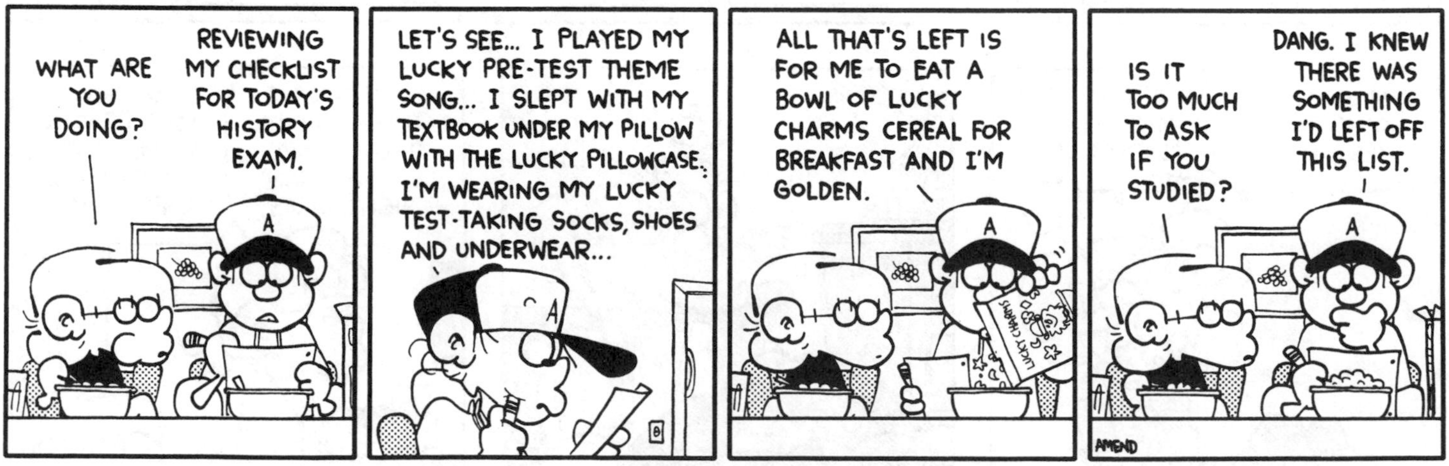
WHAT ARE YOU DOING?
REVIEWING MY CHECKLIST FOR TODAY'S HISTORY EXAM.
LET'S SEE... I PLAYED MY LUCKY PRE-TEST THEME SONG... I SLEPT WITH MY TEXTBOOK UNDER MY PILLOW WITH THE LUCKY PILLOWCASE. I'M WEARING MY LUCKY TEST-TAKING SOCKS, SHOES AND UNDERWEAR...
ALL THAT'S LEFT IS FOR ME TO EAT A BOWL OF LUCKY CHARMS CEREAL FOR BREAKFAST AND I'M GOLDEN.
LUCKY CHARMS
IS IT TOO MUCH TO ASK IF YOU STUDIED?
DANG. I KNEW THERE WAS SOMETHING I'D LEFT OFF THIS LIST.
AMEND

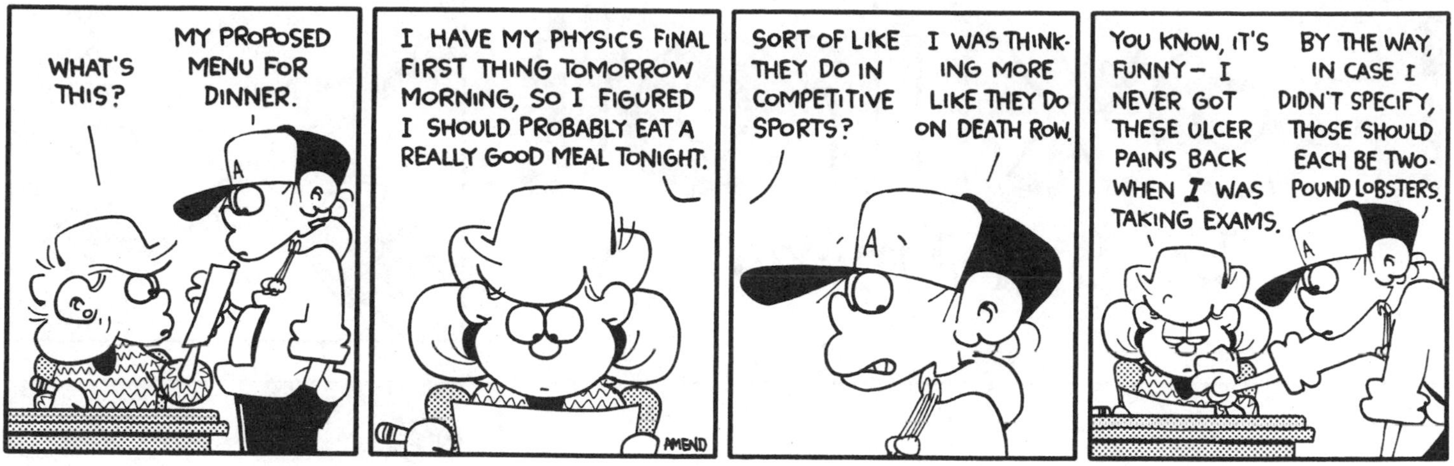
WHAT'S THIS?
MY PROPOSED MENU FOR DINNER.
I HAVE MY PHYSICS FINAL FIRST THING TOMORROW MORNING, SO I FIGURED I SHOULD PROBABLY EAT A REALLY GOOD MEAL TONIGHT.
AMEND
SORT OF LIKE THEY DO IN COMPETITIVE SPORTS?
I WAS THINKING MORE LIKE THEY DO ON DEATH ROW.
YOU KNOW, IT'S FUNNY – I NEVER GOT THESE ULCER PAINS BACK WHEN I WAS TAKING EXAMS.
BY THE WAY, IN CASE I DIDN'T SPECIFY, THOSE SHOULD EACH BE TWO-POUND LOBSTERS.

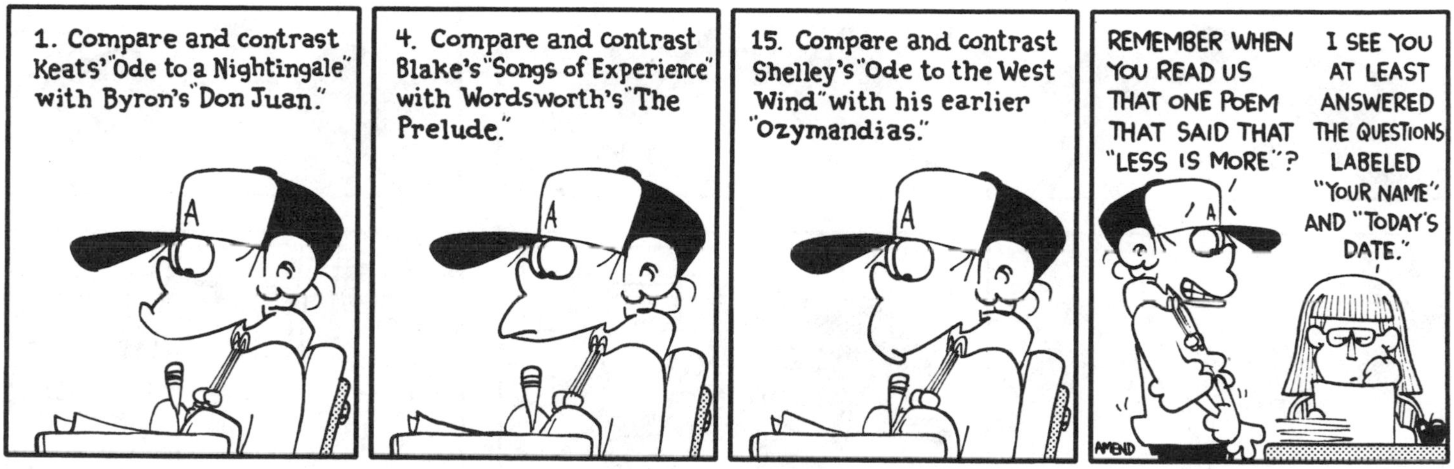
1. Compare and contrast Keats' "Ode to a Nightingale" with Byron's "Don Juan."
4. Compare and contrast Blake's "Songs of Experience" with Wordsworth's "The Prelude."
15. Compare and contrast Shelley's "Ode to the West Wind" with his earlier "Ozymandias."
REMEMBER WHEN YOU READ US THAT ONE POEM THAT SAID THAT "LESS IS MORE"?
I SEE YOU AT LEAST ANSWERED THE QUESTIONS LABELED "YOUR NAME" AND "TODAY'S DATE."
AMEND

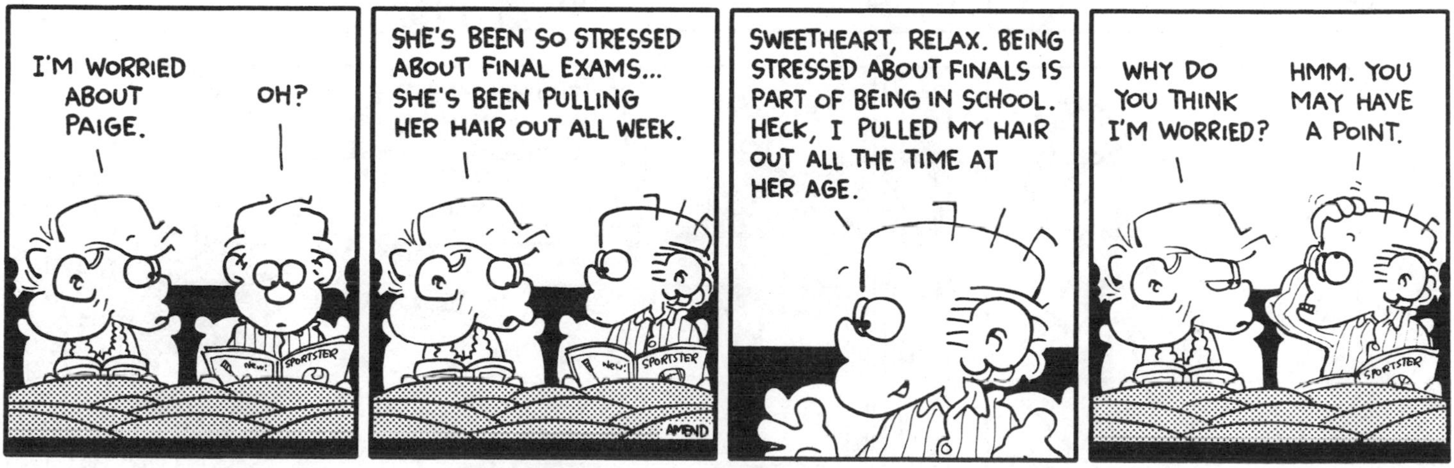
I'M WORRIED ABOUT PAIGE.
OH?
SHE'S BEEN SO STRESSED ABOUT FINAL EXAMS... SHE'S BEEN PULLING HER HAIR OUT ALL WEEK.
AMEND
SWEETHEART, RELAX. BEING STRESSED ABOUT FINALS IS PART OF BEING IN SCHOOL. HECK, I PULLED MY HAIR OUT ALL THE TIME AT HER AGE.
WHY DO YOU THINK I'M WORRIED?
HMM. YOU MAY HAVE A POINT.

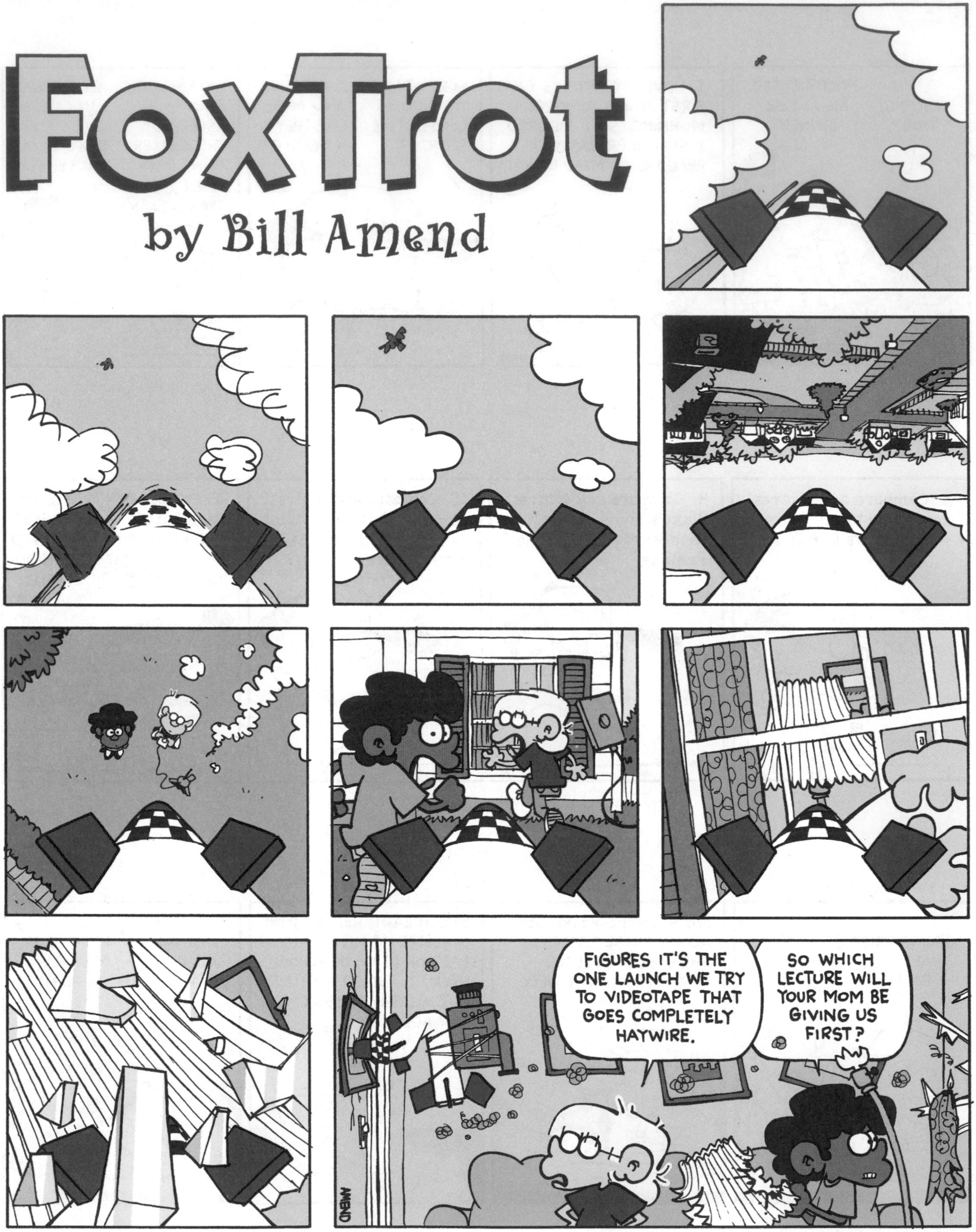
FoxTrot
by Bill Amend
FIGURES IT'S THE ONE LAUNCH WE TRY TO VIDEOTAPE THAT GOES COMPLETELY HAYWIRE.
SO WHICH LECTURE WILL YOUR MOM BE GIVING US FIRST?
AMEND

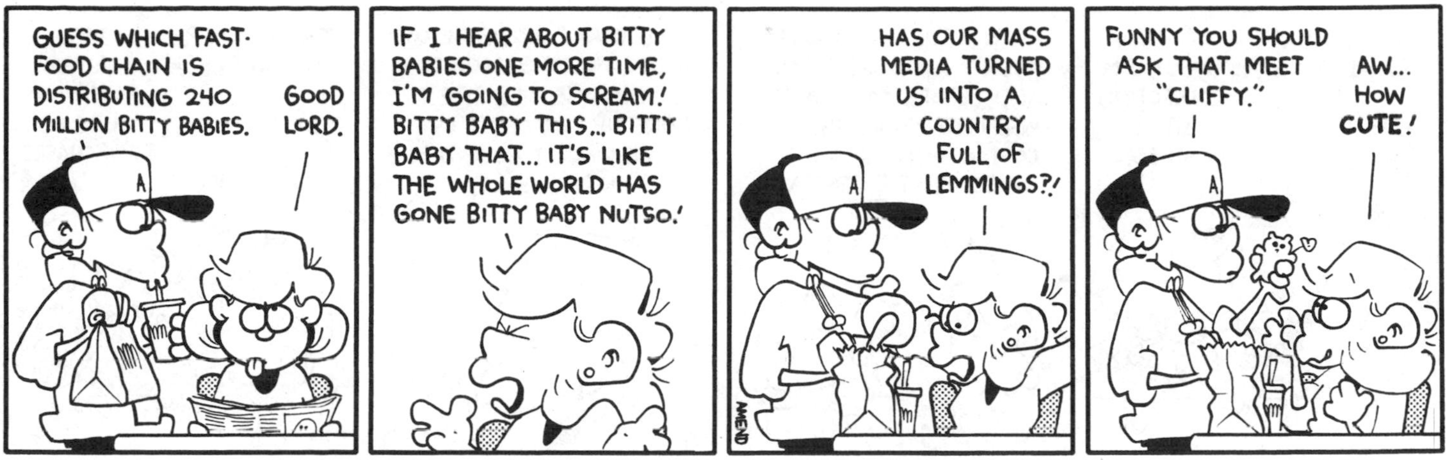
GUESS WHICH FAST-FOOD CHAIN IS DISTRIBUTING 240 MILLION BITTY BABIES.
GOOD LORD.
IF I HEAR ABOUT BITTY BABIES ONE MORE TIME, I'M GOING TO SCREAM! BITTY BABY THIS... BITTY BABY THAT... IT'S LIKE THE WHOLE WORLD HAS GONE BITTY BABY NUTSO!
HAS OUR MASS MEDIA TURNED US INTO A COUNTRY FULL OF LEMMINGS?!
AMEND
FUNNY YOU SHOULD ASK THAT. MEET "CLIFFY."
AW... HOW **CUTE**!

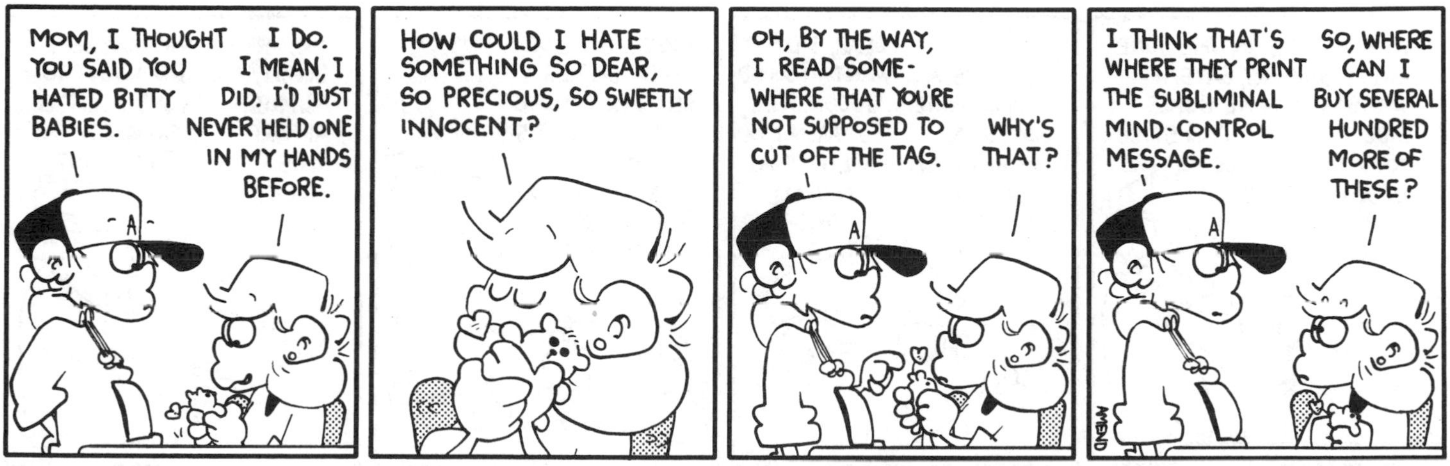
MOM, I THOUGHT YOU SAID YOU HATED BITTY BABIES.
I DO. I MEAN, I DID. I'D JUST NEVER HELD ONE IN MY HANDS BEFORE.
HOW COULD I HATE SOMETHING SO DEAR, SO PRECIOUS, SO SWEETLY INNOCENT?
OH, BY THE WAY, I READ SOMEWHERE THAT YOU'RE NOT SUPPOSED TO CUT OFF THE TAG.
WHY'S THAT?
I THINK THAT'S WHERE THEY PRINT THE SUBLIMINAL MIND-CONTROL MESSAGE.
SO, WHERE CAN I BUY SEVERAL HUNDRED MORE OF THESE?
AMEND

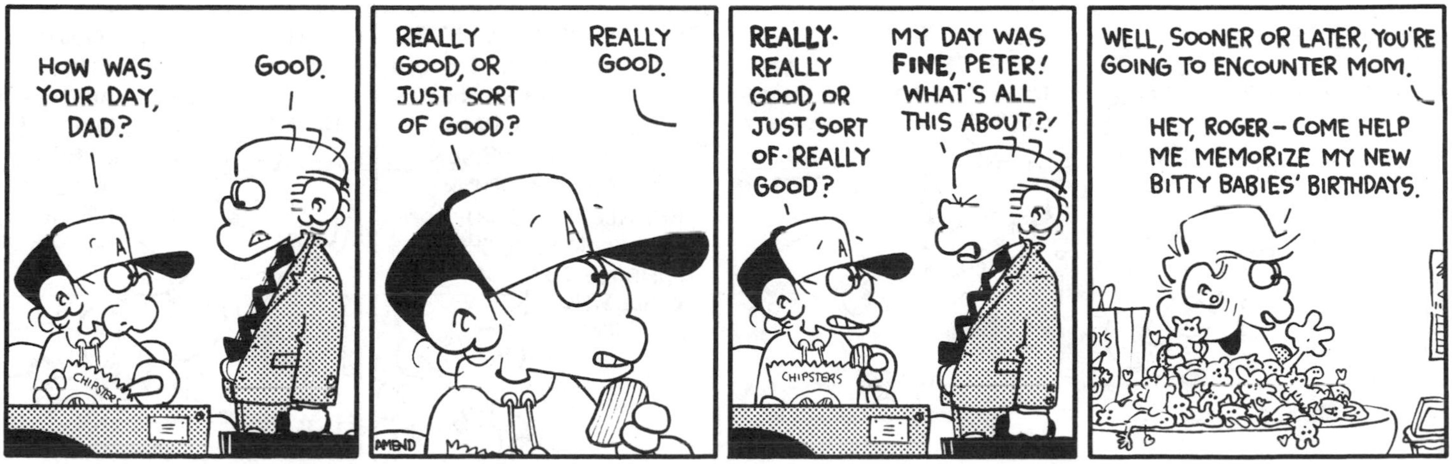
HOW WAS YOUR DAY, DAD?
GOOD.
CHIPSTERS
REALLY GOOD, OR JUST SORT OF GOOD?
REALLY GOOD.
AMEND
REALLY-REALLY GOOD, OR JUST SORT OF-REALLY GOOD?
MY DAY WAS **FINE**, PETER! WHAT'S ALL THIS ABOUT?!
CHIPSTERS
WELL, SOONER OR LATER, YOU'RE GOING TO ENCOUNTER MOM.
HEY, ROGER – COME HELP ME MEMORIZE MY NEW BITTY BABIES' BIRTHDAYS.

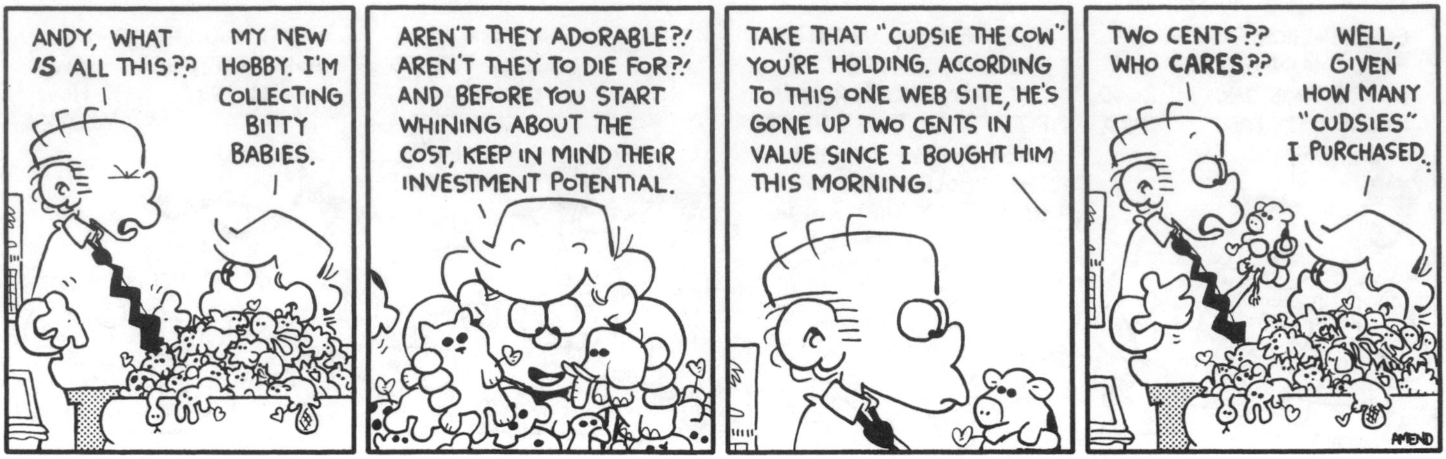
ANDY, WHAT IS ALL THIS??
MY NEW HOBBY. I'M COLLECTING BITTY BABIES.
AREN'T THEY ADORABLE?! AREN'T THEY TO DIE FOR?! AND BEFORE YOU START WHINING ABOUT THE COST, KEEP IN MIND THEIR INVESTMENT POTENTIAL.
TAKE THAT "CUDSIE THE COW" YOU'RE HOLDING. ACCORDING TO THIS ONE WEB SITE, HE'S GONE UP TWO CENTS IN VALUE SINCE I BOUGHT HIM THIS MORNING.
TWO CENTS?? WHO CARES??
WELL, GIVEN HOW MANY "CUDSIES" I PURCHASED...
AMEND

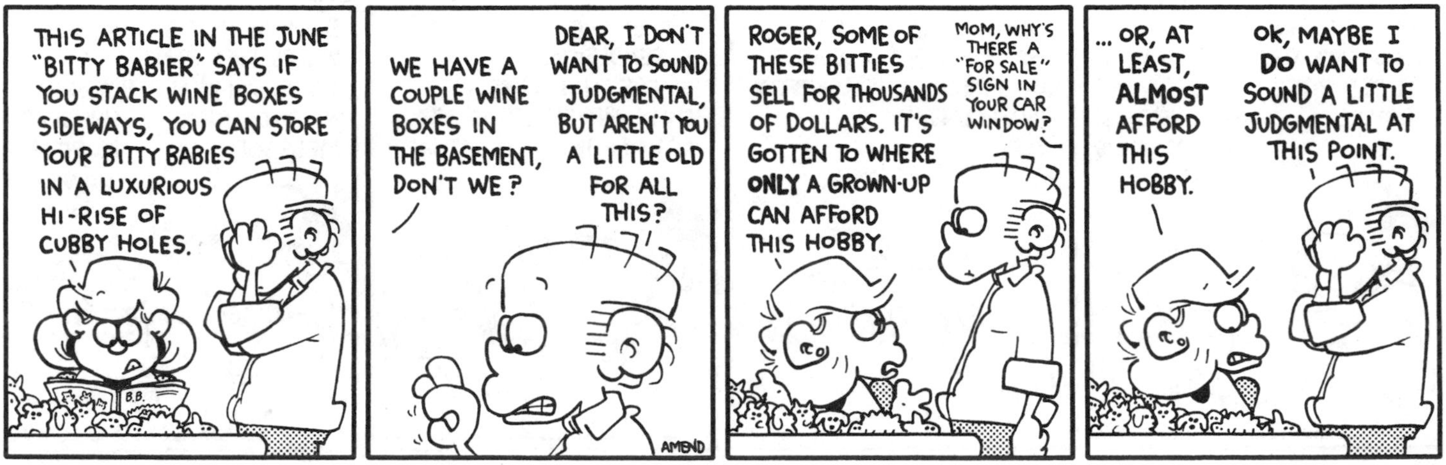
THIS ARTICLE IN THE JUNE "BITTY BABIER" SAYS IF YOU STACK WINE BOXES SIDEWAYS, YOU CAN STORE YOUR BITTY BABIES IN A LUXURIOUS HI-RISE OF CUBBY HOLES.
B.B.
WE HAVE A COUPLE WINE BOXES IN THE BASEMENT, DON'T WE?
DEAR, I DON'T WANT TO SOUND JUDGMENTAL, BUT AREN'T YOU A LITTLE OLD FOR ALL THIS?
AMEND
ROGER, SOME OF THESE BITTIES SELL FOR THOUSANDS OF DOLLARS. IT'S GOTTEN TO WHERE ONLY A GROWN-UP CAN AFFORD THIS HOBBY.
MOM, WHY'S THERE A "FOR SALE" SIGN IN YOUR CAR WINDOW?
... OR, AT LEAST, ALMOST AFFORD THIS HOBBY.
OK, MAYBE I DO WANT TO SOUND A LITTLE JUDGMENTAL AT THIS POINT.

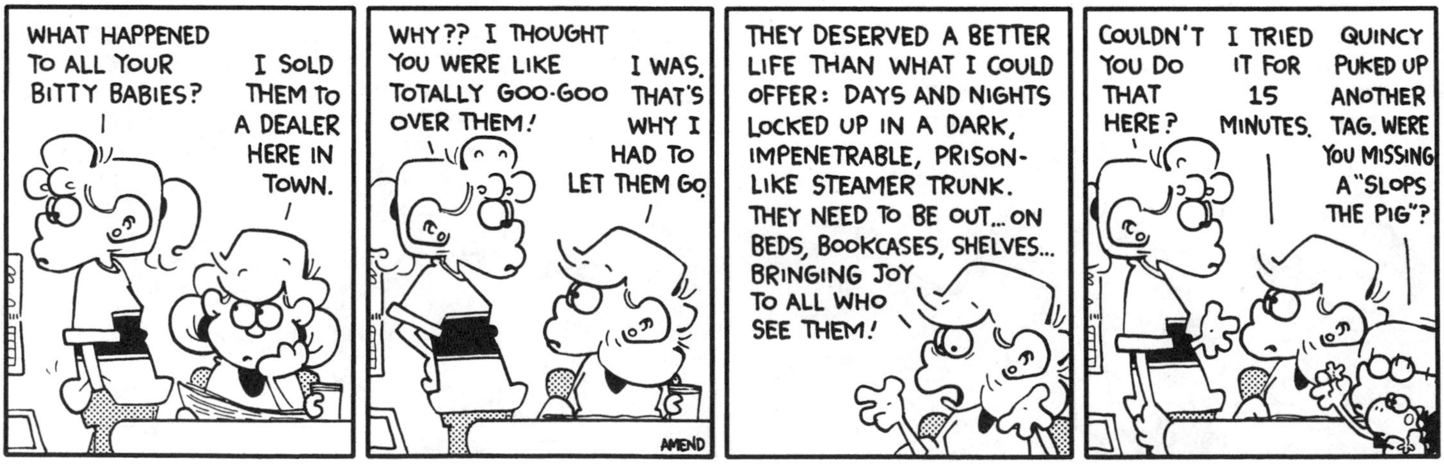
WHAT HAPPENED TO ALL YOUR BITTY BABIES?
I SOLD THEM TO A DEALER HERE IN TOWN.
WHY?? I THOUGHT YOU WERE LIKE TOTALLY GOO-GOO OVER THEM!
I WAS. THAT'S WHY I HAD TO LET THEM GO.
AMEND
THEY DESERVED A BETTER LIFE THAN WHAT I COULD OFFER: DAYS AND NIGHTS LOCKED UP IN A DARK, IMPENETRABLE, PRISON-LIKE STEAMER TRUNK. THEY NEED TO BE OUT... ON BEDS, BOOKCASES, SHELVES... BRINGING JOY TO ALL WHO SEE THEM!
COULDN'T YOU DO THAT HERE?
I TRIED IT FOR 15 MINUTES.
QUINCY PUKED UP ANOTHER TAG. WERE YOU MISSING A "SLOPS THE PIG"?

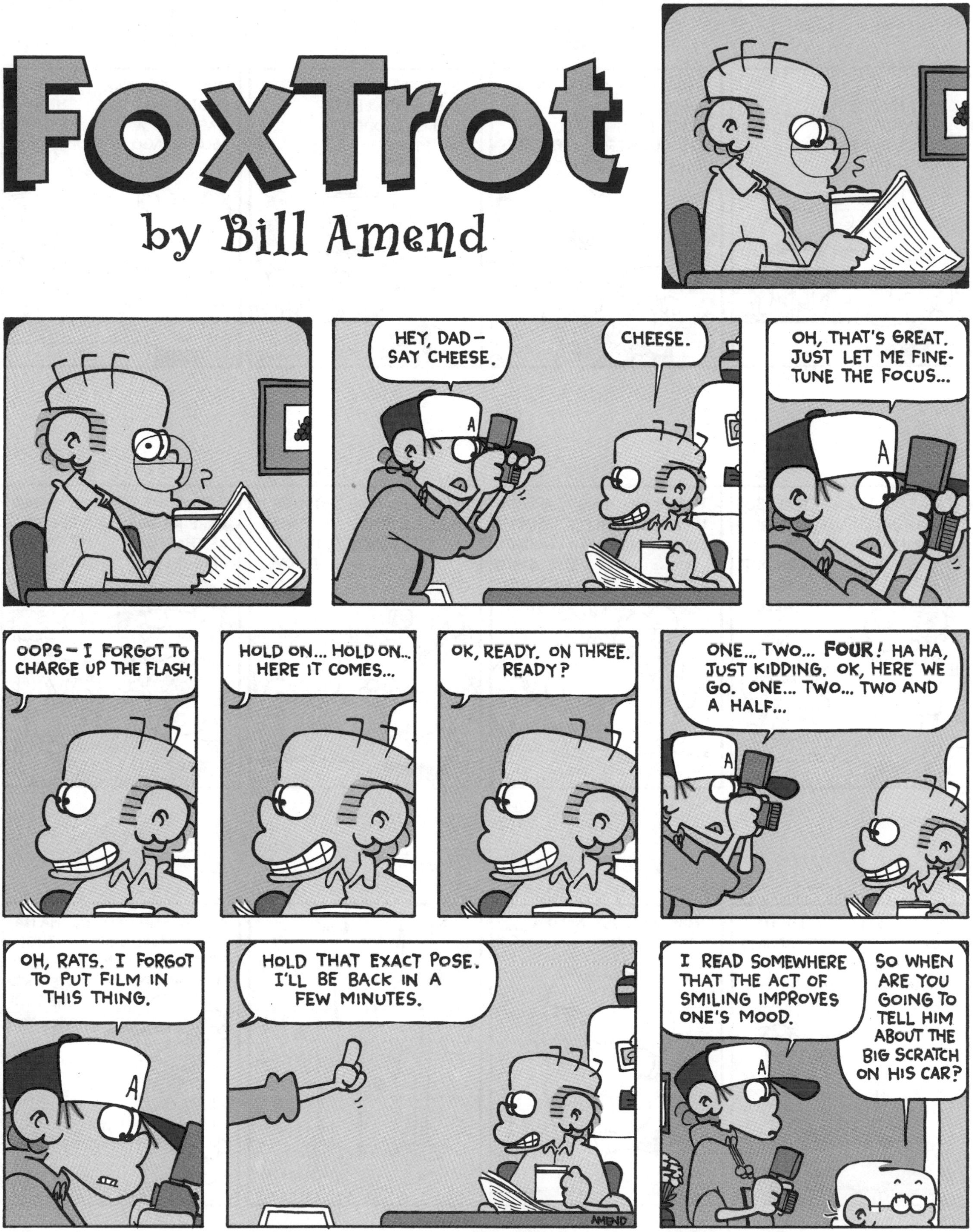
FoxTrot
by Bill Amend
HEY, DAD— SAY CHEESE.
CHEESE.
OH, THAT'S GREAT. JUST LET ME FINE-TUNE THE FOCUS...
OOPS — I FORGOT TO CHARGE UP THE FLASH.
HOLD ON... HOLD ON... HERE IT COMES...
OK, READY. ON THREE. READY?
ONE... TWO... FOUR! HA HA, JUST KIDDING. OK, HERE WE GO. ONE... TWO... TWO AND A HALF...
OH, RATS. I FORGOT TO PUT FILM IN THIS THING.
HOLD THAT EXACT POSE. I'LL BE BACK IN A FEW MINUTES.
AMEND
I READ SOMEWHERE THAT THE ACT OF SMILING IMPROVES ONE'S MOOD.
SO WHEN ARE YOU GOING TO TELL HIM ABOUT THE BIG SCRATCH ON HIS CAR?

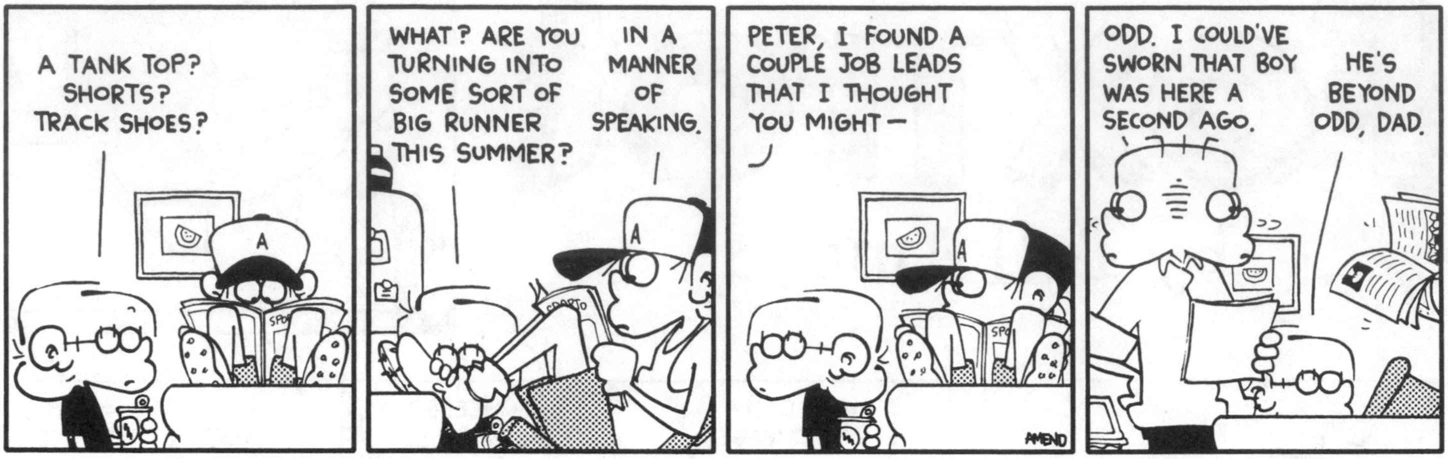
A TANK TOP? SHORTS? TRACK SHOES?
WHAT? ARE YOU TURNING INTO SOME SORT OF BIG RUNNER THIS SUMMER?
IN A MANNER OF SPEAKING.
PETER, I FOUND A COUPLE JOB LEADS THAT I THOUGHT YOU MIGHT—
ODD. I COULD'VE SWORN THAT BOY WAS HERE A SECOND AGO.
HE'S BEYOND ODD, DAD.

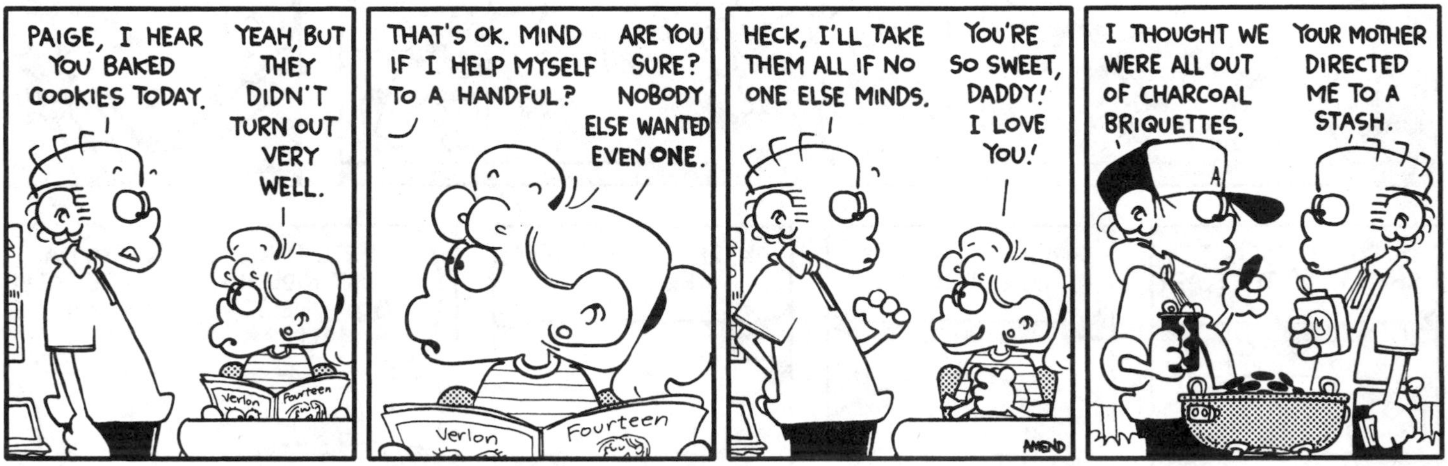
PAIGE, I HEAR YOU BAKED COOKIES TODAY.
YEAH, BUT THEY DIDN'T TURN OUT VERY WELL.
Verlon
Fourteen
THAT'S OK. MIND IF I HELP MYSELF TO A HANDFUL?
ARE YOU SURE? NOBODY ELSE WANTED EVEN ONE.
HECK, I'LL TAKE THEM ALL IF NO ONE ELSE MINDS.
YOU'RE SO SWEET, DADDY! I LOVE YOU!
I THOUGHT WE WERE ALL OUT OF CHARCOAL BRIQUETTES.
YOUR MOTHER DIRECTED ME TO A STASH.

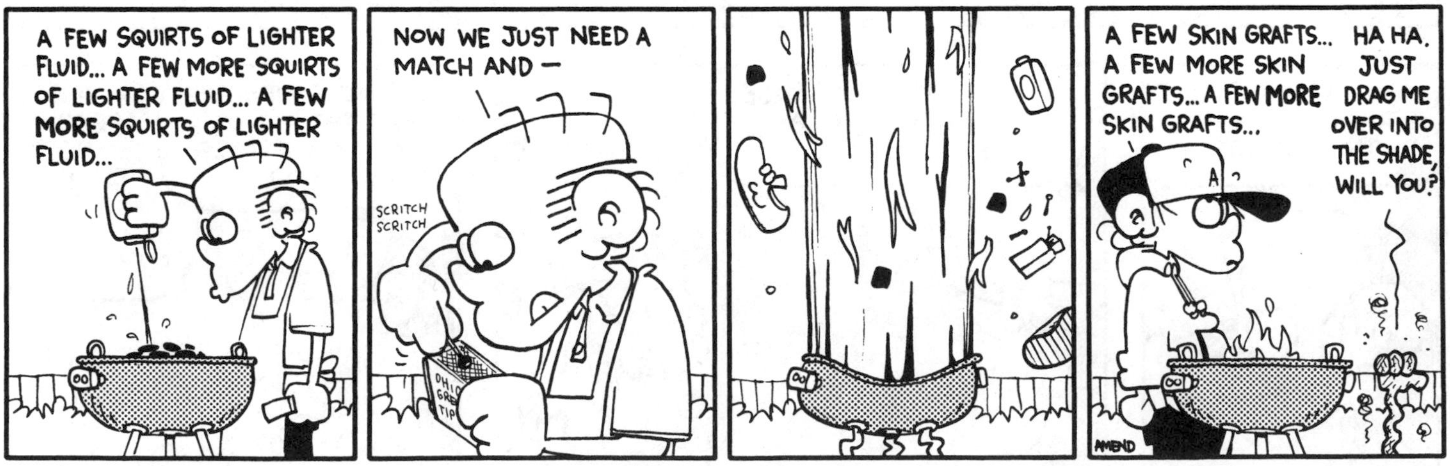
A FEW SQUIRTS OF LIGHTER FLUID... A FEW MORE SQUIRTS OF LIGHTER FLUID... A FEW MORE SQUIRTS OF LIGHTER FLUID...
NOW WE JUST NEED A MATCH AND—
SCRITCH SCRITCH
A FEW SKIN GRAFTS... A FEW MORE SKIN GRAFTS... A FEW MORE SKIN GRAFTS...
HA HA. JUST DRAG ME OVER INTO THE SHADE, WILL YOU?

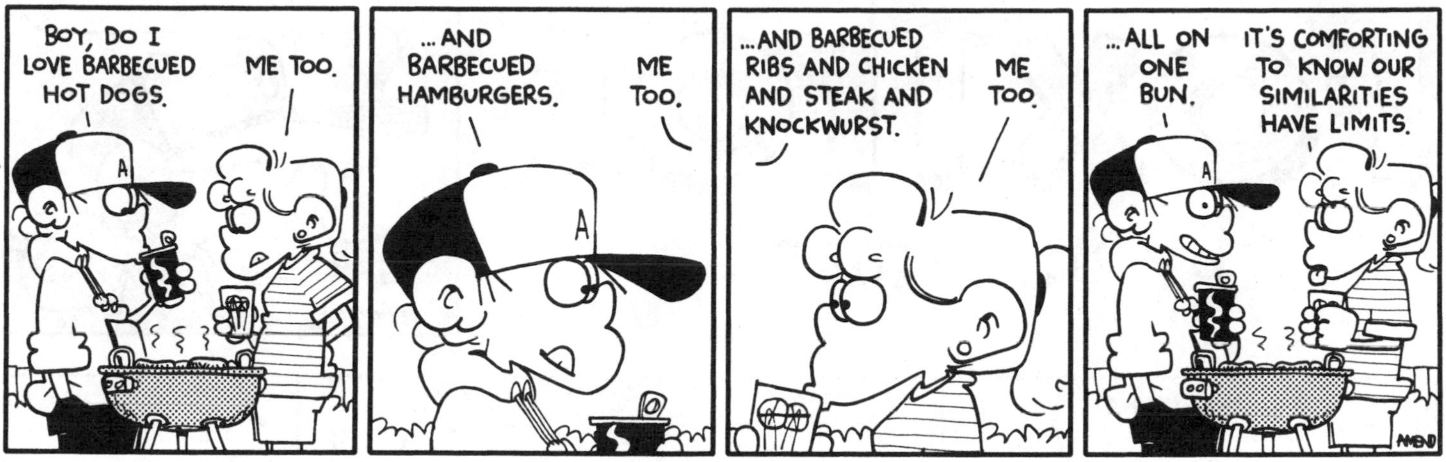

BOY, DO I LOVE BARBECUED HOT DOGS.
ME TOO.
... AND BARBECUED HAMBURGERS.
ME TOO.
... AND BARBECUED RIBS AND CHICKEN AND STEAK AND KNOCKWURST.
ME TOO.
... ALL ON ONE BUN.
IT'S COMFORTING TO KNOW OUR SIMILARITIES HAVE LIMITS.
AMEND

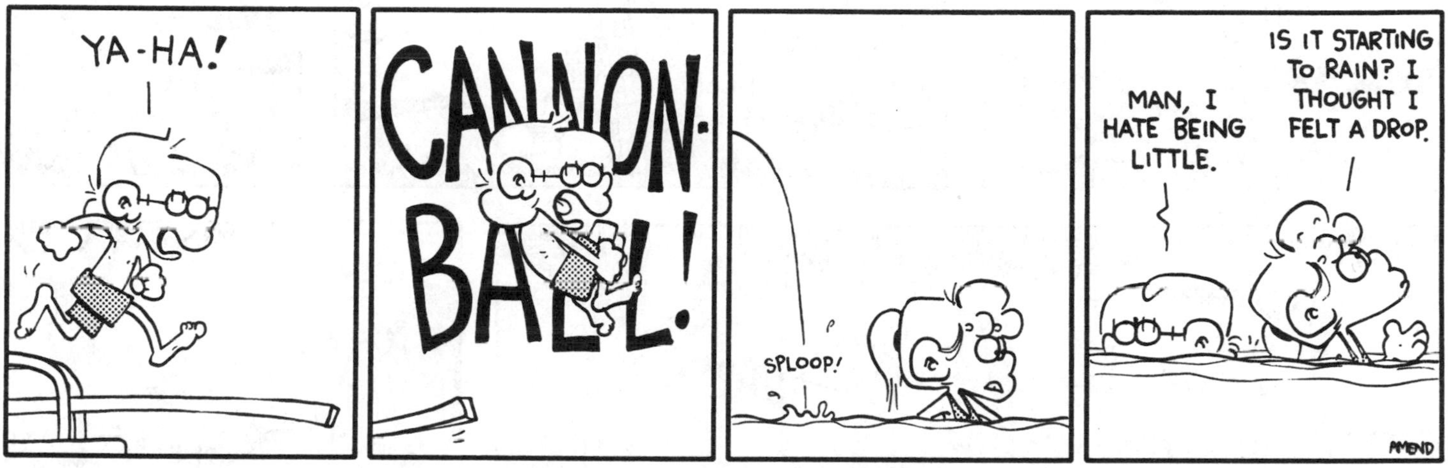

YA-HA!
CANNON-BALL!
SPLOOP!
MAN, I HATE BEING LITTLE.
IS IT STARTING TO RAIN? I THOUGHT I FELT A DROP.
AMEND

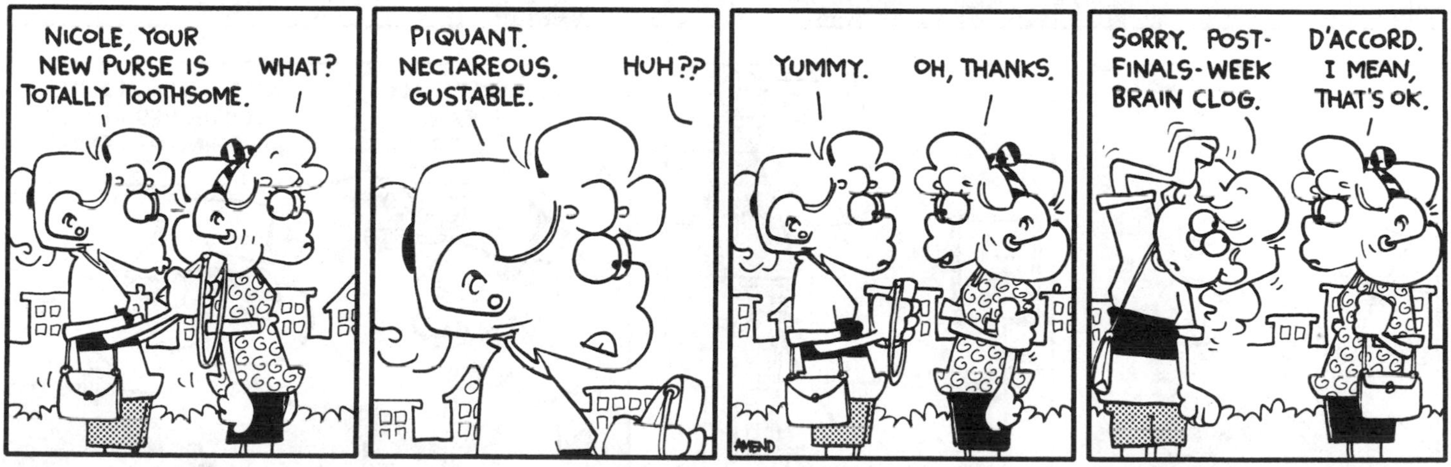

NICOLE, YOUR NEW PURSE IS TOTALLY TOOTHSOME.
WHAT?
PIQUANT. NECTAREOUS. GUSTABLE.
HUH??
YUMMY.
OH, THANKS.
AMEND
SORRY. POST-FINALS-WEEK BRAIN CLOG.
D'ACCORD. I MEAN, THAT'S OK.

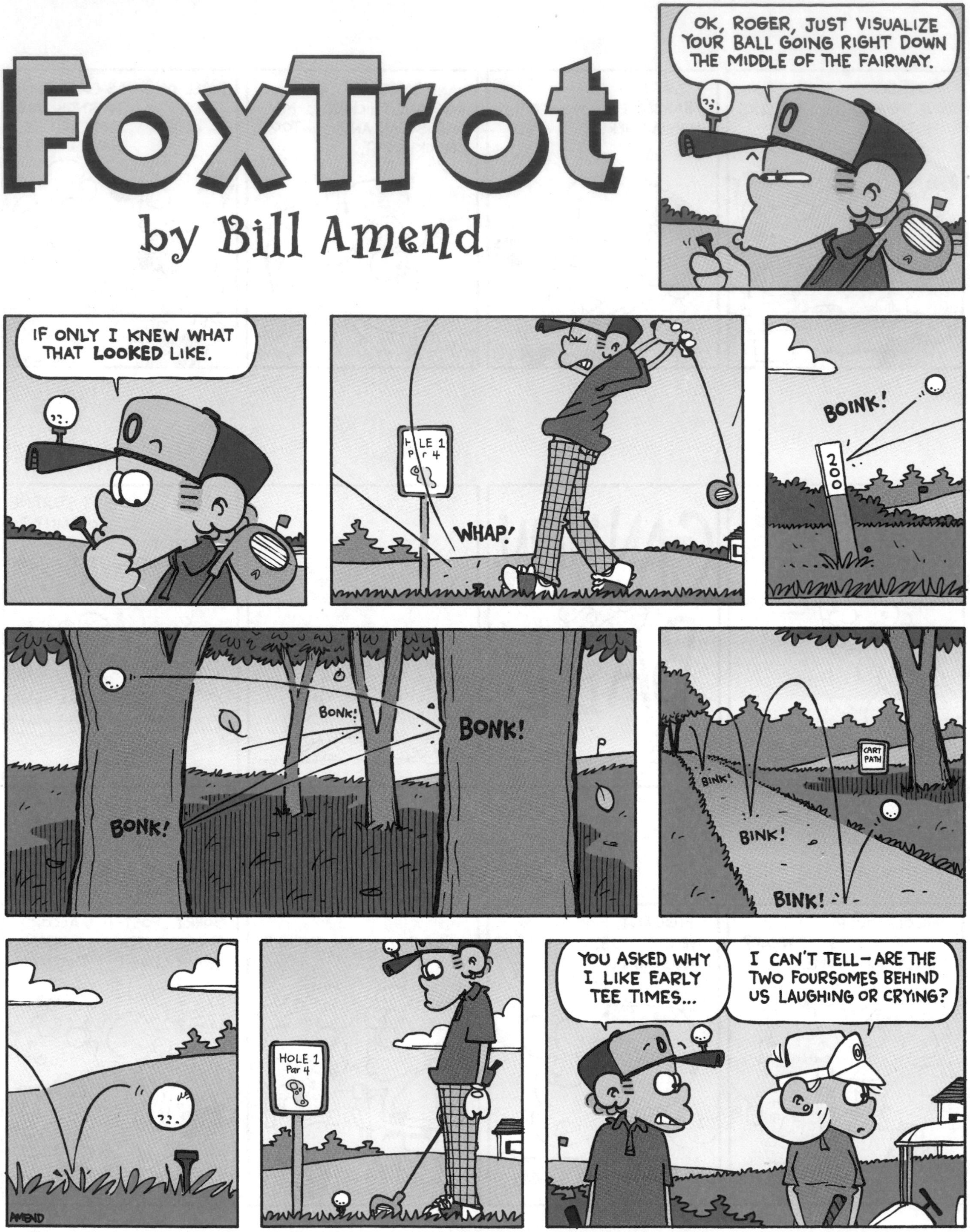
FoxTrot
by Bill Amend
OK, ROGER, JUST VISUALIZE YOUR BALL GOING RIGHT DOWN THE MIDDLE OF THE FAIRWAY.
IF ONLY I KNEW WHAT THAT LOOKED LIKE.
HOLE 1 Par 4
WHAP!
BOINK!
200
BONK!
BONK!
BONK!
CART PATH
BINK!
BINK!
BINK!
AMEND
HOLE 1 Par 4
YOU ASKED WHY I LIKE EARLY TEE TIMES...
I CAN'T TELL— ARE THE TWO FOURSOMES BEHIND US LAUGHING OR CRYING?

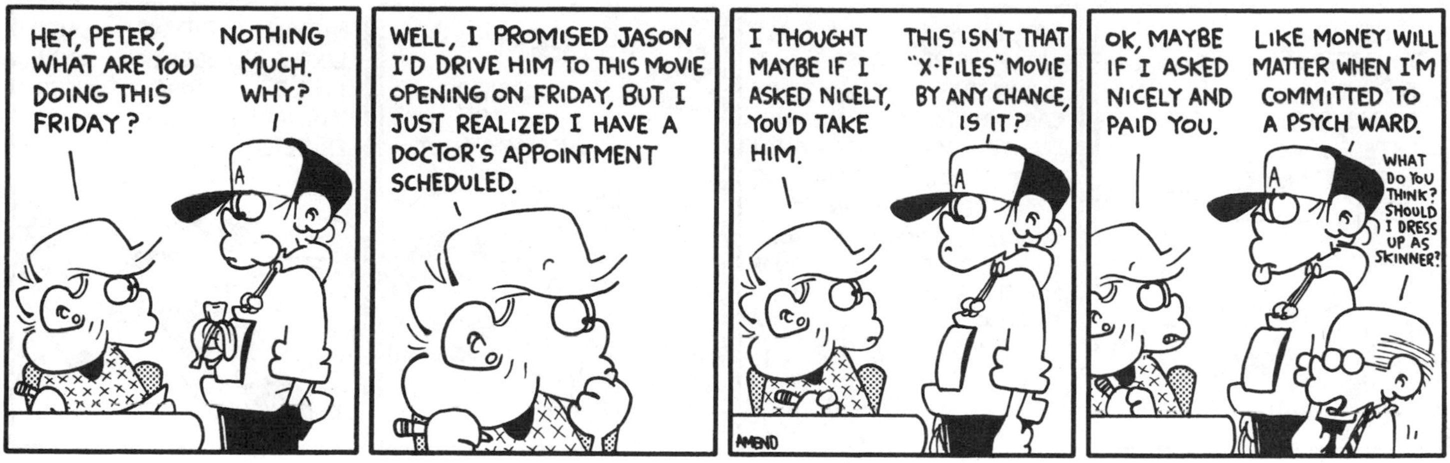
HEY, PETER, WHAT ARE YOU DOING THIS FRIDAY?
NOTHING MUCH. WHY?
WELL, I PROMISED JASON I'D DRIVE HIM TO THIS MOVIE OPENING ON FRIDAY, BUT I JUST REALIZED I HAVE A DOCTOR'S APPOINTMENT SCHEDULED.
I THOUGHT MAYBE IF I ASKED NICELY, YOU'D TAKE HIM.
THIS ISN'T THAT "X-FILES" MOVIE BY ANY CHANCE, IS IT?
OK, MAYBE IF I ASKED NICELY AND PAID YOU.
LIKE MONEY WILL MATTER WHEN I'M COMMITTED TO A PSYCH WARD.
WHAT DO YOU THINK? SHOULD I DRESS UP AS SKINNER?
AMEND

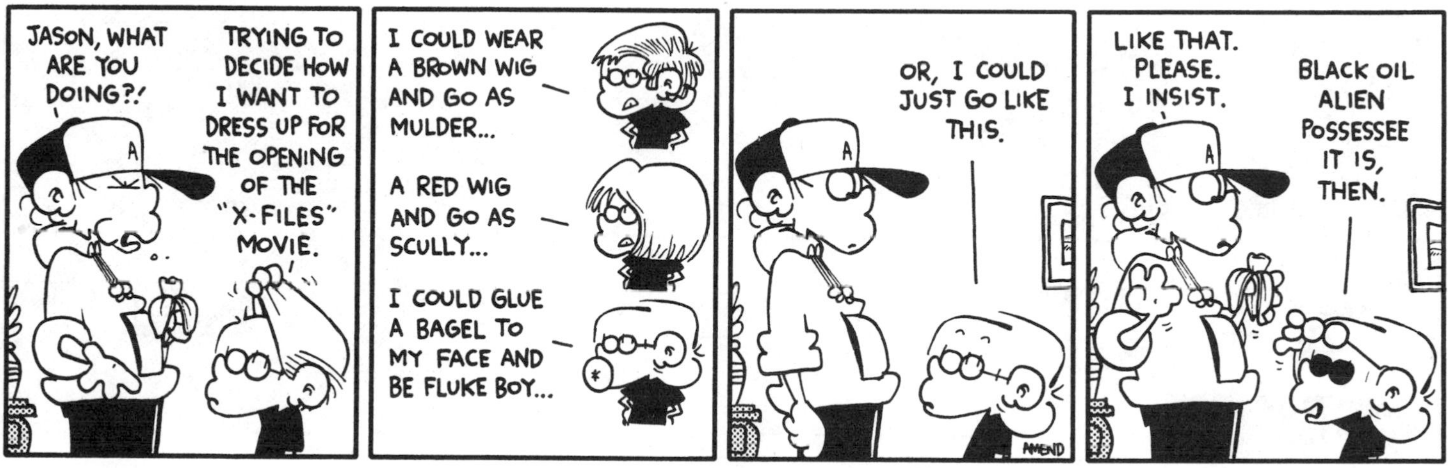
JASON, WHAT ARE YOU DOING?!
TRYING TO DECIDE HOW I WANT TO DRESS UP FOR THE OPENING OF THE "X-FILES" MOVIE.
I COULD WEAR A BROWN WIG AND GO AS MULDER...
A RED WIG AND GO AS SCULLY...
I COULD GLUE A BAGEL TO MY FACE AND BE FLUKE BOY...
OR, I COULD JUST GO LIKE THIS.
AMEND
LIKE THAT. PLEASE. I INSIST.
BLACK OIL ALIEN POSSESSEE IT IS, THEN.

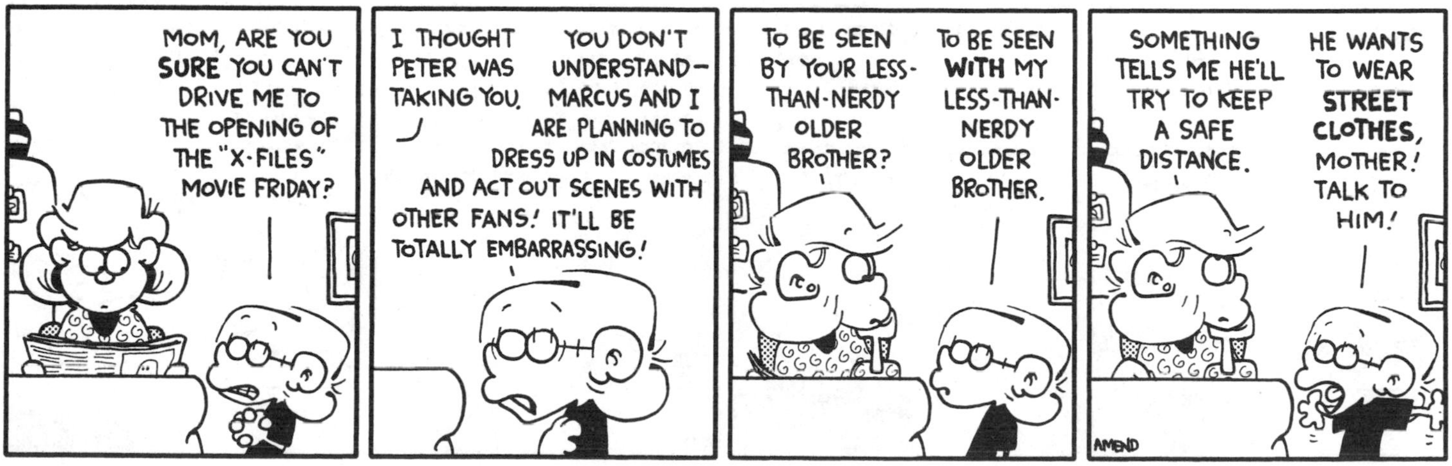
MOM, ARE YOU **SURE** YOU CAN'T DRIVE ME TO THE OPENING OF THE "X-FILES" MOVIE FRIDAY?
I THOUGHT PETER WAS TAKING YOU.
YOU DON'T UNDERSTAND— MARCUS AND I ARE PLANNING TO DRESS UP IN COSTUMES AND ACT OUT SCENES WITH OTHER FANS! IT'LL BE TOTALLY EMBARRASSING!
TO BE SEEN BY YOUR LESS-THAN-NERDY OLDER BROTHER?
TO BE SEEN **WITH** MY LESS-THAN-NERDY OLDER BROTHER.
AMEND
SOMETHING TELLS ME HE'LL TRY TO KEEP A SAFE DISTANCE.
HE WANTS TO WEAR **STREET CLOTHES**, MOTHER! TALK TO HIM!

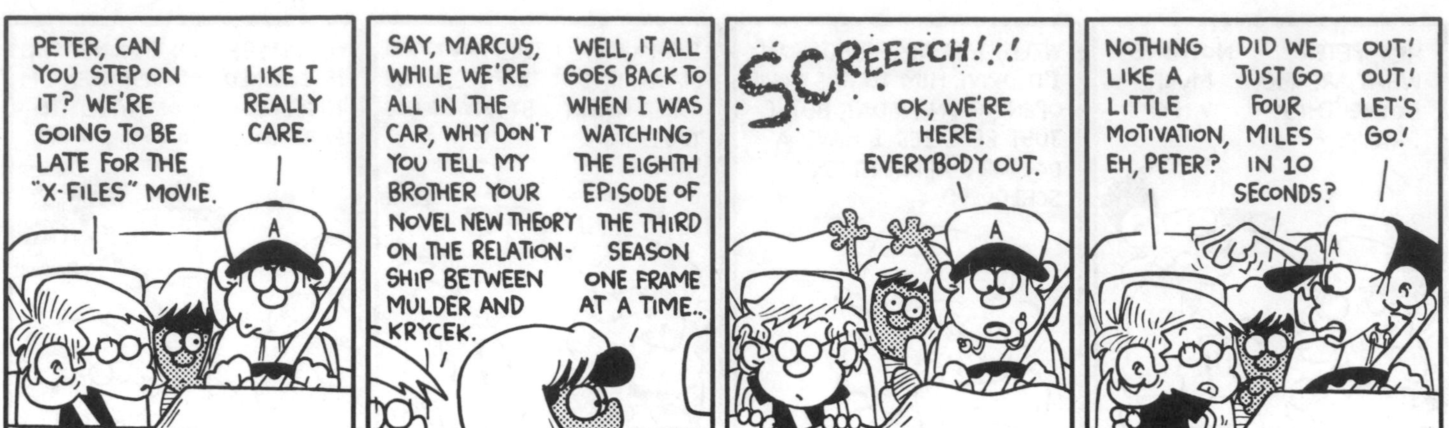
PETER, CAN YOU STEP ON IT? WE'RE GOING TO BE LATE FOR THE "X-FILES" MOVIE.
LIKE I REALLY CARE.
SAY, MARCUS, WHILE WE'RE ALL IN THE CAR, WHY DON'T YOU TELL MY BROTHER YOUR NOVEL NEW THEORY ON THE RELATIONSHIP BETWEEN MULDER AND KRYCEK.
WELL, IT ALL GOES BACK TO WHEN I WAS WATCHING THE EIGHTH EPISODE OF THE THIRD SEASON ONE FRAME AT A TIME...
SCREEECH!!!
OK, WE'RE HERE. EVERYBODY OUT.
NOTHING LIKE A LITTLE MOTIVATION, EH, PETER?
DID WE JUST GO FOUR MILES IN 10 SECONDS?
OUT! OUT! LET'S GO!
AMEND

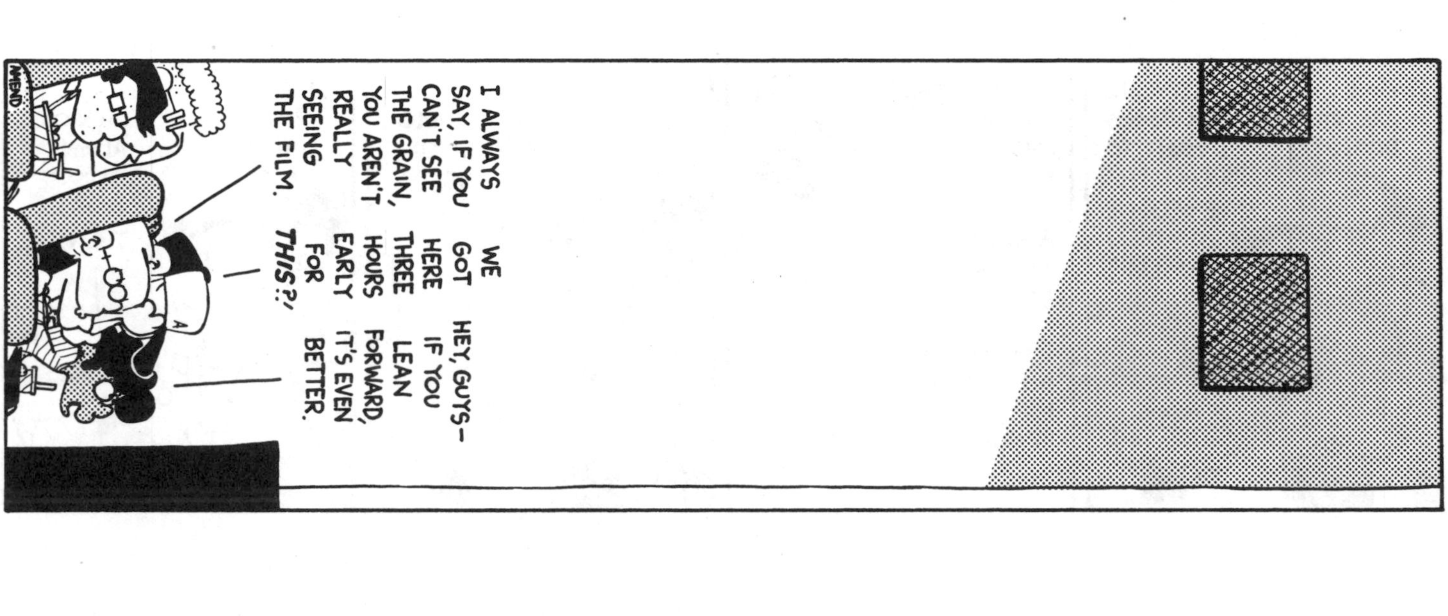
I ALWAYS SAY, IF YOU CAN'T SEE THE GRAIN, YOU AREN'T REALLY SEEING THE FILM.
WE GOT HERE THREE HOURS EARLY FOR *THIS*?!
HEY, GUYS— IF YOU LEAN FORWARD, IT'S EVEN BETTER.
AMEND

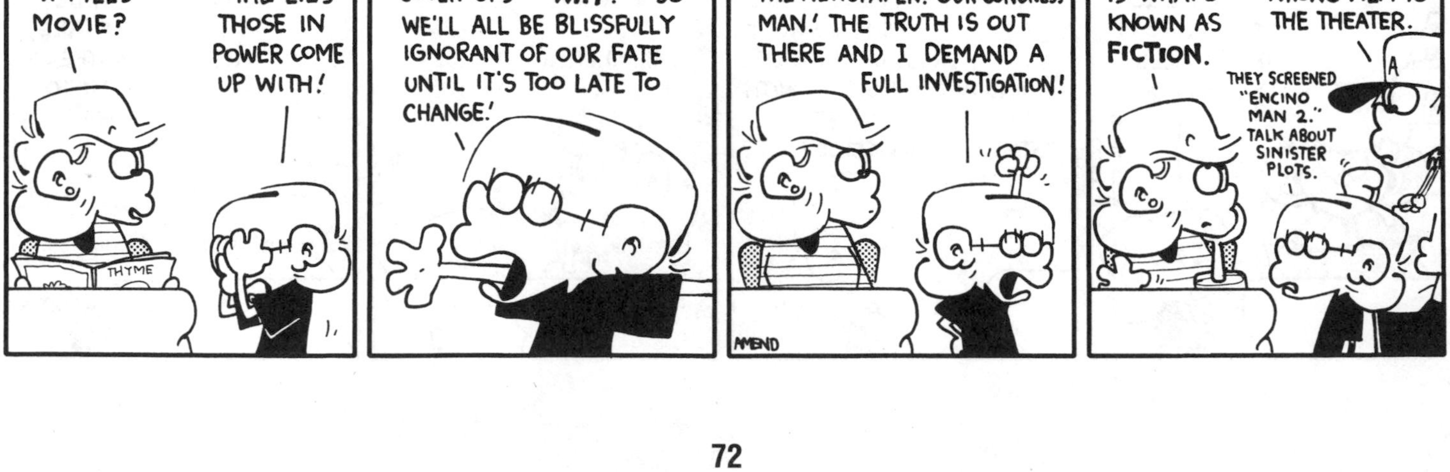
SO, HOW WAS THE BIG "X-FILES" MOVIE?
OH, MAN! THE LIES THOSE IN POWER COME UP WITH!
THYME
FIRST DENIALS, THEN HALF-TRUTHS, THEN ELABORATE COVER-UPS — *WHY?* — SO WE'LL ALL BE BLISSFULLY IGNORANT OF OUR FATE UNTIL IT'S TOO LATE TO CHANGE!
WELL, I REFUSE TO KEEP MY MOUTH SHUT! I'M WRITING THE NEWSPAPER! OUR CONGRESSMAN! THE TRUTH IS OUT THERE AND I DEMAND A FULL INVESTIGATION!
AMEND
SWEETIE, "THE X-FILES" IS WHAT'S KNOWN AS **FICTION**.
YOU MISUNDERSTAND. THEY SHIPPED THE WRONG FILM TO THE THEATER.
THEY SCREENED "ENCINO MAN 2." TALK ABOUT SINISTER PLOTS.

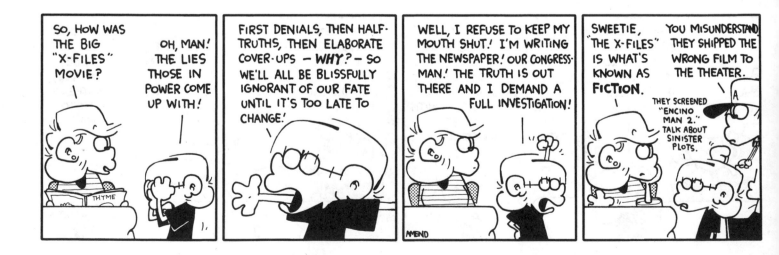

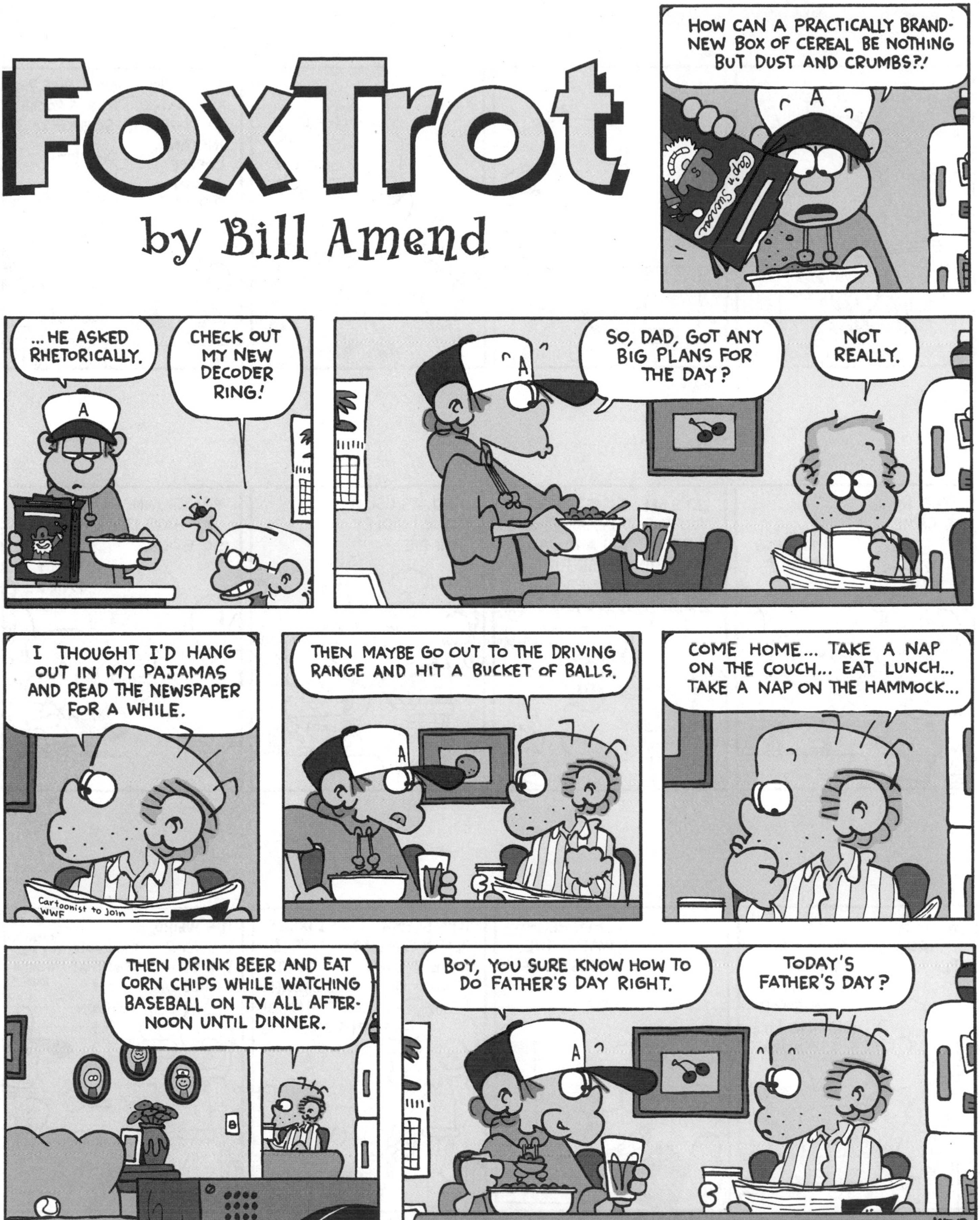
FoxTrot
by Bill Amend
HOW CAN A PRACTICALLY BRAND-NEW BOX OF CEREAL BE NOTHING BUT DUST AND CRUMBS?!
Cap'n Sucrose
...HE ASKED RHETORICALLY.
CHECK OUT MY NEW DECODER RING!
SO, DAD, GOT ANY BIG PLANS FOR THE DAY?
NOT REALLY.
I THOUGHT I'D HANG OUT IN MY PAJAMAS AND READ THE NEWSPAPER FOR A WHILE.
Cartoonist to Join WWF
THEN MAYBE GO OUT TO THE DRIVING RANGE AND HIT A BUCKET OF BALLS.
COME HOME... TAKE A NAP ON THE COUCH... EAT LUNCH... TAKE A NAP ON THE HAMMOCK...
THEN DRINK BEER AND EAT CORN CHIPS WHILE WATCHING BASEBALL ON TV ALL AFTER-NOON UNTIL DINNER.
BOY, YOU SURE KNOW HOW TO DO FATHER'S DAY RIGHT.
TODAY'S FATHER'S DAY?
AMEND

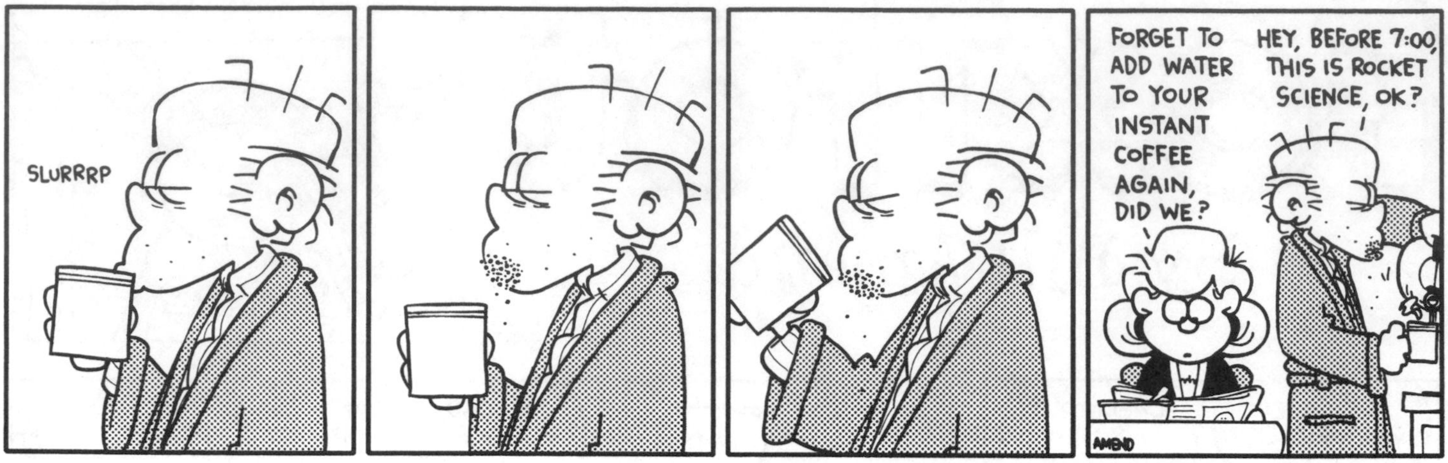
SLURRRP
FORGET TO ADD WATER TO YOUR INSTANT COFFEE AGAIN, DID WE?
HEY, BEFORE 7:00, THIS IS ROCKET SCIENCE, OK?
AMEND

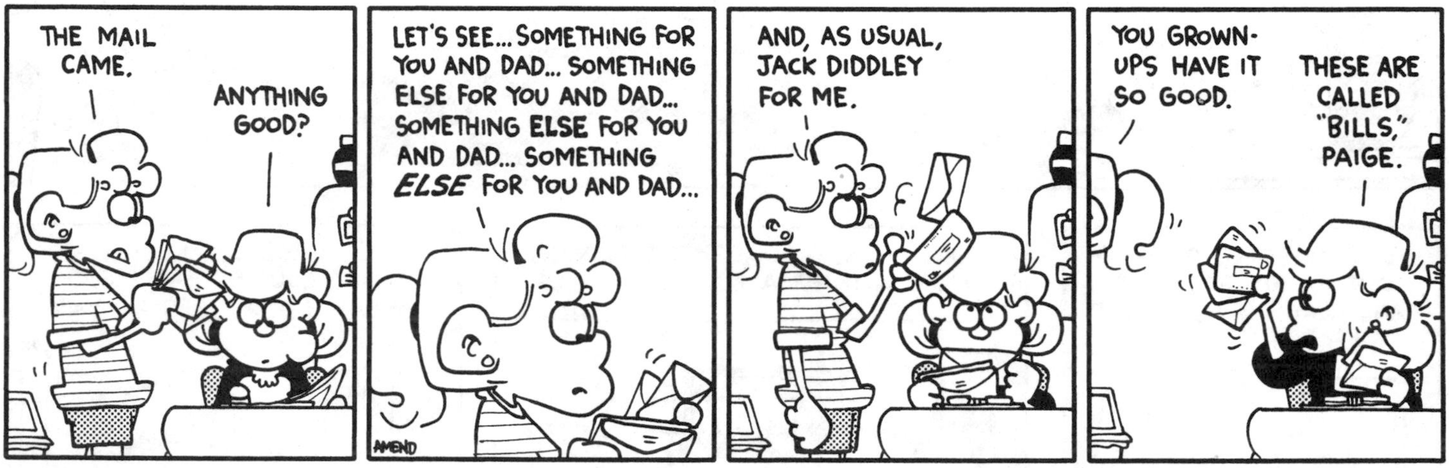
THE MAIL CAME.
ANYTHING GOOD?
LET'S SEE... SOMETHING FOR YOU AND DAD... SOMETHING ELSE FOR YOU AND DAD... SOMETHING ELSE FOR YOU AND DAD... SOMETHING ELSE FOR YOU AND DAD...
AMEND
AND, AS USUAL, JACK DIDDLEY FOR ME.
YOU GROWN-UPS HAVE IT SO GOOD.
THESE ARE CALLED "BILLS," PAIGE.

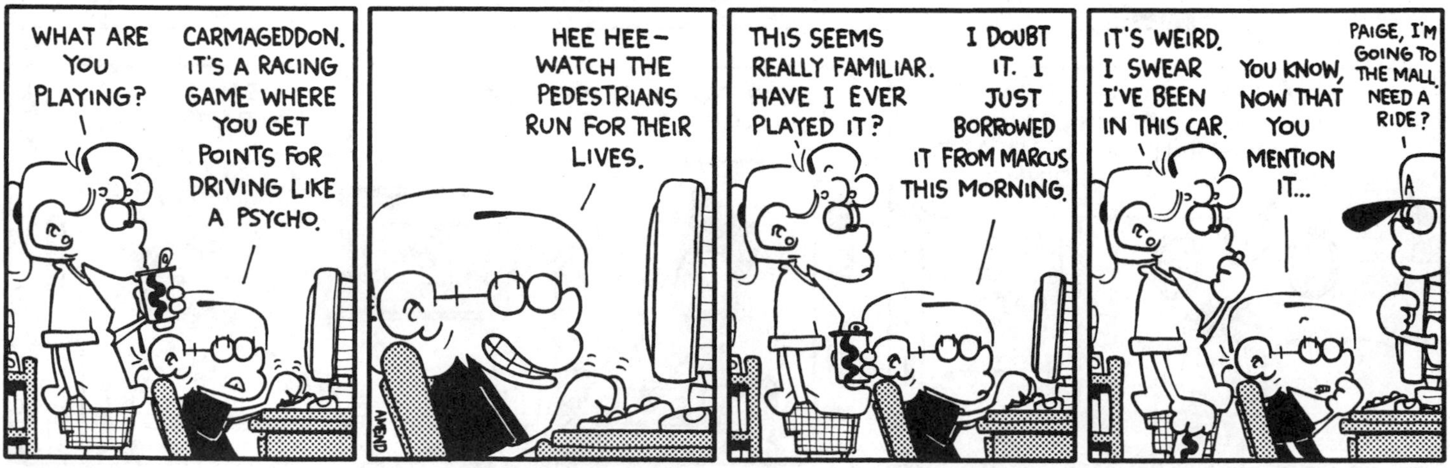
WHAT ARE YOU PLAYING?
CARMAGEDDON. IT'S A RACING GAME WHERE YOU GET POINTS FOR DRIVING LIKE A PSYCHO.
HEE HEE– WATCH THE PEDESTRIANS RUN FOR THEIR LIVES.
AMEND
THIS SEEMS REALLY FAMILIAR. HAVE I EVER PLAYED IT?
I DOUBT IT. I JUST BORROWED IT FROM MARCUS THIS MORNING.
IT'S WEIRD. I SWEAR I'VE BEEN IN THIS CAR.
YOU KNOW, NOW THAT YOU MENTION IT...
PAIGE, I'M GOING TO THE MALL. NEED A RIDE?

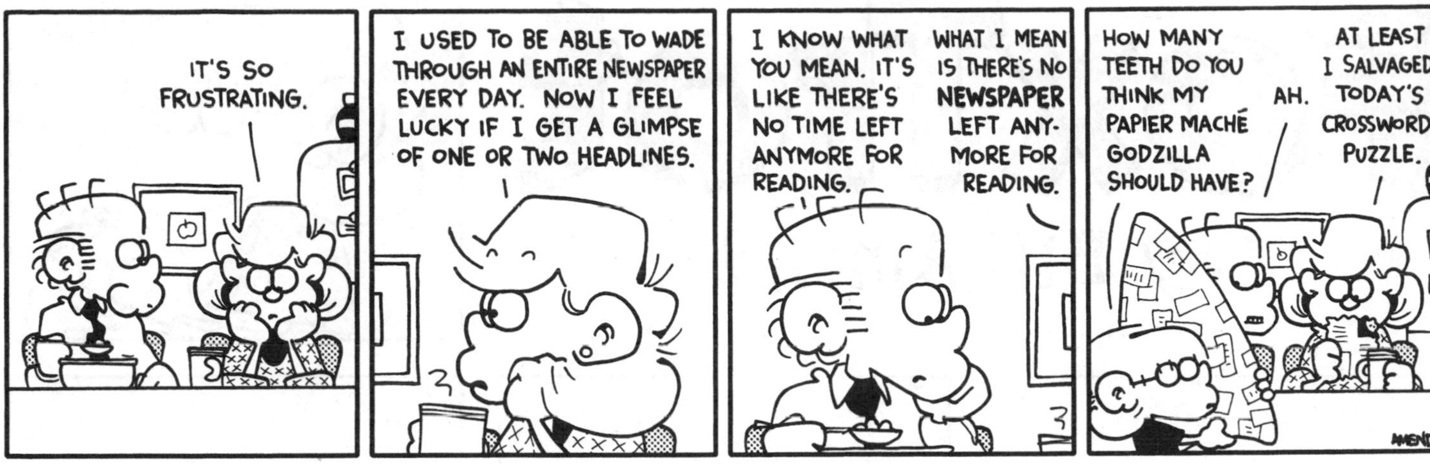
IT'S SO FRUSTRATING.
I USED TO BE ABLE TO WADE THROUGH AN ENTIRE NEWSPAPER EVERY DAY. NOW I FEEL LUCKY IF I GET A GLIMPSE OF ONE OR TWO HEADLINES.
I KNOW WHAT YOU MEAN. IT'S LIKE THERE'S NO TIME LEFT ANYMORE FOR READING.
WHAT I MEAN IS THERE'S NO **NEWSPAPER** LEFT ANYMORE FOR READING.
HOW MANY TEETH DO YOU THINK MY PAPIER MACHÉ GODZILLA SHOULD HAVE?
AH.
AT LEAST I SALVAGED TODAY'S CROSSWORD PUZZLE.
AMEND

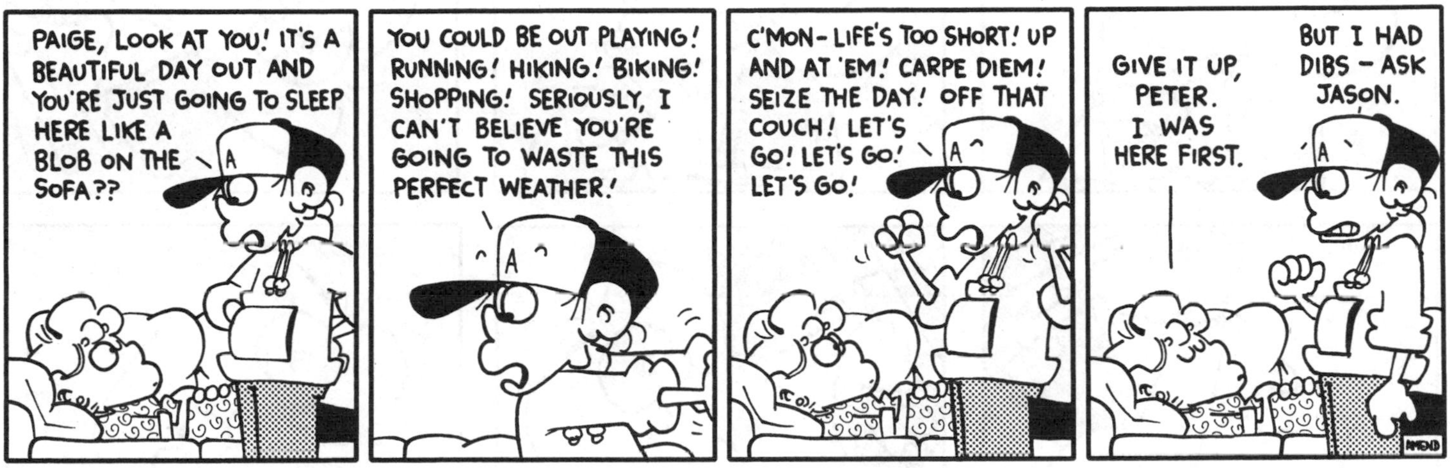
PAIGE, LOOK AT YOU! IT'S A BEAUTIFUL DAY OUT AND YOU'RE JUST GOING TO SLEEP HERE LIKE A BLOB ON THE SOFA??
YOU COULD BE OUT PLAYING! RUNNING! HIKING! BIKING! SHOPPING! SERIOUSLY, I CAN'T BELIEVE YOU'RE GOING TO WASTE THIS PERFECT WEATHER!
C'MON - LIFE'S TOO SHORT! UP AND AT 'EM! CARPE DIEM! SEIZE THE DAY! OFF THAT COUCH! LET'S GO! LET'S GO! LET'S GO!
GIVE IT UP, PETER. I WAS HERE FIRST.
BUT I HAD DIBS - ASK JASON.
AMEND

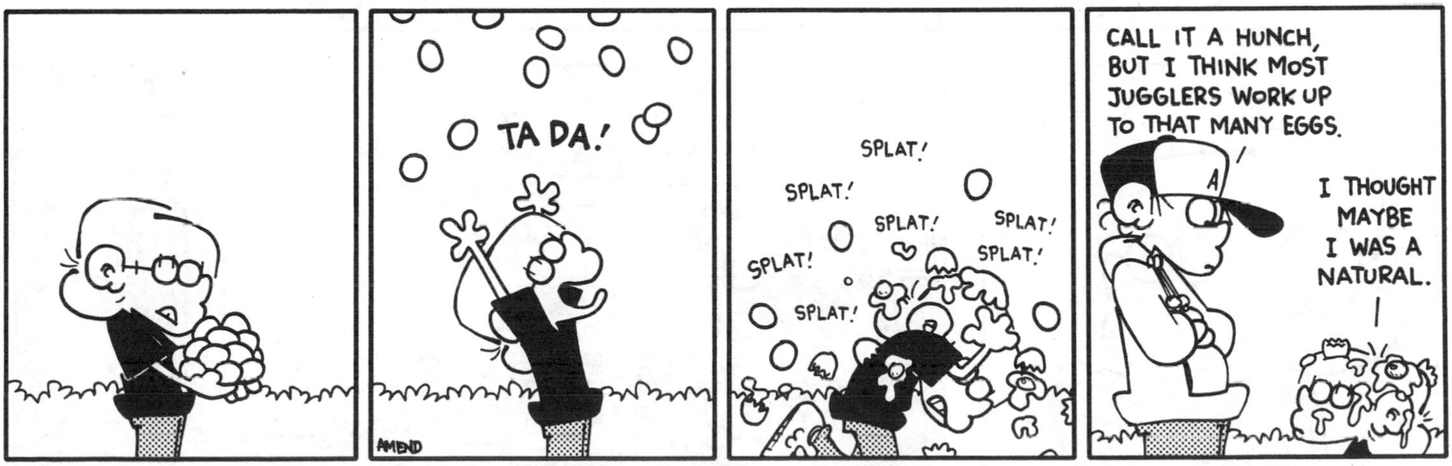
TA DA!
AMEND
SPLAT!
SPLAT!
SPLAT!
SPLAT!
SPLAT!
SPLAT!
SPLAT!
CALL IT A HUNCH, BUT I THINK MOST JUGGLERS WORK UP TO THAT MANY EGGS.
I THOUGHT MAYBE I WAS A NATURAL.

FoxTrot
by Bill Amend
TRY A LOOP-THE-LOOP.
I TOLD YOU THIS FLIGHT SIMULATOR WAS REALISTIC.
DARE I ASK WHAT HAPPENS IF I CHOOSE TO EJECT?

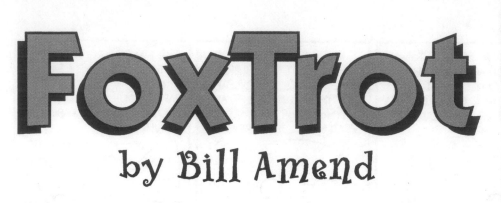

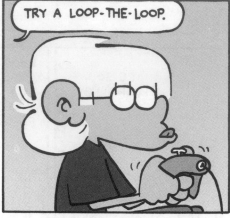

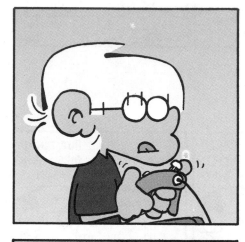

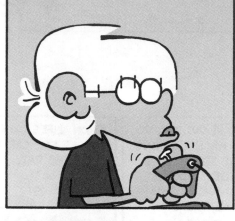

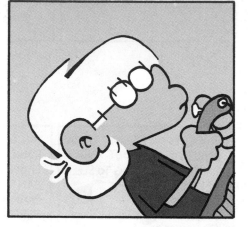

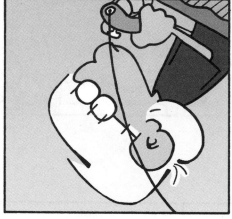

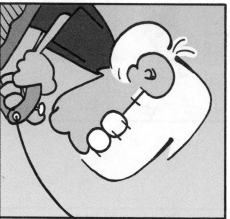

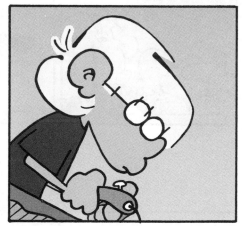

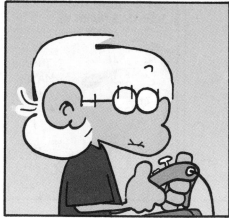

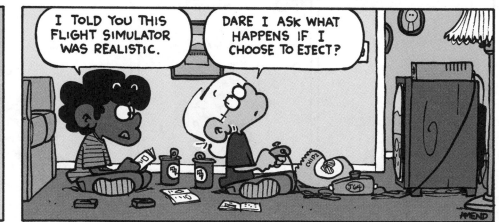

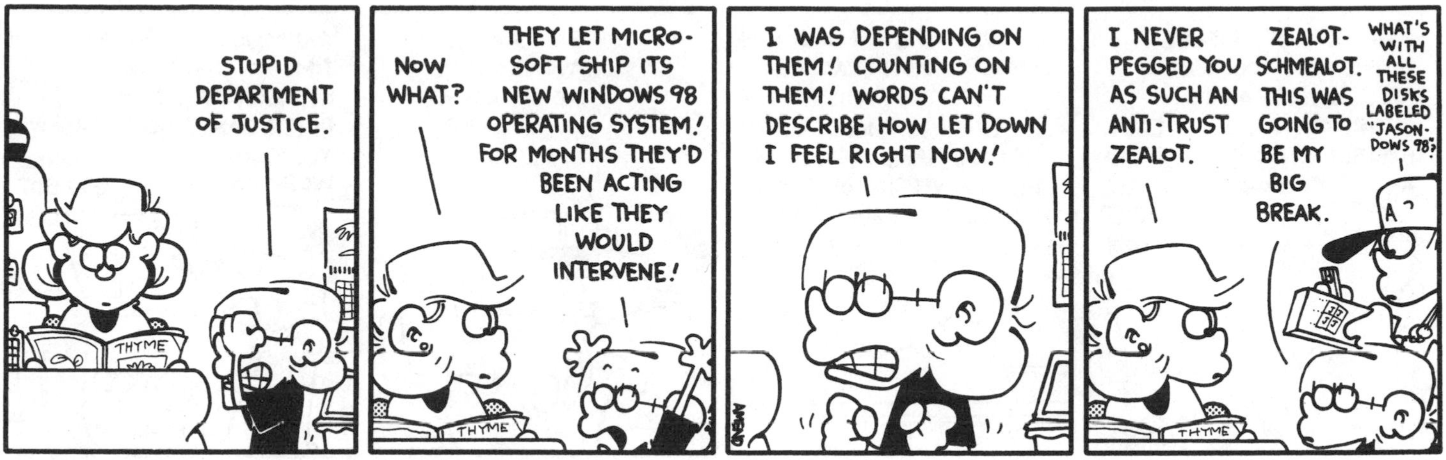
STUPID DEPARTMENT OF JUSTICE.
THYME
NOW WHAT?
THEY LET MICRO-SOFT SHIP ITS NEW WINDOWS 98 OPERATING SYSTEM! FOR MONTHS THEY'D BEEN ACTING LIKE THEY WOULD INTERVENE!
THYME
I WAS DEPENDING ON THEM! COUNTING ON THEM! WORDS CAN'T DESCRIBE HOW LET DOWN I FEEL RIGHT NOW!
I NEVER PEGGED YOU AS SUCH AN ANTI-TRUST ZEALOT.
ZEALOT-SCHMEALOT. THIS WAS GOING TO BE MY BIG BREAK.
WHAT'S WITH ALL THESE DISKS LABELED "JASON-DOWS 98"?
THYME

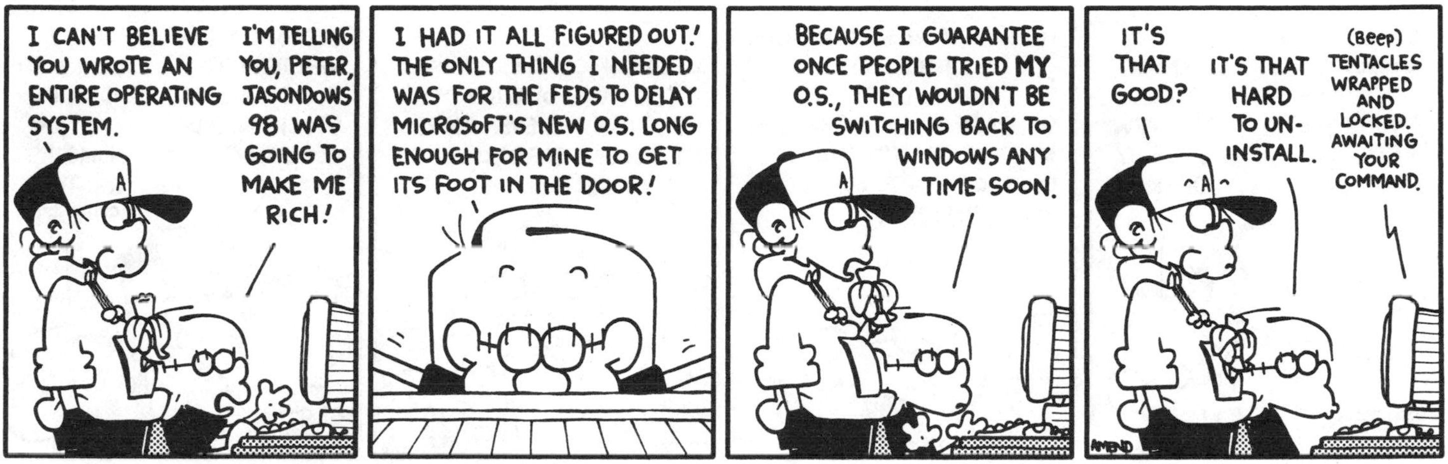
I CAN'T BELIEVE YOU WROTE AN ENTIRE OPERATING SYSTEM.
I'M TELLING YOU, PETER, JASONDOWS 98 WAS GOING TO MAKE ME RICH!
I HAD IT ALL FIGURED OUT! THE ONLY THING I NEEDED WAS FOR THE FEDS TO DELAY MICROSOFT'S NEW O.S. LONG ENOUGH FOR MINE TO GET ITS FOOT IN THE DOOR!
BECAUSE I GUARANTEE ONCE PEOPLE TRIED MY O.S., THEY WOULDN'T BE SWITCHING BACK TO WINDOWS ANY TIME SOON.
IT'S THAT GOOD?
IT'S THAT HARD TO UN-INSTALL.
(Beep) TENTACLES WRAPPED AND LOCKED. AWAITING YOUR COMMAND.
AMEND

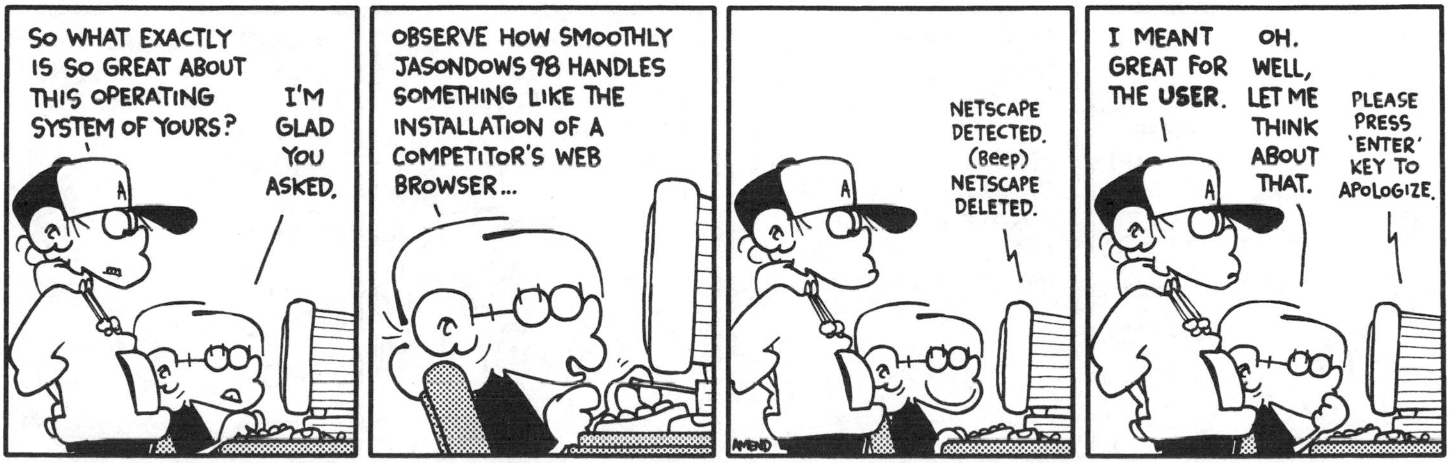
SO WHAT EXACTLY IS SO GREAT ABOUT THIS OPERATING SYSTEM OF YOURS?
I'M GLAD YOU ASKED.
OBSERVE HOW SMOOTHLY JASONDOWS 98 HANDLES SOMETHING LIKE THE INSTALLATION OF A COMPETITOR'S WEB BROWSER...
NETSCAPE DETECTED. (Beep) NETSCAPE DELETED.
AMEND
I MEANT GREAT FOR THE USER.
OH. WELL, LET ME THINK ABOUT THAT.
PLEASE PRESS 'ENTER' KEY TO APOLOGIZE.

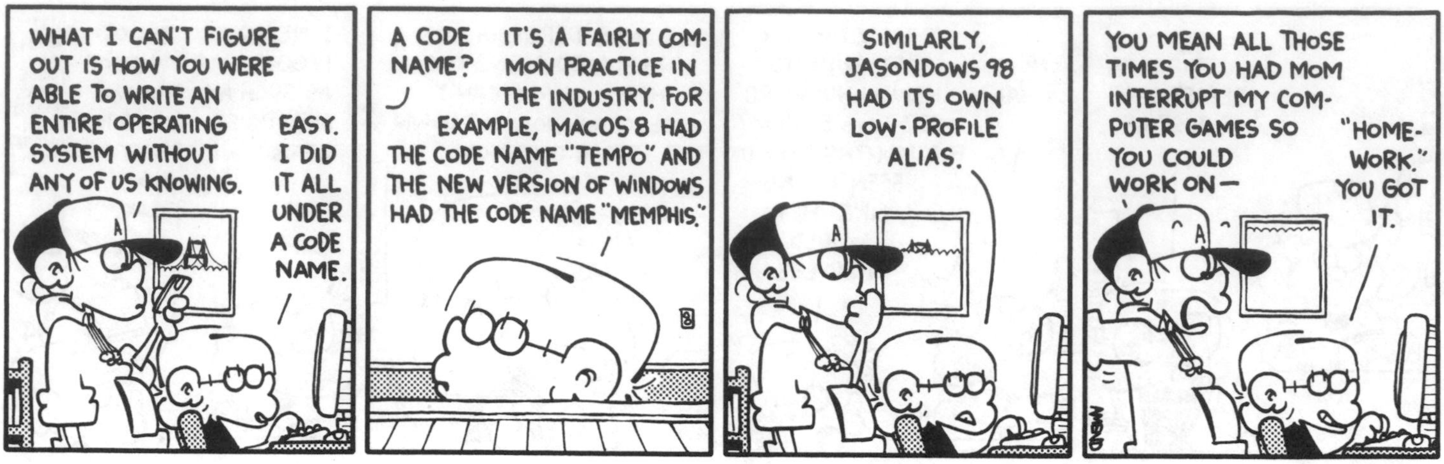
WHAT I CAN'T FIGURE OUT IS HOW YOU WERE ABLE TO WRITE AN ENTIRE OPERATING SYSTEM WITHOUT ANY OF US KNOWING.
EASY. I DID IT ALL UNDER A CODE NAME.
A CODE NAME?
IT'S A FAIRLY COMMON PRACTICE IN THE INDUSTRY. FOR EXAMPLE, MACOS 8 HAD THE CODE NAME "TEMPO" AND THE NEW VERSION OF WINDOWS HAD THE CODE NAME "MEMPHIS."
SIMILARLY, JASONDOWS 98 HAD ITS OWN LOW-PROFILE ALIAS.
YOU MEAN ALL THOSE TIMES YOU HAD MOM INTERRUPT MY COMPUTER GAMES SO YOU COULD WORK ON —
"HOMEWORK." YOU GOT IT.
AMEND

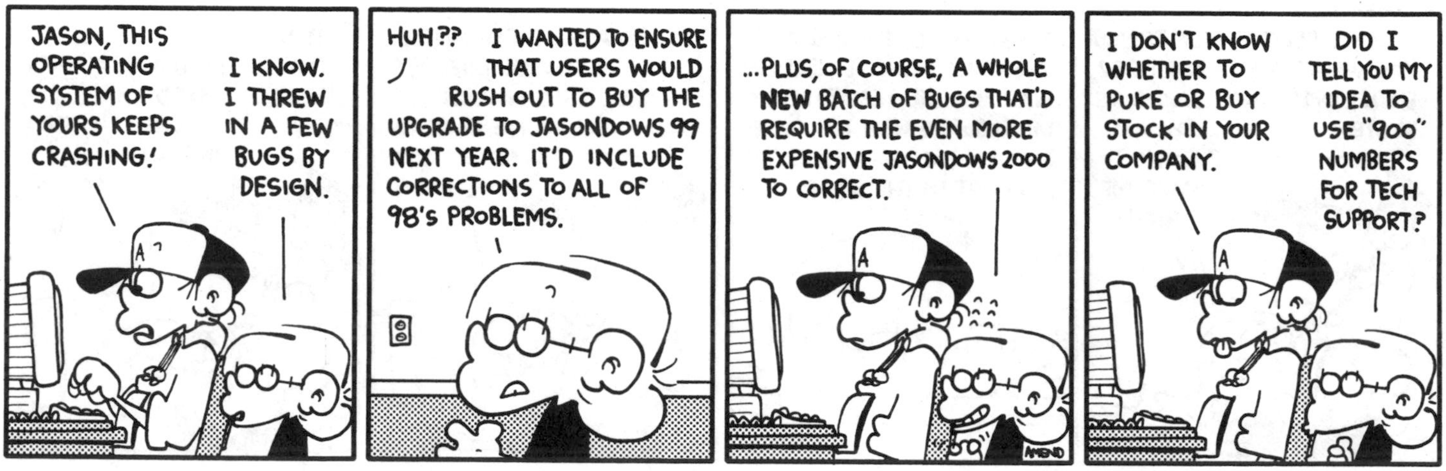
JASON, THIS OPERATING SYSTEM OF YOURS KEEPS CRASHING!
I KNOW. I THREW IN A FEW BUGS BY DESIGN.
HUH??
I WANTED TO ENSURE THAT USERS WOULD RUSH OUT TO BUY THE UPGRADE TO JASONDOWS 99 NEXT YEAR. IT'D INCLUDE CORRECTIONS TO ALL OF 98'S PROBLEMS.
...PLUS, OF COURSE, A WHOLE NEW BATCH OF BUGS THAT'D REQUIRE THE EVEN MORE EXPENSIVE JASONDOWS 2000 TO CORRECT.
AMEND
I DON'T KNOW WHETHER TO PUKE OR BUY STOCK IN YOUR COMPANY.
DID I TELL YOU MY IDEA TO USE "900" NUMBERS FOR TECH SUPPORT?

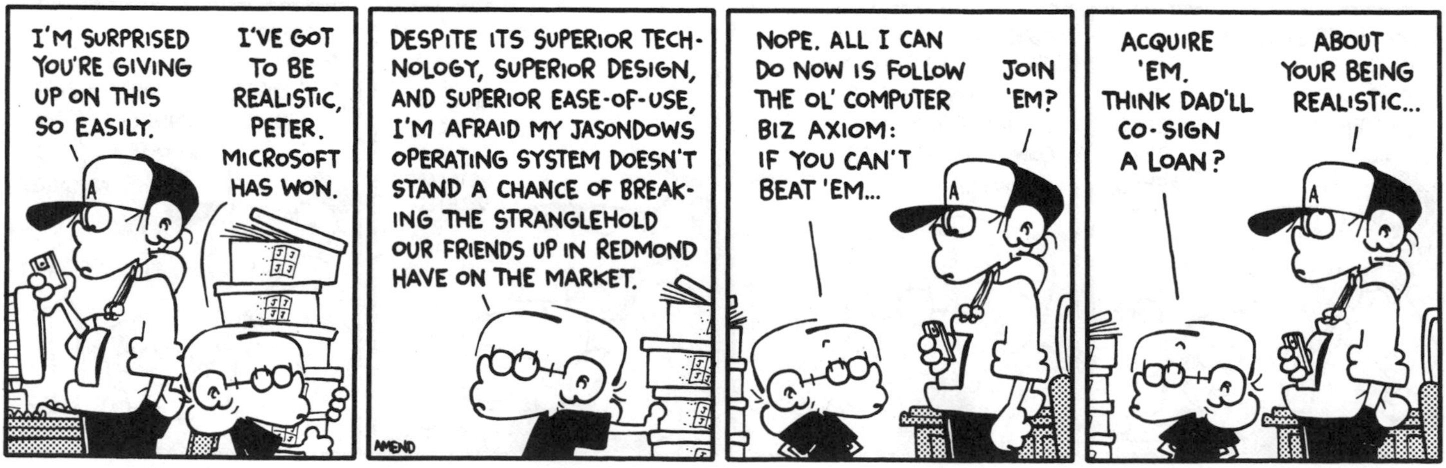
I'M SURPRISED YOU'RE GIVING UP ON THIS SO EASILY.
I'VE GOT TO BE REALISTIC, PETER. MICROSOFT HAS WON.
DESPITE ITS SUPERIOR TECHNOLOGY, SUPERIOR DESIGN, AND SUPERIOR EASE-OF-USE, I'M AFRAID MY JASONDOWS OPERATING SYSTEM DOESN'T STAND A CHANCE OF BREAKING THE STRANGLEHOLD OUR FRIENDS UP IN REDMOND HAVE ON THE MARKET.
AMEND
NOPE. ALL I CAN DO NOW IS FOLLOW THE OL' COMPUTER BIZ AXIOM: IF YOU CAN'T BEAT 'EM...
JOIN 'EM?
ACQUIRE 'EM. THINK DAD'LL CO-SIGN A LOAN?
ABOUT YOUR BEING REALISTIC...

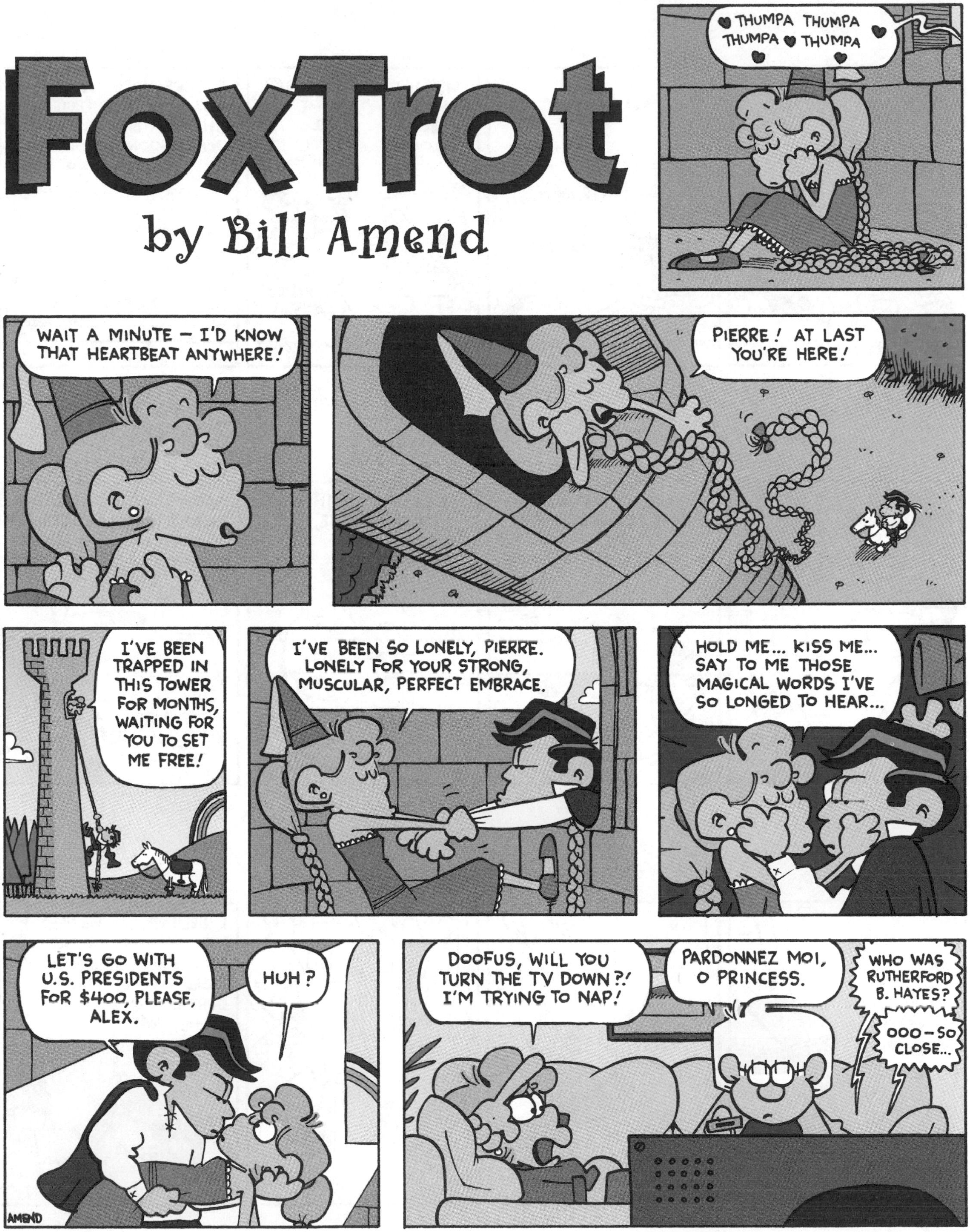
FoxTrot
by Bill Amend
THUMPA THUMPA THUMPA THUMPA
WAIT A MINUTE – I'D KNOW THAT HEARTBEAT ANYWHERE!
PIERRE! AT LAST YOU'RE HERE!
I'VE BEEN TRAPPED IN THIS TOWER FOR MONTHS, WAITING FOR YOU TO SET ME FREE!
I'VE BEEN SO LONELY, PIERRE. LONELY FOR YOUR STRONG, MUSCULAR, PERFECT EMBRACE.
HOLD ME... KISS ME... SAY TO ME THOSE MAGICAL WORDS I'VE SO LONGED TO HEAR...
LET'S GO WITH U.S. PRESIDENTS FOR $400, PLEASE, ALEX.
HUH?
AMEND
DOOFUS, WILL YOU TURN THE TV DOWN?! I'M TRYING TO NAP!
PARDONNEZ MOI, O PRINCESS.
WHO WAS RUTHERFORD B. HAYES?
OOO–SO CLOSE...

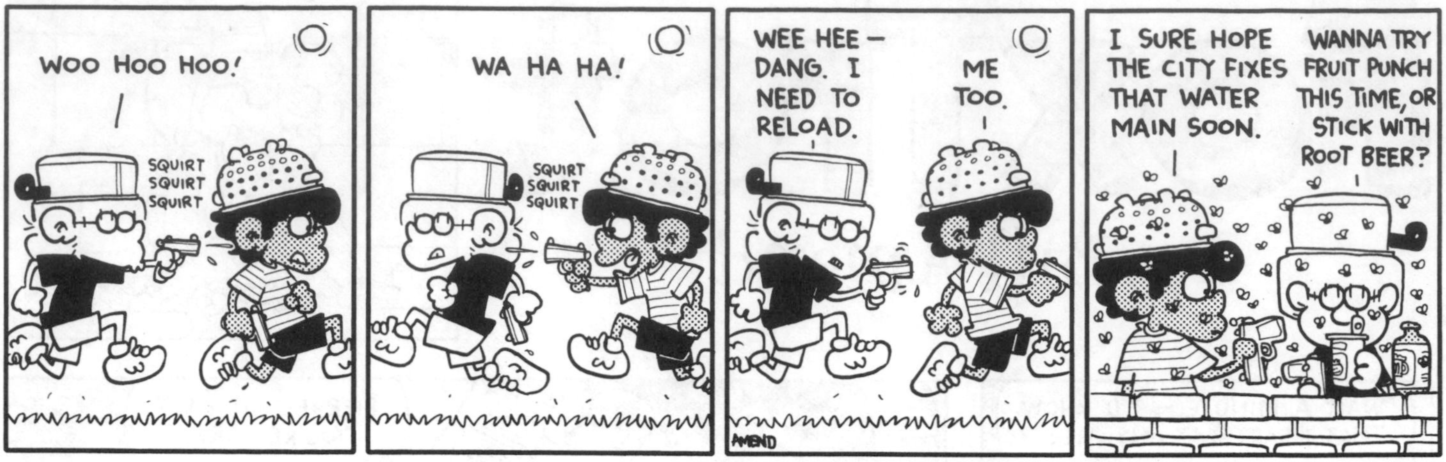
WOO HOO HOO!
SQUIRT SQUIRT SQUIRT
WA HA HA!
SQUIRT SQUIRT SQUIRT
WEE HEE— DANG. I NEED TO RELOAD.
ME TOO.
AMEND
I SURE HOPE THE CITY FIXES THAT WATER MAIN SOON.
WANNA TRY FRUIT PUNCH THIS TIME, OR STICK WITH ROOT BEER?

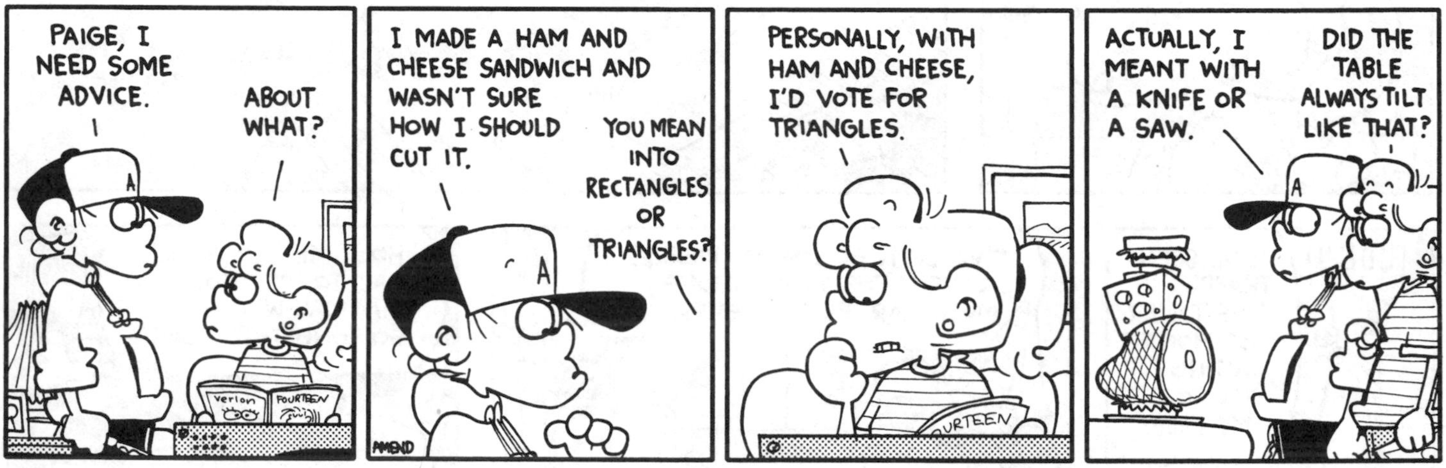
PAIGE, I NEED SOME ADVICE.
ABOUT WHAT?
I MADE A HAM AND CHEESE SANDWICH AND WASN'T SURE HOW I SHOULD CUT IT.
YOU MEAN INTO RECTANGLES OR TRIANGLES?
AMEND
PERSONALLY, WITH HAM AND CHEESE, I'D VOTE FOR TRIANGLES.
ACTUALLY, I MEANT WITH A KNIFE OR A SAW.
DID THE TABLE ALWAYS TILT LIKE THAT?

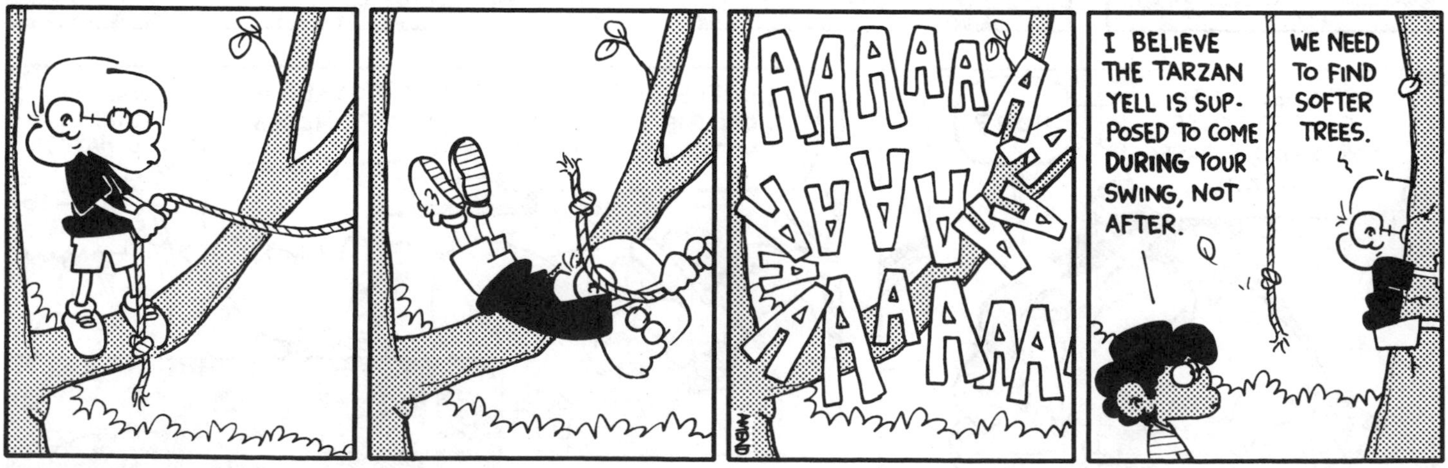
AAAAAAAAAAAAAAAAAAAAAAAAA
AMEND
I BELIEVE THE TARZAN YELL IS SUPPOSED TO COME DURING YOUR SWING, NOT AFTER.
WE NEED TO FIND SOFTER TREES.

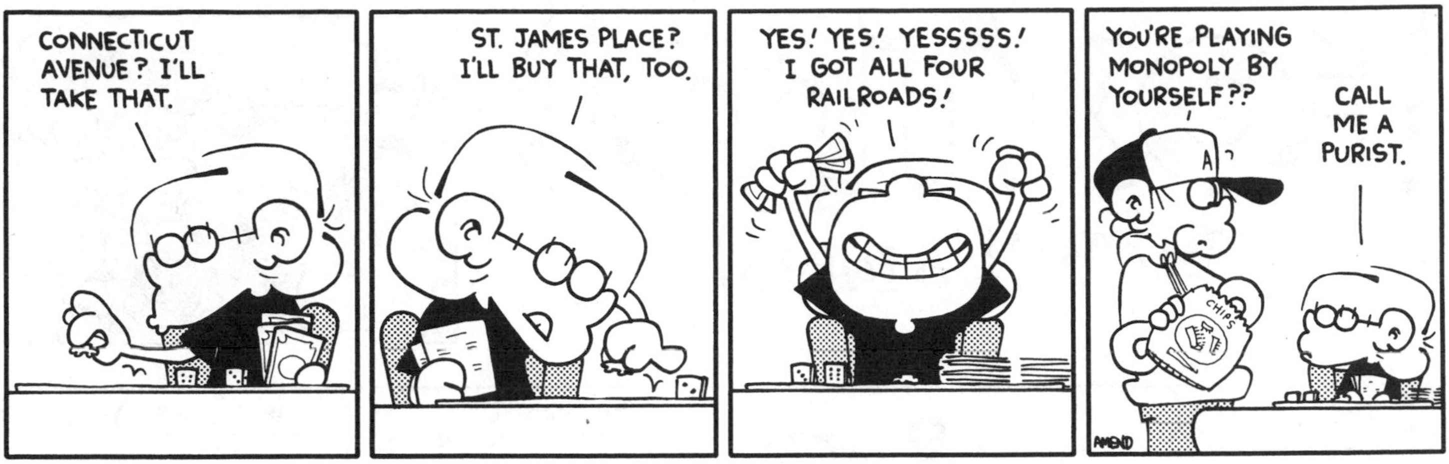
CONNECTICUT AVENUE? I'LL TAKE THAT.
ST. JAMES PLACE? I'LL BUY THAT, TOO.
YES! YES! YESSSSS! I GOT ALL FOUR RAILROADS!
YOU'RE PLAYING MONOPOLY BY YOURSELF??
CHIPS
CALL ME A PURIST.
AMEND

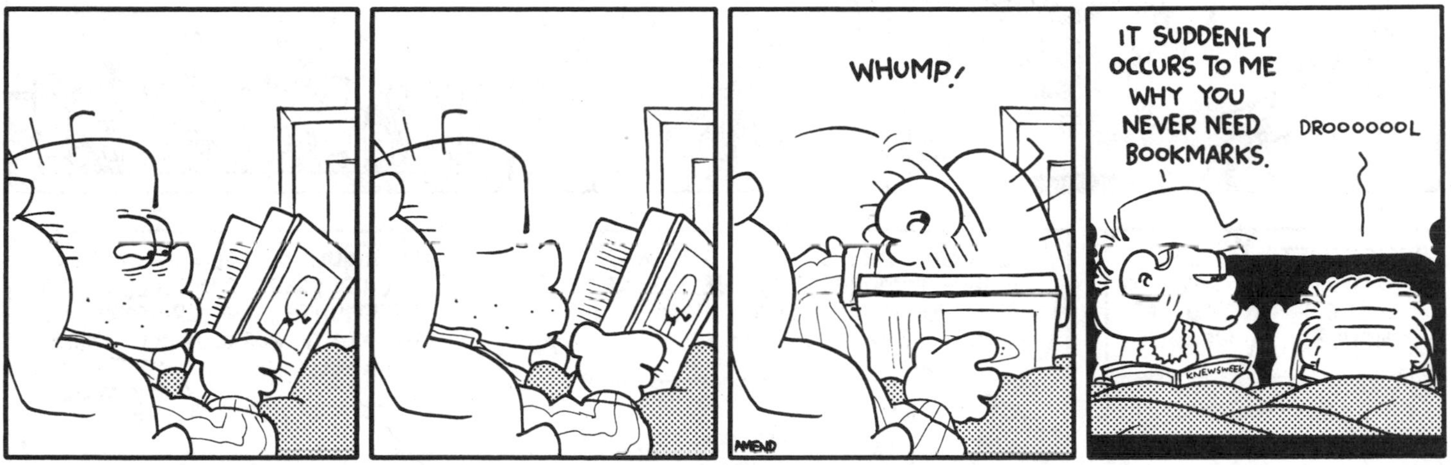
WHUMP!
AMEND
IT SUDDENLY OCCURS TO ME WHY YOU NEVER NEED BOOKMARKS.
DROOOOOOL
KNEWSWEEK

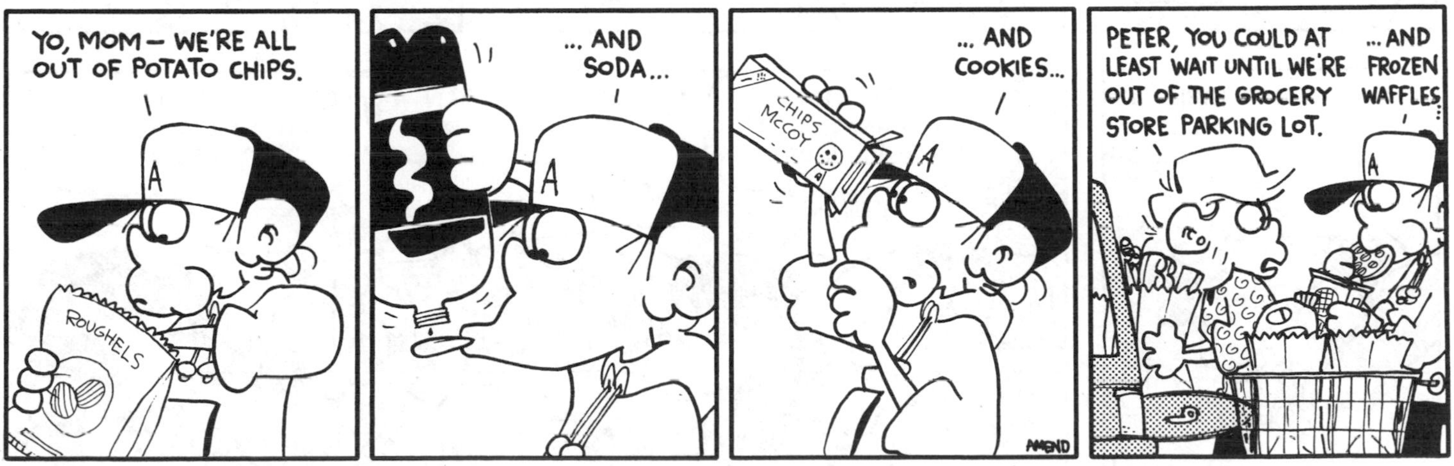
YO, MOM— WE'RE ALL OUT OF POTATO CHIPS.
ROUGHELS
... AND SODA...
... AND COOKIES...
CHIPS McCOY
AMEND
PETER, YOU COULD AT LEAST WAIT UNTIL WE'RE OUT OF THE GROCERY STORE PARKING LOT.
... AND FROZEN WAFFLES...

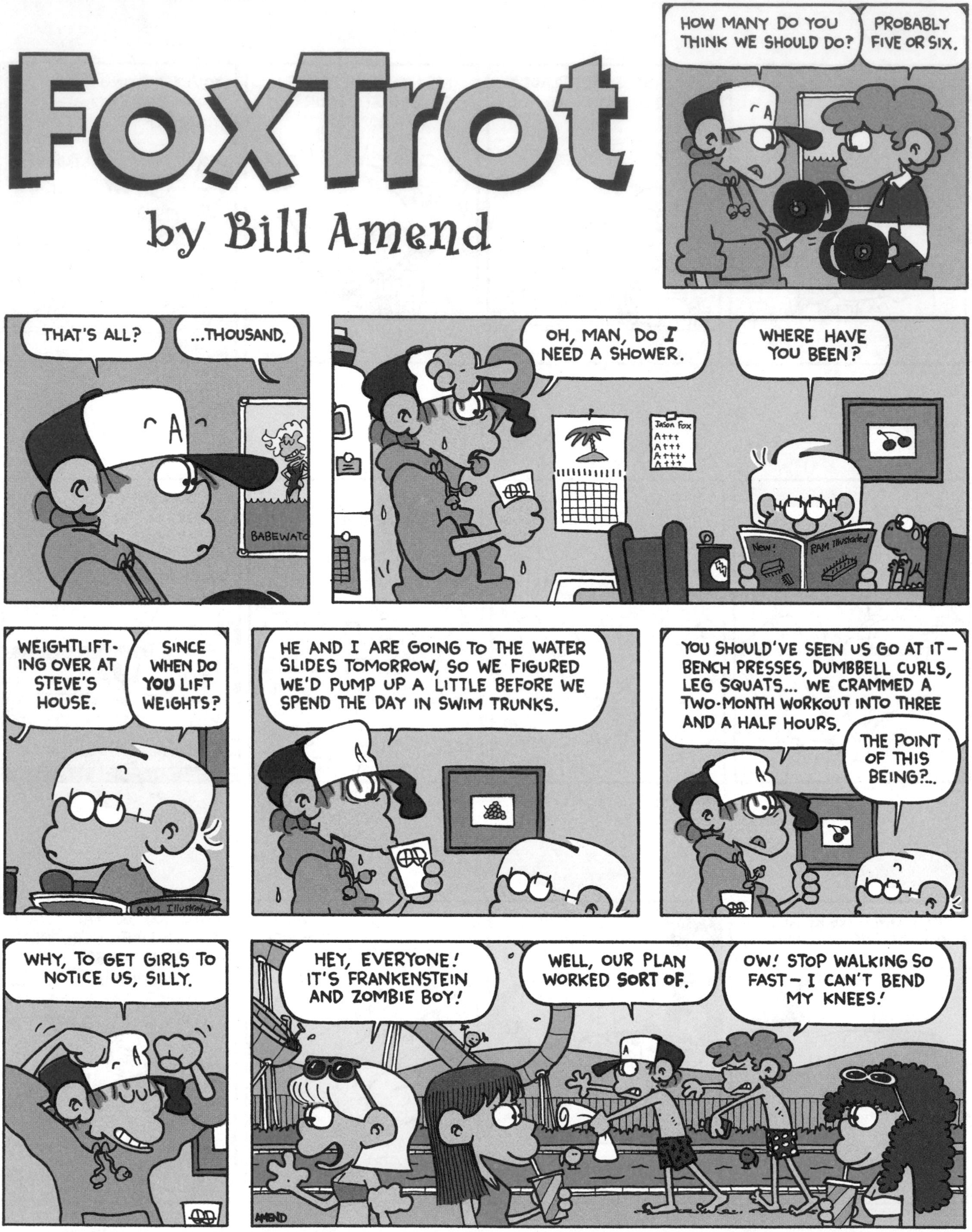
FoxTrot
by Bill Amend
HOW MANY DO YOU THINK WE SHOULD DO?
PROBABLY FIVE OR SIX.
THAT'S ALL?
...THOUSAND.
BABEWATC
OH, MAN, DO I NEED A SHOWER.
WHERE HAVE YOU BEEN?
Jason Fox
RAM Illustrated
WEIGHTLIFTING OVER AT STEVE'S HOUSE.
SINCE WHEN DO YOU LIFT WEIGHTS?
HE AND I ARE GOING TO THE WATER SLIDES TOMORROW, SO WE FIGURED WE'D PUMP UP A LITTLE BEFORE WE SPEND THE DAY IN SWIM TRUNKS.
YOU SHOULD'VE SEEN US GO AT IT – BENCH PRESSES, DUMBBELL CURLS, LEG SQUATS... WE CRAMMED A TWO-MONTH WORKOUT INTO THREE AND A HALF HOURS.
THE POINT OF THIS BEING?...
WHY, TO GET GIRLS TO NOTICE US, SILLY.
HEY, EVERYONE! IT'S FRANKENSTEIN AND ZOMBIE BOY!
WELL, OUR PLAN WORKED SORT OF.
OW! STOP WALKING SO FAST – I CAN'T BEND MY KNEES!
AMEND

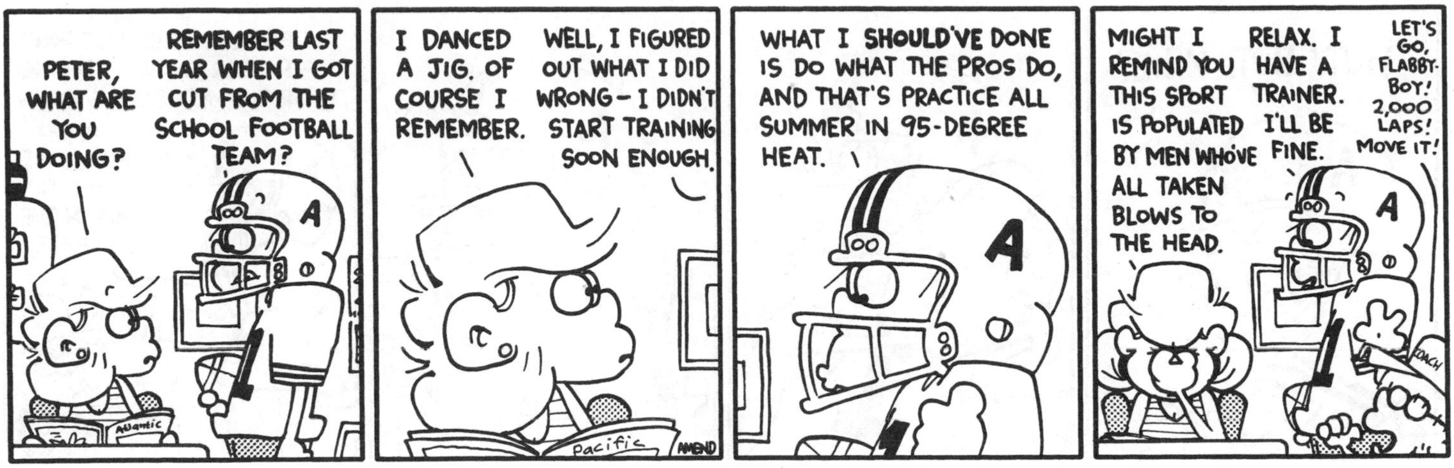
PETER, WHAT ARE YOU DOING?
REMEMBER LAST YEAR WHEN I GOT CUT FROM THE SCHOOL FOOTBALL TEAM?
I DANCED A JIG. OF COURSE I REMEMBER.
WELL, I FIGURED OUT WHAT I DID WRONG – I DIDN'T START TRAINING SOON ENOUGH.
WHAT I SHOULD'VE DONE IS DO WHAT THE PROS DO, AND THAT'S PRACTICE ALL SUMMER IN 95-DEGREE HEAT.
MIGHT I REMIND YOU THIS SPORT IS POPULATED BY MEN WHO'VE ALL TAKEN BLOWS TO THE HEAD.
RELAX. I HAVE A TRAINER. I'LL BE FINE.
LET'S GO, FLABBY-BOY! 2,000 LAPS! MOVE IT!
COACH

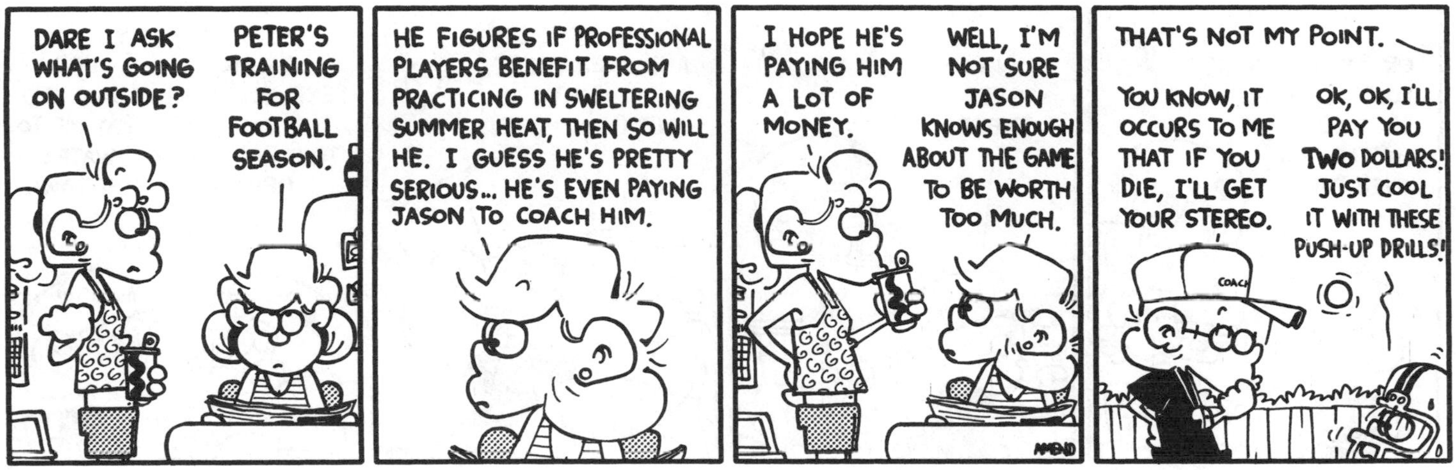
DARE I ASK WHAT'S GOING ON OUTSIDE?
PETER'S TRAINING FOR FOOTBALL SEASON.
HE FIGURES IF PROFESSIONAL PLAYERS BENEFIT FROM PRACTICING IN SWELTERING SUMMER HEAT, THEN SO WILL HE. I GUESS HE'S PRETTY SERIOUS... HE'S EVEN PAYING JASON TO COACH HIM.
I HOPE HE'S PAYING HIM A LOT OF MONEY.
WELL, I'M NOT SURE JASON KNOWS ENOUGH ABOUT THE GAME TO BE WORTH TOO MUCH.
THAT'S NOT MY POINT.
YOU KNOW, IT OCCURS TO ME THAT IF YOU DIE, I'LL GET YOUR STEREO.
OK, OK, I'LL PAY YOU TWO DOLLARS! JUST COOL IT WITH THESE PUSH-UP DRILLS!
COACH

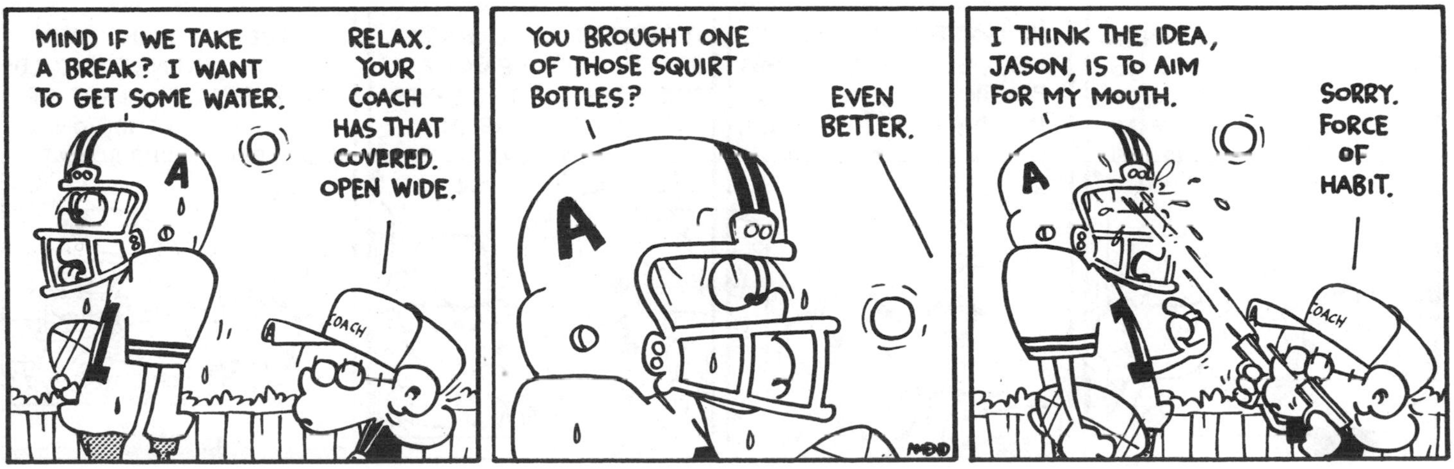
MIND IF WE TAKE A BREAK? I WANT TO GET SOME WATER.
RELAX. YOUR COACH HAS THAT COVERED. OPEN WIDE.
YOU BROUGHT ONE OF THOSE SQUIRT BOTTLES?
EVEN BETTER.
I THINK THE IDEA, JASON, IS TO AIM FOR MY MOUTH.
SORRY. FORCE OF HABIT.
COACH

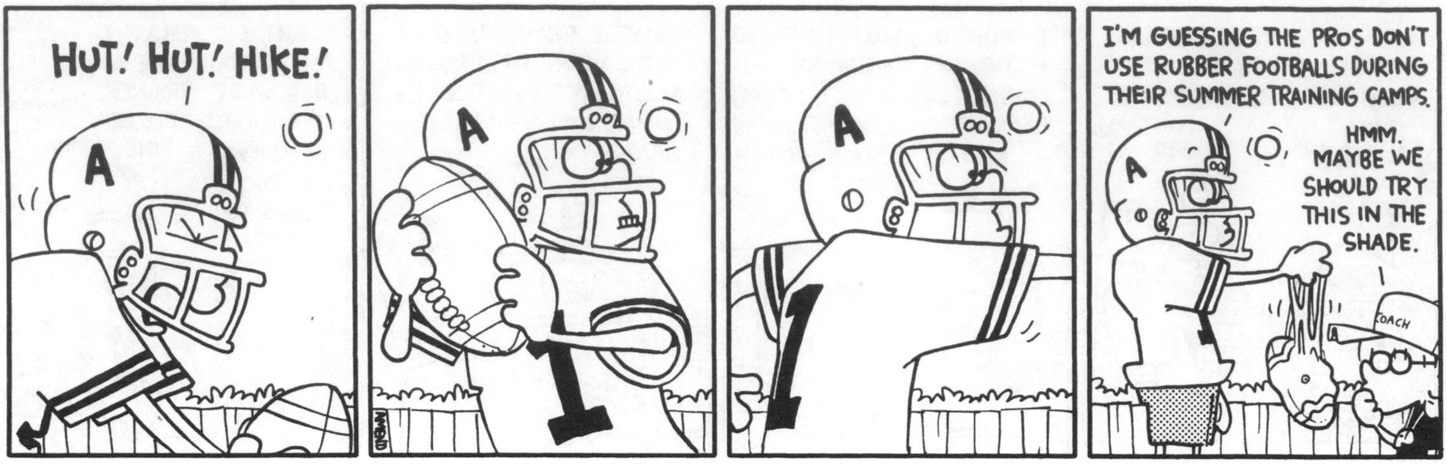
HUT! HUT! HIKE!
I'M GUESSING THE PROS DON'T USE RUBBER FOOTBALLS DURING THEIR SUMMER TRAINING CAMPS.
HMM. MAYBE WE SHOULD TRY THIS IN THE SHADE.
COACH

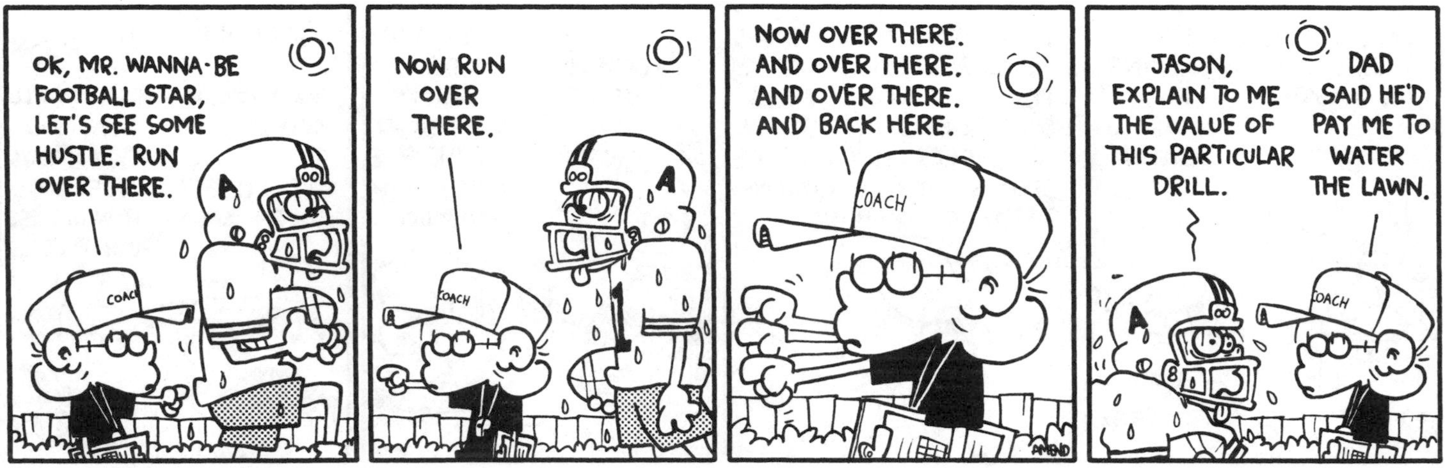
OK, MR. WANNA-BE FOOTBALL STAR, LET'S SEE SOME HUSTLE. RUN OVER THERE.
NOW RUN OVER THERE.
NOW OVER THERE. AND OVER THERE. AND OVER THERE. AND BACK HERE.
JASON, EXPLAIN TO ME THE VALUE OF THIS PARTICULAR DRILL.
DAD SAID HE'D PAY ME TO WATER THE LAWN.
AMEND

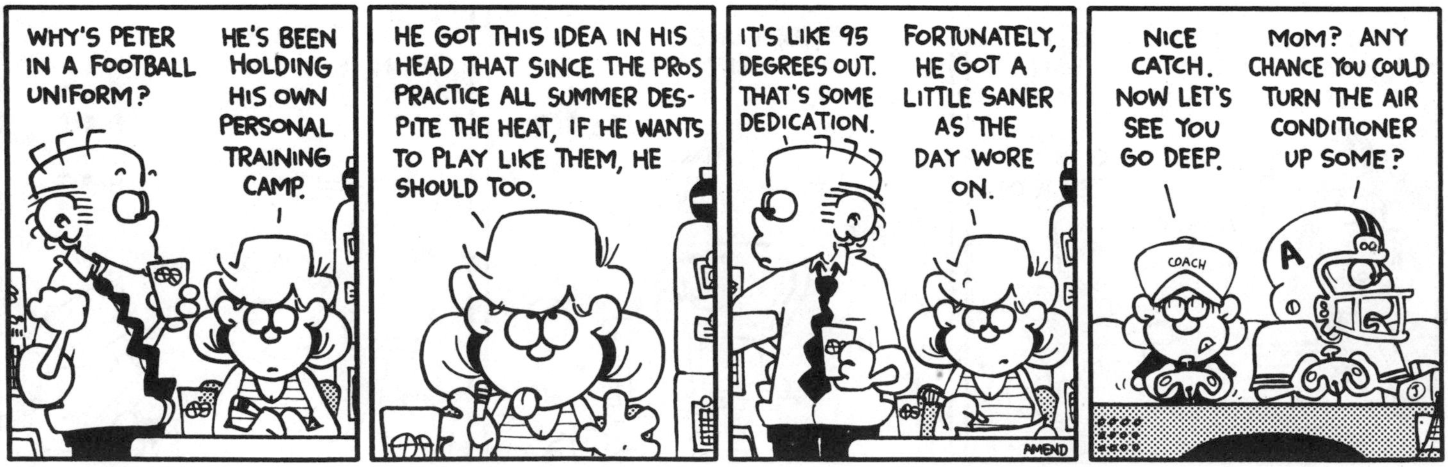
WHY'S PETER IN A FOOTBALL UNIFORM?
HE'S BEEN HOLDING HIS OWN PERSONAL TRAINING CAMP.
HE GOT THIS IDEA IN HIS HEAD THAT SINCE THE PROS PRACTICE ALL SUMMER DESPITE THE HEAT, IF HE WANTS TO PLAY LIKE THEM, HE SHOULD TOO.
IT'S LIKE 95 DEGREES OUT. THAT'S SOME DEDICATION.
FORTUNATELY, HE GOT A LITTLE SANER AS THE DAY WORE ON.
NICE CATCH. NOW LET'S SEE YOU GO DEEP.
MOM? ANY CHANCE YOU COULD TURN THE AIR CONDITIONER UP SOME?
COACH
AMEND

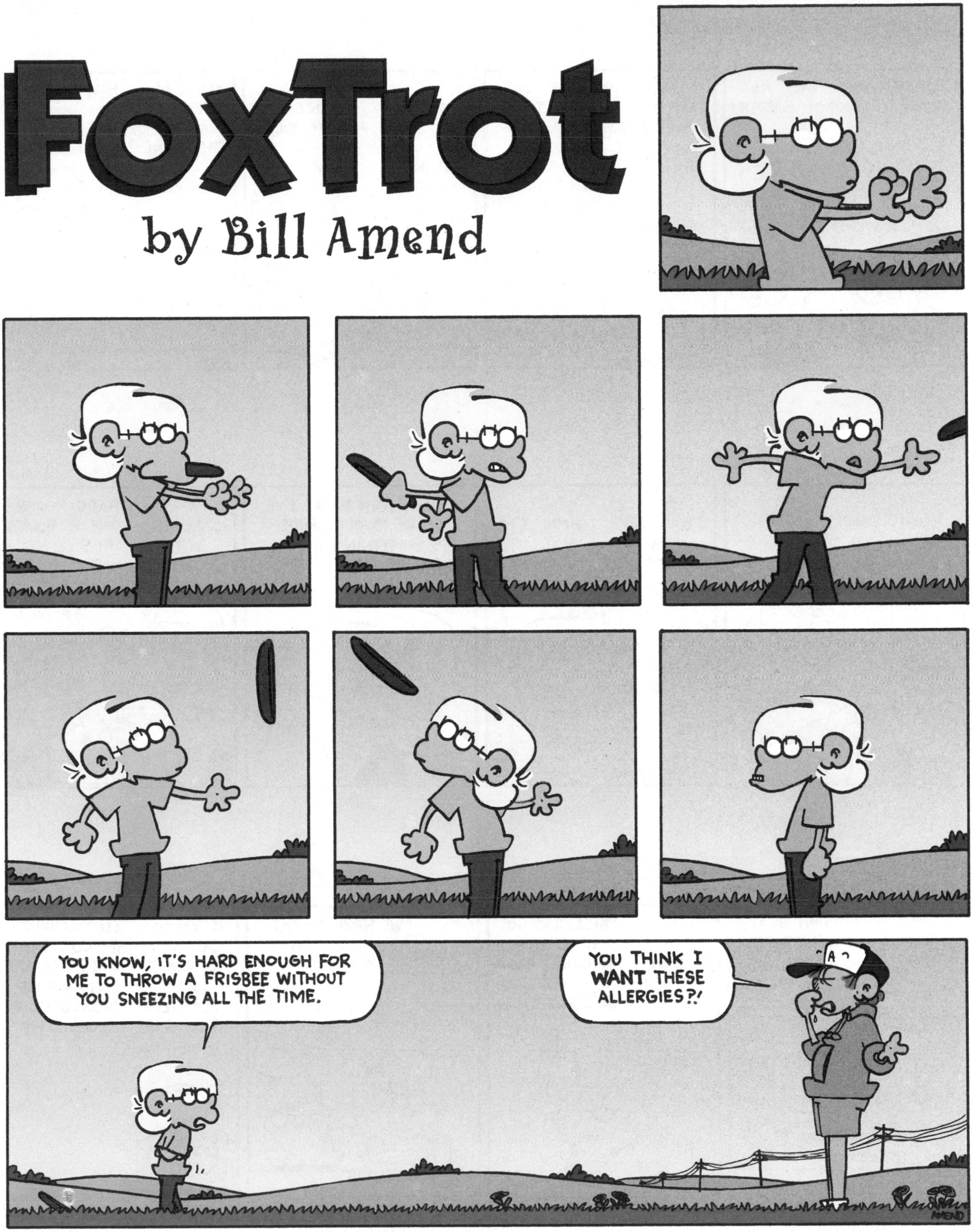
FoxTrot
by Bill Amend
YOU KNOW, IT'S HARD ENOUGH FOR ME TO THROW A FRISBEE WITHOUT YOU SNEEZING ALL THE TIME.
YOU THINK I WANT THESE ALLERGIES?!
AMEND

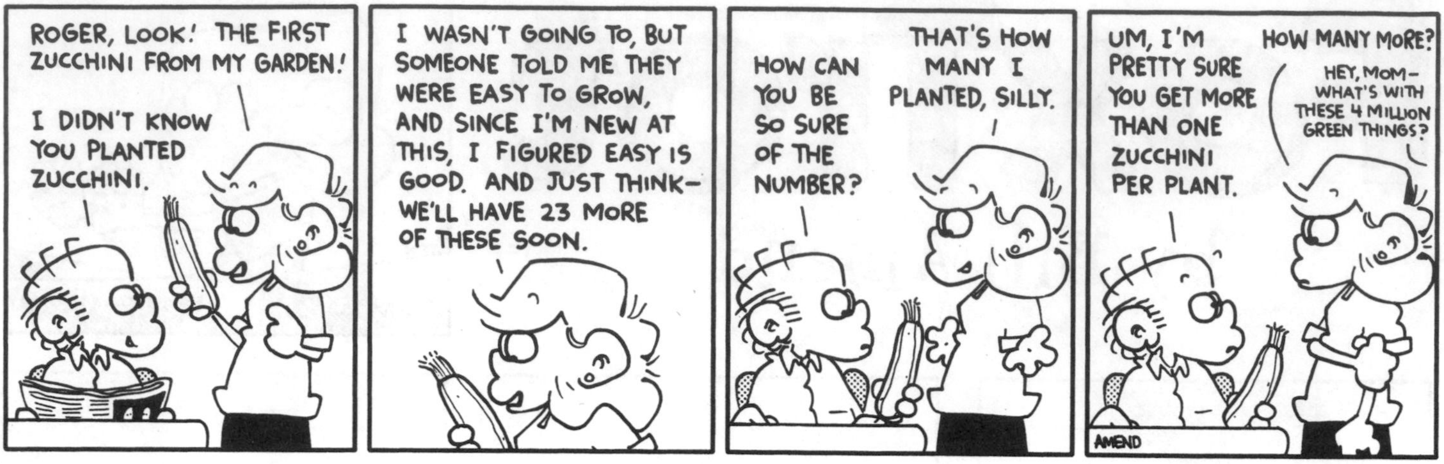
ROGER, LOOK! THE FIRST ZUCCHINI FROM MY GARDEN!
I DIDN'T KNOW YOU PLANTED ZUCCHINI.
I WASN'T GOING TO, BUT SOMEONE TOLD ME THEY WERE EASY TO GROW, AND SINCE I'M NEW AT THIS, I FIGURED EASY IS GOOD. AND JUST THINK— WE'LL HAVE 23 MORE OF THESE SOON.
HOW CAN YOU BE SO SURE OF THE NUMBER?
THAT'S HOW MANY I PLANTED, SILLY.
UM, I'M PRETTY SURE YOU GET MORE THAN ONE ZUCCHINI PER PLANT.
HOW MANY MORE?
HEY, MOM— WHAT'S WITH THESE 4 MILLION GREEN THINGS?
AMEND

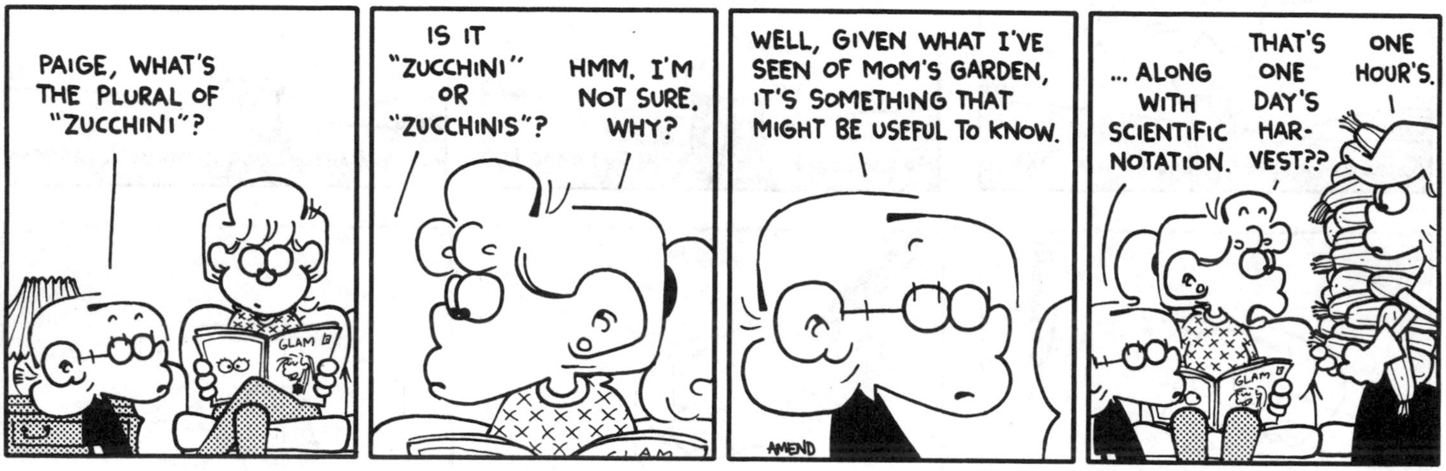
PAIGE, WHAT'S THE PLURAL OF "ZUCCHINI"?
GLAM
IS IT "ZUCCHINI" OR "ZUCCHINIS"?
HMM. I'M NOT SURE. WHY?
WELL, GIVEN WHAT I'VE SEEN OF MOM'S GARDEN, IT'S SOMETHING THAT MIGHT BE USEFUL TO KNOW.
AMEND
... ALONG WITH SCIENTIFIC NOTATION.
THAT'S ONE DAY'S HARVEST??
ONE HOUR'S.
GLAM

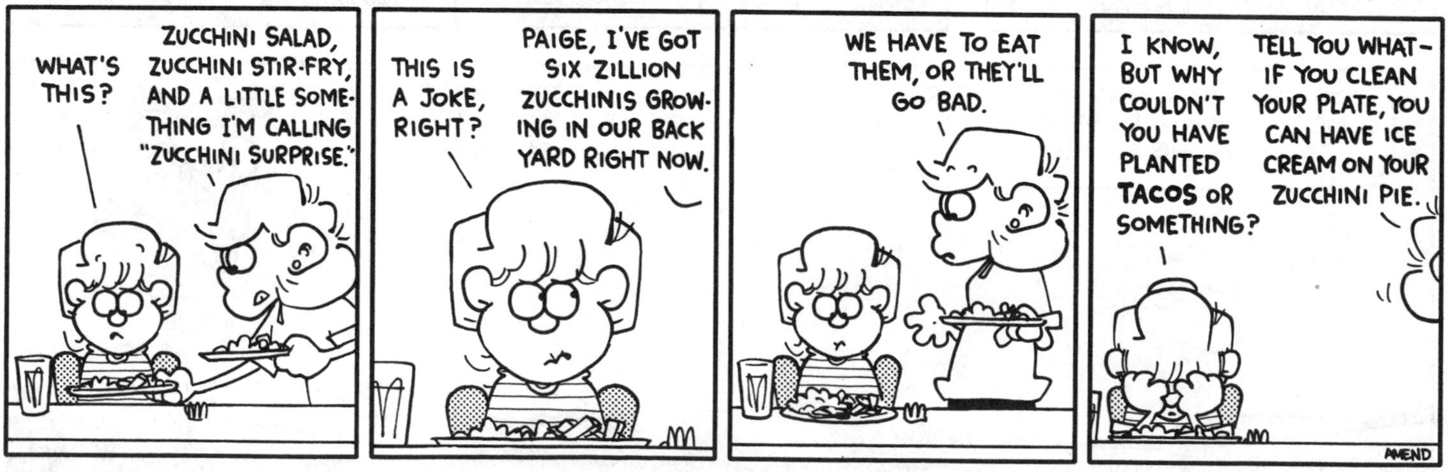
WHAT'S THIS?
ZUCCHINI SALAD, ZUCCHINI STIR-FRY, AND A LITTLE SOMETHING I'M CALLING "ZUCCHINI SURPRISE."
THIS IS A JOKE, RIGHT?
PAIGE, I'VE GOT SIX ZILLION ZUCCHINIS GROWING IN OUR BACK YARD RIGHT NOW.
WE HAVE TO EAT THEM, OR THEY'LL GO BAD.
I KNOW, BUT WHY COULDN'T YOU HAVE PLANTED TACOS OR SOMETHING?
TELL YOU WHAT— IF YOU CLEAN YOUR PLATE, YOU CAN HAVE ICE CREAM ON YOUR ZUCCHINI PIE.
AMEND

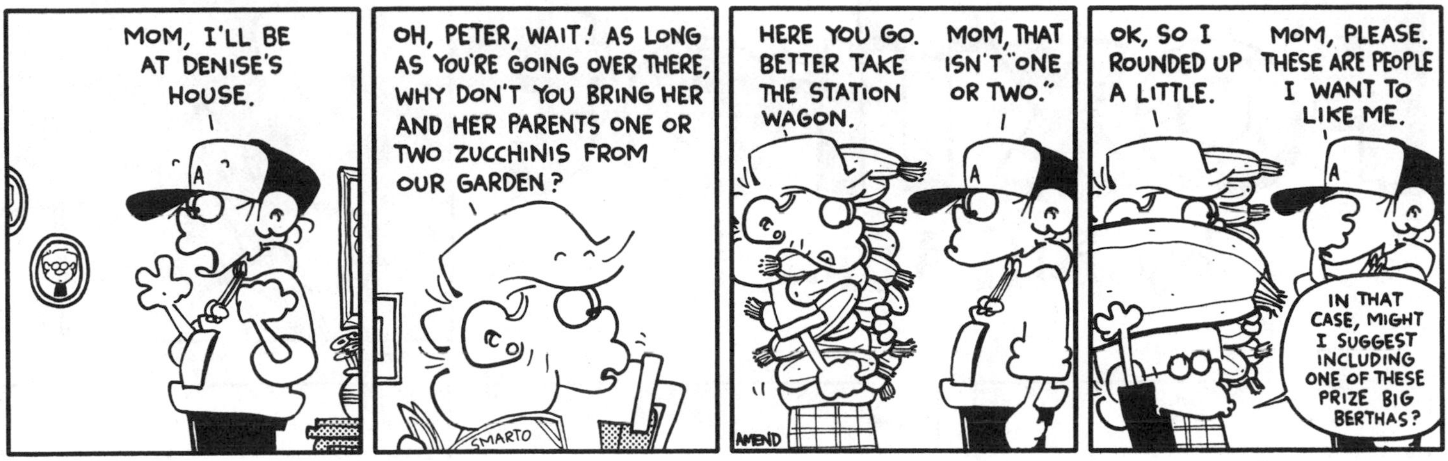
MOM, I'LL BE AT DENISE'S HOUSE.
OH, PETER, WAIT! AS LONG AS YOU'RE GOING OVER THERE, WHY DON'T YOU BRING HER AND HER PARENTS ONE OR TWO ZUCCHINIS FROM OUR GARDEN?
SMARTO
HERE YOU GO. BETTER TAKE THE STATION WAGON.
MOM, THAT ISN'T "ONE OR TWO."
OK, SO I ROUNDED UP A LITTLE.
MOM, PLEASE. THESE ARE PEOPLE I WANT TO LIKE ME.
IN THAT CASE, MIGHT I SUGGEST INCLUDING ONE OF THESE PRIZE BIG BERTHAS?

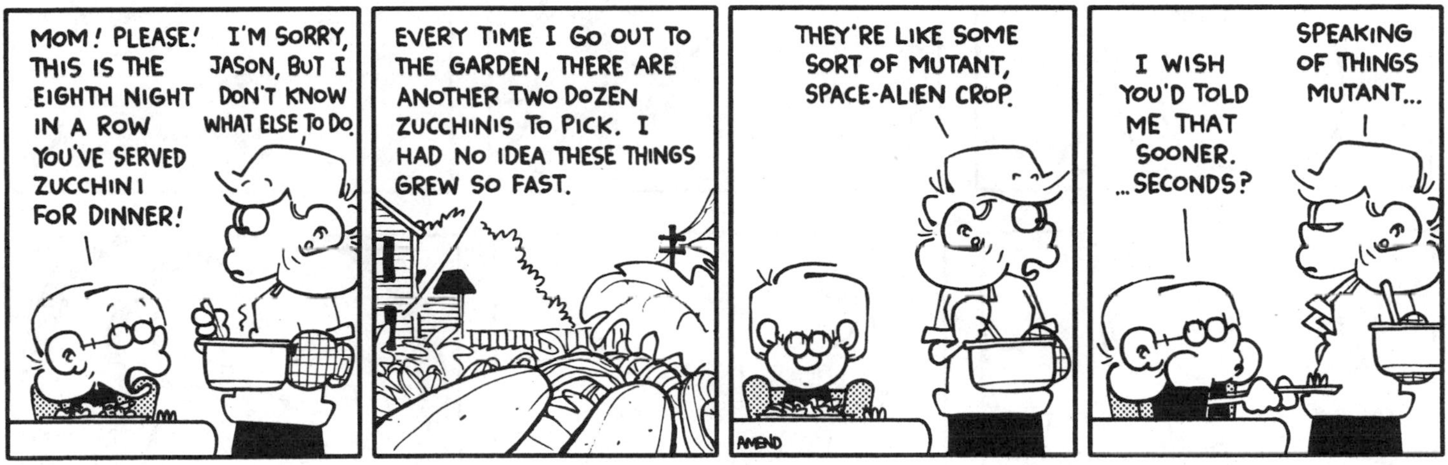
MOM! PLEASE! THIS IS THE EIGHTH NIGHT IN A ROW YOU'VE SERVED ZUCCHINI FOR DINNER!
I'M SORRY, JASON, BUT I DON'T KNOW WHAT ELSE TO DO.
EVERY TIME I GO OUT TO THE GARDEN, THERE ARE ANOTHER TWO DOZEN ZUCCHINIS TO PICK. I HAD NO IDEA THESE THINGS GREW SO FAST.
THEY'RE LIKE SOME SORT OF MUTANT, SPACE-ALIEN CROP.
I WISH YOU'D TOLD ME THAT SOONER. ...SECONDS?
SPEAKING OF THINGS MUTANT...

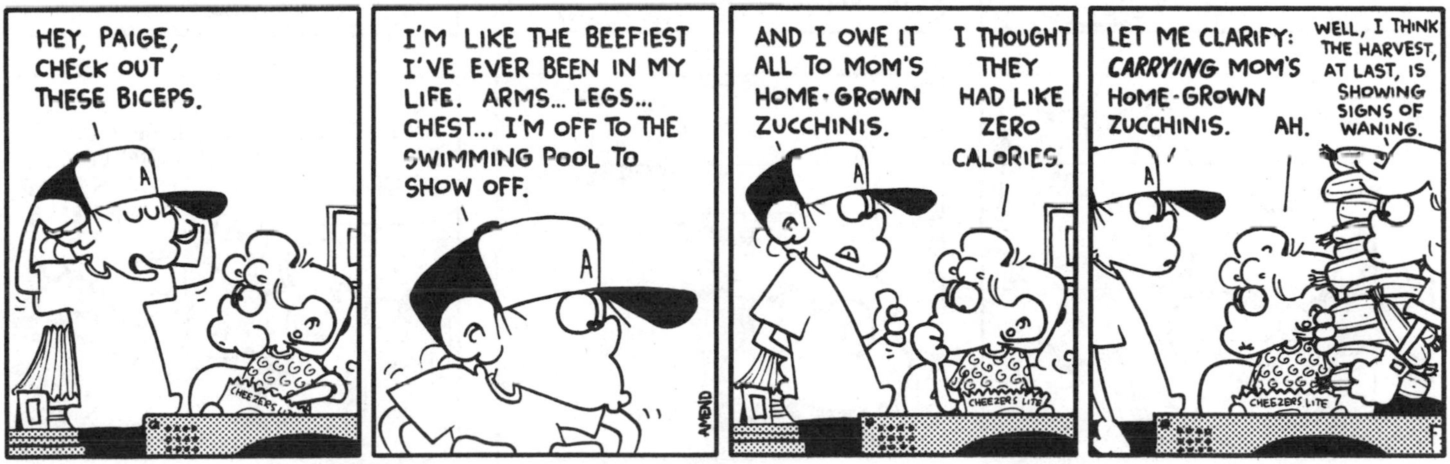
HEY, PAIGE, CHECK OUT THESE BICEPS.
I'M LIKE THE BEEFIEST I'VE EVER BEEN IN MY LIFE. ARMS... LEGS... CHEST... I'M OFF TO THE SWIMMING POOL TO SHOW OFF.
AND I OWE IT ALL TO MOM'S HOME-GROWN ZUCCHINIS.
I THOUGHT THEY HAD LIKE ZERO CALORIES.
LET ME CLARIFY: *CARRYING* MOM'S HOME-GROWN ZUCCHINIS.
AH.
WELL, I THINK THE HARVEST, AT LAST, IS SHOWING SIGNS OF WANING.

FoxTrot
by Bill Amend

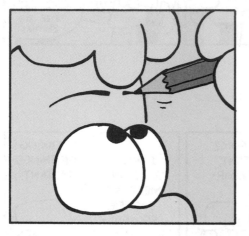

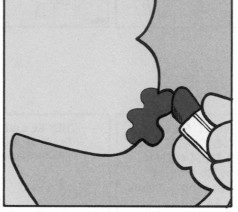

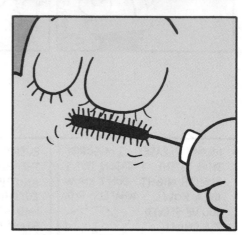

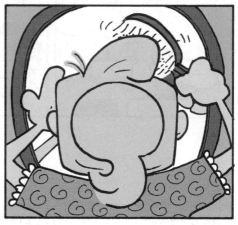

SEE YA, MOM! I'M OFF TO DENISE'S — I MEAN, THE MALL.

WOBBLE WOBBLE WOBBLE —

KEEP IT UP, PETER, AND YOU'LL BE GROUNDED ALL OF **NEXT** WEEK, TOO.

DANG. I KNEW I SHOULD'VE WORN PAIGE'S FLATS INSTEAD OF HER HEELS.

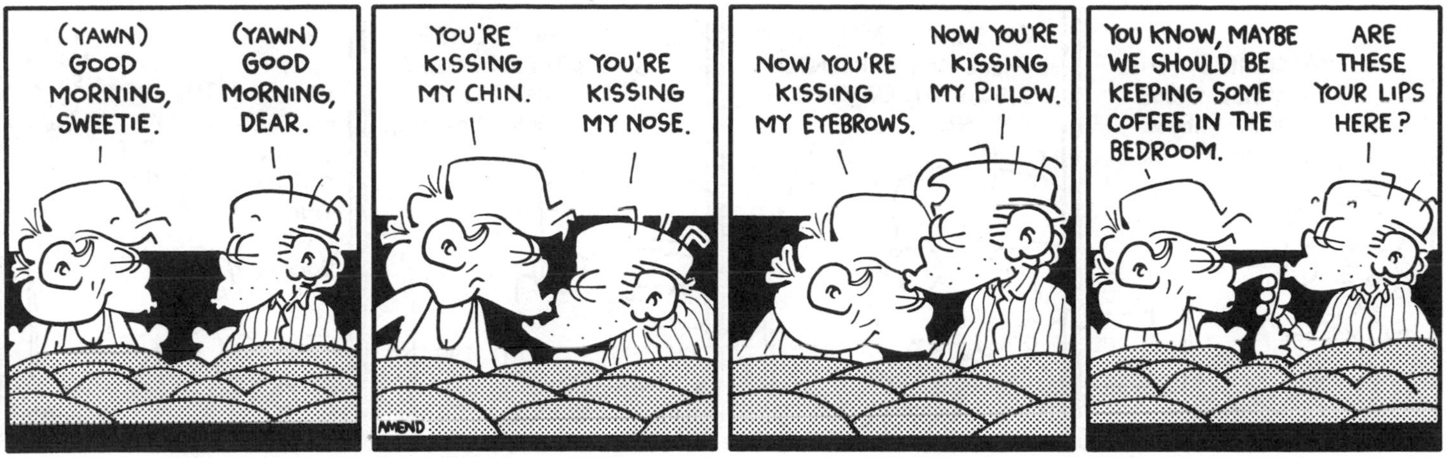
(YAWN) GOOD MORNING, SWEETIE.
(YAWN) GOOD MORNING, DEAR.
YOU'RE KISSING MY CHIN.
YOU'RE KISSING MY NOSE.
NOW YOU'RE KISSING MY EYEBROWS.
NOW YOU'RE KISSING MY PILLOW.
YOU KNOW, MAYBE WE SHOULD BE KEEPING SOME COFFEE IN THE BEDROOM.
ARE THESE YOUR LIPS HERE?
AMEND

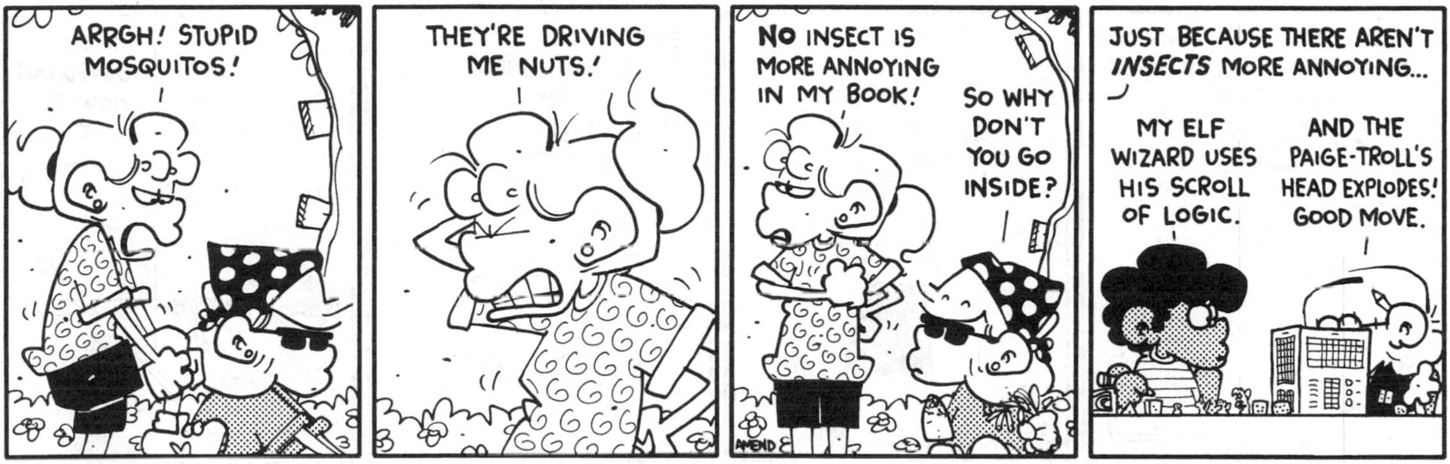
ARRGH! STUPID MOSQUITOS!
THEY'RE DRIVING ME NUTS!
NO INSECT IS MORE ANNOYING IN MY BOOK!
SO WHY DON'T YOU GO INSIDE?
JUST BECAUSE THERE AREN'T INSECTS MORE ANNOYING...
MY ELF WIZARD USES HIS SCROLL OF LOGIC.
AND THE PAIGE-TROLL'S HEAD EXPLODES! GOOD MOVE.
AMEND

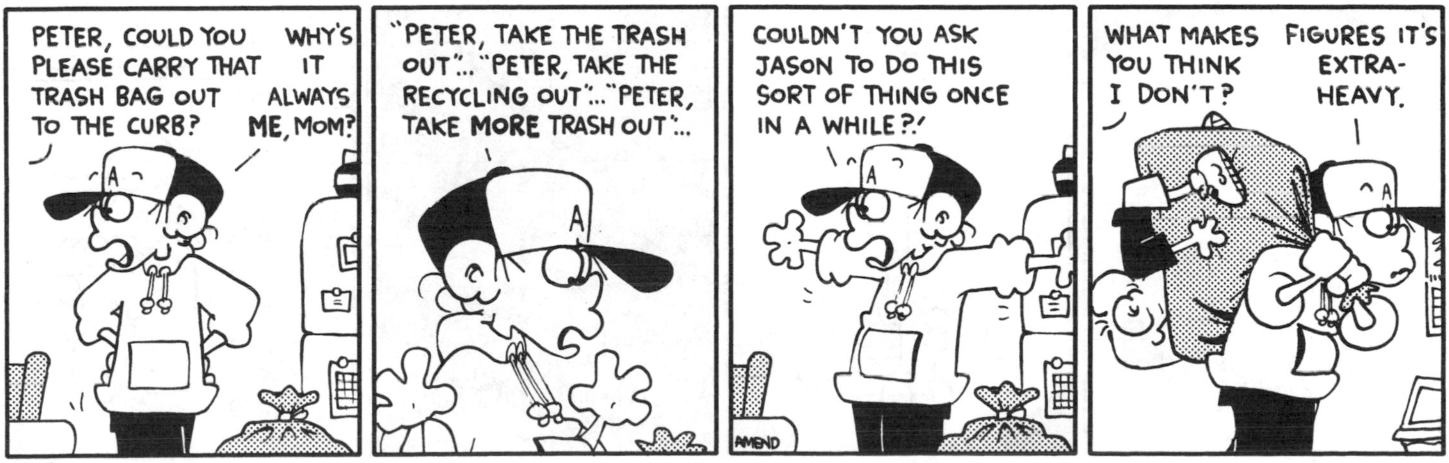
PETER, COULD YOU PLEASE CARRY THAT TRASH BAG OUT TO THE CURB?
WHY'S IT ALWAYS ME, MOM?
"PETER, TAKE THE TRASH OUT"... "PETER, TAKE THE RECYCLING OUT"... "PETER, TAKE MORE TRASH OUT"...
COULDN'T YOU ASK JASON TO DO THIS SORT OF THING ONCE IN A WHILE?!
WHAT MAKES YOU THINK I DON'T?
FIGURES IT'S EXTRA-HEAVY.
AMEND

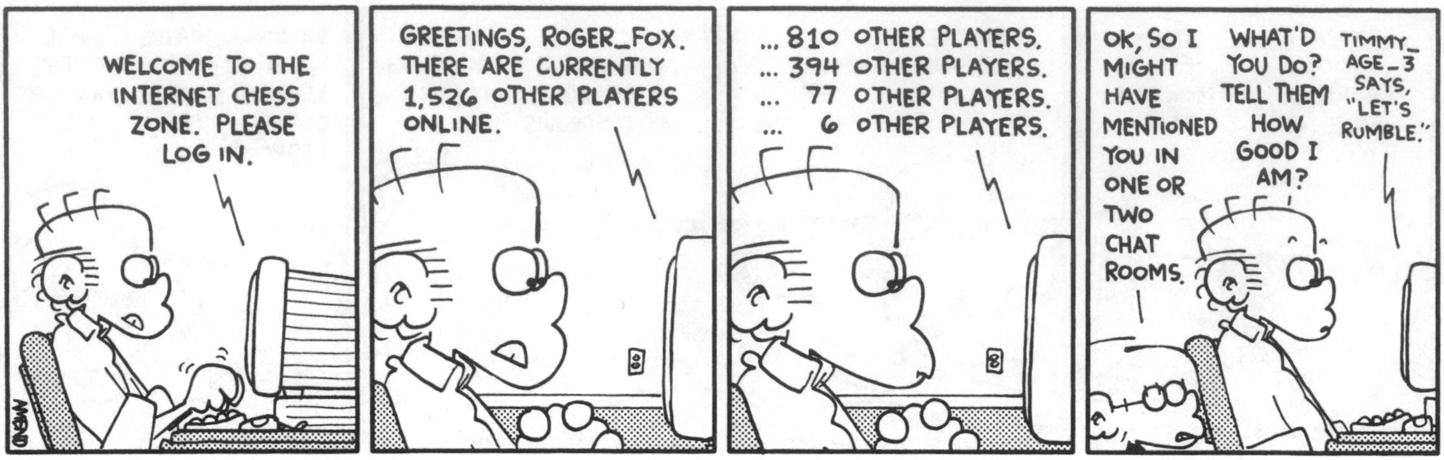
WELCOME TO THE INTERNET CHESS ZONE. PLEASE LOG IN.
GREETINGS, ROGER_FOX. THERE ARE CURRENTLY 1,526 OTHER PLAYERS ONLINE.
... 810 OTHER PLAYERS.
... 394 OTHER PLAYERS.
... 77 OTHER PLAYERS.
... 6 OTHER PLAYERS.
OK, SO I MIGHT HAVE MENTIONED YOU IN ONE OR TWO CHAT ROOMS.
WHAT'D YOU DO? TELL THEM HOW GOOD I AM?
TIMMY_AGE_3 SAYS, "LET'S RUMBLE."

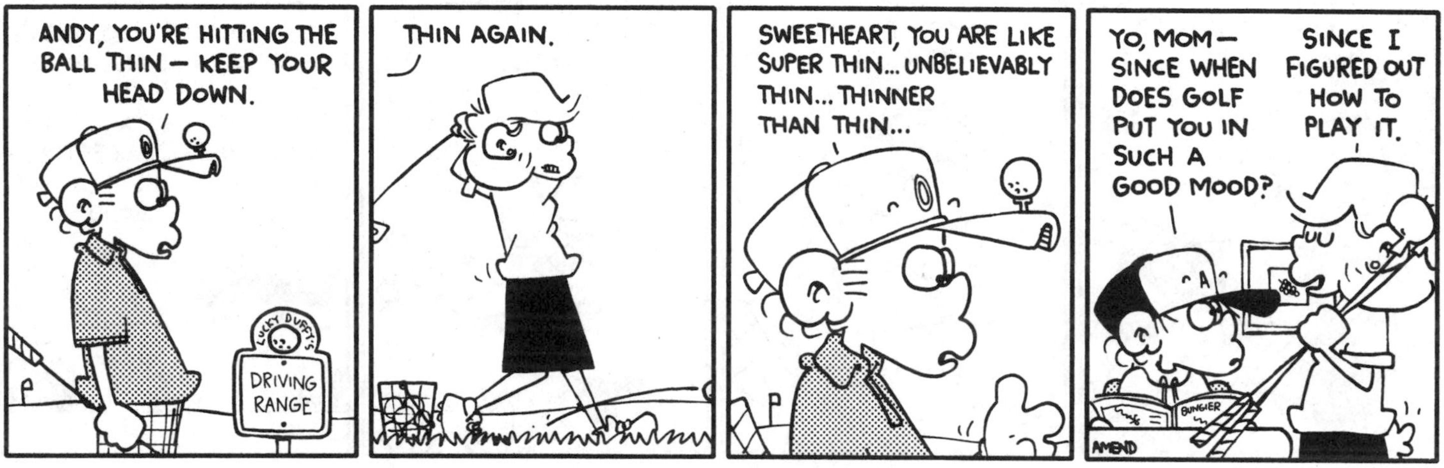
ANDY, YOU'RE HITTING THE BALL THIN – KEEP YOUR HEAD DOWN.
DRIVING RANGE
THIN AGAIN.
SWEETHEART, YOU ARE LIKE SUPER THIN... UNBELIEVABLY THIN... THINNER THAN THIN...
YO, MOM – SINCE WHEN DOES GOLF PUT YOU IN SUCH A GOOD MOOD?
SINCE I FIGURED OUT HOW TO PLAY IT.

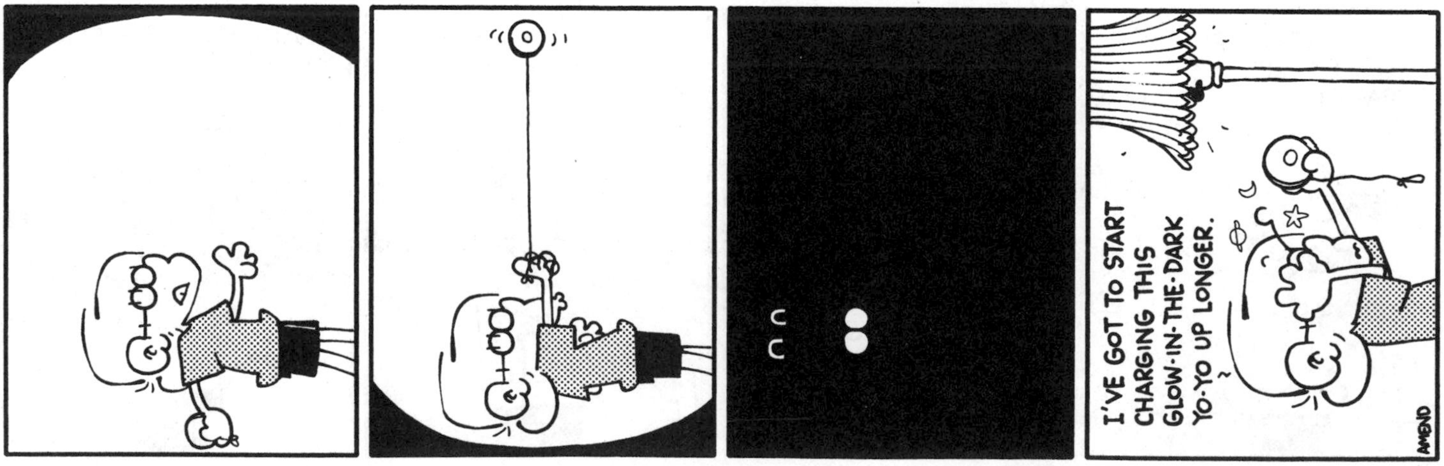
I'VE GOT TO START CHARGING THIS GLOW-IN-THE-DARK YO-YO UP LONGER.

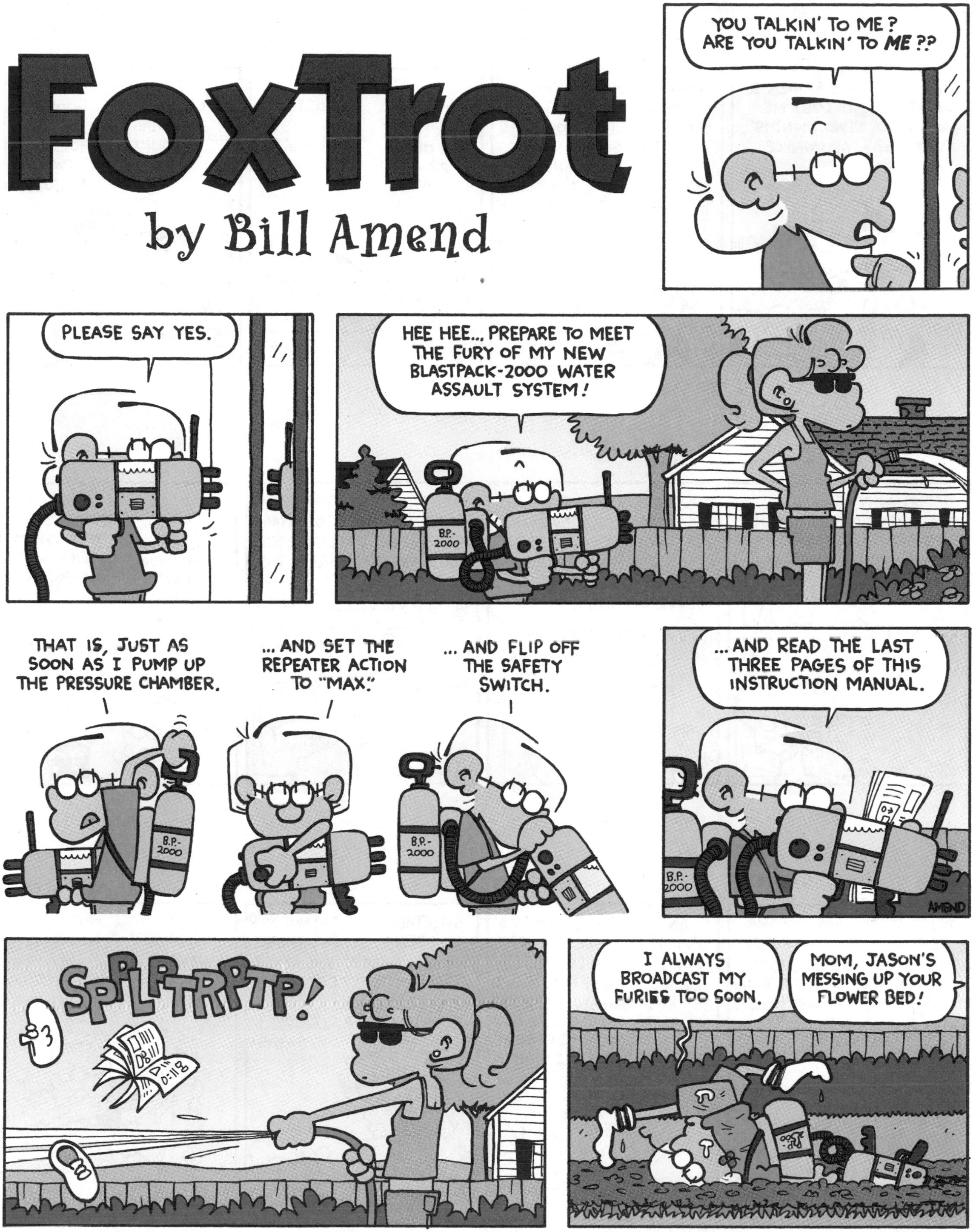
FoxTrot
by Bill Amend
YOU TALKIN' TO ME? ARE YOU TALKIN' TO *ME*??
PLEASE SAY YES.
HEE HEE... PREPARE TO MEET THE FURY OF MY NEW BLASTPACK-2000 WATER ASSAULT SYSTEM!
B.P.-2000
THAT IS, JUST AS SOON AS I PUMP UP THE PRESSURE CHAMBER.
...AND SET THE REPEATER ACTION TO "MAX."
...AND FLIP OFF THE SAFETY SWITCH.
...AND READ THE LAST THREE PAGES OF THIS INSTRUCTION MANUAL.
AMEND
SPPLPTRPTP!
I ALWAYS BROADCAST MY FURIES TOO SOON.
MOM, JASON'S MESSING UP YOUR FLOWER BED!

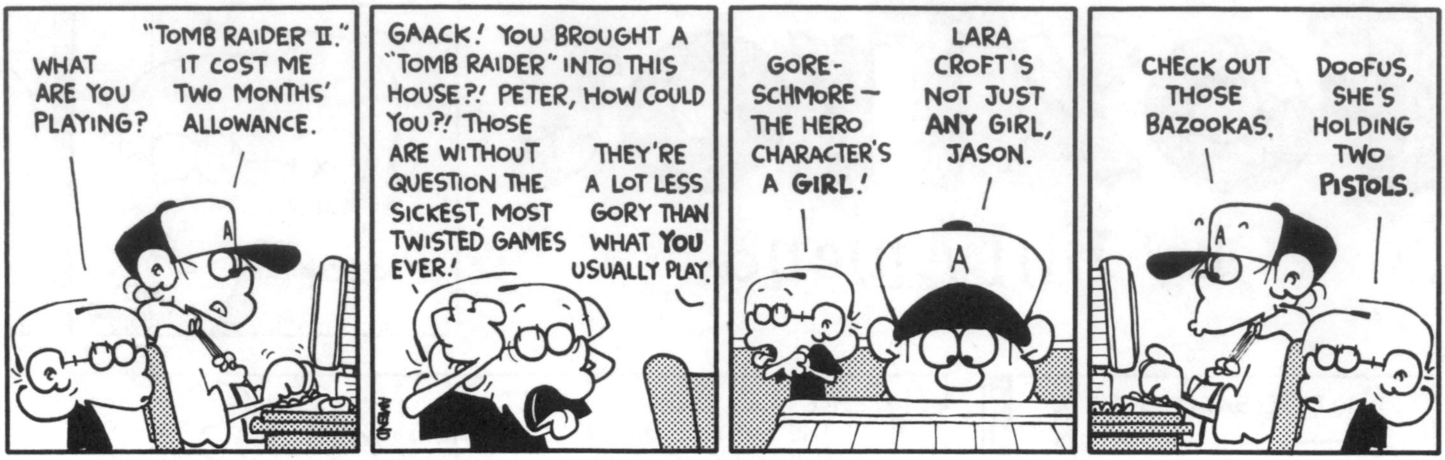
WHAT ARE YOU PLAYING?
"TOMB RAIDER II." IT COST ME TWO MONTHS' ALLOWANCE.
GAACK! YOU BROUGHT A "TOMB RAIDER" INTO THIS HOUSE?! PETER, HOW COULD YOU?! THOSE ARE WITHOUT QUESTION THE SICKEST, MOST TWISTED GAMES EVER!
THEY'RE A LOT LESS GORY THAN WHAT YOU USUALLY PLAY.
AMEND
GORE-SCHMORE— THE HERO CHARACTER'S A GIRL!
LARA CROFT'S NOT JUST ANY GIRL, JASON.
CHECK OUT THOSE BAZOOKAS.
DOOFUS, SHE'S HOLDING TWO PISTOLS.

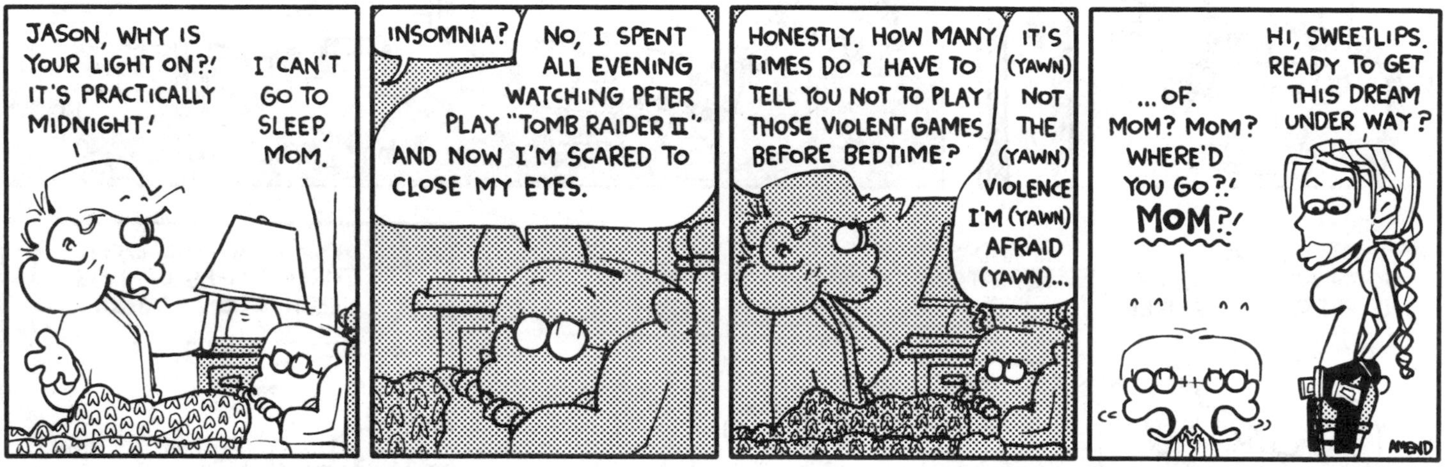
JASON, WHY IS YOUR LIGHT ON?! IT'S PRACTICALLY MIDNIGHT!
I CAN'T GO TO SLEEP, MOM.
INSOMNIA?
NO, I SPENT ALL EVENING WATCHING PETER PLAY "TOMB RAIDER II" AND NOW I'M SCARED TO CLOSE MY EYES.
HONESTLY. HOW MANY TIMES DO I HAVE TO TELL YOU NOT TO PLAY THOSE VIOLENT GAMES BEFORE BEDTIME?
IT'S (YAWN) NOT THE (YAWN) VIOLENCE I'M (YAWN) AFRAID (YAWN)...
...OF. MOM? MOM? WHERE'D YOU GO?! MOM?!
HI, SWEETLIPS. READY TO GET THIS DREAM UNDER WAY?
AMEND

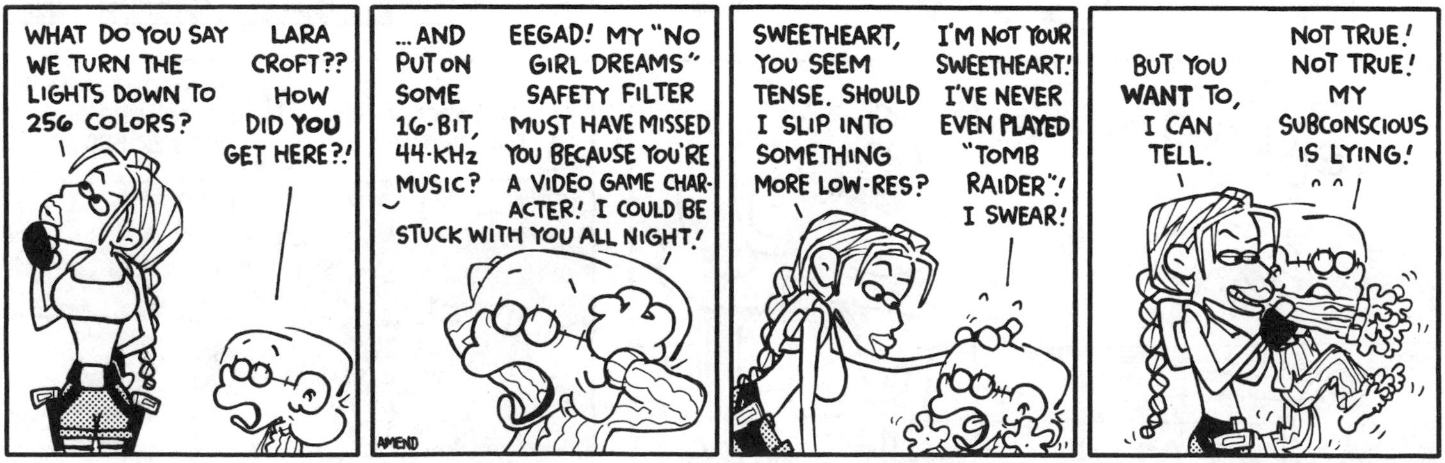
WHAT DO YOU SAY WE TURN THE LIGHTS DOWN TO 256 COLORS?
LARA CROFT?? HOW DID YOU GET HERE?!
...AND PUT ON SOME 16-BIT, 44-KHz MUSIC?
EEGAD! MY "NO GIRL DREAMS" SAFETY FILTER MUST HAVE MISSED YOU BECAUSE YOU'RE A VIDEO GAME CHARACTER! I COULD BE STUCK WITH YOU ALL NIGHT!
AMEND
SWEETHEART, YOU SEEM TENSE. SHOULD I SLIP INTO SOMETHING MORE LOW-RES?
I'M NOT YOUR SWEETHEART! I'VE NEVER EVEN PLAYED "TOMB RAIDER"! I SWEAR!
BUT YOU WANT TO, I CAN TELL.
NOT TRUE! NOT TRUE! MY SUBCONSCIOUS IS LYING!

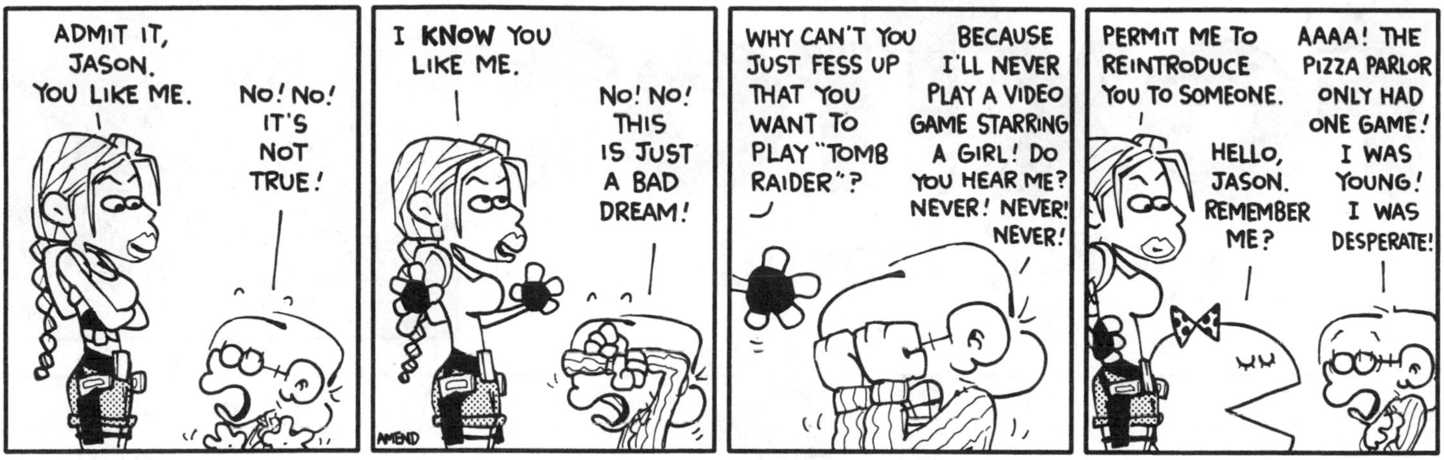
ADMIT IT, JASON. YOU LIKE ME.
NO! NO! IT'S NOT TRUE!
I KNOW YOU LIKE ME.
NO! NO! THIS IS JUST A BAD DREAM!
AMEND
WHY CAN'T YOU JUST FESS UP THAT YOU WANT TO PLAY "TOMB RAIDER"?
BECAUSE I'LL NEVER PLAY A VIDEO GAME STARRING A GIRL! DO YOU HEAR ME? NEVER! NEVER! NEVER!
PERMIT ME TO REINTRODUCE YOU TO SOMEONE.
HELLO, JASON. REMEMBER ME?
AAAA! THE PIZZA PARLOR ONLY HAD ONE GAME! I WAS YOUNG! I WAS DESPERATE!

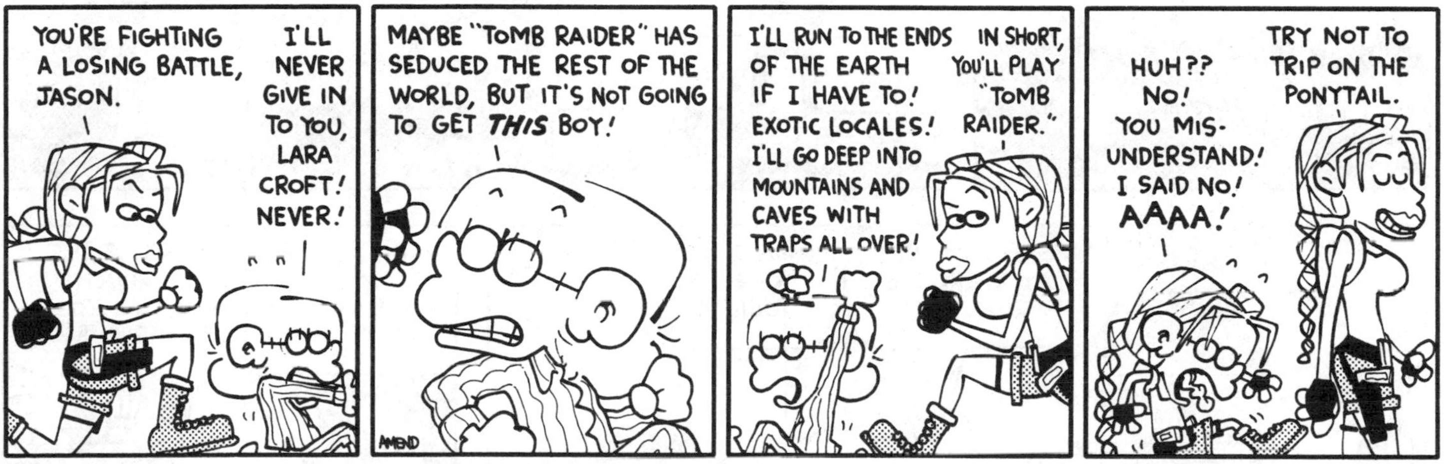
YOU'RE FIGHTING A LOSING BATTLE, JASON.
I'LL NEVER GIVE IN TO YOU, LARA CROFT! NEVER!
MAYBE "TOMB RAIDER" HAS SEDUCED THE REST OF THE WORLD, BUT IT'S NOT GOING TO GET THIS BOY!
AMEND
I'LL RUN TO THE ENDS OF THE EARTH IF I HAVE TO! EXOTIC LOCALES! I'LL GO DEEP INTO MOUNTAINS AND CAVES WITH TRAPS ALL OVER!
IN SHORT, YOU'LL PLAY "TOMB RAIDER."
HUH?? NO! YOU MISUNDERSTAND! I SAID NO! AAAA!
TRY NOT TO TRIP ON THE PONYTAIL.

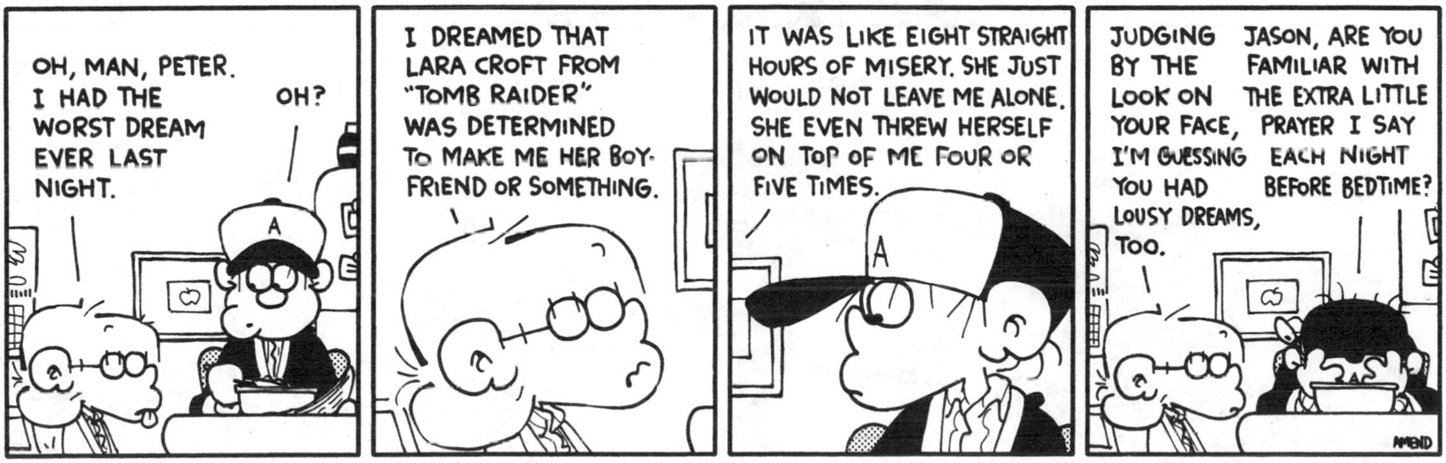
OH, MAN, PETER. I HAD THE WORST DREAM EVER LAST NIGHT.
OH?
I DREAMED THAT LARA CROFT FROM "TOMB RAIDER" WAS DETERMINED TO MAKE ME HER BOY-FRIEND OR SOMETHING.
IT WAS LIKE EIGHT STRAIGHT HOURS OF MISERY. SHE JUST WOULD NOT LEAVE ME ALONE. SHE EVEN THREW HERSELF ON TOP OF ME FOUR OR FIVE TIMES.
JUDGING BY THE LOOK ON YOUR FACE, I'M GUESSING YOU HAD LOUSY DREAMS, TOO.
JASON, ARE YOU FAMILIAR WITH THE EXTRA LITTLE PRAYER I SAY EACH NIGHT BEFORE BEDTIME?
AMEND

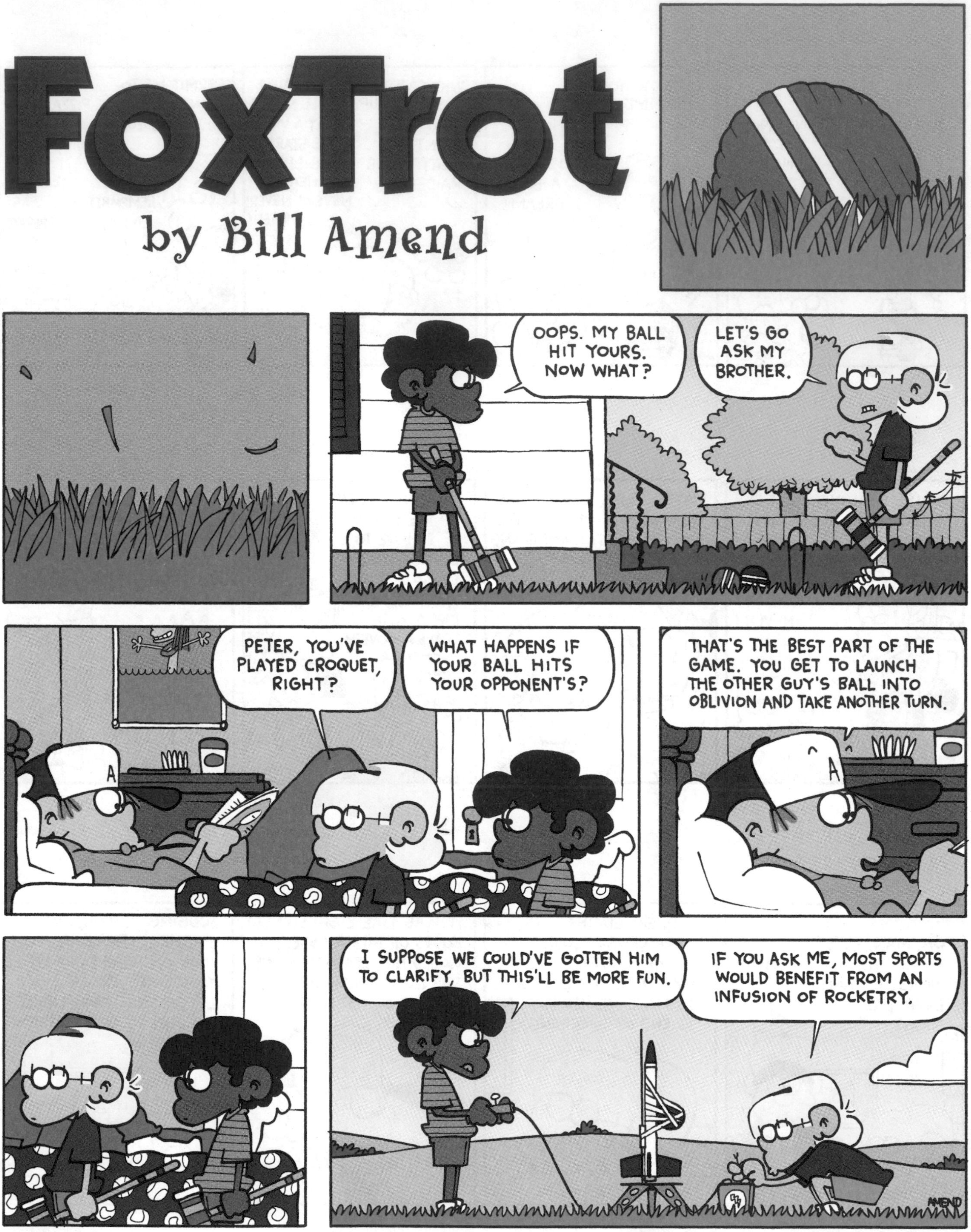
FoxTrot
by Bill Amend
OOPS. MY BALL HIT YOURS. NOW WHAT?
LET'S GO ASK MY BROTHER.
PETER, YOU'VE PLAYED CROQUET, RIGHT?
WHAT HAPPENS IF YOUR BALL HITS YOUR OPPONENT'S?
THAT'S THE BEST PART OF THE GAME. YOU GET TO LAUNCH THE OTHER GUY'S BALL INTO OBLIVION AND TAKE ANOTHER TURN.
I SUPPOSE WE COULD'VE GOTTEN HIM TO CLARIFY, BUT THIS'LL BE MORE FUN.
IF YOU ASK ME, MOST SPORTS WOULD BENEFIT FROM AN INFUSION OF ROCKETRY.
AMEND

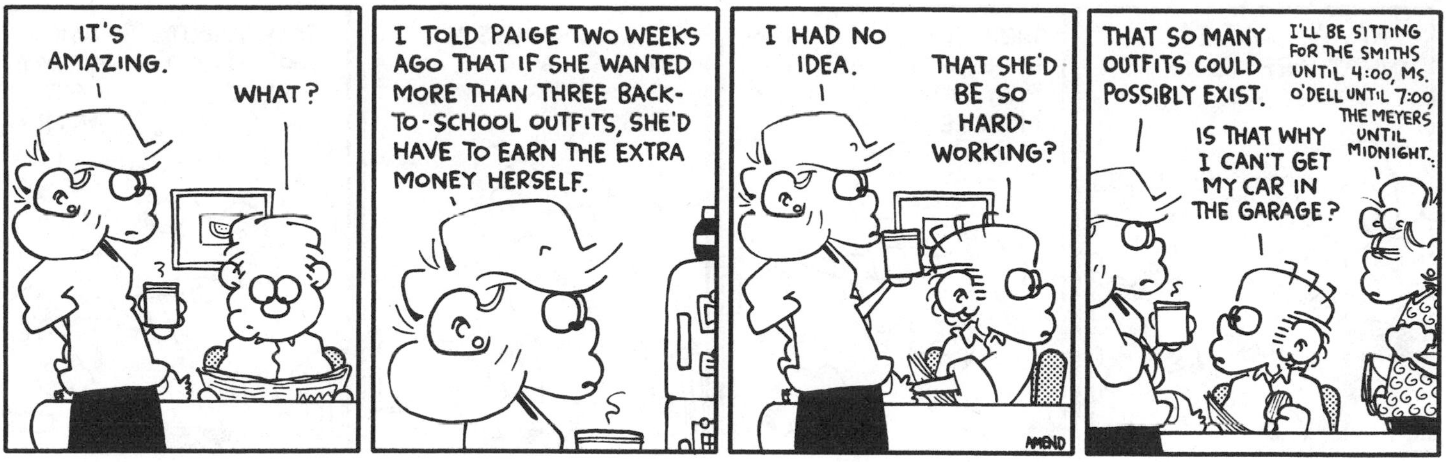
IT'S AMAZING.
WHAT?
I TOLD PAIGE TWO WEEKS AGO THAT IF SHE WANTED MORE THAN THREE BACK-TO-SCHOOL OUTFITS, SHE'D HAVE TO EARN THE EXTRA MONEY HERSELF.
I HAD NO IDEA.
THAT SHE'D BE SO HARD-WORKING?
THAT SO MANY OUTFITS COULD POSSIBLY EXIST.
I'LL BE SITTING FOR THE SMITHS UNTIL 4:00, MS. O'DELL UNTIL 7:00, THE MEYERS' UNTIL MIDNIGHT.
IS THAT WHY I CAN'T GET MY CAR IN THE GARAGE?
AMEND

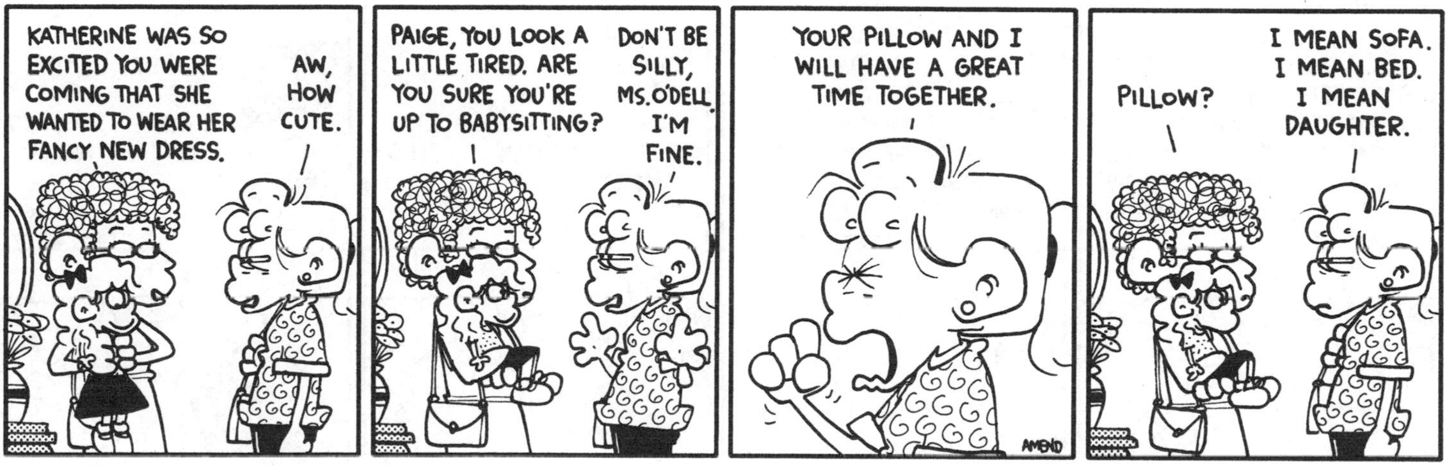
KATHERINE WAS SO EXCITED YOU WERE COMING THAT SHE WANTED TO WEAR HER FANCY NEW DRESS.
AW, HOW CUTE.
PAIGE, YOU LOOK A LITTLE TIRED. ARE YOU SURE YOU'RE UP TO BABYSITTING?
DON'T BE SILLY, MS. O'DELL. I'M FINE.
YOUR PILLOW AND I WILL HAVE A GREAT TIME TOGETHER.
PILLOW?
I MEAN SOFA. I MEAN BED. I MEAN DAUGHTER.
AMEND

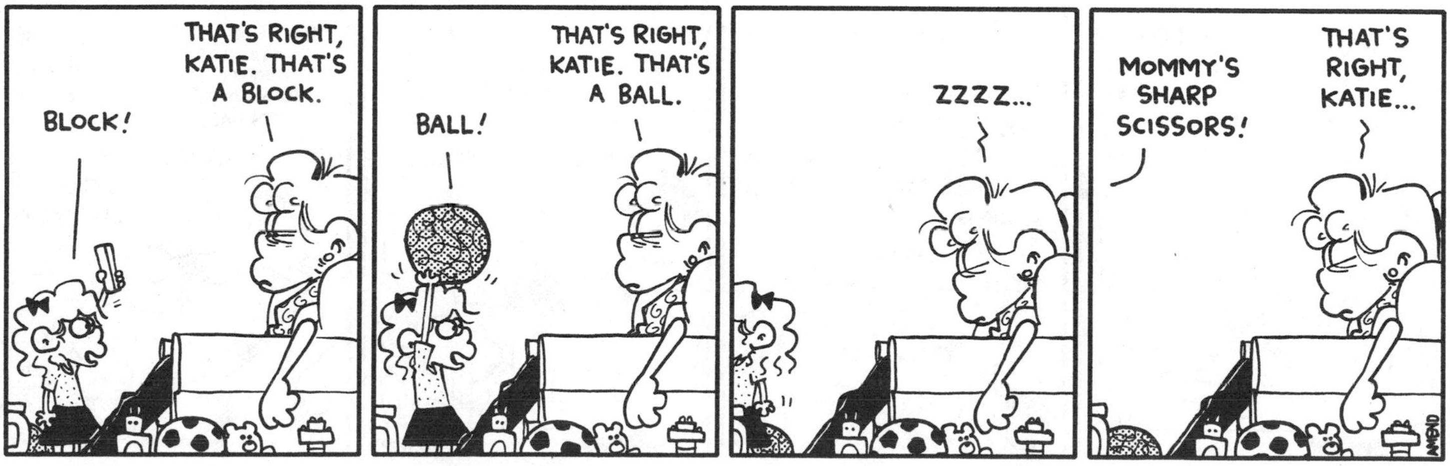
BLOCK!
THAT'S RIGHT, KATIE. THAT'S A BLOCK.
BALL!
THAT'S RIGHT, KATIE. THAT'S A BALL.
ZZZZ...
MOMMY'S SHARP SCISSORS!
THAT'S RIGHT, KATIE...
AMEND

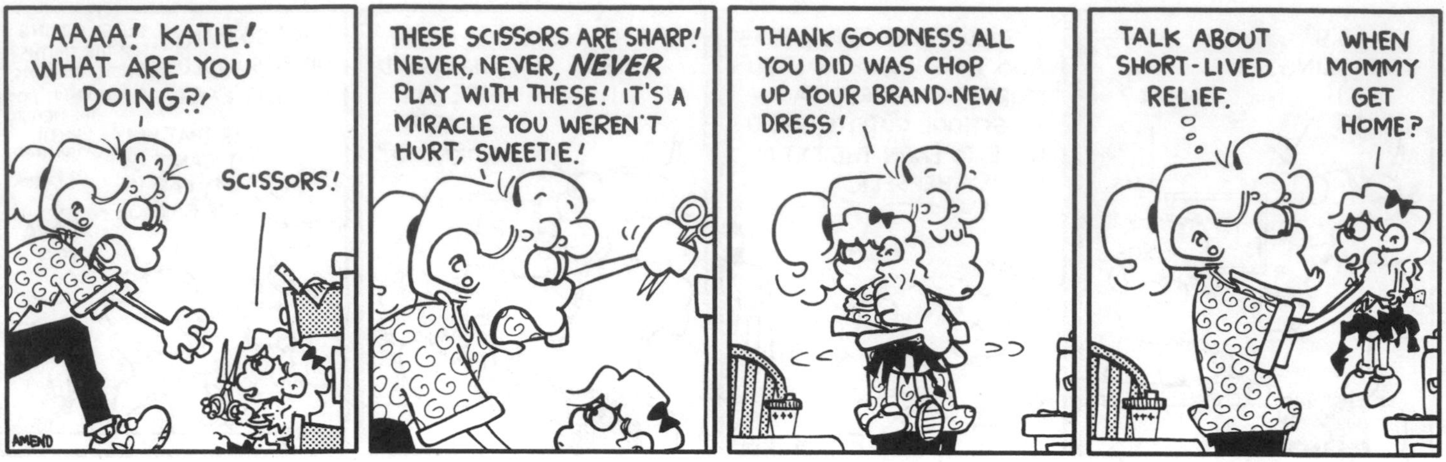
AAAA! KATIE! WHAT ARE YOU DOING?!
SCISSORS!
AMEND
THESE SCISSORS ARE SHARP! NEVER, NEVER, NEVER PLAY WITH THESE! IT'S A MIRACLE YOU WEREN'T HURT, SWEETIE!
THANK GOODNESS ALL YOU DID WAS CHOP UP YOUR BRAND-NEW DRESS!
TALK ABOUT SHORT-LIVED RELIEF.
WHEN MOMMY GET HOME?

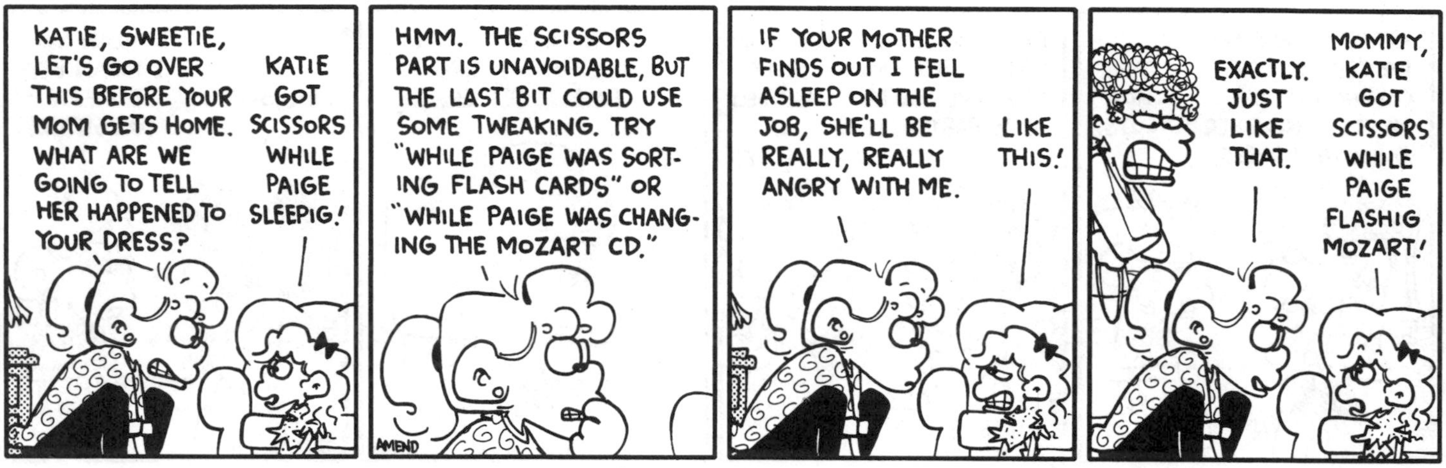
KATIE, SWEETIE, LET'S GO OVER THIS BEFORE YOUR MOM GETS HOME. WHAT ARE WE GOING TO TELL HER HAPPENED TO YOUR DRESS?
KATIE GOT SCISSORS WHILE PAIGE SLEEPIG!
HMM. THE SCISSORS PART IS UNAVOIDABLE, BUT THE LAST BIT COULD USE SOME TWEAKING. TRY "WHILE PAIGE WAS SORTING FLASH CARDS" OR "WHILE PAIGE WAS CHANGING THE MOZART CD."
AMEND
IF YOUR MOTHER FINDS OUT I FELL ASLEEP ON THE JOB, SHE'LL BE REALLY, REALLY ANGRY WITH ME.
LIKE THIS!
EXACTLY. JUST LIKE THAT.
MOMMY, KATIE GOT SCISSORS WHILE PAIGE FLASHIG MOZART!

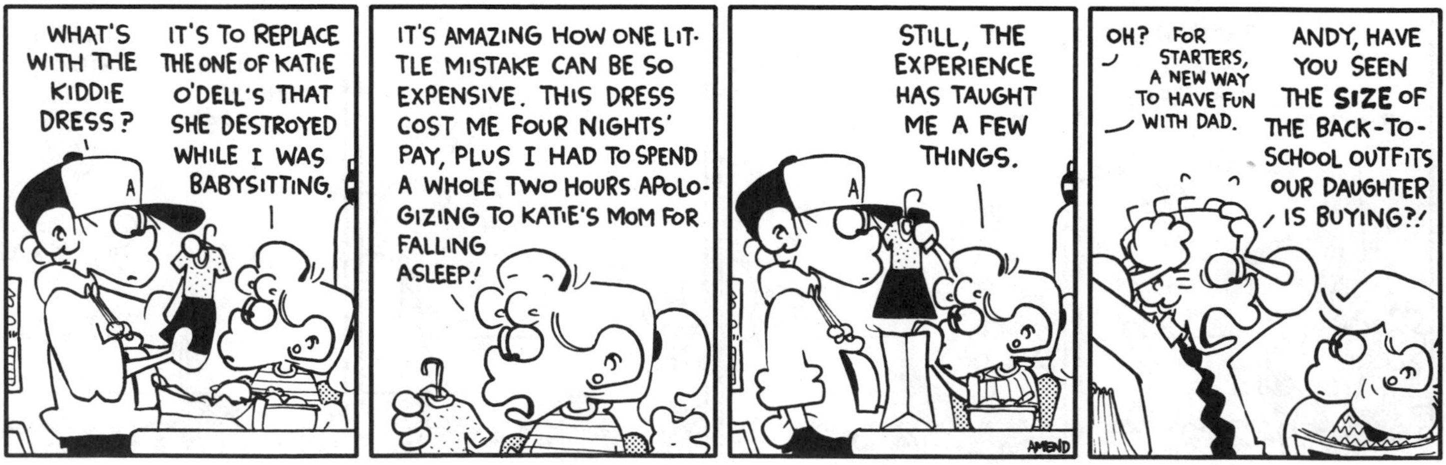
WHAT'S WITH THE KIDDIE DRESS?
IT'S TO REPLACE THE ONE OF KATIE O'DELL'S THAT SHE DESTROYED WHILE I WAS BABYSITTING.
IT'S AMAZING HOW ONE LITTLE MISTAKE CAN BE SO EXPENSIVE. THIS DRESS COST ME FOUR NIGHTS' PAY, PLUS I HAD TO SPEND A WHOLE TWO HOURS APOLOGIZING TO KATIE'S MOM FOR FALLING ASLEEP!
STILL, THE EXPERIENCE HAS TAUGHT ME A FEW THINGS.
AMEND
OH?
FOR STARTERS, A NEW WAY TO HAVE FUN WITH DAD.
ANDY, HAVE YOU SEEN THE SIZE OF THE BACK-TO-SCHOOL OUTFITS OUR DAUGHTER IS BUYING?!

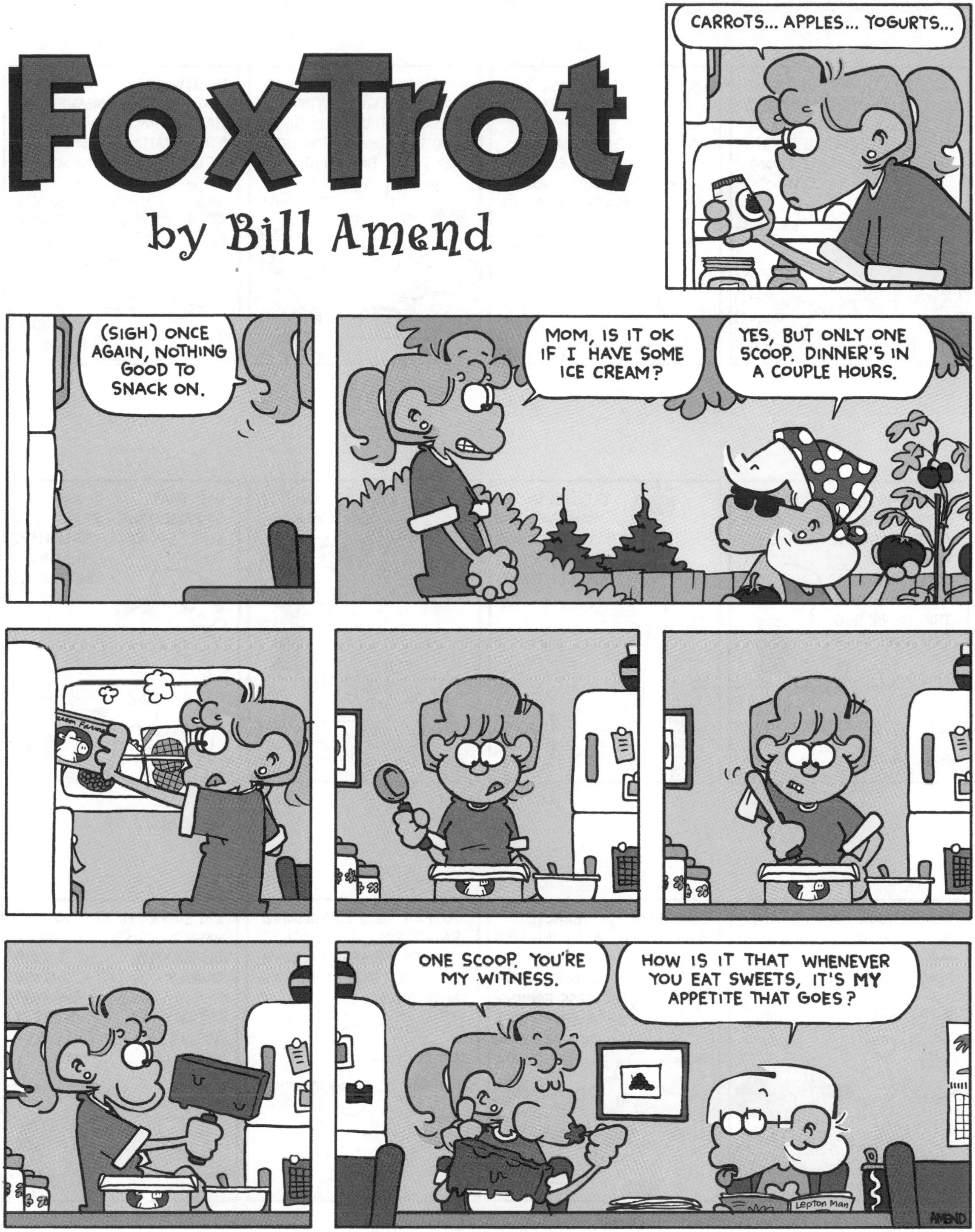
FoxTrot
by Bill Amend
CARROTS... APPLES... YOGURTS...
(SIGH) ONCE AGAIN, NOTHING GOOD TO SNACK ON.
MOM, IS IT OK IF I HAVE SOME ICE CREAM?
YES, BUT ONLY ONE SCOOP. DINNER'S IN A COUPLE HOURS.
ONE SCOOP. YOU'RE MY WITNESS.
HOW IS IT THAT WHENEVER YOU EAT SWEETS, IT'S MY APPETITE THAT GOES?
Lepton Man
AMEND

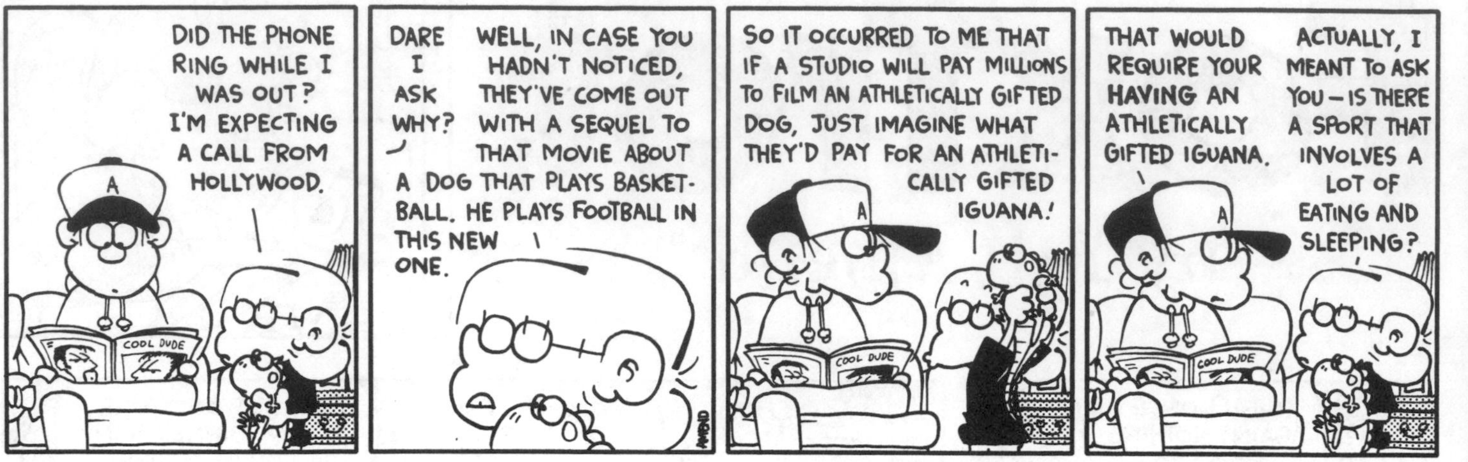
DID THE PHONE RING WHILE I WAS OUT? I'M EXPECTING A CALL FROM HOLLYWOOD.
COOL DUDE
DARE I ASK WHY?
WELL, IN CASE YOU HADN'T NOTICED, THEY'VE COME OUT WITH A SEQUEL TO THAT MOVIE ABOUT A DOG THAT PLAYS BASKETBALL. HE PLAYS FOOTBALL IN THIS NEW ONE.
SO IT OCCURRED TO ME THAT IF A STUDIO WILL PAY MILLIONS TO FILM AN ATHLETICALLY GIFTED DOG, JUST IMAGINE WHAT THEY'D PAY FOR AN ATHLETICALLY GIFTED IGUANA!
THAT WOULD REQUIRE YOUR HAVING AN ATHLETICALLY GIFTED IGUANA.
ACTUALLY, I MEANT TO ASK YOU – IS THERE A SPORT THAT INVOLVES A LOT OF EATING AND SLEEPING?

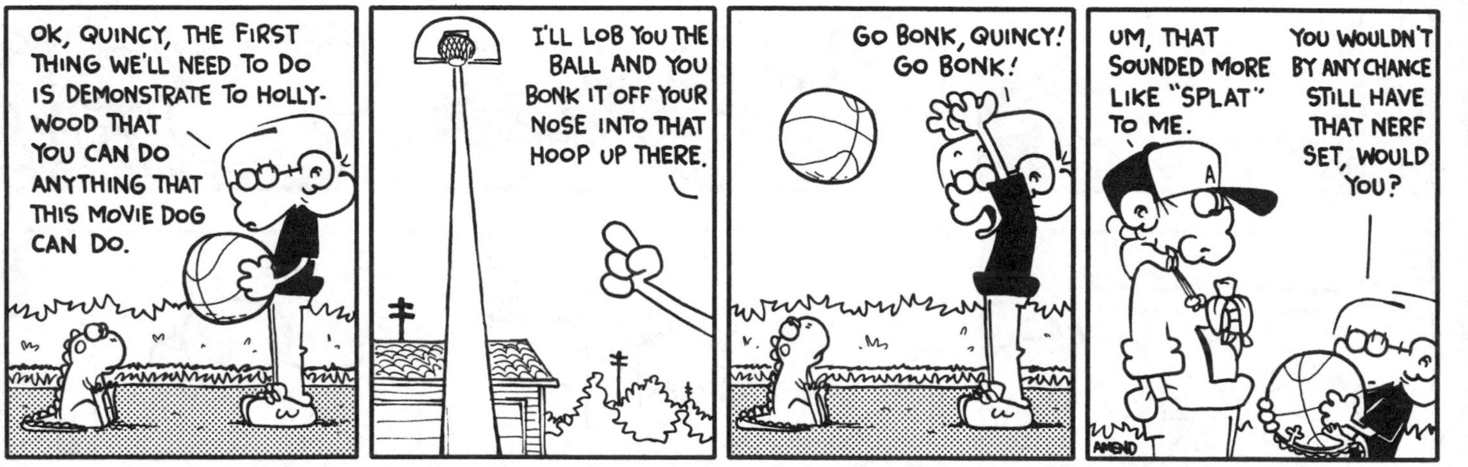
OK, QUINCY, THE FIRST THING WE'LL NEED TO DO IS DEMONSTRATE TO HOLLYWOOD THAT YOU CAN DO ANYTHING THAT THIS MOVIE DOG CAN DO.
I'LL LOB YOU THE BALL AND YOU BONK IT OFF YOUR NOSE INTO THAT HOOP UP THERE.
GO BONK, QUINCY! GO BONK!
UM, THAT SOUNDED MORE LIKE "SPLAT" TO ME.
YOU WOULDN'T BY ANY CHANCE STILL HAVE THAT NERF SET, WOULD YOU?

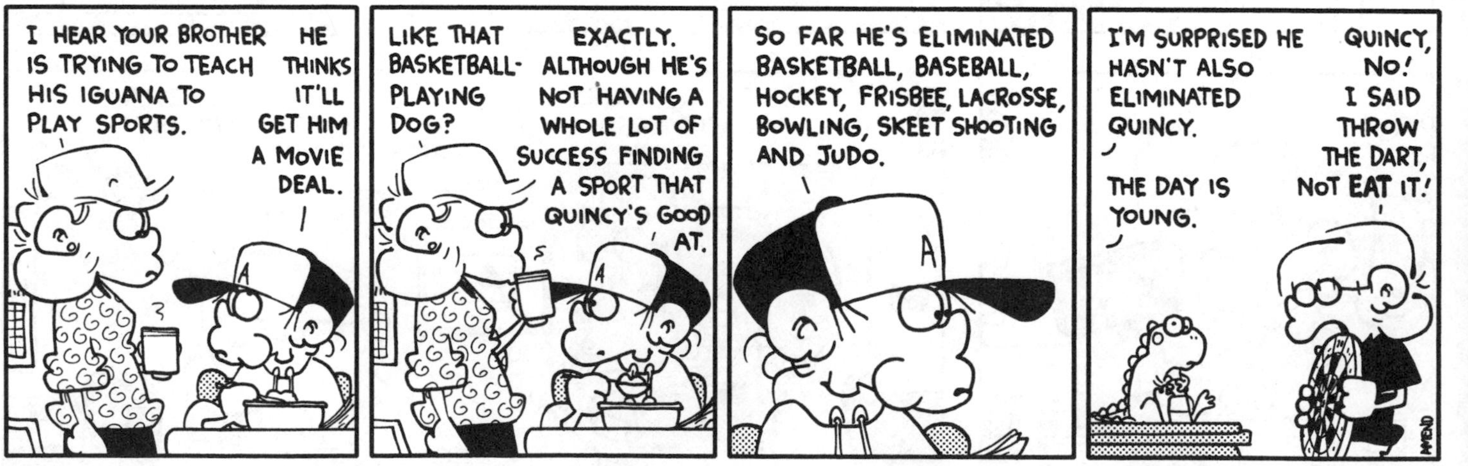
I HEAR YOUR BROTHER IS TRYING TO TEACH HIS IGUANA TO PLAY SPORTS.
HE THINKS IT'LL GET HIM A MOVIE DEAL.
LIKE THAT BASKETBALL-PLAYING DOG?
EXACTLY. ALTHOUGH HE'S NOT HAVING A WHOLE LOT OF SUCCESS FINDING A SPORT THAT QUINCY'S GOOD AT.
SO FAR HE'S ELIMINATED BASKETBALL, BASEBALL, HOCKEY, FRISBEE, LACROSSE, BOWLING, SKEET SHOOTING AND JUDO.
I'M SURPRISED HE HASN'T ALSO ELIMINATED QUINCY.
THE DAY IS YOUNG.
QUINCY, NO! I SAID THROW THE DART, NOT EAT IT!

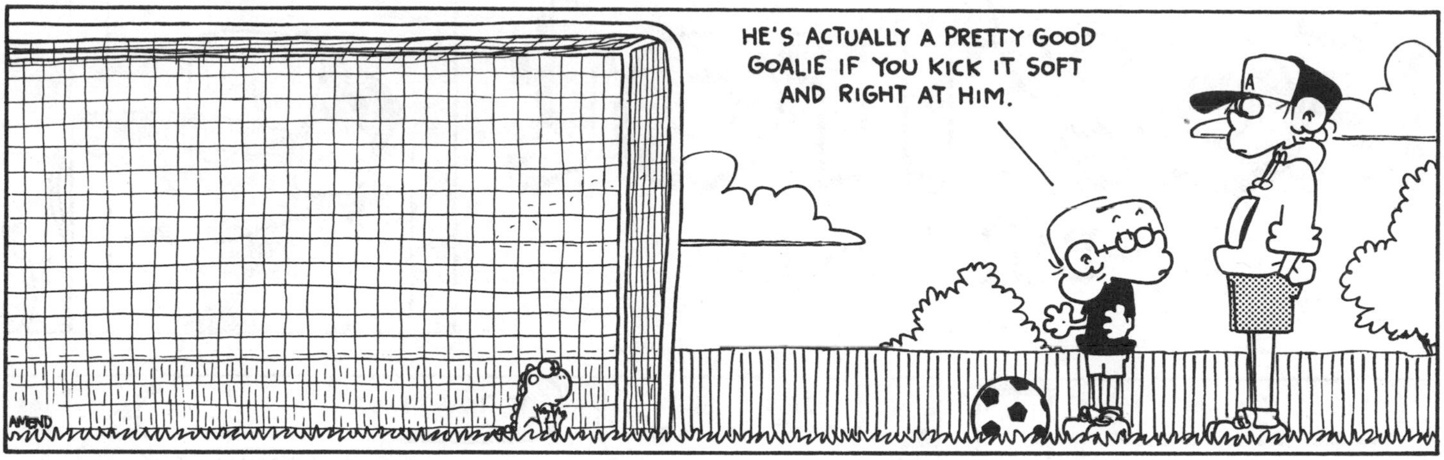
HE'S ACTUALLY A PRETTY GOOD GOALIE IF YOU KICK IT SOFT AND RIGHT AT HIM.
AMEND

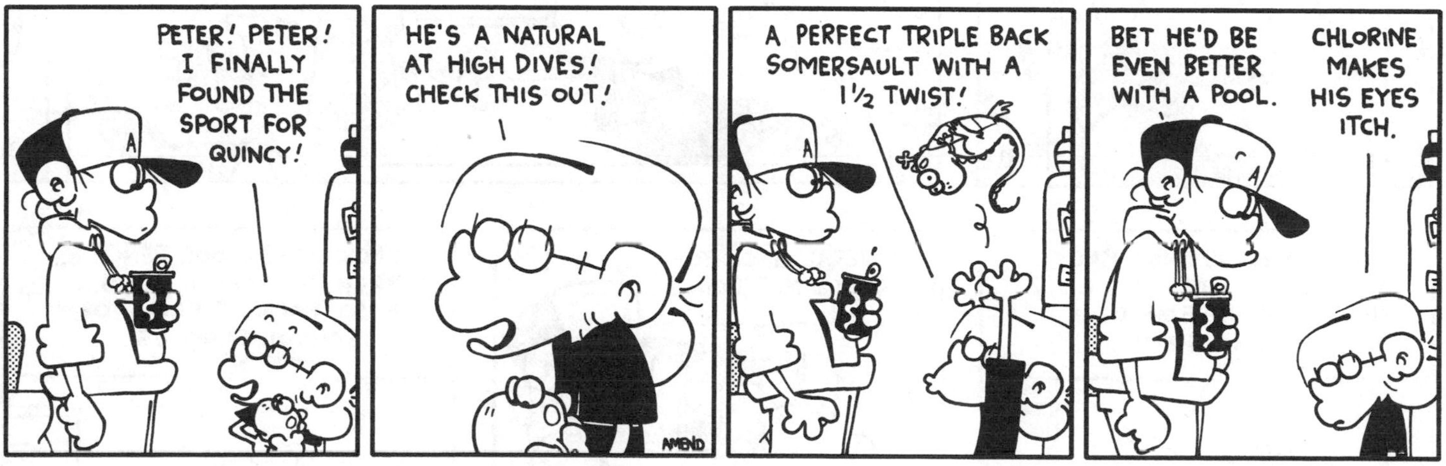
PETER! PETER! I FINALLY FOUND THE SPORT FOR QUINCY!
HE'S A NATURAL AT HIGH DIVES! CHECK THIS OUT!
AMEND
A PERFECT TRIPLE BACK SOMERSAULT WITH A 1½ TWIST!
BET HE'D BE EVEN BETTER WITH A POOL.
CHLORINE MAKES HIS EYES ITCH.

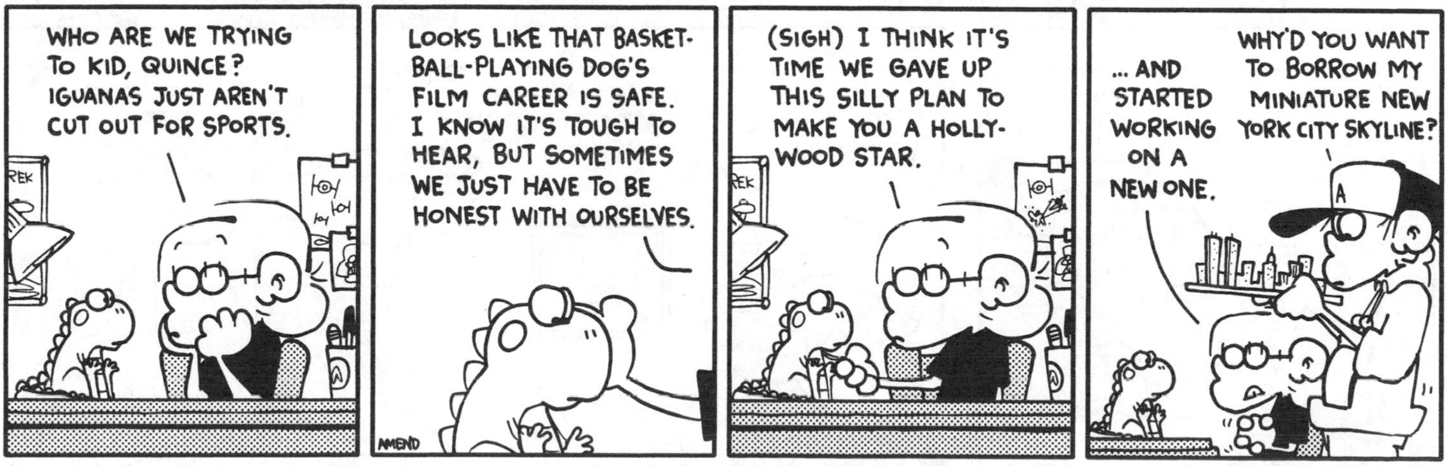
WHO ARE WE TRYING TO KID, QUINCE? IGUANAS JUST AREN'T CUT OUT FOR SPORTS.
LOOKS LIKE THAT BASKET-BALL-PLAYING DOG'S FILM CAREER IS SAFE. I KNOW IT'S TOUGH TO HEAR, BUT SOMETIMES WE JUST HAVE TO BE HONEST WITH OURSELVES.
AMEND
(SIGH) I THINK IT'S TIME WE GAVE UP THIS SILLY PLAN TO MAKE YOU A HOLLY-WOOD STAR.
WHY'D YOU WANT TO BORROW MY MINIATURE NEW YORK CITY SKYLINE?
... AND STARTED WORKING ON A NEW ONE.

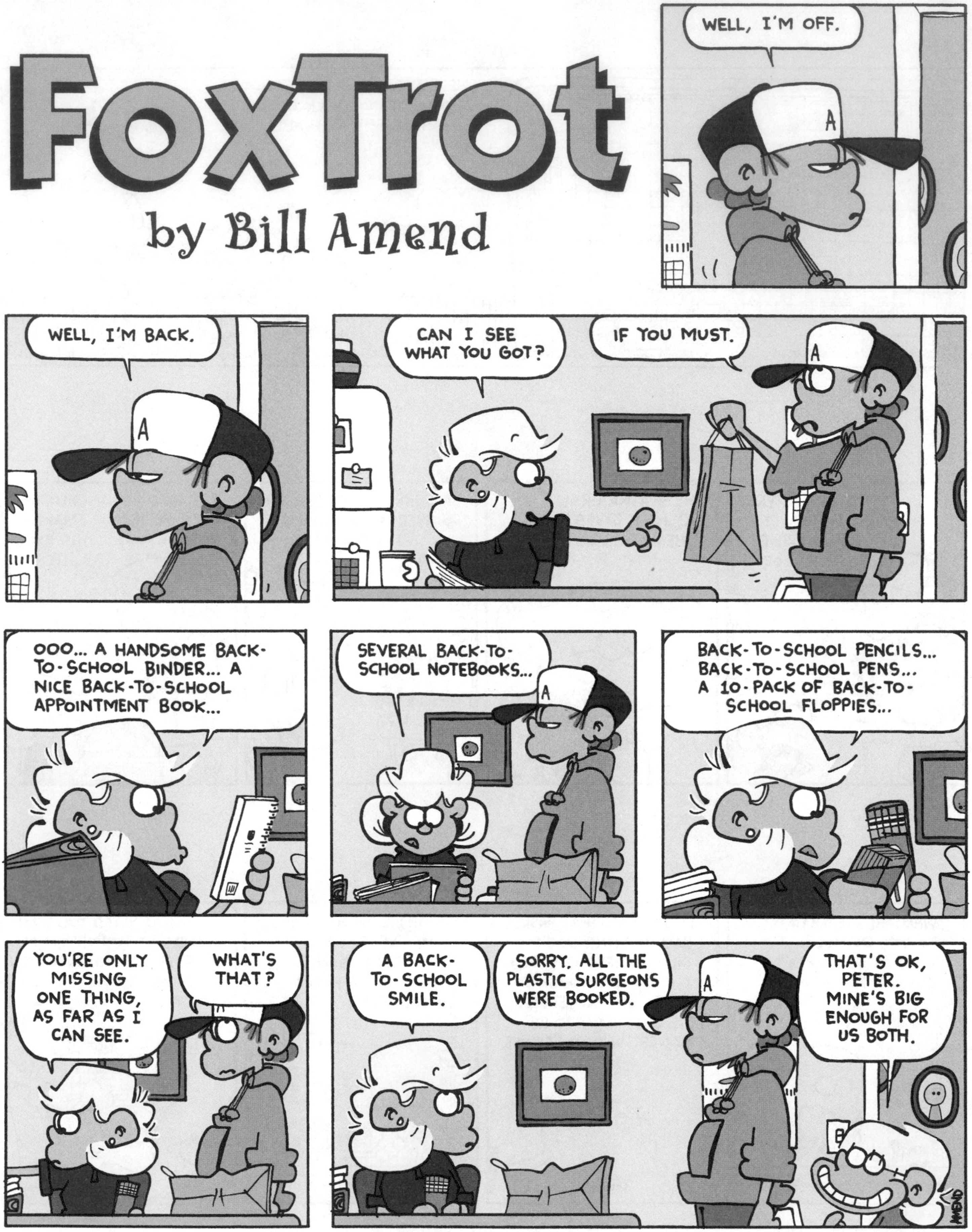
FoxTrot
by Bill Amend
WELL, I'M OFF.
WELL, I'M BACK.
CAN I SEE WHAT YOU GOT?
IF YOU MUST.
OOO... A HANDSOME BACK-TO-SCHOOL BINDER... A NICE BACK-TO-SCHOOL APPOINTMENT BOOK...
SEVERAL BACK-TO-SCHOOL NOTEBOOKS...
BACK-TO-SCHOOL PENCILS... BACK-TO-SCHOOL PENS... A 10-PACK OF BACK-TO-SCHOOL FLOPPIES...
YOU'RE ONLY MISSING ONE THING, AS FAR AS I CAN SEE.
WHAT'S THAT?
A BACK-TO-SCHOOL SMILE.
SORRY. ALL THE PLASTIC SURGEONS WERE BOOKED.
THAT'S OK, PETER. MINE'S BIG ENOUGH FOR US BOTH.
AMEND

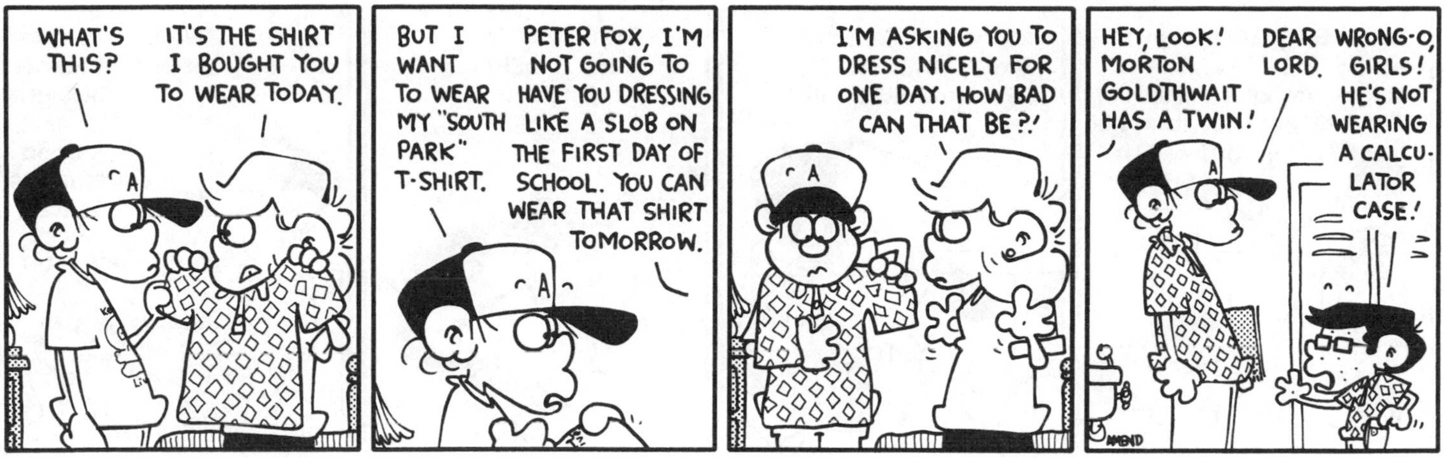
WHAT'S THIS?
IT'S THE SHIRT I BOUGHT YOU TO WEAR TODAY.
BUT I WANT TO WEAR MY "SOUTH PARK" T-SHIRT.
PETER FOX, I'M NOT GOING TO HAVE YOU DRESSING LIKE A SLOB ON THE FIRST DAY OF SCHOOL. YOU CAN WEAR THAT SHIRT TOMORROW.
I'M ASKING YOU TO DRESS NICELY FOR ONE DAY. HOW BAD CAN THAT BE?!
HEY, LOOK! MORTON GOLDTHWAIT HAS A TWIN!
DEAR LORD.
WRONG-O, GIRLS! HE'S NOT WEARING A CALCULATOR CASE!

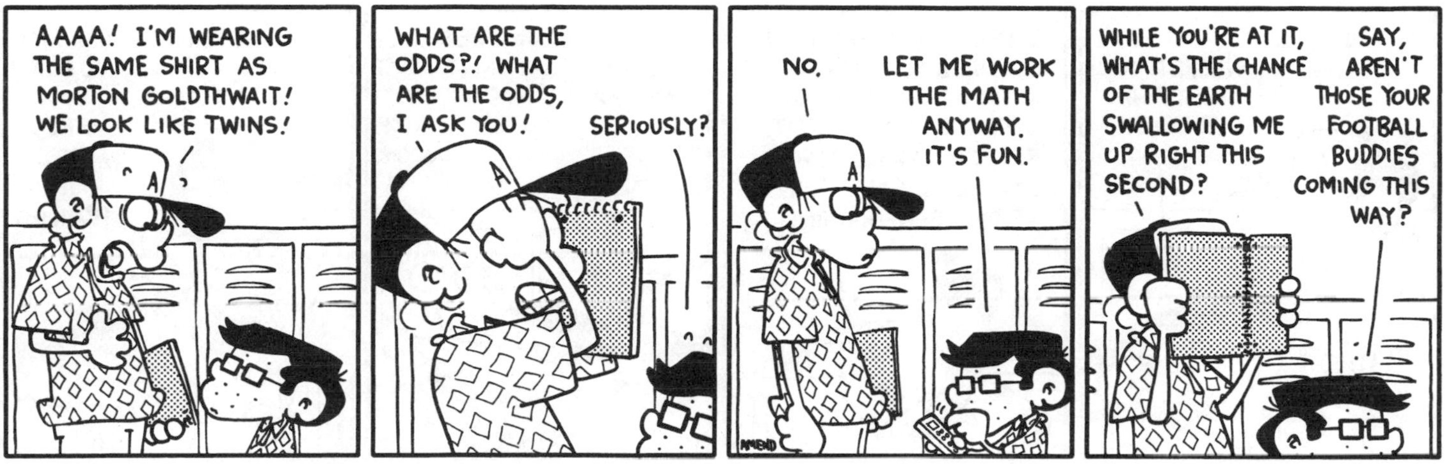
AAAA! I'M WEARING THE SAME SHIRT AS MORTON GOLDTHWAIT! WE LOOK LIKE TWINS!
WHAT ARE THE ODDS?! WHAT ARE THE ODDS, I ASK YOU!
SERIOUSLY?
NO.
LET ME WORK THE MATH ANYWAY. IT'S FUN.
WHILE YOU'RE AT IT, WHAT'S THE CHANCE OF THE EARTH SWALLOWING ME UP RIGHT THIS SECOND?
SAY, AREN'T THOSE YOUR FOOTBALL BUDDIES COMING THIS WAY?

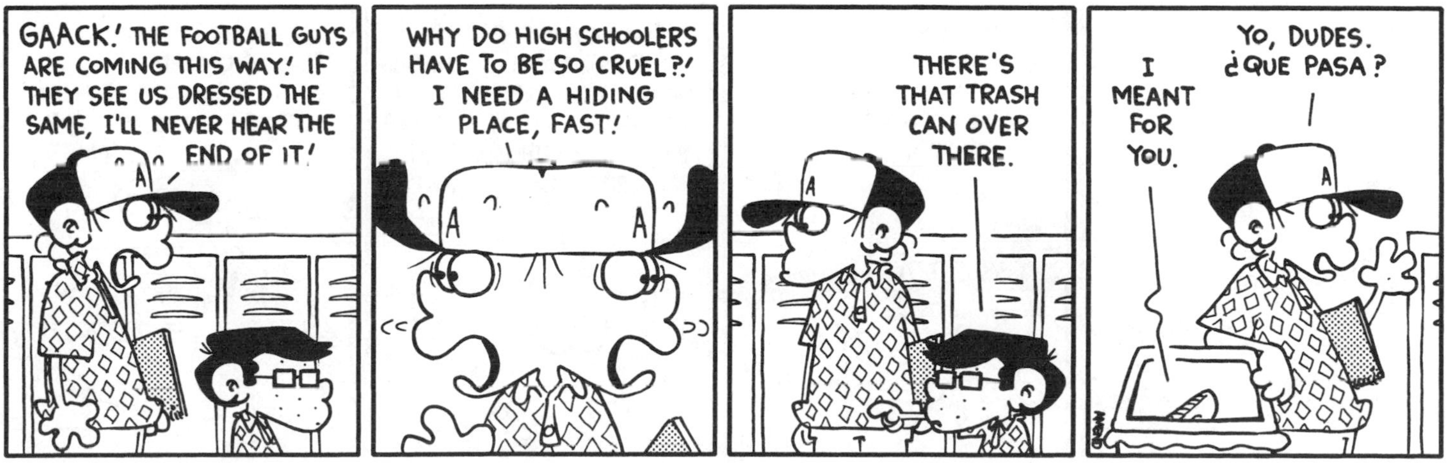
GAACK! THE FOOTBALL GUYS ARE COMING THIS WAY! IF THEY SEE US DRESSED THE SAME, I'LL NEVER HEAR THE END OF IT!
WHY DO HIGH SCHOOLERS HAVE TO BE SO CRUEL?! I NEED A HIDING PLACE, FAST!
THERE'S THAT TRASH CAN OVER THERE.
I MEANT FOR YOU.
YO, DUDES. ¿QUE PASA?

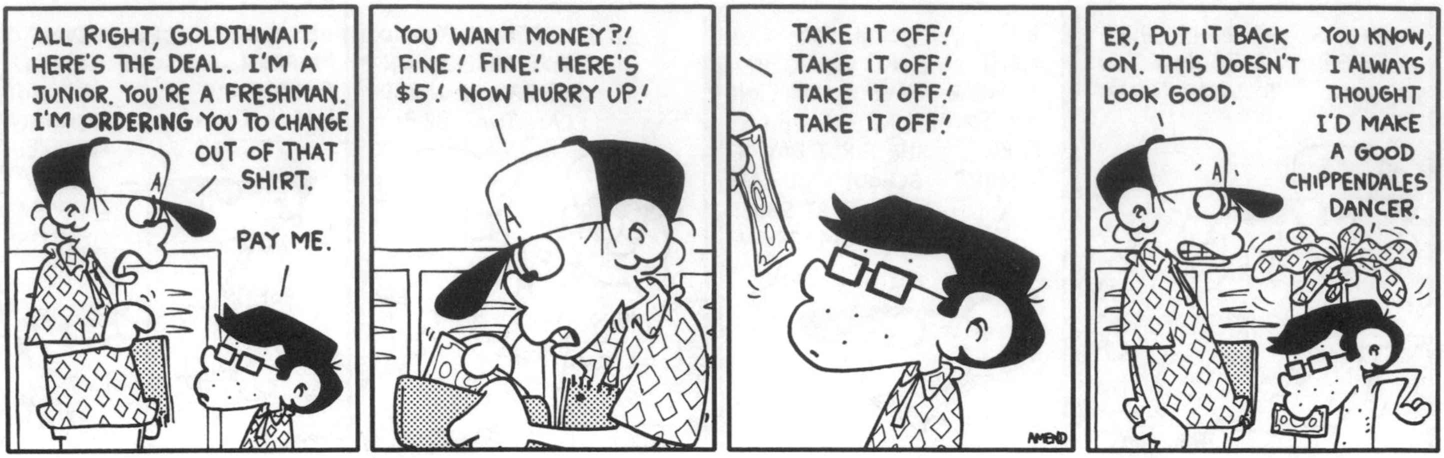
ALL RIGHT, GOLDTHWAIT, HERE'S THE DEAL. I'M A JUNIOR. YOU'RE A FRESHMAN. I'M ORDERING YOU TO CHANGE OUT OF THAT SHIRT.
PAY ME.
YOU WANT MONEY?! FINE! FINE! HERE'S $5! NOW HURRY UP!
TAKE IT OFF! TAKE IT OFF! TAKE IT OFF! TAKE IT OFF!
ER, PUT IT BACK ON. THIS DOESN'T LOOK GOOD.
YOU KNOW, I ALWAYS THOUGHT I'D MAKE A GOOD CHIPPENDALES DANCER.
AMEND

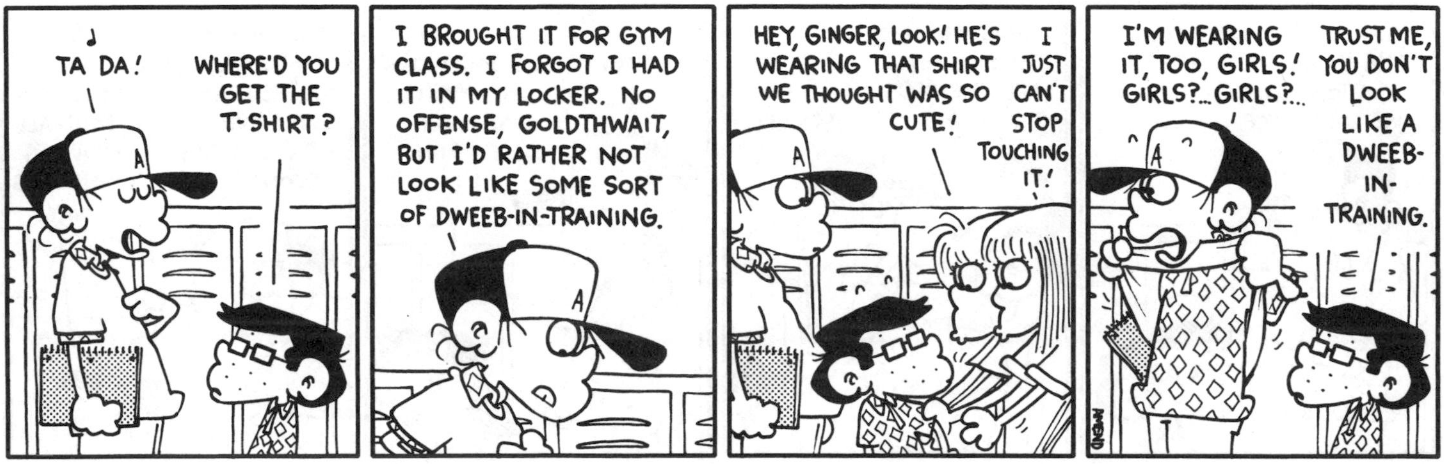
TA DA!
WHERE'D YOU GET THE T-SHIRT?
I BROUGHT IT FOR GYM CLASS. I FORGOT I HAD IT IN MY LOCKER. NO OFFENSE, GOLDTHWAIT, BUT I'D RATHER NOT LOOK LIKE SOME SORT OF DWEEB-IN-TRAINING.
HEY, GINGER, LOOK! HE'S WEARING THAT SHIRT WE THOUGHT WAS SO CUTE!
I JUST CAN'T STOP TOUCHING IT!
AMEND
I'M WEARING IT, TOO, GIRLS! GIRLS?... GIRLS?...
TRUST ME, YOU DON'T LOOK LIKE A DWEEB-IN-TRAINING.

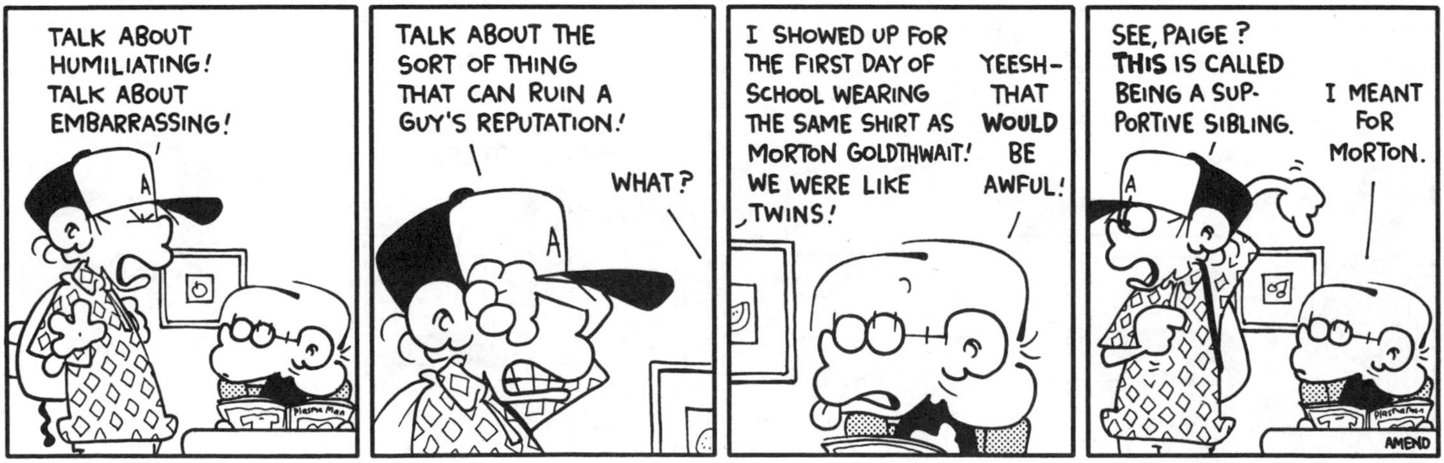
TALK ABOUT HUMILIATING! TALK ABOUT EMBARRASSING!
TALK ABOUT THE SORT OF THING THAT CAN RUIN A GUY'S REPUTATION!
WHAT?
I SHOWED UP FOR THE FIRST DAY OF SCHOOL WEARING THE SAME SHIRT AS MORTON GOLDTHWAIT! WE WERE LIKE TWINS!
YEESH— THAT WOULD BE AWFUL!
SEE, PAIGE? THIS IS CALLED BEING A SUPPORTIVE SIBLING.
I MEANT FOR MORTON.
AMEND

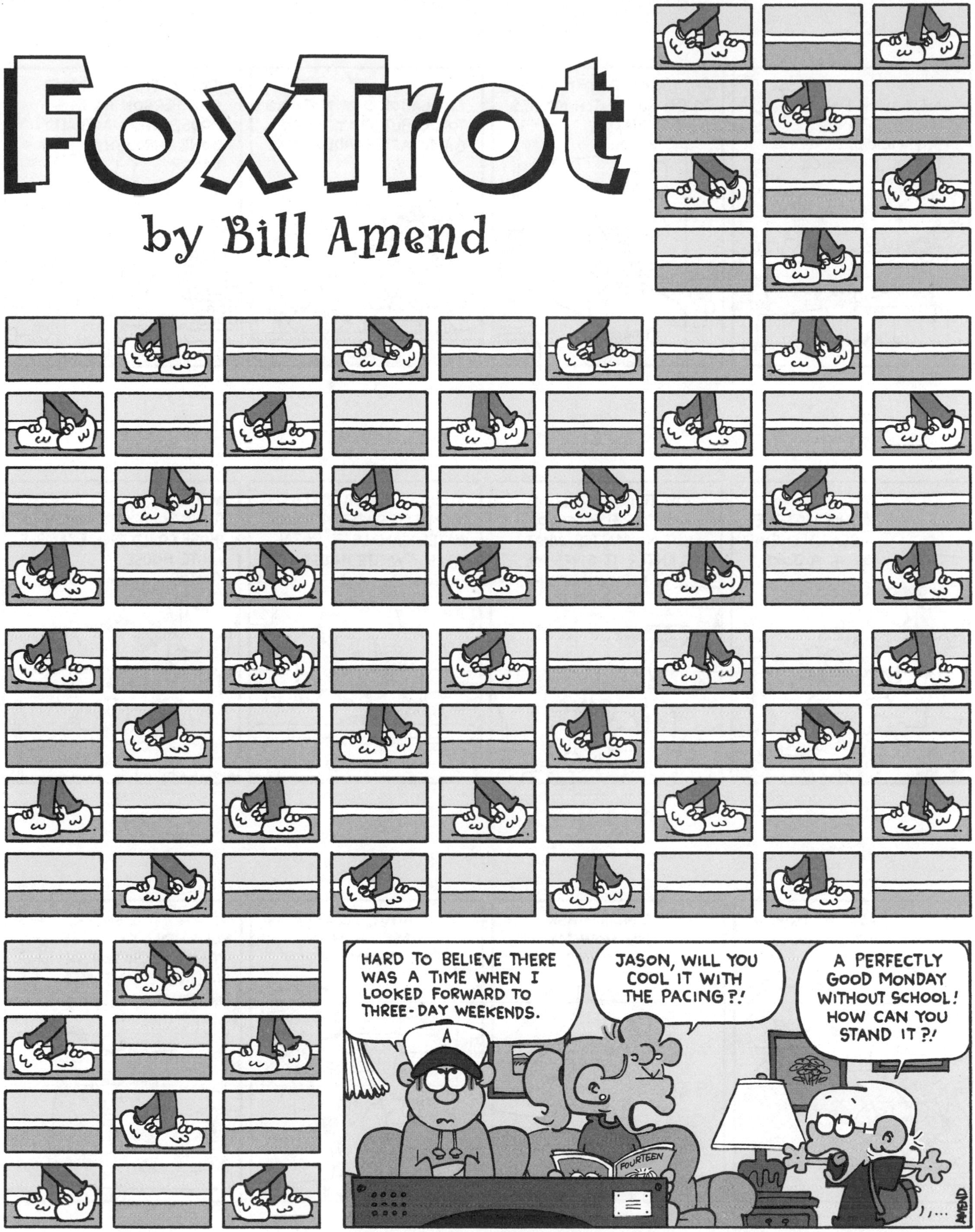
FoxTrot
by Bill Amend
HARD TO BELIEVE THERE WAS A TIME WHEN I LOOKED FORWARD TO THREE-DAY WEEKENDS.
JASON, WILL YOU COOL IT WITH THE PACING?!
A PERFECTLY GOOD MONDAY WITHOUT SCHOOL! HOW CAN YOU STAND IT?!
FOURTEEN
AMEND

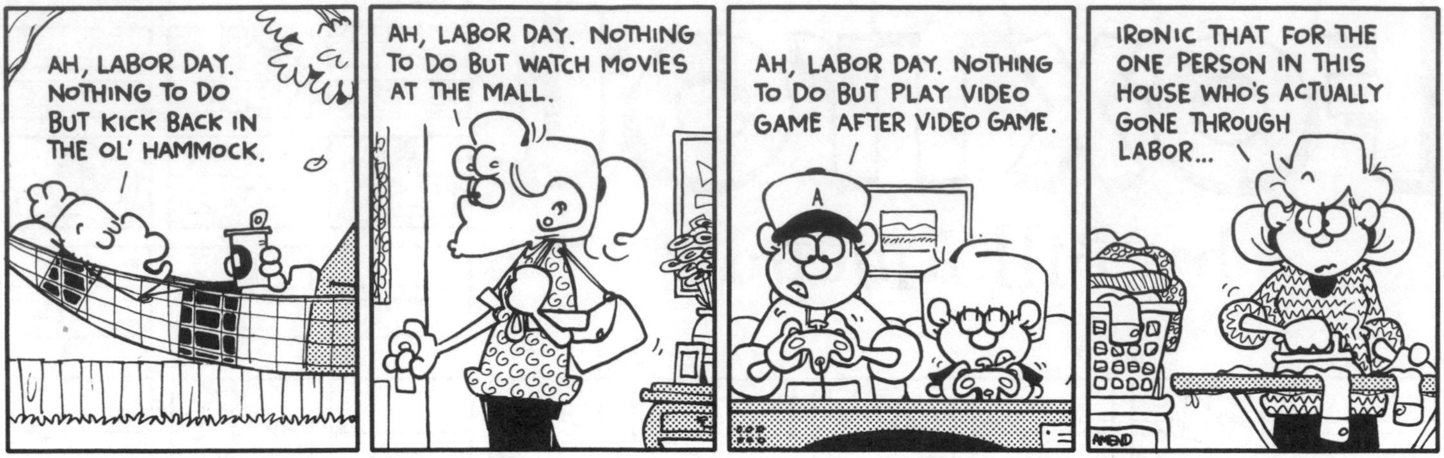
AH, LABOR DAY. NOTHING TO DO BUT KICK BACK IN THE OL' HAMMOCK.
AH, LABOR DAY. NOTHING TO DO BUT WATCH MOVIES AT THE MALL.
AH, LABOR DAY. NOTHING TO DO BUT PLAY VIDEO GAME AFTER VIDEO GAME.
IRONIC THAT FOR THE ONE PERSON IN THIS HOUSE WHO'S ACTUALLY GONE THROUGH LABOR...
AMEND

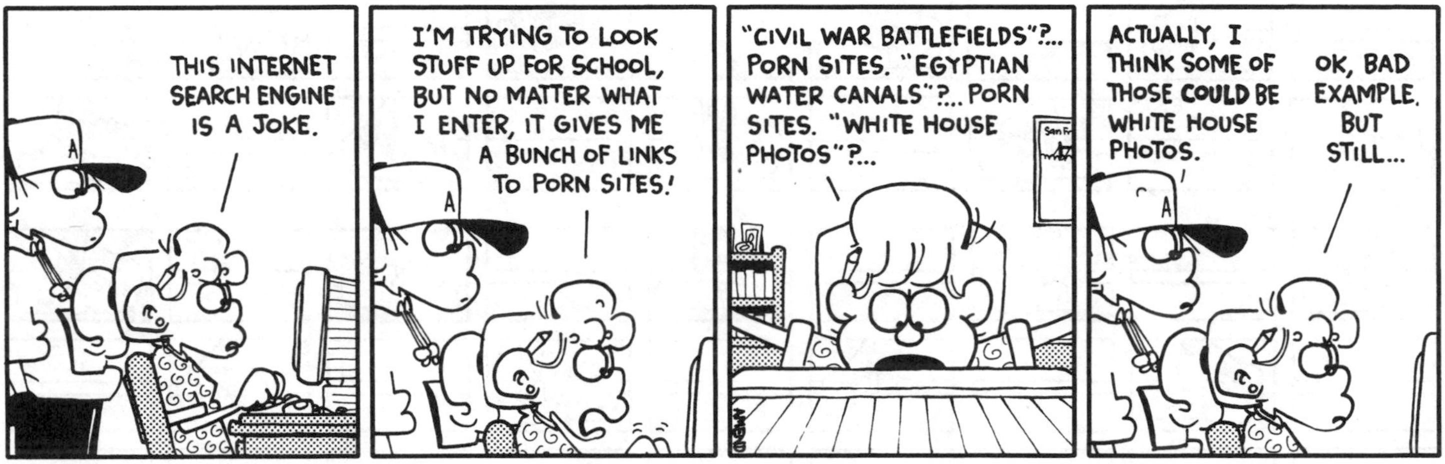
THIS INTERNET SEARCH ENGINE IS A JOKE.
I'M TRYING TO LOOK STUFF UP FOR SCHOOL, BUT NO MATTER WHAT I ENTER, IT GIVES ME A BUNCH OF LINKS TO PORN SITES!
"CIVIL WAR BATTLEFIELDS"?... PORN SITES. "EGYPTIAN WATER CANALS"?... PORN SITES. "WHITE HOUSE PHOTOS"?...
AMEND
ACTUALLY, I THINK SOME OF THOSE COULD BE WHITE HOUSE PHOTOS.
OK, BAD EXAMPLE. BUT STILL...

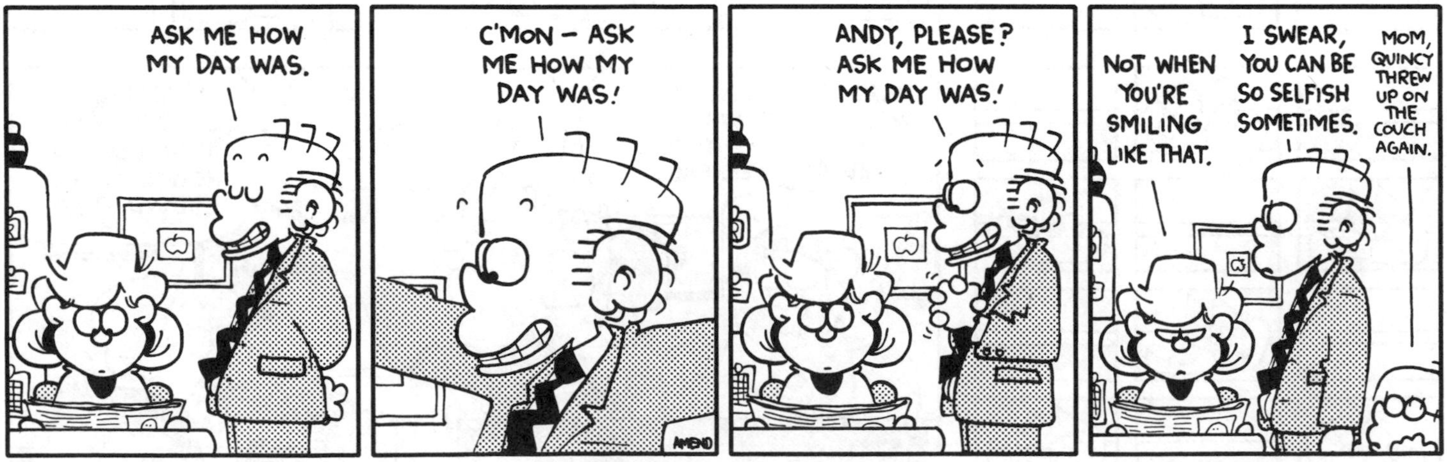
ASK ME HOW MY DAY WAS.
C'MON – ASK ME HOW MY DAY WAS!
AMEND
ANDY, PLEASE? ASK ME HOW MY DAY WAS!
NOT WHEN YOU'RE SMILING LIKE THAT.
I SWEAR, YOU CAN BE SO SELFISH SOMETIMES.
MOM, QUINCY THREW UP ON THE COUCH AGAIN.

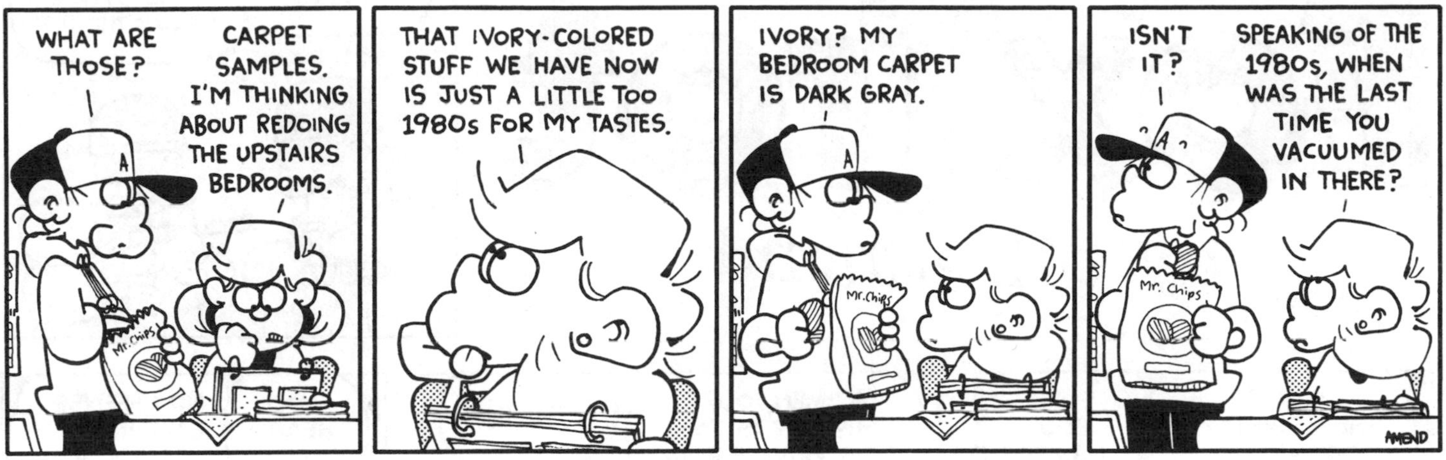
WHAT ARE THOSE?
CARPET SAMPLES. I'M THINKING ABOUT REDOING THE UPSTAIRS BEDROOMS.
Mr. Chips
THAT IVORY-COLORED STUFF WE HAVE NOW IS JUST A LITTLE TOO 1980s FOR MY TASTES.
IVORY? MY BEDROOM CARPET IS DARK GRAY.
Mr. Chips
ISN'T IT?
SPEAKING OF THE 1980s, WHEN WAS THE LAST TIME YOU VACUUMED IN THERE?
Mr. Chips
AMEND

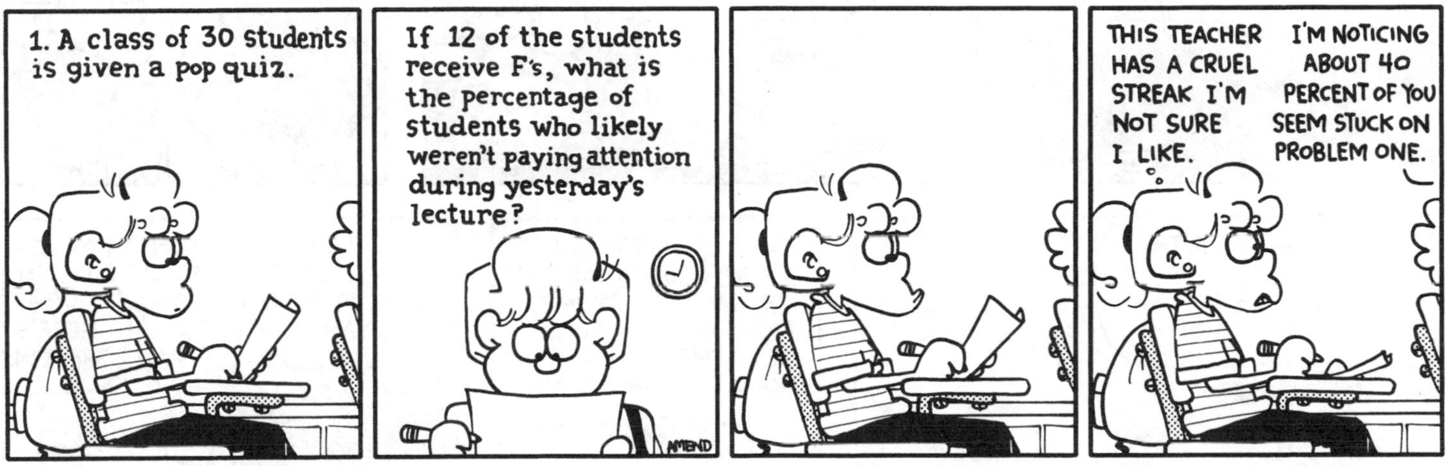
1. A class of 30 students is given a pop quiz.
If 12 of the students receive F's, what is the percentage of students who likely weren't paying attention during yesterday's lecture?
AMEND
THIS TEACHER HAS A CRUEL STREAK I'M NOT SURE I LIKE.
I'M NOTICING ABOUT 40 PERCENT OF YOU SEEM STUCK ON PROBLEM ONE.

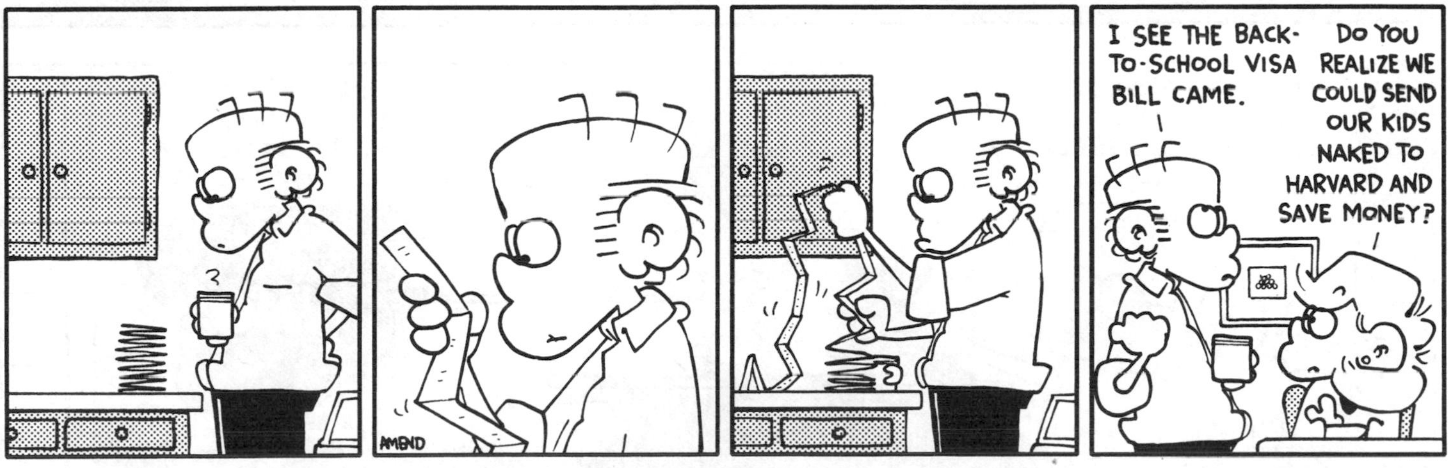
AMEND
I SEE THE BACK-TO-SCHOOL VISA BILL CAME.
DO YOU REALIZE WE COULD SEND OUR KIDS NAKED TO HARVARD AND SAVE MONEY?

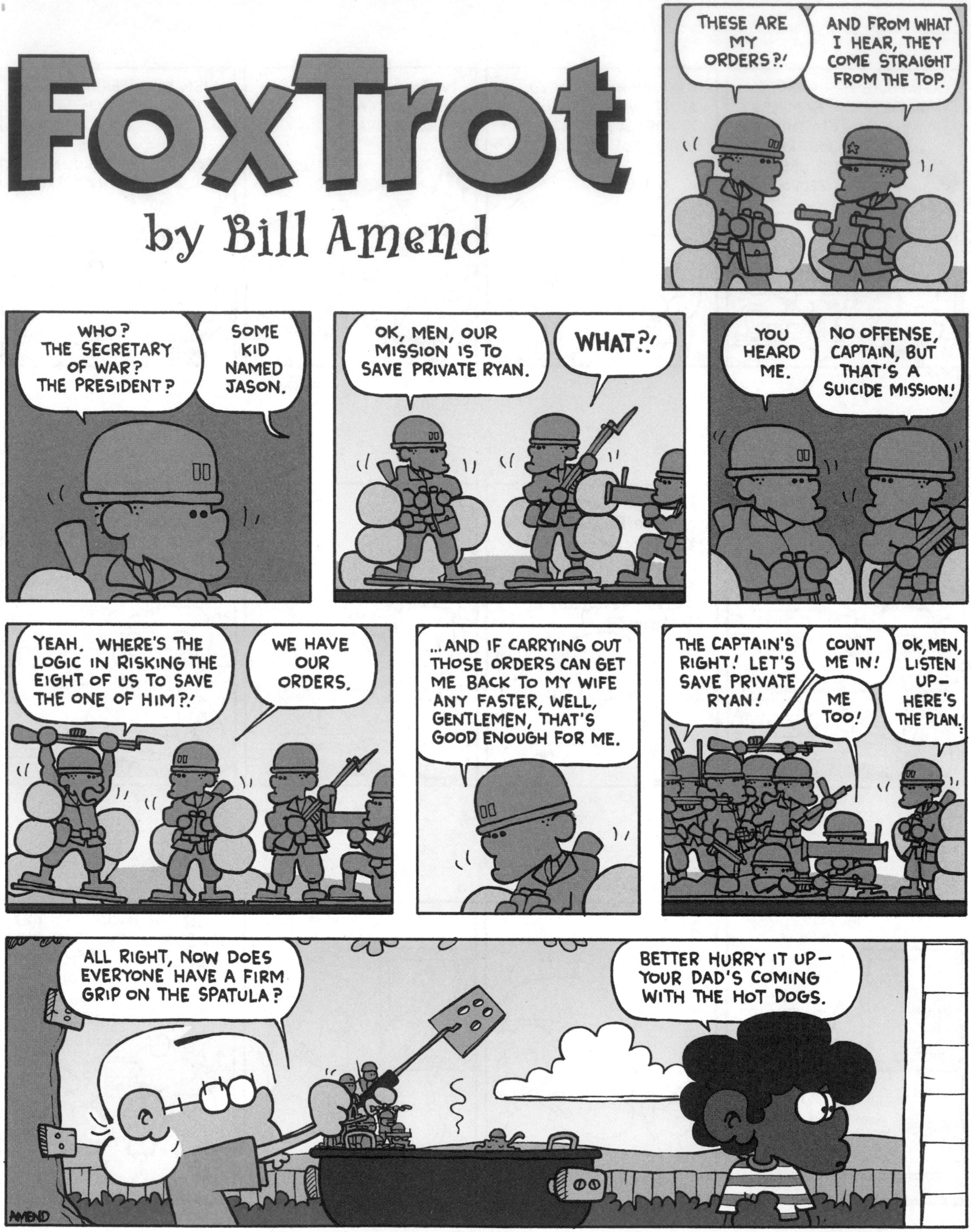
FoxTrot
by Bill Amend
THESE ARE MY ORDERS?!
AND FROM WHAT I HEAR, THEY COME STRAIGHT FROM THE TOP.
WHO? THE SECRETARY OF WAR? THE PRESIDENT?
SOME KID NAMED JASON.
OK, MEN, OUR MISSION IS TO SAVE PRIVATE RYAN.
WHAT?!
YOU HEARD ME.
NO OFFENSE, CAPTAIN, BUT THAT'S A SUICIDE MISSION!
YEAH. WHERE'S THE LOGIC IN RISKING THE EIGHT OF US TO SAVE THE ONE OF HIM?!
WE HAVE OUR ORDERS.
...AND IF CARRYING OUT THOSE ORDERS CAN GET ME BACK TO MY WIFE ANY FASTER, WELL, GENTLEMEN, THAT'S GOOD ENOUGH FOR ME.
THE CAPTAIN'S RIGHT! LET'S SAVE PRIVATE RYAN!
COUNT ME IN!
ME TOO!
OK, MEN, LISTEN UP— HERE'S THE PLAN:
ALL RIGHT, NOW DOES EVERYONE HAVE A FIRM GRIP ON THE SPATULA?
BETTER HURRY IT UP— YOUR DAD'S COMING WITH THE HOT DOGS.
AMEND

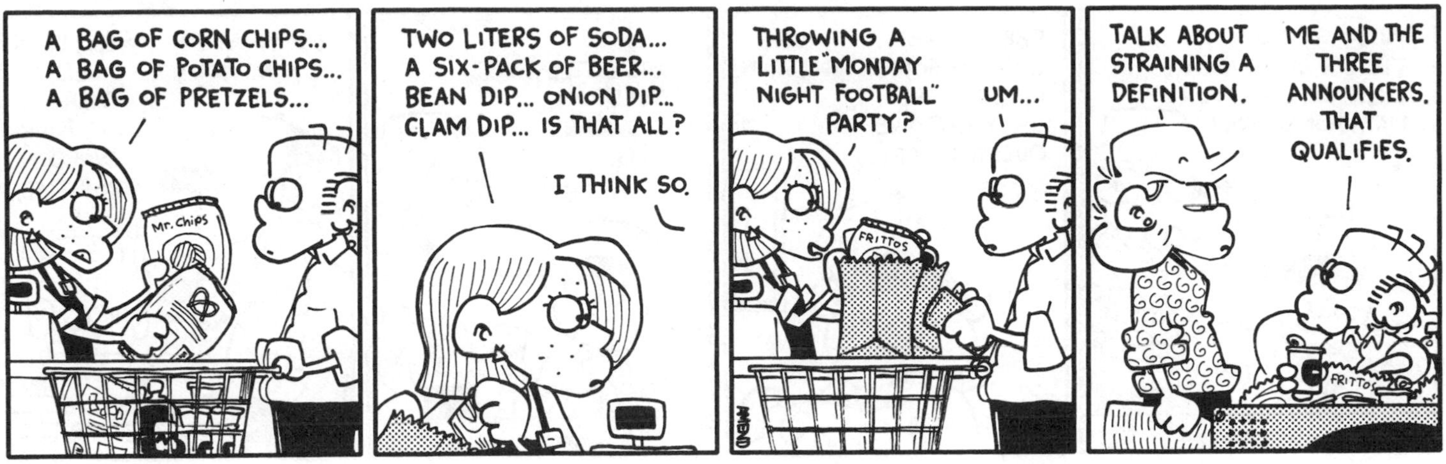
A BAG OF CORN CHIPS...
A BAG OF POTATO CHIPS...
A BAG OF PRETZELS...
Mr. Chips
TWO LITERS OF SODA...
A SIX-PACK OF BEER...
BEAN DIP... ONION DIP...
CLAM DIP... IS THAT ALL?
I THINK SO.
THROWING A LITTLE "MONDAY NIGHT FOOTBALL" PARTY?
UM...
FRITTOS
TALK ABOUT STRAINING A DEFINITION.
ME AND THE THREE ANNOUNCERS. THAT QUALIFIES.
FRITTOS

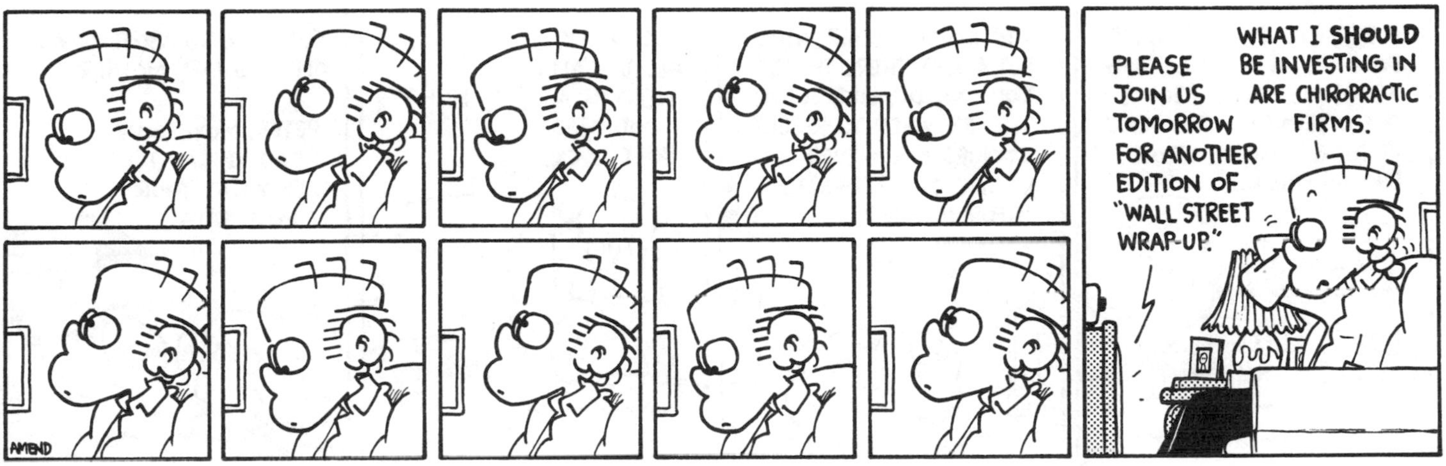
PLEASE JOIN US TOMORROW FOR ANOTHER EDITION OF "WALL STREET WRAP-UP."
WHAT I SHOULD BE INVESTING IN ARE CHIROPRACTIC FIRMS.

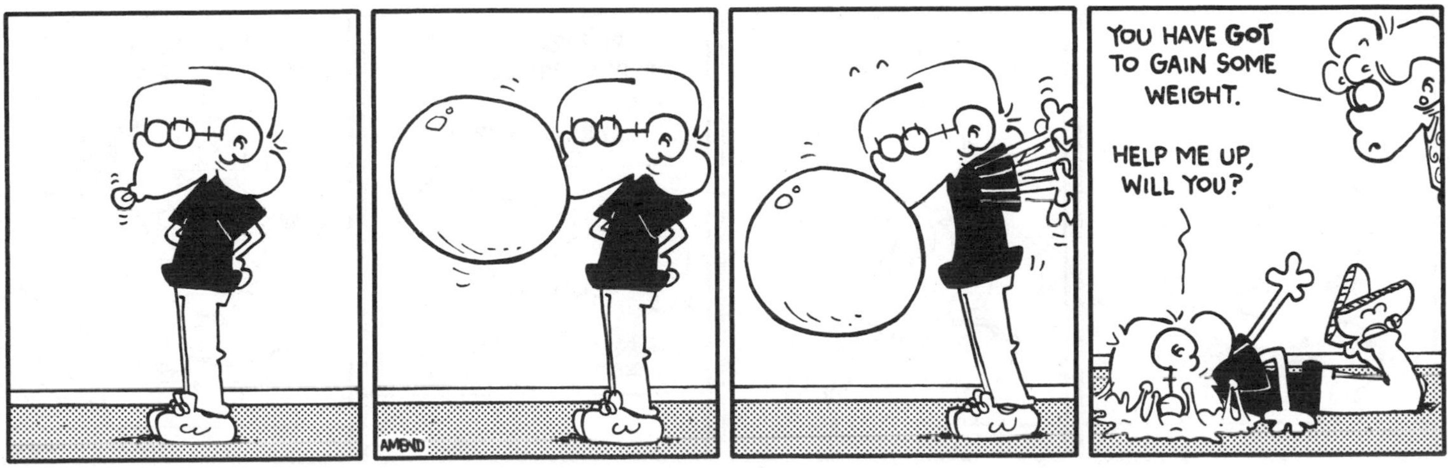
YOU HAVE GOT TO GAIN SOME WEIGHT.
HELP ME UP, WILL YOU?

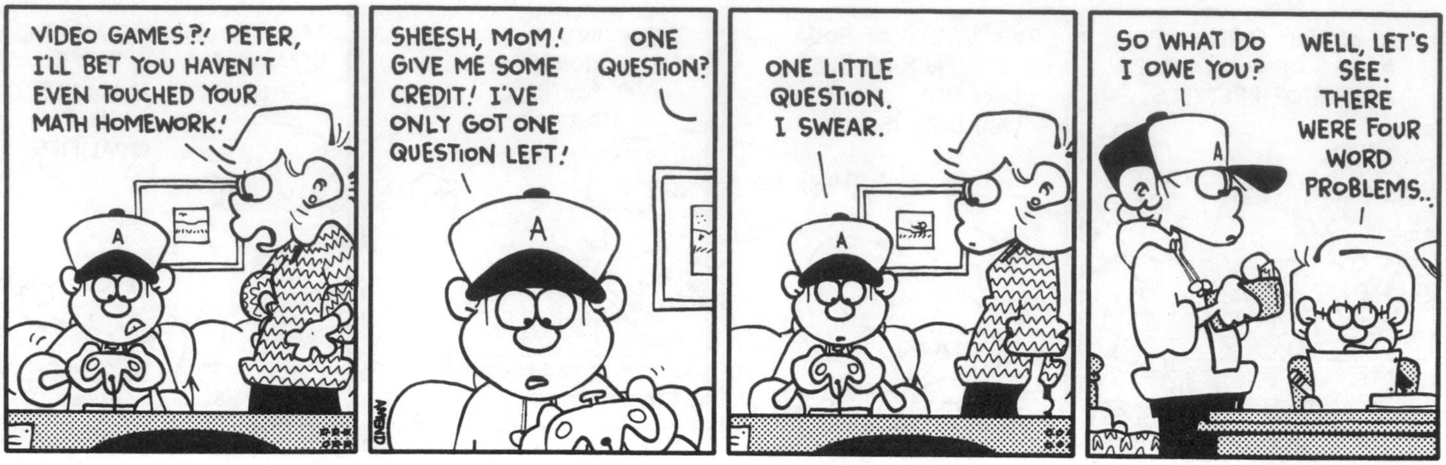
VIDEO GAMES?! PETER, I'LL BET YOU HAVEN'T EVEN TOUCHED YOUR MATH HOMEWORK!
SHEESH, MOM! GIVE ME SOME CREDIT! I'VE ONLY GOT ONE QUESTION LEFT!
ONE QUESTION?
ONE LITTLE QUESTION. I SWEAR.
SO WHAT DO I OWE YOU?
WELL, LET'S SEE. THERE WERE FOUR WORD PROBLEMS..
AMEND

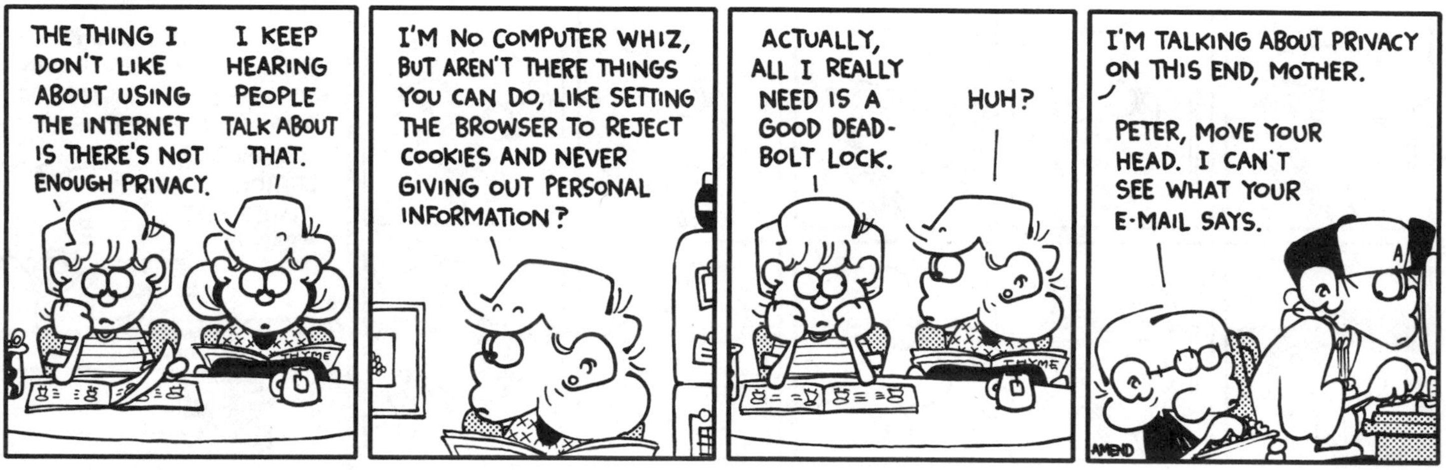
THE THING I DON'T LIKE ABOUT USING THE INTERNET IS THERE'S NOT ENOUGH PRIVACY.
I KEEP HEARING PEOPLE TALK ABOUT THAT.
I'M NO COMPUTER WHIZ, BUT AREN'T THERE THINGS YOU CAN DO, LIKE SETTING THE BROWSER TO REJECT COOKIES AND NEVER GIVING OUT PERSONAL INFORMATION?
ACTUALLY, ALL I REALLY NEED IS A GOOD DEAD-BOLT LOCK.
HUH?
I'M TALKING ABOUT PRIVACY ON THIS END, MOTHER.
PETER, MOVE YOUR HEAD. I CAN'T SEE WHAT YOUR E-MAIL SAYS.
AMEND

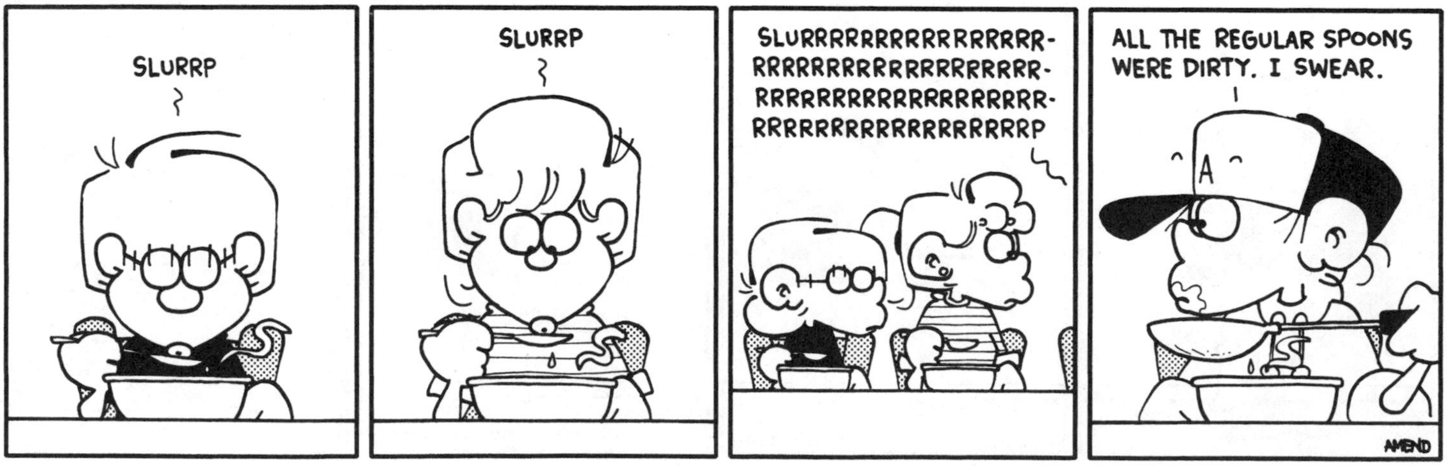
SLURRP
SLURRP
SLURRRRRRRRRRRRRRRRR-RRRRRRRRRRRRRRRRRRR-RRRRRRRRRRRRRRRRRRR-RRRRRRRRRRRRRRRRRP
ALL THE REGULAR SPOONS WERE DIRTY. I SWEAR.
AMEND

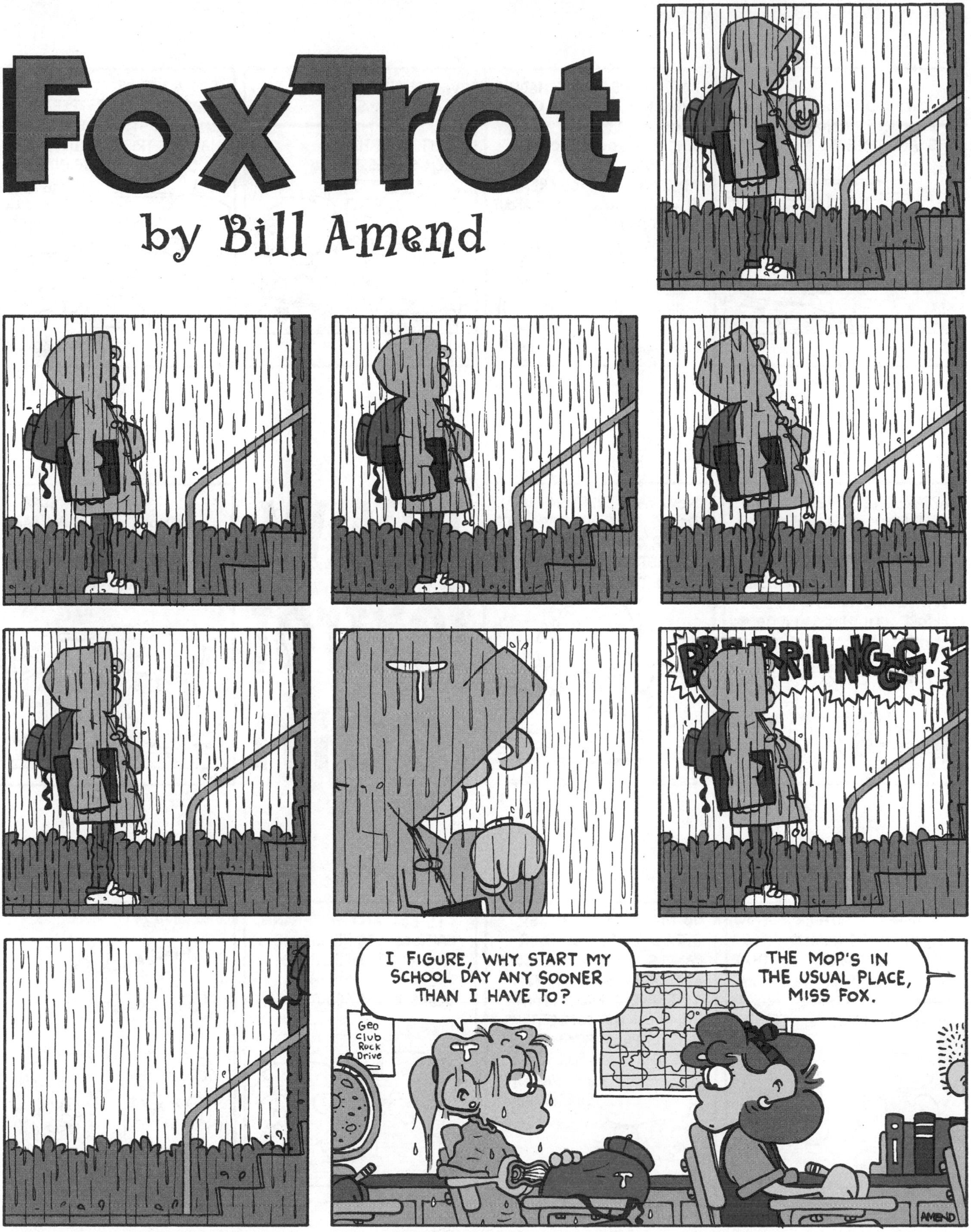
FoxTrot
by Bill Amend
I FIGURE, WHY START MY SCHOOL DAY ANY SOONER THAN I HAVE TO?
THE MOP'S IN THE USUAL PLACE, MISS FOX.
Geo Club Rock Drive
AMEND

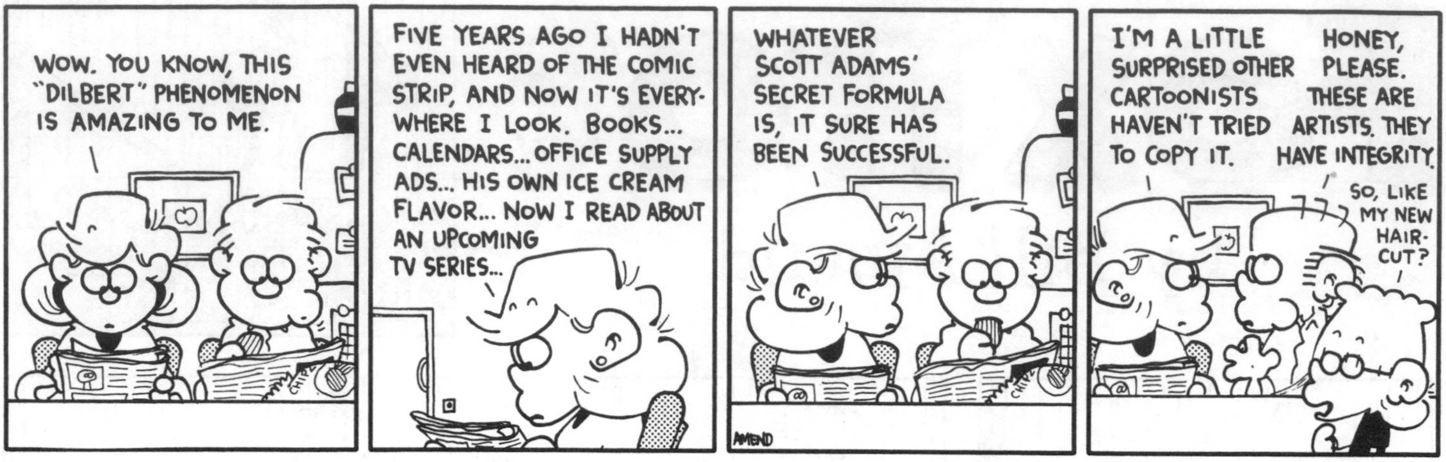
WOW. YOU KNOW, THIS "DILBERT" PHENOMENON IS AMAZING TO ME.
FIVE YEARS AGO I HADN'T EVEN HEARD OF THE COMIC STRIP, AND NOW IT'S EVERYWHERE I LOOK. BOOKS... CALENDARS... OFFICE SUPPLY ADS... HIS OWN ICE CREAM FLAVOR... NOW I READ ABOUT AN UPCOMING TV SERIES...
WHATEVER SCOTT ADAMS' SECRET FORMULA IS, IT SURE HAS BEEN SUCCESSFUL.
AMEND
I'M A LITTLE SURPRISED OTHER CARTOONISTS HAVEN'T TRIED TO COPY IT.
HONEY, PLEASE. THESE ARE ARTISTS. THEY HAVE INTEGRITY.
SO, LIKE MY NEW HAIR-CUT?

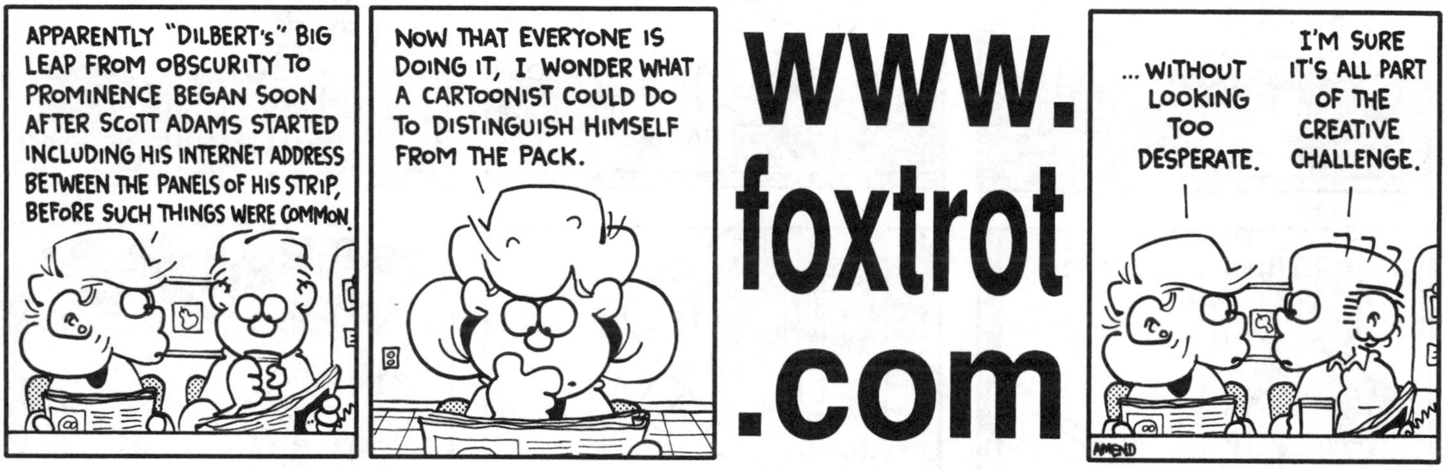
APPARENTLY "DILBERT's" BIG LEAP FROM OBSCURITY TO PROMINENCE BEGAN SOON AFTER SCOTT ADAMS STARTED INCLUDING HIS INTERNET ADDRESS BETWEEN THE PANELS OF HIS STRIP, BEFORE SUCH THINGS WERE COMMON.
NOW THAT EVERYONE IS DOING IT, I WONDER WHAT A CARTOONIST COULD DO TO DISTINGUISH HIMSELF FROM THE PACK.
www.
foxtrot
.com
...WITHOUT LOOKING TOO DESPERATE.
I'M SURE IT'S ALL PART OF THE CREATIVE CHALLENGE.
AMEND

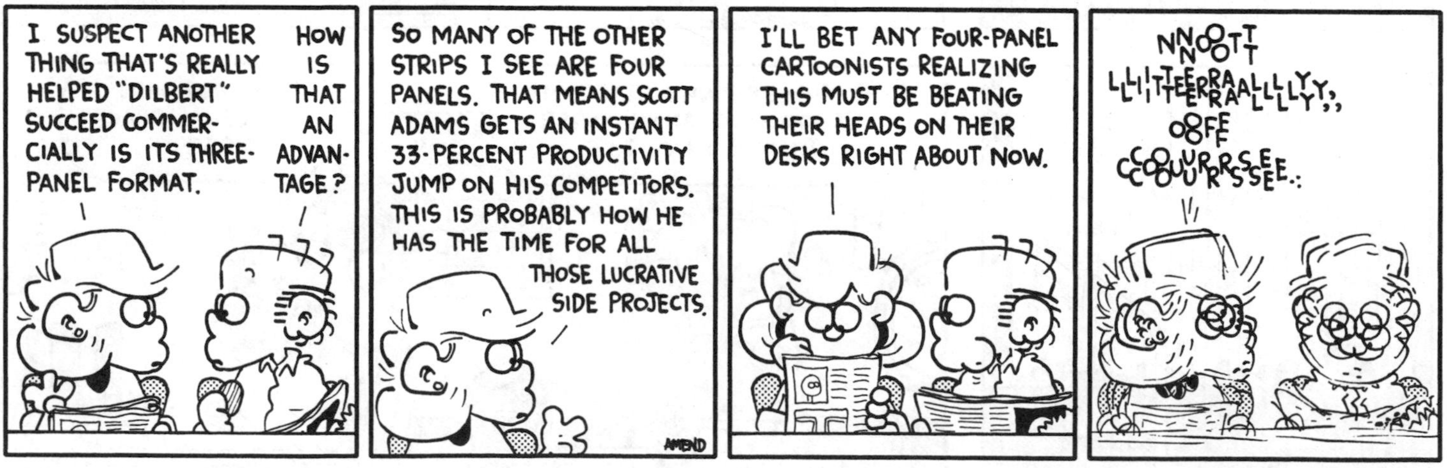
I SUSPECT ANOTHER THING THAT'S REALLY HELPED "DILBERT" SUCCEED COMMERCIALLY IS ITS THREE-PANEL FORMAT.
HOW IS THAT AN ADVANTAGE?
SO MANY OF THE OTHER STRIPS I SEE ARE FOUR PANELS. THAT MEANS SCOTT ADAMS GETS AN INSTANT 33-PERCENT PRODUCTIVITY JUMP ON HIS COMPETITORS. THIS IS PROBABLY HOW HE HAS THE TIME FOR ALL THOSE LUCRATIVE SIDE PROJECTS.
AMEND
I'LL BET ANY FOUR-PANEL CARTOONISTS REALIZING THIS MUST BE BEATING THEIR HEADS ON THEIR DESKS RIGHT ABOUT NOW.
NNOOTT LLIITTEERRAALLLLYY,, OOFF CCOOUURRSSEE.

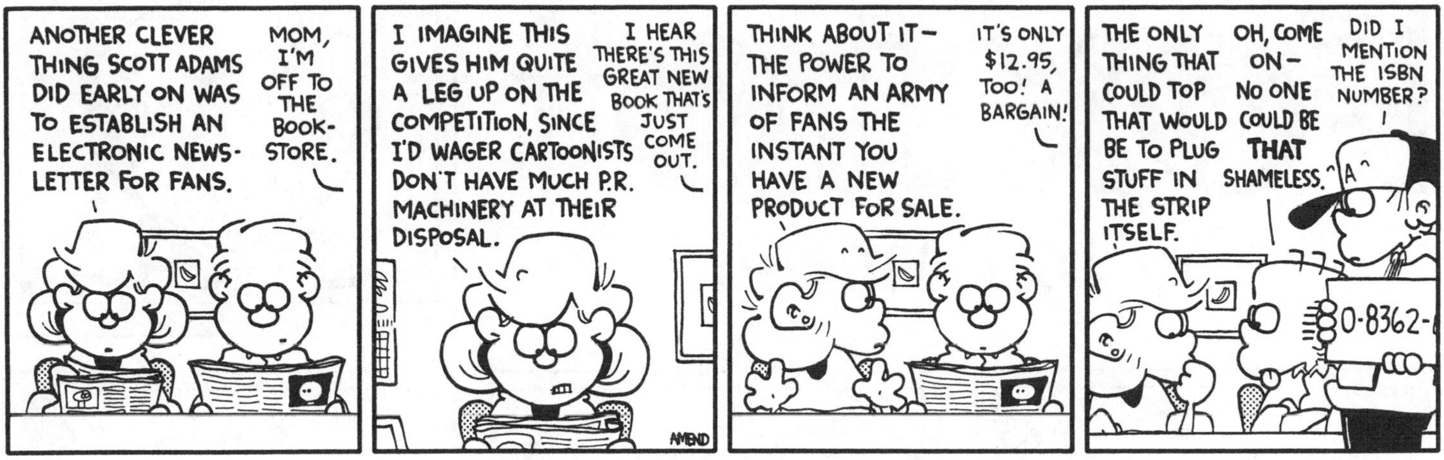
ANOTHER CLEVER THING SCOTT ADAMS DID EARLY ON WAS TO ESTABLISH AN ELECTRONIC NEWS-LETTER FOR FANS.
MOM, I'M OFF TO THE BOOK-STORE.
I IMAGINE THIS GIVES HIM QUITE A LEG UP ON THE COMPETITION, SINCE I'D WAGER CARTOONISTS DON'T HAVE MUCH P.R. MACHINERY AT THEIR DISPOSAL.
I HEAR THERE'S THIS GREAT NEW BOOK THAT'S JUST COME OUT.
AMEND
THINK ABOUT IT— THE POWER TO INFORM AN ARMY OF FANS THE INSTANT YOU HAVE A NEW PRODUCT FOR SALE.
IT'S ONLY $12.95, TOO! A BARGAIN!
THE ONLY THING THAT COULD TOP THAT WOULD BE TO PLUG STUFF IN THE STRIP ITSELF.
OH, COME ON— NO ONE COULD BE THAT SHAMELESS.
DID I MENTION THE ISBN NUMBER?
A
0-8362-

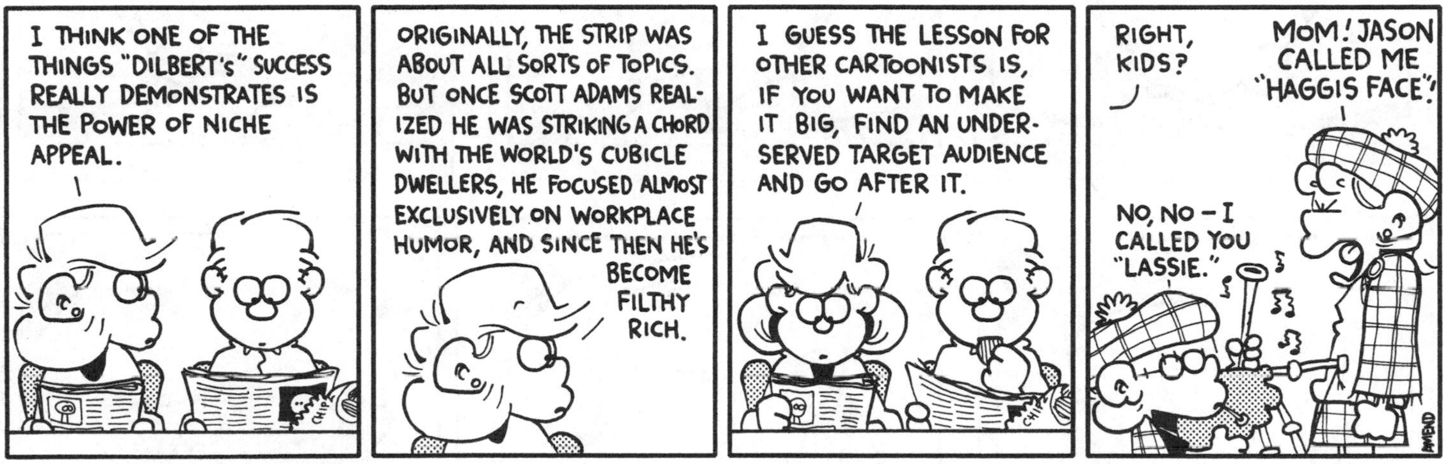
I THINK ONE OF THE THINGS "DILBERT's" SUCCESS REALLY DEMONSTRATES IS THE POWER OF NICHE APPEAL.
CHIP
ORIGINALLY, THE STRIP WAS ABOUT ALL SORTS OF TOPICS. BUT ONCE SCOTT ADAMS REAL-IZED HE WAS STRIKING A CHORD WITH THE WORLD'S CUBICLE DWELLERS, HE FOCUSED ALMOST EXCLUSIVELY ON WORKPLACE HUMOR, AND SINCE THEN HE'S BECOME FILTHY RICH.
I GUESS THE LESSON FOR OTHER CARTOONISTS IS, IF YOU WANT TO MAKE IT BIG, FIND AN UNDER-SERVED TARGET AUDIENCE AND GO AFTER IT.
CHIP
RIGHT, KIDS?
MOM! JASON CALLED ME "HAGGIS FACE"!
NO, NO—I CALLED YOU "LASSIE."
AMEND

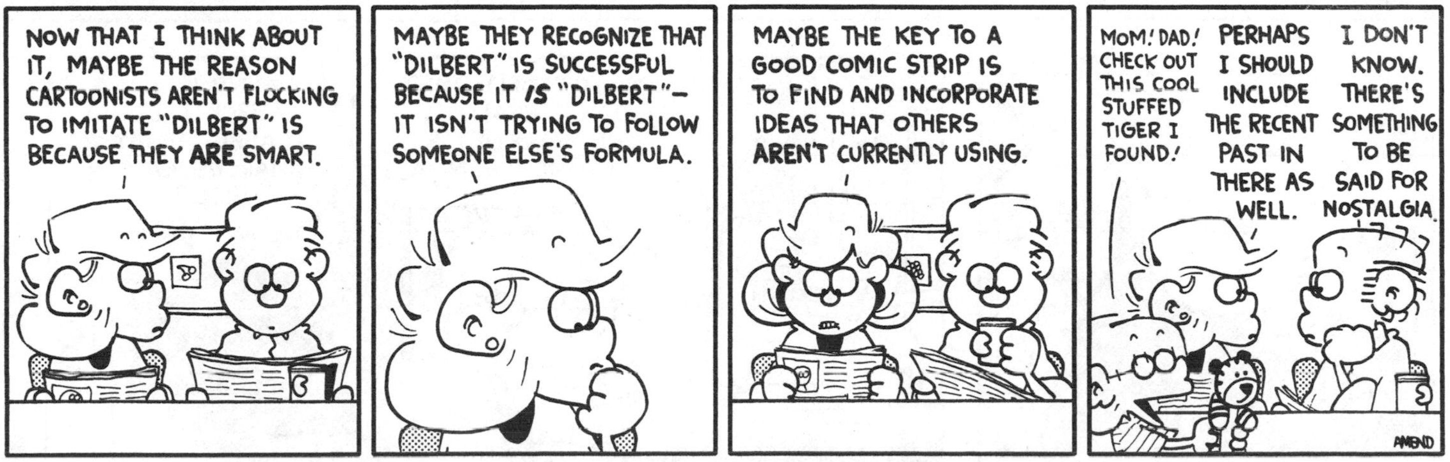
NOW THAT I THINK ABOUT IT, MAYBE THE REASON CARTOONISTS AREN'T FLOCKING TO IMITATE "DILBERT" IS BECAUSE THEY ARE SMART.
MAYBE THEY RECOGNIZE THAT "DILBERT" IS SUCCESSFUL BECAUSE IT IS "DILBERT"— IT ISN'T TRYING TO FOLLOW SOMEONE ELSE'S FORMULA.
MAYBE THE KEY TO A GOOD COMIC STRIP IS TO FIND AND INCORPORATE IDEAS THAT OTHERS AREN'T CURRENTLY USING.
MOM! DAD! CHECK OUT THIS COOL STUFFED TIGER I FOUND!
PERHAPS I SHOULD INCLUDE THE RECENT PAST IN THERE AS WELL.
I DON'T KNOW. THERE'S SOMETHING TO BE SAID FOR NOSTALGIA.
AMEND

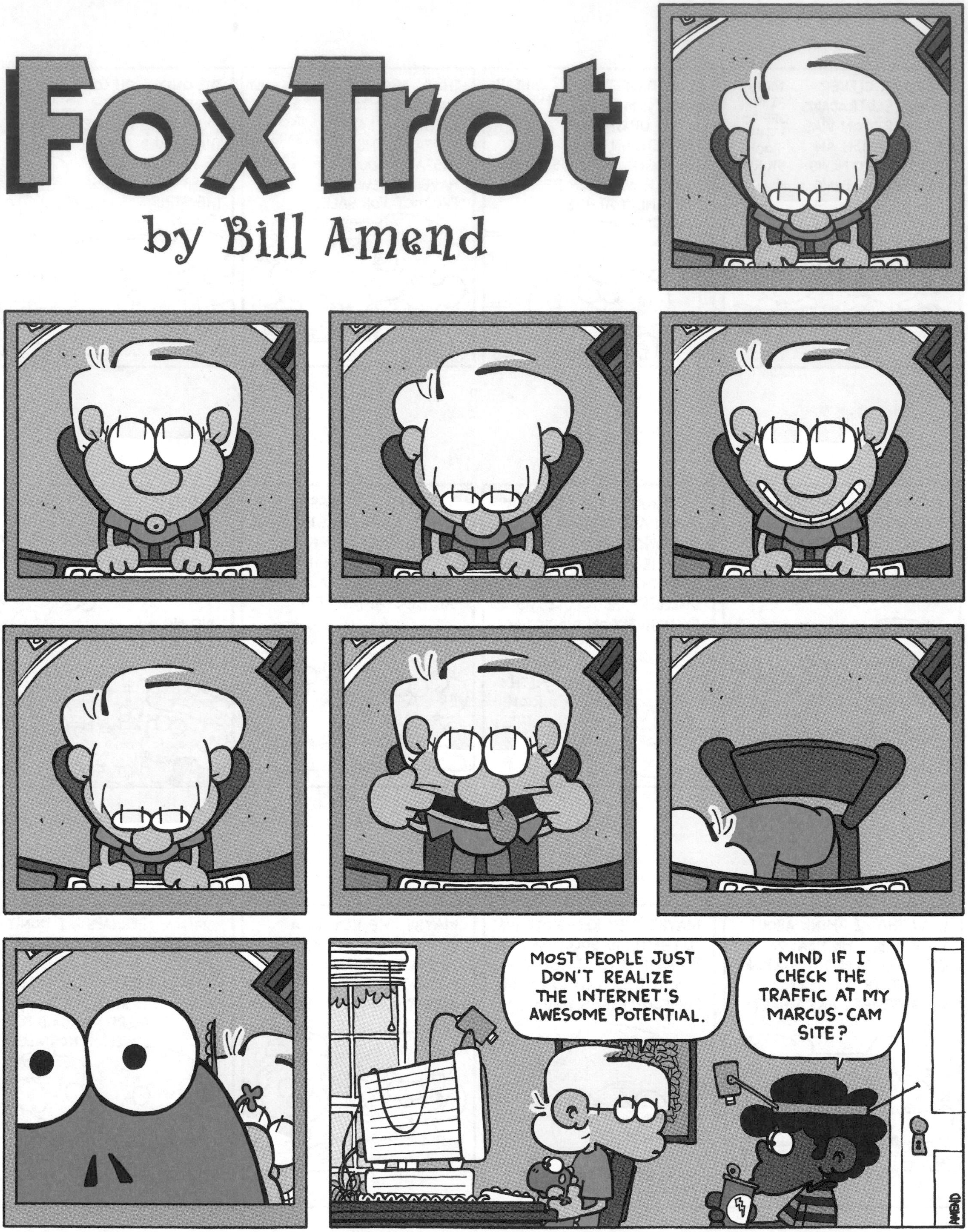
FoxTrot
by Bill Amend
MOST PEOPLE JUST DON'T REALIZE THE INTERNET'S AWESOME POTENTIAL.
MIND IF I CHECK THE TRAFFIC AT MY MARCUS-CAM SITE?
AMEND

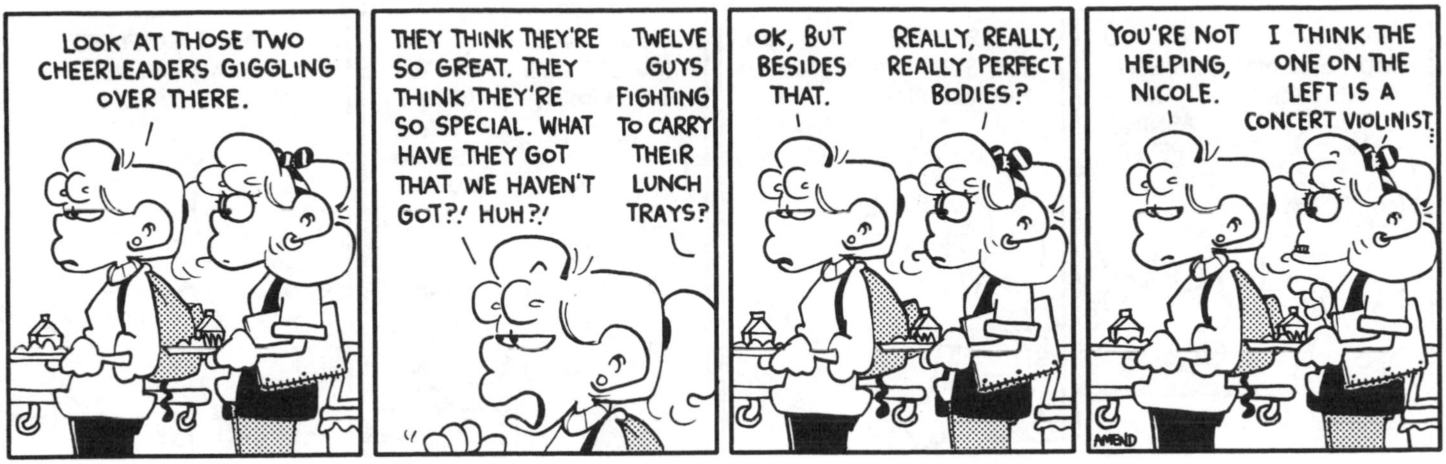
LOOK AT THOSE TWO CHEERLEADERS GIGGLING OVER THERE.
THEY THINK THEY'RE SO GREAT. THEY THINK THEY'RE SO SPECIAL. WHAT HAVE THEY GOT THAT WE HAVEN'T GOT?! HUH?!
TWELVE GUYS FIGHTING TO CARRY THEIR LUNCH TRAYS?
OK, BUT BESIDES THAT.
REALLY, REALLY, REALLY PERFECT BODIES?
YOU'RE NOT HELPING, NICOLE.
I THINK THE ONE ON THE LEFT IS A CONCERT VIOLINIST.
AMEND

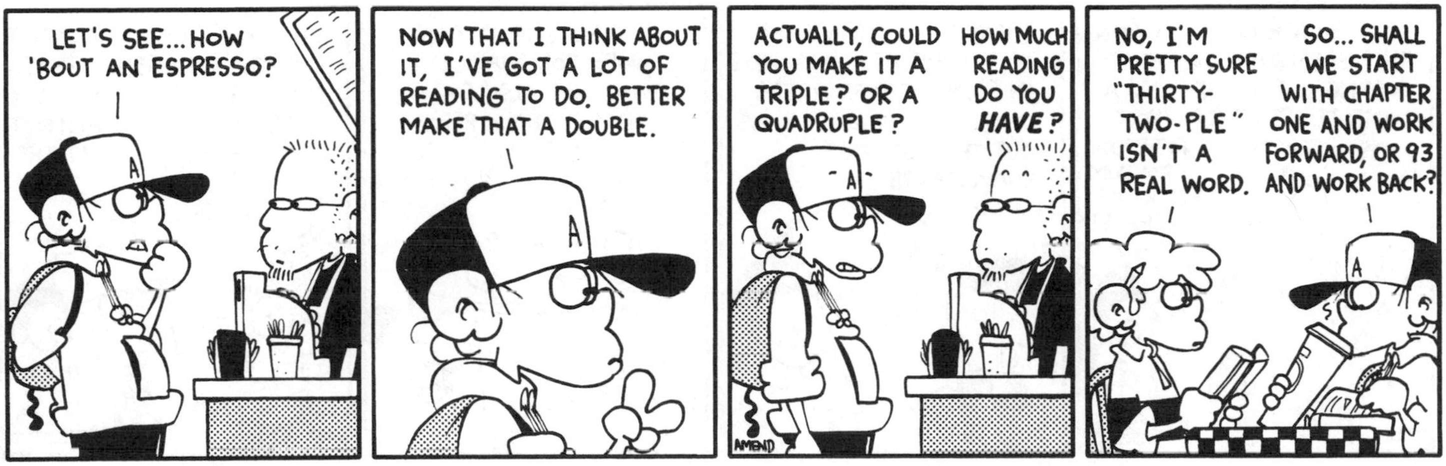
LET'S SEE... HOW 'BOUT AN ESPRESSO?
NOW THAT I THINK ABOUT IT, I'VE GOT A LOT OF READING TO DO. BETTER MAKE THAT A DOUBLE.
ACTUALLY, COULD YOU MAKE IT A TRIPLE? OR A QUADRUPLE?
HOW MUCH READING DO YOU *HAVE*?
AMEND
NO, I'M PRETTY SURE "THIRTY-TWO-PLE" ISN'T A REAL WORD.
SO... SHALL WE START WITH CHAPTER ONE AND WORK FORWARD, OR 93 AND WORK BACK?

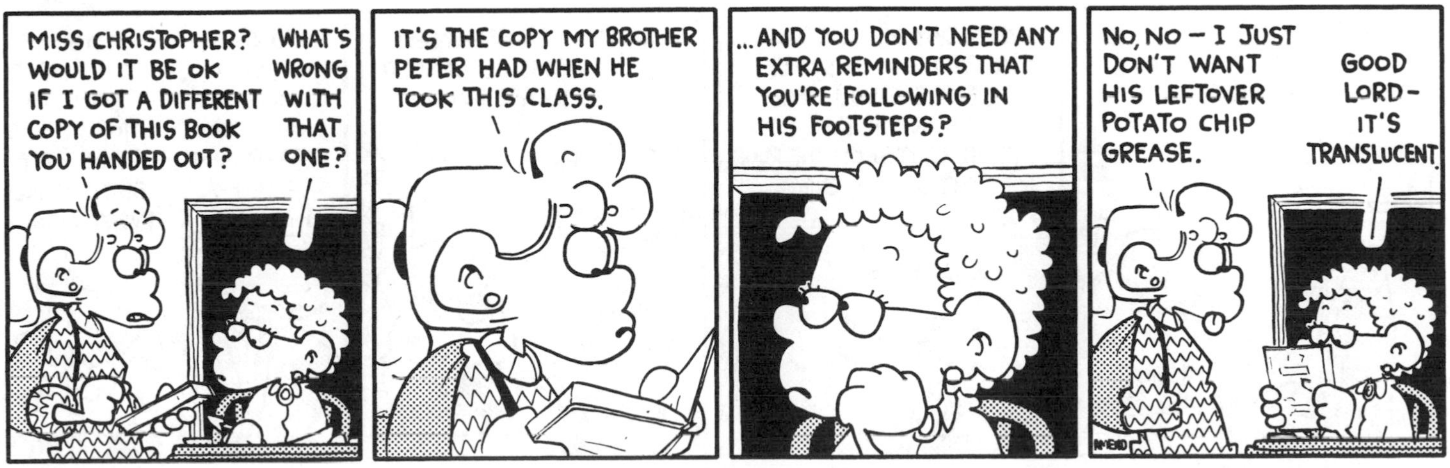
MISS CHRISTOPHER? WOULD IT BE OK IF I GOT A DIFFERENT COPY OF THIS BOOK YOU HANDED OUT?
WHAT'S WRONG WITH THAT ONE?
IT'S THE COPY MY BROTHER PETER HAD WHEN HE TOOK THIS CLASS.
...AND YOU DON'T NEED ANY EXTRA REMINDERS THAT YOU'RE FOLLOWING IN HIS FOOTSTEPS?
NO, NO – I JUST DON'T WANT HIS LEFTOVER POTATO CHIP GREASE.
GOOD LORD – IT'S TRANSLUCENT.
AMEND

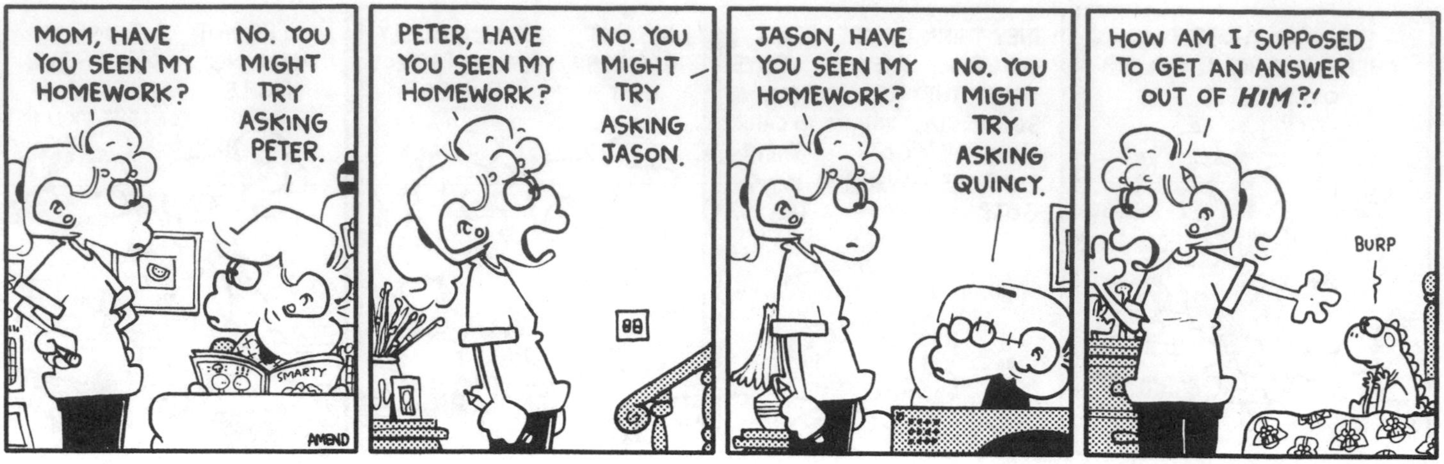
MOM, HAVE YOU SEEN MY HOMEWORK?
NO. YOU MIGHT TRY ASKING PETER.
SMARTY
AMEND
PETER, HAVE YOU SEEN MY HOMEWORK?
NO. YOU MIGHT TRY ASKING JASON.
JASON, HAVE YOU SEEN MY HOMEWORK?
NO. YOU MIGHT TRY ASKING QUINCY.
HOW AM I SUPPOSED TO GET AN ANSWER OUT OF *HIM*?!
BURP

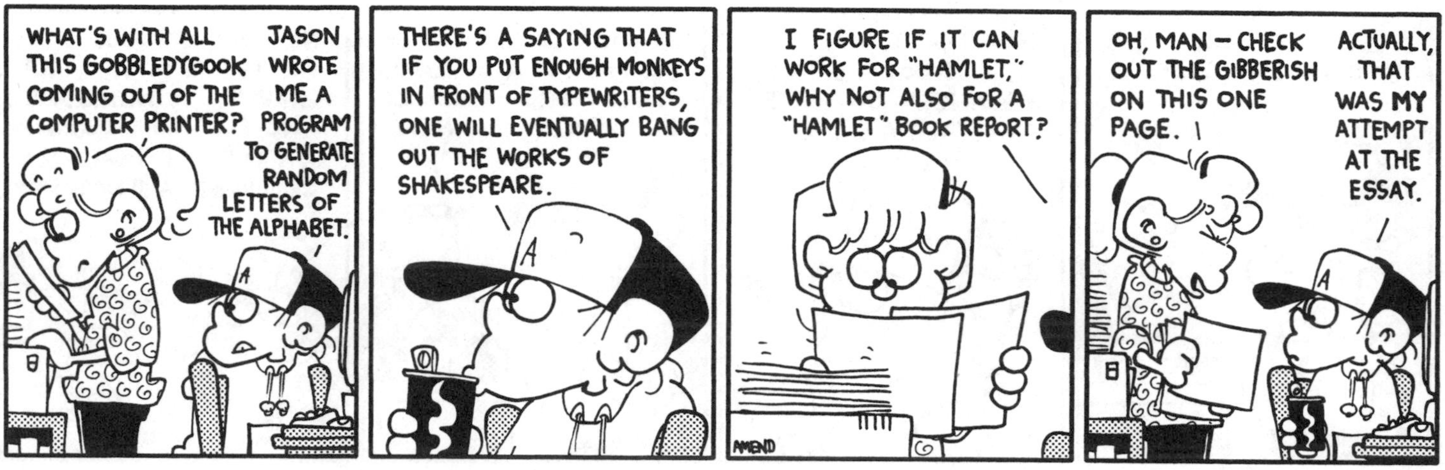
WHAT'S WITH ALL THIS GOBBLEDYGOOK COMING OUT OF THE COMPUTER PRINTER?
JASON WROTE ME A PROGRAM TO GENERATE RANDOM LETTERS OF THE ALPHABET.
THERE'S A SAYING THAT IF YOU PUT ENOUGH MONKEYS IN FRONT OF TYPEWRITERS, ONE WILL EVENTUALLY BANG OUT THE WORKS OF SHAKESPEARE.
I FIGURE IF IT CAN WORK FOR "HAMLET," WHY NOT ALSO FOR A "HAMLET" BOOK REPORT?
AMEND
OH, MAN – CHECK OUT THE GIBBERISH ON THIS ONE PAGE.
ACTUALLY, THAT WAS **MY** ATTEMPT AT THE ESSAY.

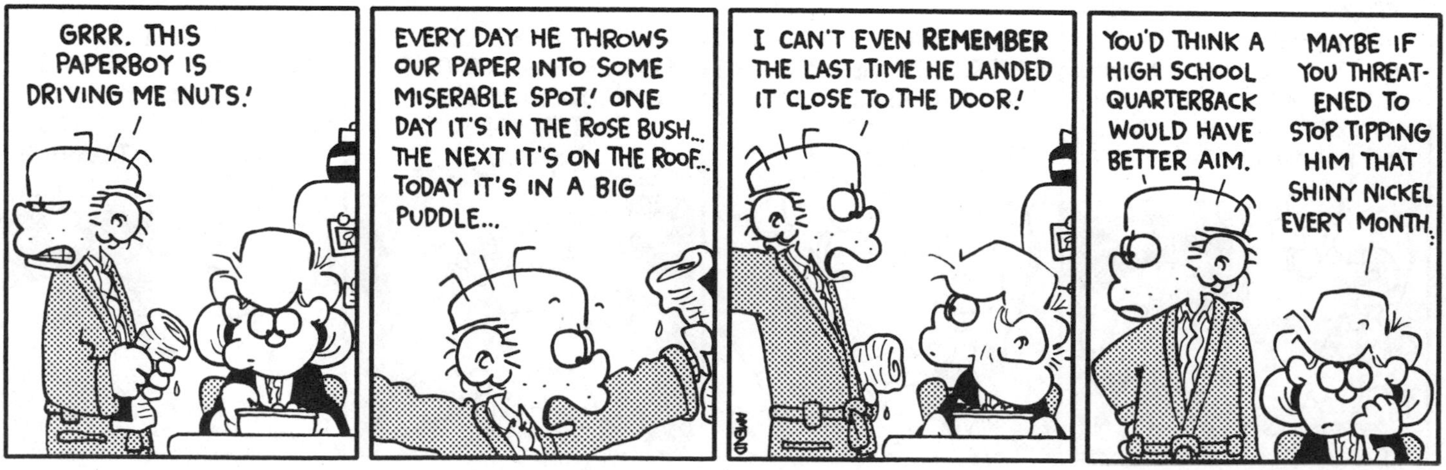
GRRR. THIS PAPERBOY IS DRIVING ME NUTS!
EVERY DAY HE THROWS OUR PAPER INTO SOME MISERABLE SPOT! ONE DAY IT'S IN THE ROSE BUSH... THE NEXT IT'S ON THE ROOF... TODAY IT'S IN A BIG PUDDLE...
I CAN'T EVEN **REMEMBER** THE LAST TIME HE LANDED IT CLOSE TO THE DOOR!
AMEND
YOU'D THINK A HIGH SCHOOL QUARTERBACK WOULD HAVE BETTER AIM.
MAYBE IF YOU THREAT-ENED TO STOP TIPPING HIM THAT SHINY NICKEL EVERY MONTH.

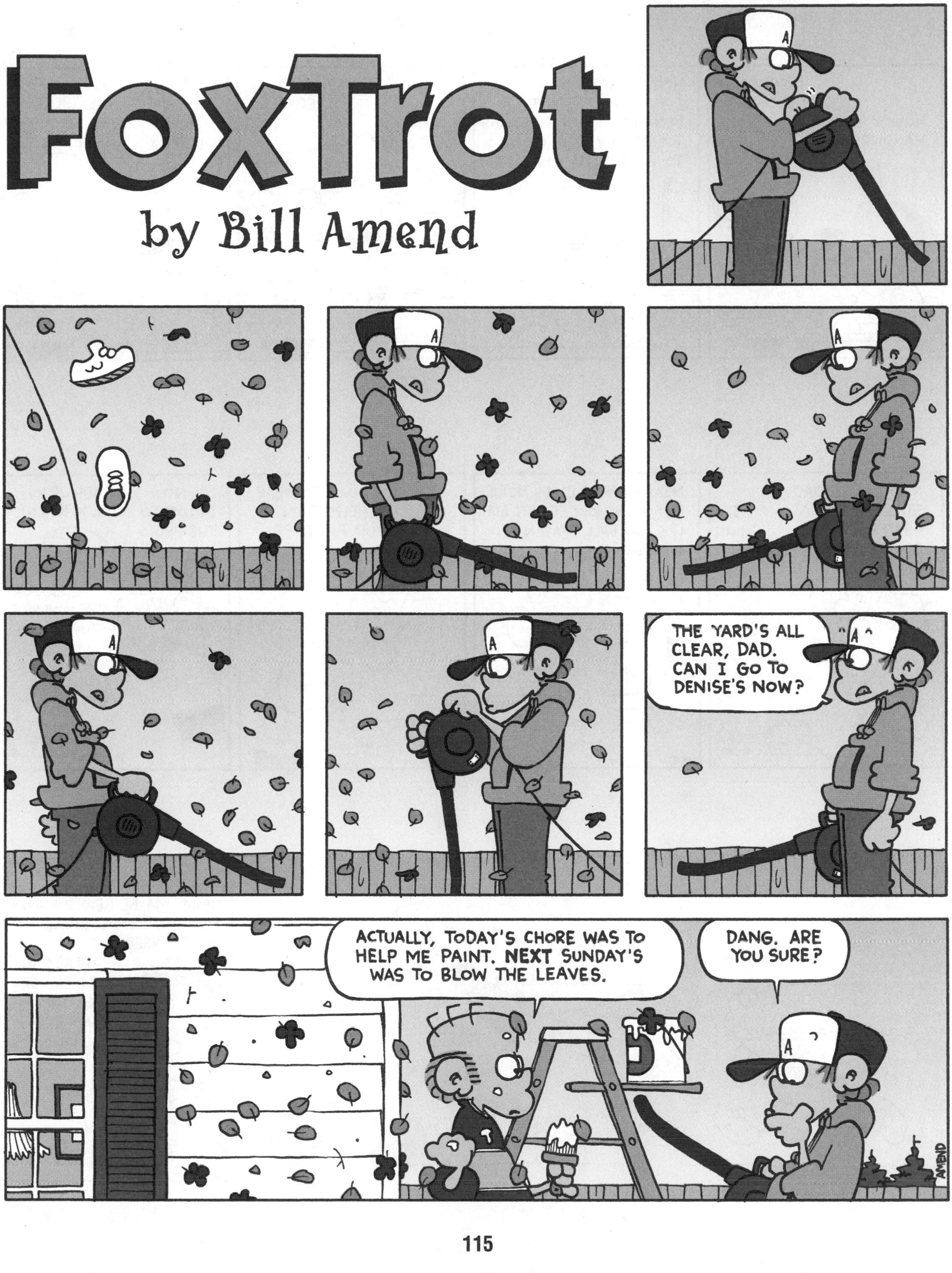
FoxTrot
by Bill Amend
THE YARD'S ALL CLEAR, DAD. CAN I GO TO DENISE'S NOW?
ACTUALLY, TODAY'S CHORE WAS TO HELP ME PAINT. NEXT SUNDAY'S WAS TO BLOW THE LEAVES.
DANG. ARE YOU SURE?
AMEND

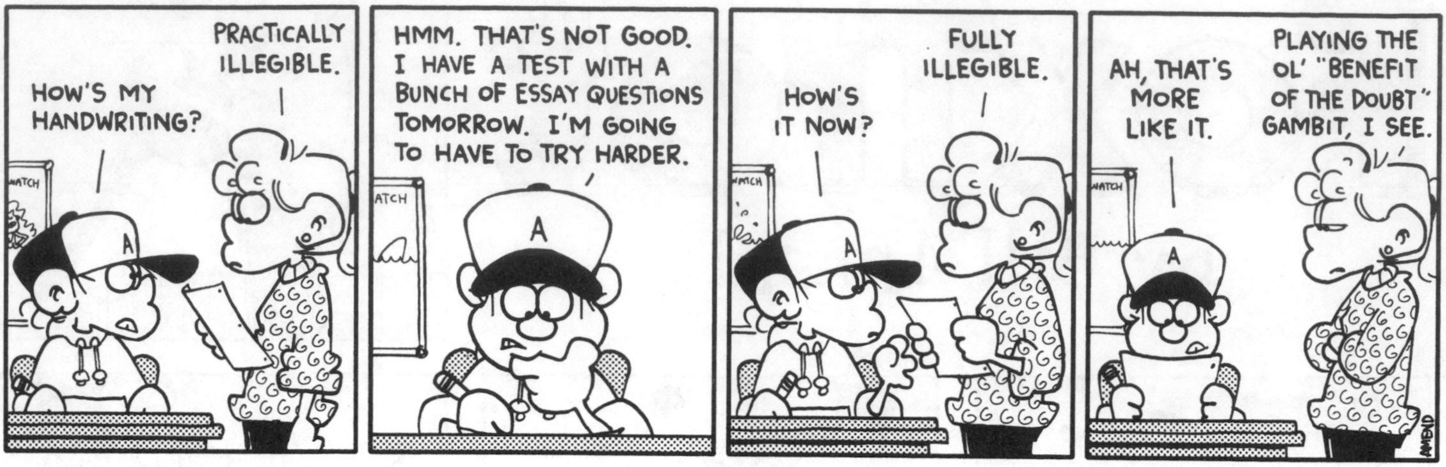
HOW'S MY HANDWRITING?
PRACTICALLY ILLEGIBLE.
HMM. THAT'S NOT GOOD. I HAVE A TEST WITH A BUNCH OF ESSAY QUESTIONS TOMORROW. I'M GOING TO HAVE TO TRY HARDER.
HOW'S IT NOW?
FULLY ILLEGIBLE.
AH, THAT'S MORE LIKE IT.
PLAYING THE OL' "BENEFIT OF THE DOUBT" GAMBIT, I SEE.
AMEND

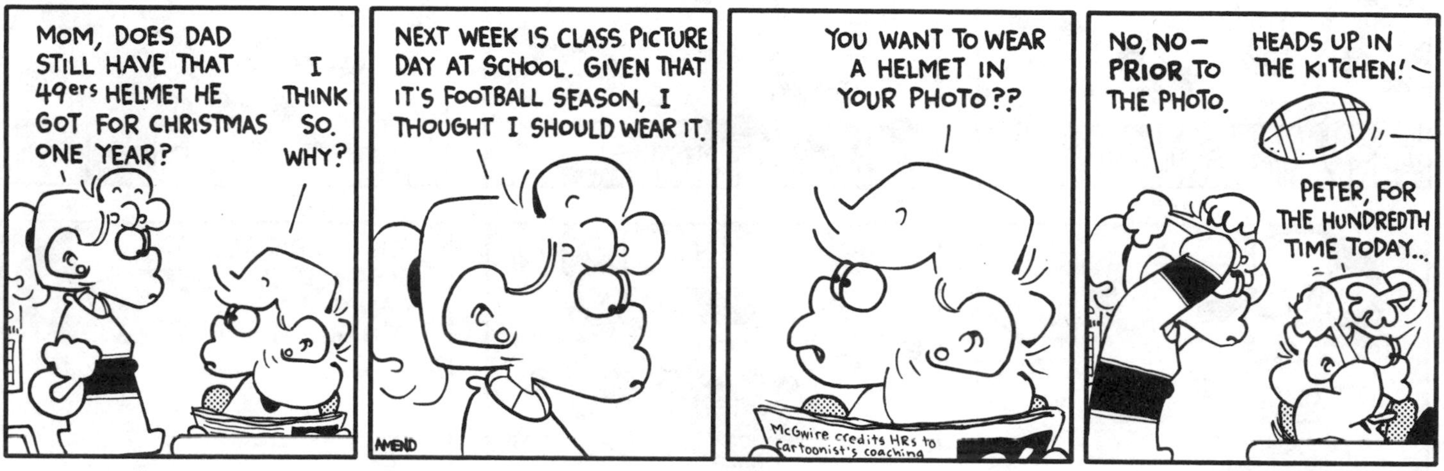
MOM, DOES DAD STILL HAVE THAT 49ers HELMET HE GOT FOR CHRISTMAS ONE YEAR?
I THINK SO. WHY?
NEXT WEEK IS CLASS PICTURE DAY AT SCHOOL. GIVEN THAT IT'S FOOTBALL SEASON, I THOUGHT I SHOULD WEAR IT.
AMEND
YOU WANT TO WEAR A HELMET IN YOUR PHOTO??
McGwire credits HRs to cartoonist's coaching
NO, NO– **PRIOR** TO THE PHOTO.
HEADS UP IN THE KITCHEN!
PETER, FOR THE HUNDREDTH TIME TODAY...

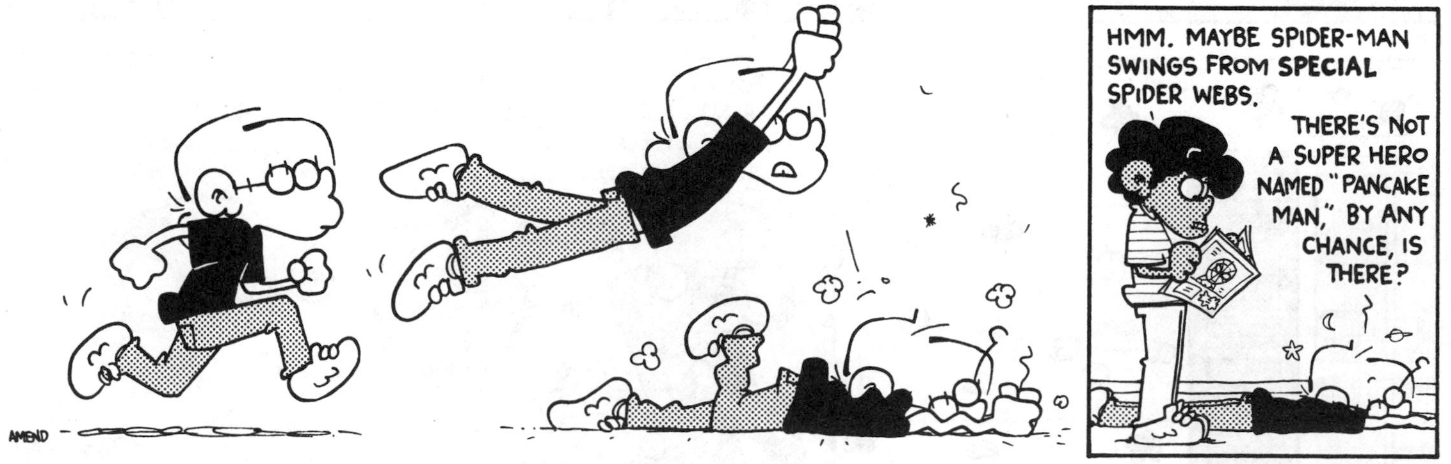
AMEND
HMM. MAYBE SPIDER-MAN SWINGS FROM **SPECIAL** SPIDER WEBS.
THERE'S NOT A SUPER HERO NAMED "PANCAKE MAN," BY ANY CHANCE, IS THERE?

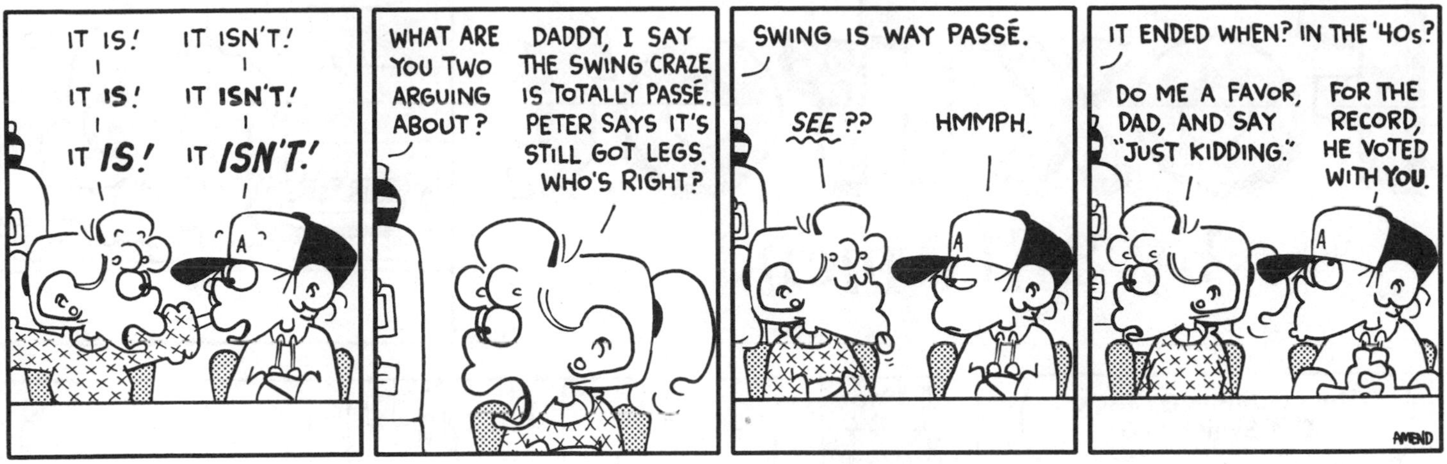
IT IS!
IT ISN'T!
IT IS!
IT ISN'T!
IT IS!
IT ISN'T!
WHAT ARE YOU TWO ARGUING ABOUT?
DADDY, I SAY THE SWING CRAZE IS TOTALLY PASSÉ. PETER SAYS IT'S STILL GOT LEGS. WHO'S RIGHT?
SWING IS WAY PASSÉ.
SEE??
HMMPH.
IT ENDED WHEN? IN THE '40s?
DO ME A FAVOR, DAD, AND SAY "JUST KIDDING."
FOR THE RECORD, HE VOTED WITH YOU.
AMEND

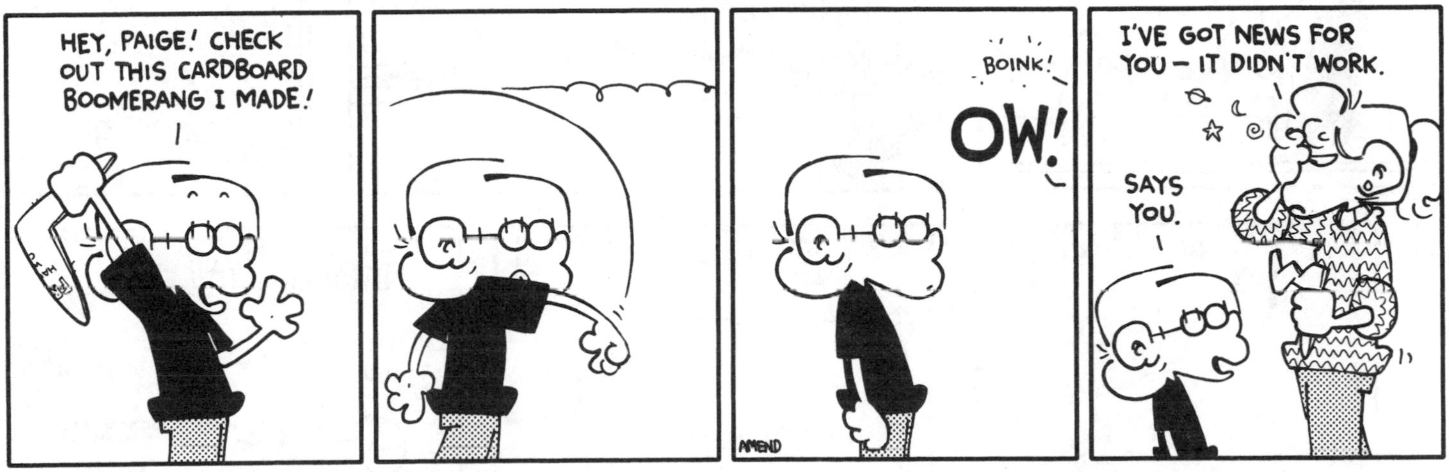
HEY, PAIGE! CHECK OUT THIS CARDBOARD BOOMERANG I MADE!
BOINK!
OW!
AMEND
I'VE GOT NEWS FOR YOU – IT DIDN'T WORK.
SAYS YOU.

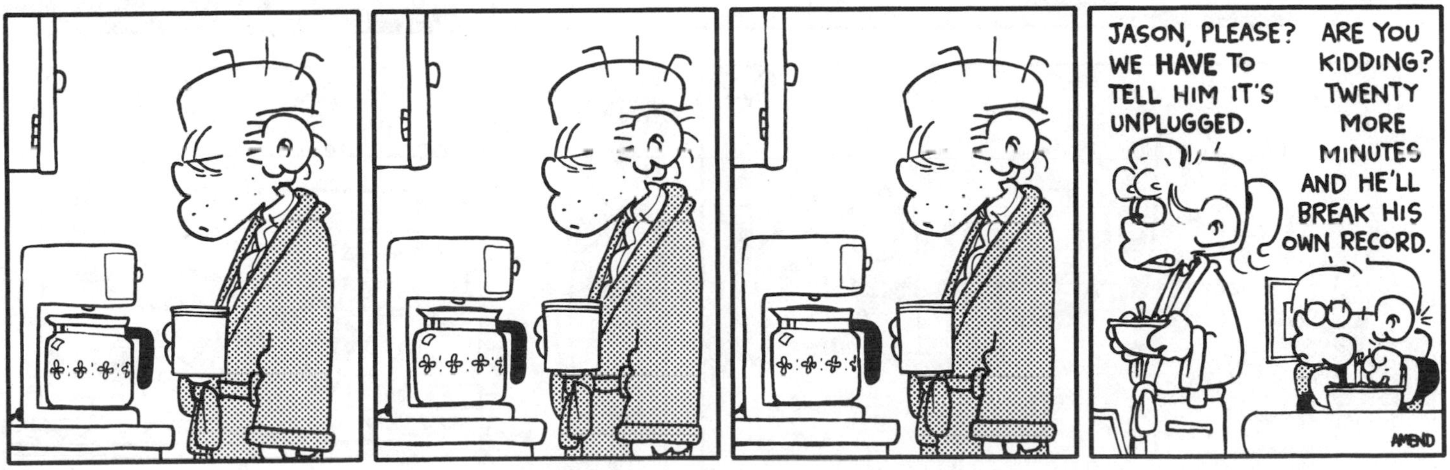
JASON, PLEASE? WE HAVE TO TELL HIM IT'S UNPLUGGED.
ARE YOU KIDDING? TWENTY MORE MINUTES AND HE'LL BREAK HIS OWN RECORD.
AMEND

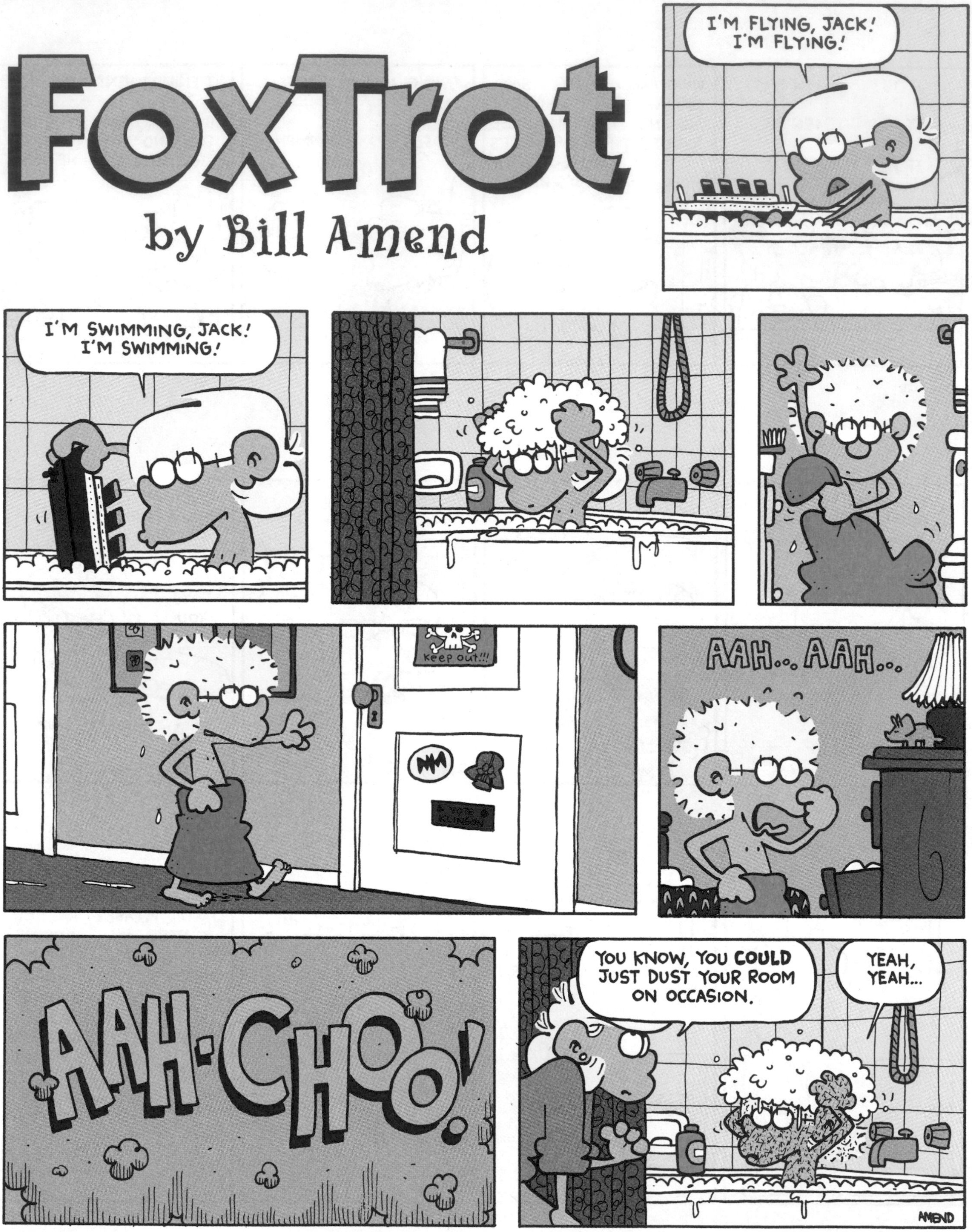
FoxTrot
by Bill Amend
I'M FLYING, JACK! I'M FLYING!
I'M SWIMMING, JACK! I'M SWIMMING!
KEEP OUT!!!
VOTE KLINGON
AAH... AAH...
AAH-CHOO!
YOU KNOW, YOU COULD JUST DUST YOUR ROOM ON OCCASION.
YEAH, YEAH...
AMEND

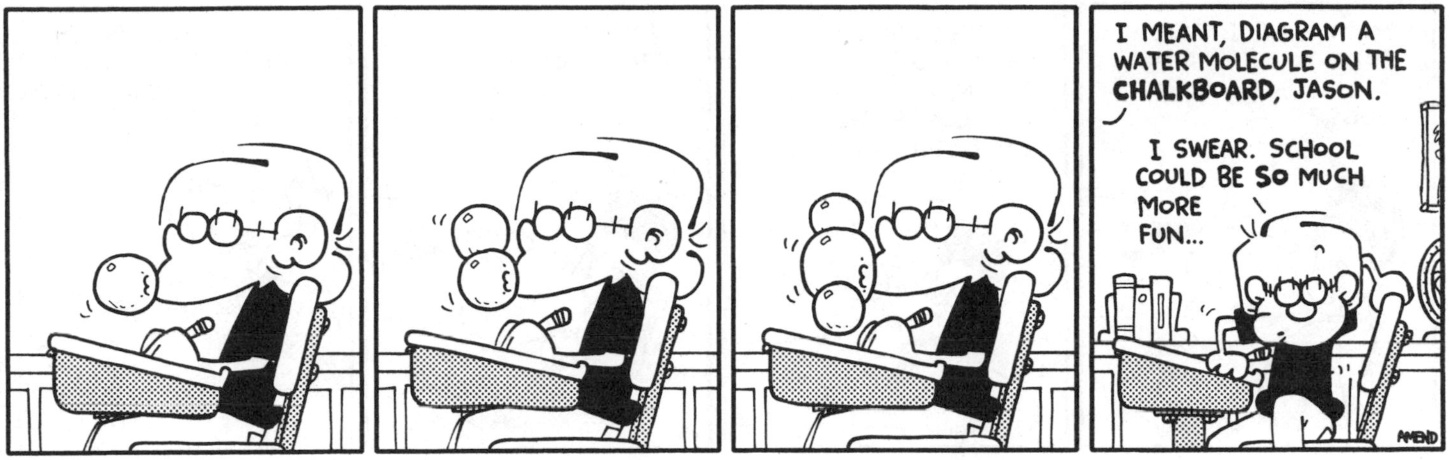
I MEANT, DIAGRAM A WATER MOLECULE ON THE CHALKBOARD, JASON.
I SWEAR. SCHOOL COULD BE SO MUCH MORE FUN...
AMEND

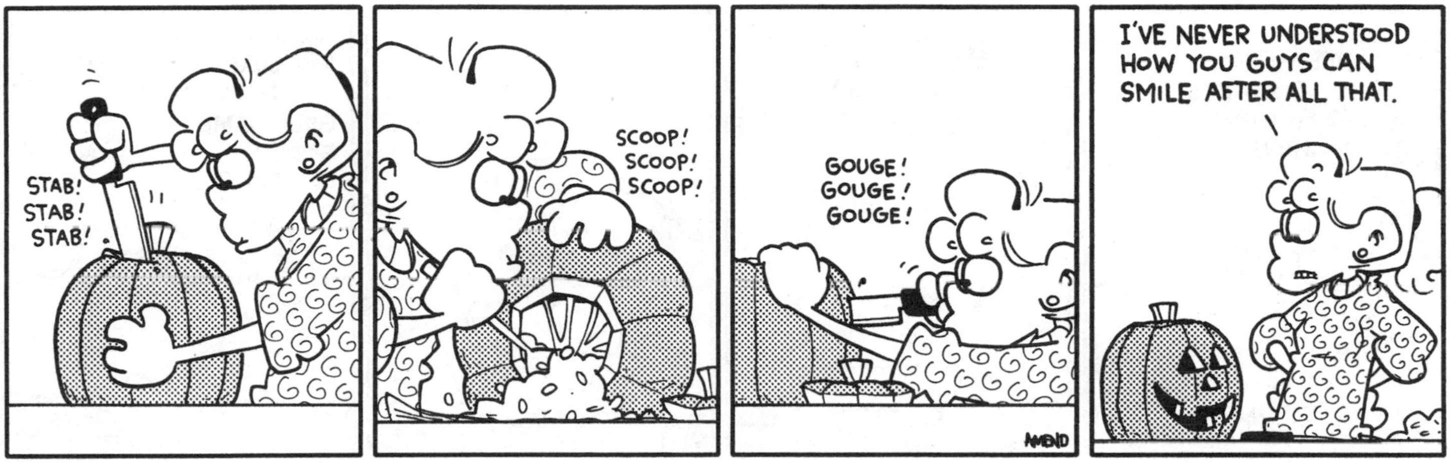
STAB! STAB! STAB!
SCOOP! SCOOP! SCOOP!
GOUGE! GOUGE! GOUGE!
AMEND
I'VE NEVER UNDERSTOOD HOW YOU GUYS CAN SMILE AFTER ALL THAT.

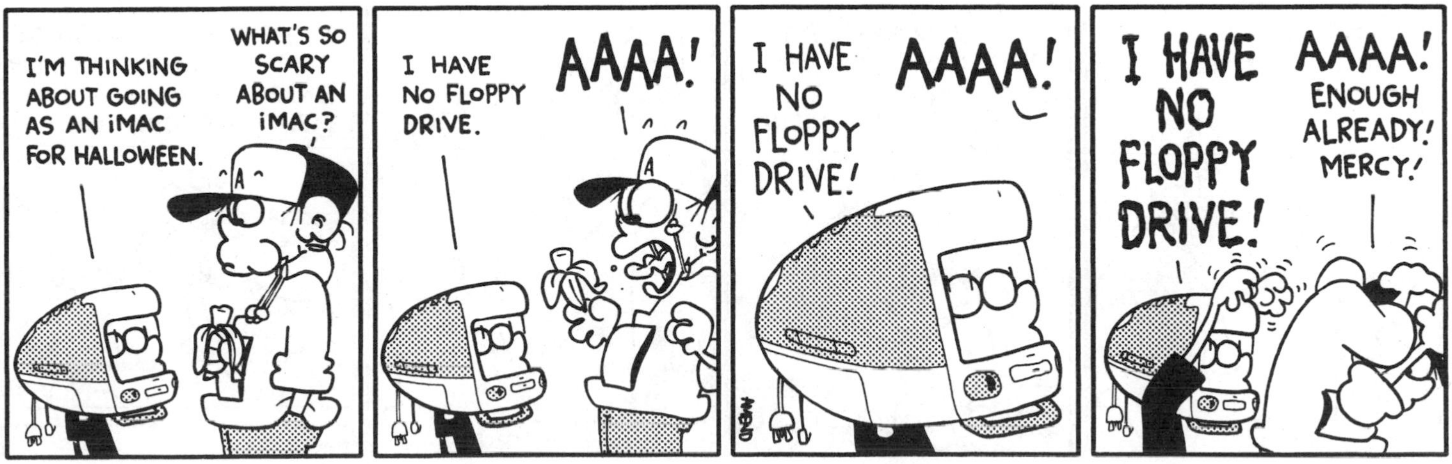
I'M THINKING ABOUT GOING AS AN iMAC FOR HALLOWEEN.
WHAT'S SO SCARY ABOUT AN iMAC?
I HAVE NO FLOPPY DRIVE.
AAAA!
AMEND
I HAVE NO FLOPPY DRIVE!
AAAA!
I HAVE NO FLOPPY DRIVE!
AAAA! ENOUGH ALREADY! MERCY!

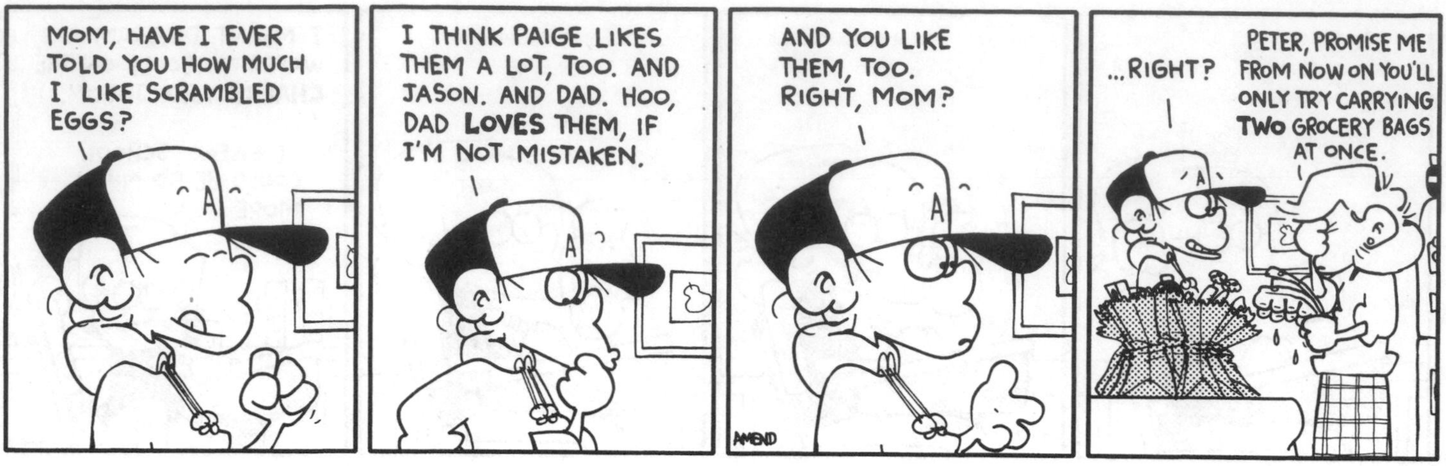
MOM, HAVE I EVER TOLD YOU HOW MUCH I LIKE SCRAMBLED EGGS?
I THINK PAIGE LIKES THEM A LOT, TOO. AND JASON. AND DAD. HOO, DAD **LOVES** THEM, IF I'M NOT MISTAKEN.
AND YOU LIKE THEM, TOO. RIGHT, MOM?
AMEND
...RIGHT?
PETER, PROMISE ME FROM NOW ON YOU'LL ONLY TRY CARRYING **TWO** GROCERY BAGS AT ONCE.

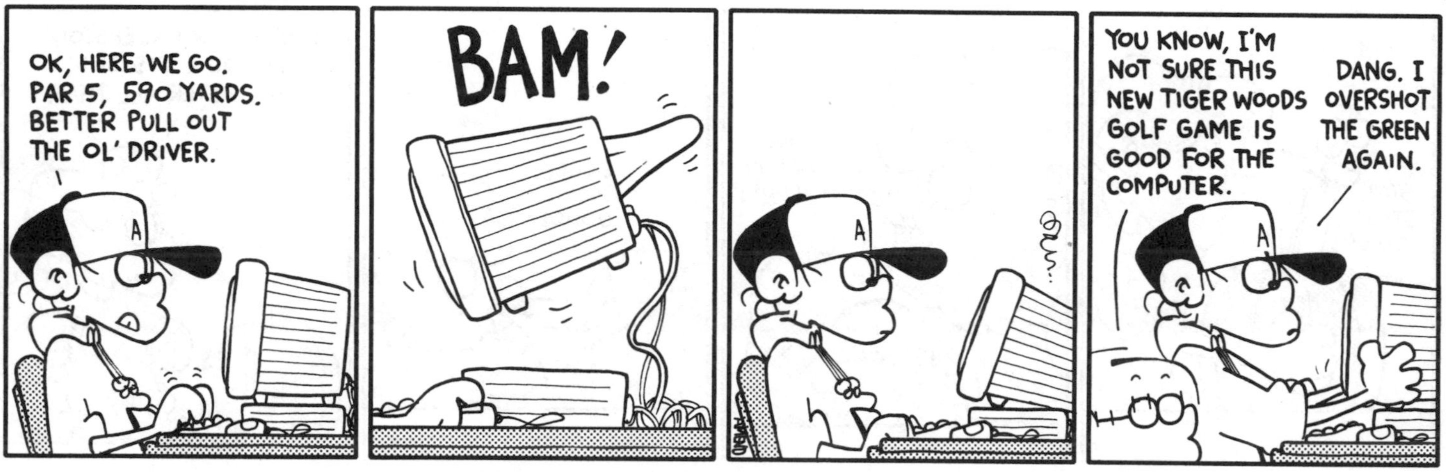
OK, HERE WE GO. PAR 5, 590 YARDS. BETTER PULL OUT THE OL' DRIVER.
BAM!
YOU KNOW, I'M NOT SURE THIS NEW TIGER WOODS GOLF GAME IS GOOD FOR THE COMPUTER.
DANG. I OVERSHOT THE GREEN AGAIN.

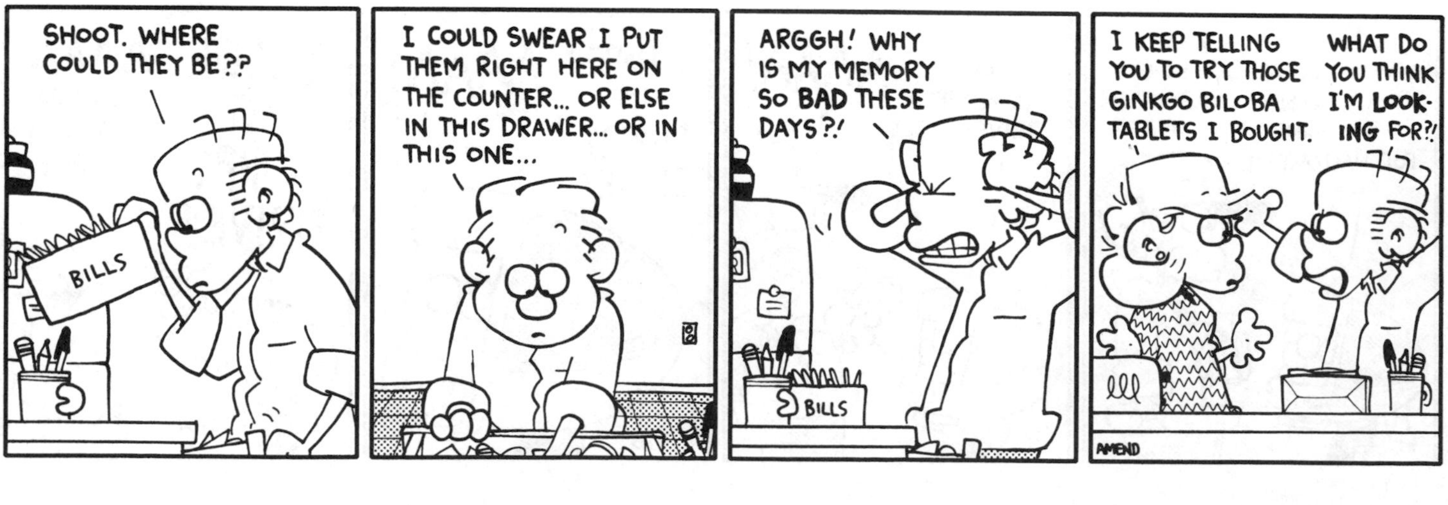
SHOOT. WHERE COULD THEY BE??
BILLS
I COULD SWEAR I PUT THEM RIGHT HERE ON THE COUNTER... OR ELSE IN THIS DRAWER... OR IN THIS ONE...
ARGGH! WHY IS MY MEMORY SO **BAD** THESE DAYS?!
BILLS
I KEEP TELLING YOU TO TRY THOSE GINKGO BILOBA TABLETS I BOUGHT.
WHAT DO YOU THINK I'M **LOOK-ING** FOR?!
AMEND

FoxTrot

by Bill Amend

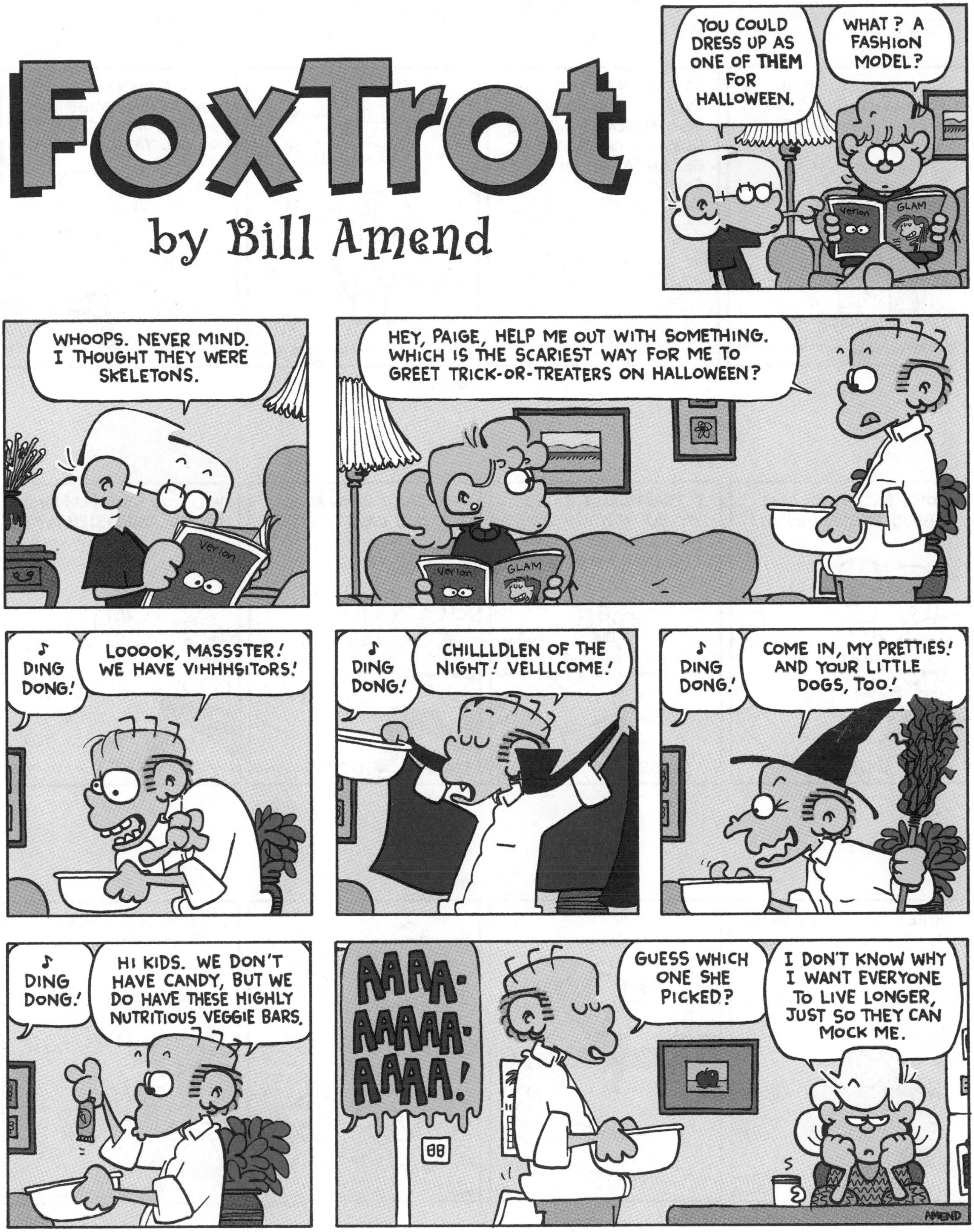
YOU COULD DRESS UP AS ONE OF THEM FOR HALLOWEEN.
WHAT? A FASHION MODEL?
Verlon
GLAM
WHOOPS. NEVER MIND. I THOUGHT THEY WERE SKELETONS.
HEY, PAIGE, HELP ME OUT WITH SOMETHING. WHICH IS THE SCARIEST WAY FOR ME TO GREET TRICK-OR-TREATERS ON HALLOWEEN?
♪ DING DONG!
LOOOOK, MASSSTER! WE HAVE VIHHHSITORS!
♪ DING DONG!
CHILLLDLEN OF THE NIGHT! VELLLCOME!
♪ DING DONG!
COME IN, MY PRETTIES! AND YOUR LITTLE DOGS, TOO!
♪ DING DONG!
HI KIDS. WE DON'T HAVE CANDY, BUT WE DO HAVE THESE HIGHLY NUTRITIOUS VEGGIE BARS.
AAAA-AAAAA-AAAA!
GUESS WHICH ONE SHE PICKED?
I DON'T KNOW WHY I WANT EVERYONE TO LIVE LONGER, JUST SO THEY CAN MOCK ME.
AMEND

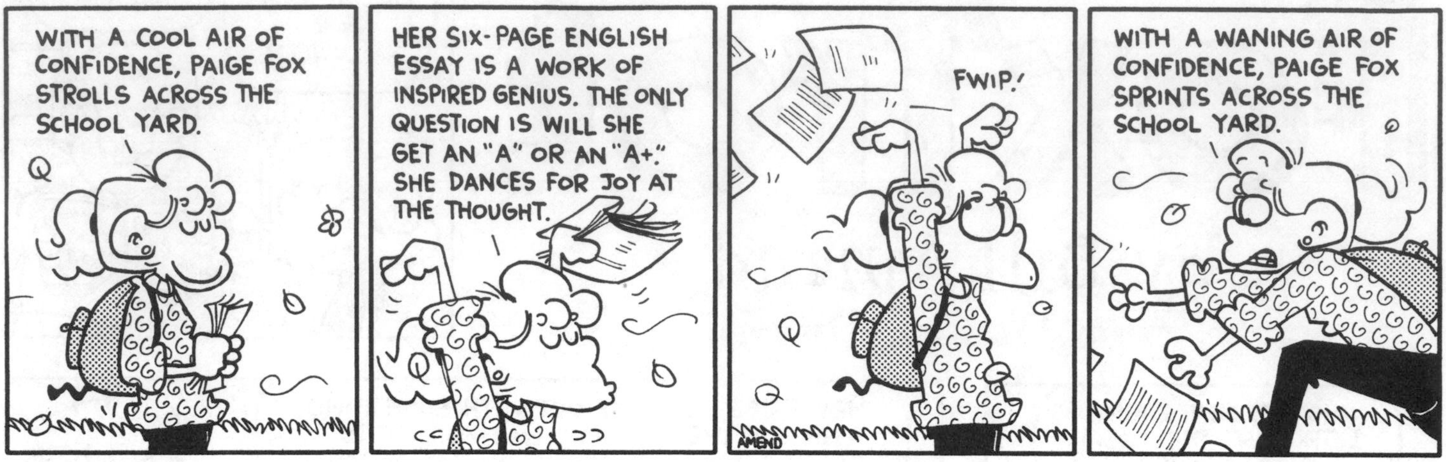
WITH A COOL AIR OF CONFIDENCE, PAIGE FOX STROLLS ACROSS THE SCHOOL YARD.
HER SIX-PAGE ENGLISH ESSAY IS A WORK OF INSPIRED GENIUS. THE ONLY QUESTION IS WILL SHE GET AN "A" OR AN "A+." SHE DANCES FOR JOY AT THE THOUGHT.
FWIP!
WITH A WANING AIR OF CONFIDENCE, PAIGE FOX SPRINTS ACROSS THE SCHOOL YARD.

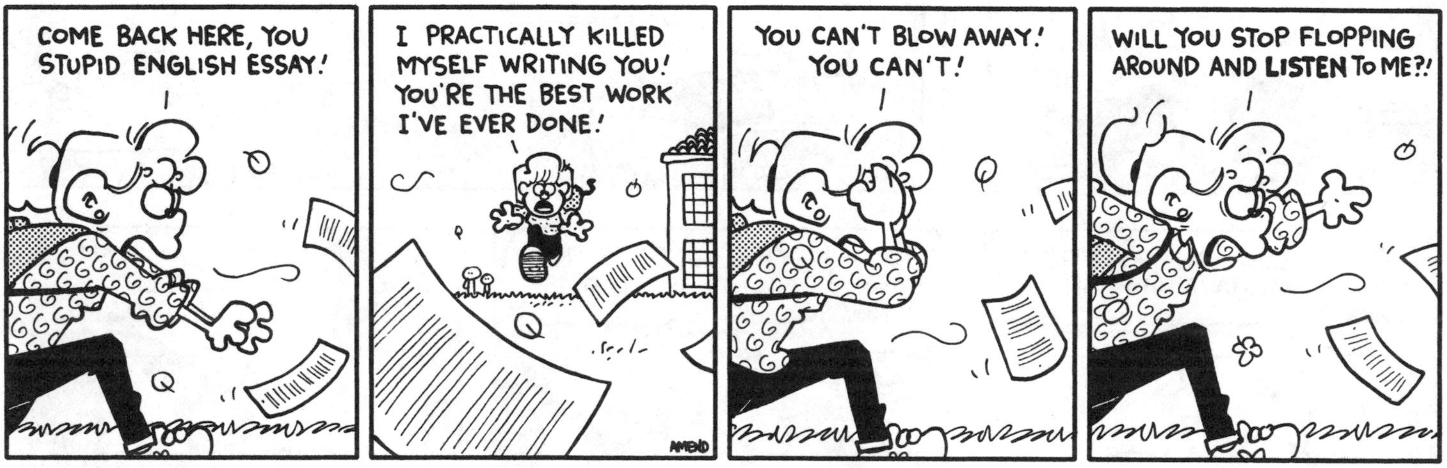
COME BACK HERE, YOU STUPID ENGLISH ESSAY!
I PRACTICALLY KILLED MYSELF WRITING YOU! YOU'RE THE BEST WORK I'VE EVER DONE!
YOU CAN'T BLOW AWAY! YOU CAN'T!
WILL YOU STOP FLOPPING AROUND AND LISTEN TO ME?!

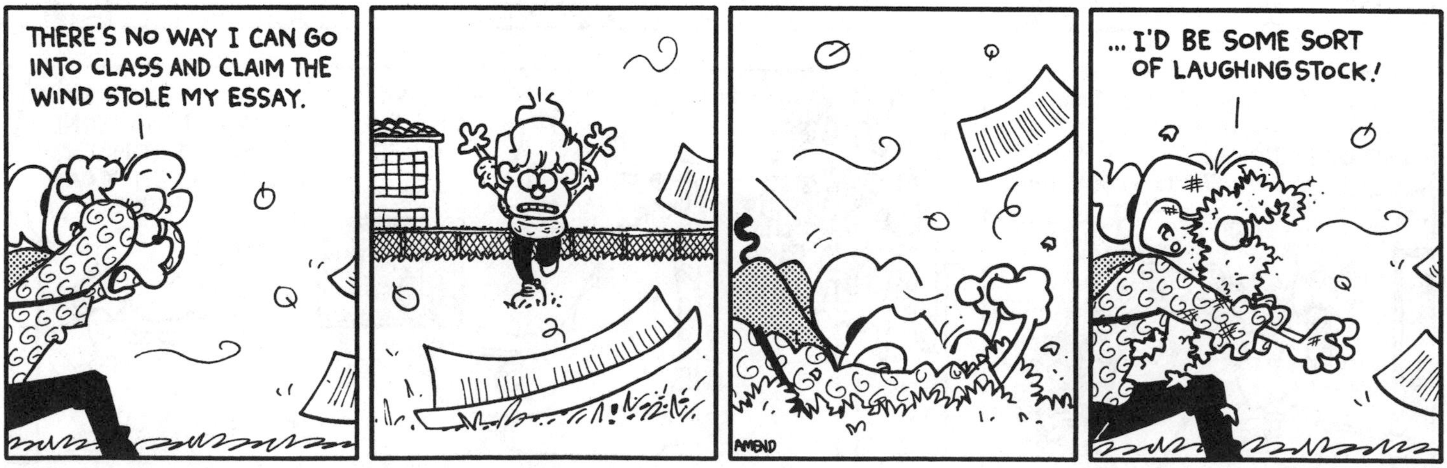
THERE'S NO WAY I CAN GO INTO CLASS AND CLAIM THE WIND STOLE MY ESSAY.
... I'D BE SOME SORT OF LAUGHINGSTOCK!

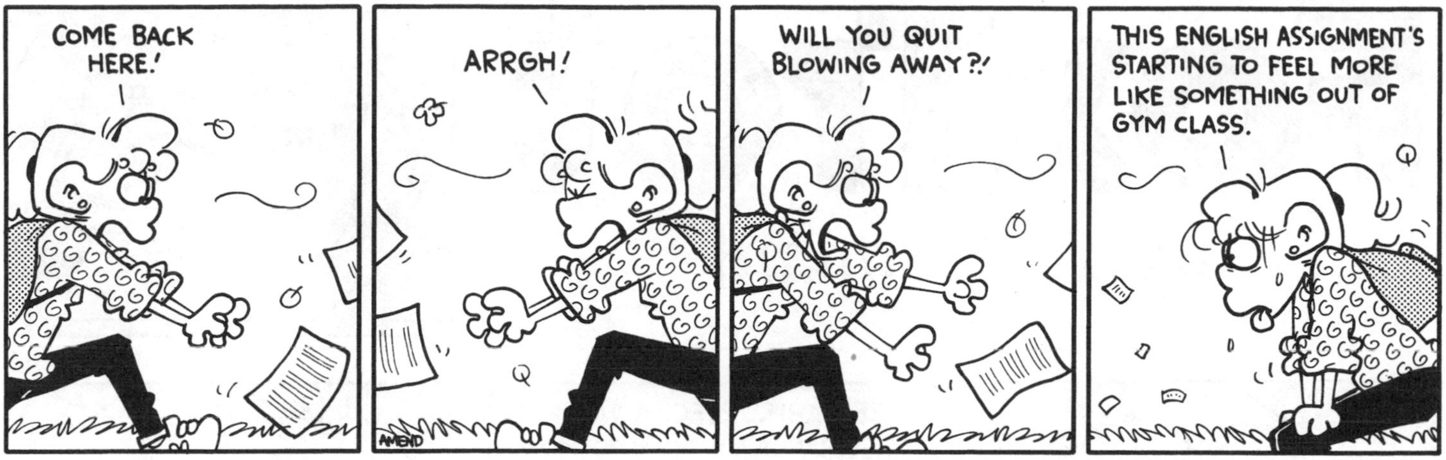
COME BACK HERE!
ARRGH!
WILL YOU QUIT BLOWING AWAY?!
THIS ENGLISH ASSIGNMENT'S STARTING TO FEEL MORE LIKE SOMETHING OUT OF GYM CLASS.

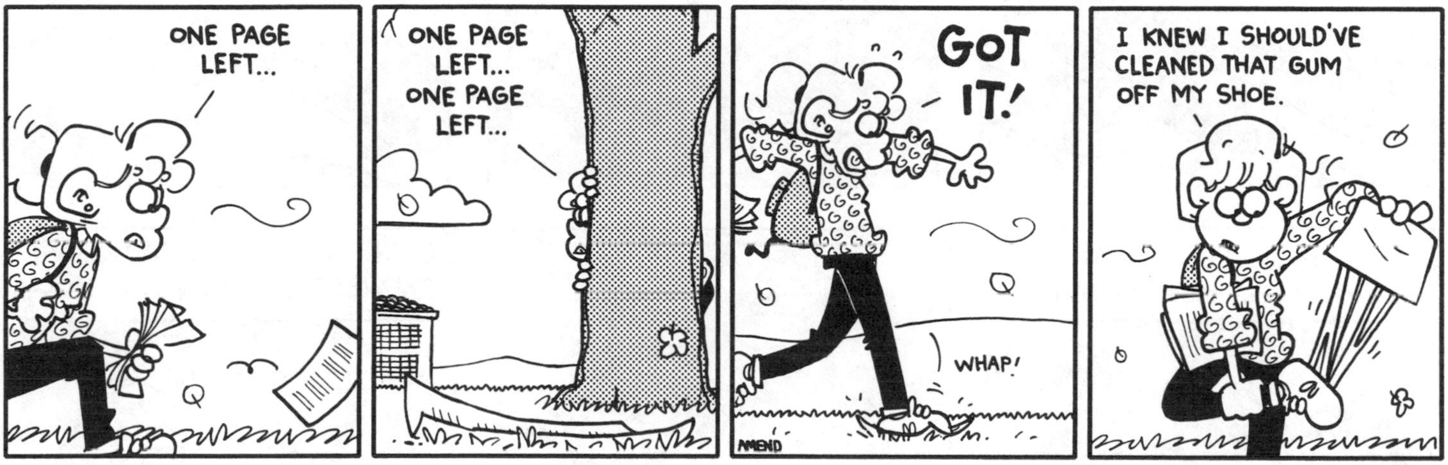
ONE PAGE LEFT...
ONE PAGE LEFT... ONE PAGE LEFT...
GOT IT!
WHAP!
I KNEW I SHOULD'VE CLEANED THAT GUM OFF MY SHOE.

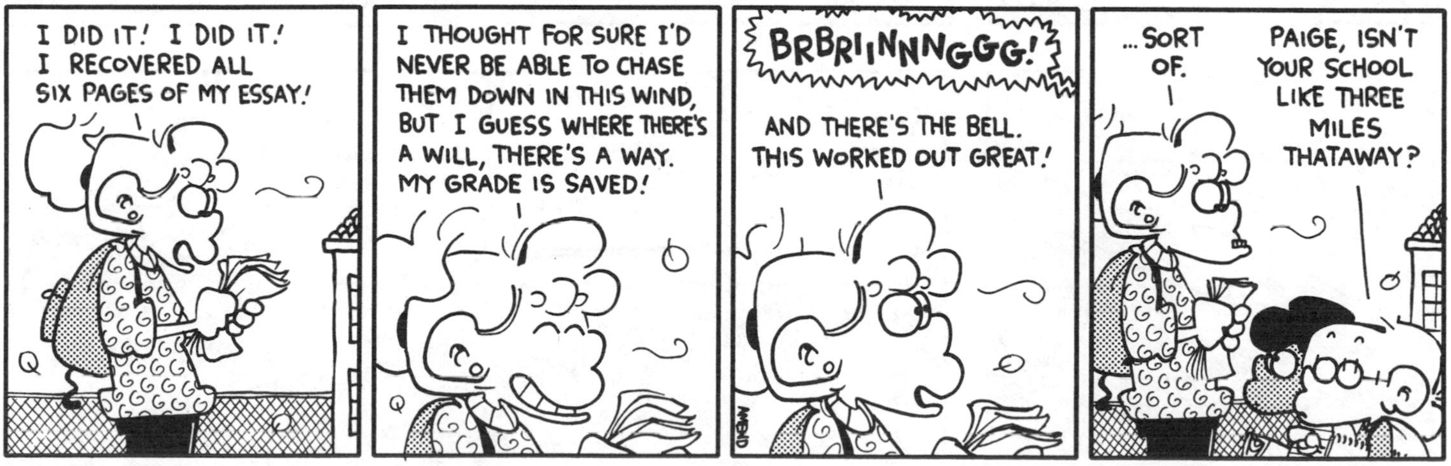
I DID IT! I DID IT! I RECOVERED ALL SIX PAGES OF MY ESSAY!
I THOUGHT FOR SURE I'D NEVER BE ABLE TO CHASE THEM DOWN IN THIS WIND, BUT I GUESS WHERE THERE'S A WILL, THERE'S A WAY. MY GRADE IS SAVED!
BRBRIINNNGGG!
AND THERE'S THE BELL. THIS WORKED OUT GREAT!
...SORT OF.
PAIGE, ISN'T YOUR SCHOOL LIKE THREE MILES THATAWAY?

FoxTrot
by Bill Amend
CHEE-SAHH... PEECHA WONKIE CHEWBACCA! WOO HOO HOO!
CHEE-SAHH... PEECHA WONKIE CHEWBACCA! WOO HOO HOO!
CHEE-SAHH... PEECHA WONKIE CHEWBACCA! WOO HOO HOO!
CHEE-SAHH... PEECHA WONKIE CHEWBACCA! WOO HOO HOO!
AMEND
I'M TELLING YOU, MARCUS, IT'S LIKE STARING INTO A MIRROR.
LOOK, YOU MAY FEEL LIKE JABBA — I FEEL LIKE THE DEATH STAR.
I SEE YOUR HALLOWEEN CANDY LASTED UNTIL MID-MORNING, AT LEAST.

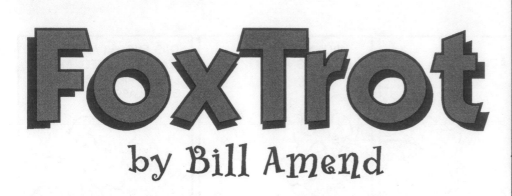

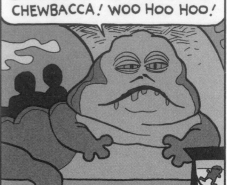

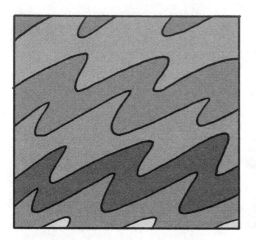

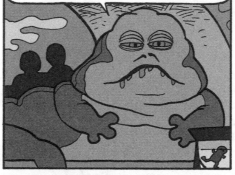

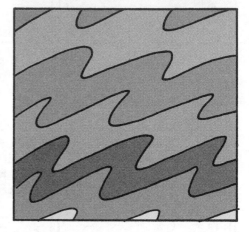

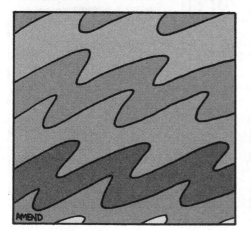

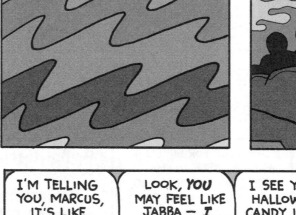

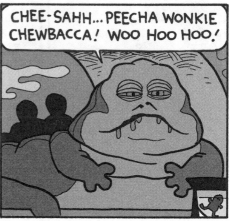

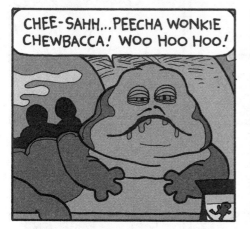

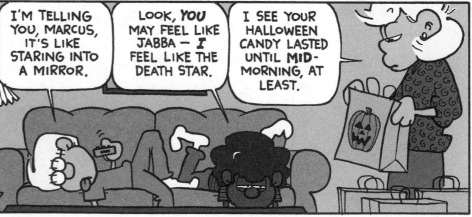

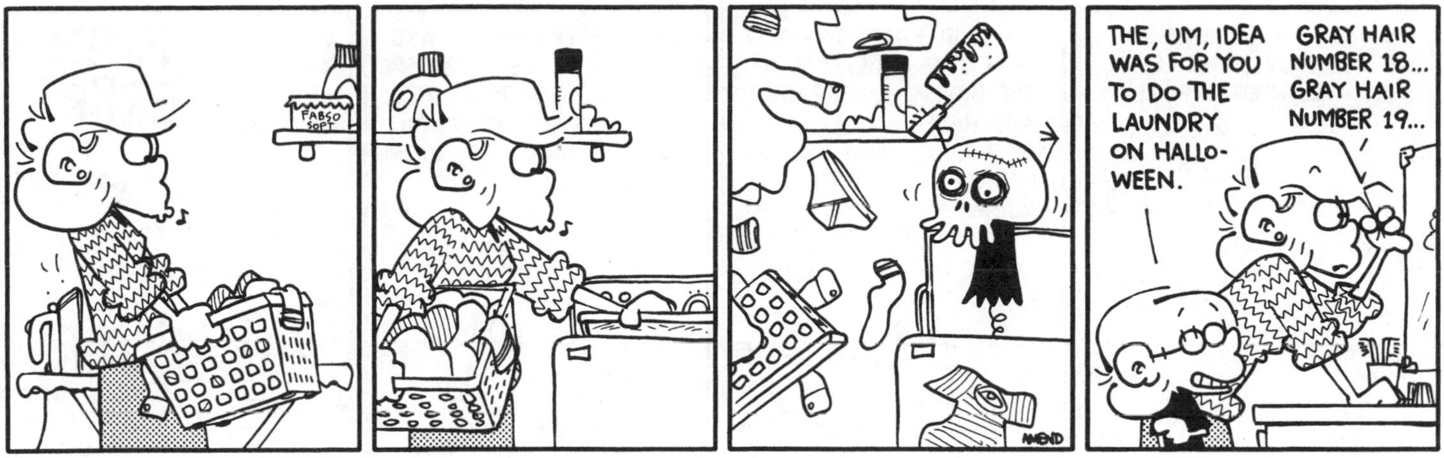
FABSO SOFT
THE, UM, IDEA WAS FOR YOU TO DO THE LAUNDRY ON HALLO-WEEN.
GRAY HAIR NUMBER 18... GRAY HAIR NUMBER 19...
AMEND

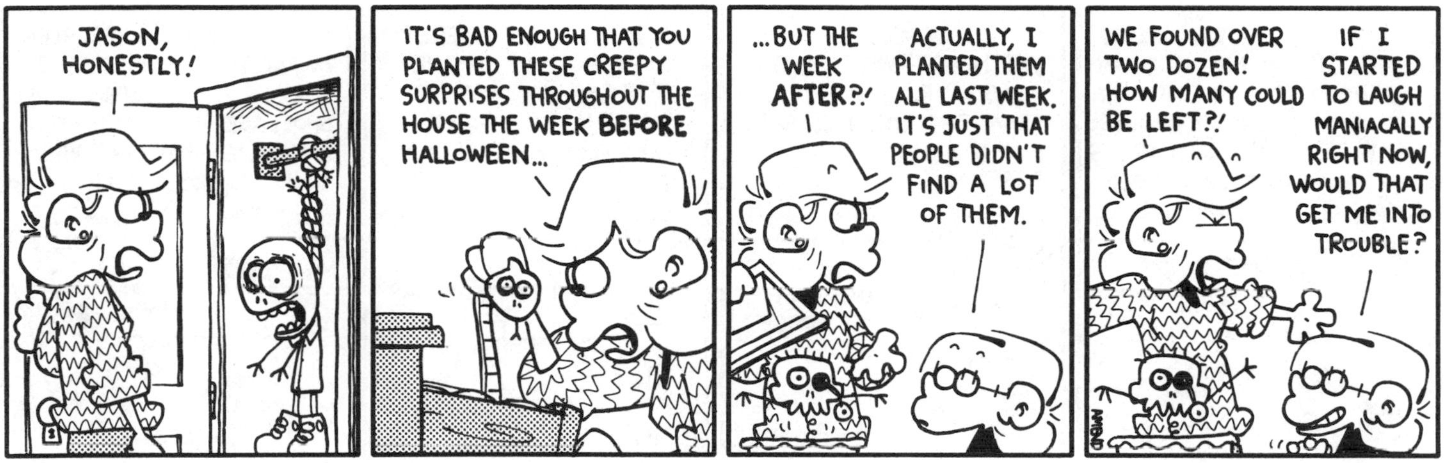
JASON, HONESTLY!
IT'S BAD ENOUGH THAT YOU PLANTED THESE CREEPY SURPRISES THROUGHOUT THE HOUSE THE WEEK BEFORE HALLOWEEN...
...BUT THE WEEK AFTER?!
ACTUALLY, I PLANTED THEM ALL LAST WEEK. IT'S JUST THAT PEOPLE DIDN'T FIND A LOT OF THEM.
WE FOUND OVER TWO DOZEN! HOW MANY COULD BE LEFT?!
IF I STARTED TO LAUGH MANIACALLY RIGHT NOW, WOULD THAT GET ME INTO TROUBLE?

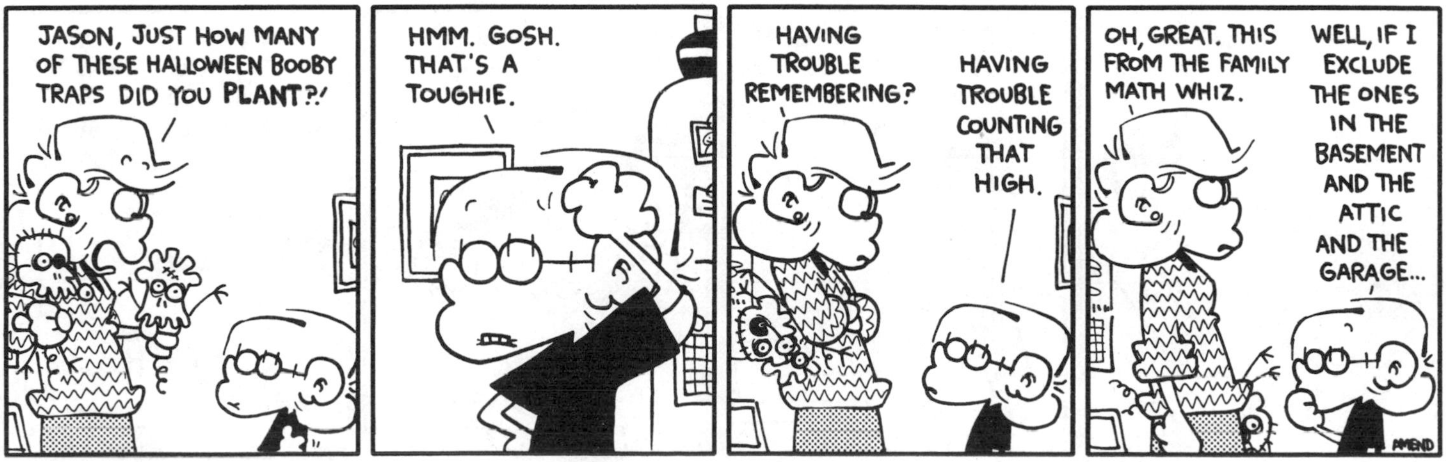
JASON, JUST HOW MANY OF THESE HALLOWEEN BOOBY TRAPS DID YOU PLANT?!
HMM. GOSH. THAT'S A TOUGHIE.
HAVING TROUBLE REMEMBERING?
HAVING TROUBLE COUNTING THAT HIGH.
OH, GREAT. THIS FROM THE FAMILY MATH WHIZ.
WELL, IF I EXCLUDE THE ONES IN THE BASEMENT AND THE ATTIC AND THE GARAGE...
AMEND

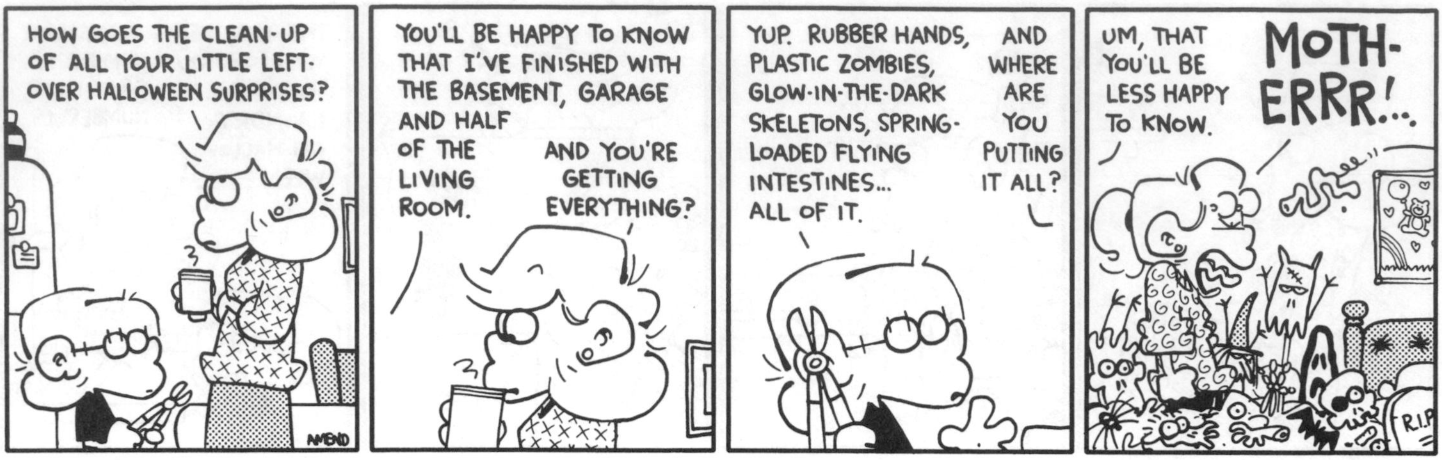
HOW GOES THE CLEAN-UP OF ALL YOUR LITTLE LEFT-OVER HALLOWEEN SURPRISES?
YOU'LL BE HAPPY TO KNOW THAT I'VE FINISHED WITH THE BASEMENT, GARAGE AND HALF OF THE LIVING ROOM.
AND YOU'RE GETTING EVERYTHING?
YUP. RUBBER HANDS, PLASTIC ZOMBIES, GLOW-IN-THE-DARK SKELETONS, SPRING-LOADED FLYING INTESTINES... ALL OF IT.
AND WHERE ARE YOU PUTTING IT ALL?
UM, THAT YOU'LL BE LESS HAPPY TO KNOW.
MOTH-ERRR!...
R.I.P.

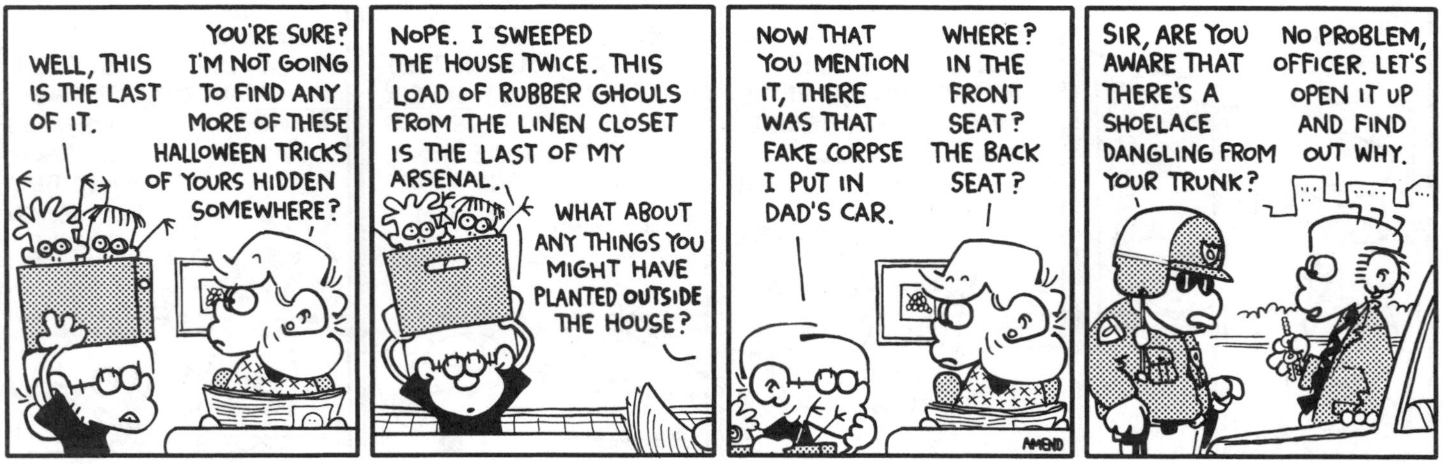
WELL, THIS IS THE LAST OF IT.
YOU'RE SURE? I'M NOT GOING TO FIND ANY MORE OF THESE HALLOWEEN TRICKS OF YOURS HIDDEN SOMEWHERE?
NOPE. I SWEEPED THE HOUSE TWICE. THIS LOAD OF RUBBER GHOULS FROM THE LINEN CLOSET IS THE LAST OF MY ARSENAL.
WHAT ABOUT ANY THINGS YOU MIGHT HAVE PLANTED OUTSIDE THE HOUSE?
NOW THAT YOU MENTION IT, THERE WAS THAT FAKE CORPSE I PUT IN DAD'S CAR.
WHERE? IN THE FRONT SEAT? THE BACK SEAT?
SIR, ARE YOU AWARE THAT THERE'S A SHOELACE DANGLING FROM YOUR TRUNK?
NO PROBLEM, OFFICER. LET'S OPEN IT UP AND FIND OUT WHY.

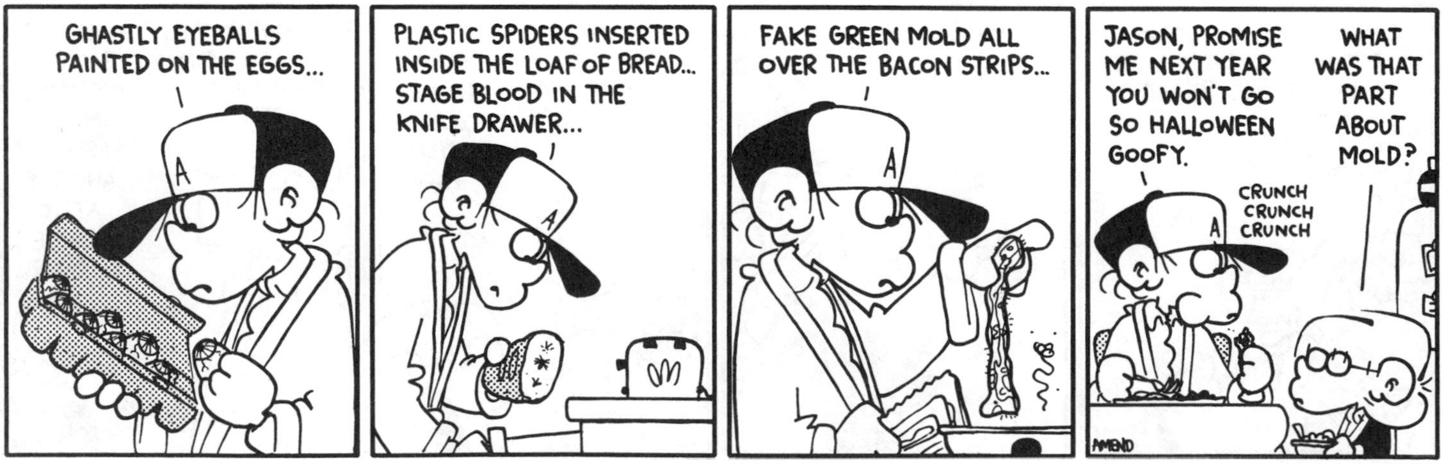
GHASTLY EYEBALLS PAINTED ON THE EGGS...
PLASTIC SPIDERS INSERTED INSIDE THE LOAF OF BREAD... STAGE BLOOD IN THE KNIFE DRAWER...
FAKE GREEN MOLD ALL OVER THE BACON STRIPS...
JASON, PROMISE ME NEXT YEAR YOU WON'T GO SO HALLOWEEN GOOFY.
CRUNCH CRUNCH CRUNCH
WHAT WAS THAT PART ABOUT MOLD?

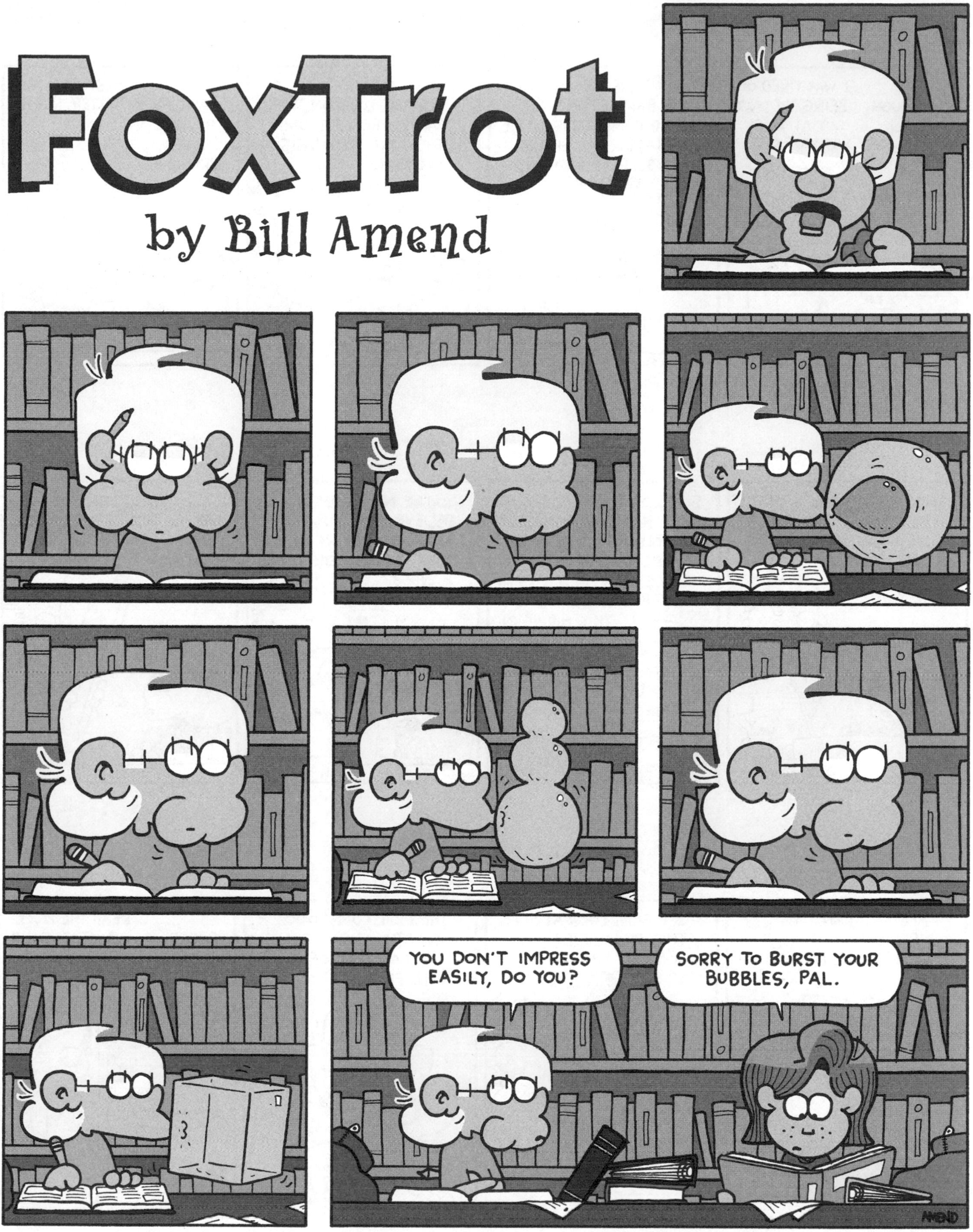
FoxTrot
by Bill Amend
YOU DON'T IMPRESS EASILY, DO YOU?
SORRY TO BURST YOUR BUBBLES, PAL.
AMEND

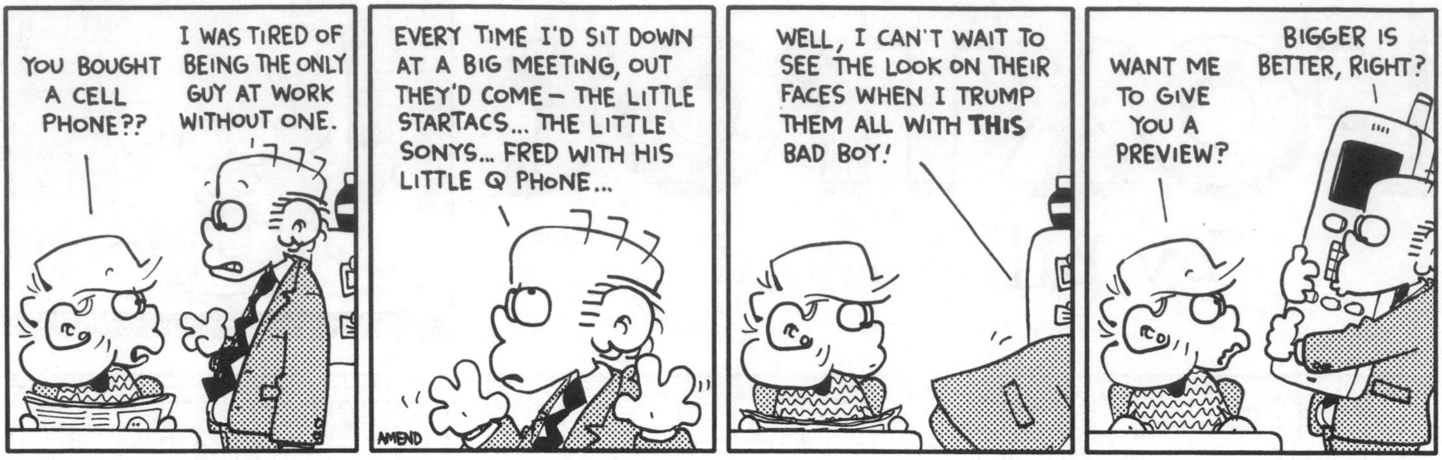
YOU BOUGHT A CELL PHONE??
I WAS TIRED OF BEING THE ONLY GUY AT WORK WITHOUT ONE.
EVERY TIME I'D SIT DOWN AT A BIG MEETING, OUT THEY'D COME – THE LITTLE STARTACS... THE LITTLE SONYS... FRED WITH HIS LITTLE Q PHONE...
AMEND
WELL, I CAN'T WAIT TO SEE THE LOOK ON THEIR FACES WHEN I TRUMP THEM ALL WITH **THIS** BAD BOY!
WANT ME TO GIVE YOU A PREVIEW?
BIGGER IS BETTER, RIGHT?

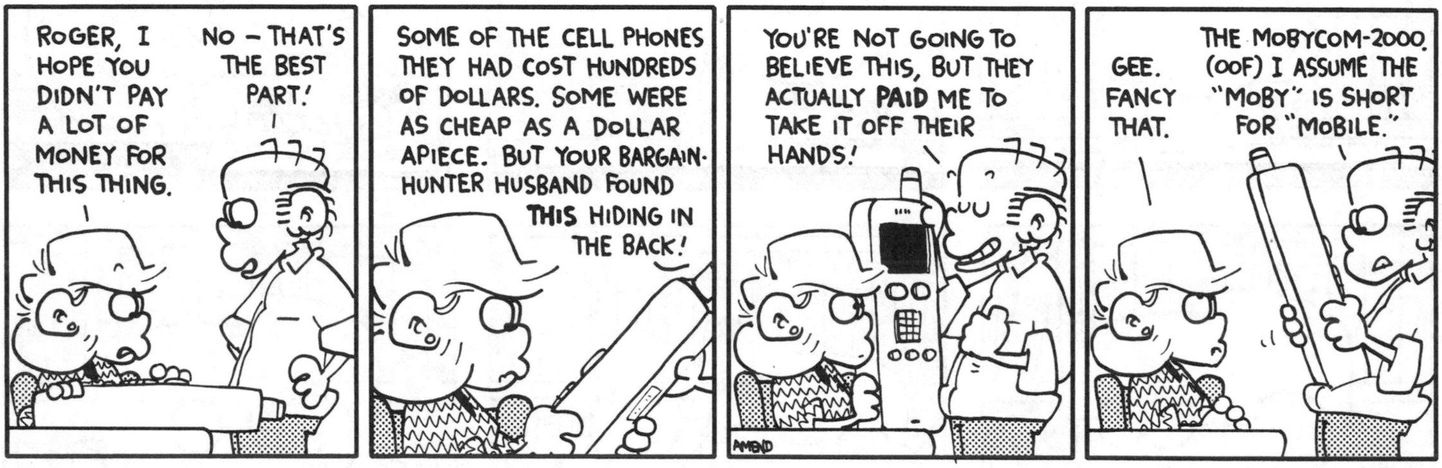
ROGER, I HOPE YOU DIDN'T PAY A LOT OF MONEY FOR THIS THING.
NO – THAT'S THE BEST PART!
SOME OF THE CELL PHONES THEY HAD COST HUNDREDS OF DOLLARS. SOME WERE AS CHEAP AS A DOLLAR APIECE. BUT YOUR BARGAIN-HUNTER HUSBAND FOUND **THIS** HIDING IN THE BACK!
YOU'RE NOT GOING TO BELIEVE THIS, BUT THEY ACTUALLY **PAID** ME TO TAKE IT OFF THEIR HANDS!
AMEND
GEE. FANCY THAT.
THE MOBYCOM-2000. (OOF) I ASSUME THE "MOBY" IS SHORT FOR "MOBILE."

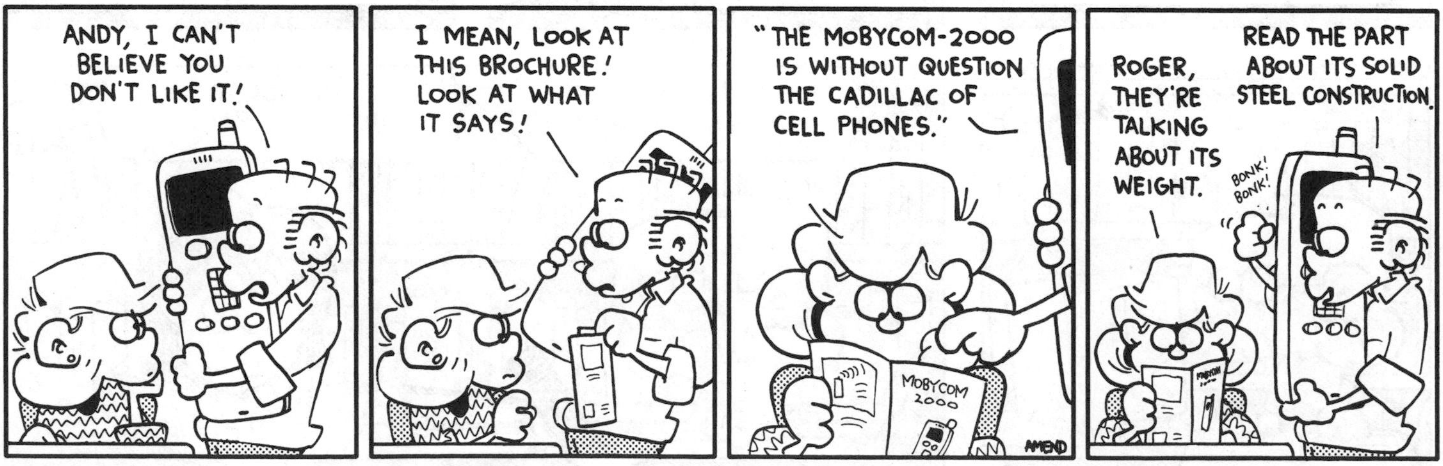
ANDY, I CAN'T BELIEVE YOU DON'T LIKE IT!
I MEAN, LOOK AT THIS BROCHURE! LOOK AT WHAT IT SAYS!
"THE MOBYCOM-2000 IS WITHOUT QUESTION THE CADILLAC OF CELL PHONES."
MOBYCOM 2000
AMEND
ROGER, THEY'RE TALKING ABOUT ITS WEIGHT.
READ THE PART ABOUT ITS SOLID STEEL CONSTRUCTION.
BONK! BONK!

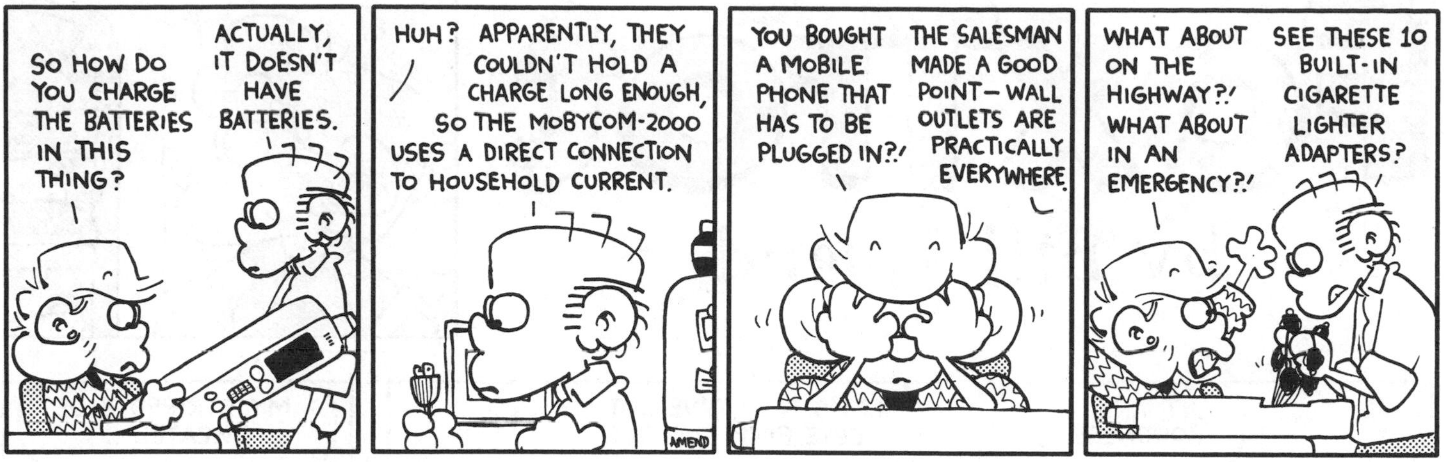
SO HOW DO YOU CHARGE THE BATTERIES IN THIS THING?
ACTUALLY, IT DOESN'T HAVE BATTERIES.
HUH?
APPARENTLY, THEY COULDN'T HOLD A CHARGE LONG ENOUGH, SO THE MOBYCOM-2000 USES A DIRECT CONNECTION TO HOUSEHOLD CURRENT.
AMEND
YOU BOUGHT A MOBILE PHONE THAT HAS TO BE PLUGGED IN?!
THE SALESMAN MADE A GOOD POINT— WALL OUTLETS ARE PRACTICALLY EVERYWHERE.
WHAT ABOUT ON THE HIGHWAY?! WHAT ABOUT IN AN EMERGENCY?!
SEE THESE 10 BUILT-IN CIGARETTE LIGHTER ADAPTERS?

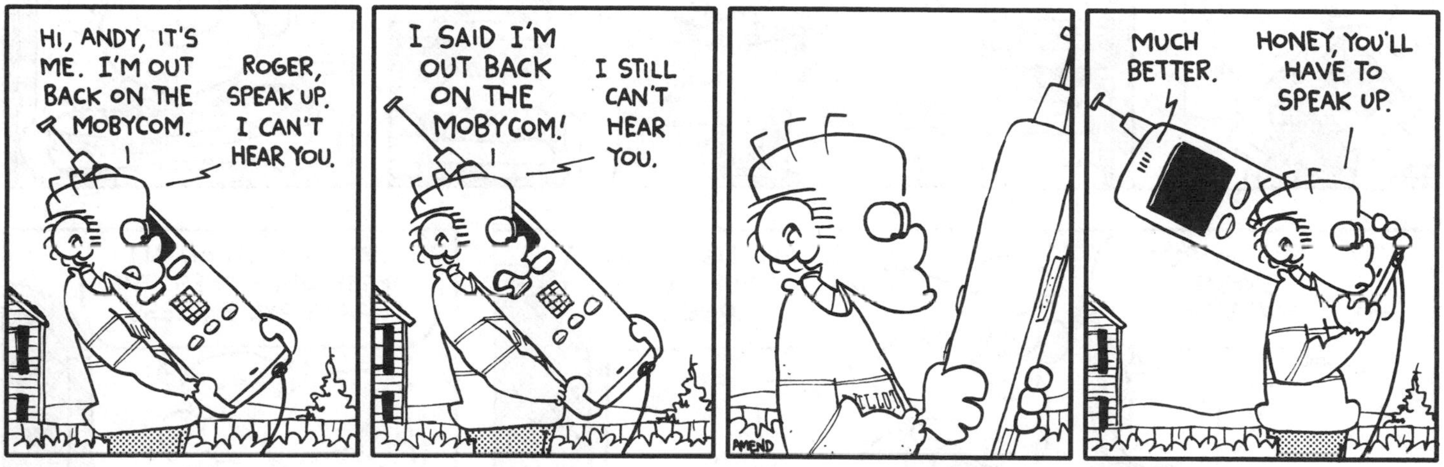
HI, ANDY, IT'S ME. I'M OUT BACK ON THE MOBYCOM.
ROGER, SPEAK UP. I CAN'T HEAR YOU.
I SAID I'M OUT BACK ON THE MOBYCOM!
I STILL CAN'T HEAR YOU.
AMEND
MUCH BETTER.
HONEY, YOU'LL HAVE TO SPEAK UP.

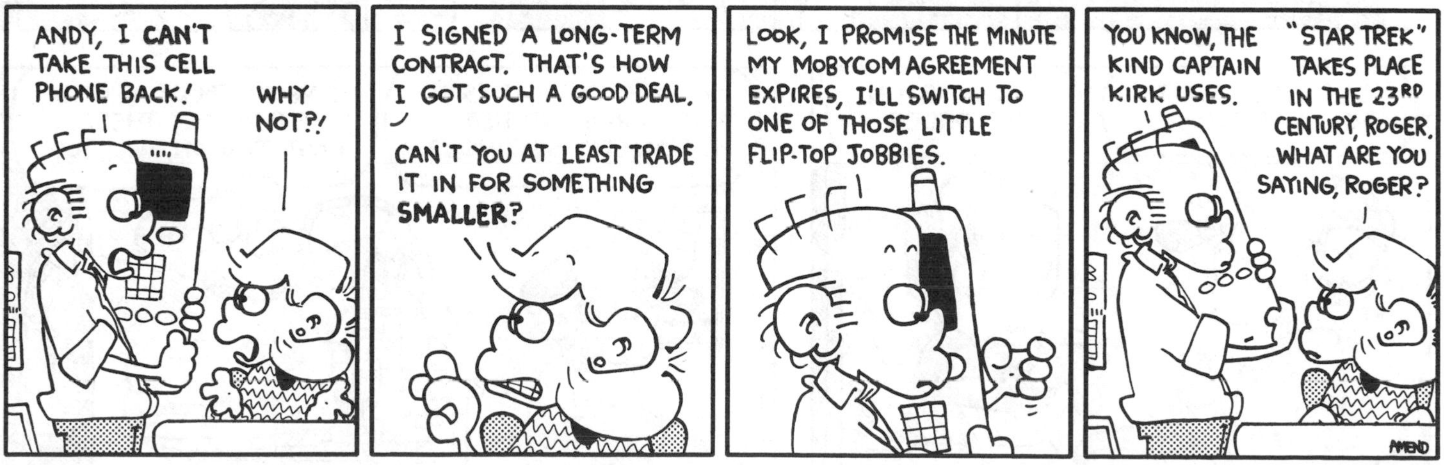
ANDY, I CAN'T TAKE THIS CELL PHONE BACK!
WHY NOT?!
I SIGNED A LONG-TERM CONTRACT. THAT'S HOW I GOT SUCH A GOOD DEAL.
CAN'T YOU AT LEAST TRADE IT IN FOR SOMETHING SMALLER?
LOOK, I PROMISE THE MINUTE MY MOBYCOM AGREEMENT EXPIRES, I'LL SWITCH TO ONE OF THOSE LITTLE FLIP-TOP JOBBIES.
YOU KNOW, THE KIND CAPTAIN KIRK USES.
"STAR TREK" TAKES PLACE IN THE 23RD CENTURY, ROGER. WHAT ARE YOU SAYING, ROGER?
AMEND

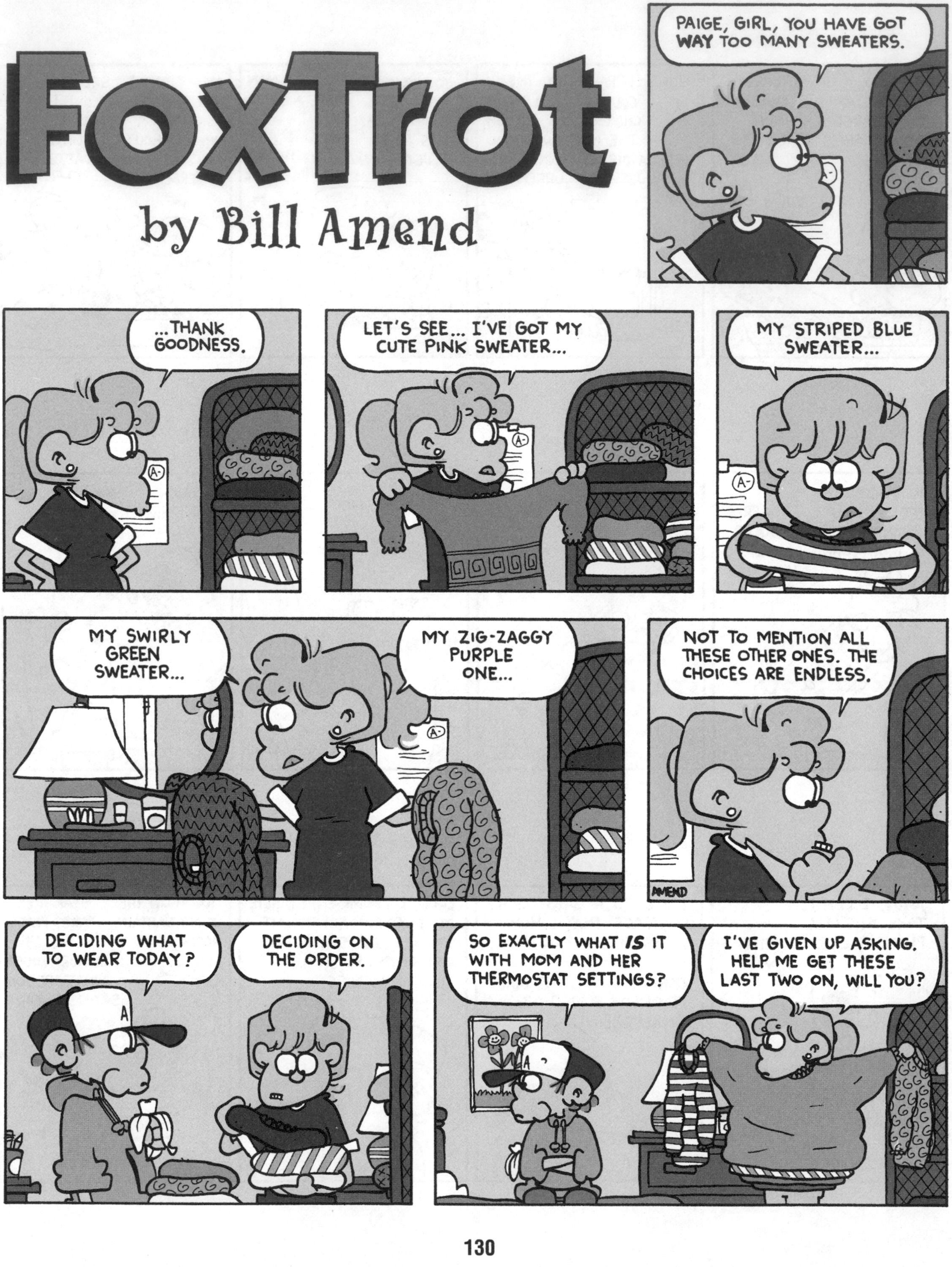
FoxTrot
by Bill Amend
PAIGE, GIRL, YOU HAVE GOT WAY TOO MANY SWEATERS.
...THANK GOODNESS.
LET'S SEE... I'VE GOT MY CUTE PINK SWEATER...
MY STRIPED BLUE SWEATER...
MY SWIRLY GREEN SWEATER...
MY ZIG-ZAGGY PURPLE ONE...
NOT TO MENTION ALL THESE OTHER ONES. THE CHOICES ARE ENDLESS.
AMEND
DECIDING WHAT TO WEAR TODAY?
DECIDING ON THE ORDER.
SO EXACTLY WHAT IS IT WITH MOM AND HER THERMOSTAT SETTINGS?
I'VE GIVEN UP ASKING. HELP ME GET THESE LAST TWO ON, WILL YOU?

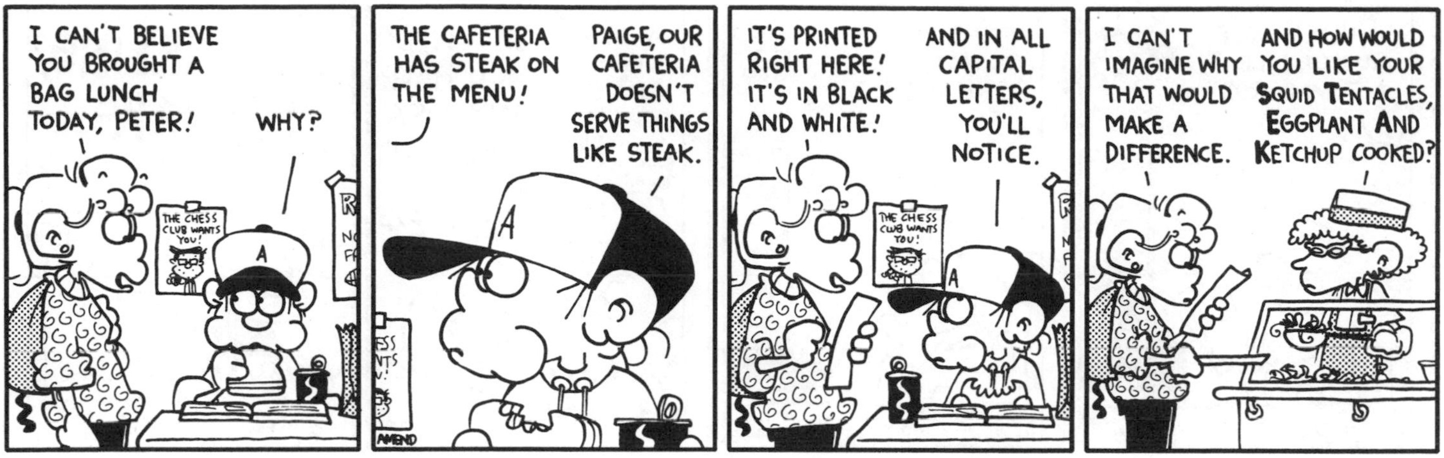
I CAN'T BELIEVE YOU BROUGHT A BAG LUNCH TODAY, PETER!
WHY?
THE CHESS CLUB WANTS YOU!
THE CAFETERIA HAS STEAK ON THE MENU!
PAIGE, OUR CAFETERIA DOESN'T SERVE THINGS LIKE STEAK.
AMEND
IT'S PRINTED RIGHT HERE! IT'S IN BLACK AND WHITE!
AND IN ALL CAPITAL LETTERS, YOU'LL NOTICE.
THE CHESS CLUB WANTS YOU!
I CAN'T IMAGINE WHY THAT WOULD MAKE A DIFFERENCE.
AND HOW WOULD YOU LIKE YOUR SQUID TENTACLES, EGGPLANT AND KETCHUP COOKED?

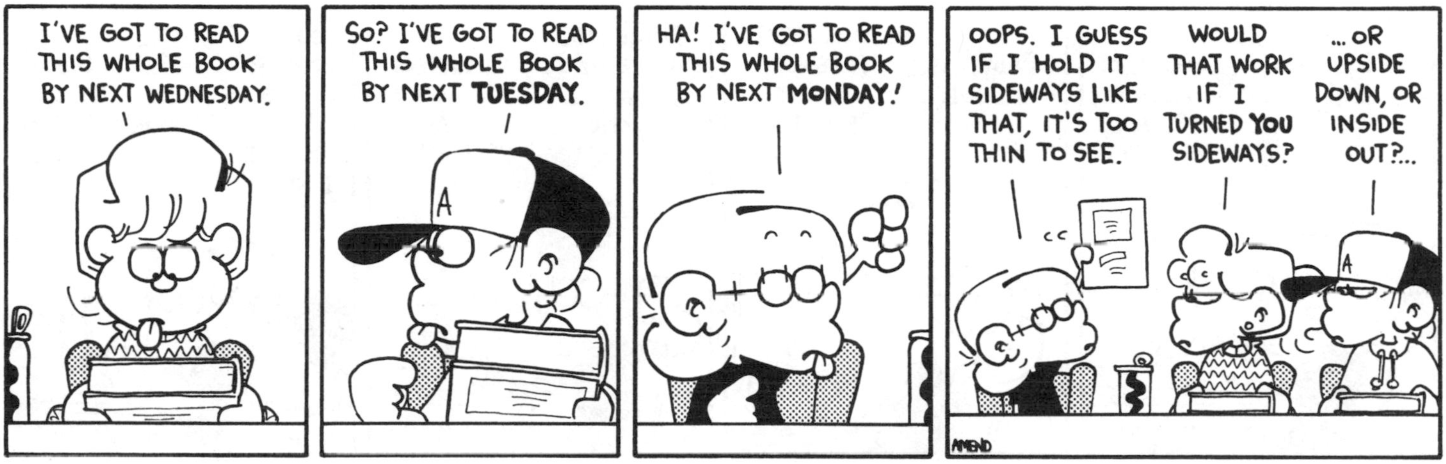
I'VE GOT TO READ THIS WHOLE BOOK BY NEXT WEDNESDAY.
SO? I'VE GOT TO READ THIS WHOLE BOOK BY NEXT TUESDAY.
HA! I'VE GOT TO READ THIS WHOLE BOOK BY NEXT MONDAY!
OOPS. I GUESS IF I HOLD IT SIDEWAYS LIKE THAT, IT'S TOO THIN TO SEE.
WOULD THAT WORK IF I TURNED YOU SIDEWAYS?
...OR UPSIDE DOWN, OR INSIDE OUT?...
AMEND

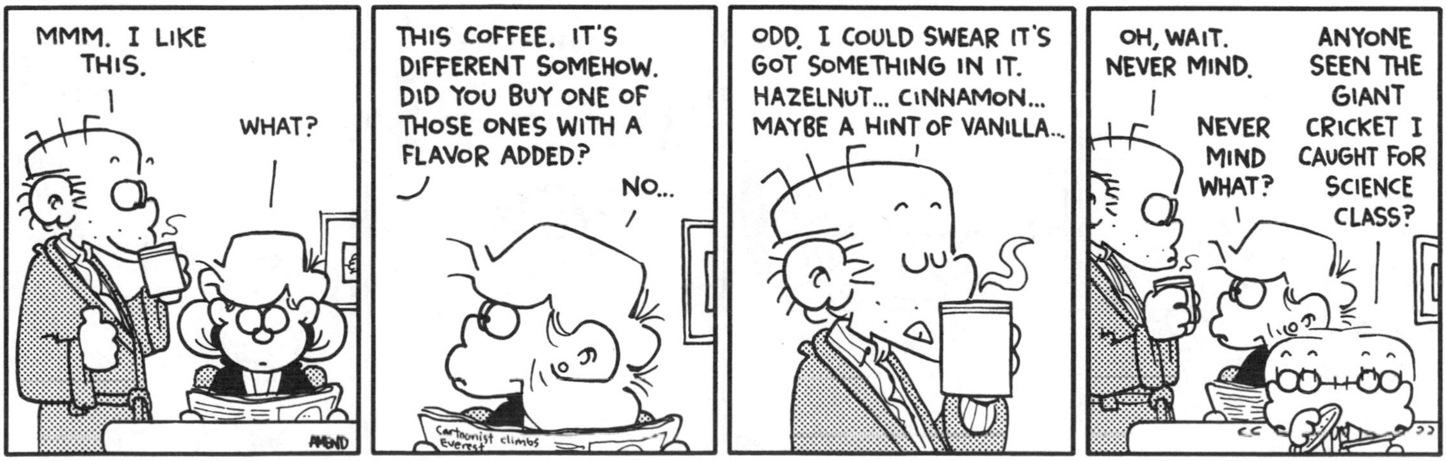
MMM. I LIKE THIS.
WHAT?
AMEND
THIS COFFEE. IT'S DIFFERENT SOMEHOW. DID YOU BUY ONE OF THOSE ONES WITH A FLAVOR ADDED?
NO...
Cartoonist climbs Everest
ODD. I COULD SWEAR IT'S GOT SOMETHING IN IT. HAZELNUT... CINNAMON... MAYBE A HINT OF VANILLA...
OH, WAIT. NEVER MIND.
NEVER MIND WHAT?
ANYONE SEEN THE GIANT CRICKET I CAUGHT FOR SCIENCE CLASS?

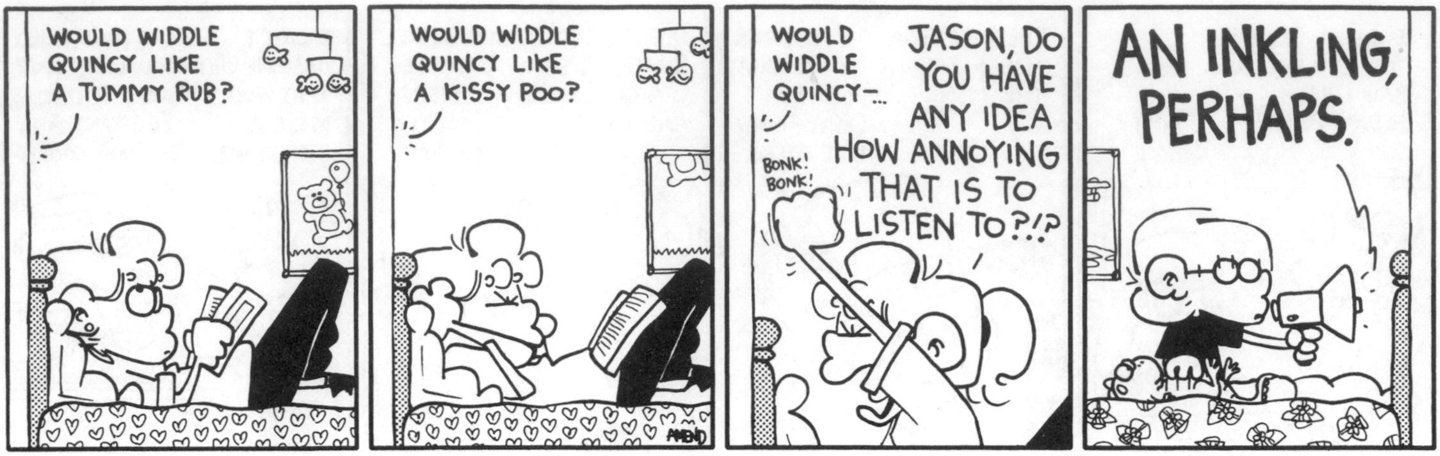
WOULD WIDDLE QUINCY LIKE A TUMMY RUB?
WOULD WIDDLE QUINCY LIKE A KISSY POO?
WOULD WIDDLE QUINCY–...
BONK! BONK!
JASON, DO YOU HAVE ANY IDEA HOW ANNOYING THAT IS TO LISTEN TO?!?
AN INKLING, PERHAPS.

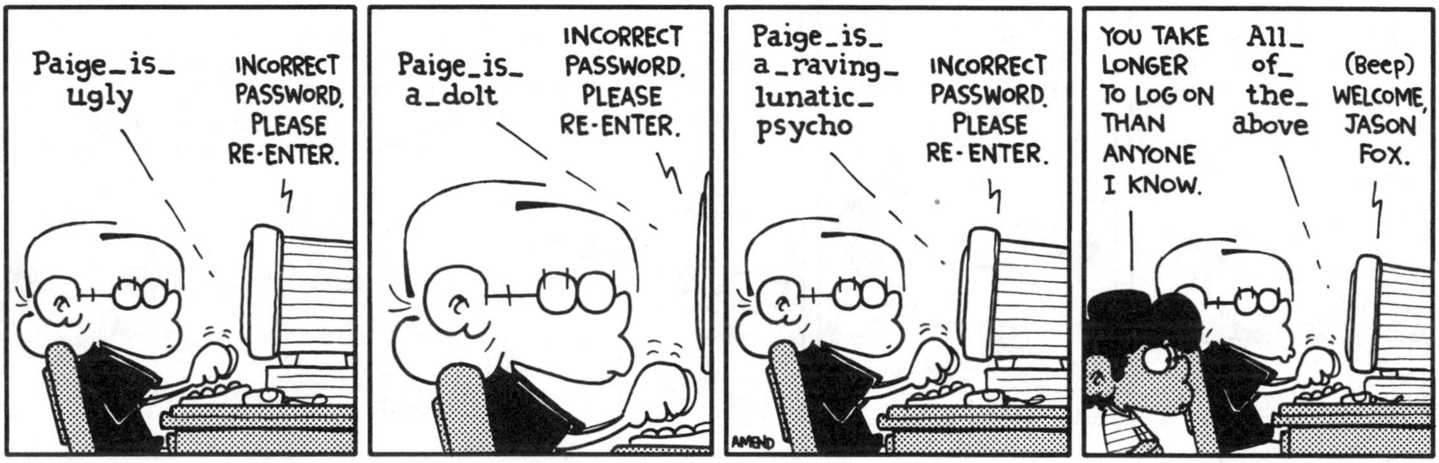
Paige_is_ ugly
INCORRECT PASSWORD. PLEASE RE-ENTER.
Paige_is_ a_dolt
INCORRECT PASSWORD. PLEASE RE-ENTER.
Paige_is_ a_raving_ lunatic_ psycho
INCORRECT PASSWORD. PLEASE RE-ENTER.
YOU TAKE LONGER TO LOG ON THAN ANYONE I KNOW.
All_ of_ the_ above
(Beep) WELCOME, JASON FOX.

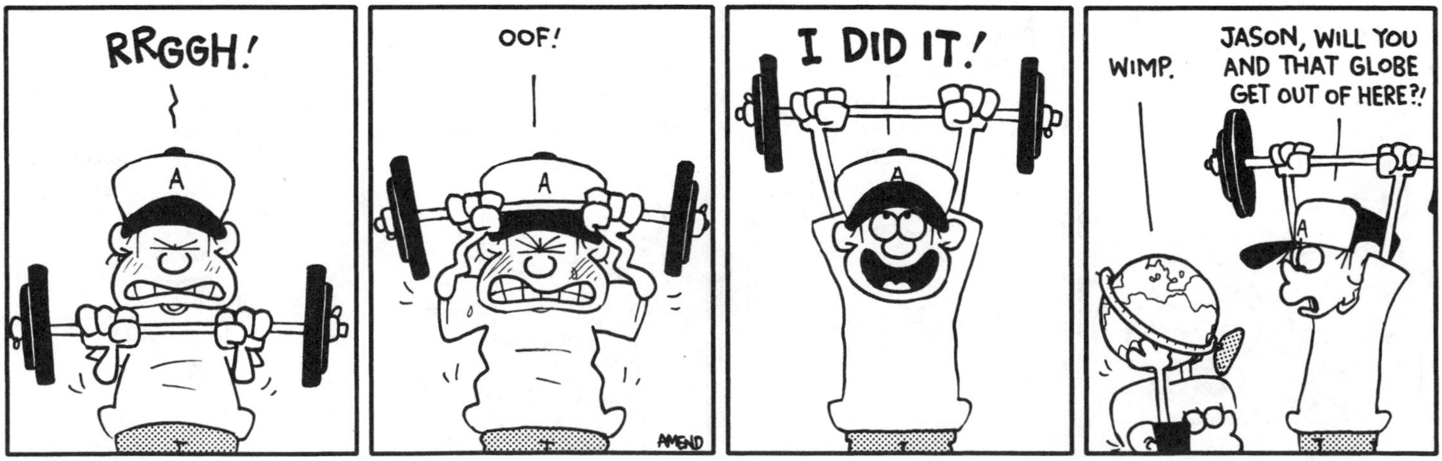
RRGGH!
OOF!
I DID IT!
WIMP.
JASON, WILL YOU AND THAT GLOBE GET OUT OF HERE?!

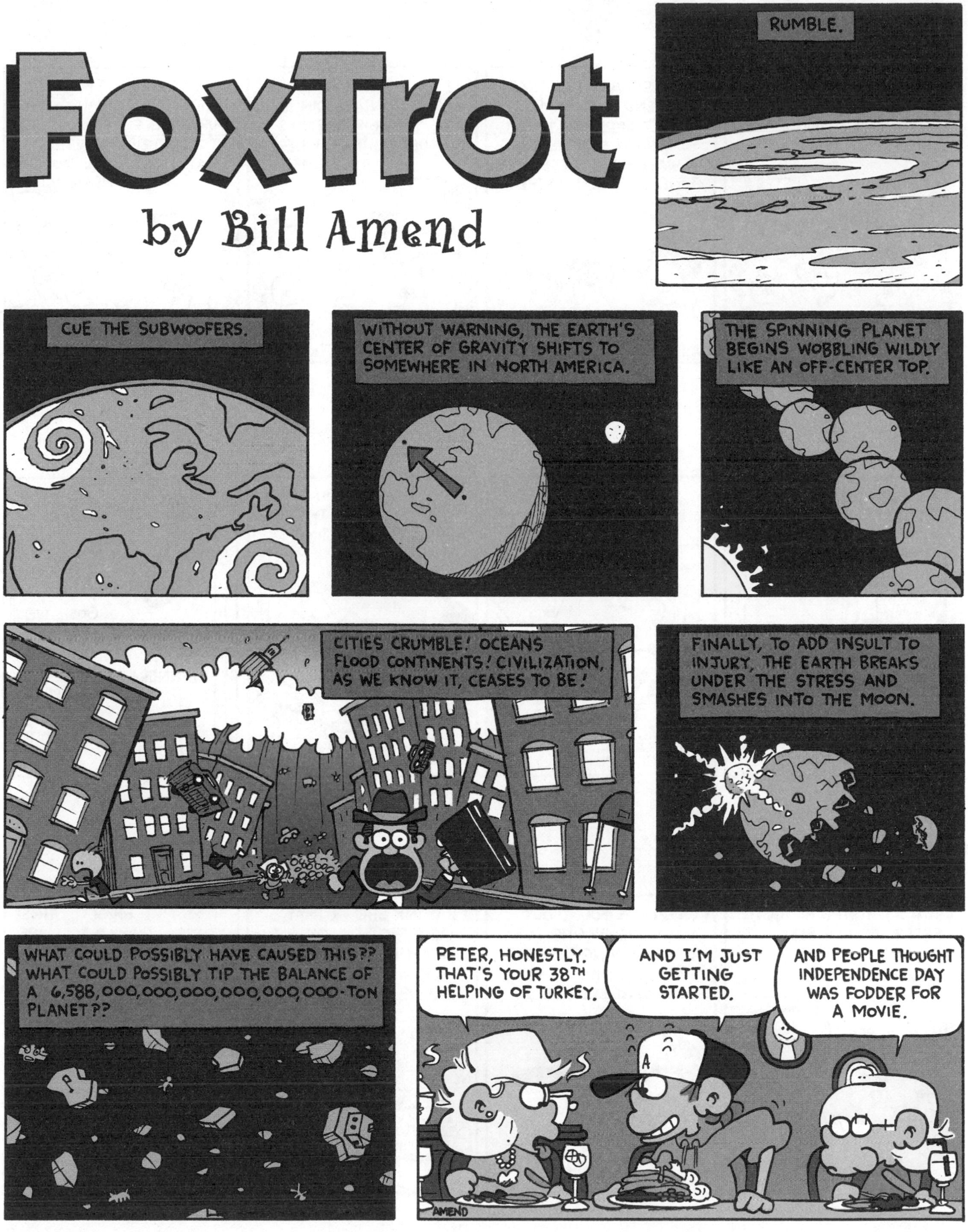
FoxTrot
by Bill Amend
RUMBLE.
CUE THE SUBWOOFERS.
WITHOUT WARNING, THE EARTH'S CENTER OF GRAVITY SHIFTS TO SOMEWHERE IN NORTH AMERICA.
THE SPINNING PLANET BEGINS WOBBLING WILDLY LIKE AN OFF-CENTER TOP.
CITIES CRUMBLE! OCEANS FLOOD CONTINENTS! CIVILIZATION, AS WE KNOW IT, CEASES TO BE!
FINALLY, TO ADD INSULT TO INJURY, THE EARTH BREAKS UNDER THE STRESS AND SMASHES INTO THE MOON.
WHAT COULD POSSIBLY HAVE CAUSED THIS?? WHAT COULD POSSIBLY TIP THE BALANCE OF A 6,588,000,000,000,000,000,000-TON PLANET??
PETER, HONESTLY. THAT'S YOUR 38TH HELPING OF TURKEY.
AND I'M JUST GETTING STARTED.
AND PEOPLE THOUGHT INDEPENDENCE DAY WAS FODDER FOR A MOVIE.
AMEND

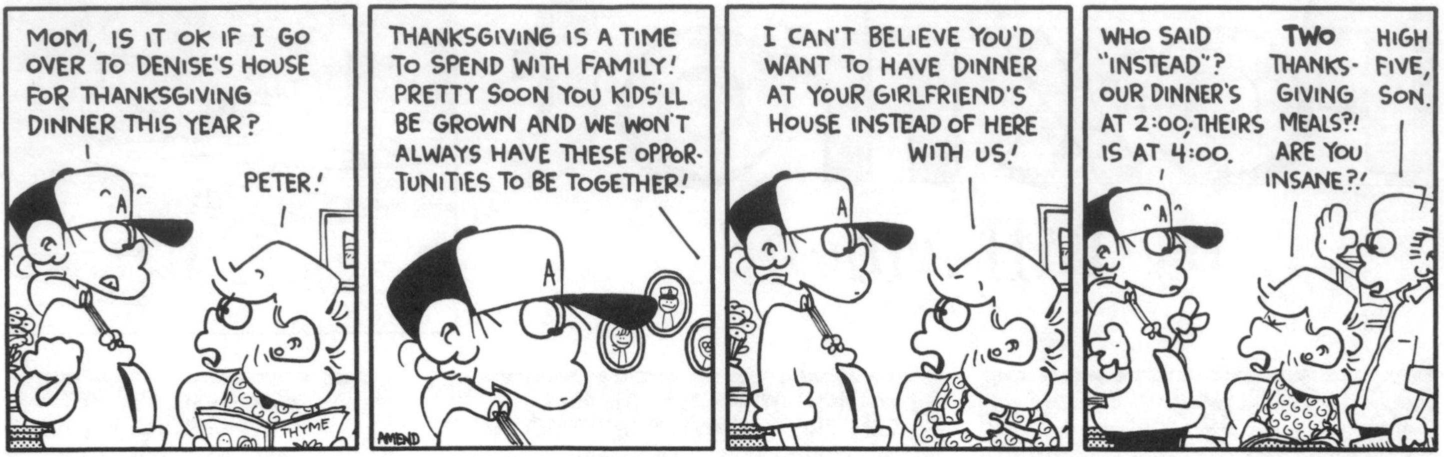
MOM, IS IT OK IF I GO OVER TO DENISE'S HOUSE FOR THANKSGIVING DINNER THIS YEAR?
PETER!
THYME
THANKSGIVING IS A TIME TO SPEND WITH FAMILY! PRETTY SOON YOU KIDS'LL BE GROWN AND WE WON'T ALWAYS HAVE THESE OPPORTUNITIES TO BE TOGETHER!
AMEND
I CAN'T BELIEVE YOU'D WANT TO HAVE DINNER AT YOUR GIRLFRIEND'S HOUSE INSTEAD OF HERE WITH US!
WHO SAID "INSTEAD"? OUR DINNER'S AT 2:00; THEIRS IS AT 4:00.
TWO THANKSGIVING MEALS?! ARE YOU INSANE?!
HIGH FIVE, SON.

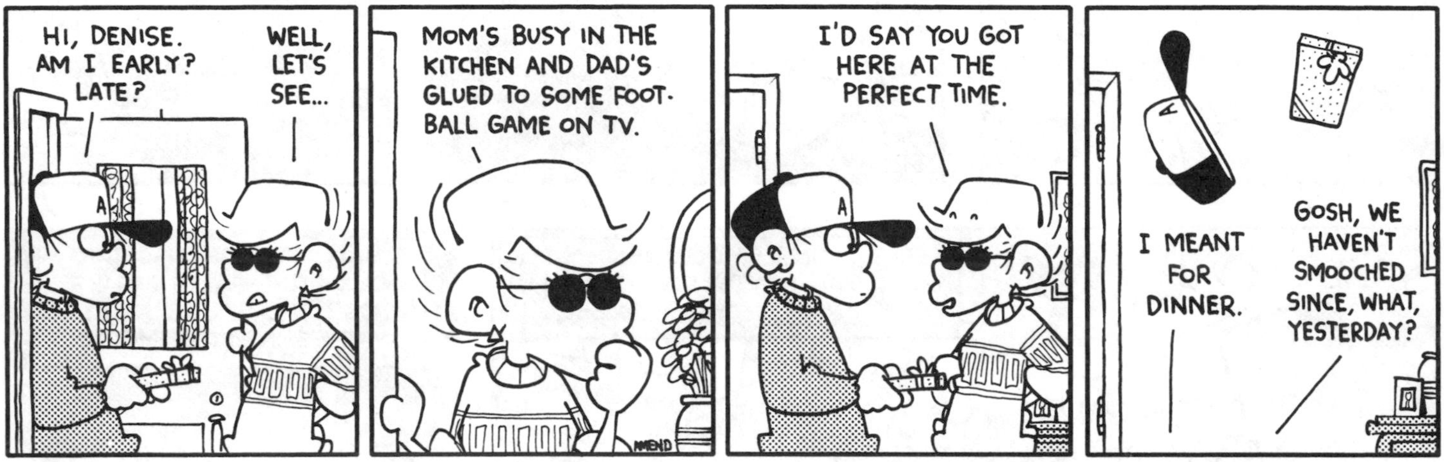
HI, DENISE. AM I EARLY? LATE?
WELL, LET'S SEE...
MOM'S BUSY IN THE KITCHEN AND DAD'S GLUED TO SOME FOOTBALL GAME ON TV.
AMEND
I'D SAY YOU GOT HERE AT THE PERFECT TIME.
I MEANT FOR DINNER.
GOSH, WE HAVEN'T SMOOCHED SINCE, WHAT, YESTERDAY?

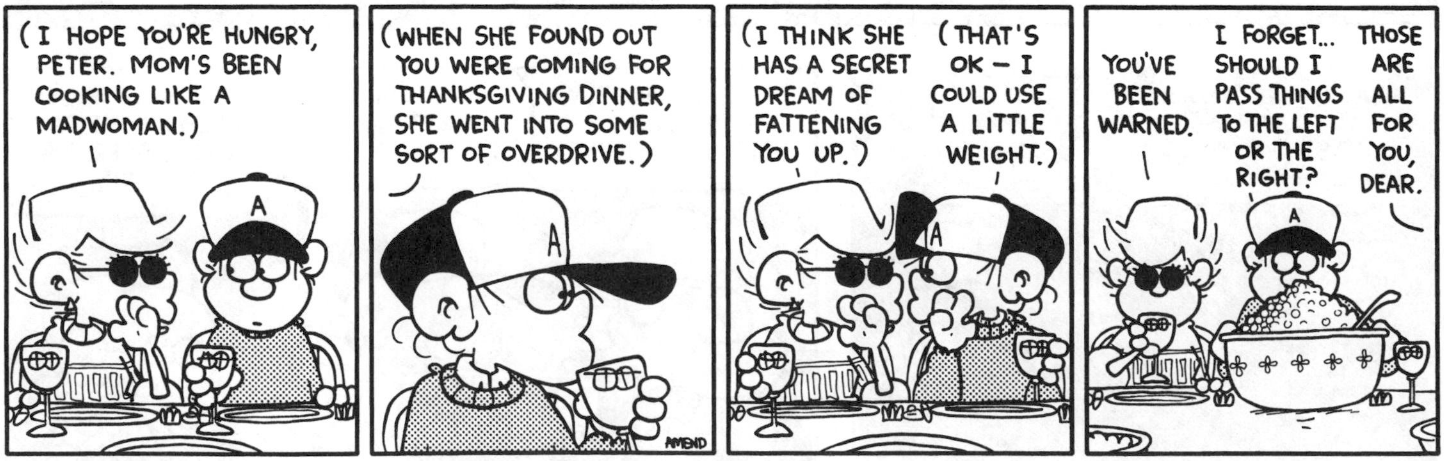
(I HOPE YOU'RE HUNGRY, PETER. MOM'S BEEN COOKING LIKE A MADWOMAN.)
(WHEN SHE FOUND OUT YOU WERE COMING FOR THANKSGIVING DINNER, SHE WENT INTO SOME SORT OF OVERDRIVE.)
AMEND
(I THINK SHE HAS A SECRET DREAM OF FATTENING YOU UP.)
(THAT'S OK – I COULD USE A LITTLE WEIGHT.)
YOU'VE BEEN WARNED.
I FORGET... SHOULD I PASS THINGS TO THE LEFT OR THE RIGHT?
THOSE ARE ALL FOR YOU, DEAR.

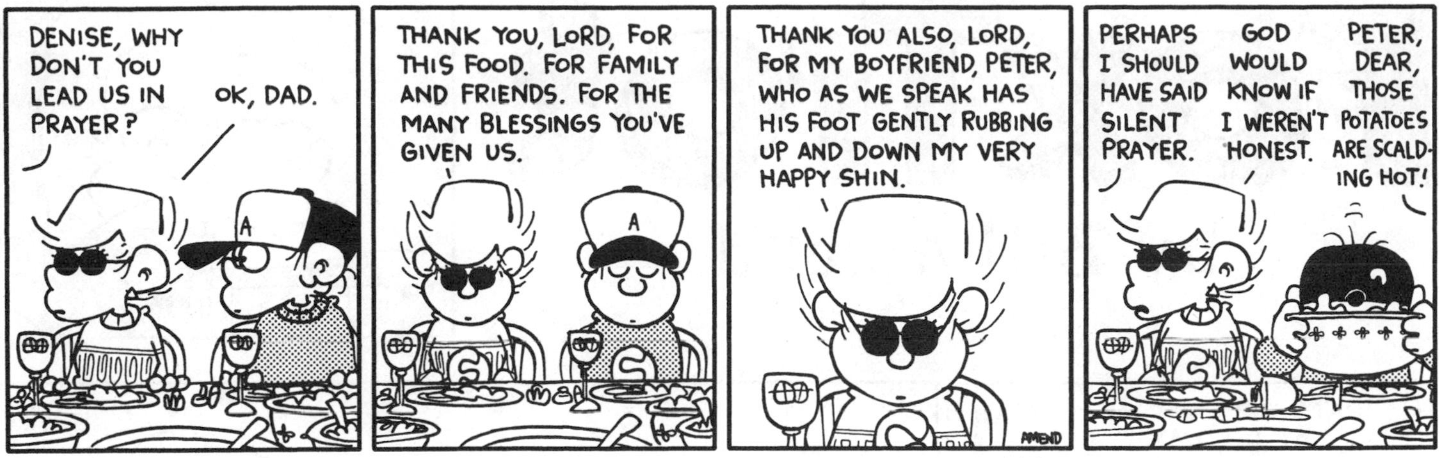
DENISE, WHY DON'T YOU LEAD US IN PRAYER?
OK, DAD.
THANK YOU, LORD, FOR THIS FOOD. FOR FAMILY AND FRIENDS. FOR THE MANY BLESSINGS YOU'VE GIVEN US.
THANK YOU ALSO, LORD, FOR MY BOYFRIEND, PETER, WHO AS WE SPEAK HAS HIS FOOT GENTLY RUBBING UP AND DOWN MY VERY HAPPY SHIN.
AMEND
PERHAPS I SHOULD HAVE SAID SILENT PRAYER.
GOD WOULD KNOW IF I WEREN'T HONEST.
PETER, DEAR, THOSE POTATOES ARE SCALDING HOT!

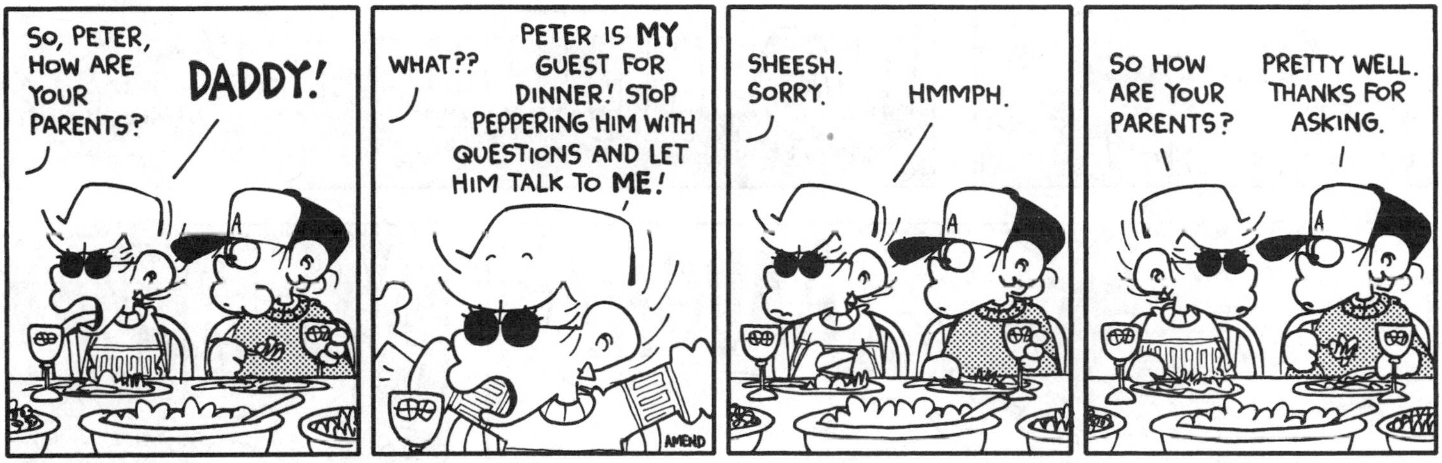
SO, PETER, HOW ARE YOUR PARENTS?
DADDY!
WHAT??
PETER IS MY GUEST FOR DINNER! STOP PEPPERING HIM WITH QUESTIONS AND LET HIM TALK TO ME!
AMEND
SHEESH. SORRY.
HMMPH.
SO HOW ARE YOUR PARENTS?
PRETTY WELL. THANKS FOR ASKING.

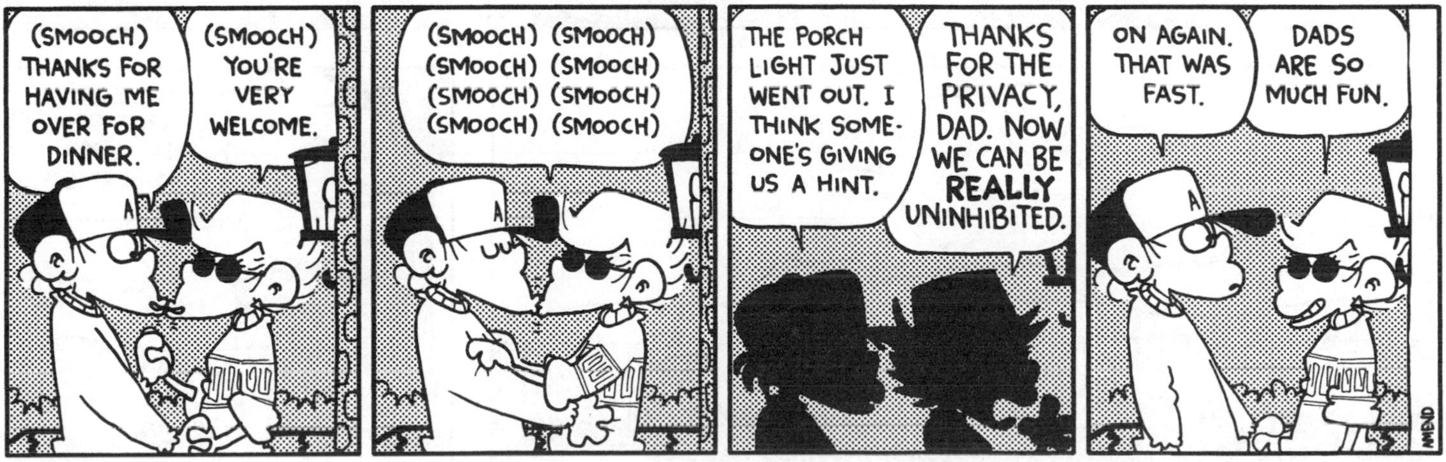
(SMOOCH) THANKS FOR HAVING ME OVER FOR DINNER.
(SMOOCH) YOU'RE VERY WELCOME.
(SMOOCH) (SMOOCH) (SMOOCH) (SMOOCH) (SMOOCH) (SMOOCH) (SMOOCH) (SMOOCH)
THE PORCH LIGHT JUST WENT OUT. I THINK SOMEONE'S GIVING US A HINT.
THANKS FOR THE PRIVACY, DAD. NOW WE CAN BE REALLY UNINHIBITED.
ON AGAIN. THAT WAS FAST.
DADS ARE SO MUCH FUN.
AMEND

FoxTrot

by Bill Amend

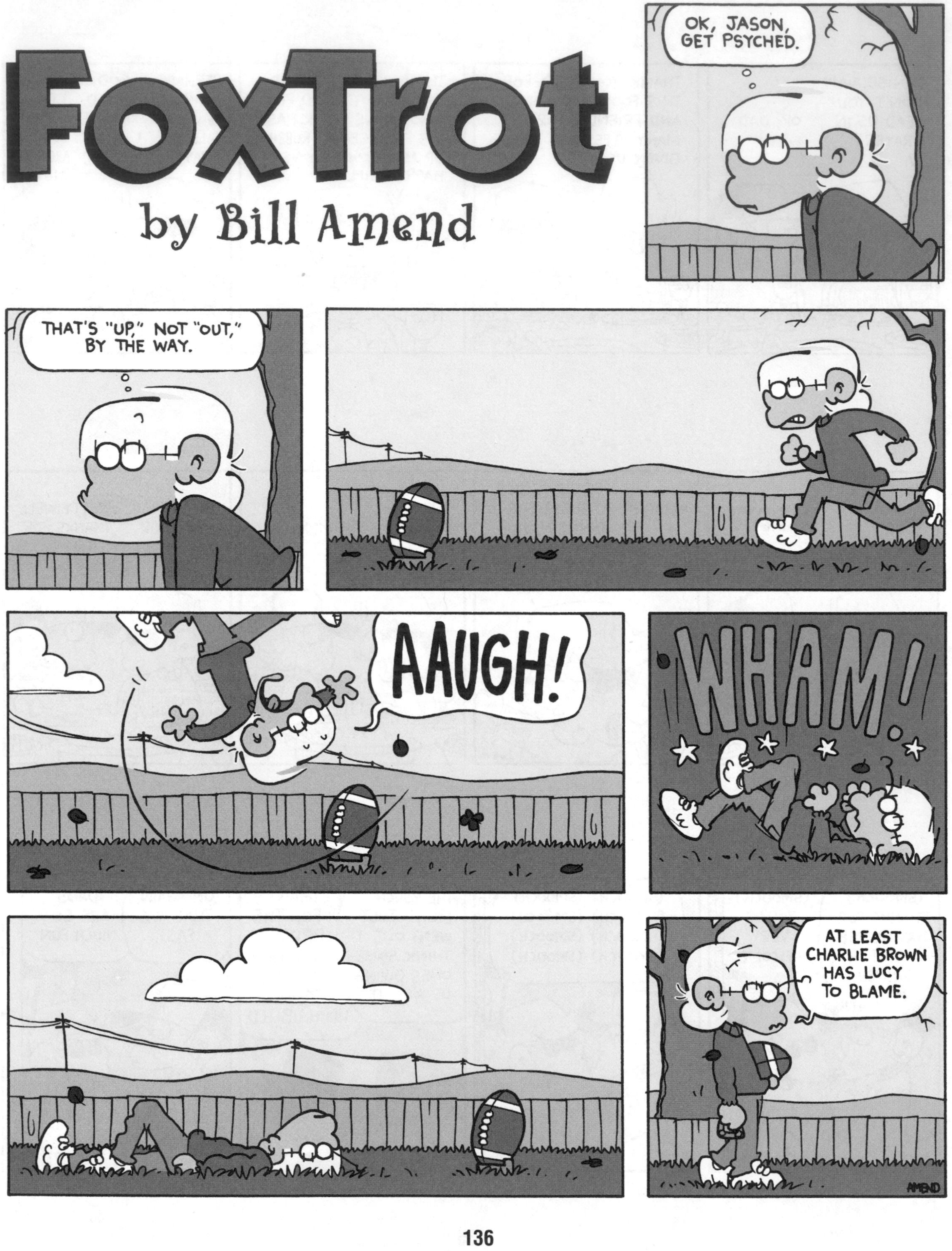

OK, JASON, GET PSYCHED.
THAT'S "UP," NOT "OUT," BY THE WAY.
AAUGH!
WHAM!
AT LEAST CHARLIE BROWN HAS LUCY TO BLAME.
AMEND

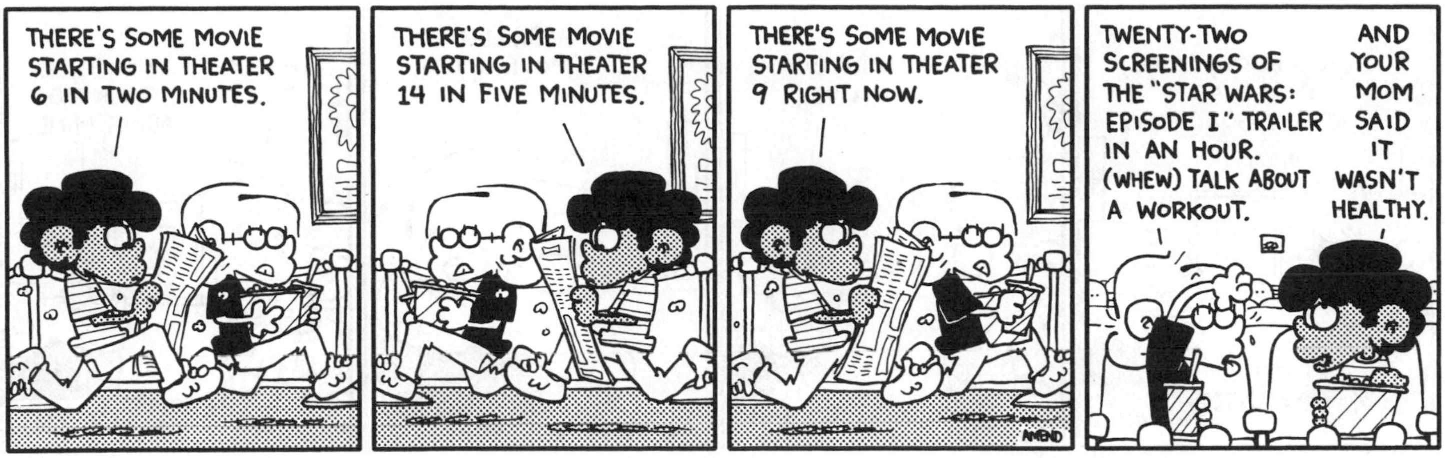
THERE'S SOME MOVIE STARTING IN THEATER 6 IN TWO MINUTES.
THERE'S SOME MOVIE STARTING IN THEATER 14 IN FIVE MINUTES.
THERE'S SOME MOVIE STARTING IN THEATER 9 RIGHT NOW.
AMEND
TWENTY-TWO SCREENINGS OF THE "STAR WARS: EPISODE I" TRAILER IN AN HOUR. (WHEW) TALK ABOUT A WORKOUT.
AND YOUR MOM SAID IT WASN'T HEALTHY.

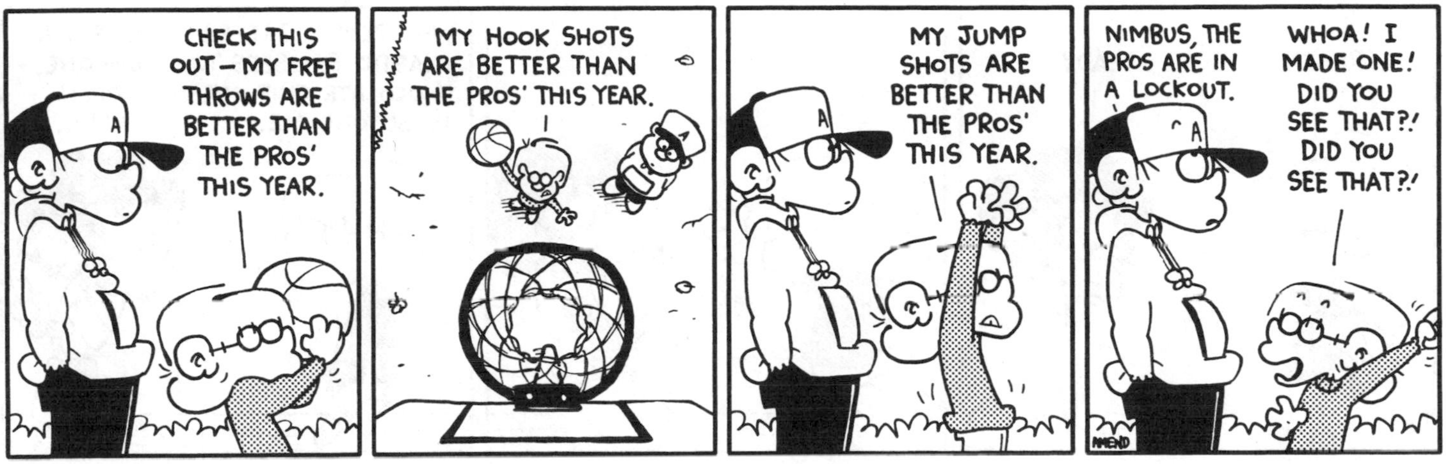
CHECK THIS OUT – MY FREE THROWS ARE BETTER THAN THE PROS' THIS YEAR.
MY HOOK SHOTS ARE BETTER THAN THE PROS' THIS YEAR.
MY JUMP SHOTS ARE BETTER THAN THE PROS' THIS YEAR.
NIMBUS, THE PROS ARE IN A LOCKOUT.
WHOA! I MADE ONE! DID YOU SEE THAT?! DID YOU SEE THAT?!
AMEND

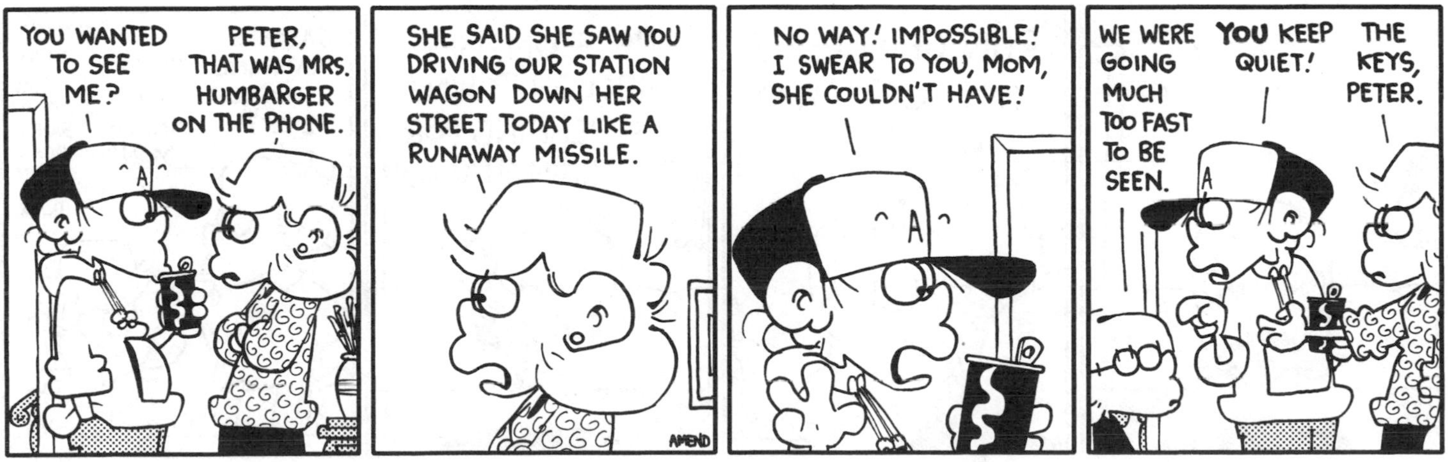
YOU WANTED TO SEE ME?
PETER, THAT WAS MRS. HUMBARGER ON THE PHONE.
SHE SAID SHE SAW YOU DRIVING OUR STATION WAGON DOWN HER STREET TODAY LIKE A RUNAWAY MISSILE.
AMEND
NO WAY! IMPOSSIBLE! I SWEAR TO YOU, MOM, SHE COULDN'T HAVE!
WE WERE GOING MUCH TOO FAST TO BE SEEN.
YOU KEEP QUIET!
THE KEYS, PETER.

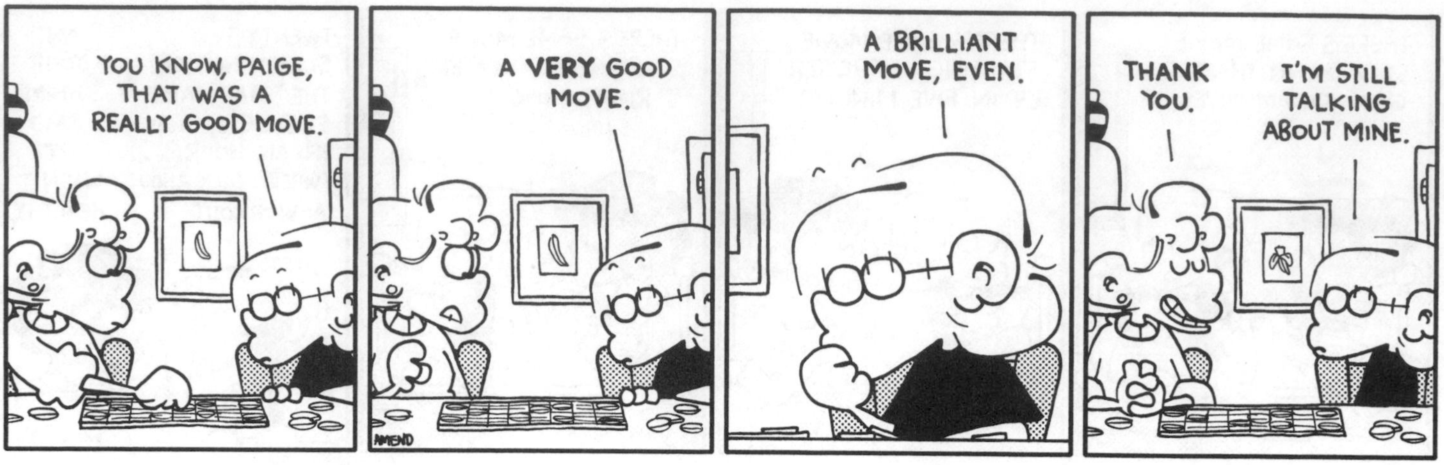
YOU KNOW, PAIGE, THAT WAS A REALLY GOOD MOVE.
A VERY GOOD MOVE.
AMEND
A BRILLIANT MOVE, EVEN.
THANK YOU.
I'M STILL TALKING ABOUT MINE.

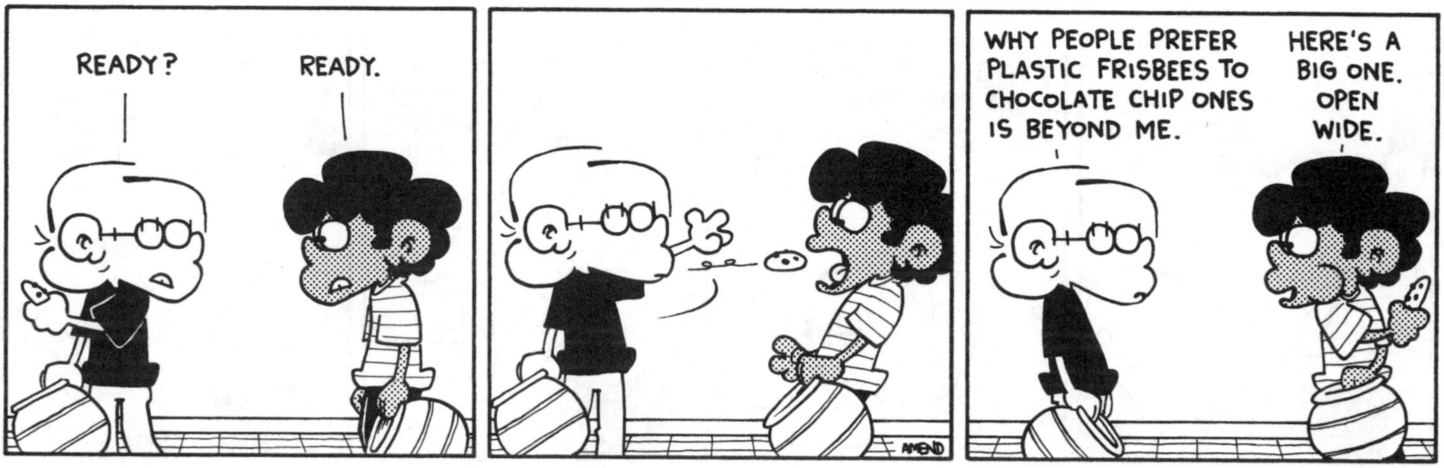
READY?
READY.
AMEND
WHY PEOPLE PREFER PLASTIC FRISBEES TO CHOCOLATE CHIP ONES IS BEYOND ME.
HERE'S A BIG ONE. OPEN WIDE.

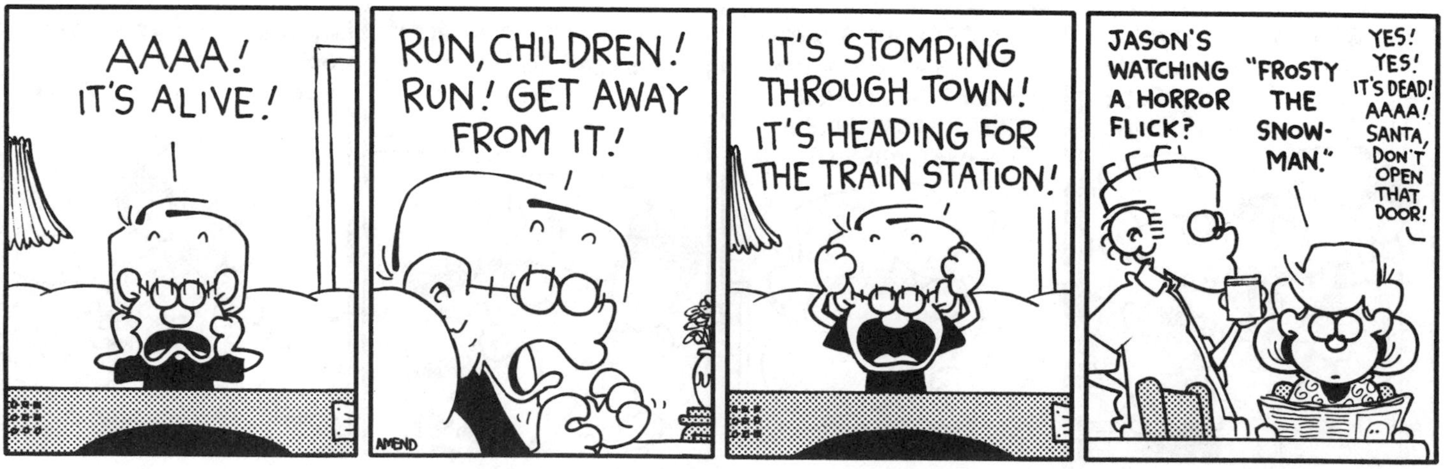
AAAA! IT'S ALIVE!
RUN, CHILDREN! RUN! GET AWAY FROM IT!
AMEND
IT'S STOMPING THROUGH TOWN! IT'S HEADING FOR THE TRAIN STATION!
JASON'S WATCHING A HORROR FLICK?
"FROSTY THE SNOW-MAN."
YES! YES! IT'S DEAD! AAAA! SANTA, DON'T OPEN THAT DOOR!

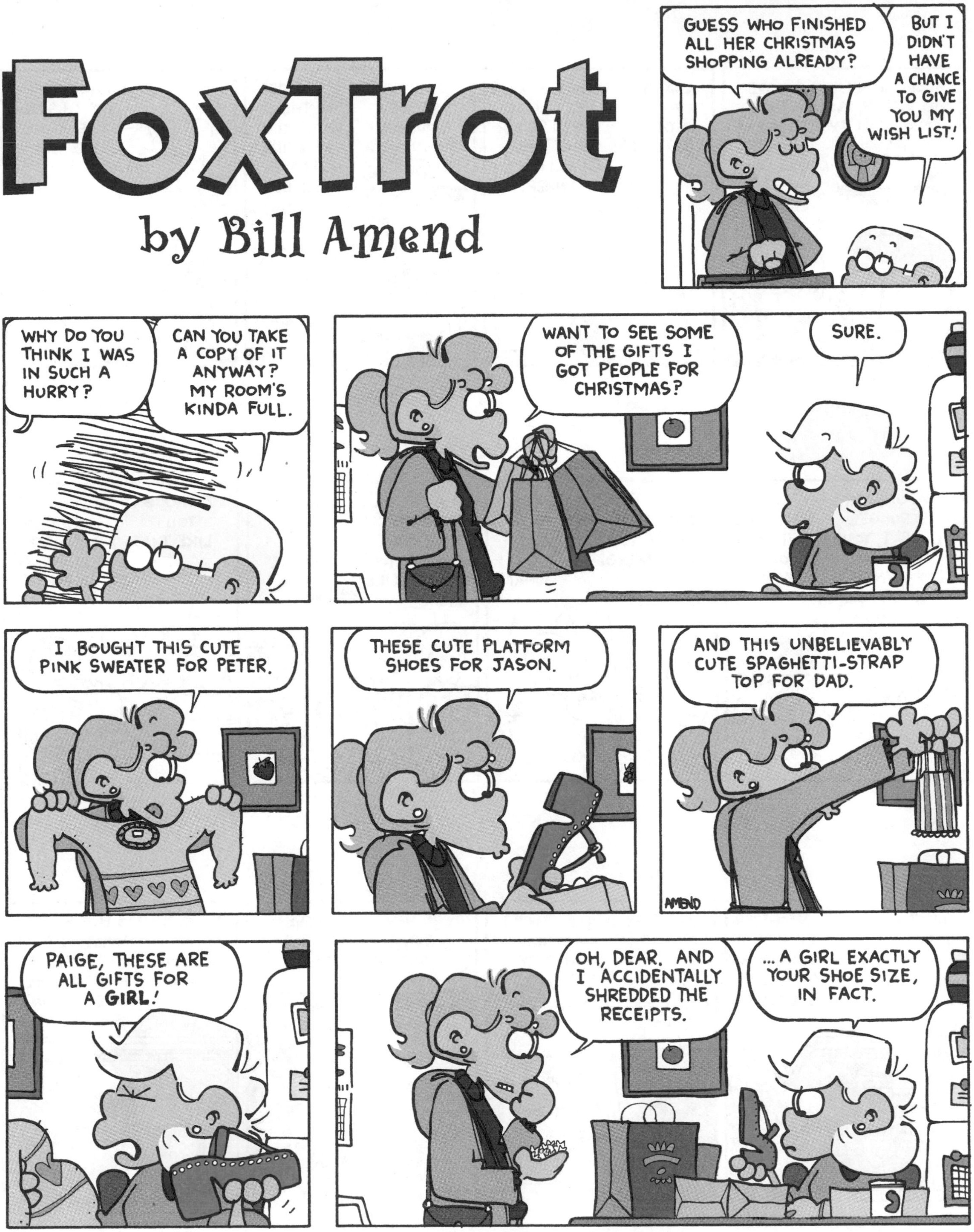
FoxTrot
by Bill Amend
GUESS WHO FINISHED ALL HER CHRISTMAS SHOPPING ALREADY?
BUT I DIDN'T HAVE A CHANCE TO GIVE YOU MY WISH LIST!
WHY DO YOU THINK I WAS IN SUCH A HURRY?
CAN YOU TAKE A COPY OF IT ANYWAY? MY ROOM'S KINDA FULL.
WANT TO SEE SOME OF THE GIFTS I GOT PEOPLE FOR CHRISTMAS?
SURE.
I BOUGHT THIS CUTE PINK SWEATER FOR PETER.
THESE CUTE PLATFORM SHOES FOR JASON.
AND THIS UNBELIEVABLY CUTE SPAGHETTI-STRAP TOP FOR DAD.
AMEND
PAIGE, THESE ARE ALL GIFTS FOR A **GIRL**!
OH, DEAR. AND I ACCIDENTALLY SHREDDED THE RECEIPTS.
... A GIRL EXACTLY YOUR SHOE SIZE, IN FACT.

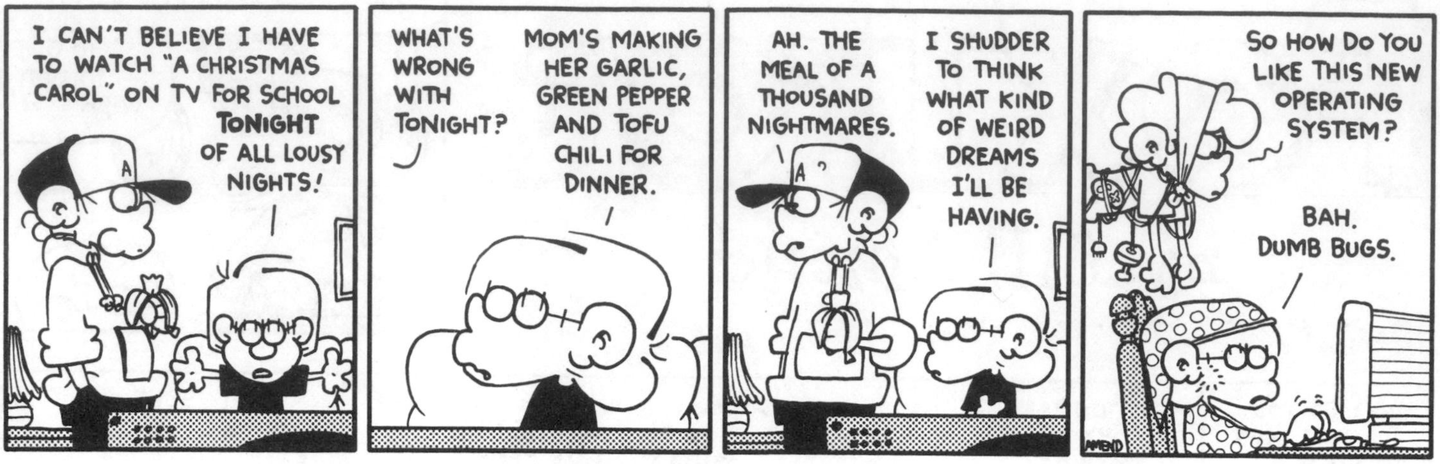
I CAN'T BELIEVE I HAVE TO WATCH "A CHRISTMAS CAROL" ON TV FOR SCHOOL TONIGHT OF ALL LOUSY NIGHTS!
WHAT'S WRONG WITH TONIGHT?
MOM'S MAKING HER GARLIC, GREEN PEPPER AND TOFU CHILI FOR DINNER.
AH. THE MEAL OF A THOUSAND NIGHTMARES.
I SHUDDER TO THINK WHAT KIND OF WEIRD DREAMS I'LL BE HAVING.
SO HOW DO YOU LIKE THIS NEW OPERATING SYSTEM?
BAH. DUMB BUGS.

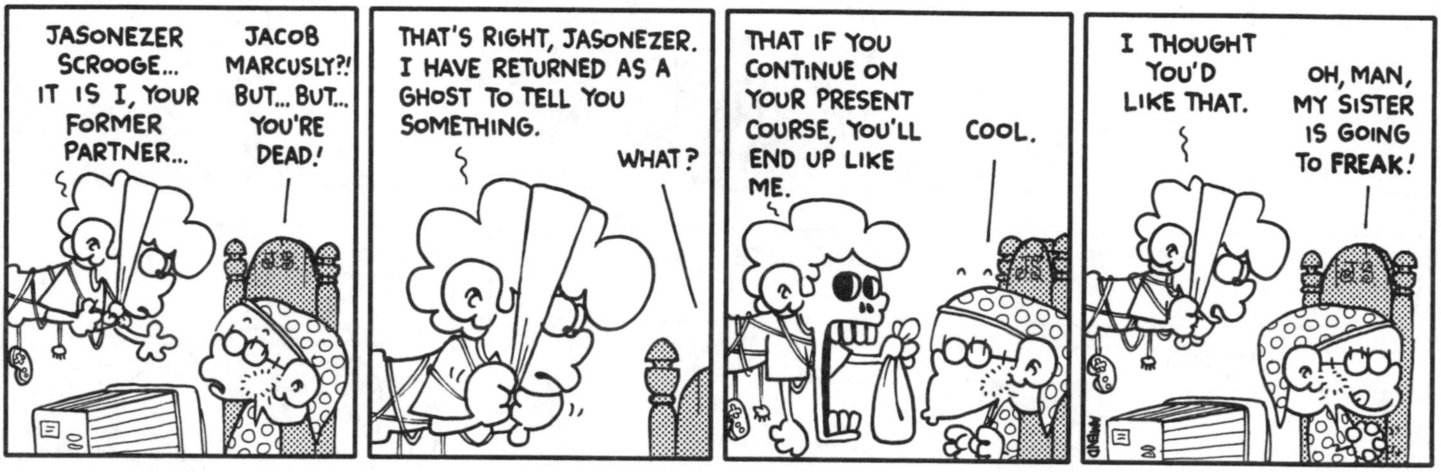
JASONEZER SCROOGE... IT IS I, YOUR FORMER PARTNER...
JACOB MARCUSLY?! BUT... BUT... YOU'RE DEAD!
THAT'S RIGHT, JASONEZER. I HAVE RETURNED AS A GHOST TO TELL YOU SOMETHING.
WHAT?
THAT IF YOU CONTINUE ON YOUR PRESENT COURSE, YOU'LL END UP LIKE ME.
COOL.
I THOUGHT YOU'D LIKE THAT.
OH, MAN, MY SISTER IS GOING TO FREAK!

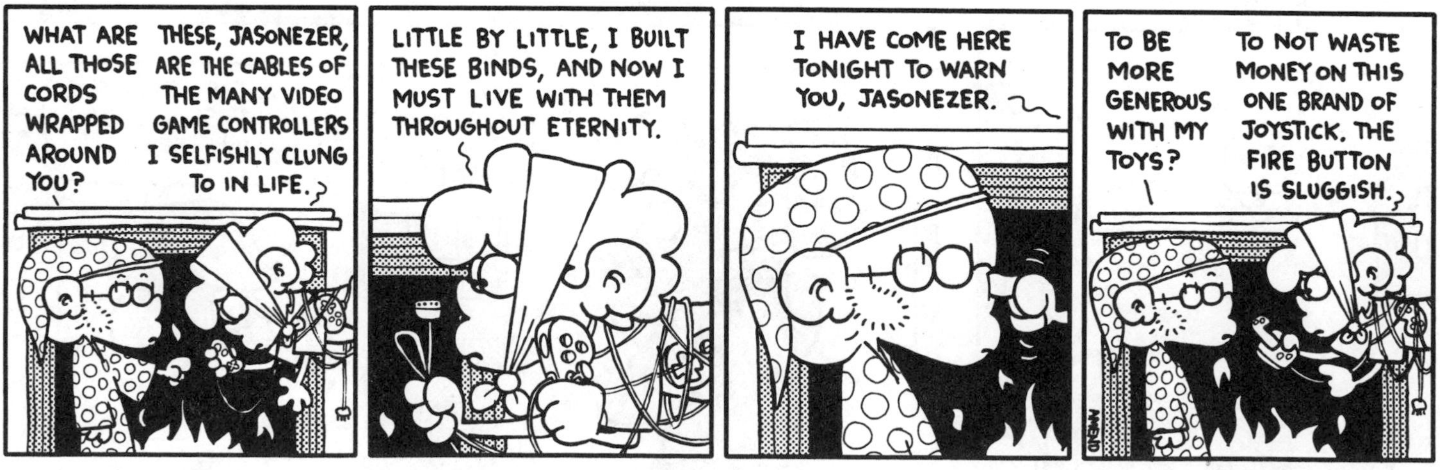
WHAT ARE ALL THOSE CORDS WRAPPED AROUND YOU?
THESE, JASONEZER, ARE THE CABLES OF THE MANY VIDEO GAME CONTROLLERS I SELFISHLY CLUNG TO IN LIFE.
LITTLE BY LITTLE, I BUILT THESE BINDS, AND NOW I MUST LIVE WITH THEM THROUGHOUT ETERNITY.
I HAVE COME HERE TONIGHT TO WARN YOU, JASONEZER.
TO BE MORE GENEROUS WITH MY TOYS?
TO NOT WASTE MONEY ON THIS ONE BRAND OF JOYSTICK. THE FIRE BUTTON IS SLUGGISH.

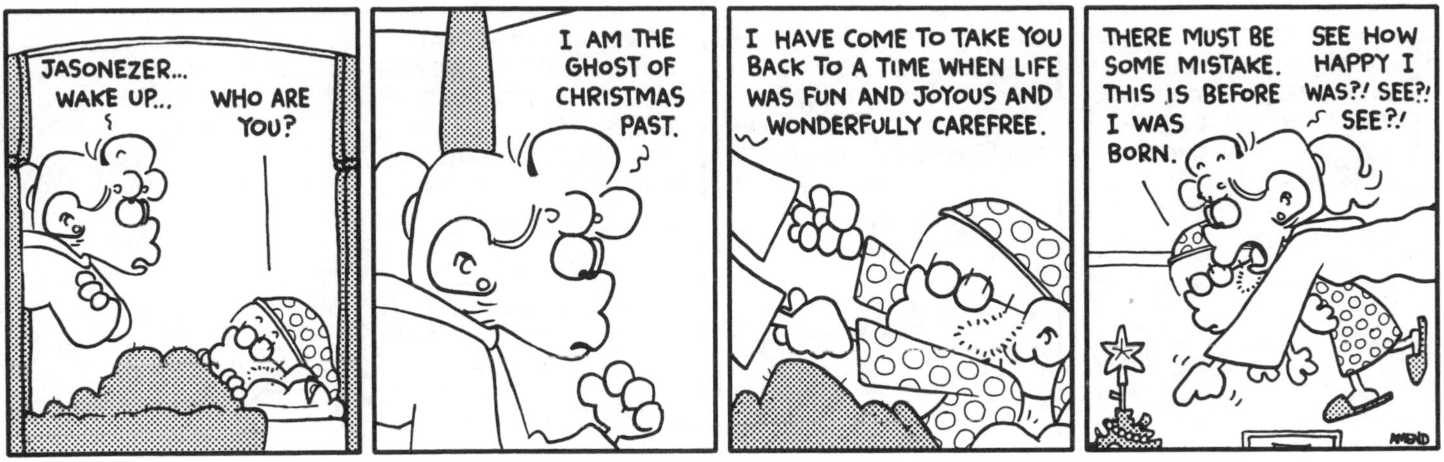
JASONEZER... WAKE UP...
WHO ARE YOU?
I AM THE GHOST OF CHRISTMAS PAST.
I HAVE COME TO TAKE YOU BACK TO A TIME WHEN LIFE WAS FUN AND JOYOUS AND WONDERFULLY CAREFREE.
THERE MUST BE SOME MISTAKE. THIS IS BEFORE I WAS BORN.
SEE HOW HAPPY I WAS?! SEE?! SEE?!
AMEND

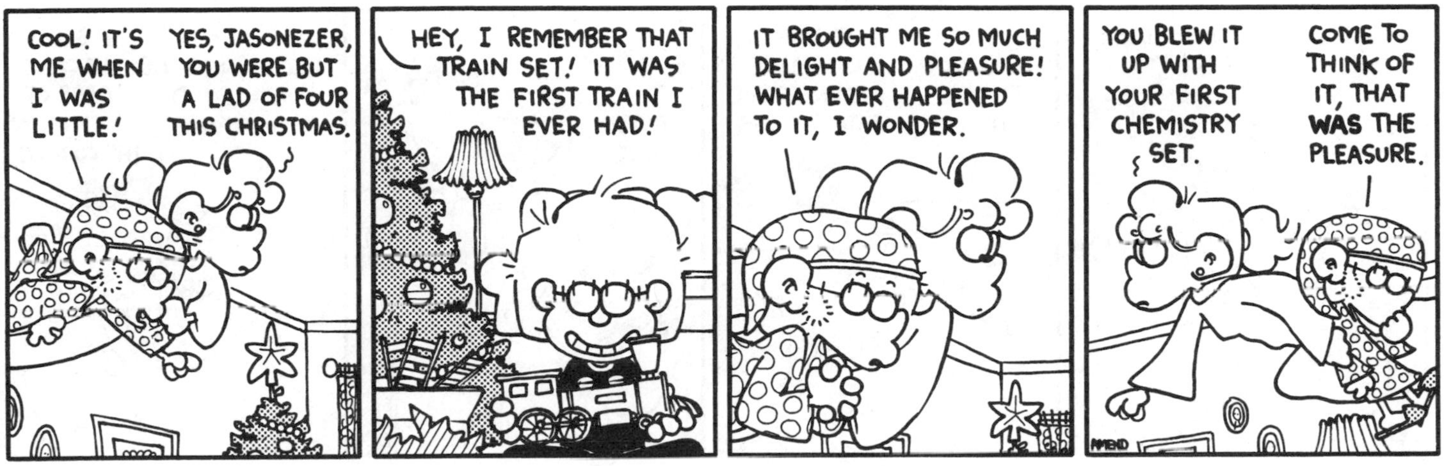
COOL! IT'S ME WHEN I WAS LITTLE!
YES, JASONEZER, YOU WERE BUT A LAD OF FOUR THIS CHRISTMAS.
HEY, I REMEMBER THAT TRAIN SET! IT WAS THE FIRST TRAIN I EVER HAD!
IT BROUGHT ME SO MUCH DELIGHT AND PLEASURE! WHAT EVER HAPPENED TO IT, I WONDER.
YOU BLEW IT UP WITH YOUR FIRST CHEMISTRY SET.
COME TO THINK OF IT, THAT **WAS** THE PLEASURE.
AMEND

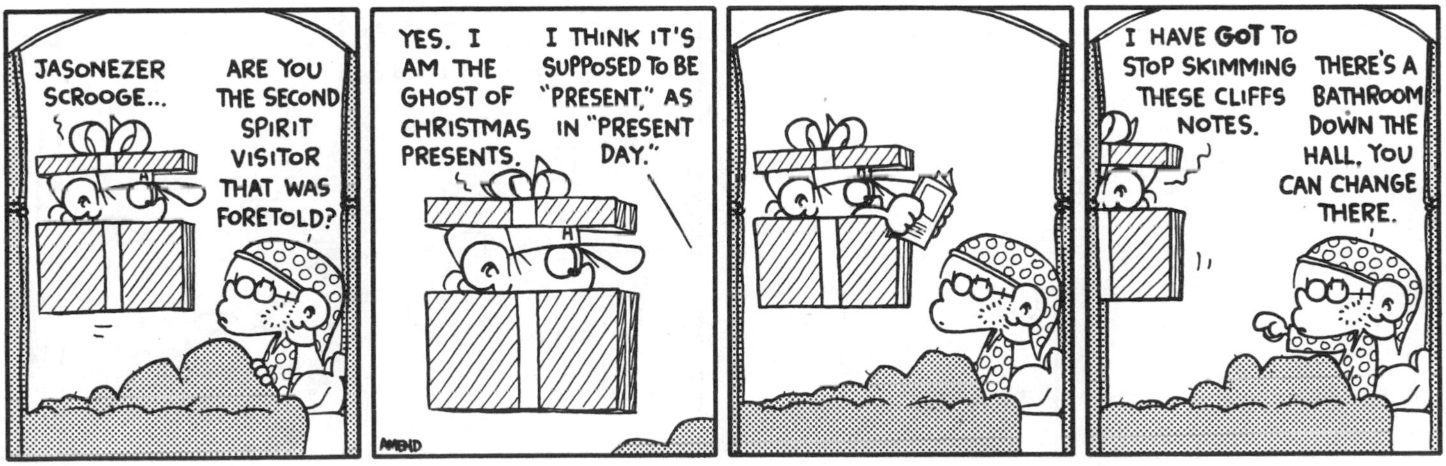
JASONEZER SCROOGE...
ARE YOU THE SECOND SPIRIT VISITOR THAT WAS FORETOLD?
YES. I AM THE GHOST OF CHRISTMAS PRESENTS.
I THINK IT'S SUPPOSED TO BE "PRESENT," AS IN "PRESENT DAY."
AMEND
I HAVE **GOT** TO STOP SKIMMING THESE CLIFFS NOTES.
THERE'S A BATHROOM DOWN THE HALL. YOU CAN CHANGE THERE.

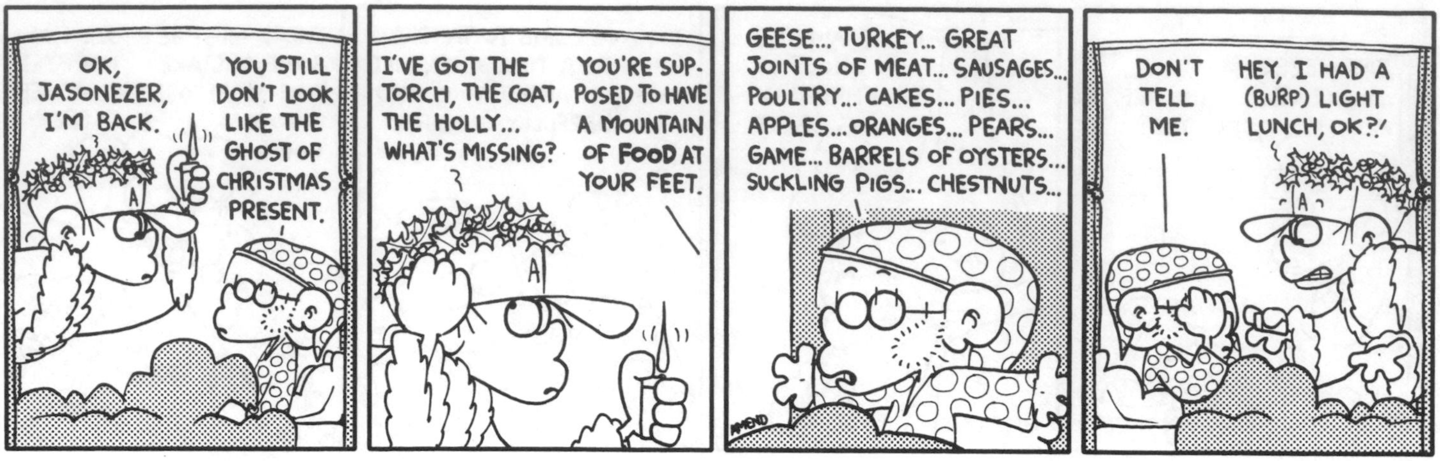
OK, JASONEZER, I'M BACK.
YOU STILL DON'T LOOK LIKE THE GHOST OF CHRISTMAS PRESENT.
I'VE GOT THE TORCH, THE COAT, THE HOLLY... WHAT'S MISSING?
YOU'RE SUP-POSED TO HAVE A MOUNTAIN OF FOOD AT YOUR FEET.
GEESE... TURKEY... GREAT JOINTS OF MEAT... SAUSAGES... POULTRY... CAKES... PIES... APPLES...ORANGES... PEARS... GAME... BARRELS OF OYSTERS... SUCKLING PIGS... CHESTNUTS...
DON'T TELL ME.
HEY, I HAD A (BURP) LIGHT LUNCH, OK?!

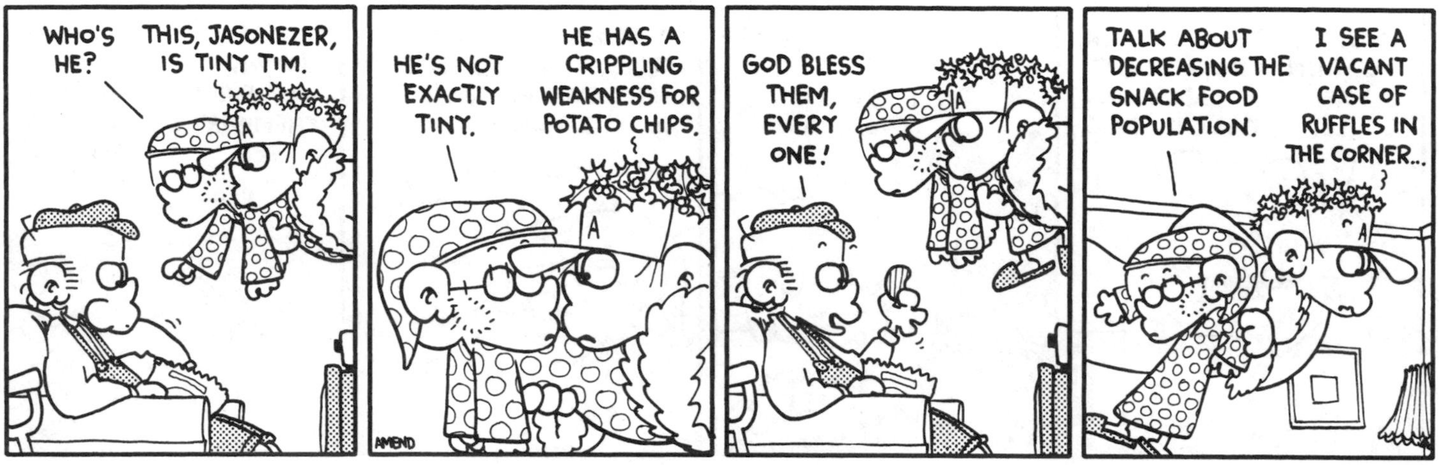
WHO'S HE?
THIS, JASONEZER, IS TINY TIM.
HE'S NOT EXACTLY TINY.
HE HAS A CRIPPLING WEAKNESS FOR POTATO CHIPS.
GOD BLESS THEM, EVERY ONE!
TALK ABOUT DECREASING THE SNACK FOOD POPULATION.
I SEE A VACANT CASE OF RUFFLES IN THE CORNER...

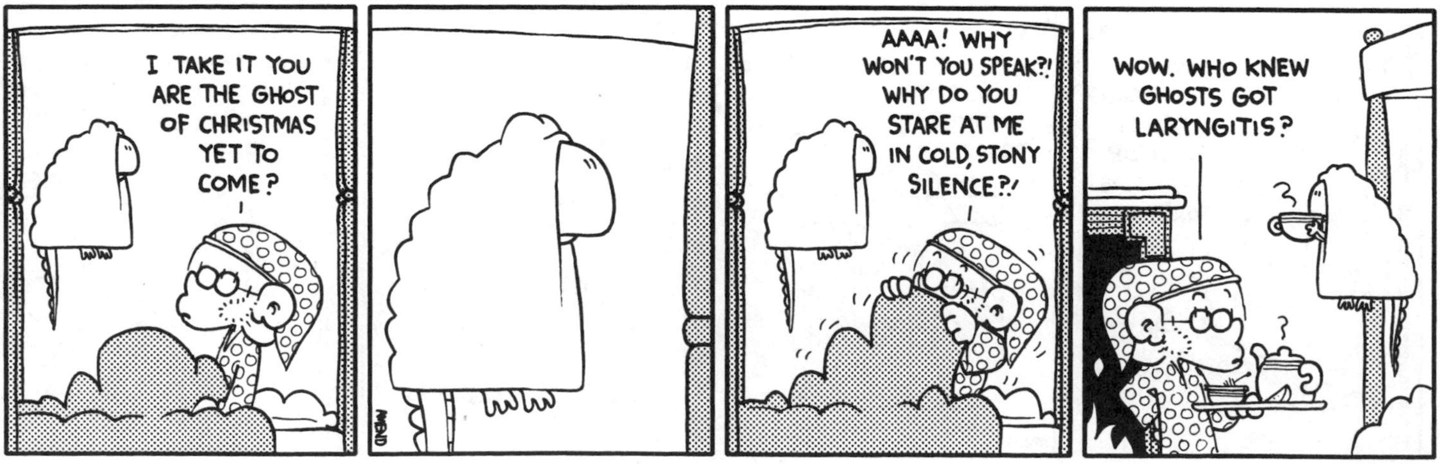
I TAKE IT YOU ARE THE GHOST OF CHRISTMAS YET TO COME?
AAAA! WHY WON'T YOU SPEAK?! WHY DO YOU STARE AT ME IN COLD, STONY SILENCE?!
WOW. WHO KNEW GHOSTS GOT LARYNGITIS?

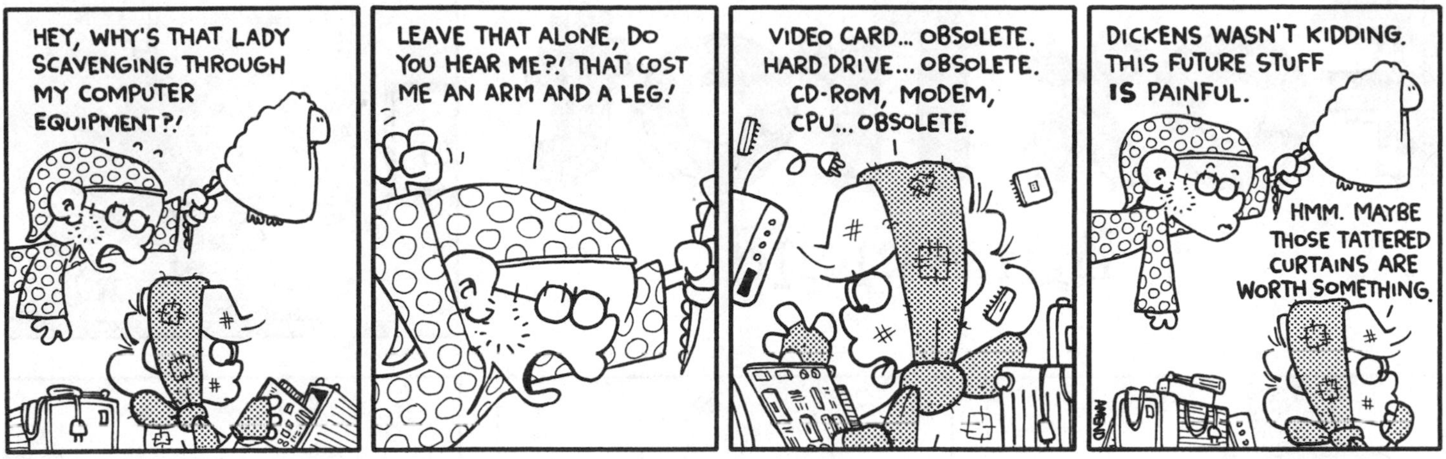
HEY, WHY'S THAT LADY SCAVENGING THROUGH MY COMPUTER EQUIPMENT?!
LEAVE THAT ALONE, DO YOU HEAR ME?! THAT COST ME AN ARM AND A LEG!
VIDEO CARD... OBSOLETE. HARD DRIVE... OBSOLETE. CD-ROM, MODEM, CPU... OBSOLETE.
DICKENS WASN'T KIDDING. THIS FUTURE STUFF **IS** PAINFUL.
HMM. MAYBE THOSE TATTERED CURTAINS ARE WORTH SOMETHING.
AMEND

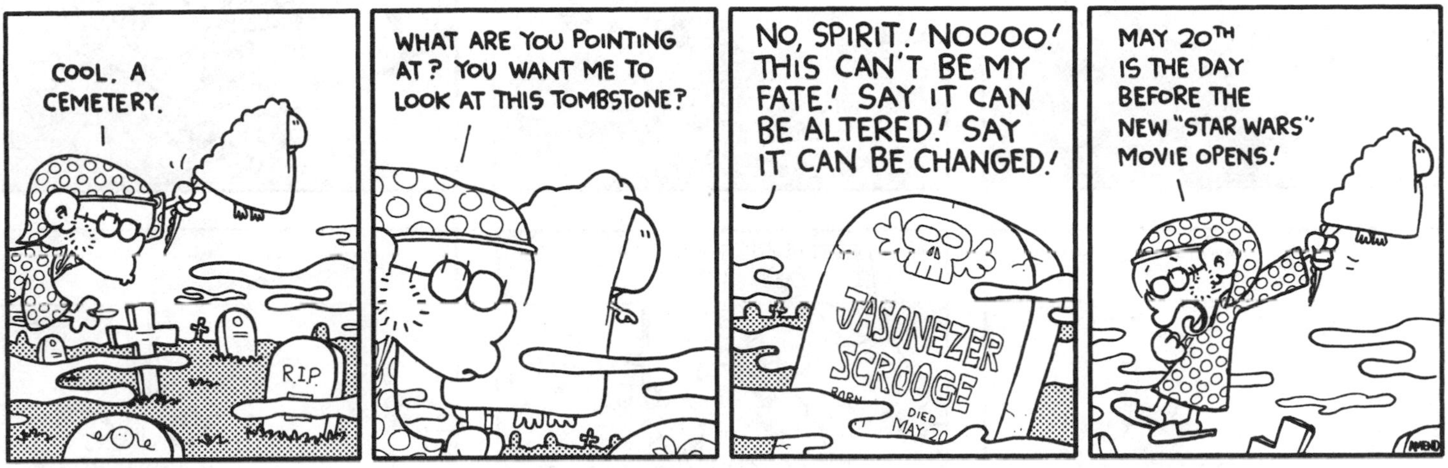
COOL. A CEMETERY.
R.I.P.
WHAT ARE YOU POINTING AT? YOU WANT ME TO LOOK AT THIS TOMBSTONE?
NO, SPIRIT! NOOOO! THIS CAN'T BE MY FATE! SAY IT CAN BE ALTERED! SAY IT CAN BE CHANGED!
JASONEZER SCROOGE
BORN
DIED MAY 20
MAY 20TH IS THE DAY BEFORE THE NEW "STAR WARS" MOVIE OPENS!
AMEND

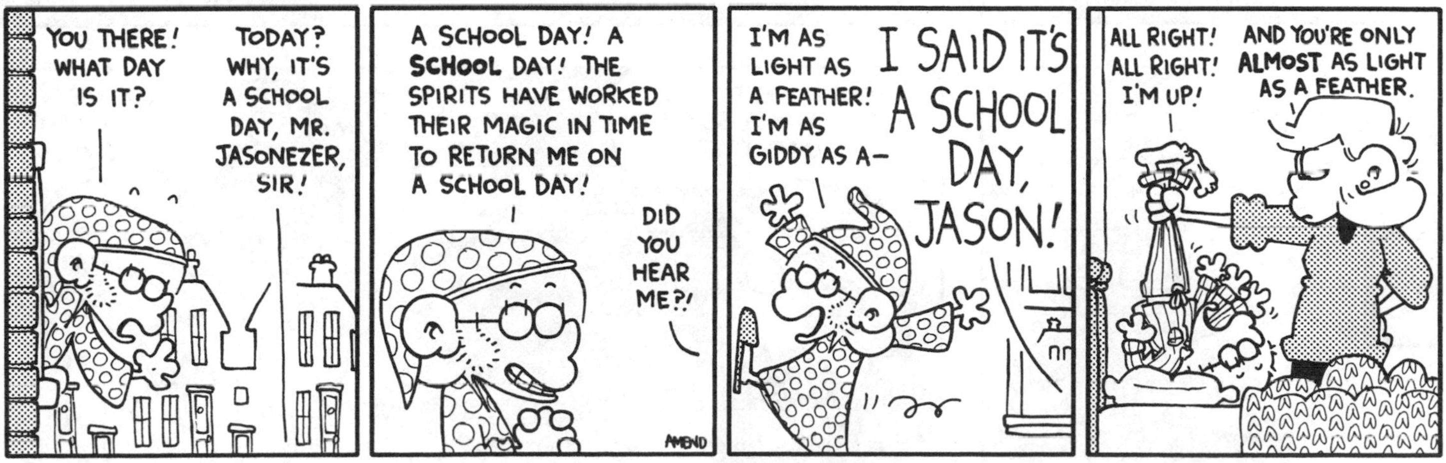
YOU THERE! WHAT DAY IS IT?
TODAY? WHY, IT'S A SCHOOL DAY, MR. JASONEZER, SIR!
A SCHOOL DAY! A **SCHOOL** DAY! THE SPIRITS HAVE WORKED THEIR MAGIC IN TIME TO RETURN ME ON A SCHOOL DAY!
DID YOU HEAR ME?!
AMEND
I'M AS LIGHT AS A FEATHER! I'M AS GIDDY AS A–
I SAID IT'S A SCHOOL DAY, JASON!
ALL RIGHT! ALL RIGHT! I'M UP!
AND YOU'RE ONLY **ALMOST** AS LIGHT AS A FEATHER.

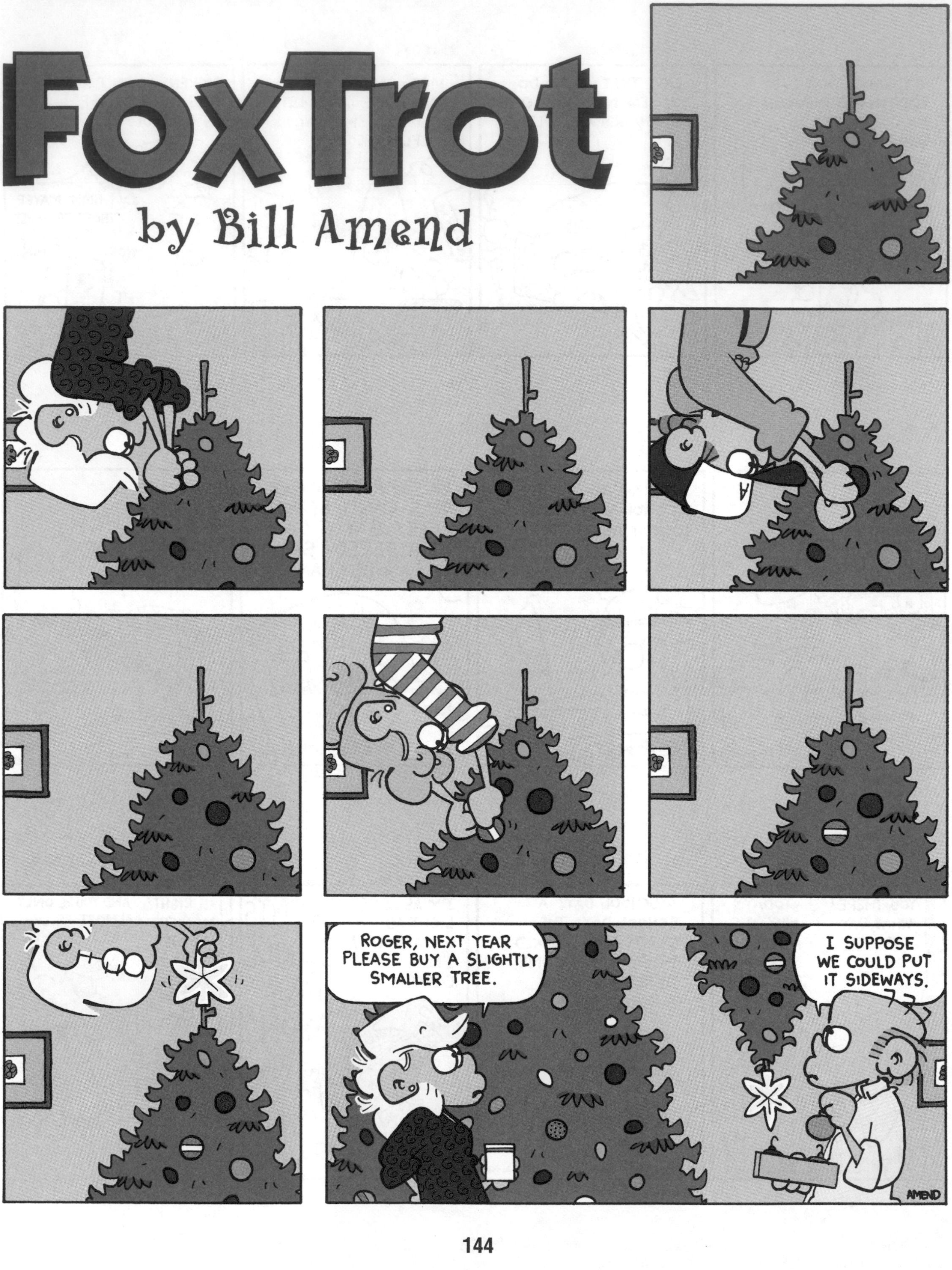
FoxTrot
by Bill Amend
ROGER, NEXT YEAR PLEASE BUY A SLIGHTLY SMALLER TREE.
I SUPPOSE WE COULD PUT IT SIDEWAYS.
AMEND

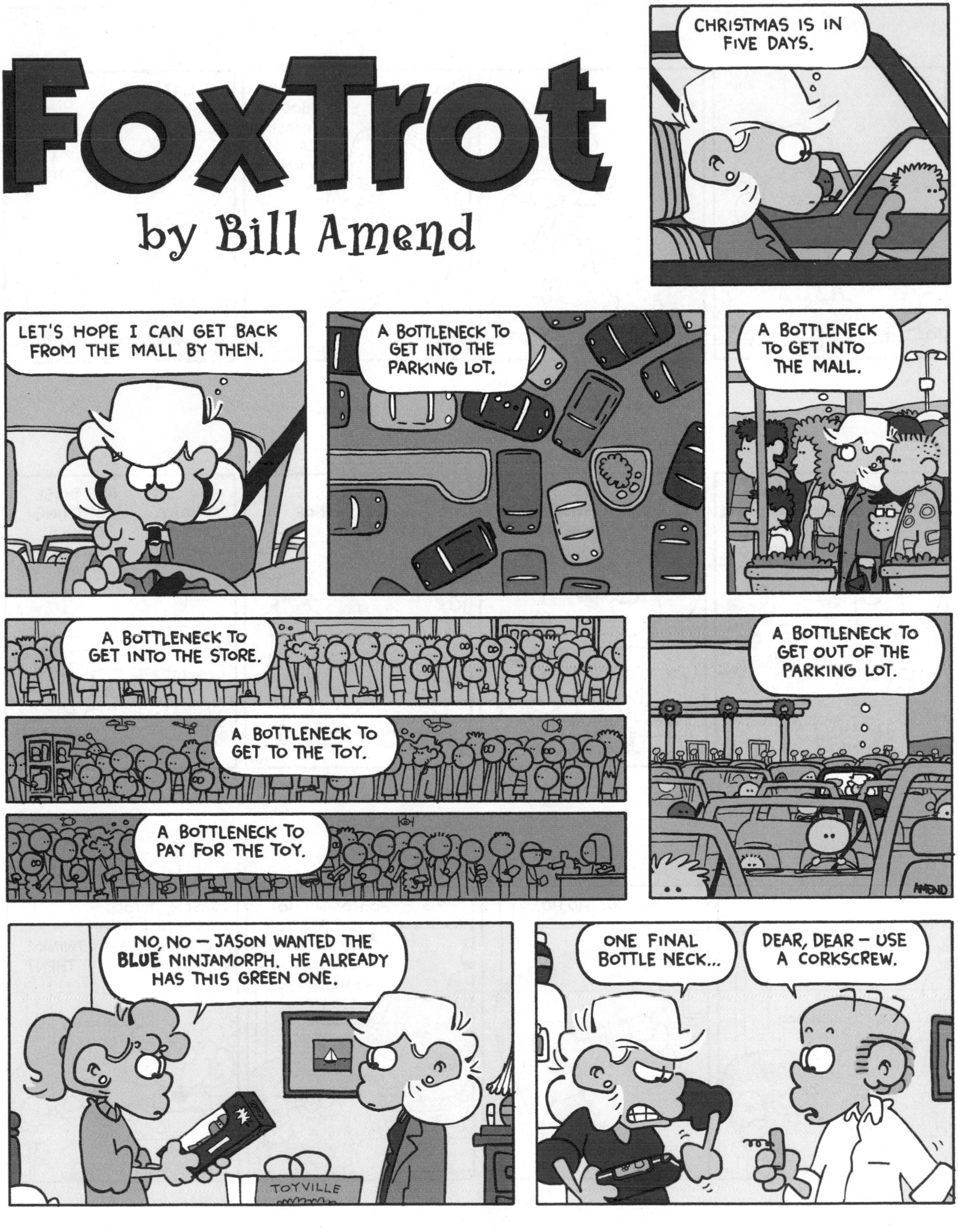
FoxTrot
by Bill Amend
CHRISTMAS IS IN FIVE DAYS.
LET'S HOPE I CAN GET BACK FROM THE MALL BY THEN.
A BOTTLENECK TO GET INTO THE PARKING LOT.
A BOTTLENECK TO GET INTO THE MALL.
A BOTTLENECK TO GET INTO THE STORE.
A BOTTLENECK TO GET TO THE TOY.
A BOTTLENECK TO PAY FOR THE TOY.
A BOTTLENECK TO GET OUT OF THE PARKING LOT.
AMEND
NO, NO – JASON WANTED THE **BLUE** NINJAMORPH. HE ALREADY HAS THIS GREEN ONE.
TOYVILLE
ONE FINAL BOTTLE NECK...
DEAR, DEAR – USE A CORKSCREW.

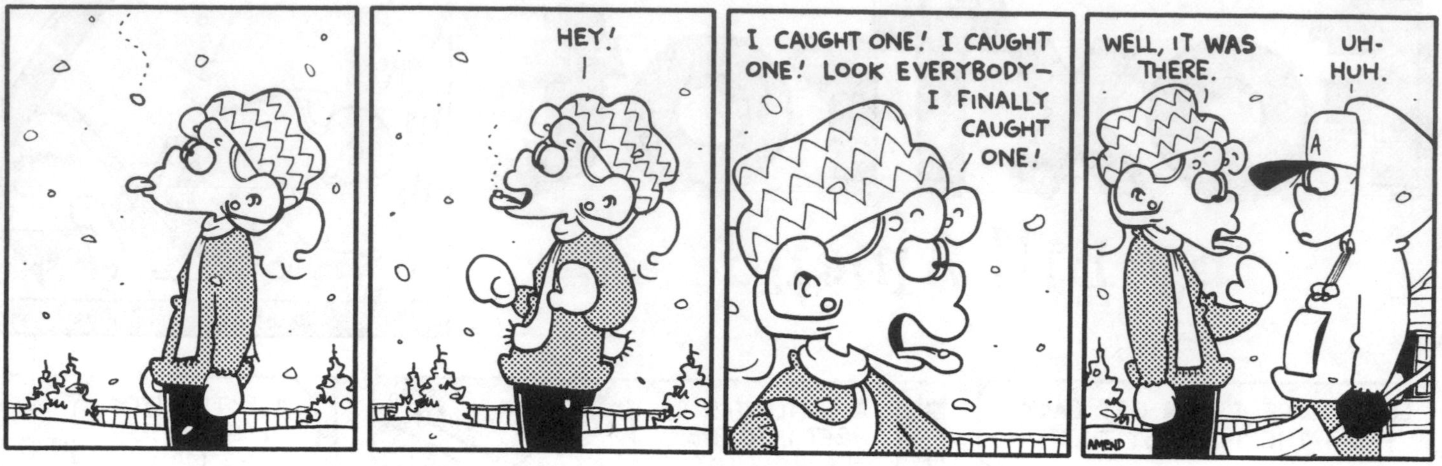
HEY!
I CAUGHT ONE! I CAUGHT ONE! LOOK EVERYBODY— I FINALLY CAUGHT ONE!
WELL, IT WAS THERE.
UH-HUH.
AMEND

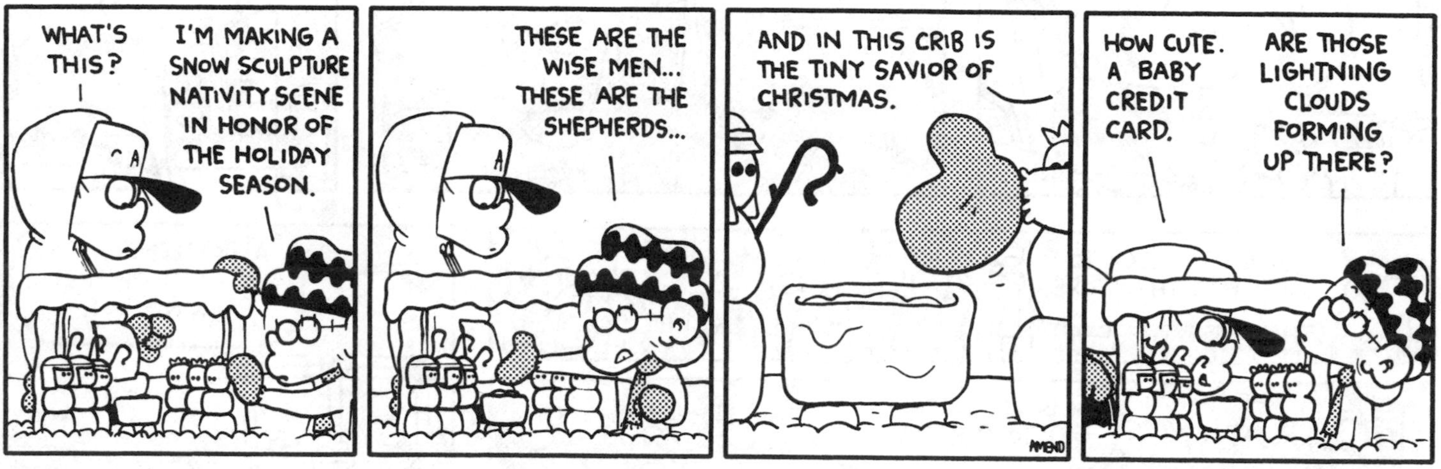
WHAT'S THIS?
I'M MAKING A SNOW SCULPTURE NATIVITY SCENE IN HONOR OF THE HOLIDAY SEASON.
THESE ARE THE WISE MEN... THESE ARE THE SHEPHERDS...
AND IN THIS CRIB IS THE TINY SAVIOR OF CHRISTMAS.
AMEND
HOW CUTE. A BABY CREDIT CARD.
ARE THOSE LIGHTNING CLOUDS FORMING UP THERE?

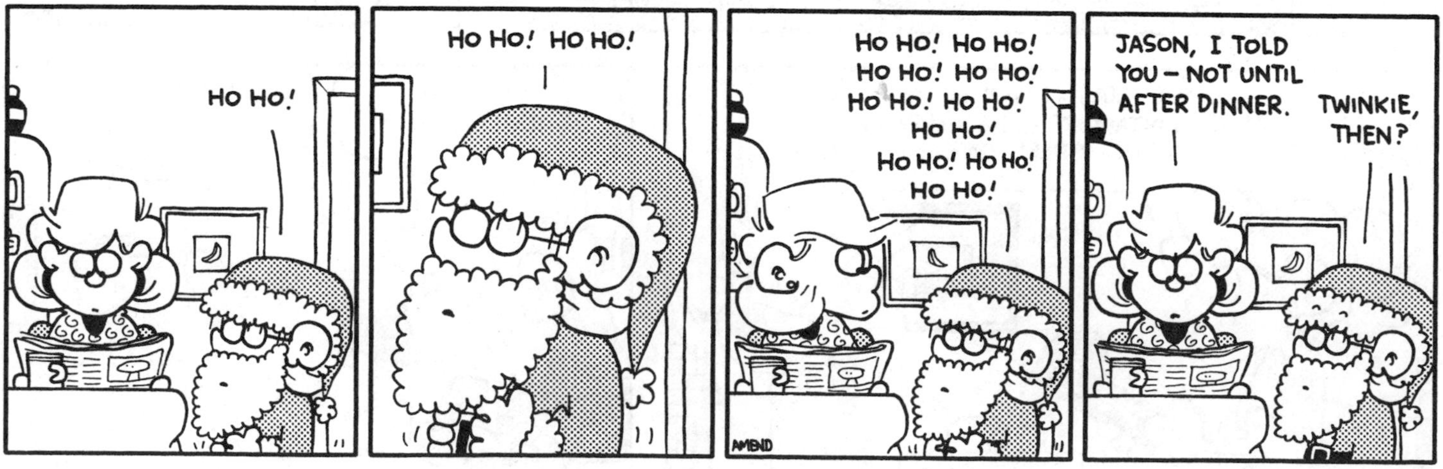
HO HO!
HO HO! HO HO!
HO HO! HO HO! HO HO! HO HO! HO HO! HO HO! HO HO! HO HO! HO HO! HO HO!
AMEND
JASON, I TOLD YOU – NOT UNTIL AFTER DINNER.
TWINKIE, THEN?

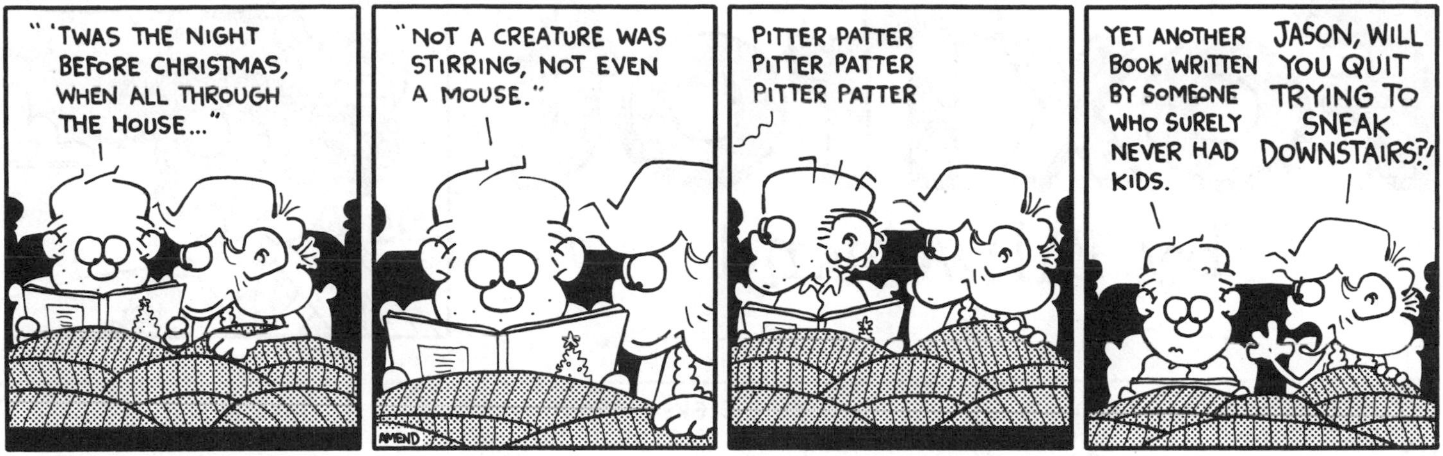
"'TWAS THE NIGHT BEFORE CHRISTMAS, WHEN ALL THROUGH THE HOUSE..."
"NOT A CREATURE WAS STIRRING, NOT EVEN A MOUSE."
PITTER PATTER
PITTER PATTER
PITTER PATTER
YET ANOTHER BOOK WRITTEN BY SOMEONE WHO SURELY NEVER HAD KIDS.
JASON, WILL YOU QUIT TRYING TO SNEAK DOWNSTAIRS?!

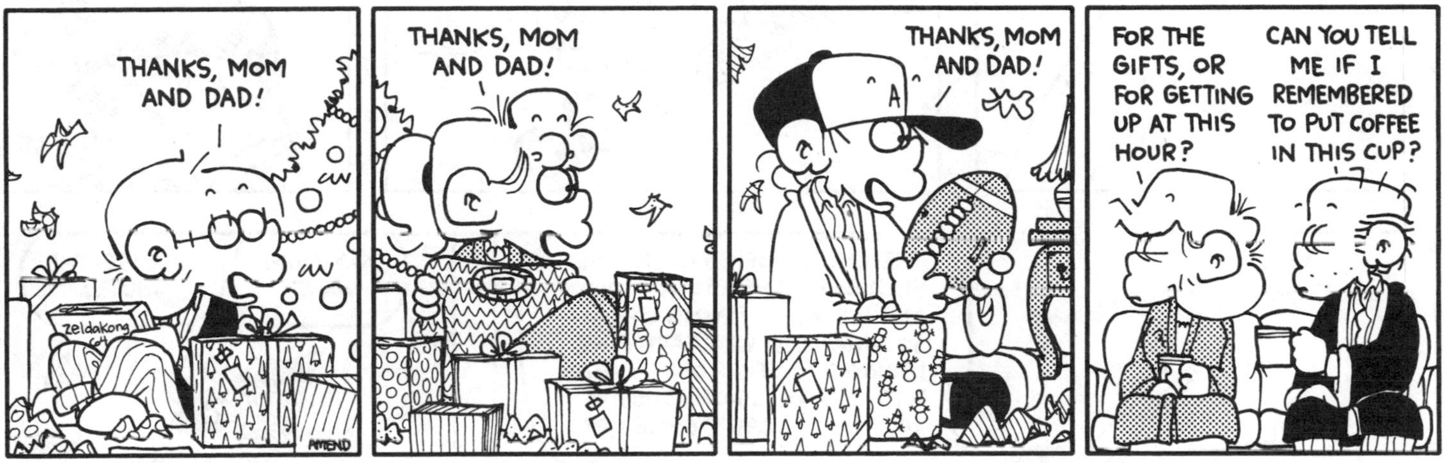
THANKS, MOM AND DAD!
Zeldakong
THANKS, MOM AND DAD!
THANKS, MOM AND DAD!
FOR THE GIFTS, OR FOR GETTING UP AT THIS HOUR?
CAN YOU TELL ME IF I REMEMBERED TO PUT COFFEE IN THIS CUP?

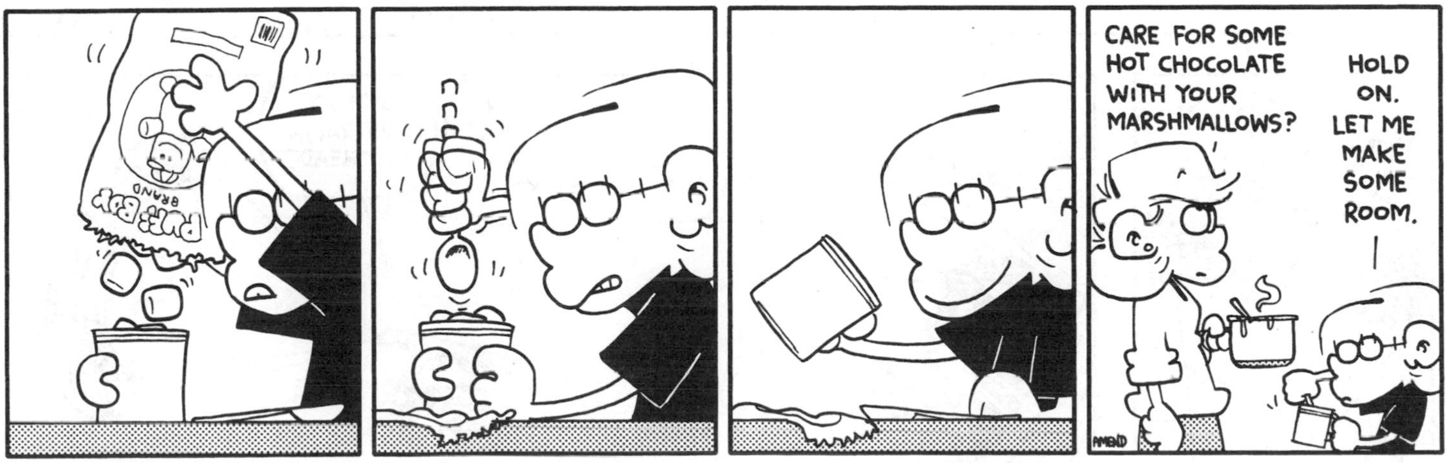
CARE FOR SOME HOT CHOCOLATE WITH YOUR MARSHMALLOWS?
HOLD ON. LET ME MAKE SOME ROOM.

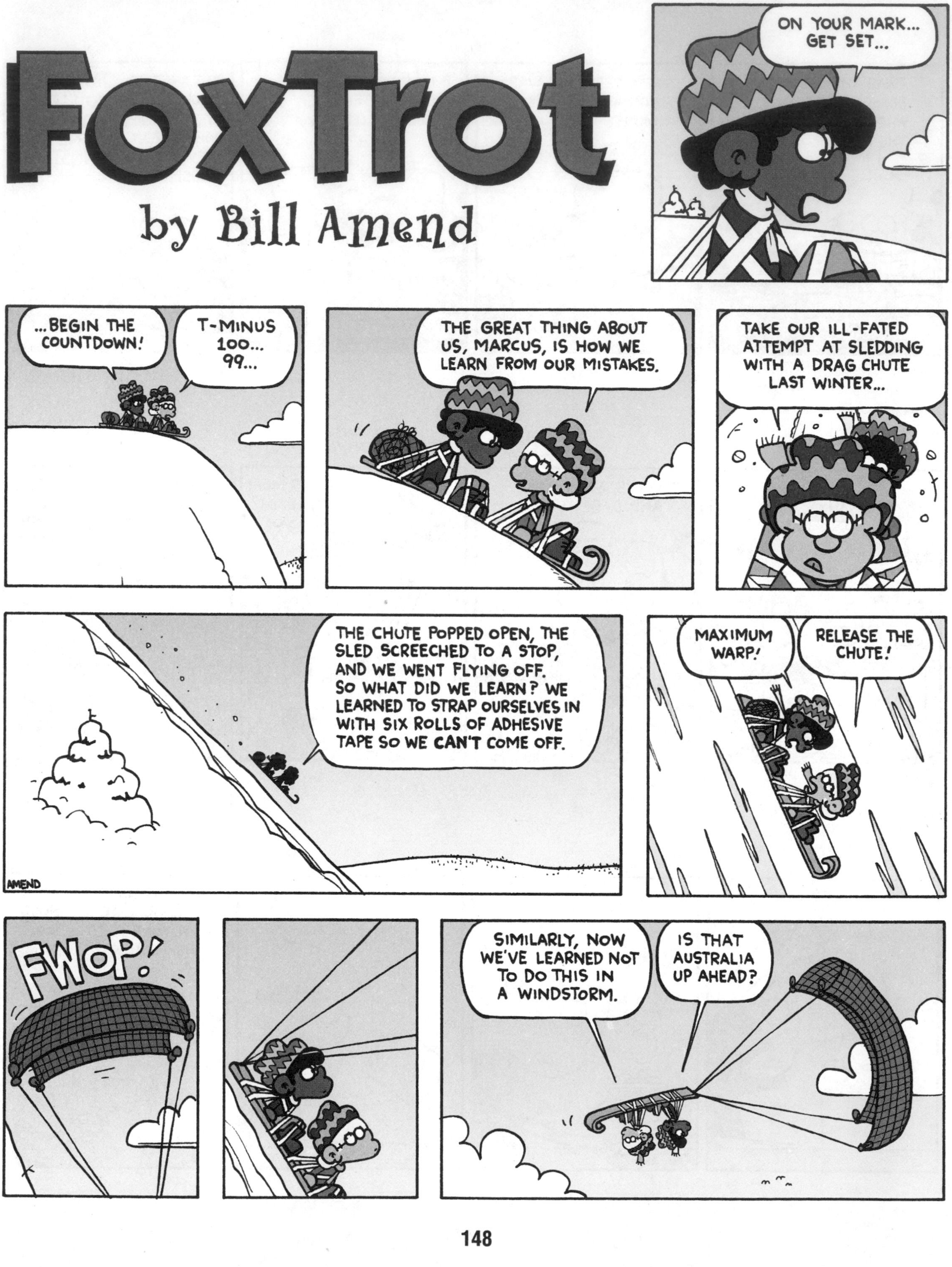
FoxTrot
by Bill Amend
ON YOUR MARK... GET SET...
...BEGIN THE COUNTDOWN!
T-MINUS 100... 99...
THE GREAT THING ABOUT US, MARCUS, IS HOW WE LEARN FROM OUR MISTAKES.
TAKE OUR ILL-FATED ATTEMPT AT SLEDDING WITH A DRAG CHUTE LAST WINTER...
THE CHUTE POPPED OPEN, THE SLED SCREECHED TO A STOP, AND WE WENT FLYING OFF. SO WHAT DID WE LEARN? WE LEARNED TO STRAP OURSELVES IN WITH SIX ROLLS OF ADHESIVE TAPE SO WE CAN'T COME OFF.
AMEND
MAXIMUM WARP!
RELEASE THE CHUTE!
FWOP!
SIMILARLY, NOW WE'VE LEARNED NOT TO DO THIS IN A WINDSTORM.
IS THAT AUSTRALIA UP AHEAD?

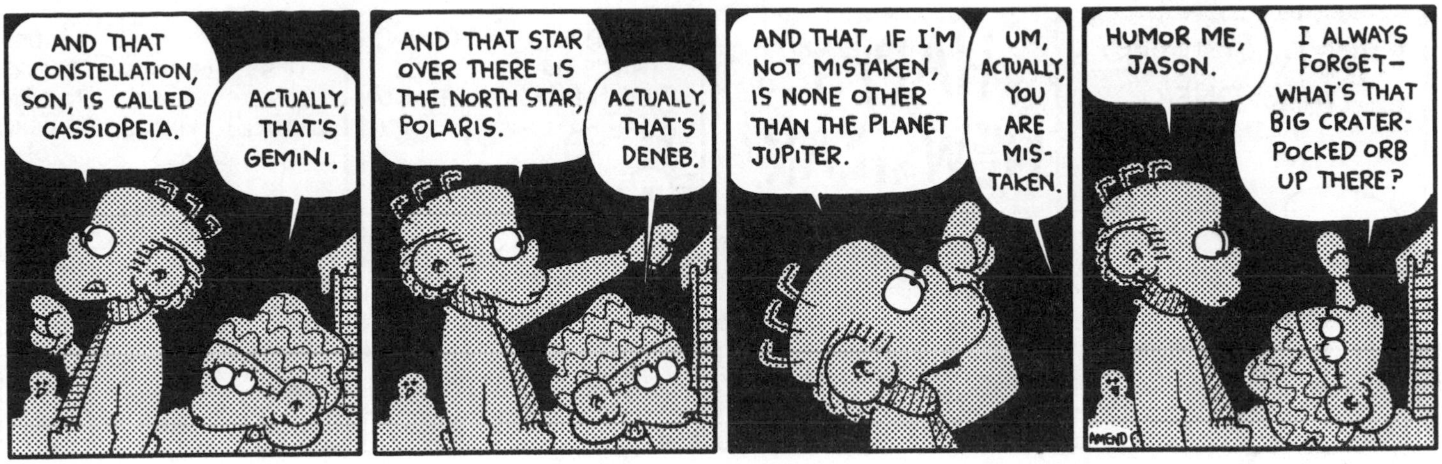
AND THAT CONSTELLATION, SON, IS CALLED CASSIOPEIA.
ACTUALLY, THAT'S GEMINI.
AND THAT STAR OVER THERE IS THE NORTH STAR, POLARIS.
ACTUALLY, THAT'S DENEB.
AND THAT, IF I'M NOT MISTAKEN, IS NONE OTHER THAN THE PLANET JUPITER.
UM, ACTUALLY, YOU ARE MIS-TAKEN.
HUMOR ME, JASON.
I ALWAYS FORGET— WHAT'S THAT BIG CRATER-POCKED ORB UP THERE?
AMEND

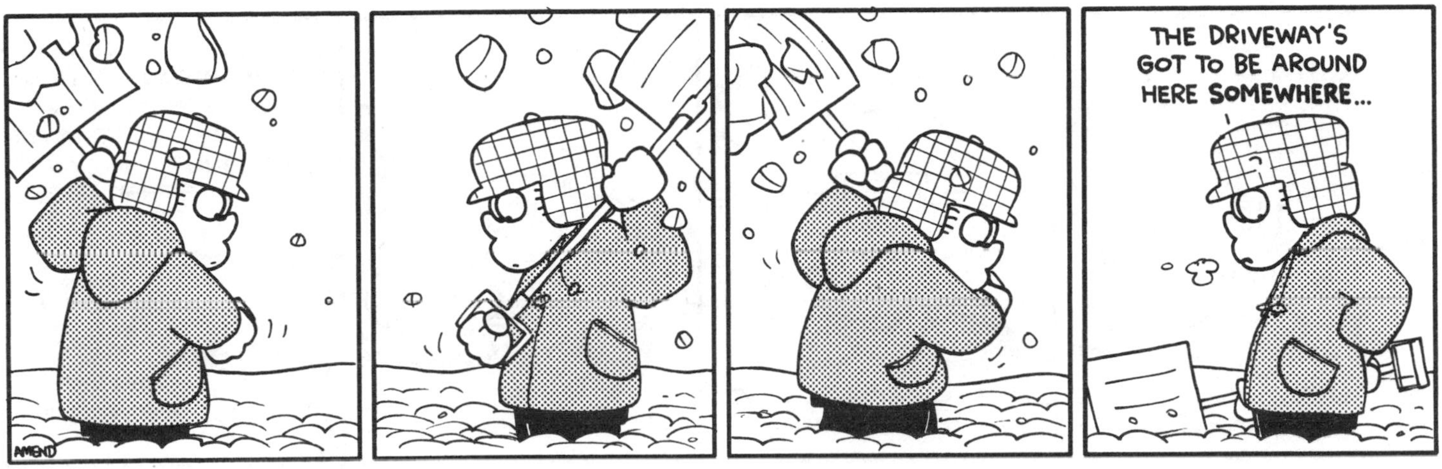
AMEND
THE DRIVEWAY'S GOT TO BE AROUND HERE **SOMEWHERE**...

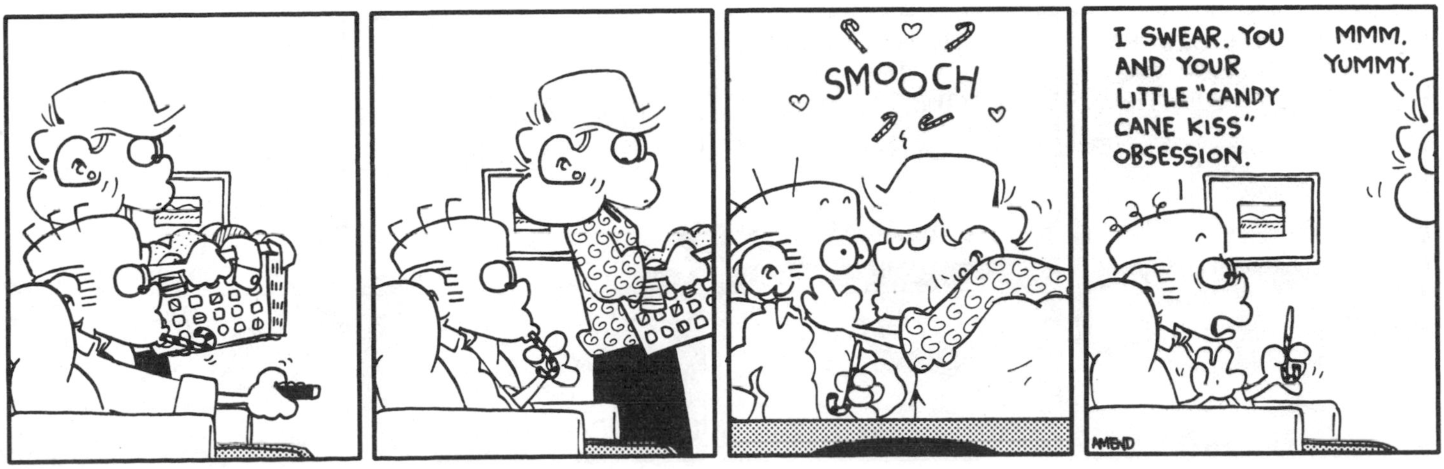
SMOOCH
I SWEAR. YOU AND YOUR LITTLE "CANDY CANE KISS" OBSESSION.
MMM. YUMMY.
AMEND

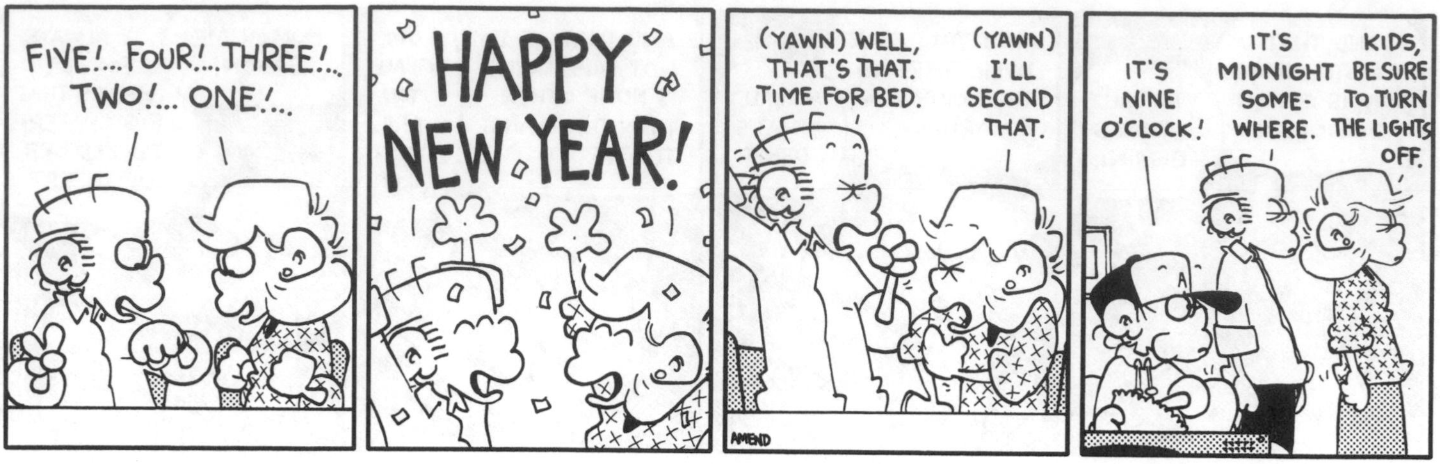
FIVE!... FOUR!... THREE!... TWO!... ONE!...
HAPPY NEW YEAR!
(YAWN) WELL, THAT'S THAT. TIME FOR BED.
(YAWN) I'LL SECOND THAT.
IT'S NINE O'CLOCK!
IT'S MIDNIGHT SOME-WHERE.
KIDS, BE SURE TO TURN THE LIGHTS OFF.
AMEND

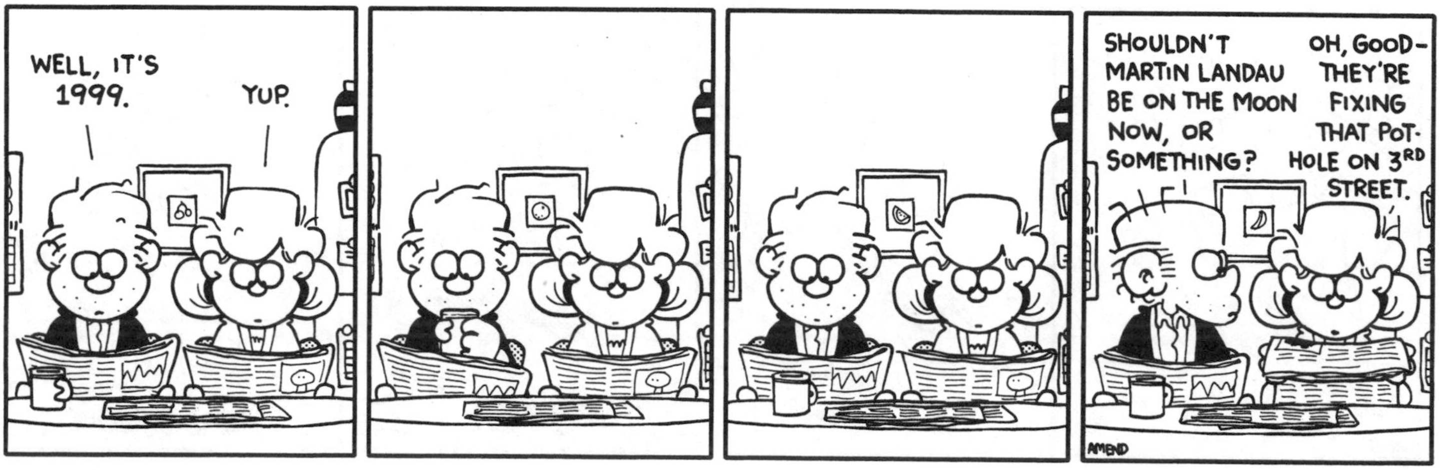
WELL, IT'S 1999.
YUP.
SHOULDN'T MARTIN LANDAU BE ON THE MOON NOW, OR SOMETHING?
OH, GOOD-THEY'RE FIXING THAT POT-HOLE ON 3RD STREET.
AMEND

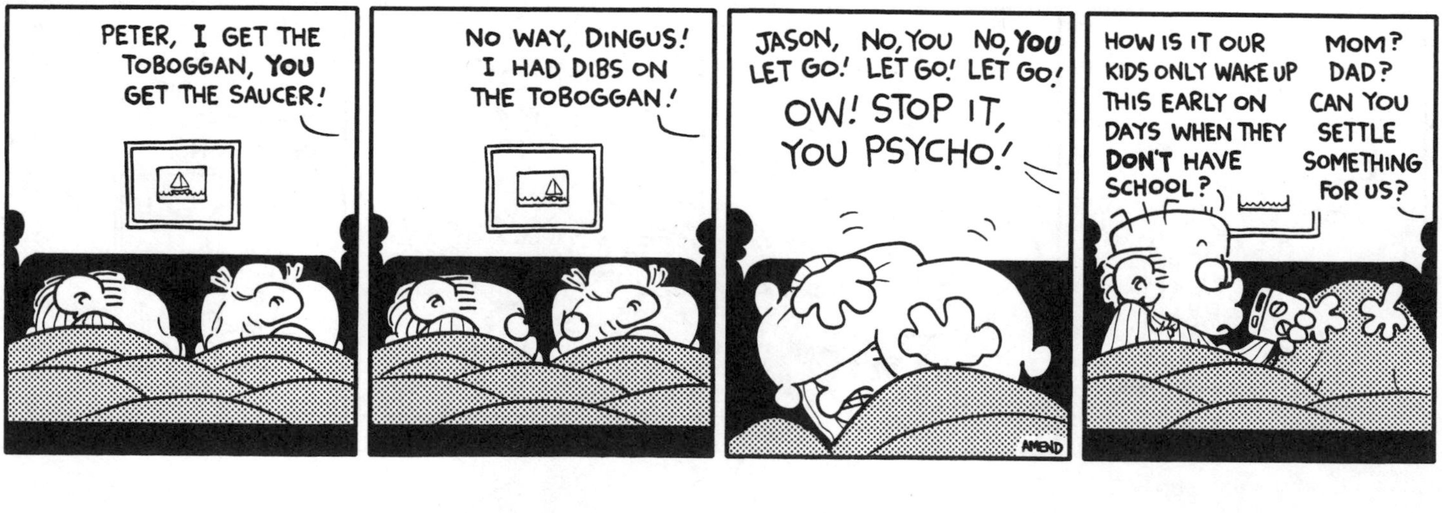
PETER, I GET THE TOBOGGAN, YOU GET THE SAUCER!
NO WAY, DINGUS! I HAD DIBS ON THE TOBOGGAN!
JASON, LET GO!
NO, YOU LET GO!
NO, YOU LET GO!
OW! STOP IT, YOU PSYCHO!
AMEND
HOW IS IT OUR KIDS ONLY WAKE UP THIS EARLY ON DAYS WHEN THEY DON'T HAVE SCHOOL?
MOM? DAD? CAN YOU SETTLE SOMETHING FOR US?

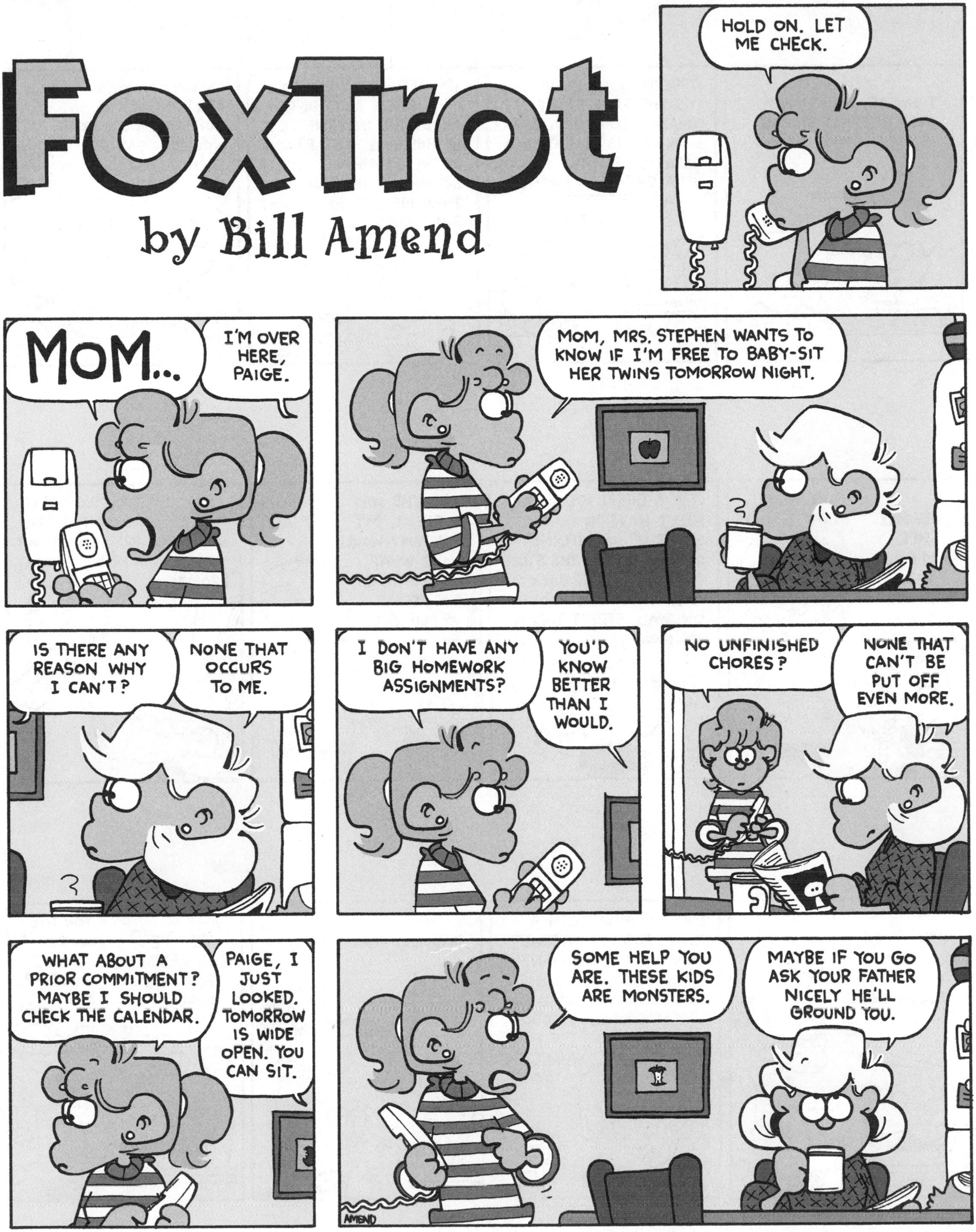
FoxTrot
by Bill Amend
HOLD ON. LET ME CHECK.
MOM...
I'M OVER HERE, PAIGE.
MOM, MRS. STEPHEN WANTS TO KNOW IF I'M FREE TO BABY-SIT HER TWINS TOMORROW NIGHT.
IS THERE ANY REASON WHY I CAN'T?
NONE THAT OCCURS TO ME.
I DON'T HAVE ANY BIG HOMEWORK ASSIGNMENTS?
YOU'D KNOW BETTER THAN I WOULD.
NO UNFINISHED CHORES?
NONE THAT CAN'T BE PUT OFF EVEN MORE.
WHAT ABOUT A PRIOR COMMITMENT? MAYBE I SHOULD CHECK THE CALENDAR.
PAIGE, I JUST LOOKED. TOMORROW IS WIDE OPEN. YOU CAN SIT.
SOME HELP YOU ARE. THESE KIDS ARE MONSTERS.
MAYBE IF YOU GO ASK YOUR FATHER NICELY HE'LL GROUND YOU.
AMEND

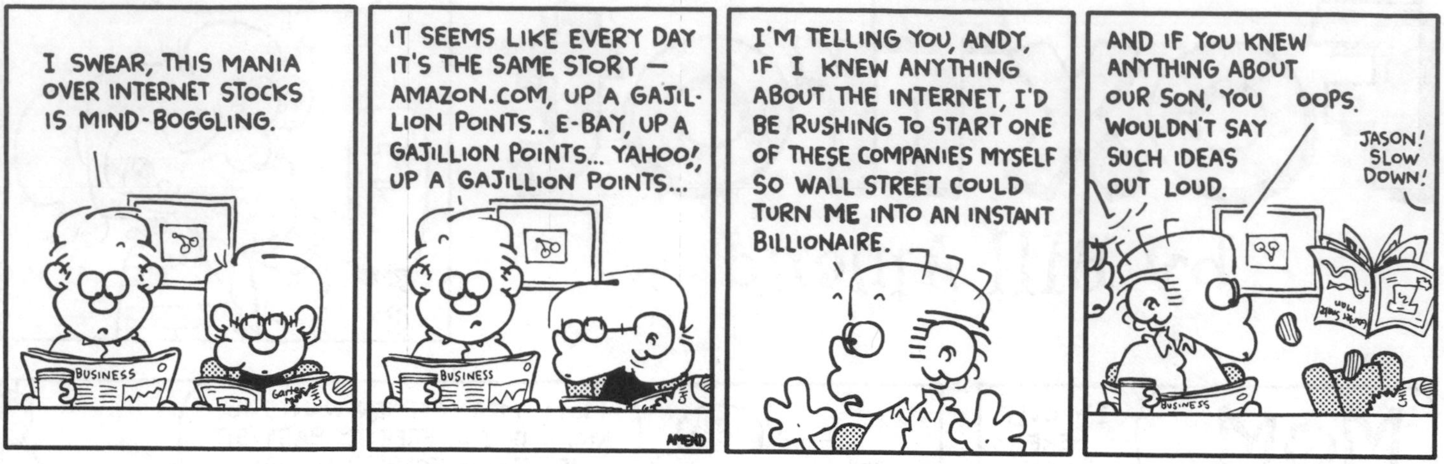
I SWEAR, THIS MANIA OVER INTERNET STOCKS IS MIND-BOGGLING.
IT SEEMS LIKE EVERY DAY IT'S THE SAME STORY — AMAZON.COM, UP A GAJILLION POINTS... E-BAY, UP A GAJILLION POINTS... YAHOO!, UP A GAJILLION POINTS...
I'M TELLING YOU, ANDY, IF I KNEW ANYTHING ABOUT THE INTERNET, I'D BE RUSHING TO START ONE OF THESE COMPANIES MYSELF SO WALL STREET COULD TURN ME INTO AN INSTANT BILLIONAIRE.
AND IF YOU KNEW ANYTHING ABOUT OUR SON, YOU WOULDN'T SAY SUCH IDEAS OUT LOUD.
OOPS.
JASON! SLOW DOWN!

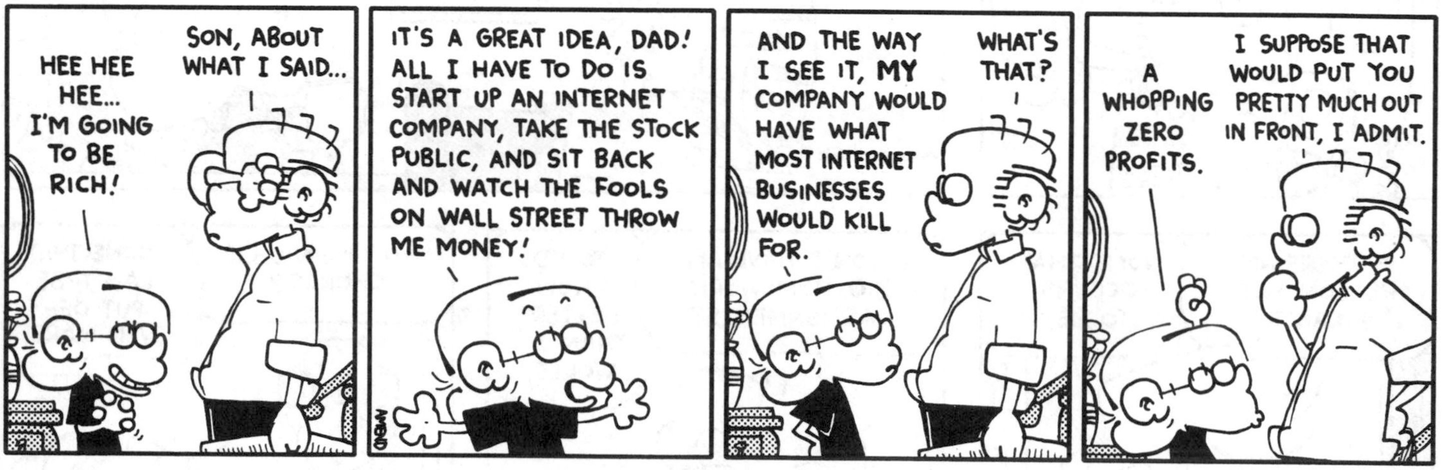
HEE HEE HEE... I'M GOING TO BE RICH!
SON, ABOUT WHAT I SAID...
IT'S A GREAT IDEA, DAD! ALL I HAVE TO DO IS START UP AN INTERNET COMPANY, TAKE THE STOCK PUBLIC, AND SIT BACK AND WATCH THE FOOLS ON WALL STREET THROW ME MONEY!
AND THE WAY I SEE IT, MY COMPANY WOULD HAVE WHAT MOST INTERNET BUSINESSES WOULD KILL FOR.
WHAT'S THAT?
A WHOPPING ZERO PROFITS.
I SUPPOSE THAT WOULD PUT YOU PRETTY MUCH OUT IN FRONT, I ADMIT.

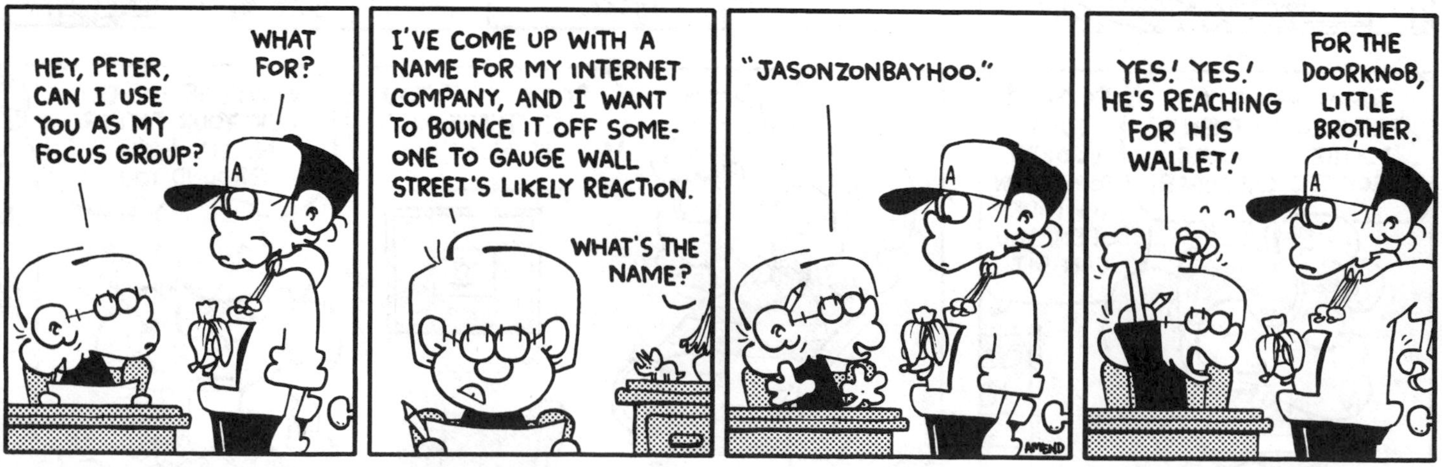
HEY, PETER, CAN I USE YOU AS MY FOCUS GROUP?
WHAT FOR?
I'VE COME UP WITH A NAME FOR MY INTERNET COMPANY, AND I WANT TO BOUNCE IT OFF SOMEONE TO GAUGE WALL STREET'S LIKELY REACTION.
WHAT'S THE NAME?
"JASONZONBAYHOO."
YES! YES! HE'S REACHING FOR HIS WALLET!
FOR THE DOORKNOB, LITTLE BROTHER.

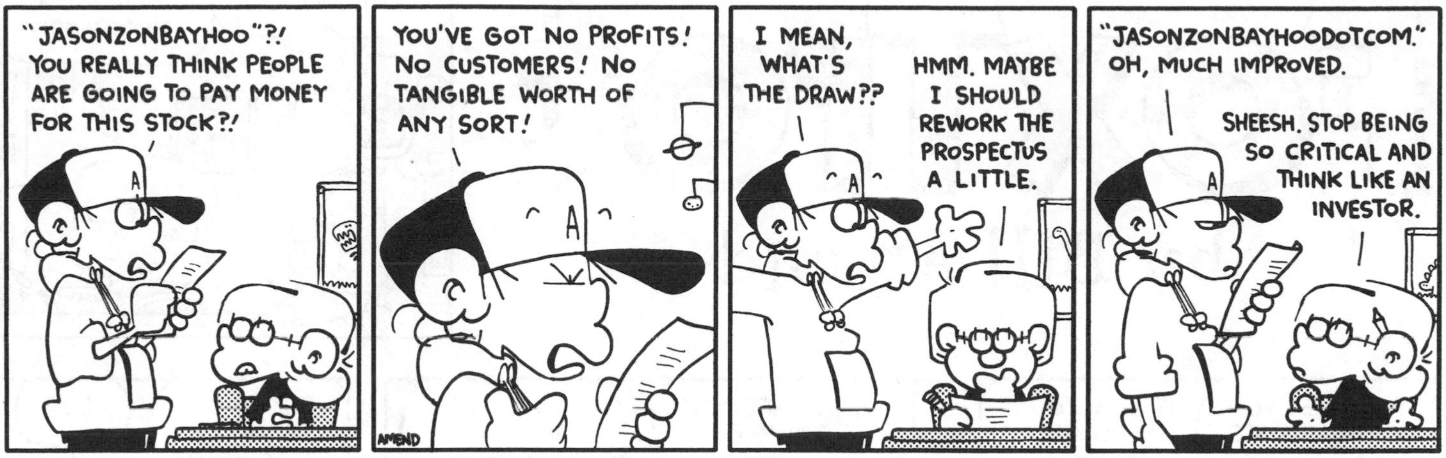

"JASONZONBAYHOO"?! YOU REALLY THINK PEOPLE ARE GOING TO PAY MONEY FOR THIS STOCK?!
YOU'VE GOT NO PROFITS! NO CUSTOMERS! NO TANGIBLE WORTH OF ANY SORT!
AMEND
I MEAN, WHAT'S THE DRAW??
HMM. MAYBE I SHOULD REWORK THE PROSPECTUS A LITTLE.
"JASONZONBAYHOODOTCOM." OH, MUCH IMPROVED.
SHEESH. STOP BEING SO CRITICAL AND THINK LIKE AN INVESTOR.

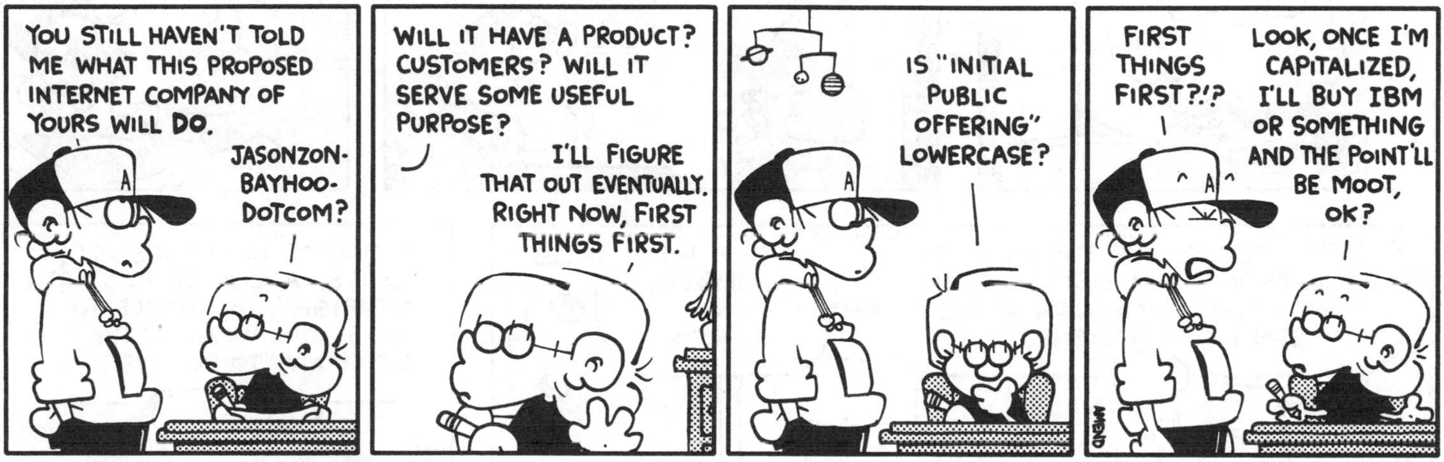

YOU STILL HAVEN'T TOLD ME WHAT THIS PROPOSED INTERNET COMPANY OF YOURS WILL DO.
JASONZON-BAYHOO-DOTCOM?
WILL IT HAVE A PRODUCT? CUSTOMERS? WILL IT SERVE SOME USEFUL PURPOSE?
I'LL FIGURE THAT OUT EVENTUALLY. RIGHT NOW, FIRST THINGS FIRST.
IS "INITIAL PUBLIC OFFERING" LOWERCASE?
FIRST THINGS FIRST?!?
LOOK, ONCE I'M CAPITALIZED, I'LL BUY IBM OR SOMETHING AND THE POINT'LL BE MOOT, OK?
AMEND

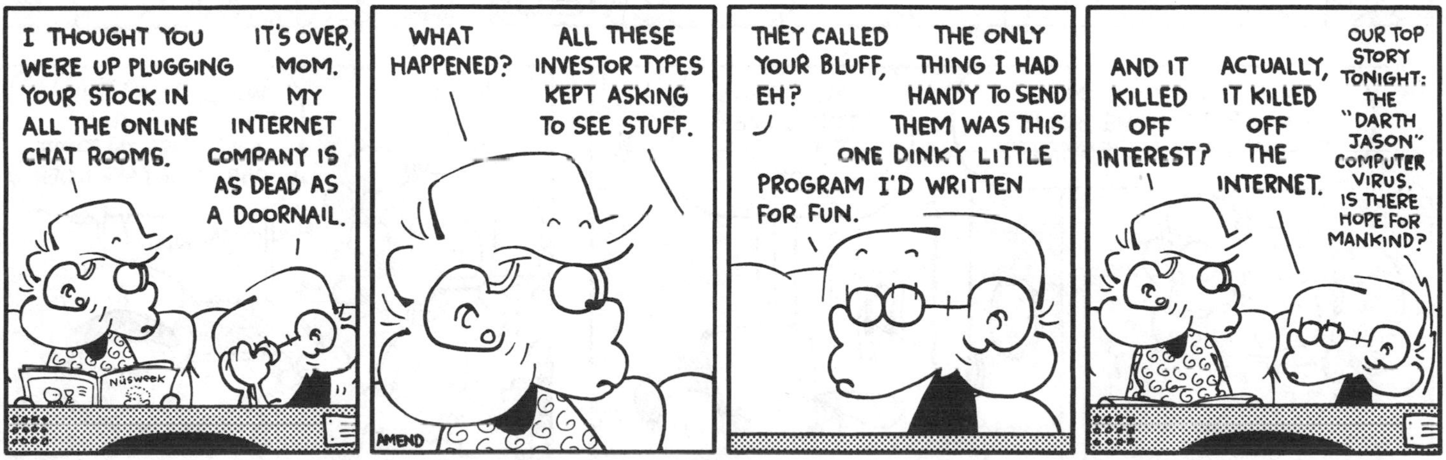

I THOUGHT YOU WERE UP PLUGGING YOUR STOCK IN ALL THE ONLINE CHAT ROOMS.
IT'S OVER, MOM. MY INTERNET COMPANY IS AS DEAD AS A DOORNAIL.
Nüsweek
WHAT HAPPENED?
ALL THESE INVESTOR TYPES KEPT ASKING TO SEE STUFF.
AMEND
THEY CALLED YOUR BLUFF, EH?
THE ONLY THING I HAD HANDY TO SEND THEM WAS THIS ONE DINKY LITTLE PROGRAM I'D WRITTEN FOR FUN.
AND IT KILLED OFF INTEREST?
ACTUALLY, IT KILLED OFF THE INTERNET.
OUR TOP STORY TONIGHT: THE "DARTH JASON" COMPUTER VIRUS. IS THERE HOPE FOR MANKIND?

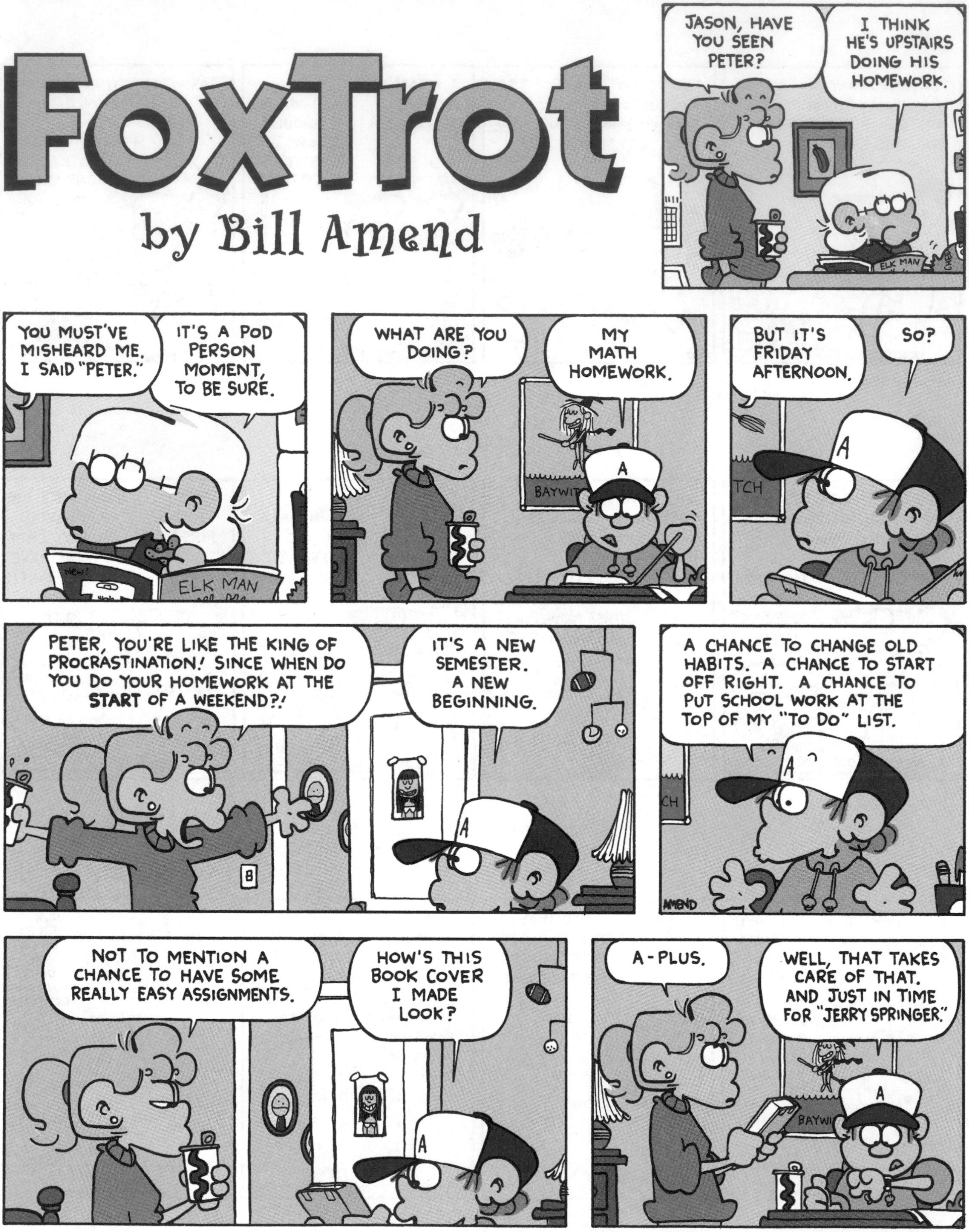

FoxTrot
by Bill Amend
JASON, HAVE YOU SEEN PETER?
I THINK HE'S UPSTAIRS DOING HIS HOMEWORK.
ELK MAN
YOU MUST'VE MISHEARD ME. I SAID "PETER."
IT'S A POD PERSON MOMENT, TO BE SURE.
ELK MAN
WHAT ARE YOU DOING?
MY MATH HOMEWORK.
BUT IT'S FRIDAY AFTERNOON.
SO?
PETER, YOU'RE LIKE THE KING OF PROCRASTINATION! SINCE WHEN DO YOU DO YOUR HOMEWORK AT THE START OF A WEEKEND?!
IT'S A NEW SEMESTER. A NEW BEGINNING.
A CHANCE TO CHANGE OLD HABITS. A CHANCE TO START OFF RIGHT. A CHANCE TO PUT SCHOOL WORK AT THE TOP OF MY "TO DO" LIST.
AMEND
NOT TO MENTION A CHANCE TO HAVE SOME REALLY EASY ASSIGNMENTS.
HOW'S THIS BOOK COVER I MADE LOOK?
A-PLUS.
WELL, THAT TAKES CARE OF THAT. AND JUST IN TIME FOR "JERRY SPRINGER."

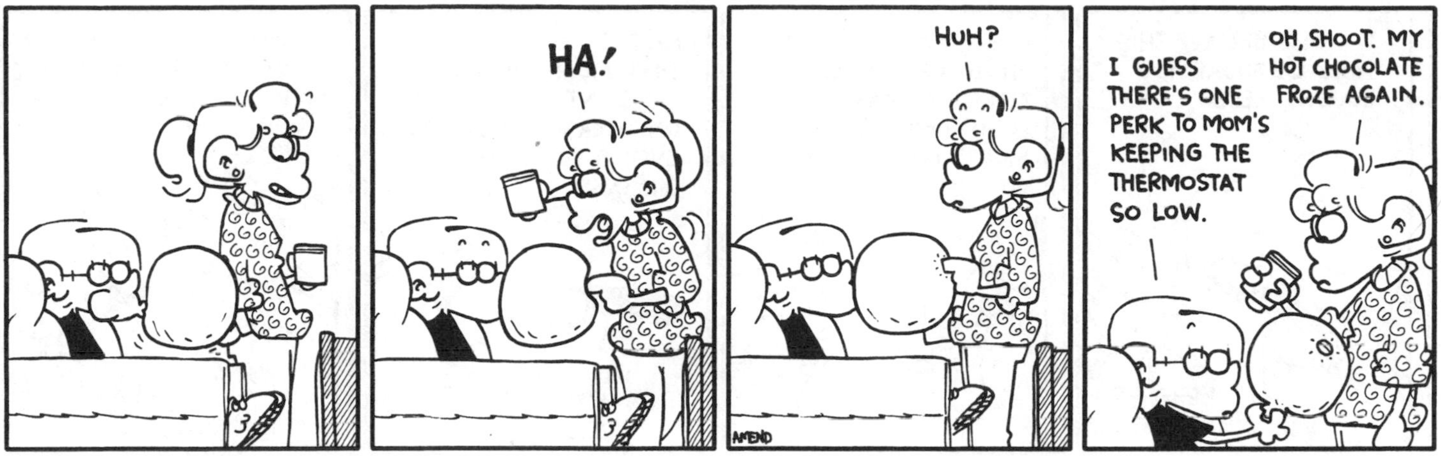
HA!
HUH?
I GUESS THERE'S ONE PERK TO MOM'S KEEPING THE THERMOSTAT SO LOW.
OH, SHOOT. MY HOT CHOCOLATE FROZE AGAIN.

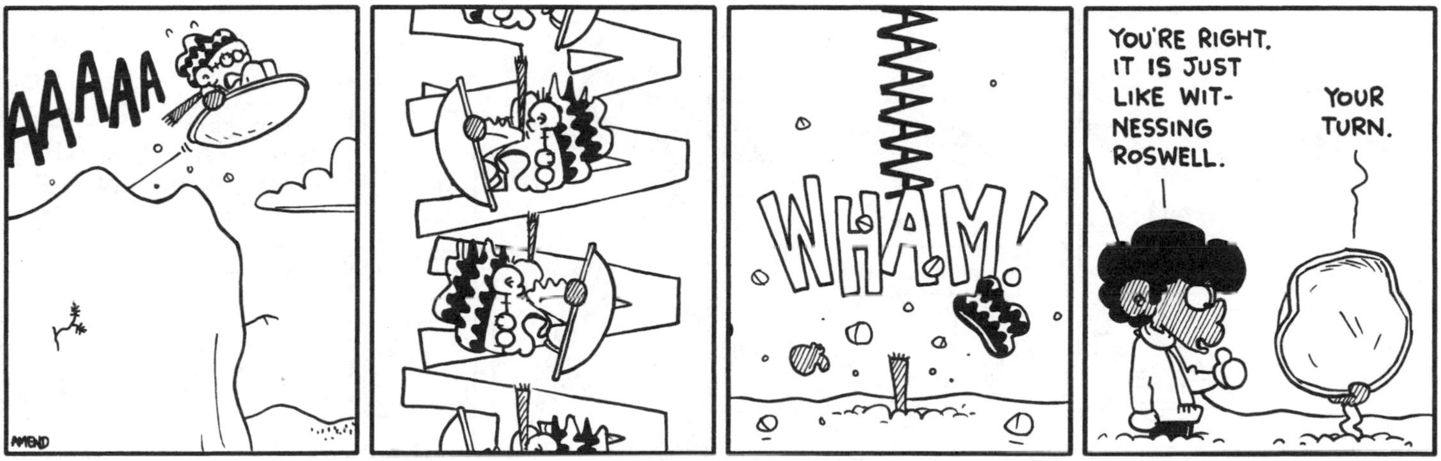
AAAAA
AAAAAAAA
WHAM!
YOU'RE RIGHT. IT IS JUST LIKE WIT- NESSING ROSWELL.
YOUR TURN.

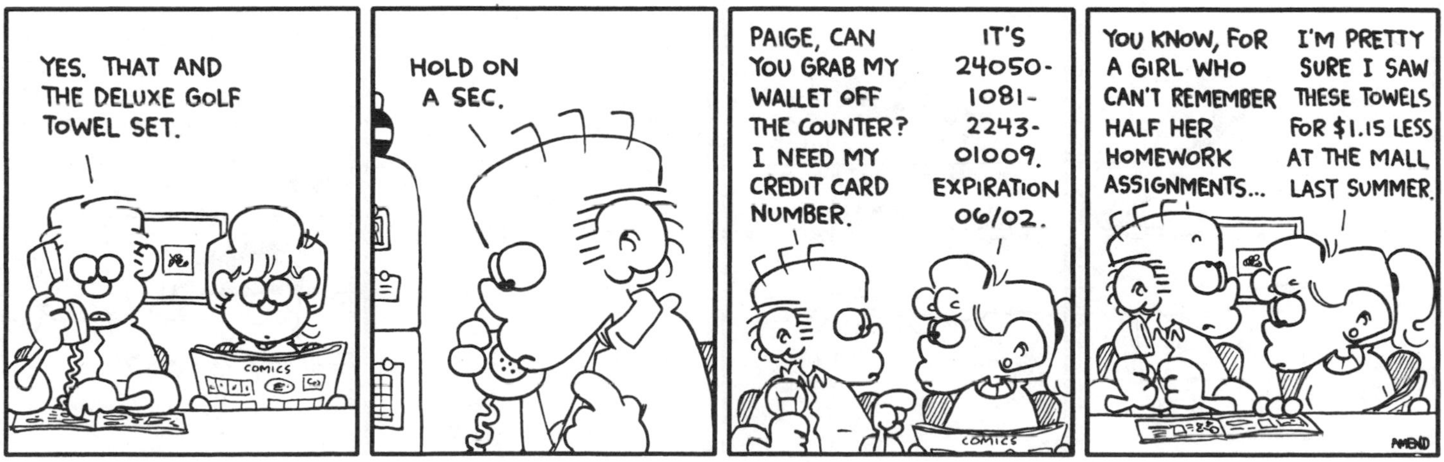
YES. THAT AND THE DELUXE GOLF TOWEL SET.
HOLD ON A SEC.
PAIGE, CAN YOU GRAB MY WALLET OFF THE COUNTER? I NEED MY CREDIT CARD NUMBER.
IT'S 24050-1081-2243-01009. EXPIRATION 06/02.
YOU KNOW, FOR A GIRL WHO CAN'T REMEMBER HALF HER HOMEWORK ASSIGNMENTS...
I'M PRETTY SURE I SAW THESE TOWELS FOR $1.15 LESS AT THE MALL LAST SUMMER.

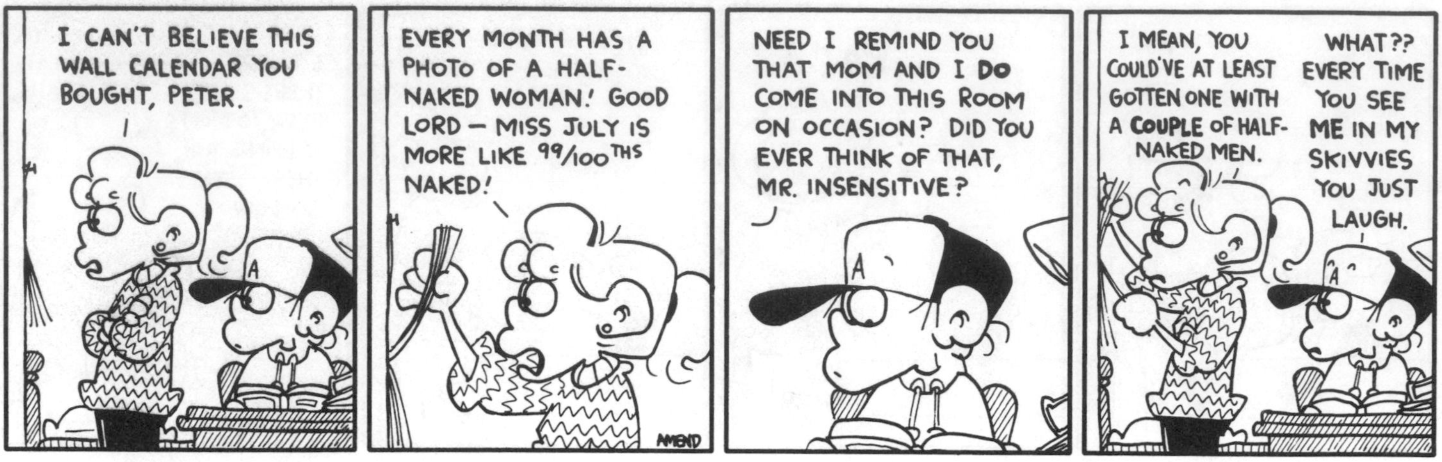
I CAN'T BELIEVE THIS WALL CALENDAR YOU BOUGHT, PETER.
EVERY MONTH HAS A PHOTO OF A HALF-NAKED WOMAN! GOOD LORD — MISS JULY IS MORE LIKE 99/100THS NAKED!
AMEND
NEED I REMIND YOU THAT MOM AND I DO COME INTO THIS ROOM ON OCCASION? DID YOU EVER THINK OF THAT, MR. INSENSITIVE?
I MEAN, YOU COULD'VE AT LEAST GOTTEN ONE WITH A COUPLE OF HALF-NAKED MEN.
WHAT?? EVERY TIME YOU SEE ME IN MY SKIVVIES YOU JUST LAUGH.

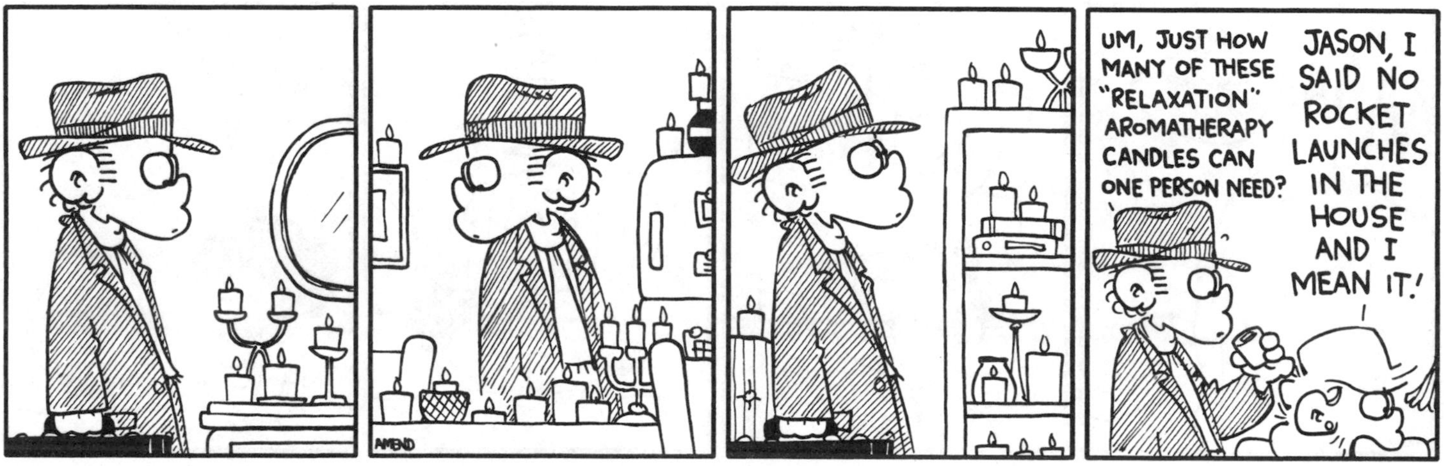
AMEND
UM, JUST HOW MANY OF THESE "RELAXATION" AROMATHERAPY CANDLES CAN ONE PERSON NEED?
JASON, I SAID NO ROCKET LAUNCHES IN THE HOUSE AND I MEAN IT!

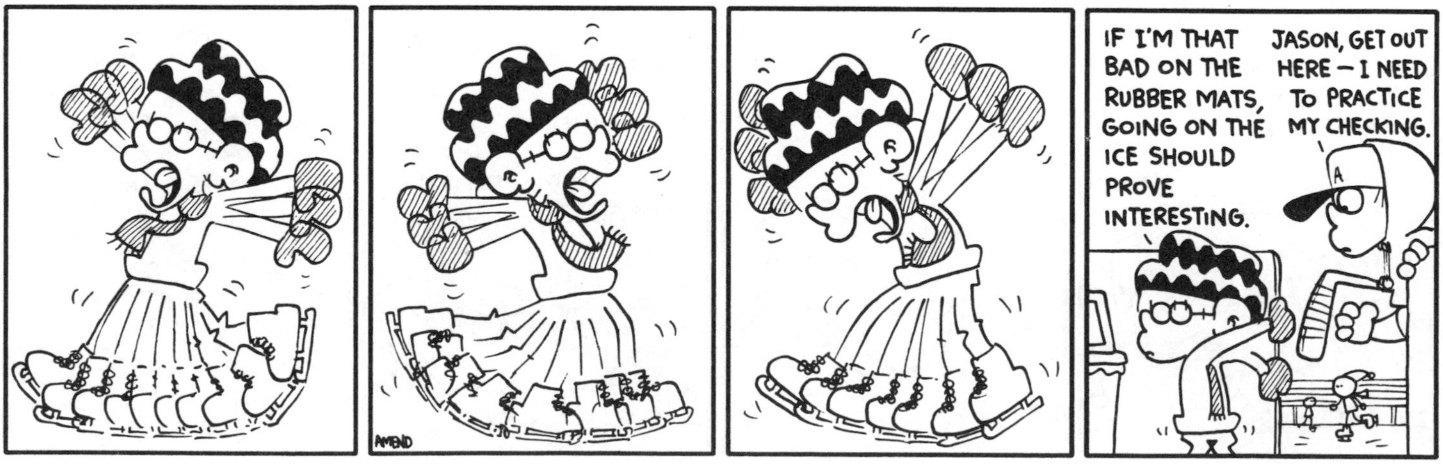
AMEND
IF I'M THAT BAD ON THE RUBBER MATS, GOING ON THE ICE SHOULD PROVE INTERESTING.
JASON, GET OUT HERE — I NEED TO PRACTICE MY CHECKING.

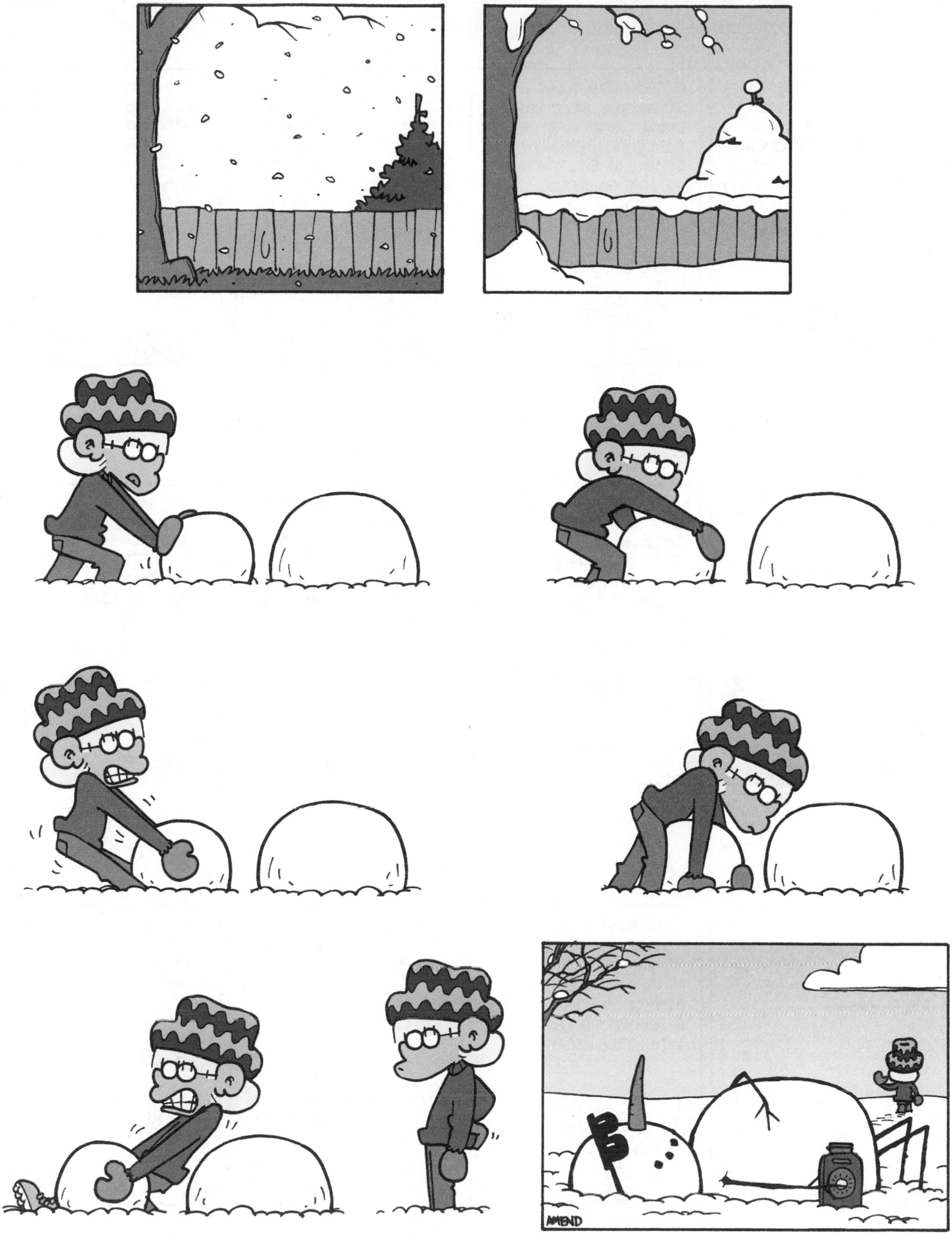
AMEND

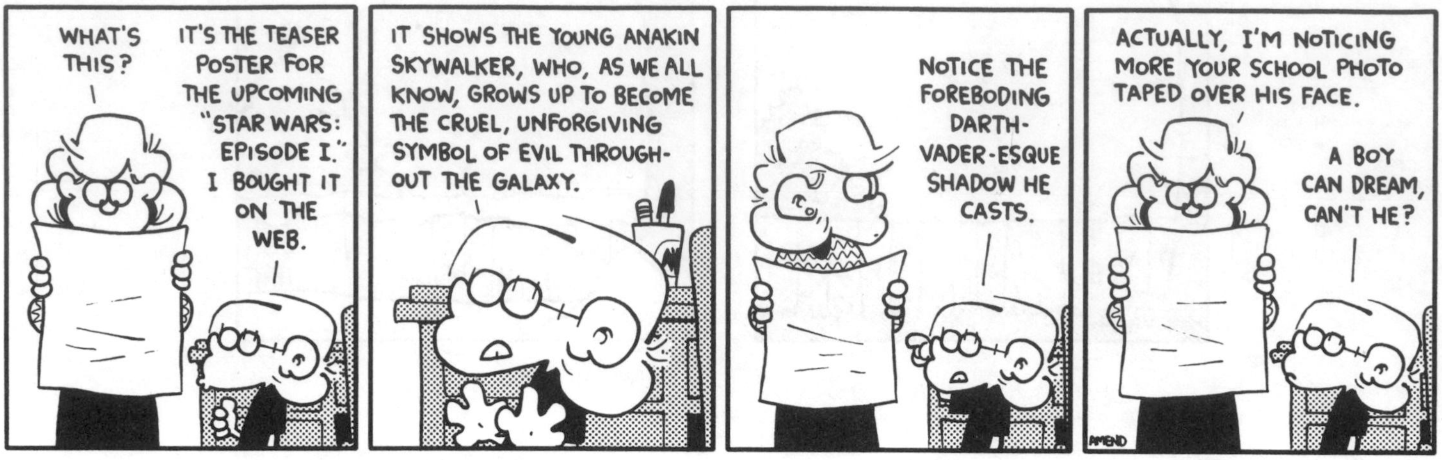
WHAT'S THIS?
IT'S THE TEASER POSTER FOR THE UPCOMING "STAR WARS: EPISODE I." I BOUGHT IT ON THE WEB.
IT SHOWS THE YOUNG ANAKIN SKYWALKER, WHO, AS WE ALL KNOW, GROWS UP TO BECOME THE CRUEL, UNFORGIVING SYMBOL OF EVIL THROUGH-OUT THE GALAXY.
NOTICE THE FOREBODING DARTH-VADER-ESQUE SHADOW HE CASTS.
ACTUALLY, I'M NOTICING MORE YOUR SCHOOL PHOTO TAPED OVER HIS FACE.
A BOY CAN DREAM, CAN'T HE?

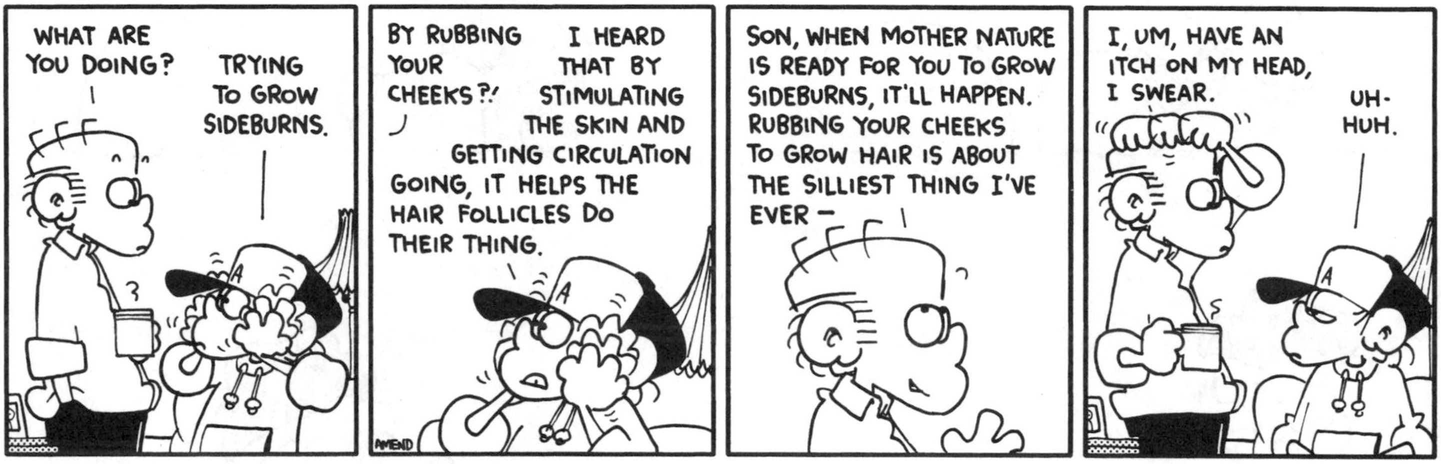
WHAT ARE YOU DOING?
TRYING TO GROW SIDEBURNS.
BY RUBBING YOUR CHEEKS?!
I HEARD THAT BY STIMULATING THE SKIN AND GETTING CIRCULATION GOING, IT HELPS THE HAIR FOLLICLES DO THEIR THING.
SON, WHEN MOTHER NATURE IS READY FOR YOU TO GROW SIDEBURNS, IT'LL HAPPEN. RUBBING YOUR CHEEKS TO GROW HAIR IS ABOUT THE SILLIEST THING I'VE EVER —
I, UM, HAVE AN ITCH ON MY HEAD, I SWEAR.
UH-HUH.

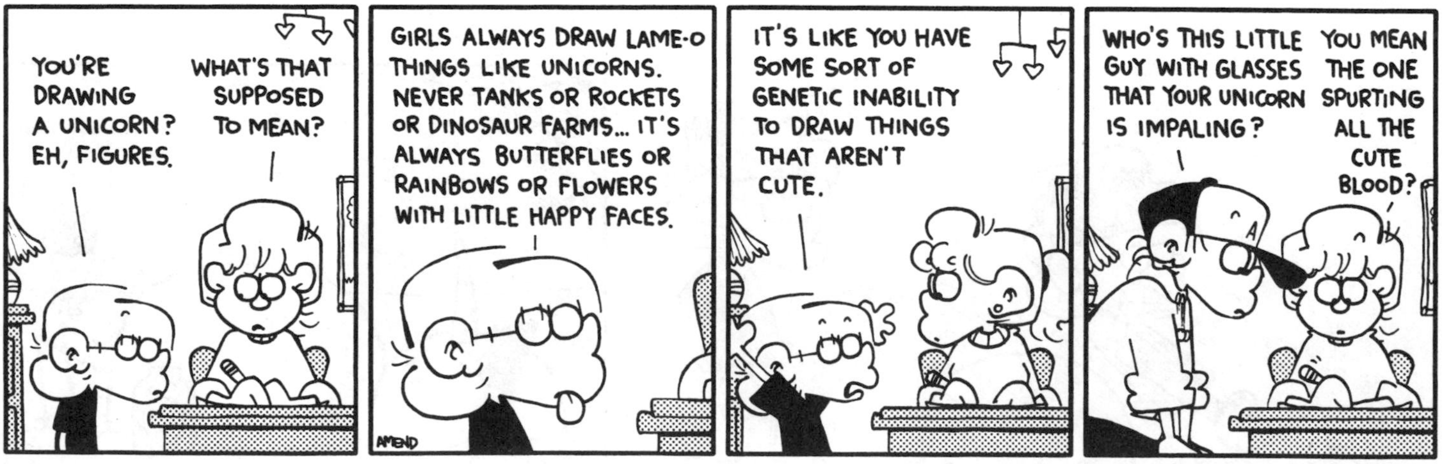
YOU'RE DRAWING A UNICORN? EH, FIGURES.
WHAT'S THAT SUPPOSED TO MEAN?
GIRLS ALWAYS DRAW LAME-O THINGS LIKE UNICORNS. NEVER TANKS OR ROCKETS OR DINOSAUR FARMS... IT'S ALWAYS BUTTERFLIES OR RAINBOWS OR FLOWERS WITH LITTLE HAPPY FACES.
IT'S LIKE YOU HAVE SOME SORT OF GENETIC INABILITY TO DRAW THINGS THAT AREN'T CUTE.
WHO'S THIS LITTLE GUY WITH GLASSES THAT YOUR UNICORN IS IMPALING?
YOU MEAN THE ONE SPURTING ALL THE CUTE BLOOD?

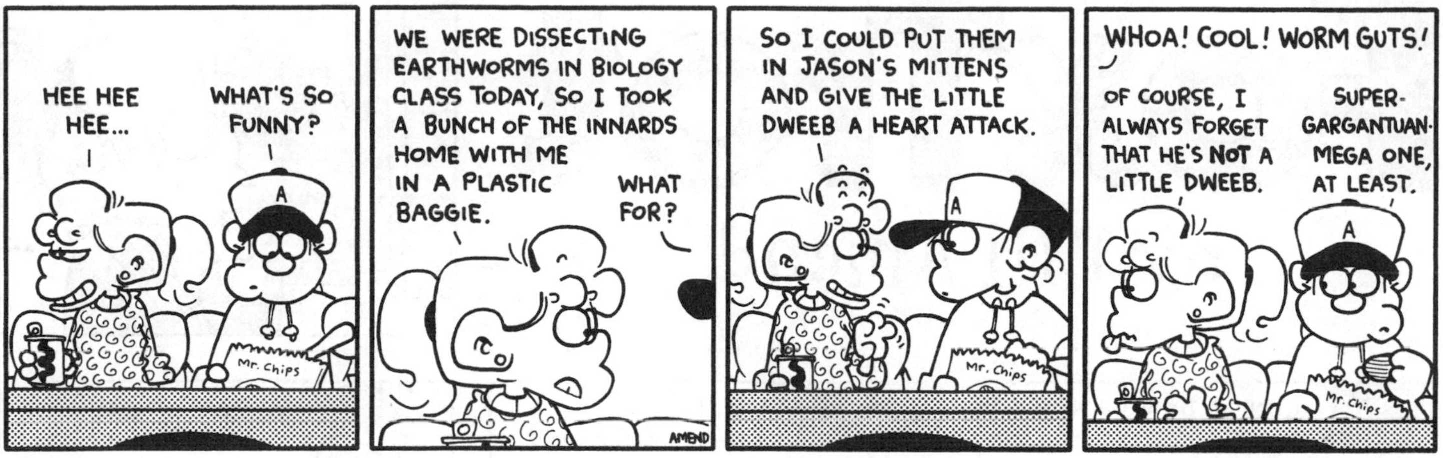
HEE HEE HEE...
WHAT'S SO FUNNY?
WE WERE DISSECTING EARTHWORMS IN BIOLOGY CLASS TODAY, SO I TOOK A BUNCH OF THE INNARDS HOME WITH ME IN A PLASTIC BAGGIE.
WHAT FOR?
SO I COULD PUT THEM IN JASON'S MITTENS AND GIVE THE LITTLE DWEEB A HEART ATTACK.
WHOA! COOL! WORM GUTS!
OF COURSE, I ALWAYS FORGET THAT HE'S NOT A LITTLE DWEEB.
SUPER-GARGANTUAN-MEGA ONE, AT LEAST.
Mr. Chips
AMEND

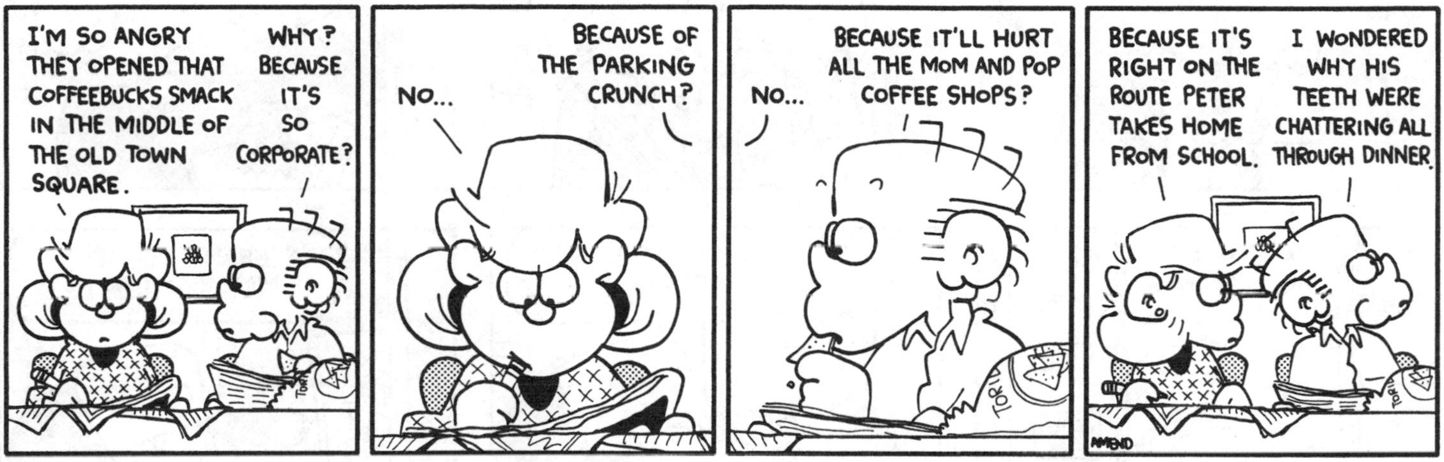
I'M SO ANGRY THEY OPENED THAT COFFEEBUCKS SMACK IN THE MIDDLE OF THE OLD TOWN SQUARE.
WHY? BECAUSE IT'S SO CORPORATE?
NO...
BECAUSE OF THE PARKING CRUNCH?
NO...
BECAUSE IT'LL HURT ALL THE MOM AND POP COFFEE SHOPS?
BECAUSE IT'S RIGHT ON THE ROUTE PETER TAKES HOME FROM SCHOOL.
I WONDERED WHY HIS TEETH WERE CHATTERING ALL THROUGH DINNER.
AMEND

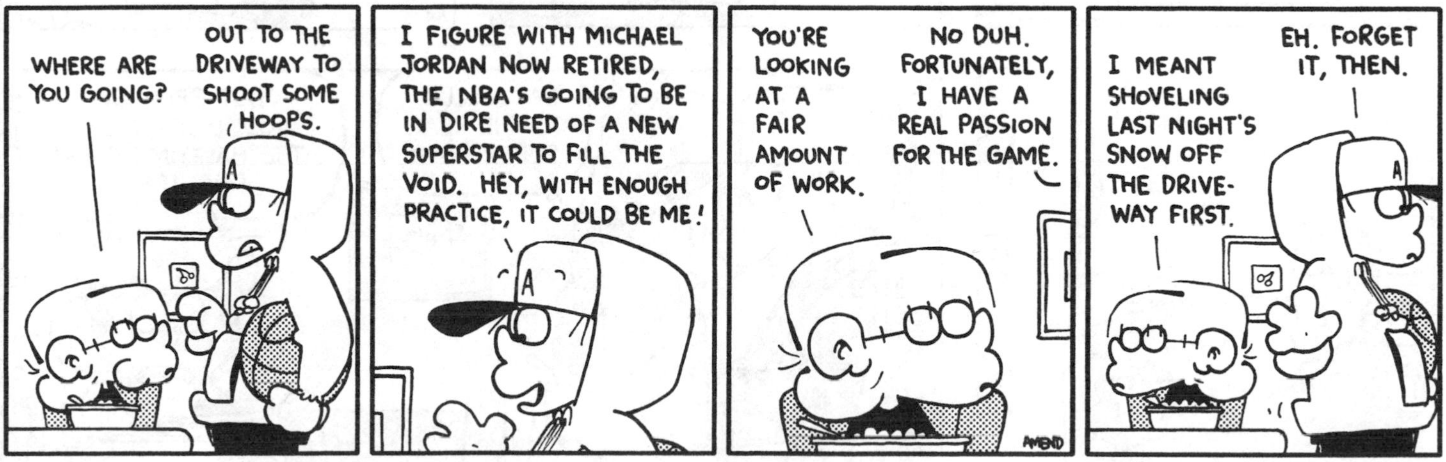
WHERE ARE YOU GOING?
OUT TO THE DRIVEWAY TO SHOOT SOME HOOPS.
I FIGURE WITH MICHAEL JORDAN NOW RETIRED, THE NBA'S GOING TO BE IN DIRE NEED OF A NEW SUPERSTAR TO FILL THE VOID. HEY, WITH ENOUGH PRACTICE, IT COULD BE ME!
YOU'RE LOOKING AT A FAIR AMOUNT OF WORK.
NO DUH. FORTUNATELY, I HAVE A REAL PASSION FOR THE GAME.
I MEANT SHOVELING LAST NIGHT'S SNOW OFF THE DRIVEWAY FIRST.
EH. FORGET IT, THEN.
AMEND

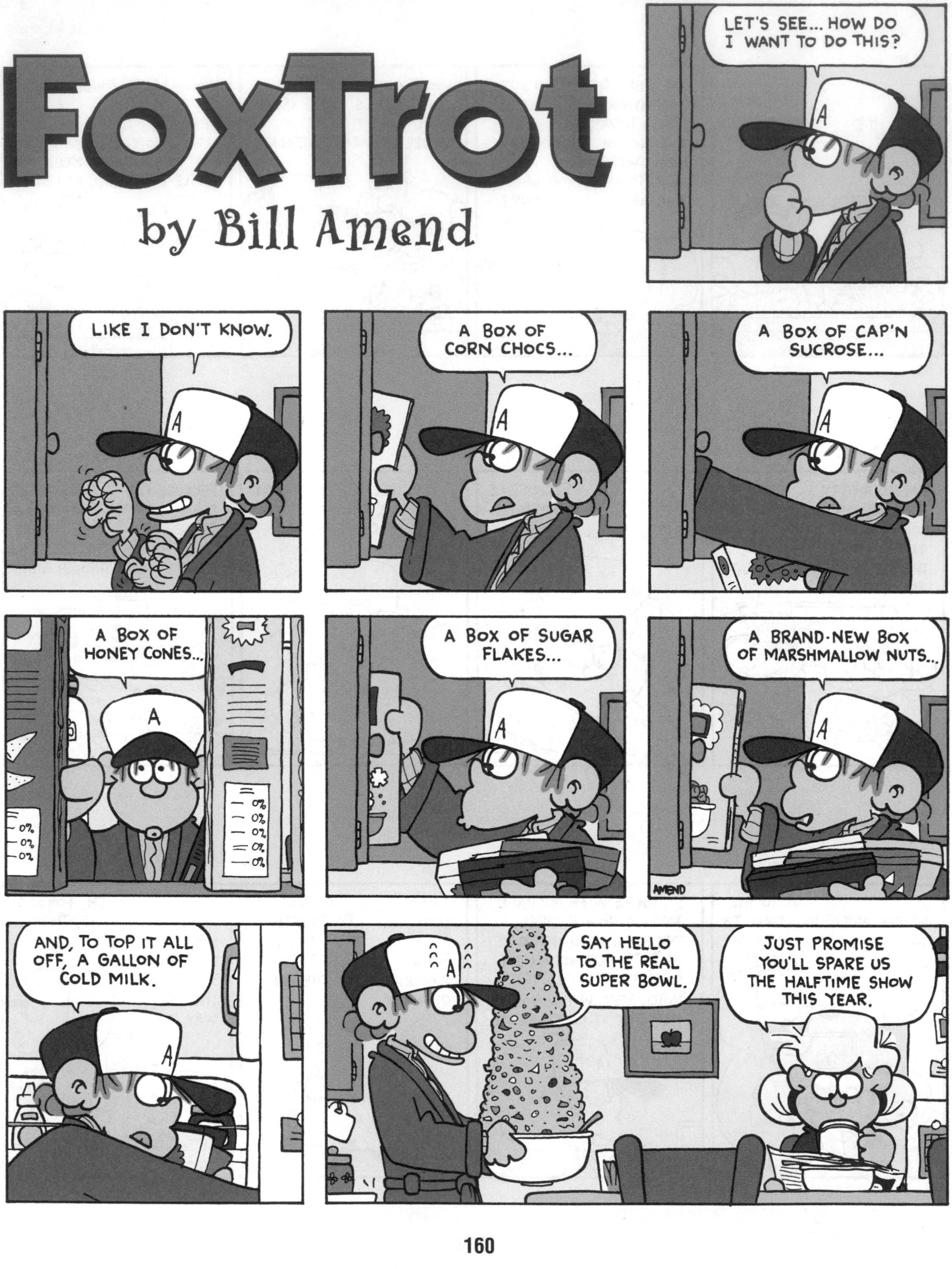
FoxTrot
by Bill Amend
LET'S SEE... HOW DO I WANT TO DO THIS?
LIKE I DON'T KNOW.
A BOX OF CORN CHOCS...
A BOX OF CAP'N SUCROSE...
A BOX OF HONEY CONES...
A BOX OF SUGAR FLAKES...
A BRAND-NEW BOX OF MARSHMALLOW NUTS...
AND, TO TOP IT ALL OFF, A GALLON OF COLD MILK.
SAY HELLO TO THE REAL SUPER BOWL.
JUST PROMISE YOU'LL SPARE US THE HALFTIME SHOW THIS YEAR.

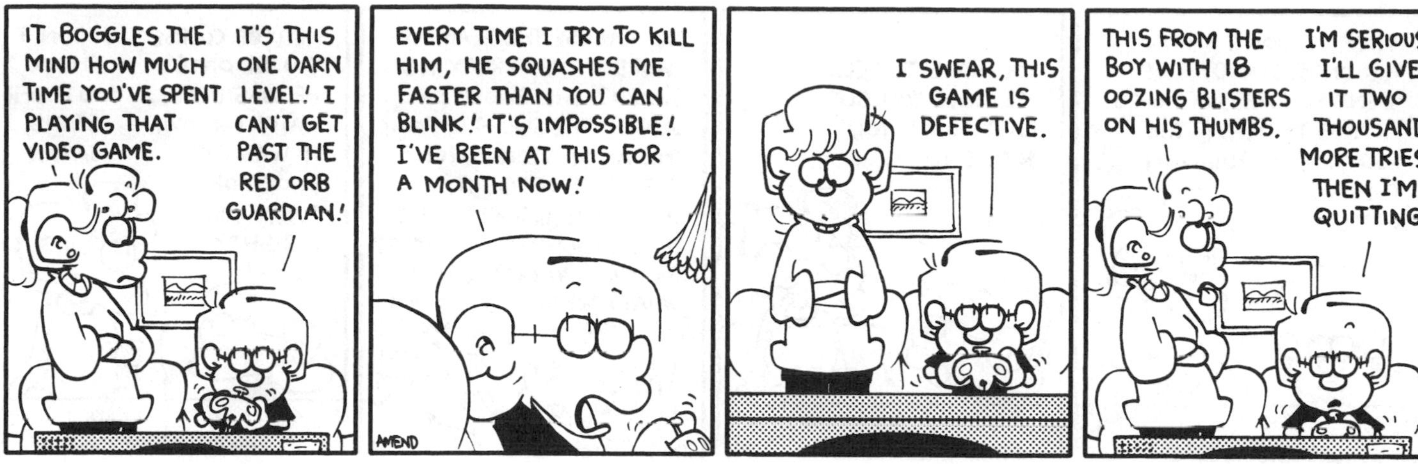
IT BOGGLES THE MIND HOW MUCH TIME YOU'VE SPENT PLAYING THAT VIDEO GAME.
IT'S THIS ONE DARN LEVEL! I CAN'T GET PAST THE RED ORB GUARDIAN!
EVERY TIME I TRY TO KILL HIM, HE SQUASHES ME FASTER THAN YOU CAN BLINK! IT'S IMPOSSIBLE! I'VE BEEN AT THIS FOR A MONTH NOW!
I SWEAR, THIS GAME IS DEFECTIVE.
THIS FROM THE BOY WITH 18 OOZING BLISTERS ON HIS THUMBS.
I'M SERIOUS. I'LL GIVE IT TWO THOUSAND MORE TRIES, THEN I'M QUITTING.

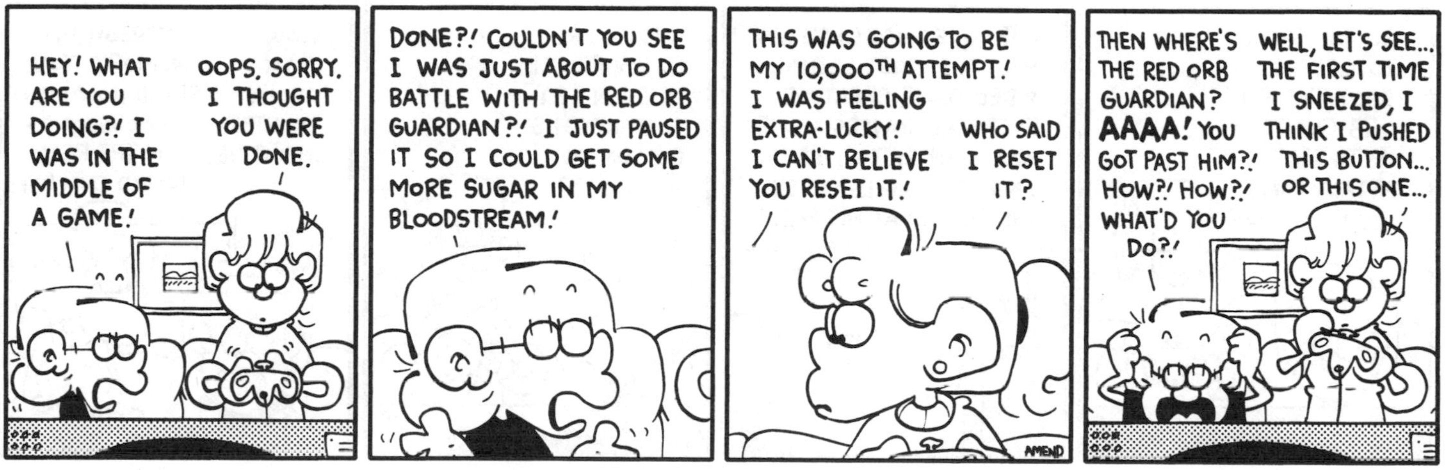
HEY! WHAT ARE YOU DOING?! I WAS IN THE MIDDLE OF A GAME!
OOPS, SORRY. I THOUGHT YOU WERE DONE.
DONE?! COULDN'T YOU SEE I WAS JUST ABOUT TO DO BATTLE WITH THE RED ORB GUARDIAN?! I JUST PAUSED IT SO I COULD GET SOME MORE SUGAR IN MY BLOODSTREAM!
THIS WAS GOING TO BE MY 10,000TH ATTEMPT! I WAS FEELING EXTRA-LUCKY! I CAN'T BELIEVE YOU RESET IT!
WHO SAID I RESET IT?
THEN WHERE'S THE RED ORB GUARDIAN? AAAA! YOU GOT PAST HIM?! HOW?! HOW?! WHAT'D YOU DO?!
WELL, LET'S SEE... THE FIRST TIME I SNEEZED, I THINK I PUSHED THIS BUTTON... OR THIS ONE...

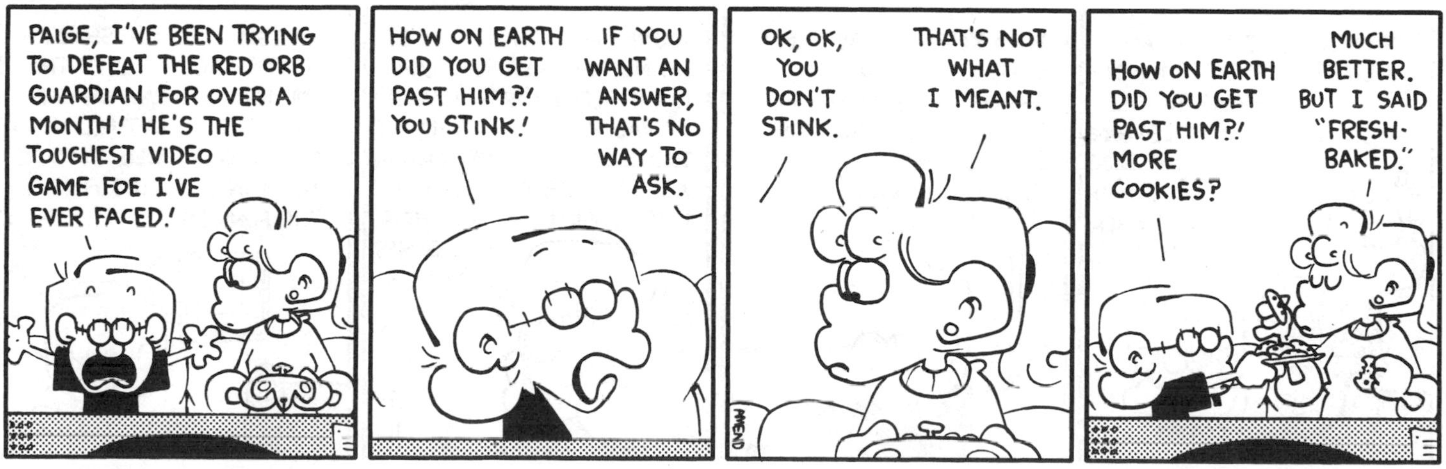
PAIGE, I'VE BEEN TRYING TO DEFEAT THE RED ORB GUARDIAN FOR OVER A MONTH! HE'S THE TOUGHEST VIDEO GAME FOE I'VE EVER FACED!
HOW ON EARTH DID YOU GET PAST HIM?! YOU STINK!
IF YOU WANT AN ANSWER, THAT'S NO WAY TO ASK.
OK, OK, YOU DON'T STINK.
THAT'S NOT WHAT I MEANT.
HOW ON EARTH DID YOU GET PAST HIM?! MORE COOKIES?
MUCH BETTER. BUT I SAID "FRESH-BAKED."

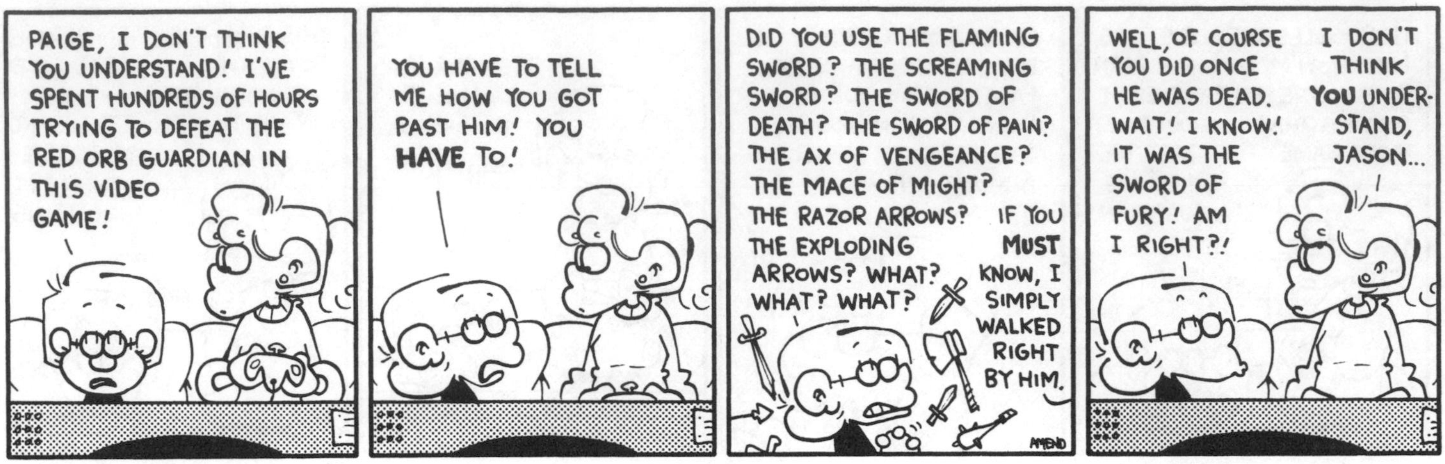
PAIGE, I DON'T THINK YOU UNDERSTAND! I'VE SPENT HUNDREDS OF HOURS TRYING TO DEFEAT THE RED ORB GUARDIAN IN THIS VIDEO GAME!
YOU HAVE TO TELL ME HOW YOU GOT PAST HIM! YOU HAVE TO!
DID YOU USE THE FLAMING SWORD? THE SCREAMING SWORD? THE SWORD OF DEATH? THE SWORD OF PAIN? THE AX OF VENGEANCE? THE MACE OF MIGHT? THE RAZOR ARROWS? THE EXPLODING ARROWS? WHAT? WHAT? WHAT?
IF YOU MUST KNOW, I SIMPLY WALKED RIGHT BY HIM.
AMEND
WELL, OF COURSE YOU DID ONCE HE WAS DEAD. WAIT! I KNOW! IT WAS THE SWORD OF FURY! AM I RIGHT?!
I DON'T THINK YOU UNDERSTAND, JASON...

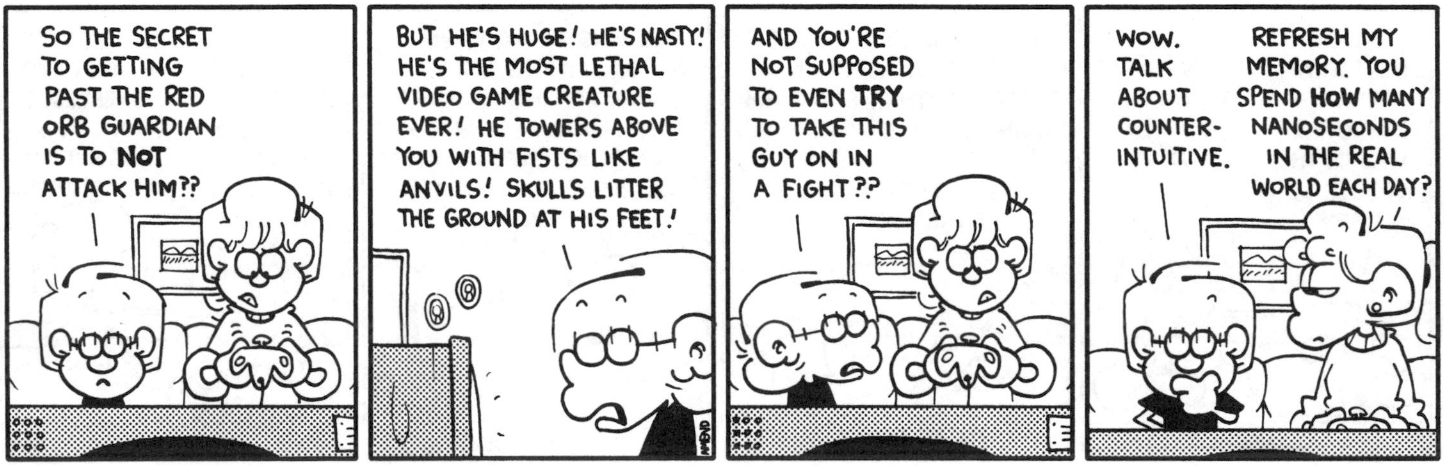
SO THE SECRET TO GETTING PAST THE RED ORB GUARDIAN IS TO NOT ATTACK HIM??
BUT HE'S HUGE! HE'S NASTY! HE'S THE MOST LETHAL VIDEO GAME CREATURE EVER! HE TOWERS ABOVE YOU WITH FISTS LIKE ANVILS! SKULLS LITTER THE GROUND AT HIS FEET!
AMEND
AND YOU'RE NOT SUPPOSED TO EVEN TRY TO TAKE THIS GUY ON IN A FIGHT??
WOW. TALK ABOUT COUNTER-INTUITIVE.
REFRESH MY MEMORY. YOU SPEND HOW MANY NANOSECONDS IN THE REAL WORLD EACH DAY?

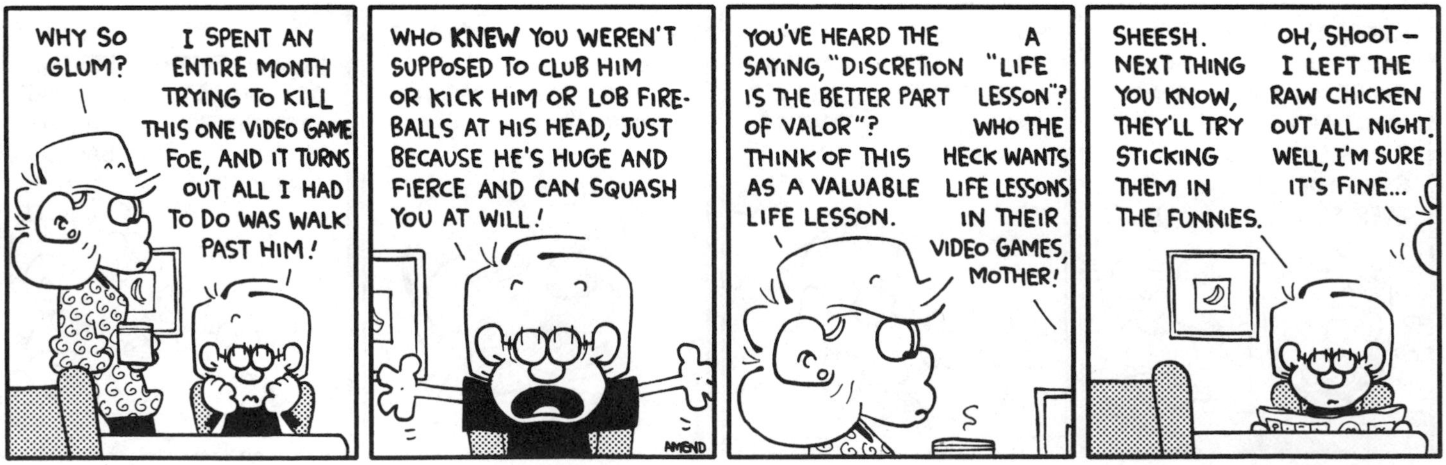
WHY SO GLUM?
I SPENT AN ENTIRE MONTH TRYING TO KILL THIS ONE VIDEO GAME FOE, AND IT TURNS OUT ALL I HAD TO DO WAS WALK PAST HIM!
WHO KNEW YOU WEREN'T SUPPOSED TO CLUB HIM OR KICK HIM OR LOB FIRE-BALLS AT HIS HEAD, JUST BECAUSE HE'S HUGE AND FIERCE AND CAN SQUASH YOU AT WILL!
AMEND
YOU'VE HEARD THE SAYING, "DISCRETION IS THE BETTER PART OF VALOR"? THINK OF THIS AS A VALUABLE LIFE LESSON.
A "LIFE LESSON"? WHO THE HECK WANTS LIFE LESSONS IN THEIR VIDEO GAMES, MOTHER!
SHEESH. NEXT THING YOU KNOW, THEY'LL TRY STICKING THEM IN THE FUNNIES.
OH, SHOOT — I LEFT THE RAW CHICKEN OUT ALL NIGHT. WELL, I'M SURE IT'S FINE...

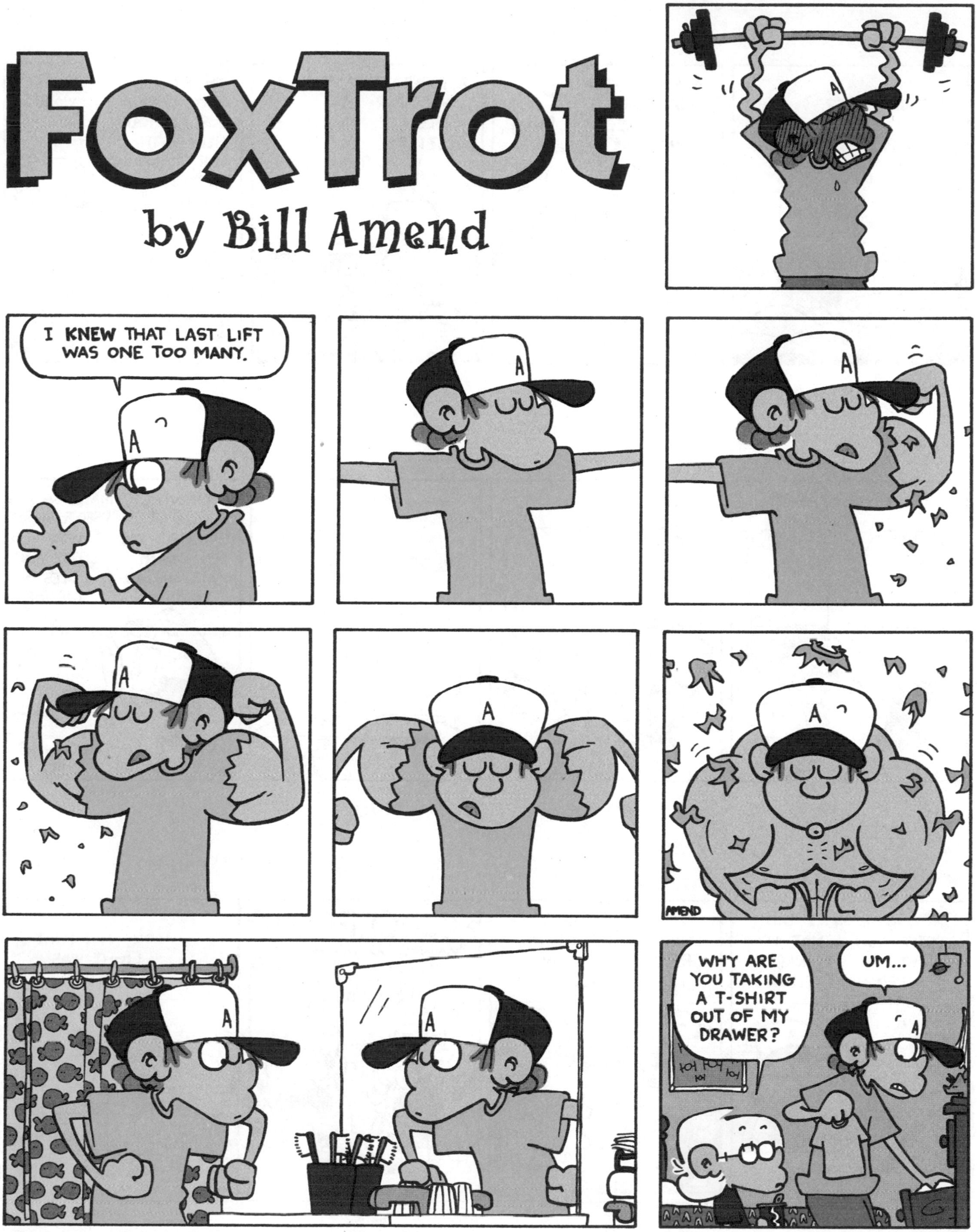
FoxTrot
by Bill Amend
I KNEW THAT LAST LIFT WAS ONE TOO MANY.
AMEND
WHY ARE YOU TAKING A T-SHIRT OUT OF MY DRAWER?
UM...

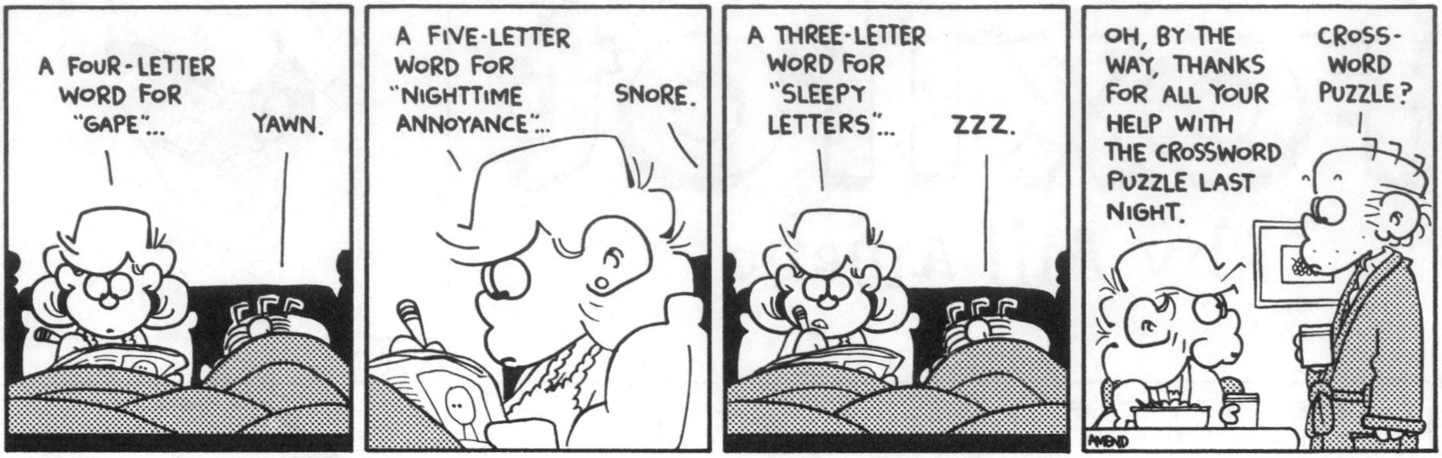
A FOUR-LETTER WORD FOR "GAPE"...
YAWN.
A FIVE-LETTER WORD FOR "NIGHTTIME ANNOYANCE"...
SNORE.
A THREE-LETTER WORD FOR "SLEEPY LETTERS"...
ZZZ.
OH, BY THE WAY, THANKS FOR ALL YOUR HELP WITH THE CROSSWORD PUZZLE LAST NIGHT.
CROSSWORD PUZZLE?
AMEND

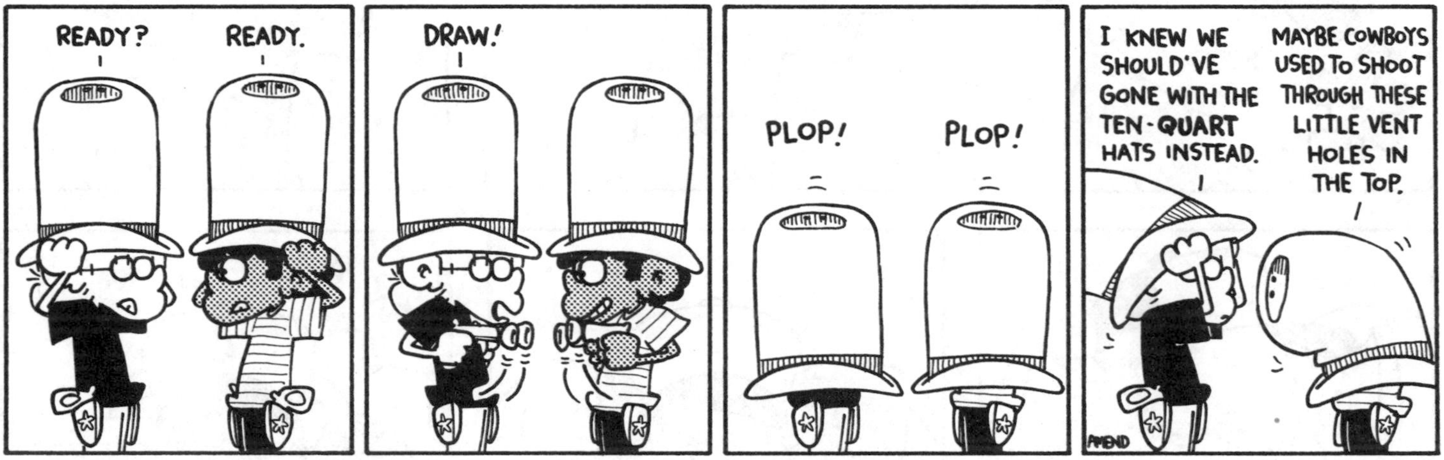
READY?
READY.
DRAW!
PLOP!
PLOP!
I KNEW WE SHOULD'VE GONE WITH THE TEN-QUART HATS INSTEAD.
MAYBE COWBOYS USED TO SHOOT THROUGH THESE LITTLE VENT HOLES IN THE TOP.
AMEND

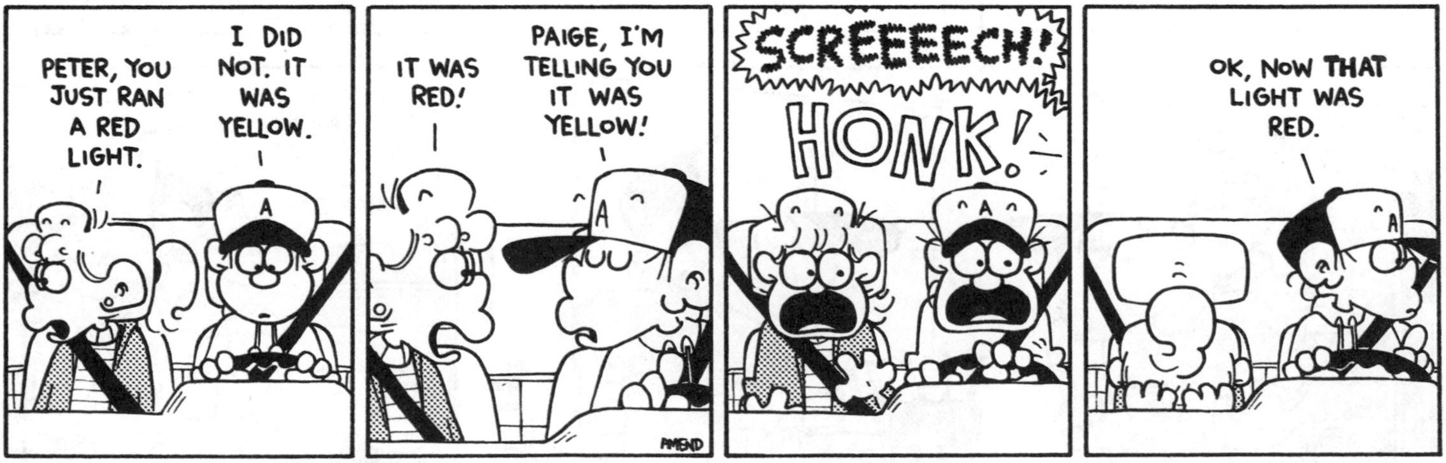
PETER, YOU JUST RAN A RED LIGHT.
I DID NOT. IT WAS YELLOW.
IT WAS RED!
PAIGE, I'M TELLING YOU IT WAS YELLOW!
AMEND
SCREEEECH!
HONK!
OK, NOW THAT LIGHT WAS RED.

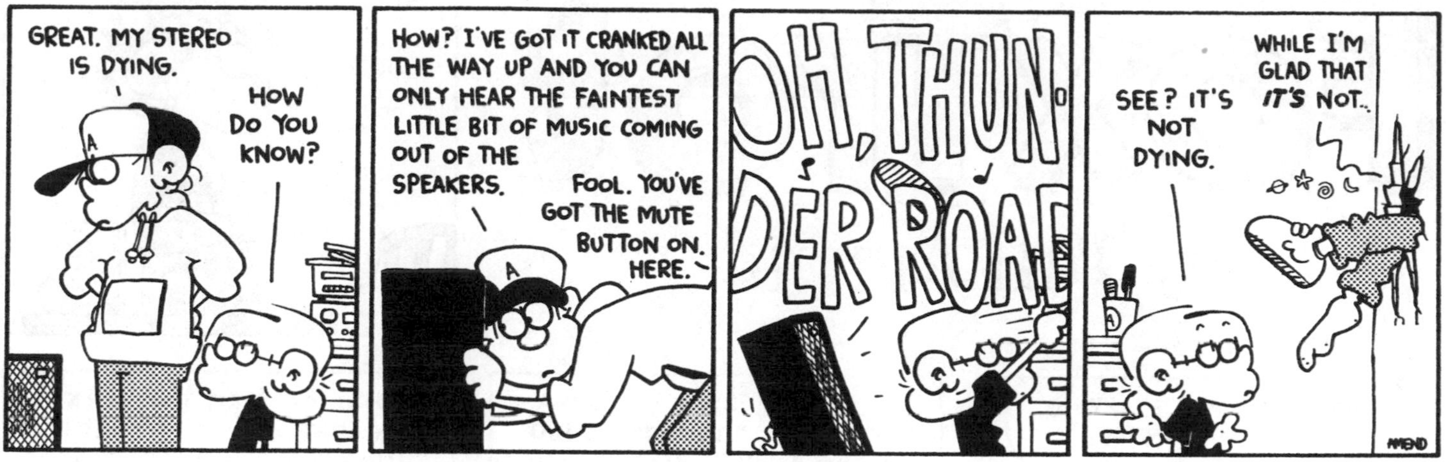
GREAT. MY STEREO IS DYING.
HOW DO YOU KNOW?
HOW? I'VE GOT IT CRANKED ALL THE WAY UP AND YOU CAN ONLY HEAR THE FAINTEST LITTLE BIT OF MUSIC COMING OUT OF THE SPEAKERS.
FOOL. YOU'VE GOT THE MUTE BUTTON ON. HERE.
OH, THUNDER ROAD
SEE? IT'S NOT DYING.
WHILE I'M GLAD THAT *IT'S* NOT..
AMEND

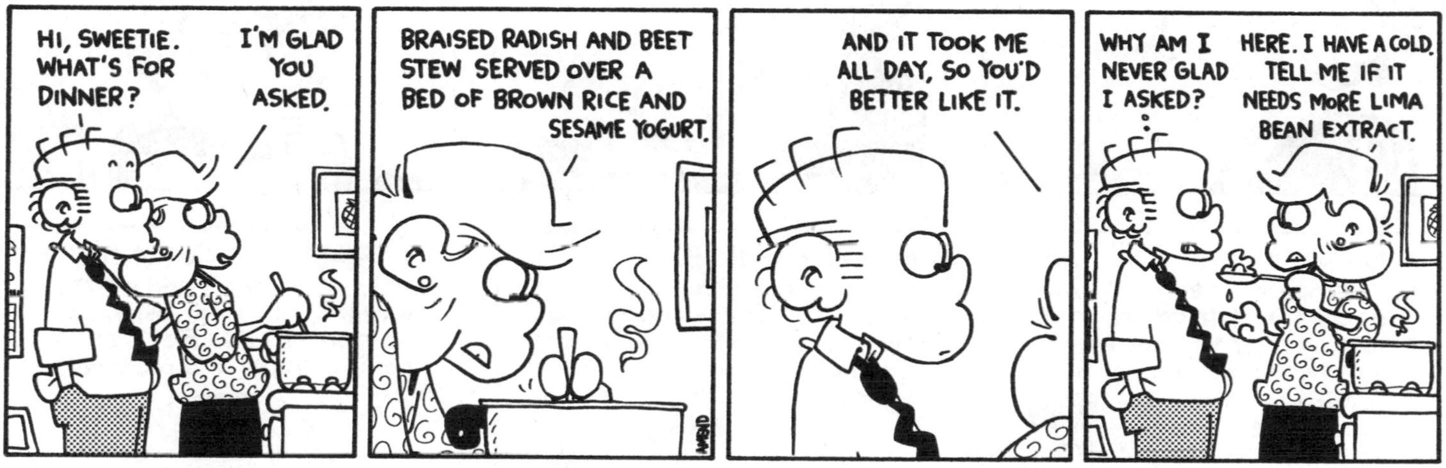
HI, SWEETIE. WHAT'S FOR DINNER?
I'M GLAD YOU ASKED.
BRAISED RADISH AND BEET STEW SERVED OVER A BED OF BROWN RICE AND SESAME YOGURT.
AMEND
AND IT TOOK ME ALL DAY, SO YOU'D BETTER LIKE IT.
WHY AM I NEVER GLAD I ASKED?
HERE. I HAVE A COLD. TELL ME IF IT NEEDS MORE LIMA BEAN EXTRACT.

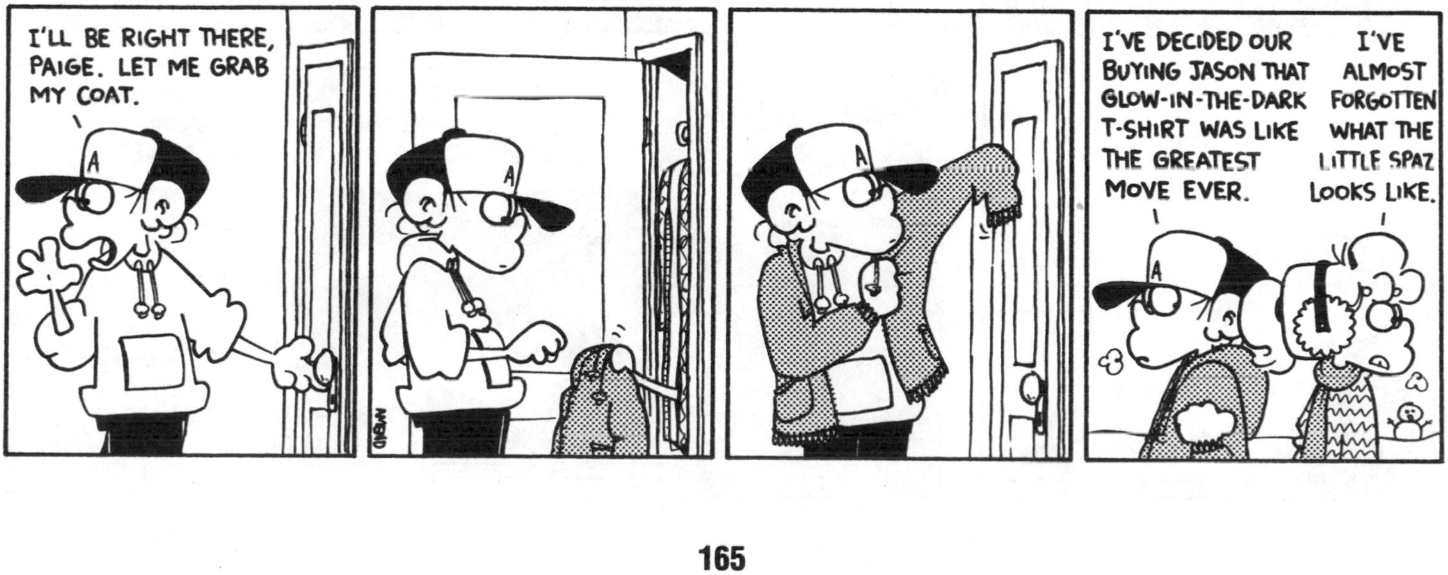
I'LL BE RIGHT THERE, PAIGE. LET ME GRAB MY COAT.
AMEND
I'VE DECIDED OUR BUYING JASON THAT GLOW-IN-THE-DARK T-SHIRT WAS LIKE THE GREATEST MOVE EVER.
I'VE ALMOST FORGOTTEN WHAT THE LITTLE SPAZ LOOKS LIKE.

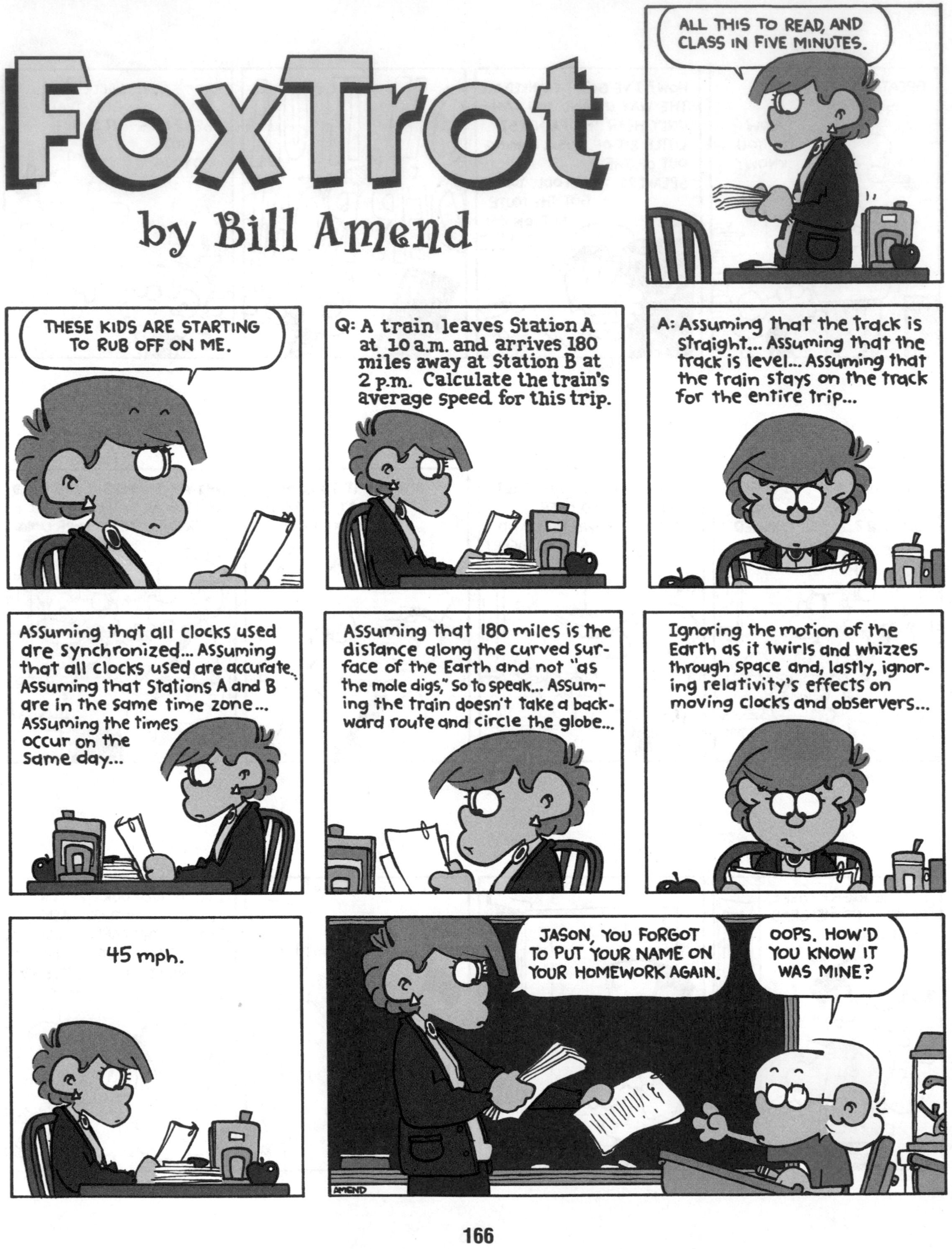
FoxTrot
by Bill Amend
ALL THIS TO READ, AND CLASS IN FIVE MINUTES.
THESE KIDS ARE STARTING TO RUB OFF ON ME.
Q: A train leaves Station A at 10 a.m. and arrives 180 miles away at Station B at 2 p.m. Calculate the train's average speed for this trip.
A: Assuming that the track is straight... Assuming that the track is level... Assuming that the train stays on the track for the entire trip...
Assuming that all clocks used are synchronized... Assuming that all clocks used are accurate... Assuming that Stations A and B are in the same time zone... Assuming the times occur on the same day...
Assuming that 180 miles is the distance along the curved surface of the Earth and not "as the mole digs," so to speak... Assuming the train doesn't take a backward route and circle the globe...
Ignoring the motion of the Earth as it twirls and whizzes through space and, lastly, ignoring relativity's effects on moving clocks and observers...
45 mph.
JASON, YOU FORGOT TO PUT YOUR NAME ON YOUR HOMEWORK AGAIN.
OOPS. HOW'D YOU KNOW IT WAS MINE?
AMEND

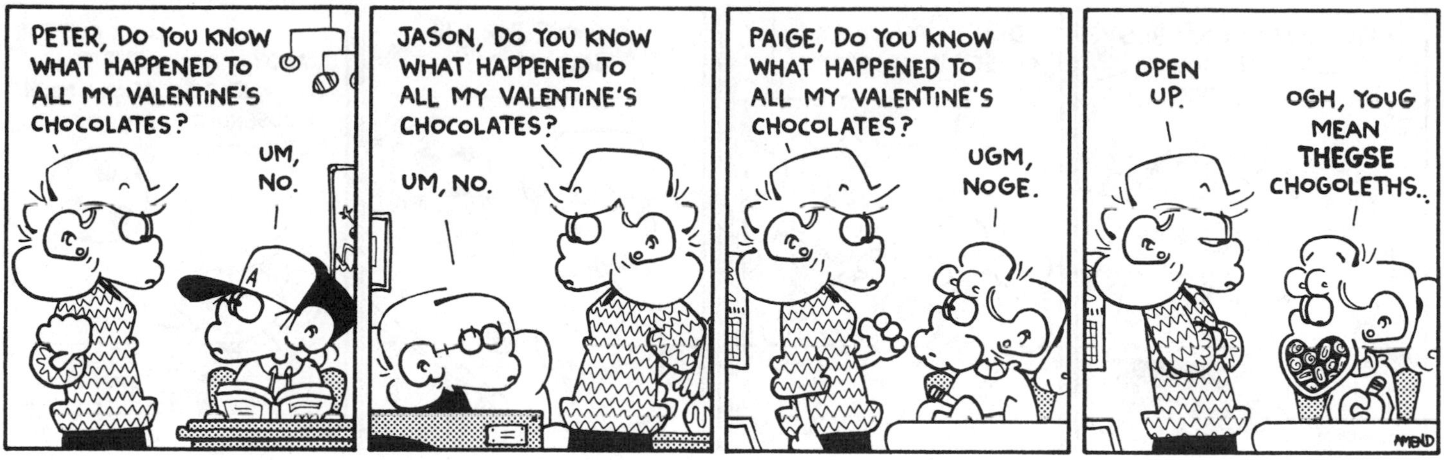
PETER, DO YOU KNOW WHAT HAPPENED TO ALL MY VALENTINE'S CHOCOLATES?
UM, NO.
JASON, DO YOU KNOW WHAT HAPPENED TO ALL MY VALENTINE'S CHOCOLATES?
UM, NO.
PAIGE, DO YOU KNOW WHAT HAPPENED TO ALL MY VALENTINE'S CHOCOLATES?
UGM, NOGE.
OPEN UP.
OGH, YOUG MEAN **THEGSE** CHOGOLETHS..

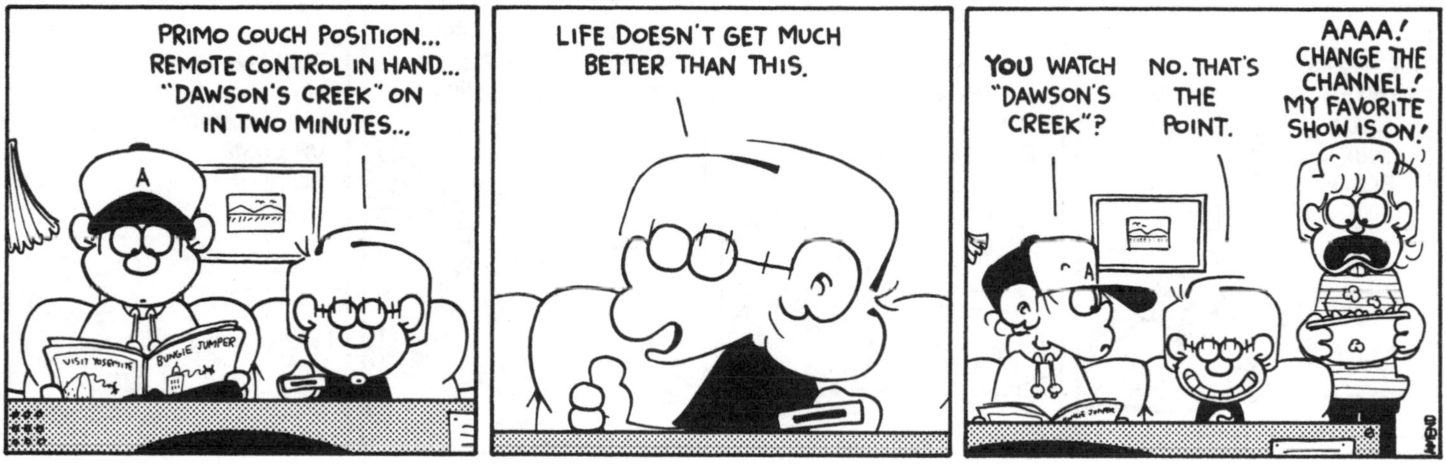
PRIMO COUCH POSITION... REMOTE CONTROL IN HAND... "DAWSON'S CREEK" ON IN TWO MINUTES...
LIFE DOESN'T GET MUCH BETTER THAN THIS.
YOU WATCH "DAWSON'S CREEK"?
NO. THAT'S THE POINT.
AAAA! CHANGE THE CHANNEL! MY FAVORITE SHOW IS ON!

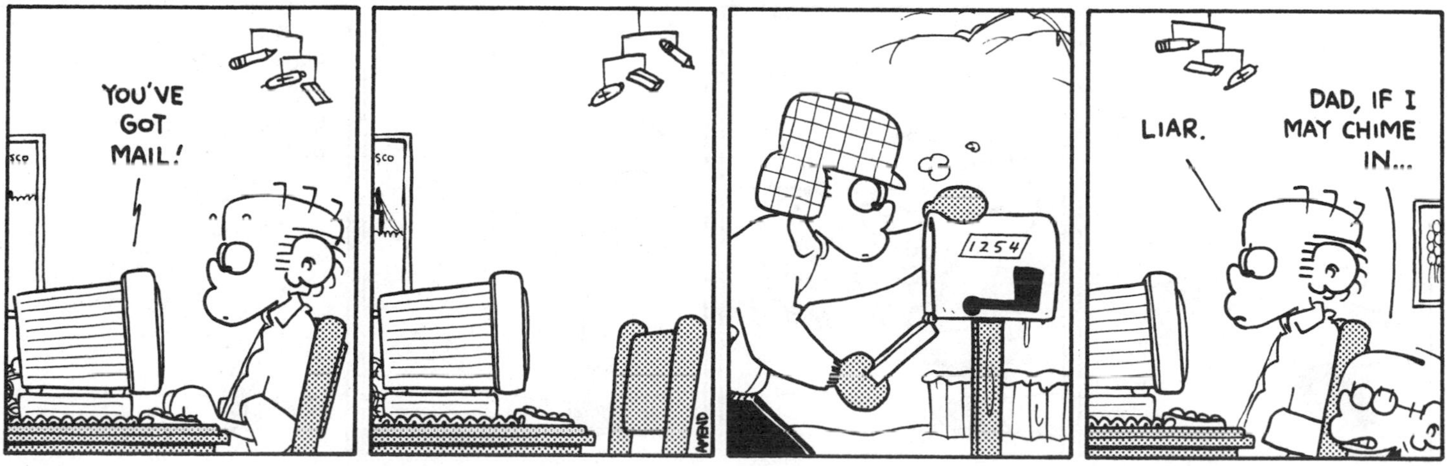
YOU'VE GOT MAIL!
LIAR.
DAD, IF I MAY CHIME IN...

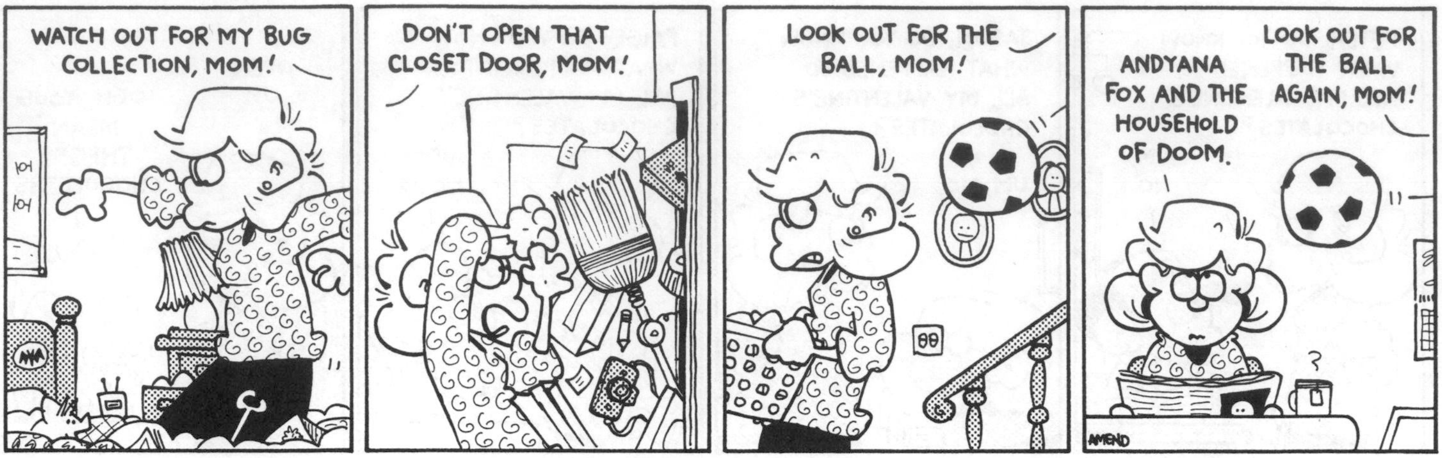
WATCH OUT FOR MY BUG COLLECTION, MOM!
DON'T OPEN THAT CLOSET DOOR, MOM!
LOOK OUT FOR THE BALL, MOM!
ANDYANA FOX AND THE HOUSEHOLD OF DOOM.
LOOK OUT FOR THE BALL AGAIN, MOM!
AMEND

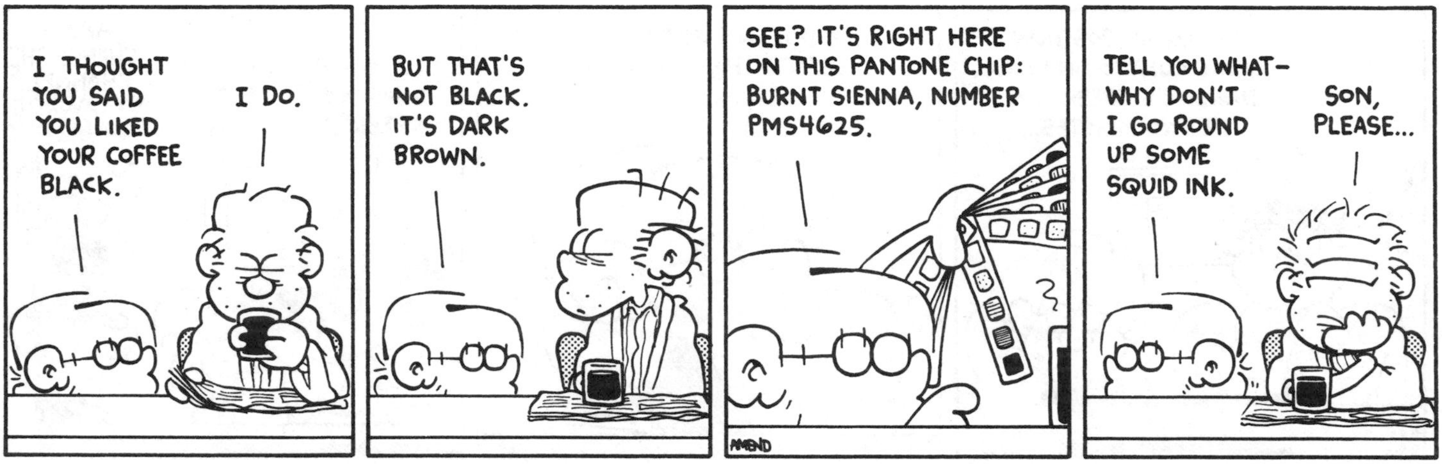
I THOUGHT YOU SAID YOU LIKED YOUR COFFEE BLACK.
I DO.
BUT THAT'S NOT BLACK. IT'S DARK BROWN.
SEE? IT'S RIGHT HERE ON THIS PANTONE CHIP: BURNT SIENNA, NUMBER PMS4625.
AMEND
TELL YOU WHAT— WHY DON'T I GO ROUND UP SOME SQUID INK.
SON, PLEASE...

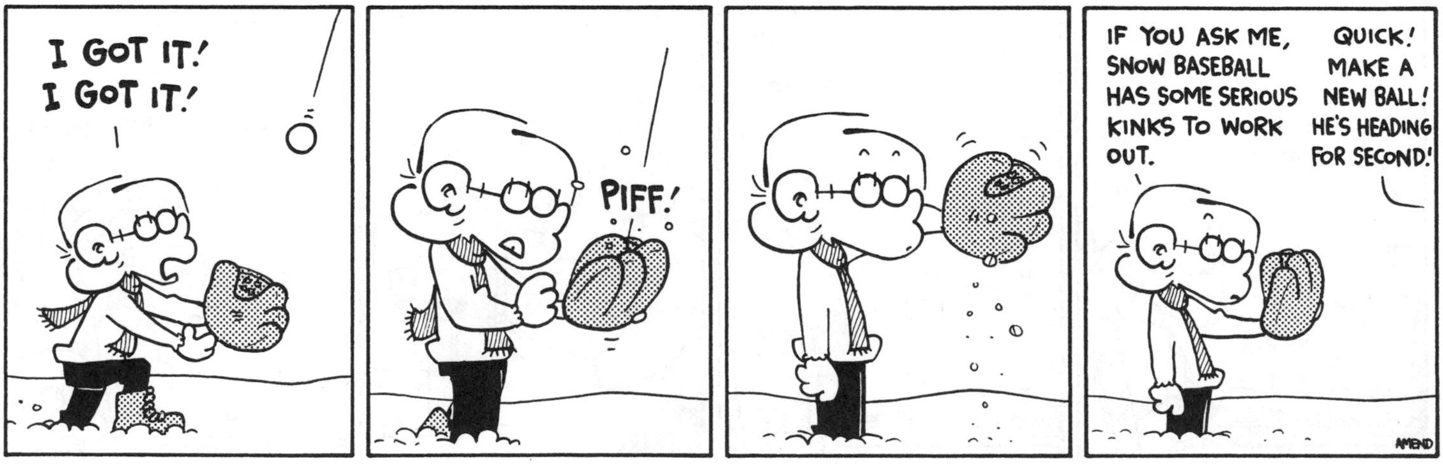
I GOT IT! I GOT IT!
PIFF!
IF YOU ASK ME, SNOW BASEBALL HAS SOME SERIOUS KINKS TO WORK OUT.
QUICK! MAKE A NEW BALL! HE'S HEADING FOR SECOND!
AMEND

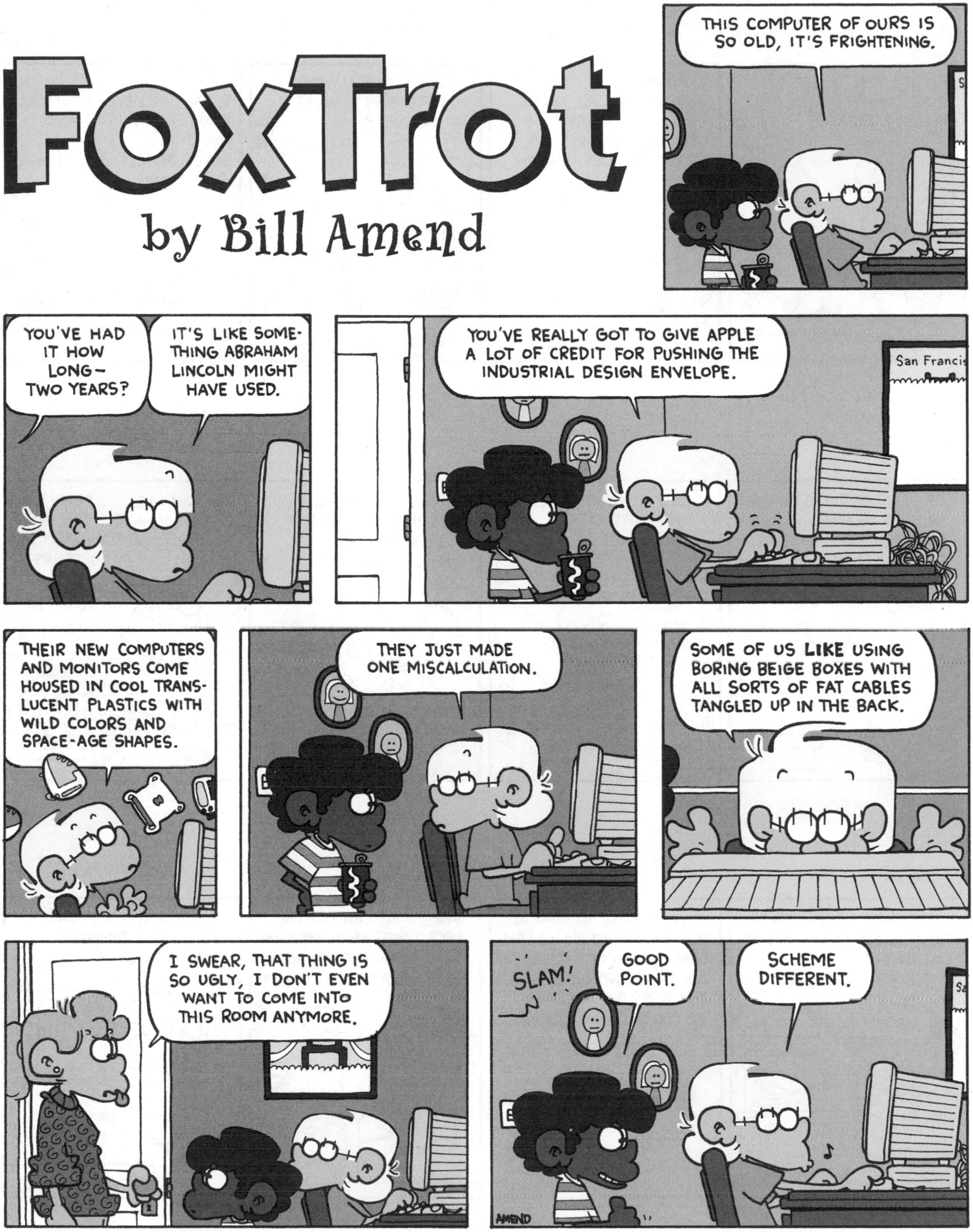
FoxTrot
by Bill Amend
THIS COMPUTER OF OURS IS SO OLD, IT'S FRIGHTENING.
YOU'VE HAD IT HOW LONG— TWO YEARS?
IT'S LIKE SOMETHING ABRAHAM LINCOLN MIGHT HAVE USED.
YOU'VE REALLY GOT TO GIVE APPLE A LOT OF CREDIT FOR PUSHING THE INDUSTRIAL DESIGN ENVELOPE.
San Francis
THEIR NEW COMPUTERS AND MONITORS COME HOUSED IN COOL TRANSLUCENT PLASTICS WITH WILD COLORS AND SPACE-AGE SHAPES.
THEY JUST MADE ONE MISCALCULATION.
SOME OF US LIKE USING BORING BEIGE BOXES WITH ALL SORTS OF FAT CABLES TANGLED UP IN THE BACK.
I SWEAR, THAT THING IS SO UGLY, I DON'T EVEN WANT TO COME INTO THIS ROOM ANYMORE.
SLAM!
GOOD POINT.
SCHEME DIFFERENT.
AMEND

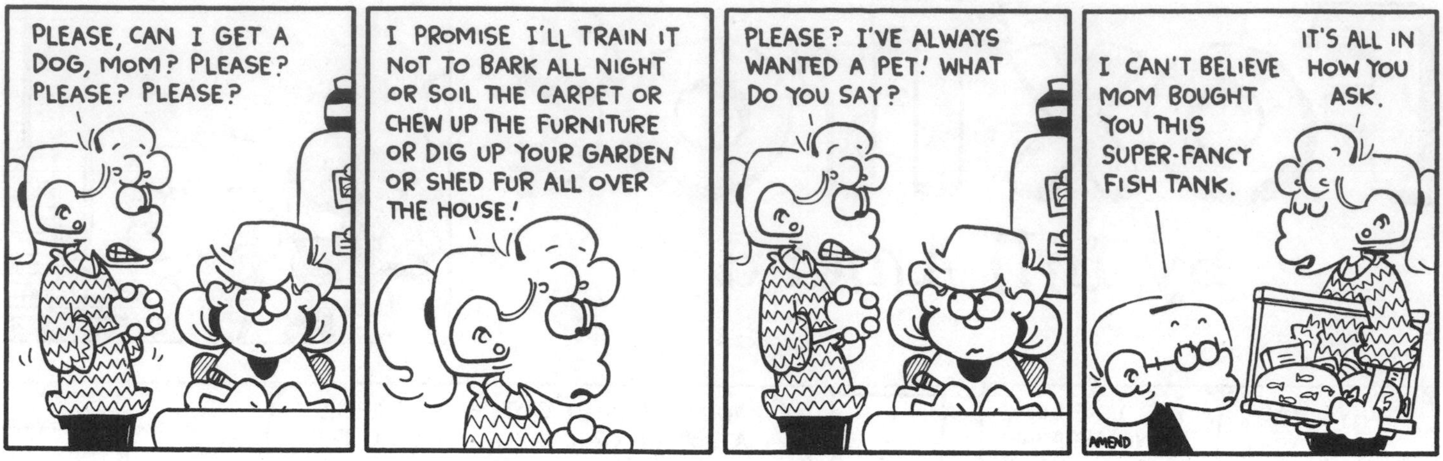
PLEASE, CAN I GET A DOG, MOM? PLEASE? PLEASE? PLEASE?
I PROMISE I'LL TRAIN IT NOT TO BARK ALL NIGHT OR SOIL THE CARPET OR CHEW UP THE FURNITURE OR DIG UP YOUR GARDEN OR SHED FUR ALL OVER THE HOUSE!
PLEASE? I'VE ALWAYS WANTED A PET! WHAT DO YOU SAY?
I CAN'T BELIEVE MOM BOUGHT YOU THIS SUPER-FANCY FISH TANK.
IT'S ALL IN HOW YOU ASK.
AMEND

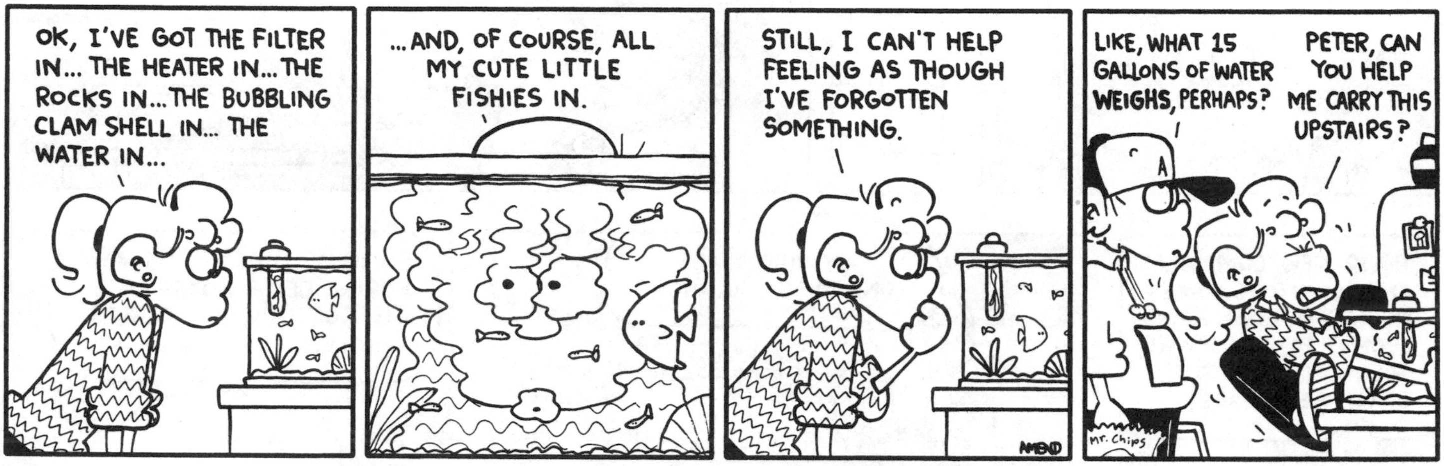
OK, I'VE GOT THE FILTER IN... THE HEATER IN... THE ROCKS IN... THE BUBBLING CLAM SHELL IN... THE WATER IN...
...AND, OF COURSE, ALL MY CUTE LITTLE FISHIES IN.
STILL, I CAN'T HELP FEELING AS THOUGH I'VE FORGOTTEN SOMETHING.
AMEND
PETER, CAN YOU HELP ME CARRY THIS UPSTAIRS?
LIKE, WHAT 15 GALLONS OF WATER WEIGHS, PERHAPS?
Mr. Chips

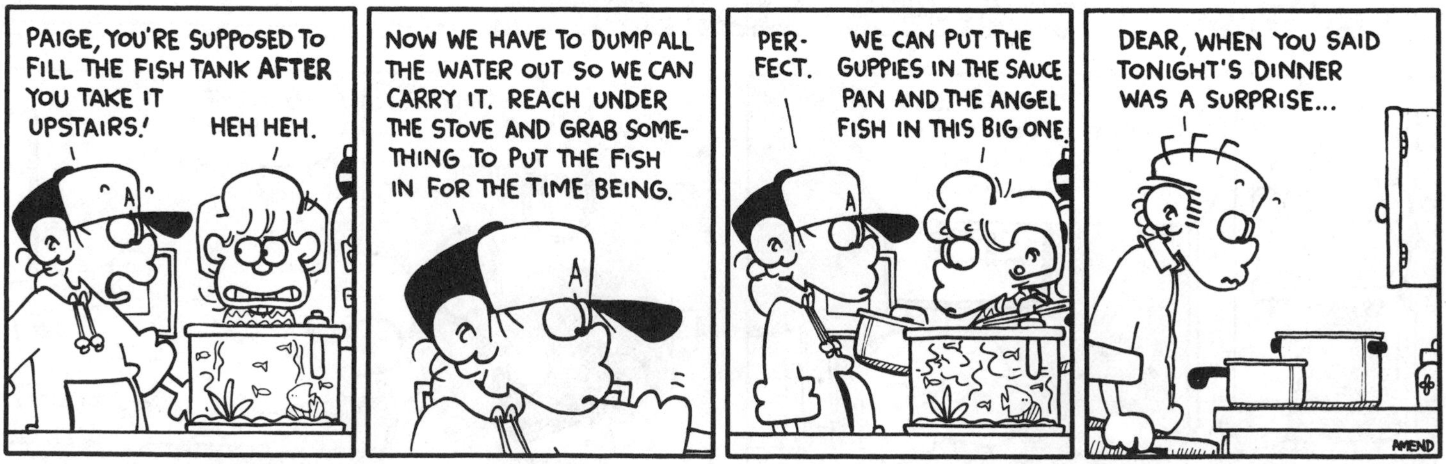
PAIGE, YOU'RE SUPPOSED TO FILL THE FISH TANK AFTER YOU TAKE IT UPSTAIRS!
HEH HEH.
NOW WE HAVE TO DUMP ALL THE WATER OUT SO WE CAN CARRY IT. REACH UNDER THE STOVE AND GRAB SOMETHING TO PUT THE FISH IN FOR THE TIME BEING.
PER-FECT.
WE CAN PUT THE GUPPIES IN THE SAUCE PAN AND THE ANGEL FISH IN THIS BIG ONE.
DEAR, WHEN YOU SAID TONIGHT'S DINNER WAS A SURPRISE...
AMEND

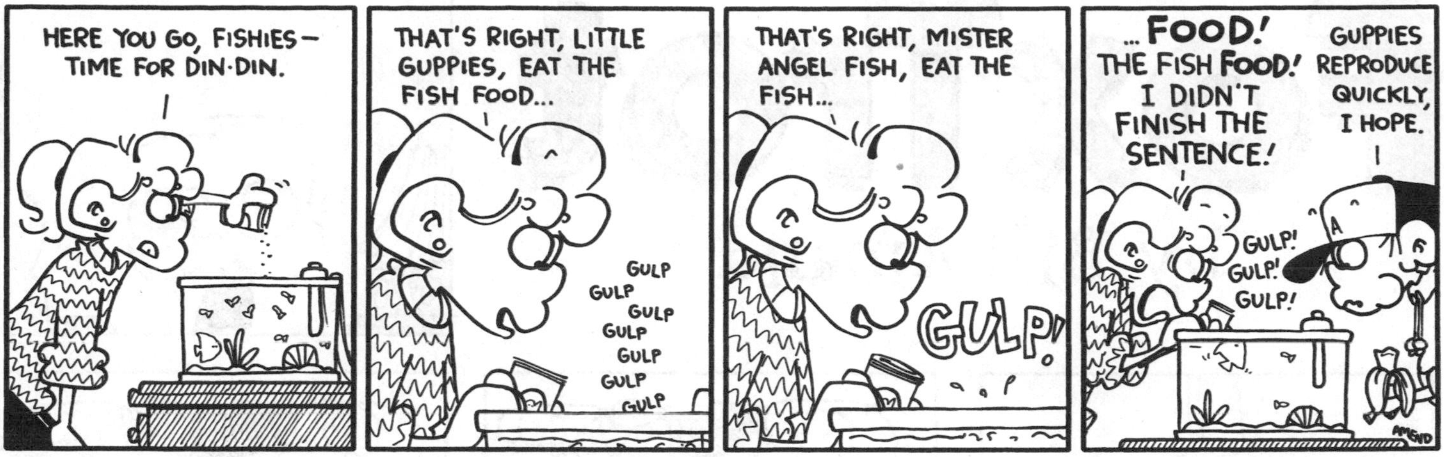
HERE YOU GO, FISHIES— TIME FOR DIN·DIN.
THAT'S RIGHT, LITTLE GUPPIES, EAT THE FISH FOOD...
GULP GULP GULP GULP GULP GULP GULP
THAT'S RIGHT, MISTER ANGEL FISH, EAT THE FISH...
GULP!
...FOOD! THE FISH FOOD! I DIDN'T FINISH THE SENTENCE!
GULP! GULP! GULP!
GUPPIES REPRODUCE QUICKLY, I HOPE.
AMEND

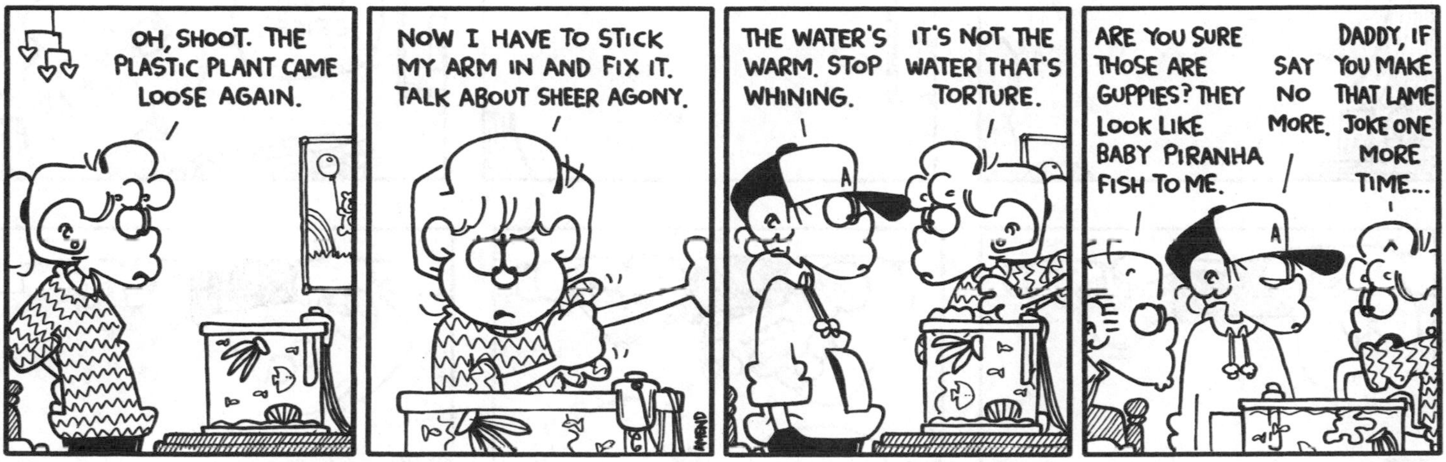
OH, SHOOT. THE PLASTIC PLANT CAME LOOSE AGAIN.
NOW I HAVE TO STICK MY ARM IN AND FIX IT. TALK ABOUT SHEER AGONY.
AMEND
THE WATER'S WARM. STOP WHINING.
IT'S NOT THE WATER THAT'S TORTURE.
ARE YOU SURE THOSE ARE GUPPIES? THEY LOOK LIKE BABY PIRANHA FISH TO ME.
SAY NO MORE.
DADDY, IF YOU MAKE THAT LAME JOKE ONE MORE TIME...

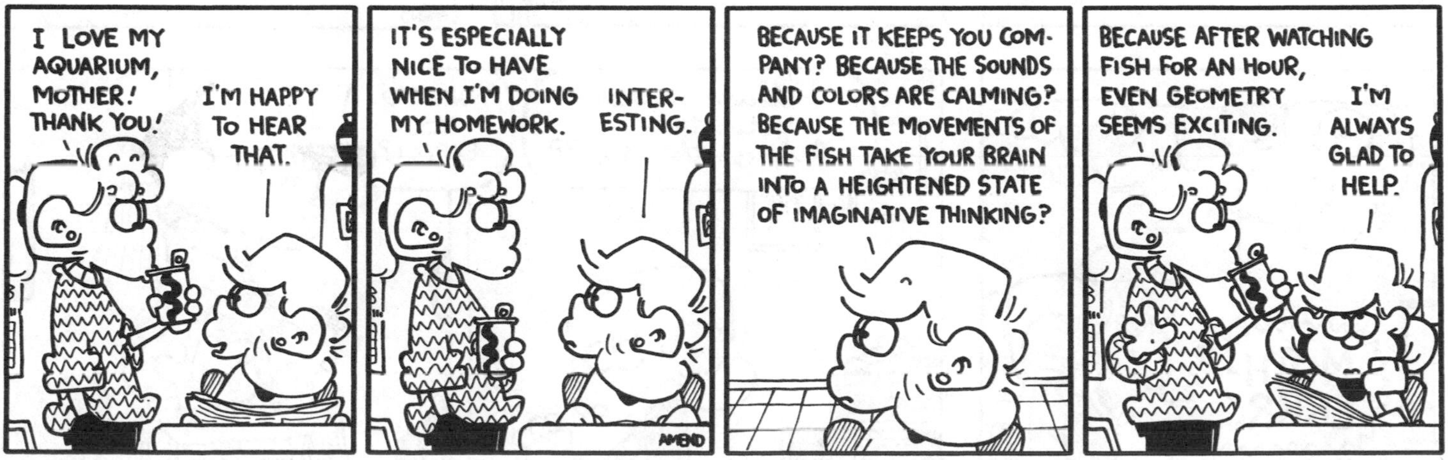
I LOVE MY AQUARIUM, MOTHER! THANK YOU!
I'M HAPPY TO HEAR THAT.
IT'S ESPECIALLY NICE TO HAVE WHEN I'M DOING MY HOMEWORK.
INTER-ESTING.
AMEND
BECAUSE IT KEEPS YOU COMPANY? BECAUSE THE SOUNDS AND COLORS ARE CALMING? BECAUSE THE MOVEMENTS OF THE FISH TAKE YOUR BRAIN INTO A HEIGHTENED STATE OF IMAGINATIVE THINKING?
BECAUSE AFTER WATCHING FISH FOR AN HOUR, EVEN GEOMETRY SEEMS EXCITING.
I'M ALWAYS GLAD TO HELP.

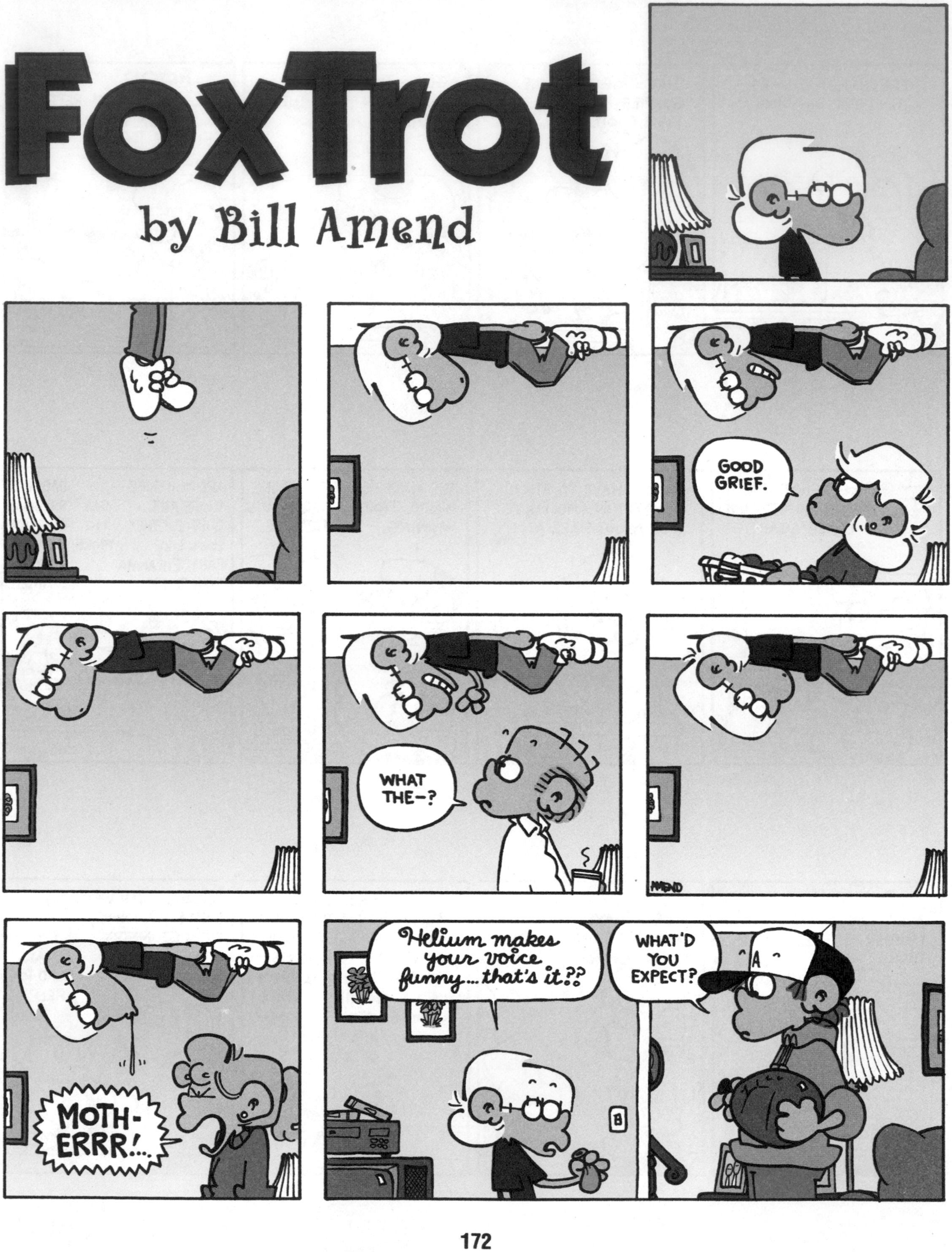
FoxTrot
by Bill Amend
GOOD GRIEF.
WHAT THE-?
AMEND
MOTH-ERRR!...
Helium makes your voice funny... that's it??
WHAT'D YOU EXPECT?

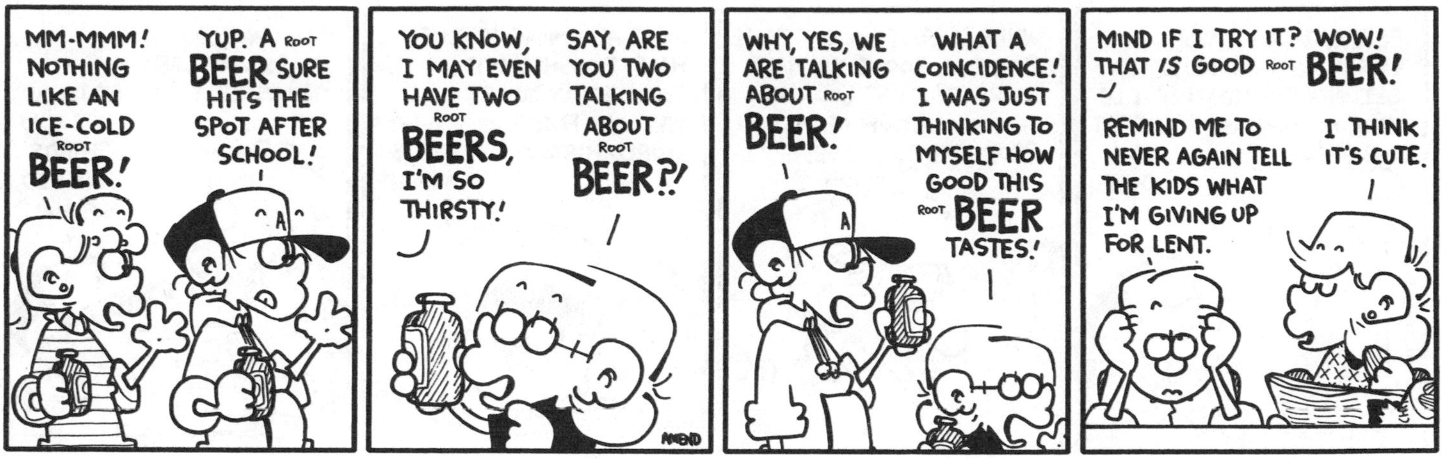
MM-MMM! NOTHING LIKE AN ICE-COLD ROOT BEER!
YUP. A ROOT BEER SURE HITS THE SPOT AFTER SCHOOL!
YOU KNOW, I MAY EVEN HAVE TWO ROOT BEERS, I'M SO THIRSTY!
SAY, ARE YOU TWO TALKING ABOUT ROOT BEER?!
WHY, YES, WE ARE TALKING ABOUT ROOT BEER!
WHAT A COINCIDENCE! I WAS JUST THINKING TO MYSELF HOW GOOD THIS ROOT BEER TASTES!
MIND IF I TRY IT?
WOW! THAT IS GOOD ROOT BEER!
REMIND ME TO NEVER AGAIN TELL THE KIDS WHAT I'M GIVING UP FOR LENT.
I THINK IT'S CUTE.

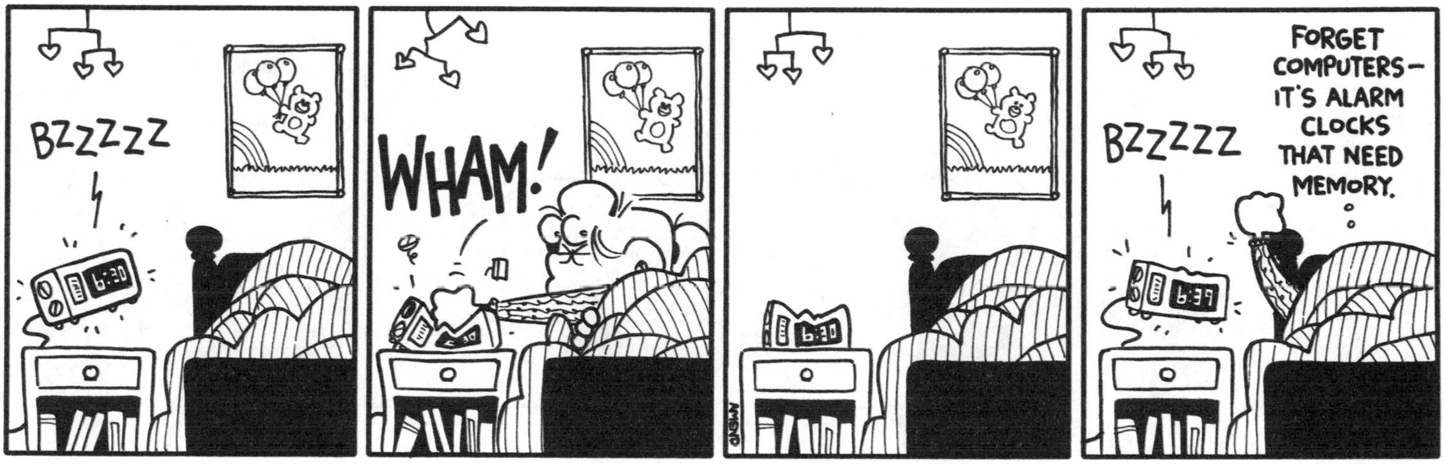
BZZZZZ
WHAM!
BZZZZZ
FORGET COMPUTERS– IT'S ALARM CLOCKS THAT NEED MEMORY.

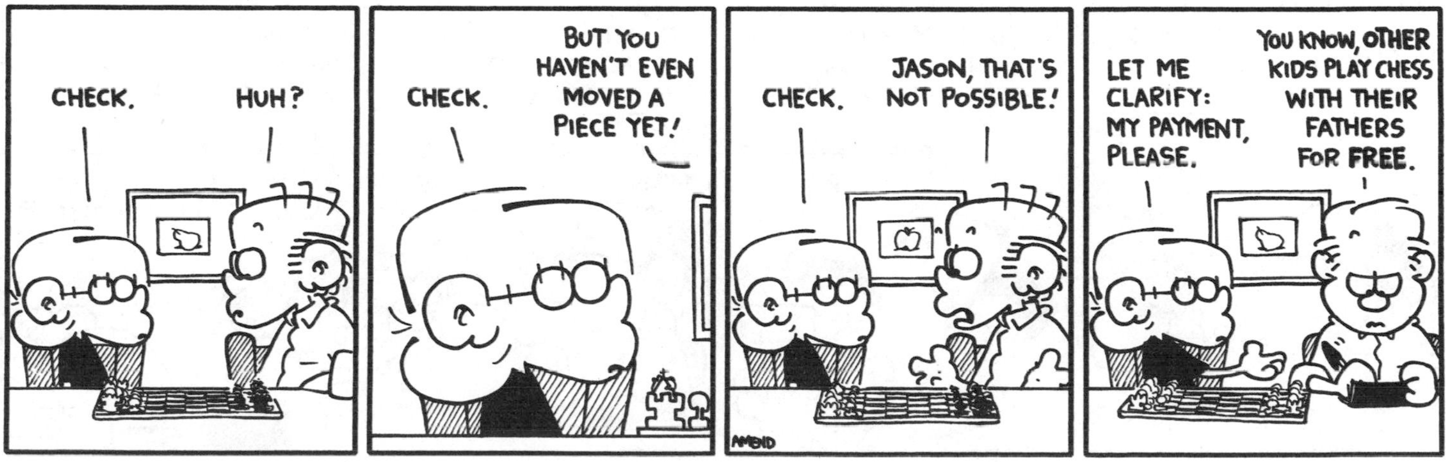
CHECK.
HUH?
CHECK.
BUT YOU HAVEN'T EVEN MOVED A PIECE YET!
CHECK.
JASON, THAT'S NOT POSSIBLE!
LET ME CLARIFY: MY PAYMENT, PLEASE.
YOU KNOW, OTHER KIDS PLAY CHESS WITH THEIR FATHERS FOR FREE.

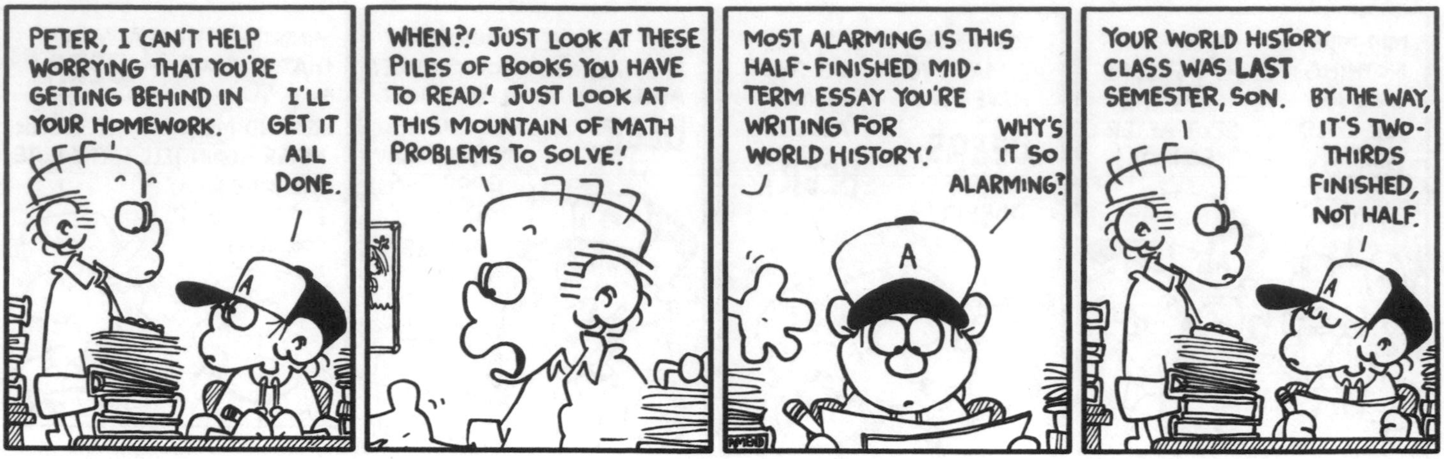
PETER, I CAN'T HELP WORRYING THAT YOU'RE GETTING BEHIND IN YOUR HOMEWORK.
I'LL GET IT ALL DONE.
WHEN?! JUST LOOK AT THESE PILES OF BOOKS YOU HAVE TO READ! JUST LOOK AT THIS MOUNTAIN OF MATH PROBLEMS TO SOLVE!
MOST ALARMING IS THIS HALF-FINISHED MID-TERM ESSAY YOU'RE WRITING FOR WORLD HISTORY!
WHY'S IT SO ALARMING?
YOUR WORLD HISTORY CLASS WAS LAST SEMESTER, SON.
BY THE WAY, IT'S TWO-THIRDS FINISHED, NOT HALF.

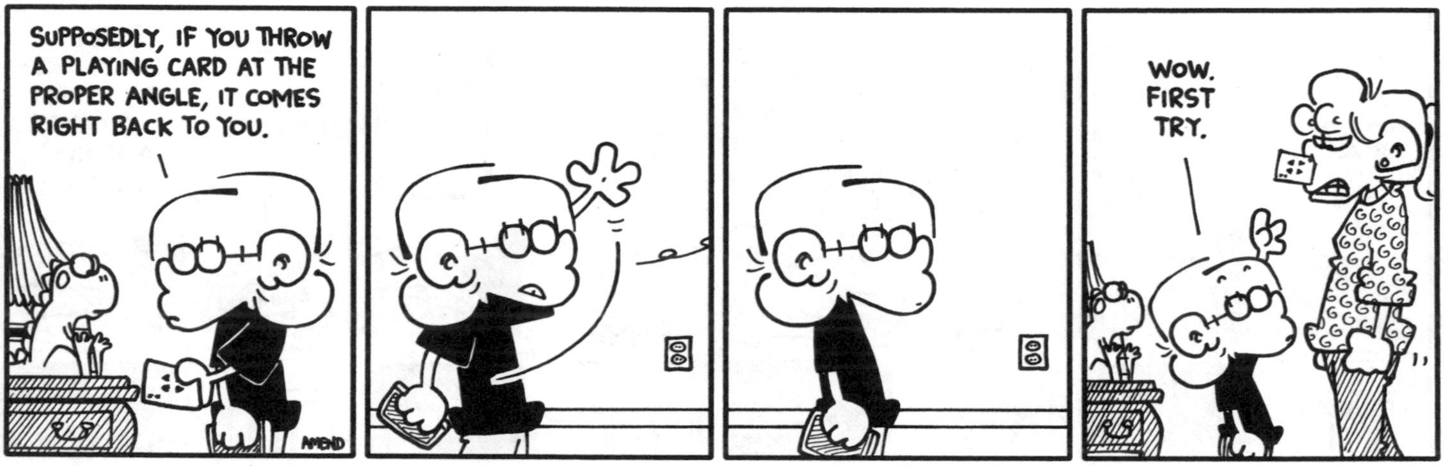
SUPPOSEDLY, IF YOU THROW A PLAYING CARD AT THE PROPER ANGLE, IT COMES RIGHT BACK TO YOU.
WOW. FIRST TRY.

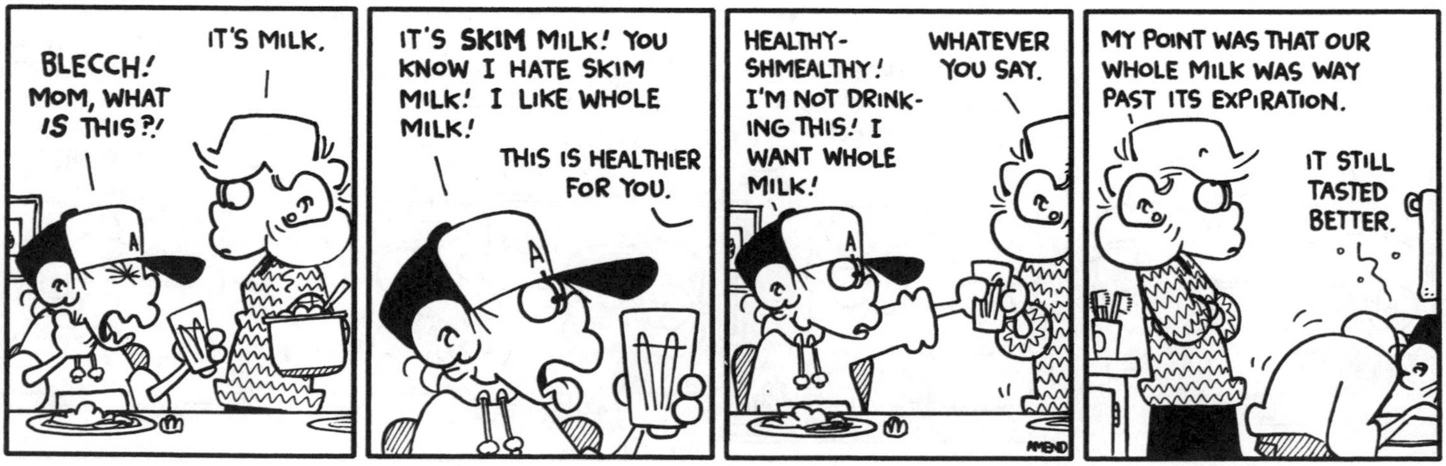
BLECCH! MOM, WHAT IS THIS?!
IT'S MILK.
IT'S SKIM MILK! YOU KNOW I HATE SKIM MILK! I LIKE WHOLE MILK!
THIS IS HEALTHIER FOR YOU.
HEALTHY-SHMEALTHY! I'M NOT DRINKING THIS! I WANT WHOLE MILK!
WHATEVER YOU SAY.
MY POINT WAS THAT OUR WHOLE MILK WAS WAY PAST ITS EXPIRATION.
IT STILL TASTED BETTER.

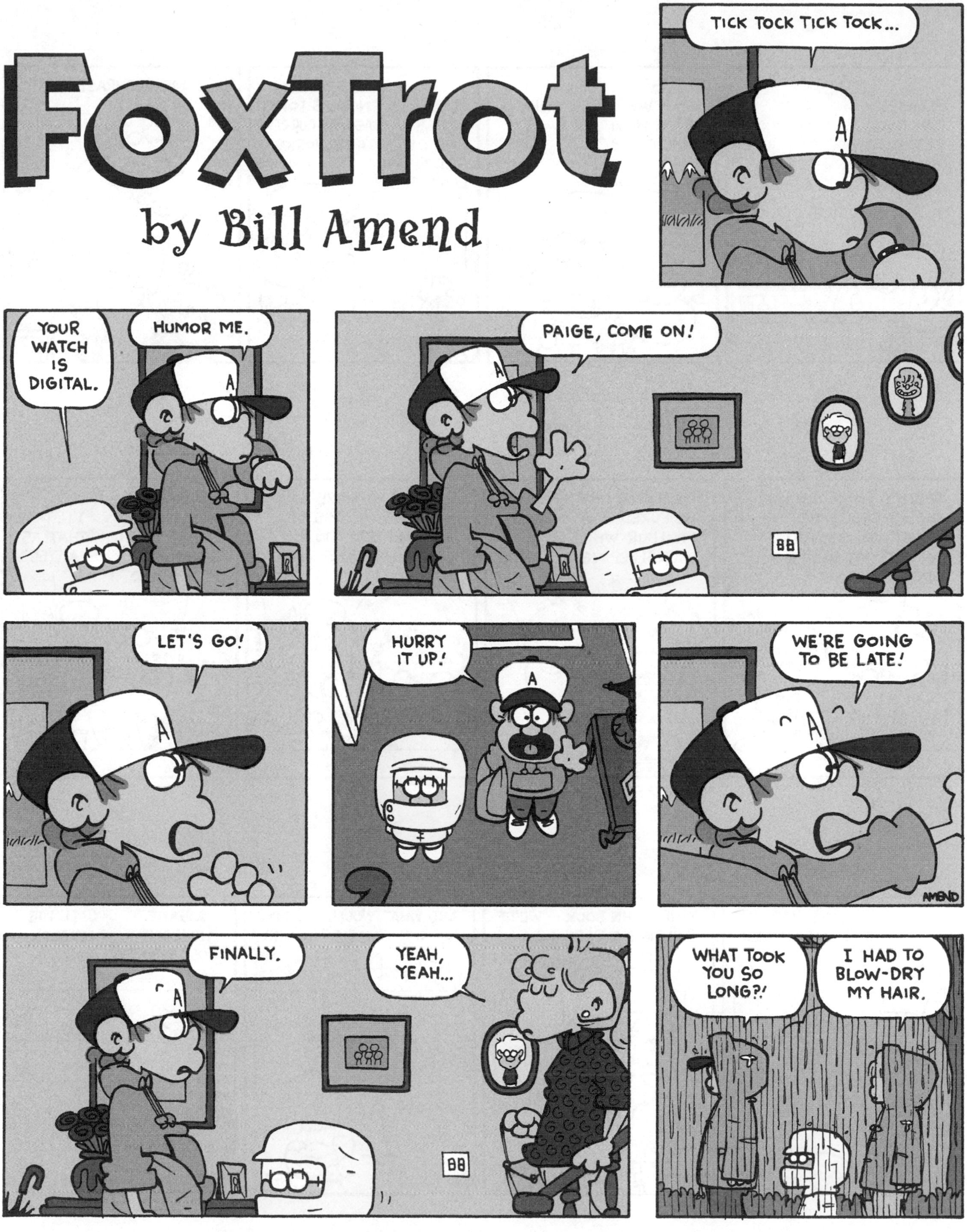
FoxTrot
by Bill Amend
TICK TOCK TICK TOCK...
YOUR WATCH IS DIGITAL.
HUMOR ME.
PAIGE, COME ON!
LET'S GO!
HURRY IT UP!
WE'RE GOING TO BE LATE!
AMEND
FINALLY.
YEAH, YEAH...
WHAT TOOK YOU SO LONG?!
I HAD TO BLOW-DRY MY HAIR.

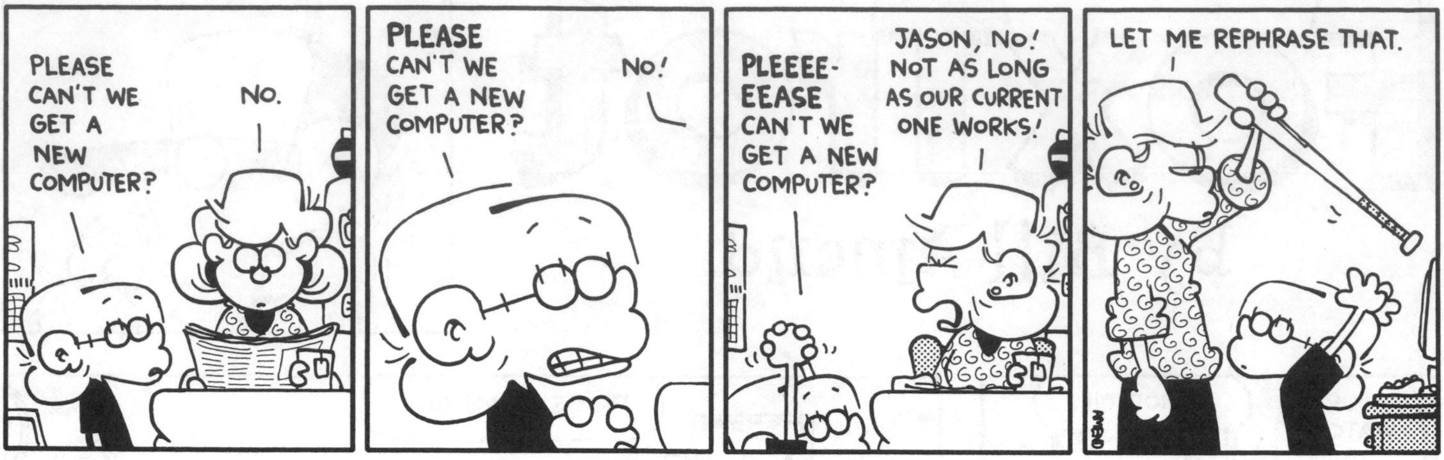
PLEASE CAN'T WE GET A NEW COMPUTER?
NO.
PLEASE CAN'T WE GET A NEW COMPUTER?
NO!
PLEEEE-EEASE CAN'T WE GET A NEW COMPUTER?
JASON, NO! NOT AS LONG AS OUR CURRENT ONE WORKS!
LET ME REPHRASE THAT.

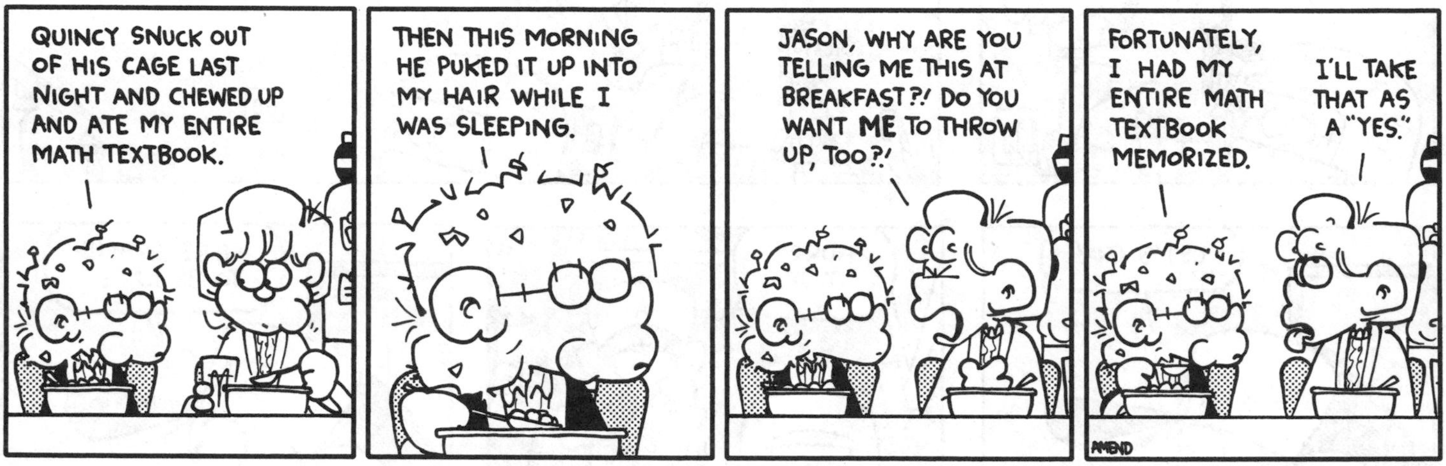
QUINCY SNUCK OUT OF HIS CAGE LAST NIGHT AND CHEWED UP AND ATE MY ENTIRE MATH TEXTBOOK.
THEN THIS MORNING HE PUKED IT UP INTO MY HAIR WHILE I WAS SLEEPING.
JASON, WHY ARE YOU TELLING ME THIS AT BREAKFAST?! DO YOU WANT ME TO THROW UP, TOO?!
FORTUNATELY, I HAD MY ENTIRE MATH TEXTBOOK MEMORIZED.
I'LL TAKE THAT AS A "YES."
AMEND

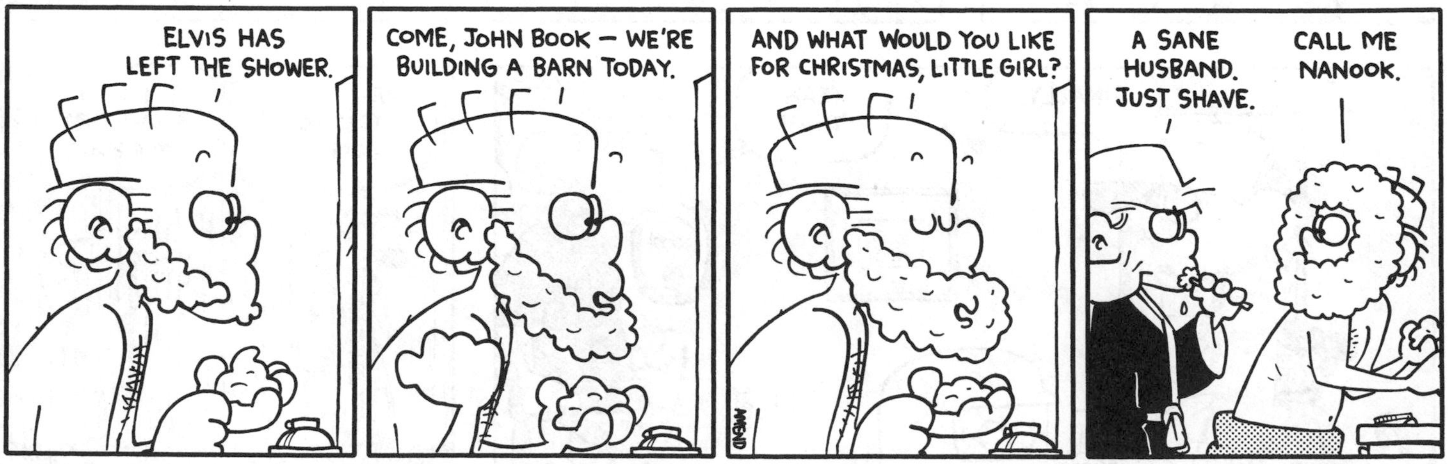
ELVIS HAS LEFT THE SHOWER.
COME, JOHN BOOK — WE'RE BUILDING A BARN TODAY.
AND WHAT WOULD YOU LIKE FOR CHRISTMAS, LITTLE GIRL?
A SANE HUSBAND. JUST SHAVE.
CALL ME NANOOK.

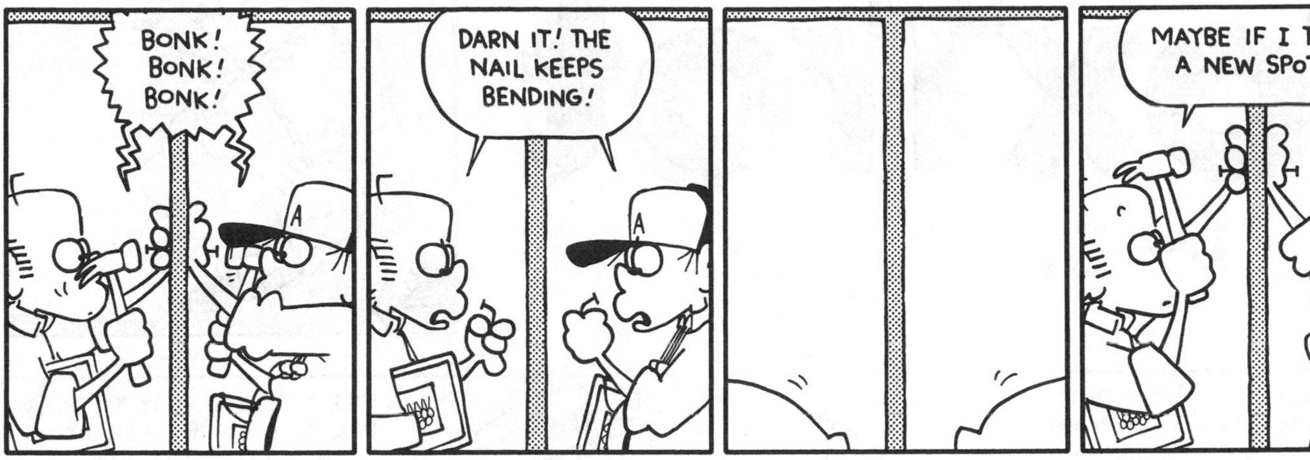
BONK! BONK! BONK!
DARN IT! THE NAIL KEEPS BENDING!
MAYBE IF I TRY A NEW SPOT...
AMEND

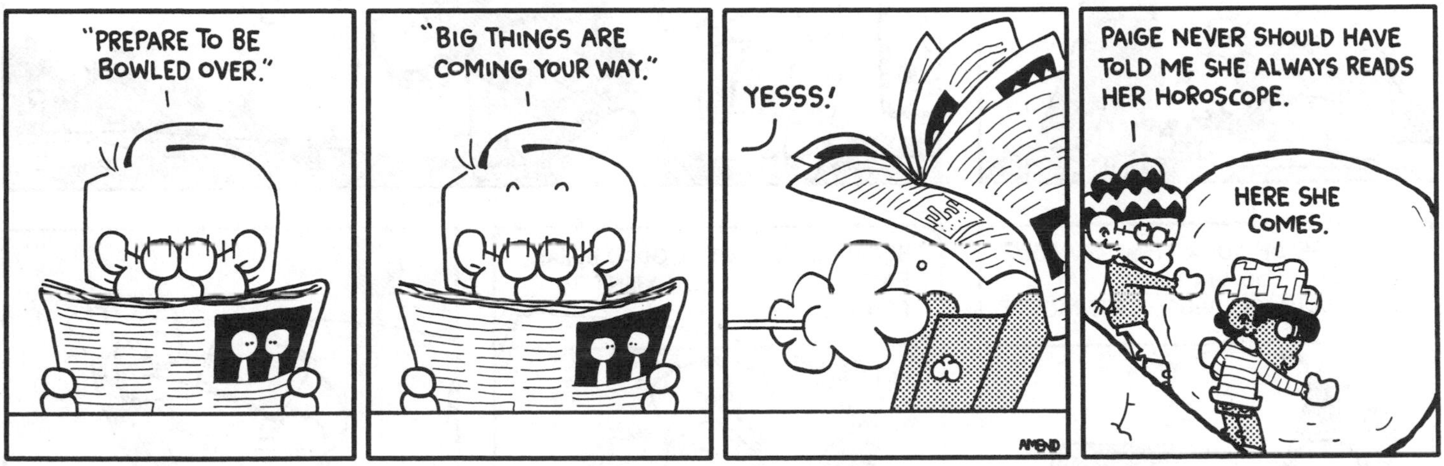
"PREPARE TO BE BOWLED OVER."
"BIG THINGS ARE COMING YOUR WAY."
YESSS!
AMEND
PAIGE NEVER SHOULD HAVE TOLD ME SHE ALWAYS READS HER HOROSCOPE.
HERE SHE COMES.

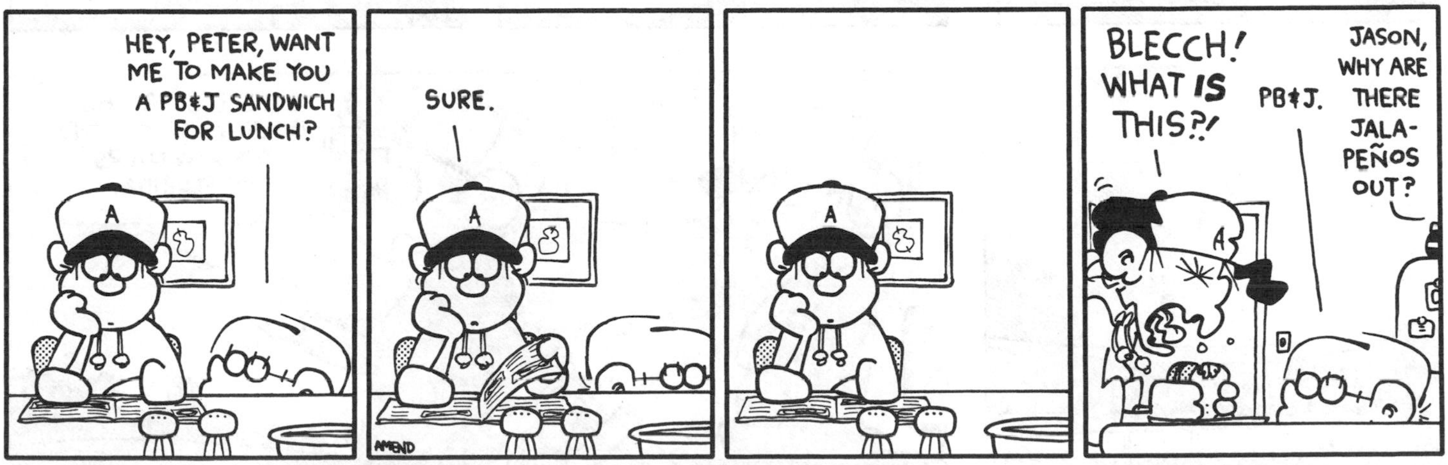
HEY, PETER, WANT ME TO MAKE YOU A PB&J SANDWICH FOR LUNCH?
AMEND
SURE.
BLECCH! WHAT IS THIS?!
PB&J.
JASON, WHY ARE THERE JALAPEÑOS OUT?

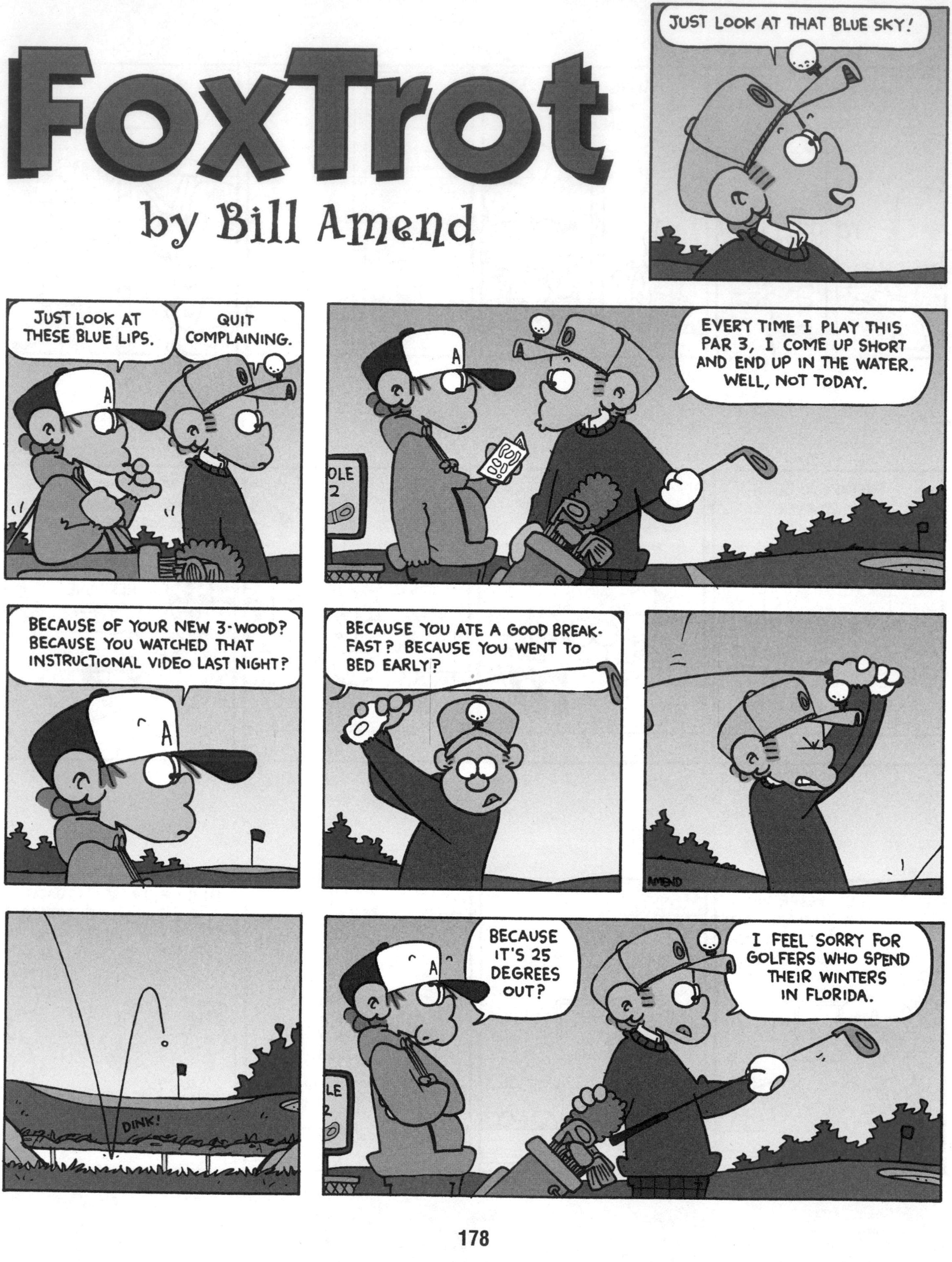
FoxTrot
by Bill Amend
JUST LOOK AT THAT BLUE SKY!
JUST LOOK AT THESE BLUE LIPS.
QUIT COMPLAINING.
EVERY TIME I PLAY THIS PAR 3, I COME UP SHORT AND END UP IN THE WATER. WELL, NOT TODAY.
BECAUSE OF YOUR NEW 3-WOOD? BECAUSE YOU WATCHED THAT INSTRUCTIONAL VIDEO LAST NIGHT?
BECAUSE YOU ATE A GOOD BREAK-FAST? BECAUSE YOU WENT TO BED EARLY?
AMEND
DINK!
BECAUSE IT'S 25 DEGREES OUT?
I FEEL SORRY FOR GOLFERS WHO SPEND THEIR WINTERS IN FLORIDA.

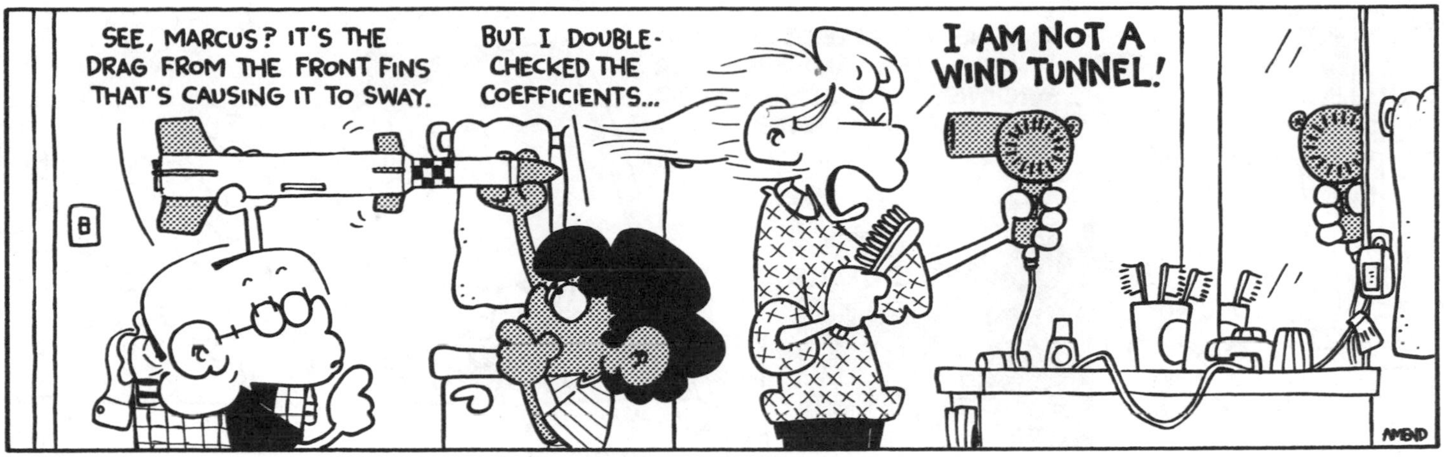
SEE, MARCUS? IT'S THE DRAG FROM THE FRONT FINS THAT'S CAUSING IT TO SWAY.
BUT I DOUBLE-CHECKED THE COEFFICIENTS...
I AM NOT A WIND TUNNEL!
AMEND

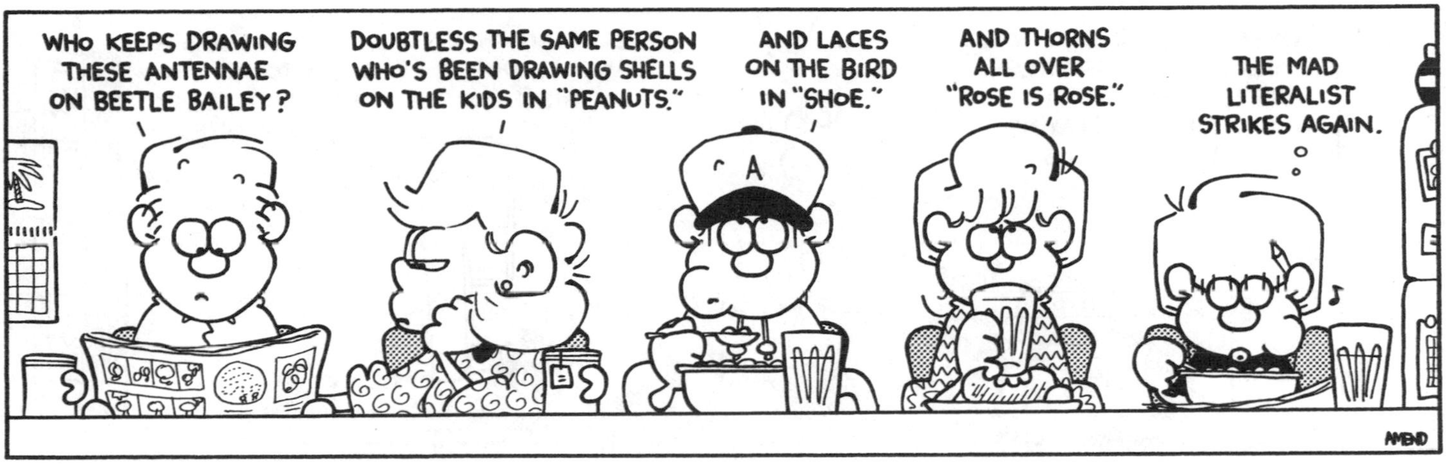
WHO KEEPS DRAWING THESE ANTENNAE ON BEETLE BAILEY?
DOUBTLESS THE SAME PERSON WHO'S BEEN DRAWING SHELLS ON THE KIDS IN "PEANUTS."
AND LACES ON THE BIRD IN "SHOE."
AND THORNS ALL OVER "ROSE IS ROSE."
THE MAD LITERALIST STRIKES AGAIN.
AMEND

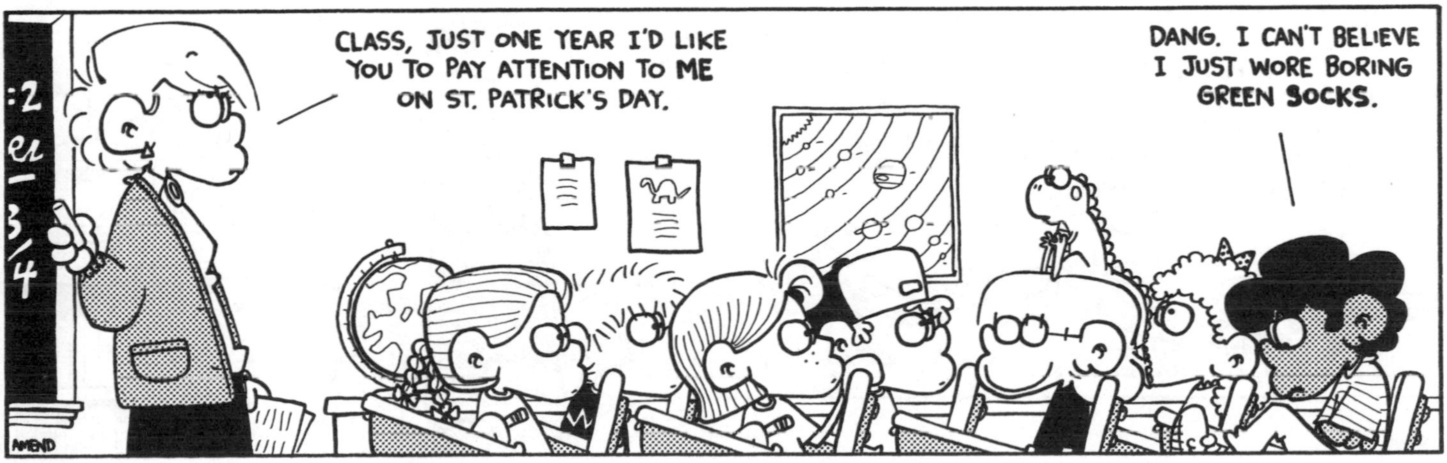
CLASS, JUST ONE YEAR I'D LIKE YOU TO PAY ATTENTION TO ME ON ST. PATRICK'S DAY.
DANG. I CAN'T BELIEVE I JUST WORE BORING GREEN SOCKS.
AMEND

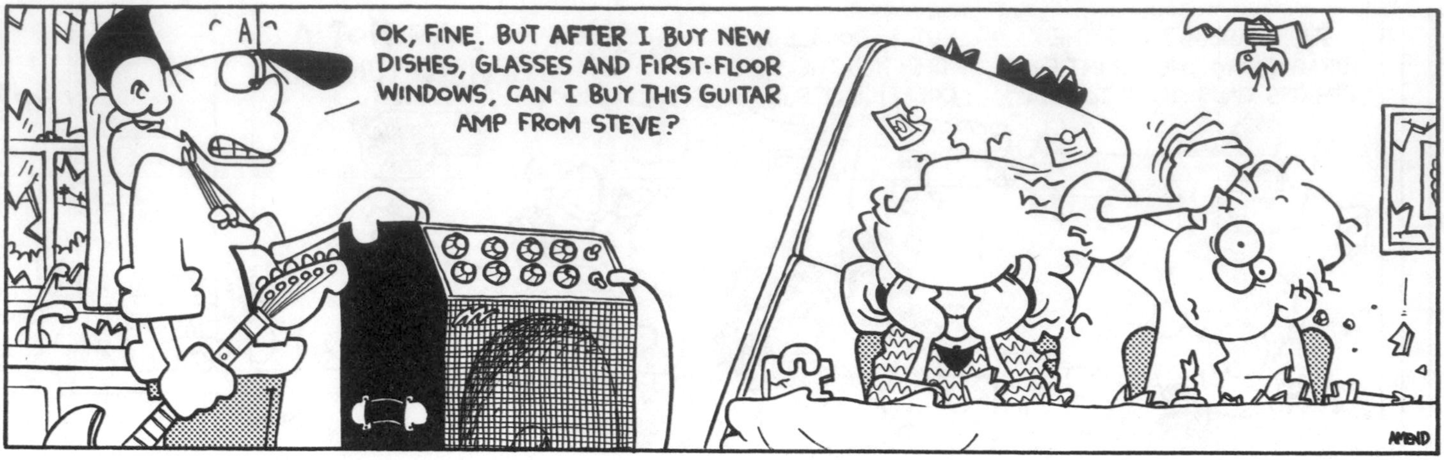
OK, FINE. BUT AFTER I BUY NEW DISHES, GLASSES AND FIRST-FLOOR WINDOWS, CAN I BUY THIS GUITAR AMP FROM STEVE?
AMEND

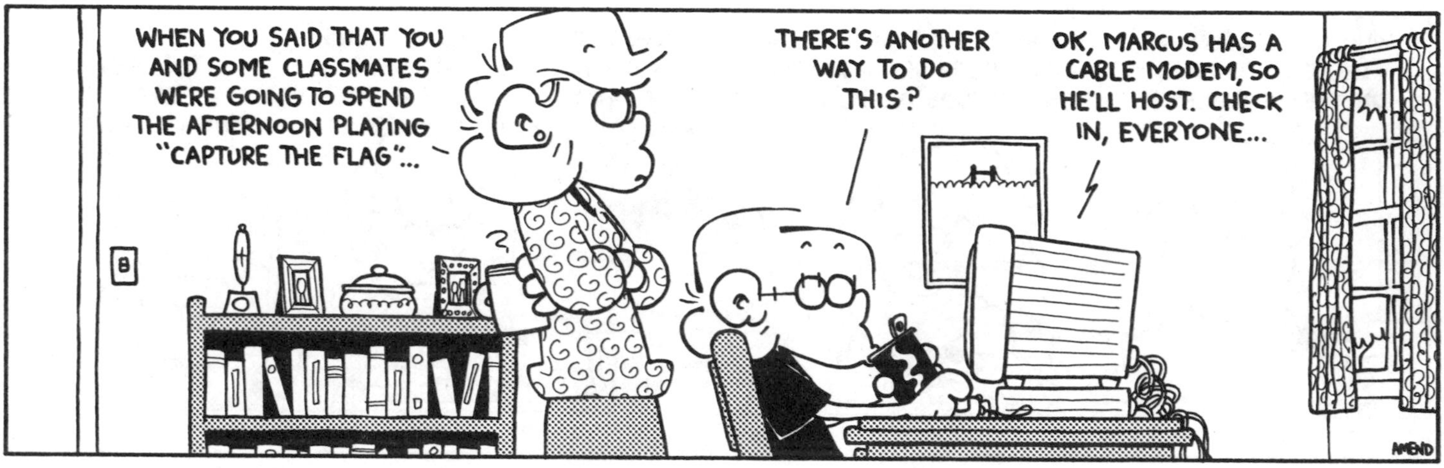
WHEN YOU SAID THAT YOU AND SOME CLASSMATES WERE GOING TO SPEND THE AFTERNOON PLAYING "CAPTURE THE FLAG"...
THERE'S ANOTHER WAY TO DO THIS?
OK, MARCUS HAS A CABLE MODEM, SO HE'LL HOST. CHECK IN, EVERYONE...
AMEND

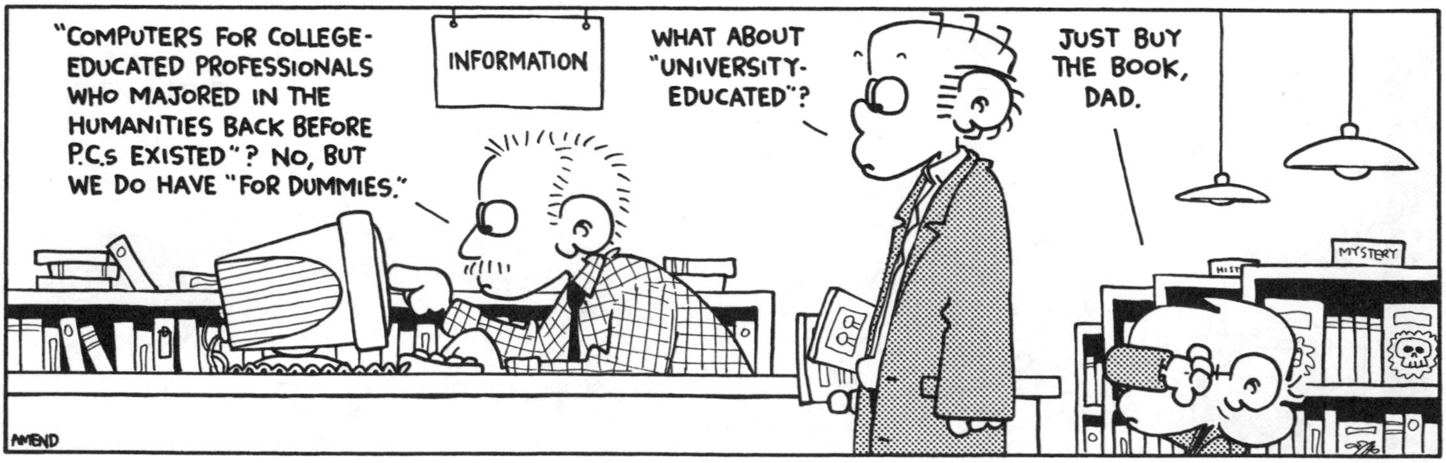
"COMPUTERS FOR COLLEGE-EDUCATED PROFESSIONALS WHO MAJORED IN THE HUMANITIES BACK BEFORE P.C.s EXISTED"? NO, BUT WE DO HAVE "FOR DUMMIES."
INFORMATION
WHAT ABOUT "UNIVERSITY-EDUCATED"?
JUST BUY THE BOOK, DAD.
MYSTERY
AMEND

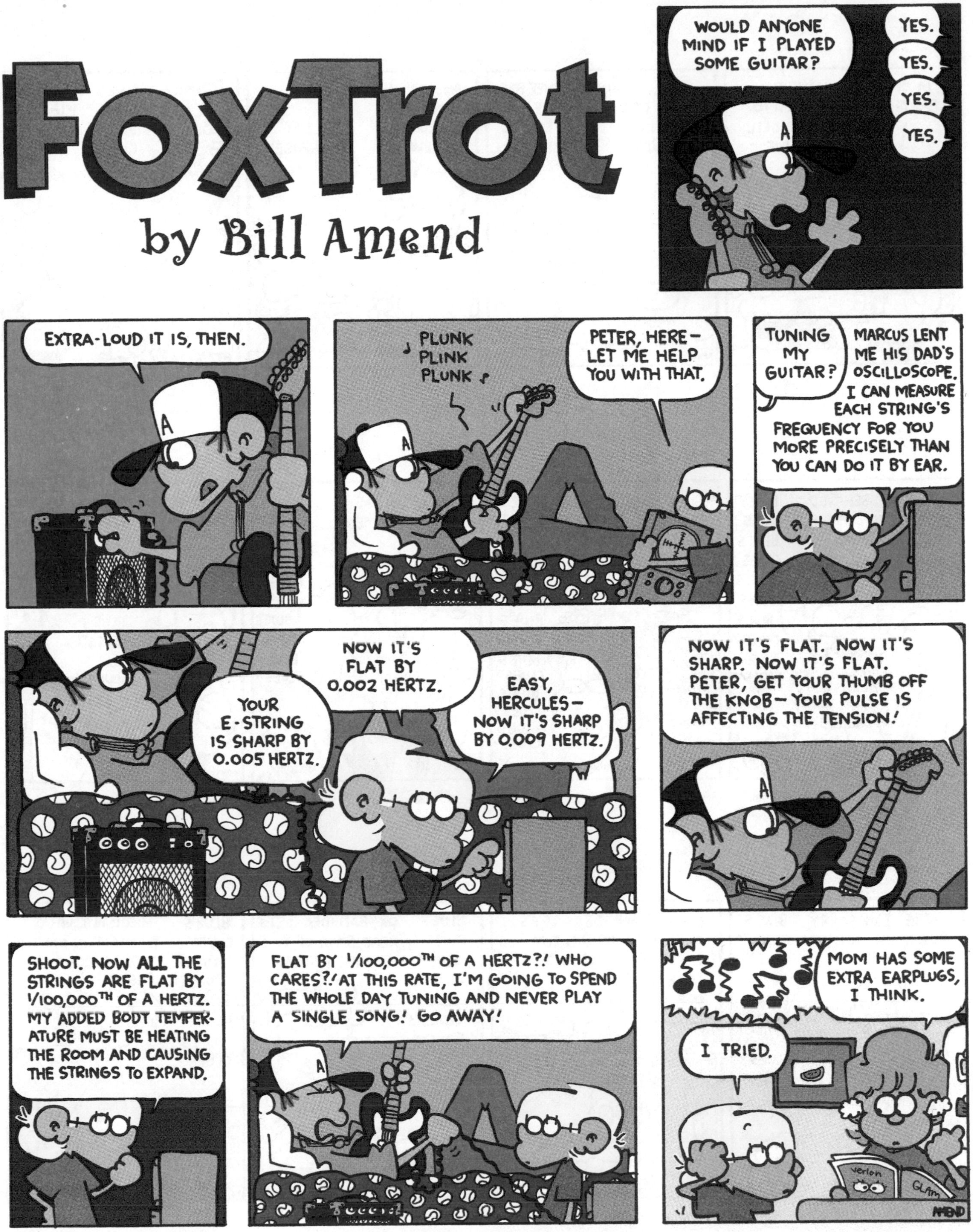
FoxTrot
by Bill Amend
WOULD ANYONE MIND IF I PLAYED SOME GUITAR?
YES.
YES.
YES.
YES.
EXTRA-LOUD IT IS, THEN.
PLUNK PLINK PLUNK
PETER, HERE— LET ME HELP YOU WITH THAT.
TUNING MY GUITAR?
MARCUS LENT ME HIS DAD'S OSCILLOSCOPE. I CAN MEASURE EACH STRING'S FREQUENCY FOR YOU MORE PRECISELY THAN YOU CAN DO IT BY EAR.
YOUR E-STRING IS SHARP BY 0.005 HERTZ.
NOW IT'S FLAT BY 0.002 HERTZ.
EASY, HERCULES— NOW IT'S SHARP BY 0.009 HERTZ.
NOW IT'S FLAT. NOW IT'S SHARP. NOW IT'S FLAT. PETER, GET YOUR THUMB OFF THE KNOB— YOUR PULSE IS AFFECTING THE TENSION!
SHOOT. NOW ALL THE STRINGS ARE FLAT BY 1/100,000TH OF A HERTZ. MY ADDED BODY TEMPERATURE MUST BE HEATING THE ROOM AND CAUSING THE STRINGS TO EXPAND.
FLAT BY 1/100,000TH OF A HERTZ?! WHO CARES?! AT THIS RATE, I'M GOING TO SPEND THE WHOLE DAY TUNING AND NEVER PLAY A SINGLE SONG! GO AWAY!
MOM HAS SOME EXTRA EARPLUGS, I THINK.
I TRIED.
AMEND

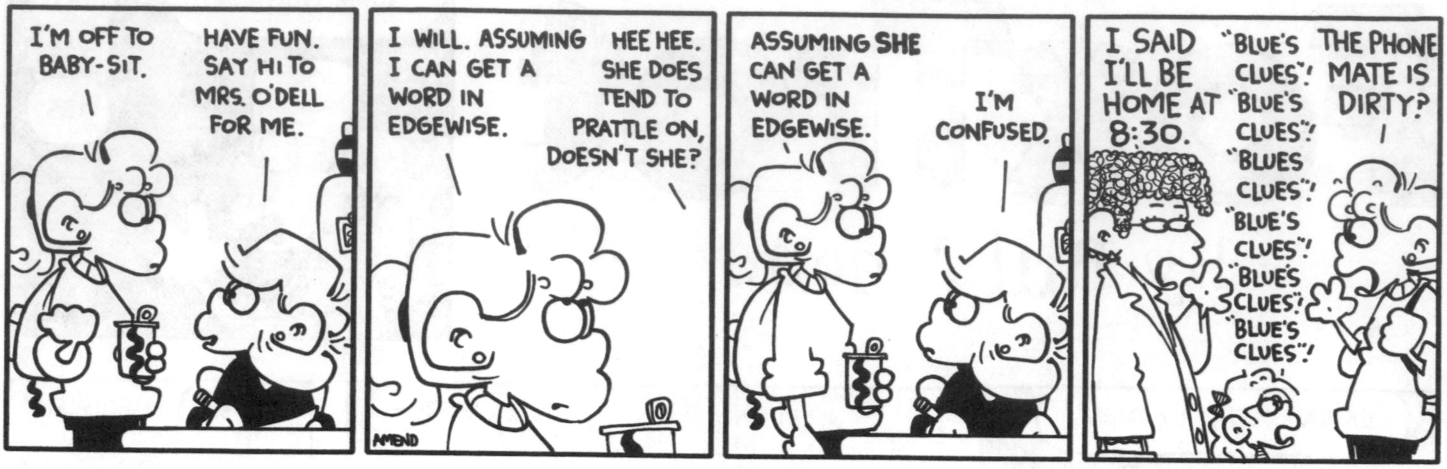
I'M OFF TO BABY-SIT.
HAVE FUN. SAY HI TO MRS. O'DELL FOR ME.
I WILL. ASSUMING I CAN GET A WORD IN EDGEWISE.
HEE HEE. SHE DOES TEND TO PRATTLE ON, DOESN'T SHE?
AMEND
ASSUMING SHE CAN GET A WORD IN EDGEWISE.
I'M CONFUSED.
I SAID I'LL BE HOME AT 8:30.
"BLUE'S CLUES"! "BLUE'S CLUES"! "BLUES CLUES"! "BLUE'S CLUES"! "BLUES CLUES"! "BLUE'S CLUES"!
THE PHONE MATE IS DIRTY?

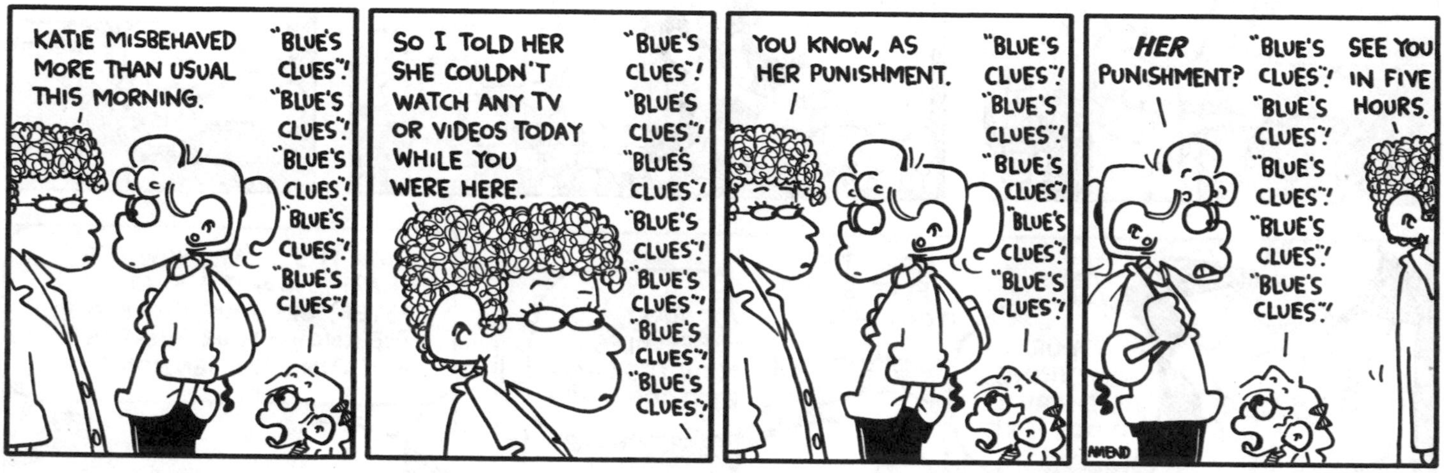
KATIE MISBEHAVED MORE THAN USUAL THIS MORNING.
"BLUE'S CLUES"! "BLUE'S CLUES"! "BLUE'S CLUES"! "BLUE'S CLUES"! "BLUE'S CLUES"!
SO I TOLD HER SHE COULDN'T WATCH ANY TV OR VIDEOS TODAY WHILE YOU WERE HERE.
"BLUE'S CLUES"! "BLUE'S CLUES"! "BLUES CLUES"! "BLUE'S CLUES"! "BLUE'S CLUES"! "BLUE'S CLUES"! "BLUE'S CLUES"!
YOU KNOW, AS HER PUNISHMENT.
"BLUE'S CLUES"! "BLUE'S CLUES"! "BLUE'S CLUES"! "BLUE'S CLUES"! "BLUE'S CLUES"!
HER PUNISHMENT?
"BLUE'S CLUES"! "BLUE'S CLUES"! "BLUE'S CLUES"! "BLUE'S CLUES"! "BLUE'S CLUES"!
SEE YOU IN FIVE HOURS.
AMEND

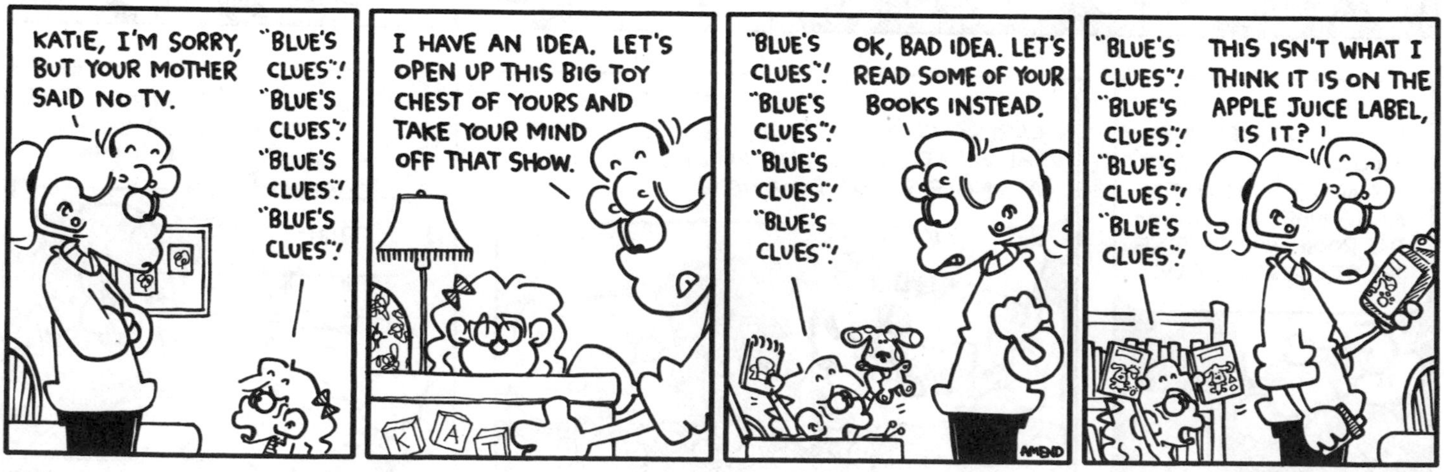
KATIE, I'M SORRY, BUT YOUR MOTHER SAID NO TV.
"BLUE'S CLUES"! "BLUE'S CLUES"! "BLUE'S CLUES"! "BLUE'S CLUES"!
I HAVE AN IDEA. LET'S OPEN UP THIS BIG TOY CHEST OF YOURS AND TAKE YOUR MIND OFF THAT SHOW.
K A T
"BLUE'S CLUES"! "BLUE'S CLUES"! "BLUE'S CLUES"! "BLUE'S CLUES"!
OK, BAD IDEA. LET'S READ SOME OF YOUR BOOKS INSTEAD.
AMEND
"BLUE'S CLUES"! "BLUE'S CLUES"! "BLUE'S CLUES"! "BLUE'S CLUES"!
THIS ISN'T WHAT I THINK IT IS ON THE APPLE JUICE LABEL, IS IT?

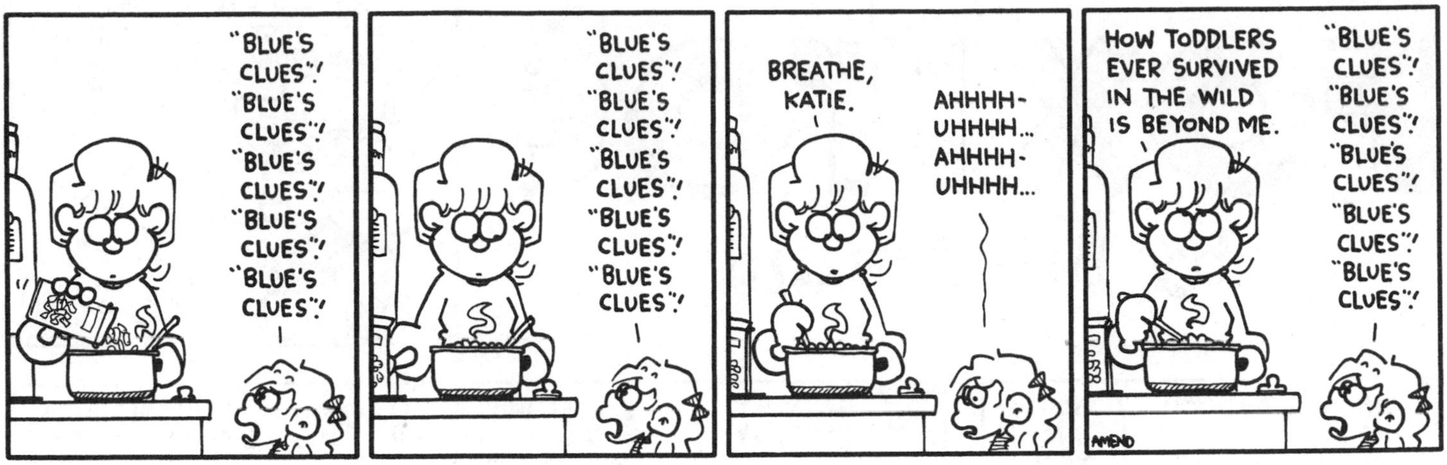
"BLUE'S CLUES"! "BLUE'S CLUES"! "BLUE'S CLUES"! "BLUE'S CLUES"! "BLUE'S CLUES"!
"BLUE'S CLUES"! "BLUE'S CLUES"! "BLUE'S CLUES"! "BLUE'S CLUES"!
BREATHE, KATIE.
AHHHH-UHHHH... AHHHH-UHHHH...
HOW TODDLERS EVER SURVIVED IN THE WILD IS BEYOND ME.
"BLUE'S CLUES"! "BLUE'S CLUES"! "BLUE'S CLUES"! "BLUE'S CLUES"! "BLUE'S CLUES"!
AMEND

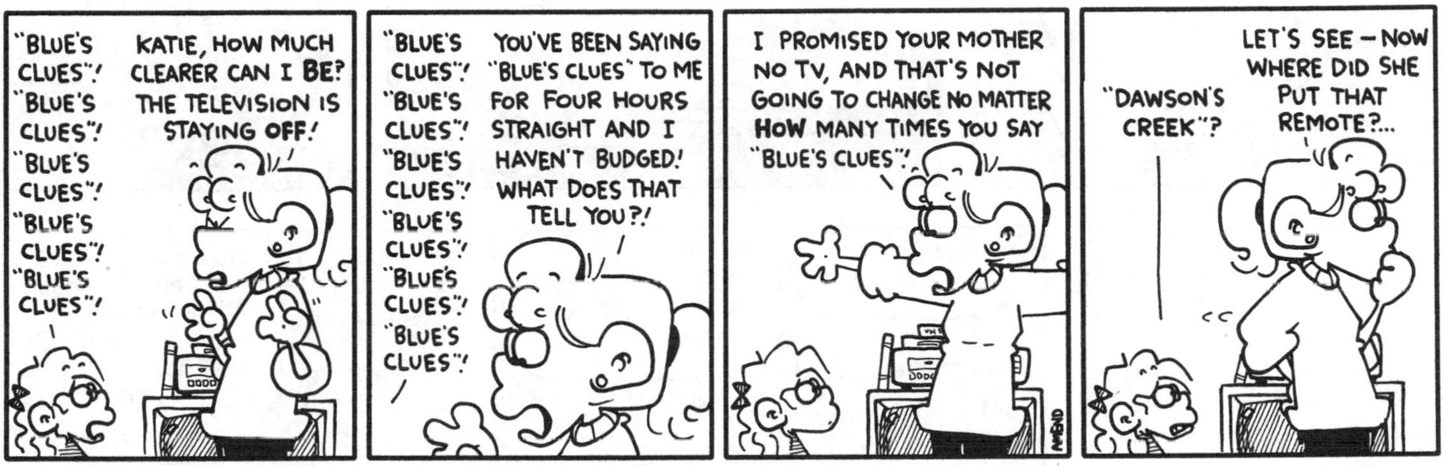
"BLUE'S CLUES"! "BLUE'S CLUES"! "BLUE'S CLUES"! "BLUE'S CLUES"! "BLUE'S CLUES"!
KATIE, HOW MUCH CLEARER CAN I BE? THE TELEVISION IS STAYING OFF!
"BLUE'S CLUES"! "BLUE'S CLUES"! "BLUE'S CLUES"! "BLUE'S CLUES"! "BLUE'S CLUES"! "BLUE'S CLUES"!
YOU'VE BEEN SAYING "BLUE'S CLUES" TO ME FOR FOUR HOURS STRAIGHT AND I HAVEN'T BUDGED! WHAT DOES THAT TELL YOU?!
I PROMISED YOUR MOTHER NO TV, AND THAT'S NOT GOING TO CHANGE NO MATTER HOW MANY TIMES YOU SAY "BLUE'S CLUES"!
AMEND
"DAWSON'S CREEK"?
LET'S SEE – NOW WHERE DID SHE PUT THAT REMOTE?...

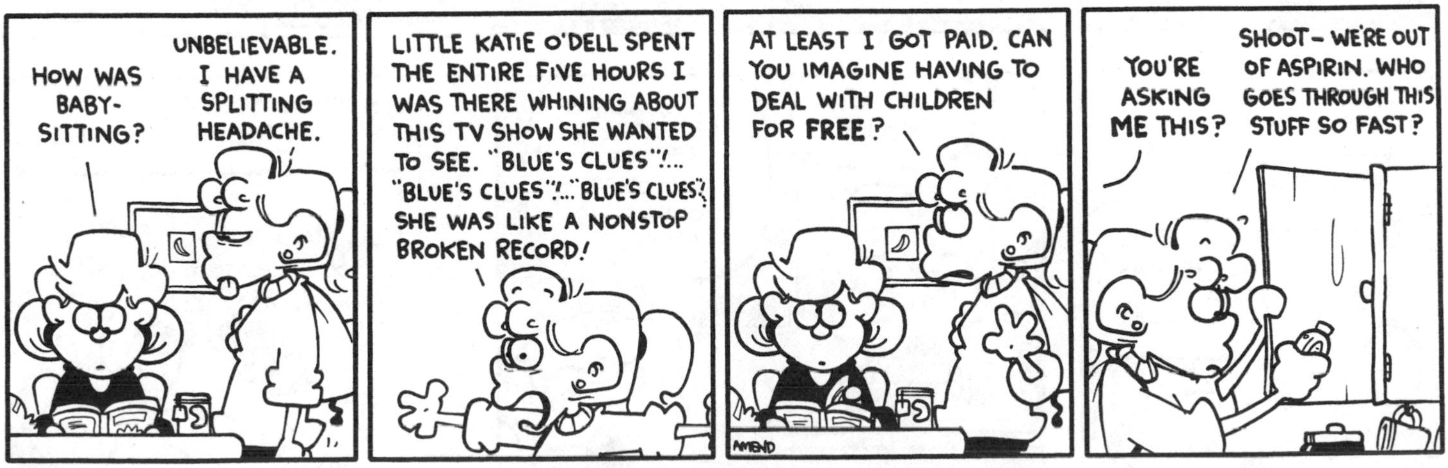
HOW WAS BABY-SITTING?
UNBELIEVABLE. I HAVE A SPLITTING HEADACHE.
LITTLE KATIE O'DELL SPENT THE ENTIRE FIVE HOURS I WAS THERE WHINING ABOUT THIS TV SHOW SHE WANTED TO SEE. "BLUE'S CLUES"!... "BLUE'S CLUES"!... "BLUE'S CLUES"! SHE WAS LIKE A NONSTOP BROKEN RECORD!
AT LEAST I GOT PAID. CAN YOU IMAGINE HAVING TO DEAL WITH CHILDREN FOR FREE?
AMEND
YOU'RE ASKING ME THIS?
SHOOT – WE'RE OUT OF ASPIRIN. WHO GOES THROUGH THIS STUFF SO FAST?

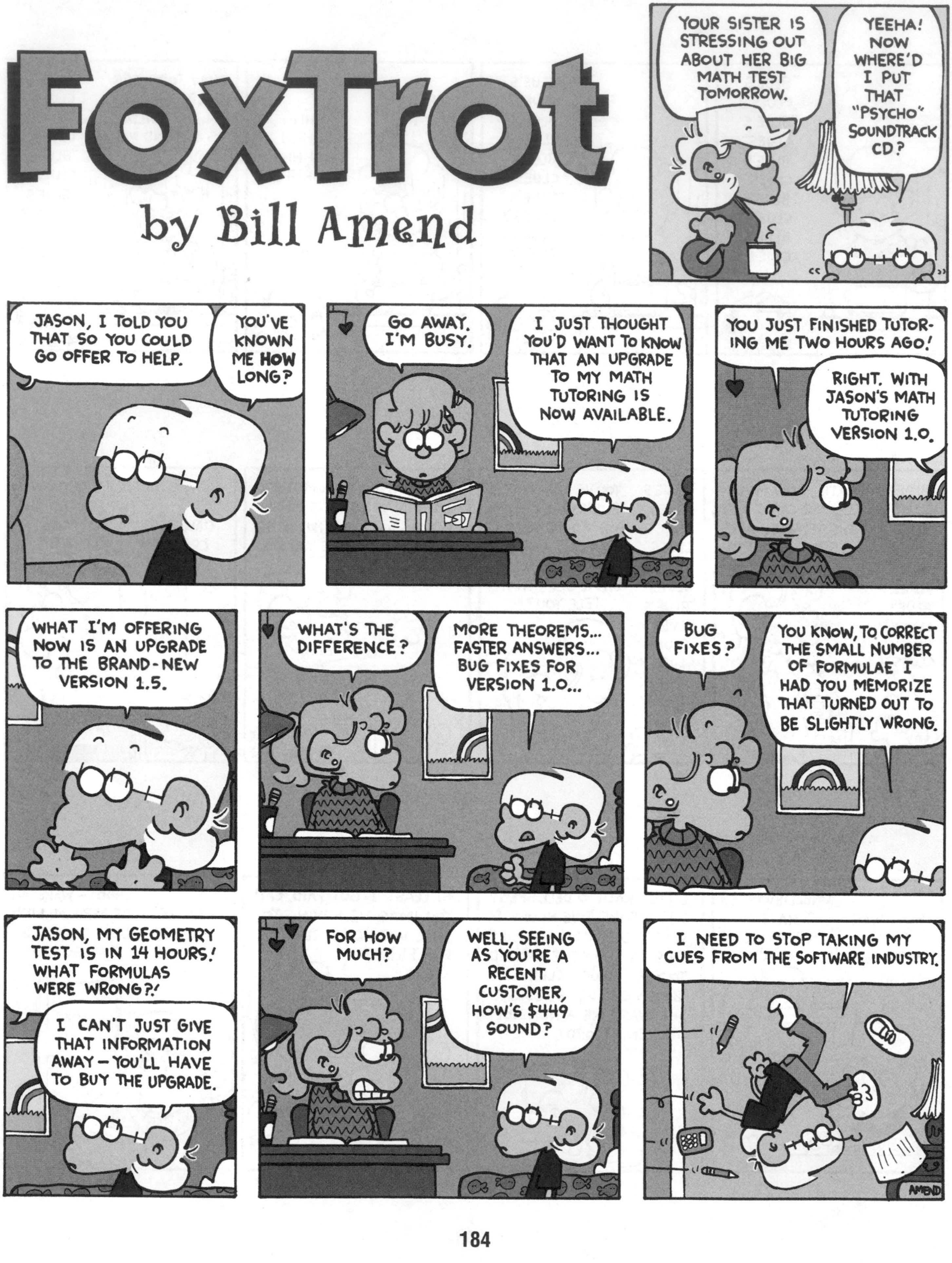
FoxTrot
by Bill Amend
YOUR SISTER IS STRESSING OUT ABOUT HER BIG MATH TEST TOMORROW.
YEEHA! NOW WHERE'D I PUT THAT "PSYCHO" SOUNDTRACK CD?
JASON, I TOLD YOU THAT SO YOU COULD GO OFFER TO HELP.
YOU'VE KNOWN ME HOW LONG?
GO AWAY. I'M BUSY.
I JUST THOUGHT YOU'D WANT TO KNOW THAT AN UPGRADE TO MY MATH TUTORING IS NOW AVAILABLE.
YOU JUST FINISHED TUTORING ME TWO HOURS AGO!
RIGHT. WITH JASON'S MATH TUTORING VERSION 1.0.
WHAT I'M OFFERING NOW IS AN UPGRADE TO THE BRAND-NEW VERSION 1.5.
WHAT'S THE DIFFERENCE?
MORE THEOREMS... FASTER ANSWERS... BUG FIXES FOR VERSION 1.0...
BUG FIXES?
YOU KNOW, TO CORRECT THE SMALL NUMBER OF FORMULAE I HAD YOU MEMORIZE THAT TURNED OUT TO BE SLIGHTLY WRONG.
JASON, MY GEOMETRY TEST IS IN 14 HOURS! WHAT FORMULAS WERE WRONG?!
I CAN'T JUST GIVE THAT INFORMATION AWAY – YOU'LL HAVE TO BUY THE UPGRADE.
FOR HOW MUCH?
WELL, SEEING AS YOU'RE A RECENT CUSTOMER, HOW'S $449 SOUND?
I NEED TO STOP TAKING MY CUES FROM THE SOFTWARE INDUSTRY.
AMEND

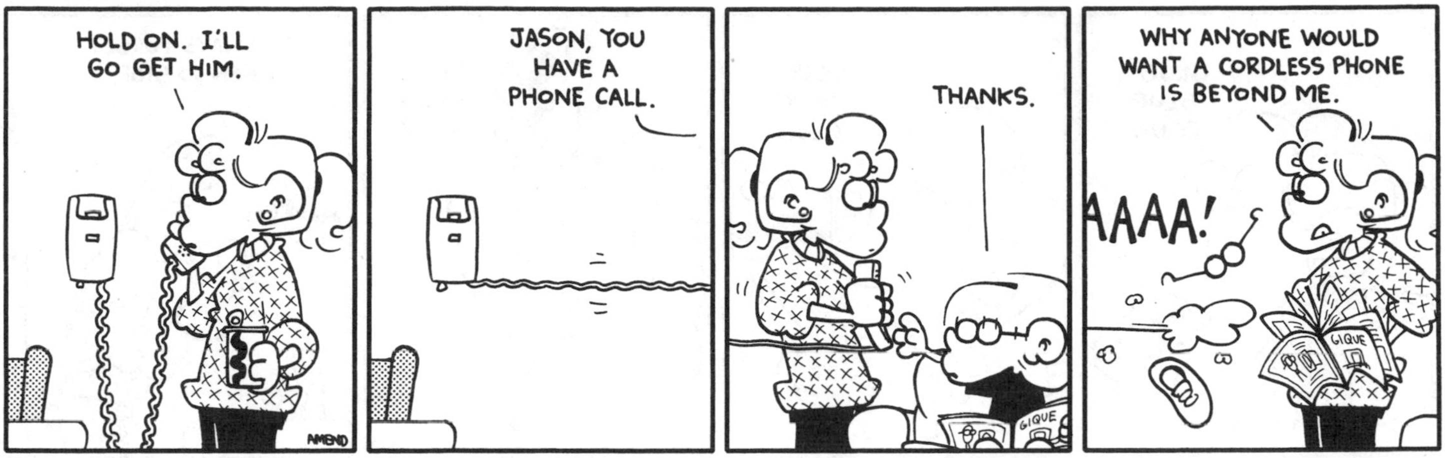
HOLD ON. I'LL GO GET HIM.
JASON, YOU HAVE A PHONE CALL.
THANKS.
GIQUE
AAAA!
WHY ANYONE WOULD WANT A CORDLESS PHONE IS BEYOND ME.
GIQUE
AMEND

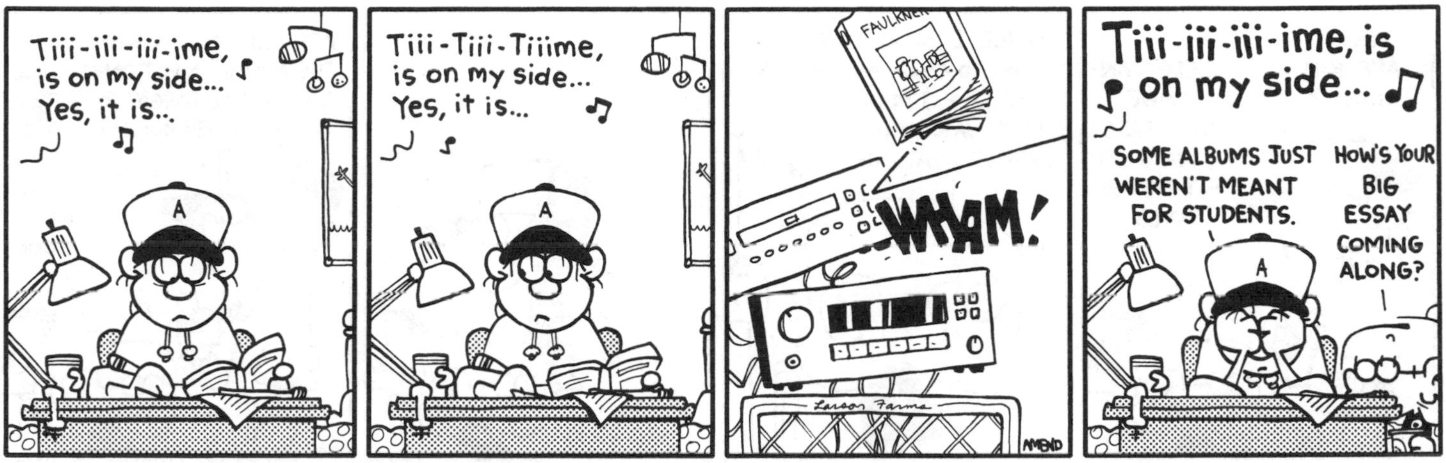
Tiii-iii-iii-ime, is on my side... Yes, it is...
Tiii-Tiii-Tiiime, is on my side... Yes, it is...
FAULKNER
WHAM!
AMEND
Tiii-iii-iii-ime, is on my side...
SOME ALBUMS JUST WEREN'T MEANT FOR STUDENTS.
HOW'S YOUR BIG ESSAY COMING ALONG?

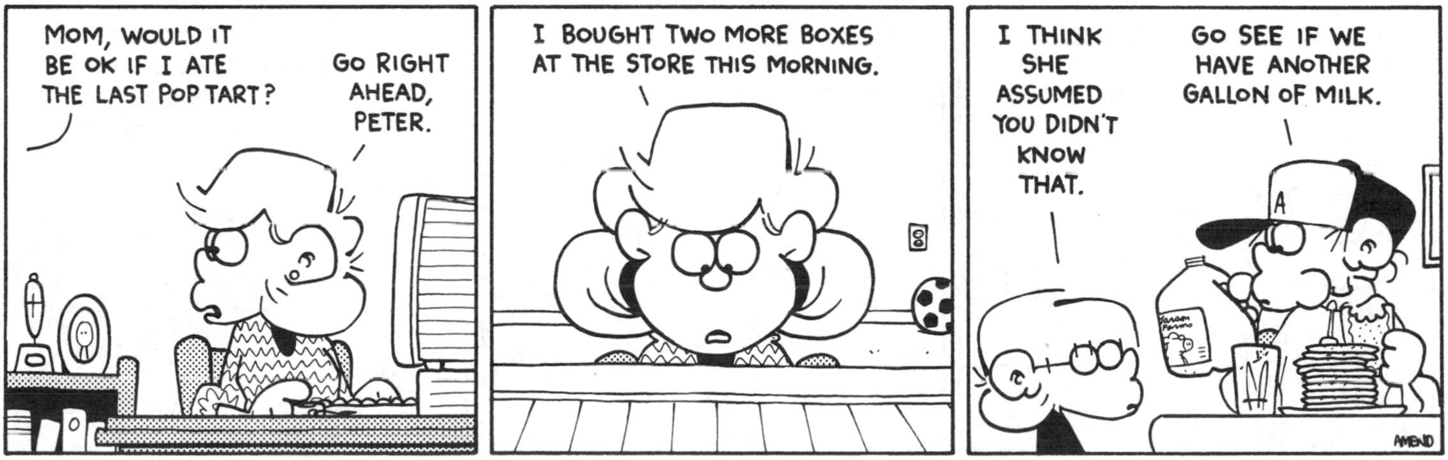
MOM, WOULD IT BE OK IF I ATE THE LAST POP TART?
GO RIGHT AHEAD, PETER.
I BOUGHT TWO MORE BOXES AT THE STORE THIS MORNING.
I THINK SHE ASSUMED YOU DIDN'T KNOW THAT.
GO SEE IF WE HAVE ANOTHER GALLON OF MILK.
AMEND

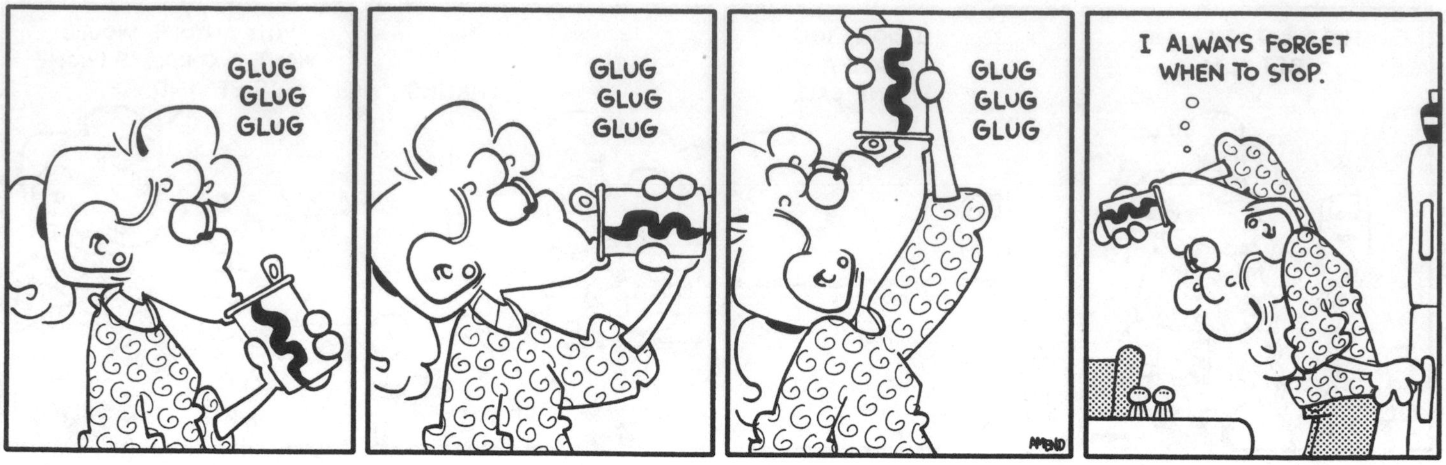
GLUG
GLUG
GLUG
GLUG
GLUG
GLUG
GLUG
GLUG
GLUG
I ALWAYS FORGET WHEN TO STOP.
AMEND

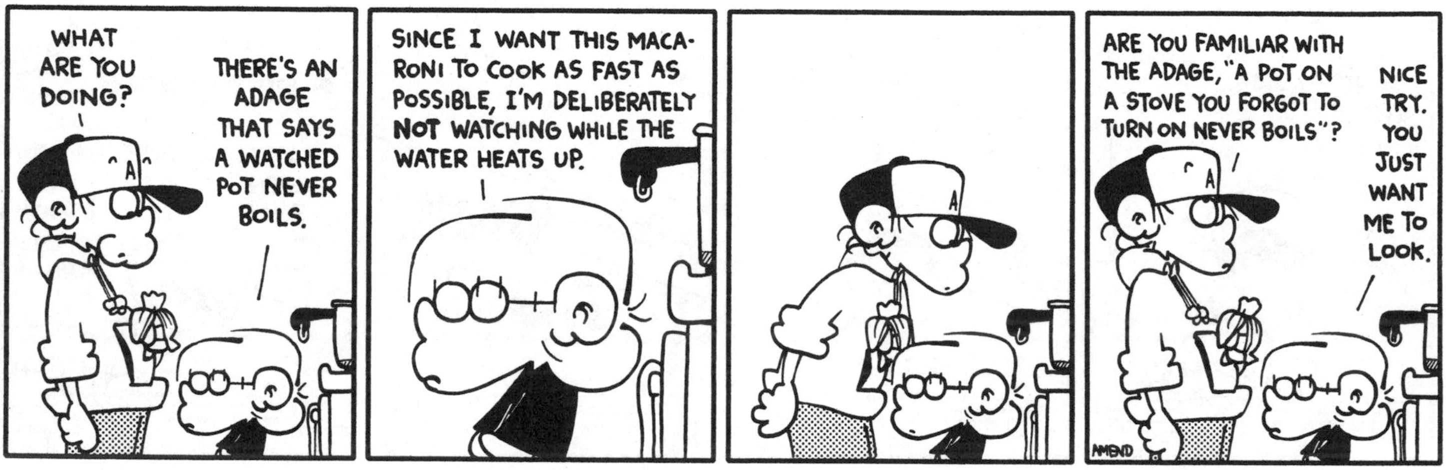
WHAT ARE YOU DOING?
THERE'S AN ADAGE THAT SAYS A WATCHED POT NEVER BOILS.
SINCE I WANT THIS MACARONI TO COOK AS FAST AS POSSIBLE, I'M DELIBERATELY NOT WATCHING WHILE THE WATER HEATS UP.
ARE YOU FAMILIAR WITH THE ADAGE, "A POT ON A STOVE YOU FORGOT TO TURN ON NEVER BOILS"?
NICE TRY. YOU JUST WANT ME TO LOOK.
AMEND

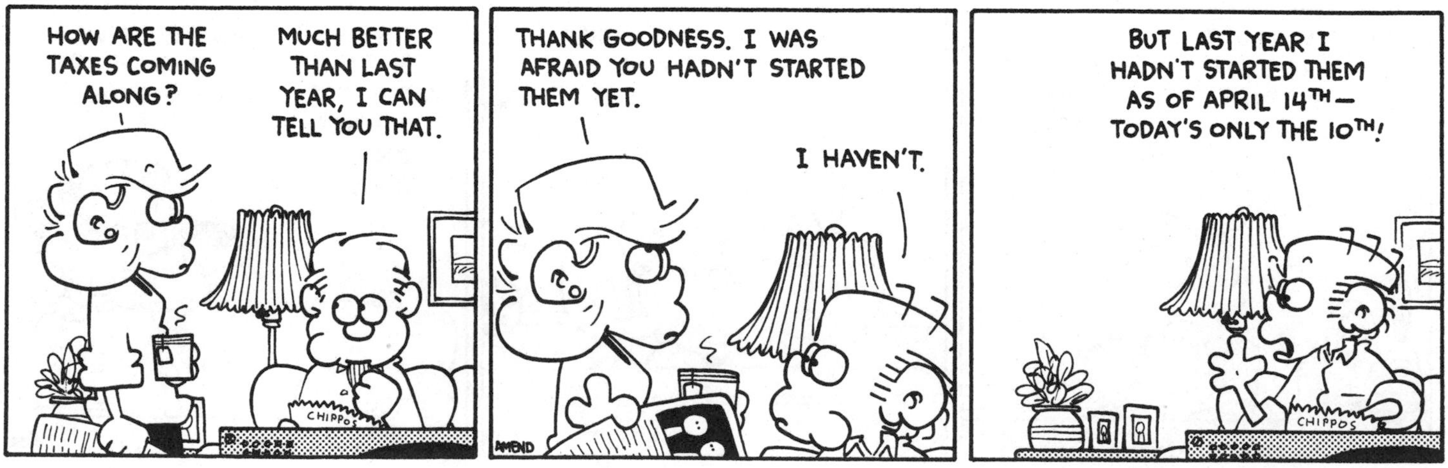
HOW ARE THE TAXES COMING ALONG?
MUCH BETTER THAN LAST YEAR, I CAN TELL YOU THAT.
CHIPPOS
THANK GOODNESS. I WAS AFRAID YOU HADN'T STARTED THEM YET.
I HAVEN'T.
AMEND
BUT LAST YEAR I HADN'T STARTED THEM AS OF APRIL 14TH— TODAY'S ONLY THE 10TH!
CHIPPOS

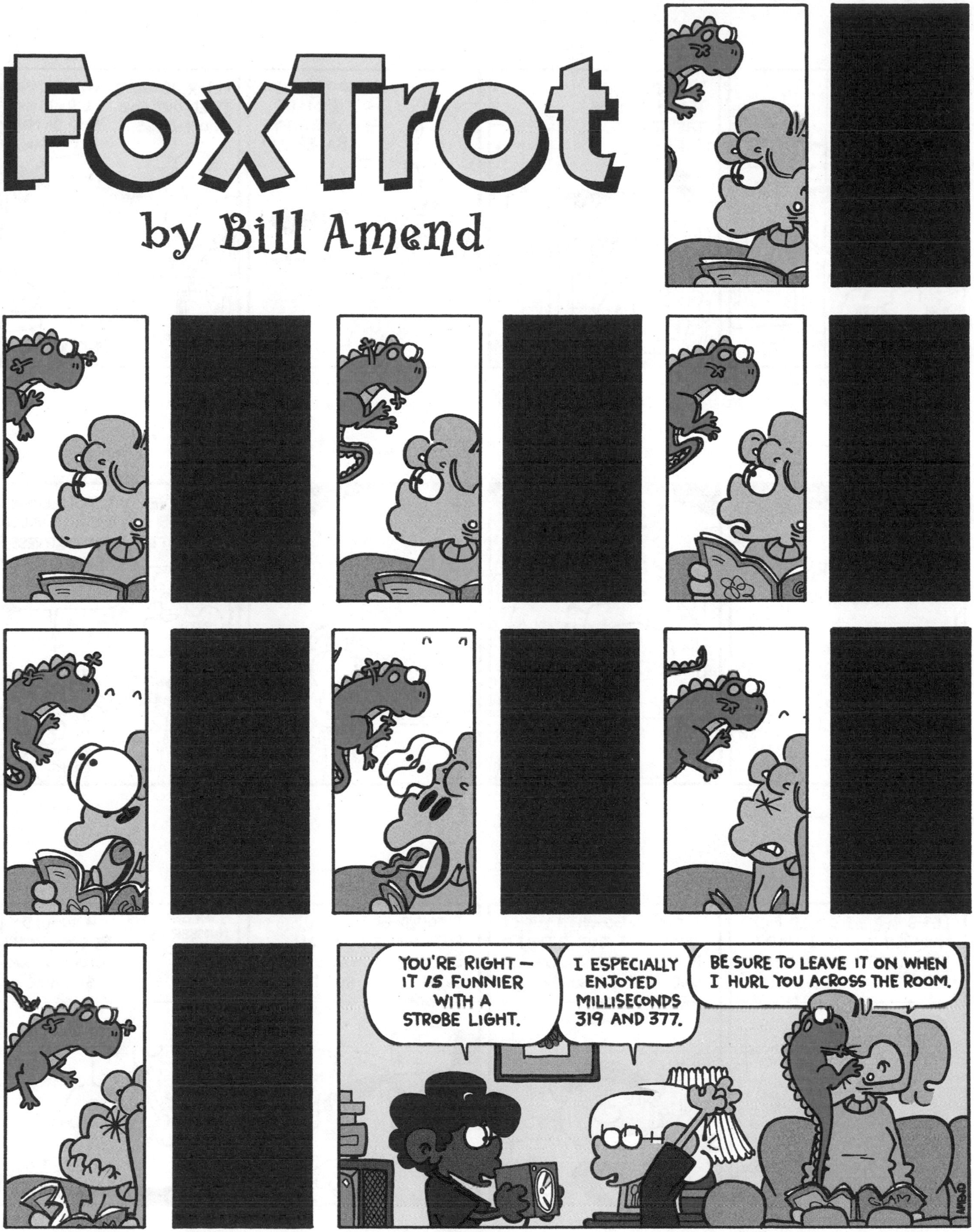
FoxTrot
by Bill Amend
YOU'RE RIGHT — IT IS FUNNIER WITH A STROBE LIGHT.
I ESPECIALLY ENJOYED MILLISECONDS 319 AND 377.
BE SURE TO LEAVE IT ON WHEN I HURL YOU ACROSS THE ROOM.

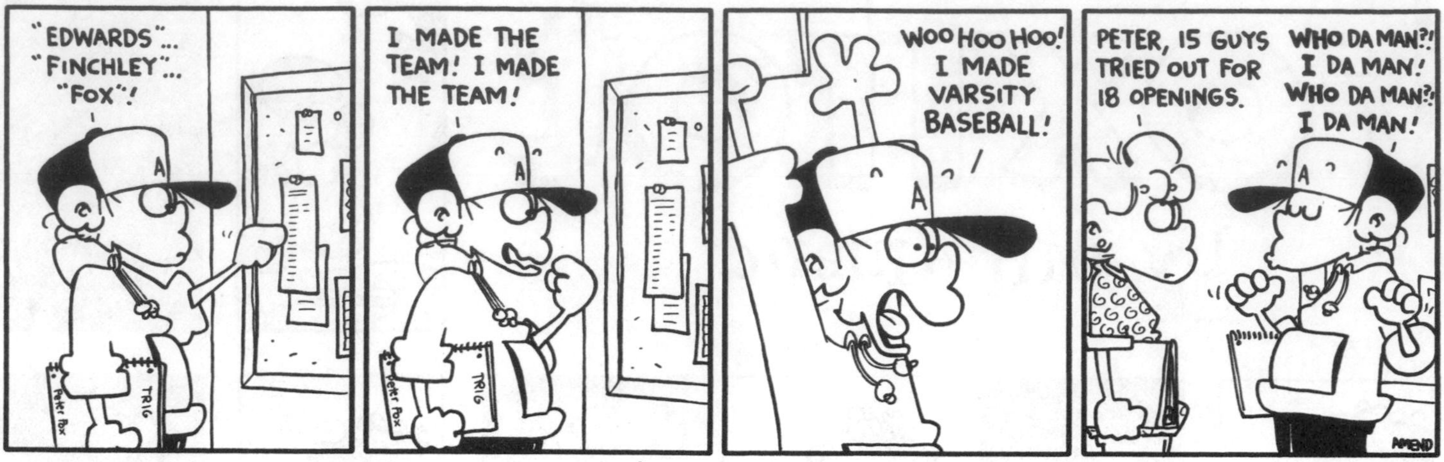
"EDWARDS"... "FINCHLEY"... "FOX"!
I MADE THE TEAM! I MADE THE TEAM!
WOO HOO HOO! I MADE VARSITY BASEBALL!
PETER, 15 GUYS TRIED OUT FOR 18 OPENINGS.
WHO DA MAN?! I DA MAN! WHO DA MAN?! I DA MAN!
AMEND

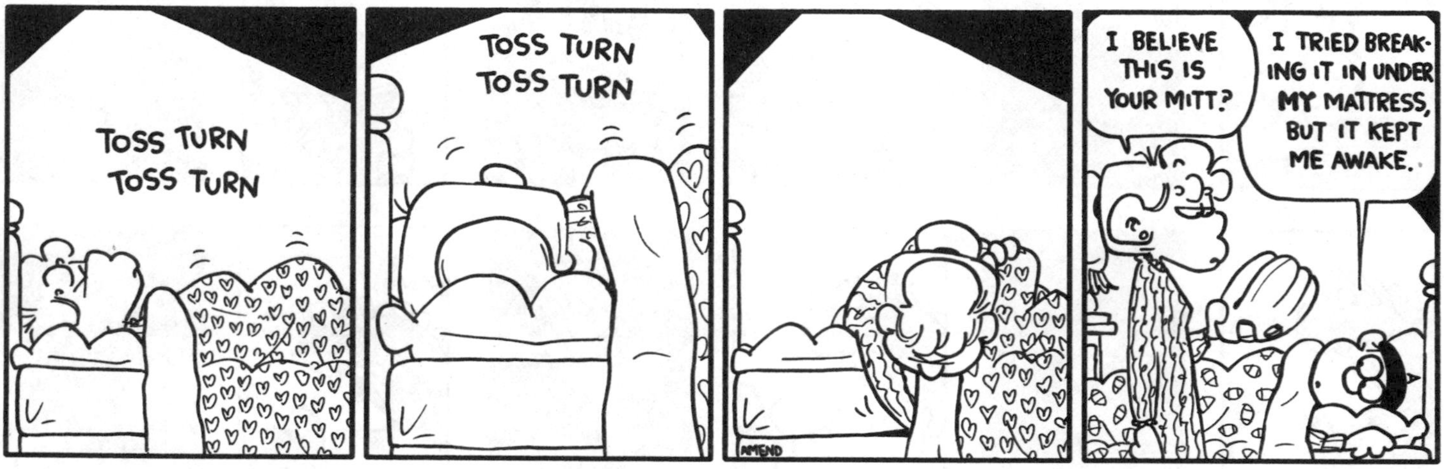
TOSS TURN TOSS TURN
TOSS TURN TOSS TURN
AMEND
I BELIEVE THIS IS YOUR MITT?
I TRIED BREAKING IT IN UNDER MY MATTRESS, BUT IT KEPT ME AWAKE.

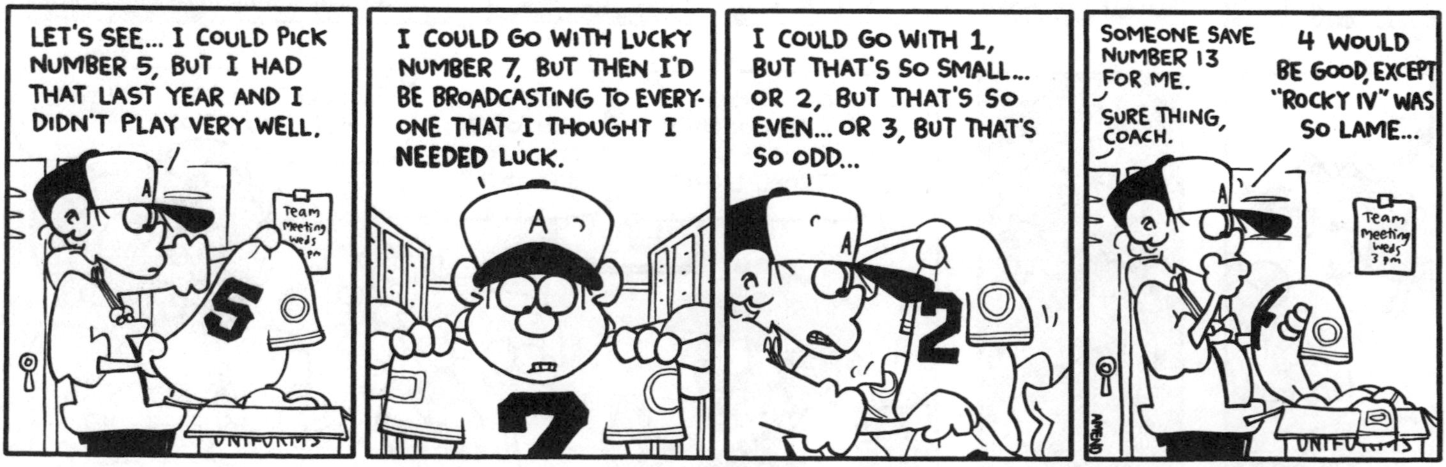
LET'S SEE... I COULD PICK NUMBER 5, BUT I HAD THAT LAST YEAR AND I DIDN'T PLAY VERY WELL.
Team Meeting weds 3pm
I COULD GO WITH LUCKY NUMBER 7, BUT THEN I'D BE BROADCASTING TO EVERYONE THAT I THOUGHT I NEEDED LUCK.
I COULD GO WITH 1, BUT THAT'S SO SMALL... OR 2, BUT THAT'S SO EVEN... OR 3, BUT THAT'S SO ODD...
SOMEONE SAVE NUMBER 13 FOR ME.
SURE THING, COACH.
4 WOULD BE GOOD, EXCEPT "ROCKY IV" WAS SO LAME...
Team Meeting weds 3pm
AMEND

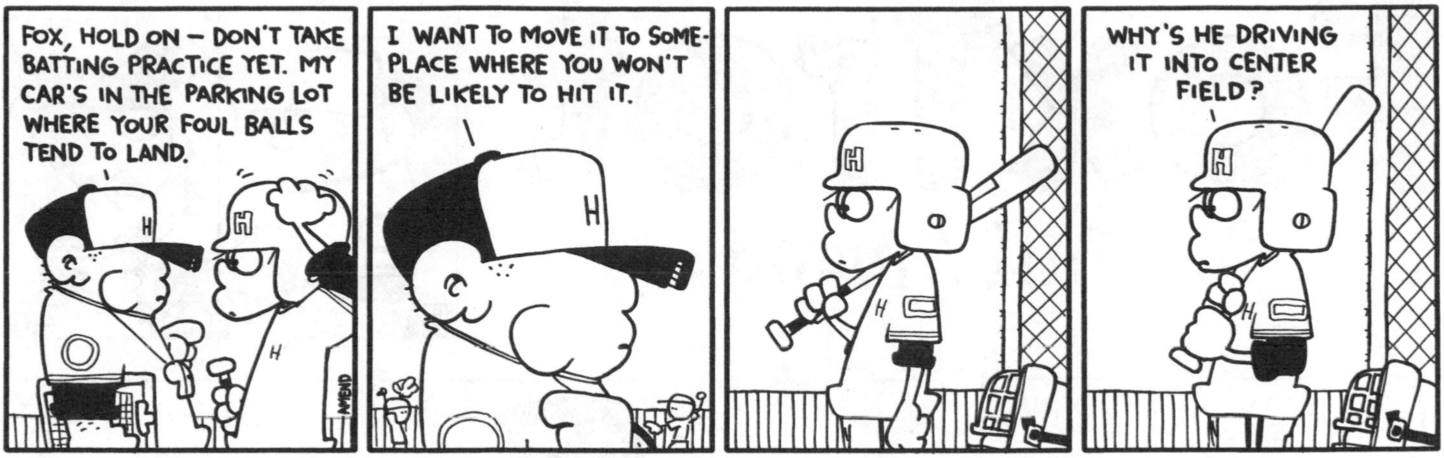
FOX, HOLD ON — DON'T TAKE BATTING PRACTICE YET. MY CAR'S IN THE PARKING LOT WHERE YOUR FOUL BALLS TEND TO LAND.
I WANT TO MOVE IT TO SOME-PLACE WHERE YOU WON'T BE LIKELY TO HIT IT.
WHY'S HE DRIVING IT INTO CENTER FIELD?

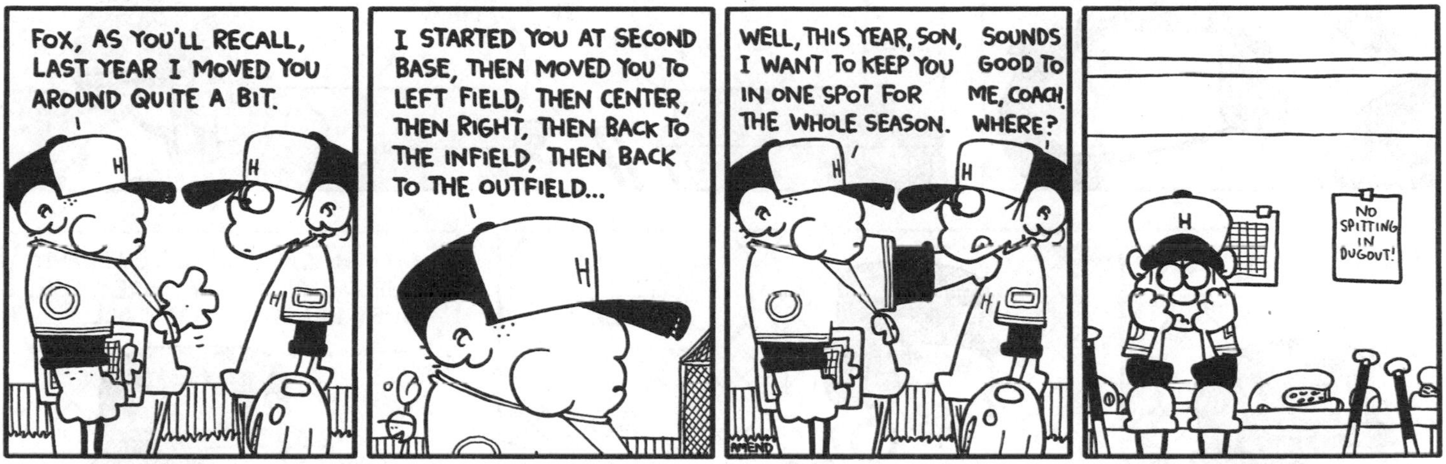
FOX, AS YOU'LL RECALL, LAST YEAR I MOVED YOU AROUND QUITE A BIT.
I STARTED YOU AT SECOND BASE, THEN MOVED YOU TO LEFT FIELD, THEN CENTER, THEN RIGHT, THEN BACK TO THE INFIELD, THEN BACK TO THE OUTFIELD...
WELL, THIS YEAR, SON, I WANT TO KEEP YOU IN ONE SPOT FOR THE WHOLE SEASON.
SOUNDS GOOD TO ME, COACH. WHERE?
NO SPITTING IN DUGOUT!

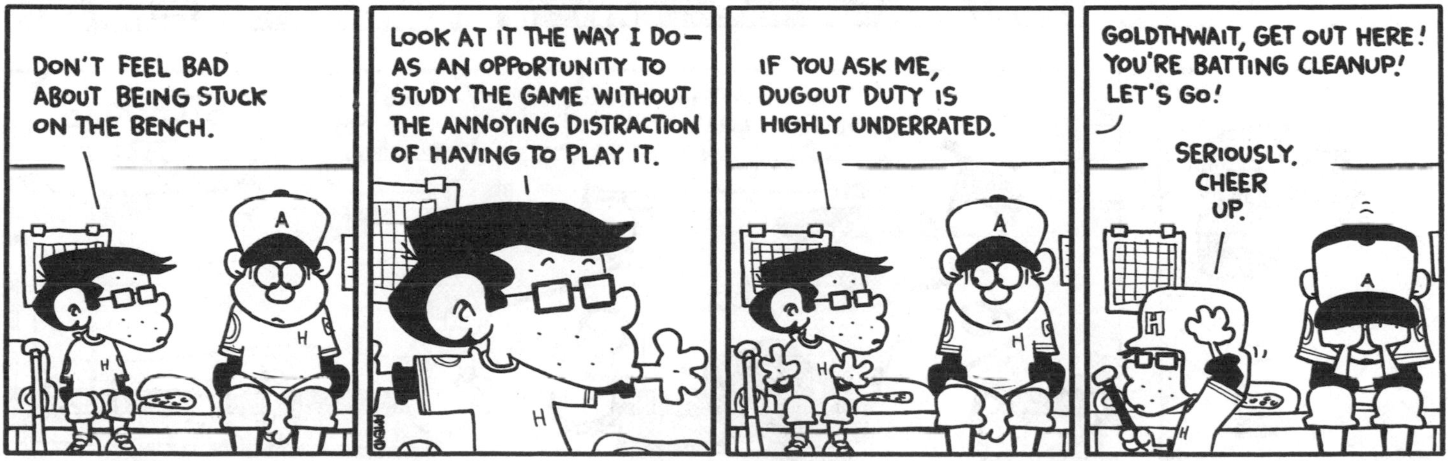
DON'T FEEL BAD ABOUT BEING STUCK ON THE BENCH.
LOOK AT IT THE WAY I DO — AS AN OPPORTUNITY TO STUDY THE GAME WITHOUT THE ANNOYING DISTRACTION OF HAVING TO PLAY IT.
IF YOU ASK ME, DUGOUT DUTY IS HIGHLY UNDERRATED.
GOLDTHWAIT, GET OUT HERE! YOU'RE BATTING CLEANUP! LET'S GO!
SERIOUSLY. CHEER UP.

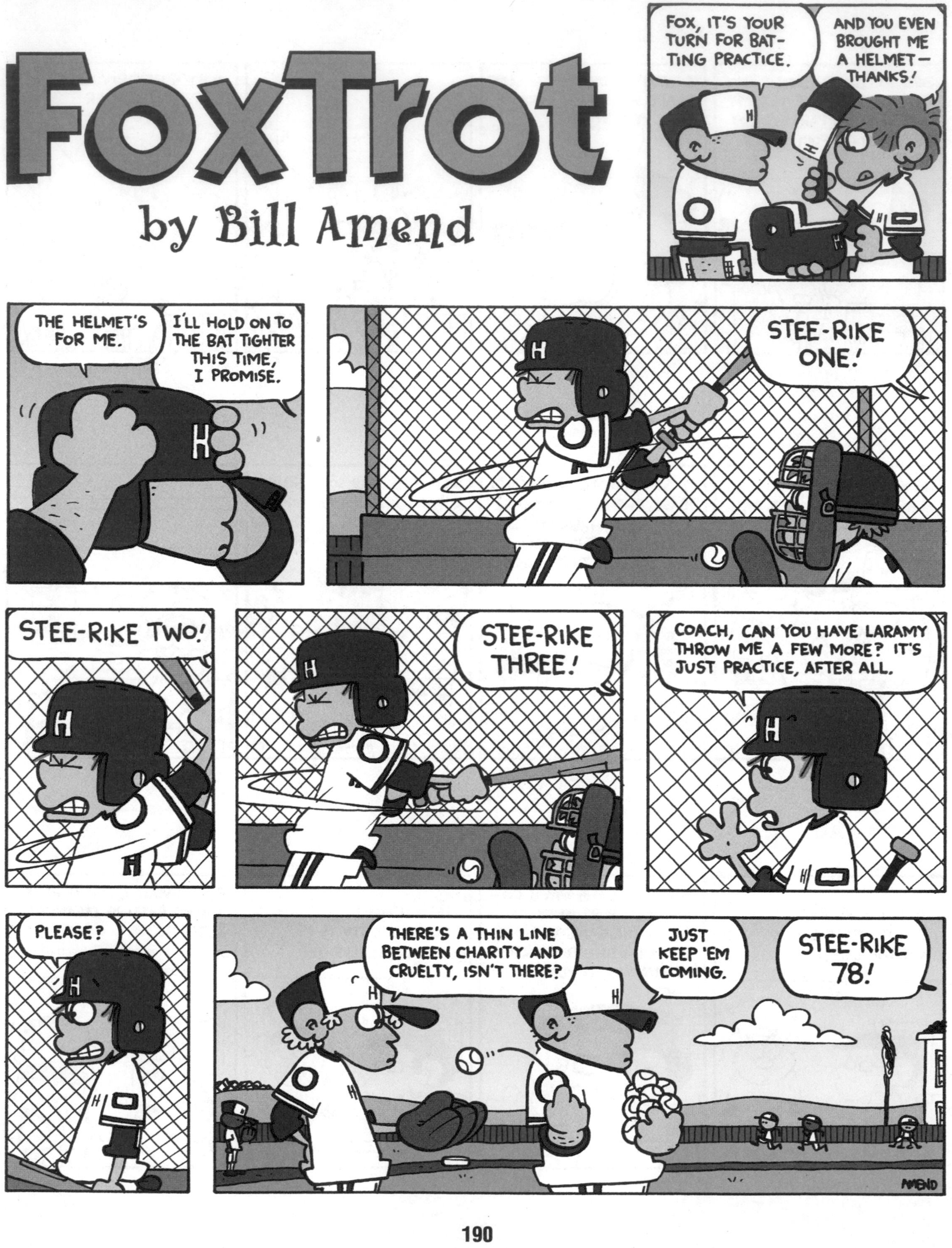
FoxTrot
by Bill Amend
FOX, IT'S YOUR TURN FOR BAT-TING PRACTICE.
AND YOU EVEN BROUGHT ME A HELMET— THANKS!
THE HELMET'S FOR ME.
I'LL HOLD ON TO THE BAT TIGHTER THIS TIME, I PROMISE.
STEE-RIKE ONE!
STEE-RIKE TWO!
STEE-RIKE THREE!
COACH, CAN YOU HAVE LARAMY THROW ME A FEW MORE? IT'S JUST PRACTICE, AFTER ALL.
PLEASE?
THERE'S A THIN LINE BETWEEN CHARITY AND CRUELTY, ISN'T THERE?
JUST KEEP 'EM COMING.
STEE-RIKE 78!
AMEND

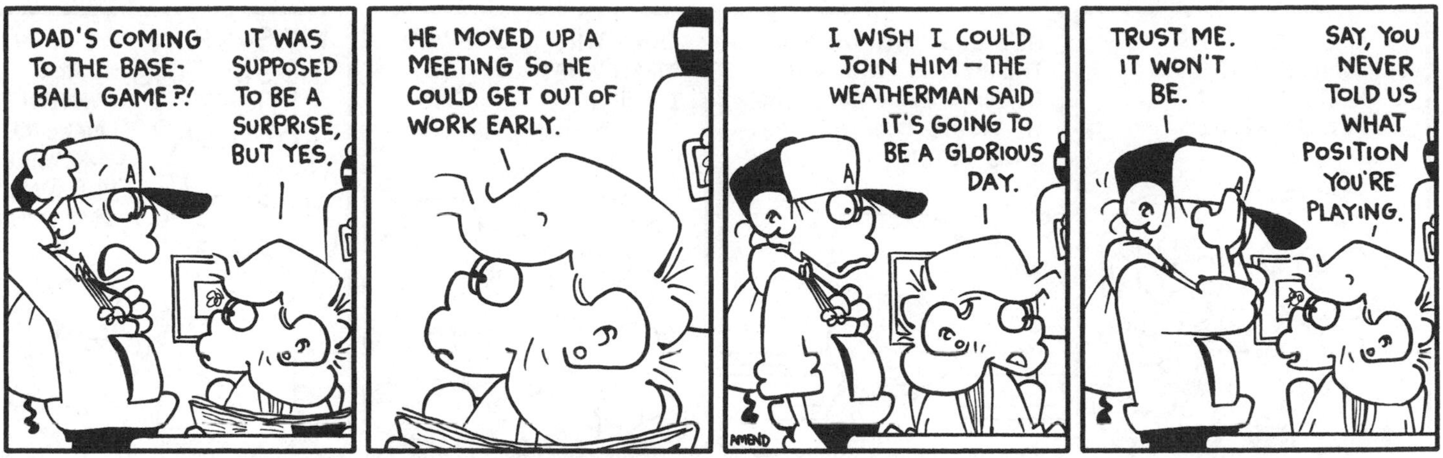
DAD'S COMING TO THE BASE-BALL GAME?!
IT WAS SUPPOSED TO BE A SURPRISE, BUT YES.
HE MOVED UP A MEETING SO HE COULD GET OUT OF WORK EARLY.
I WISH I COULD JOIN HIM — THE WEATHERMAN SAID IT'S GOING TO BE A GLORIOUS DAY.
TRUST ME. IT WON'T BE.
SAY, YOU NEVER TOLD US WHAT POSITION YOU'RE PLAYING.
AMEND

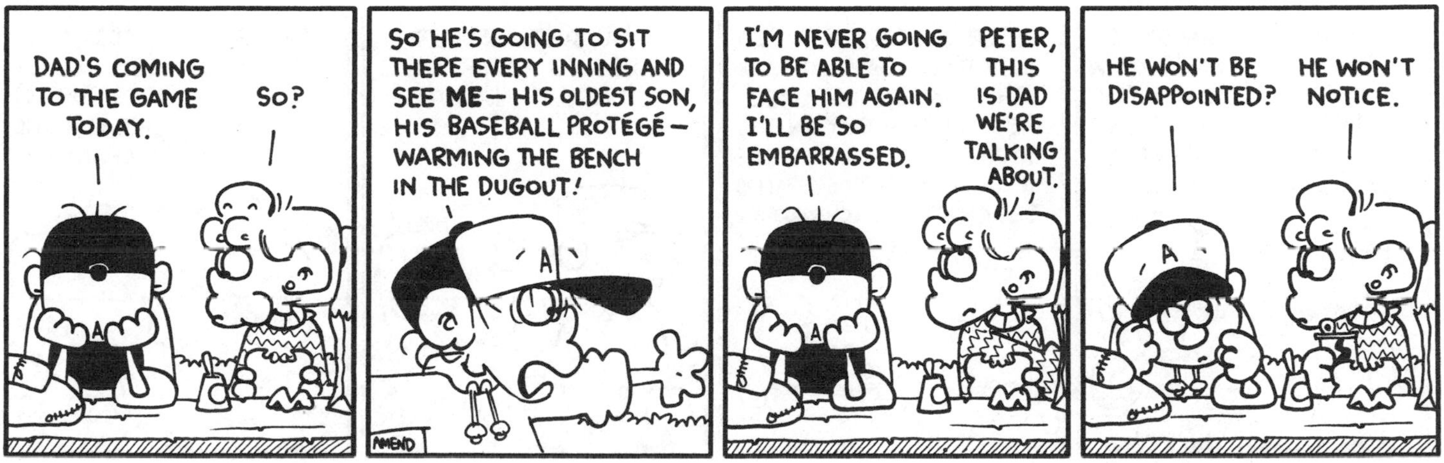
DAD'S COMING TO THE GAME TODAY.
SO?
SO HE'S GOING TO SIT THERE EVERY INNING AND SEE ME — HIS OLDEST SON, HIS BASEBALL PROTÉGÉ — WARMING THE BENCH IN THE DUGOUT!
AMEND
I'M NEVER GOING TO BE ABLE TO FACE HIM AGAIN. I'LL BE SO EMBARRASSED.
PETER, THIS IS DAD WE'RE TALKING ABOUT.
HE WON'T BE DISAPPOINTED?
HE WON'T NOTICE.

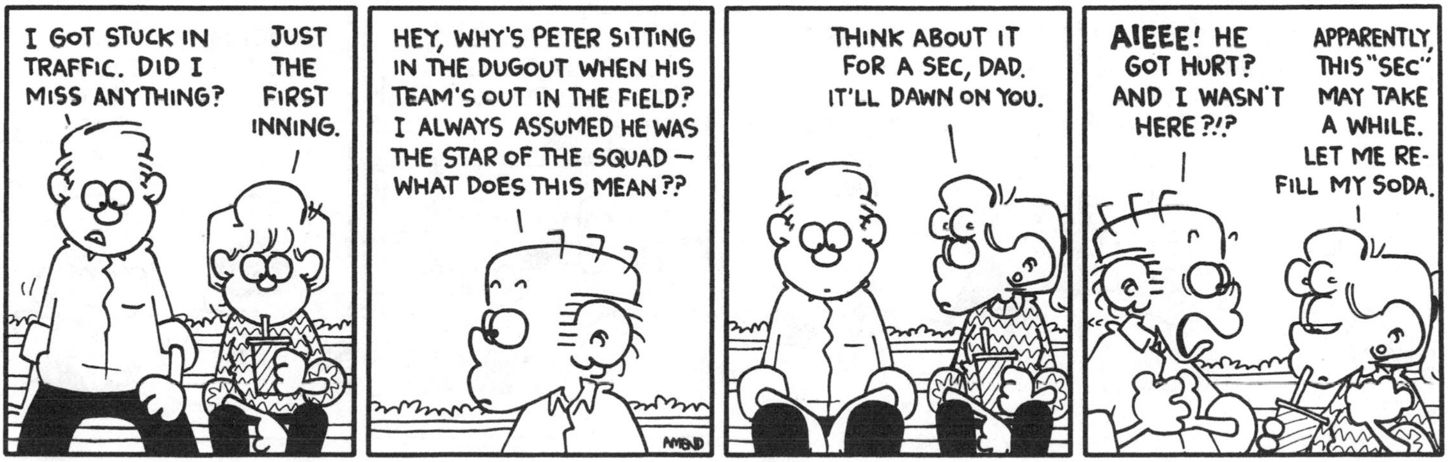
I GOT STUCK IN TRAFFIC. DID I MISS ANYTHING?
JUST THE FIRST INNING.
HEY, WHY'S PETER SITTING IN THE DUGOUT WHEN HIS TEAM'S OUT IN THE FIELD? I ALWAYS ASSUMED HE WAS THE STAR OF THE SQUAD — WHAT DOES THIS MEAN??
AMEND
THINK ABOUT IT FOR A SEC, DAD. IT'LL DAWN ON YOU.
AIEEE! HE GOT HURT? AND I WASN'T HERE?!?
APPARENTLY, THIS "SEC" MAY TAKE A WHILE. LET ME RE-FILL MY SODA.

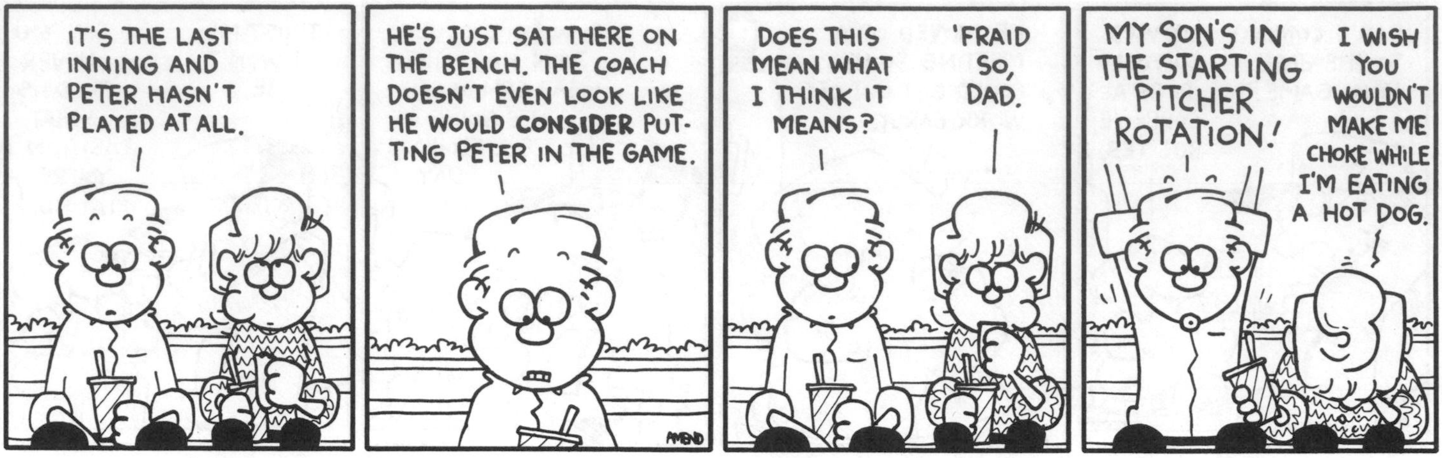
IT'S THE LAST INNING AND PETER HASN'T PLAYED AT ALL.
HE'S JUST SAT THERE ON THE BENCH. THE COACH DOESN'T EVEN LOOK LIKE HE WOULD CONSIDER PUTTING PETER IN THE GAME.
AMEND
DOES THIS MEAN WHAT I THINK IT MEANS?
'FRAID SO, DAD.
MY SON'S IN THE STARTING PITCHER ROTATION!
I WISH YOU WOULDN'T MAKE ME CHOKE WHILE I'M EATING A HOT DOG.

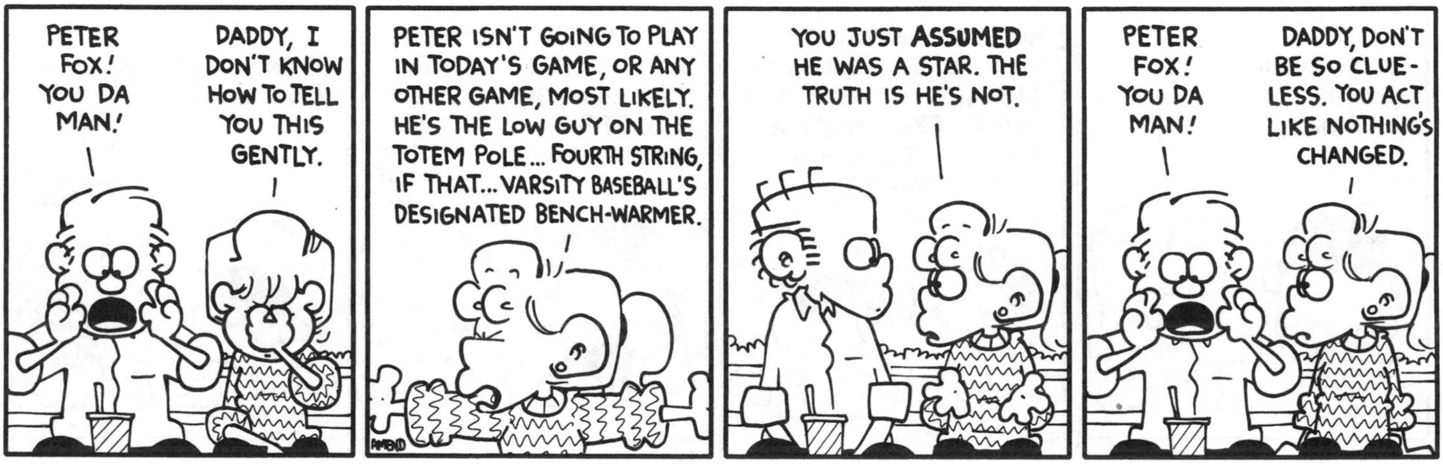
PETER FOX! YOU DA MAN!
DADDY, I DON'T KNOW HOW TO TELL YOU THIS GENTLY.
PETER ISN'T GOING TO PLAY IN TODAY'S GAME, OR ANY OTHER GAME, MOST LIKELY. HE'S THE LOW GUY ON THE TOTEM POLE... FOURTH STRING, IF THAT... VARSITY BASEBALL'S DESIGNATED BENCH-WARMER.
AMEND
YOU JUST ASSUMED HE WAS A STAR. THE TRUTH IS HE'S NOT.
PETER FOX! YOU DA MAN!
DADDY, DON'T BE SO CLUELESS. YOU ACT LIKE NOTHING'S CHANGED.

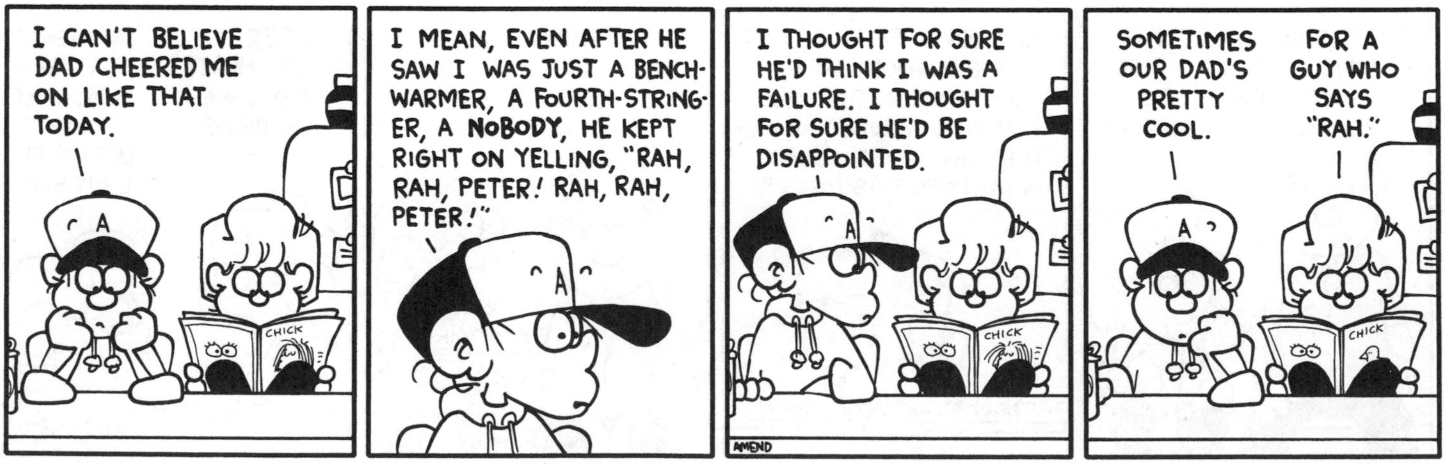
I CAN'T BELIEVE DAD CHEERED ME ON LIKE THAT TODAY.
CHICK
I MEAN, EVEN AFTER HE SAW I WAS JUST A BENCHWARMER, A FOURTH-STRINGER, A NOBODY, HE KEPT RIGHT ON YELLING, "RAH, RAH, PETER! RAH, RAH, PETER!"
I THOUGHT FOR SURE HE'D THINK I WAS A FAILURE. I THOUGHT FOR SURE HE'D BE DISAPPOINTED.
CHICK
AMEND
SOMETIMES OUR DAD'S PRETTY COOL.
FOR A GUY WHO SAYS "RAH."
CHICK

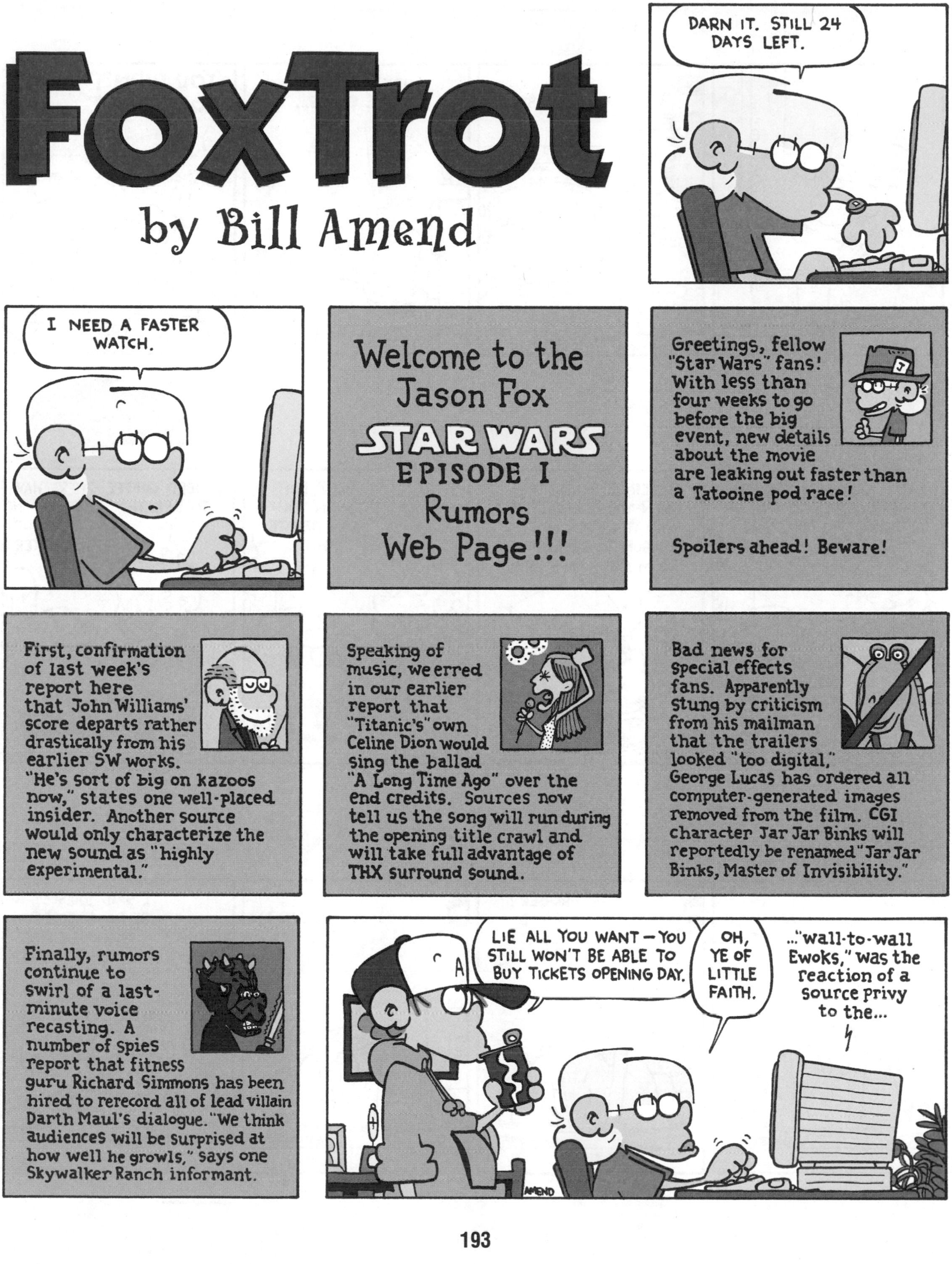
FoxTrot
by Bill Amend
DARN IT. STILL 24 DAYS LEFT.
I NEED A FASTER WATCH.
Welcome to the Jason Fox STAR WARS EPISODE I Rumors Web Page!!!
Greetings, fellow "Star Wars" fans! With less than four weeks to go before the big event, new details about the movie are leaking out faster than a Tatooine pod race!
Spoilers ahead! Beware!
First, confirmation of last week's report here that John Williams' score departs rather drastically from his earlier SW works. "He's sort of big on kazoos now," states one well-placed insider. Another source would only characterize the new sound as "highly experimental."
Speaking of music, we erred in our earlier report that "Titanic's" own Celine Dion would sing the ballad "A Long Time Ago" over the end credits. Sources now tell us the song will run during the opening title crawl and will take full advantage of THX surround sound.
Bad news for special effects fans. Apparently stung by criticism from his mailman that the trailers looked "too digital," George Lucas has ordered all computer-generated images removed from the film. CGI character Jar Jar Binks will reportedly be renamed "Jar Jar Binks, Master of Invisibility."
Finally, rumors continue to swirl of a last-minute voice recasting. A number of spies report that fitness guru Richard Simmons has been hired to rerecord all of lead villain Darth Maul's dialogue. "We think audiences will be surprised at how well he growls," says one Skywalker Ranch informant.
LIE ALL YOU WANT — YOU STILL WON'T BE ABLE TO BUY TICKETS OPENING DAY.
OH, YE OF LITTLE FAITH.
..."wall-to-wall Ewoks," was the reaction of a source privy to the...
AMEND

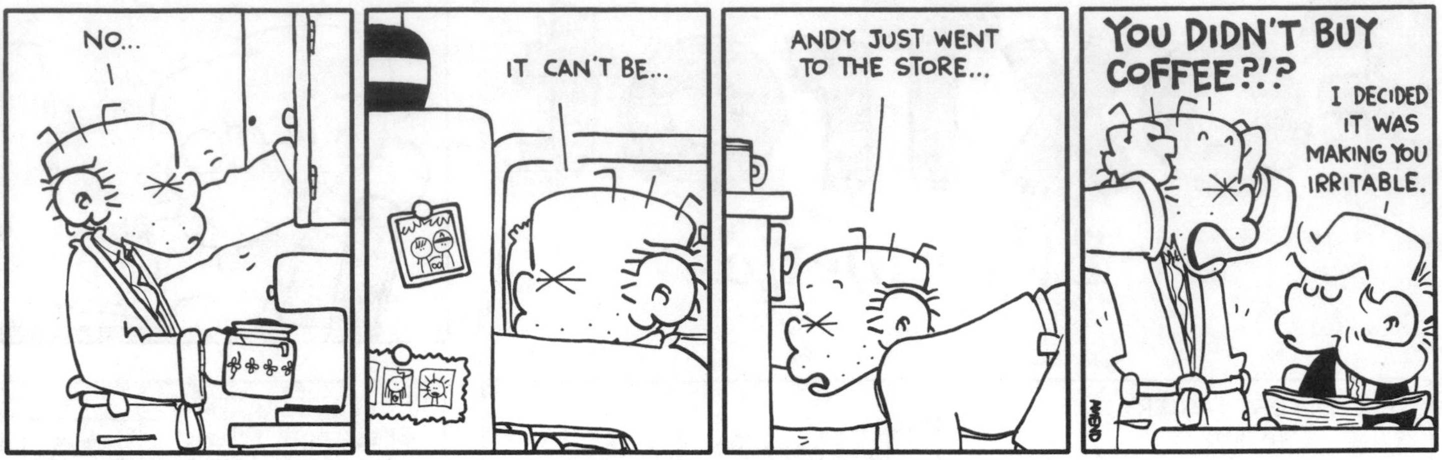
NO...
IT CAN'T BE...
ANDY JUST WENT TO THE STORE...
YOU DIDN'T BUY COFFEE?!?
I DECIDED IT WAS MAKING YOU IRRITABLE.

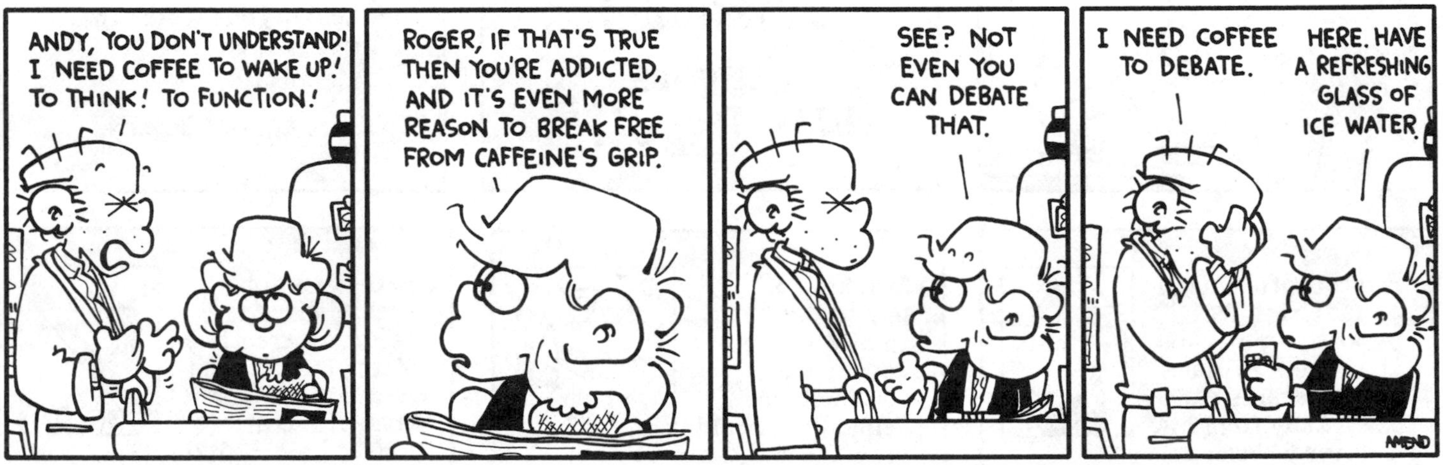
ANDY, YOU DON'T UNDERSTAND! I NEED COFFEE TO WAKE UP! TO THINK! TO FUNCTION!
ROGER, IF THAT'S TRUE THEN YOU'RE ADDICTED, AND IT'S EVEN MORE REASON TO BREAK FREE FROM CAFFEINE'S GRIP.
SEE? NOT EVEN YOU CAN DEBATE THAT.
I NEED COFFEE TO DEBATE.
HERE. HAVE A REFRESHING GLASS OF ICE WATER.

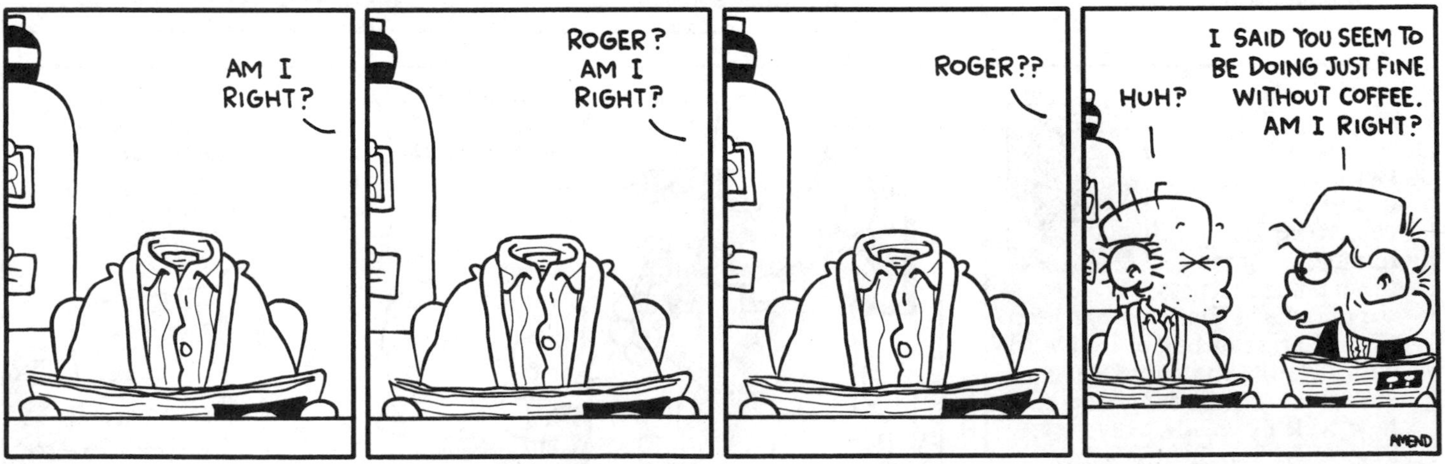
AM I RIGHT?
ROGER? AM I RIGHT?
ROGER??
HUH?
I SAID YOU SEEM TO BE DOING JUST FINE WITHOUT COFFEE. AM I RIGHT?

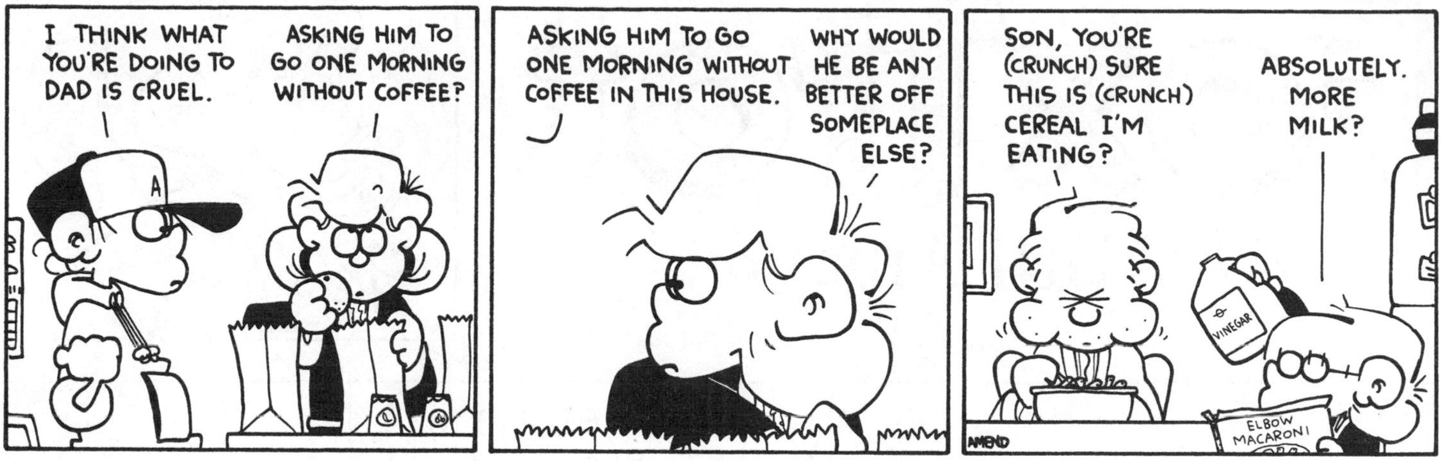
I THINK WHAT YOU'RE DOING TO DAD IS CRUEL.
ASKING HIM TO GO ONE MORNING WITHOUT COFFEE?
ASKING HIM TO GO ONE MORNING WITHOUT COFFEE IN THIS HOUSE.
WHY WOULD HE BE ANY BETTER OFF SOMEPLACE ELSE?
SON, YOU'RE (CRUNCH) SURE THIS IS (CRUNCH) CEREAL I'M EATING?
ABSOLUTELY. MORE MILK?
VINEGAR
ELBOW MACARONI
AMEND

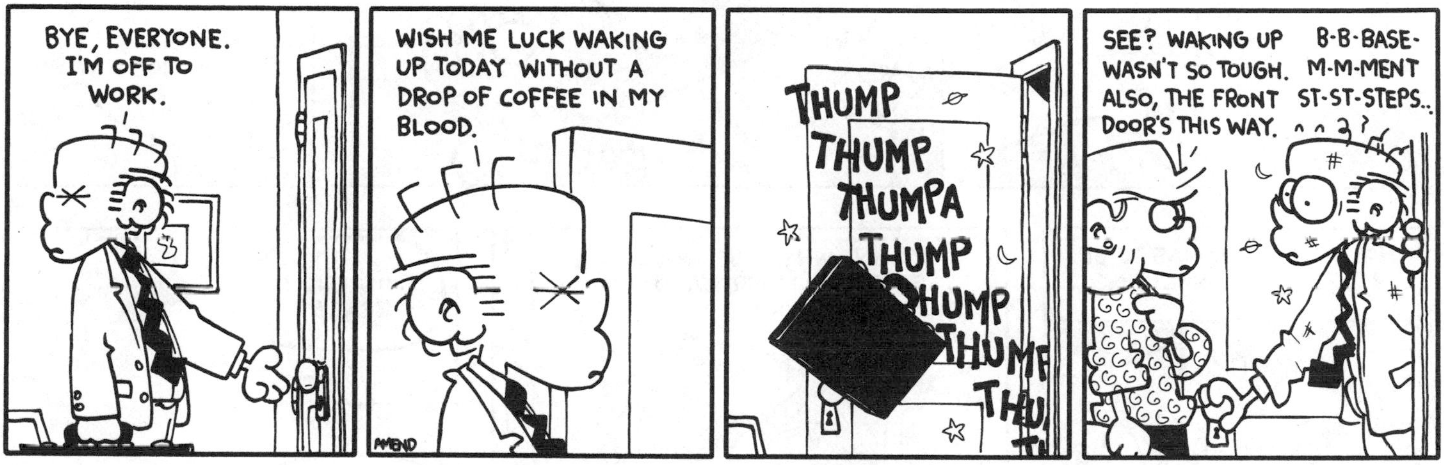
BYE, EVERYONE. I'M OFF TO WORK.
WISH ME LUCK WAKING UP TODAY WITHOUT A DROP OF COFFEE IN MY BLOOD.
AMEND
THUMP
THUMP
THUMPA
THUMP
SEE? WAKING UP WASN'T SO TOUGH. ALSO, THE FRONT DOOR'S THIS WAY.
B-B-BASE-M-M-MENT ST-ST-STEPS..

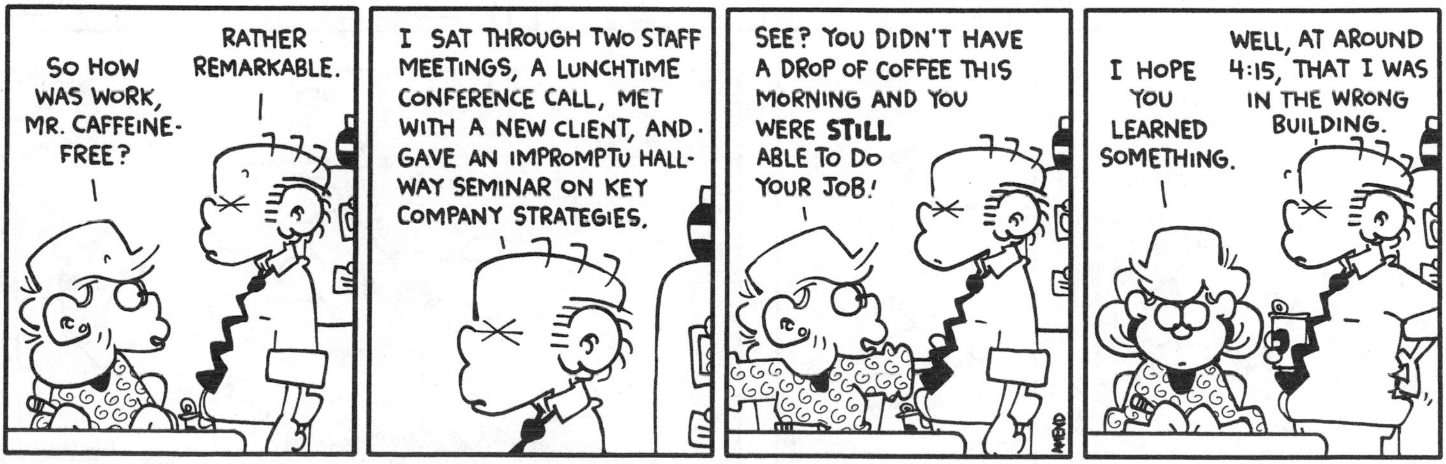
SO HOW WAS WORK, MR. CAFFEINE-FREE?
RATHER REMARKABLE.
I SAT THROUGH TWO STAFF MEETINGS, A LUNCHTIME CONFERENCE CALL, MET WITH A NEW CLIENT, AND GAVE AN IMPROMPTU HALLWAY SEMINAR ON KEY COMPANY STRATEGIES.
SEE? YOU DIDN'T HAVE A DROP OF COFFEE THIS MORNING AND YOU WERE STILL ABLE TO DO YOUR JOB!
AMEND
I HOPE YOU LEARNED SOMETHING.
WELL, AT AROUND 4:15, THAT I WAS IN THE WRONG BUILDING.

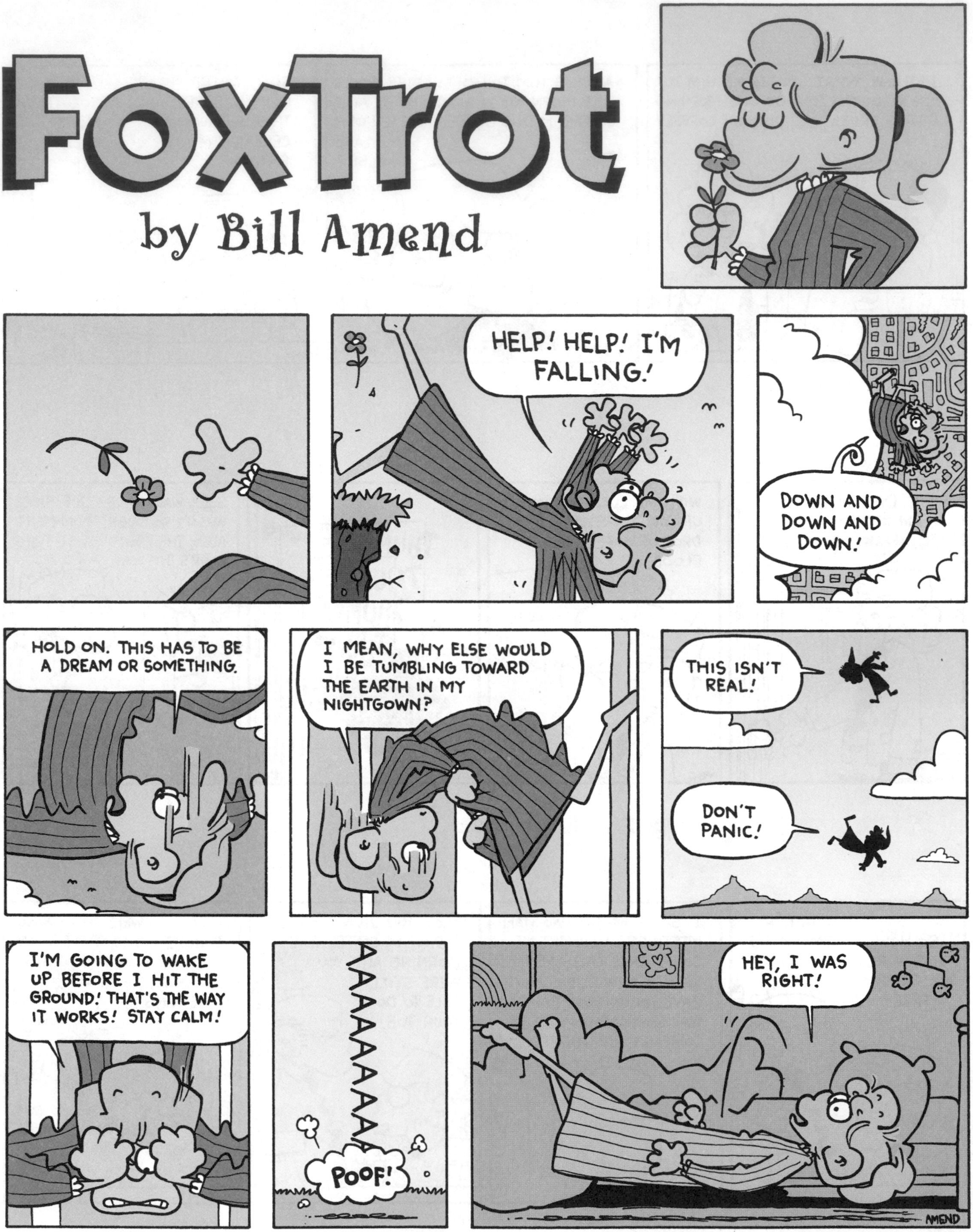
FoxTrot
by Bill Amend
HELP! HELP! I'M FALLING!
DOWN AND DOWN AND DOWN!
HOLD ON. THIS HAS TO BE A DREAM OR SOMETHING.
I MEAN, WHY ELSE WOULD I BE TUMBLING TOWARD THE EARTH IN MY NIGHTGOWN?
THIS ISN'T REAL!
DON'T PANIC!
I'M GOING TO WAKE UP BEFORE I HIT THE GROUND! THAT'S THE WAY IT WORKS! STAY CALM!
AAAAAAAAAAAA
POOF!
HEY, I WAS RIGHT!
AMEND

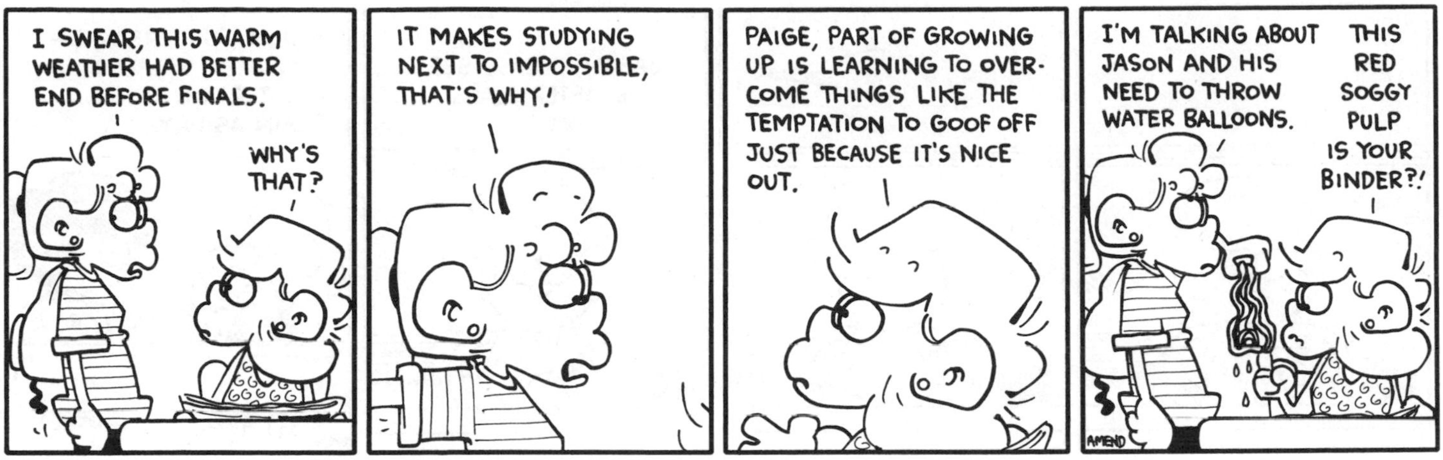
I SWEAR, THIS WARM WEATHER HAD BETTER END BEFORE FINALS.
WHY'S THAT?
IT MAKES STUDYING NEXT TO IMPOSSIBLE, THAT'S WHY!
PAIGE, PART OF GROWING UP IS LEARNING TO OVERCOME THINGS LIKE THE TEMPTATION TO GOOF OFF JUST BECAUSE IT'S NICE OUT.
I'M TALKING ABOUT JASON AND HIS NEED TO THROW WATER BALLOONS.
THIS RED SOGGY PULP IS YOUR BINDER?!
AMEND

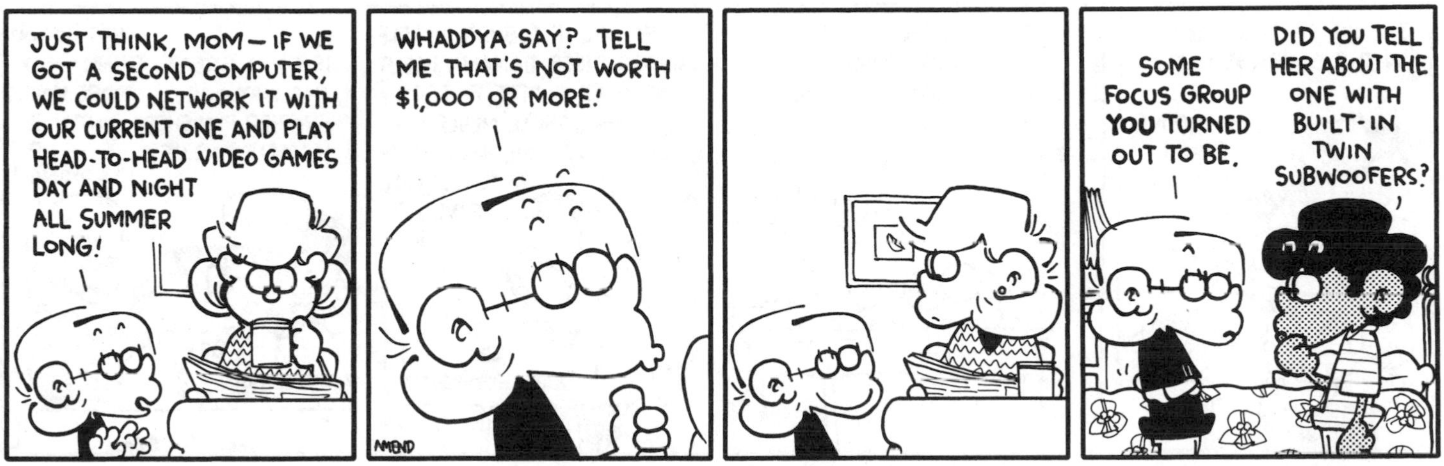
JUST THINK, MOM — IF WE GOT A SECOND COMPUTER, WE COULD NETWORK IT WITH OUR CURRENT ONE AND PLAY HEAD-TO-HEAD VIDEO GAMES DAY AND NIGHT ALL SUMMER LONG!
WHADDYA SAY? TELL ME THAT'S NOT WORTH $1,000 OR MORE!
AMEND
SOME FOCUS GROUP YOU TURNED OUT TO BE.
DID YOU TELL HER ABOUT THE ONE WITH BUILT-IN TWIN SUBWOOFERS?

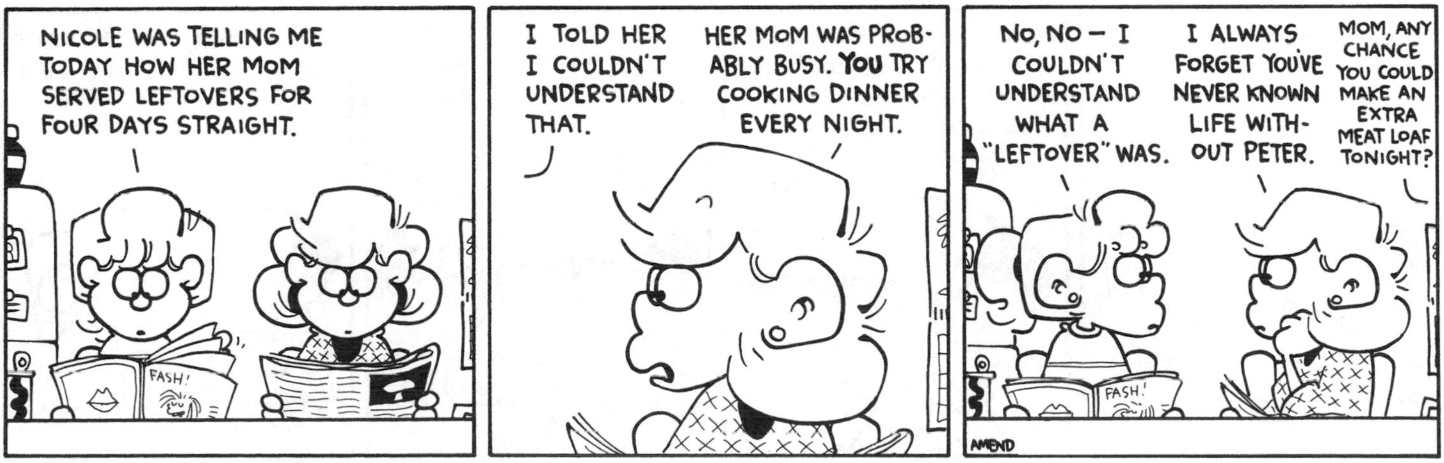
NICOLE WAS TELLING ME TODAY HOW HER MOM SERVED LEFTOVERS FOR FOUR DAYS STRAIGHT.
FASH!
I TOLD HER I COULDN'T UNDERSTAND THAT.
HER MOM WAS PROBABLY BUSY. YOU TRY COOKING DINNER EVERY NIGHT.
NO, NO — I COULDN'T UNDERSTAND WHAT A "LEFTOVER" WAS.
I ALWAYS FORGET YOU'VE NEVER KNOWN LIFE WITHOUT PETER.
MOM, ANY CHANCE YOU COULD MAKE AN EXTRA MEAT LOAF TONIGHT?
FASH!
AMEND

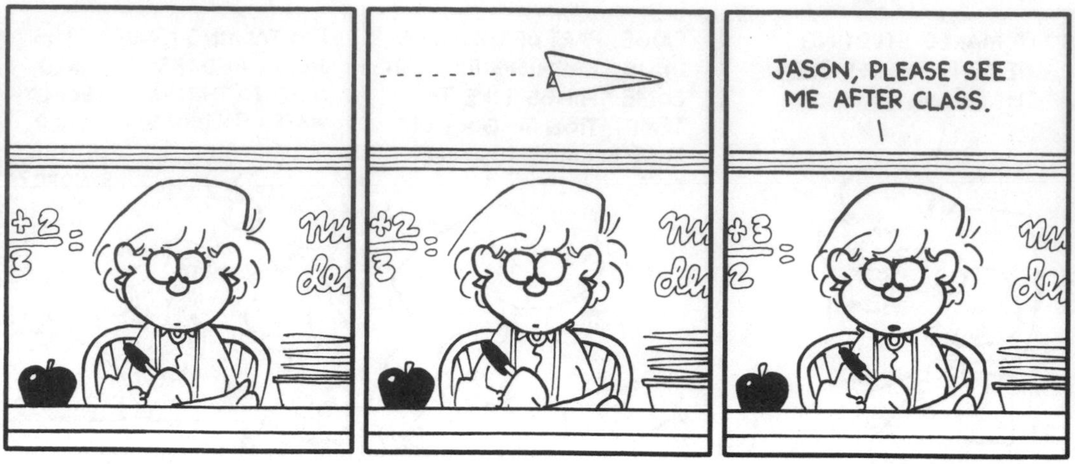
JASON, PLEASE SEE ME AFTER CLASS.
I DON'T UNDERSTAND— I WROTE "STEALTH FIGHTER" ON THIS PLAIN AS DAY.
AMEND

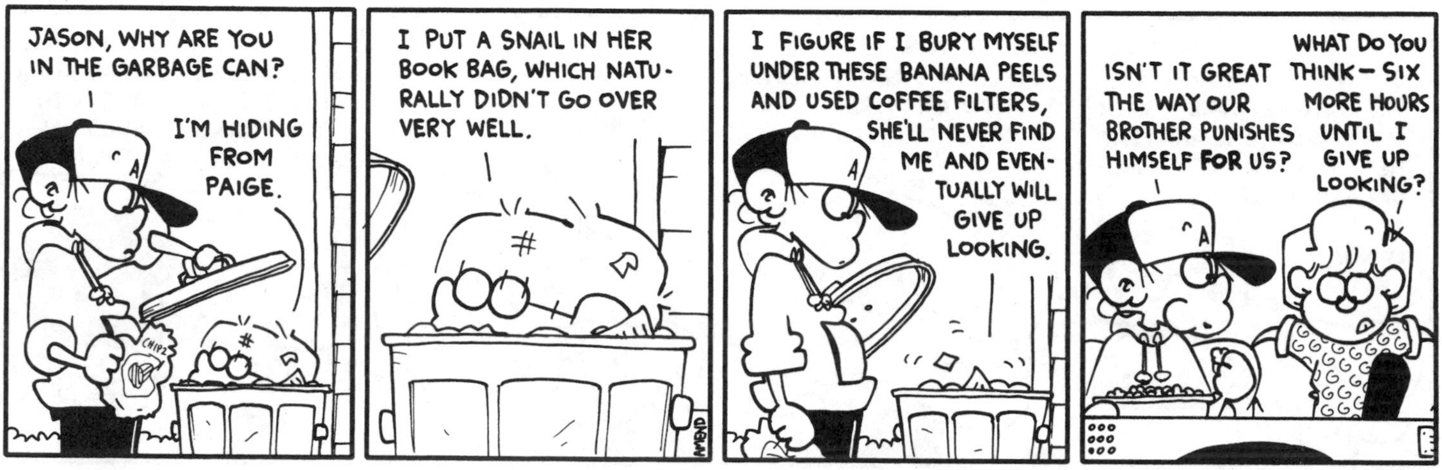
JASON, WHY ARE YOU IN THE GARBAGE CAN?
I'M HIDING FROM PAIGE.
CHIPS
I PUT A SNAIL IN HER BOOK BAG, WHICH NATURALLY DIDN'T GO OVER VERY WELL.
AMEND
I FIGURE IF I BURY MYSELF UNDER THESE BANANA PEELS AND USED COFFEE FILTERS, SHE'LL NEVER FIND ME AND EVENTUALLY WILL GIVE UP LOOKING.
ISN'T IT GREAT THE WAY OUR BROTHER PUNISHES HIMSELF FOR US?
WHAT DO YOU THINK— SIX MORE HOURS UNTIL I GIVE UP LOOKING?

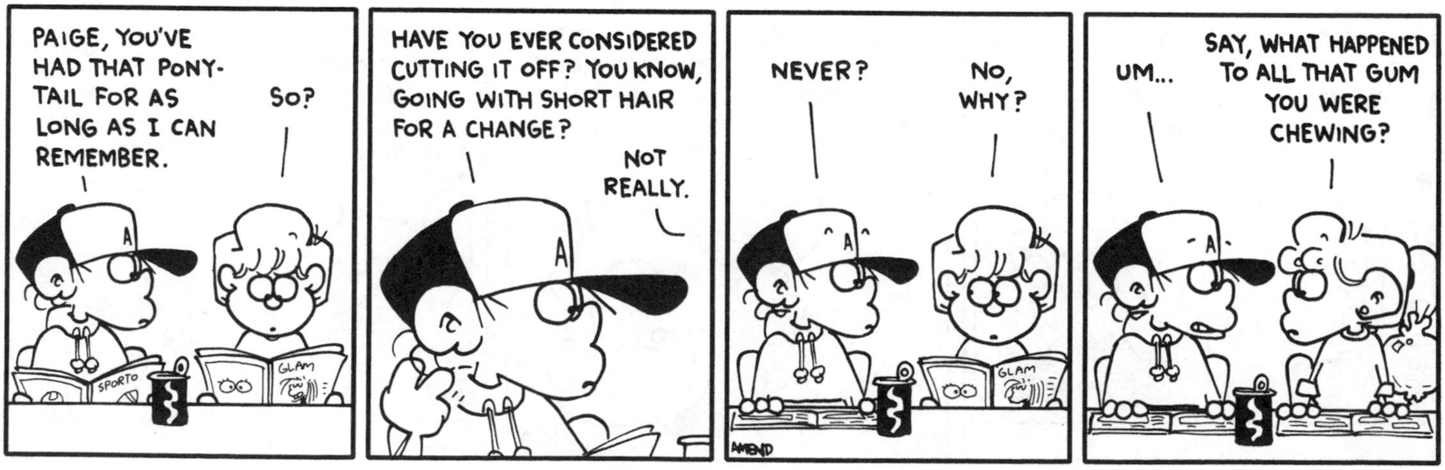
PAIGE, YOU'VE HAD THAT PONYTAIL FOR AS LONG AS I CAN REMEMBER.
SO?
SPORTO
GLAM
HAVE YOU EVER CONSIDERED CUTTING IT OFF? YOU KNOW, GOING WITH SHORT HAIR FOR A CHANGE?
NOT REALLY.
NEVER?
NO, WHY?
GLAM
AMEND
UM...
SAY, WHAT HAPPENED TO ALL THAT GUM YOU WERE CHEWING?

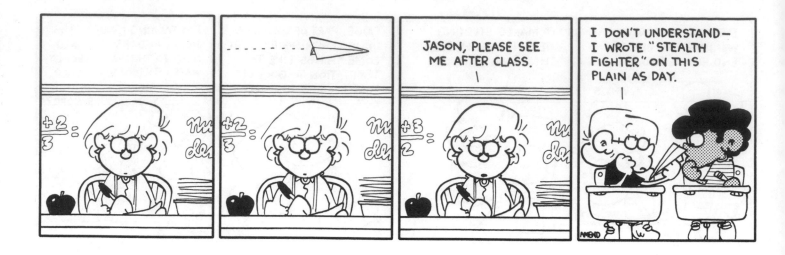

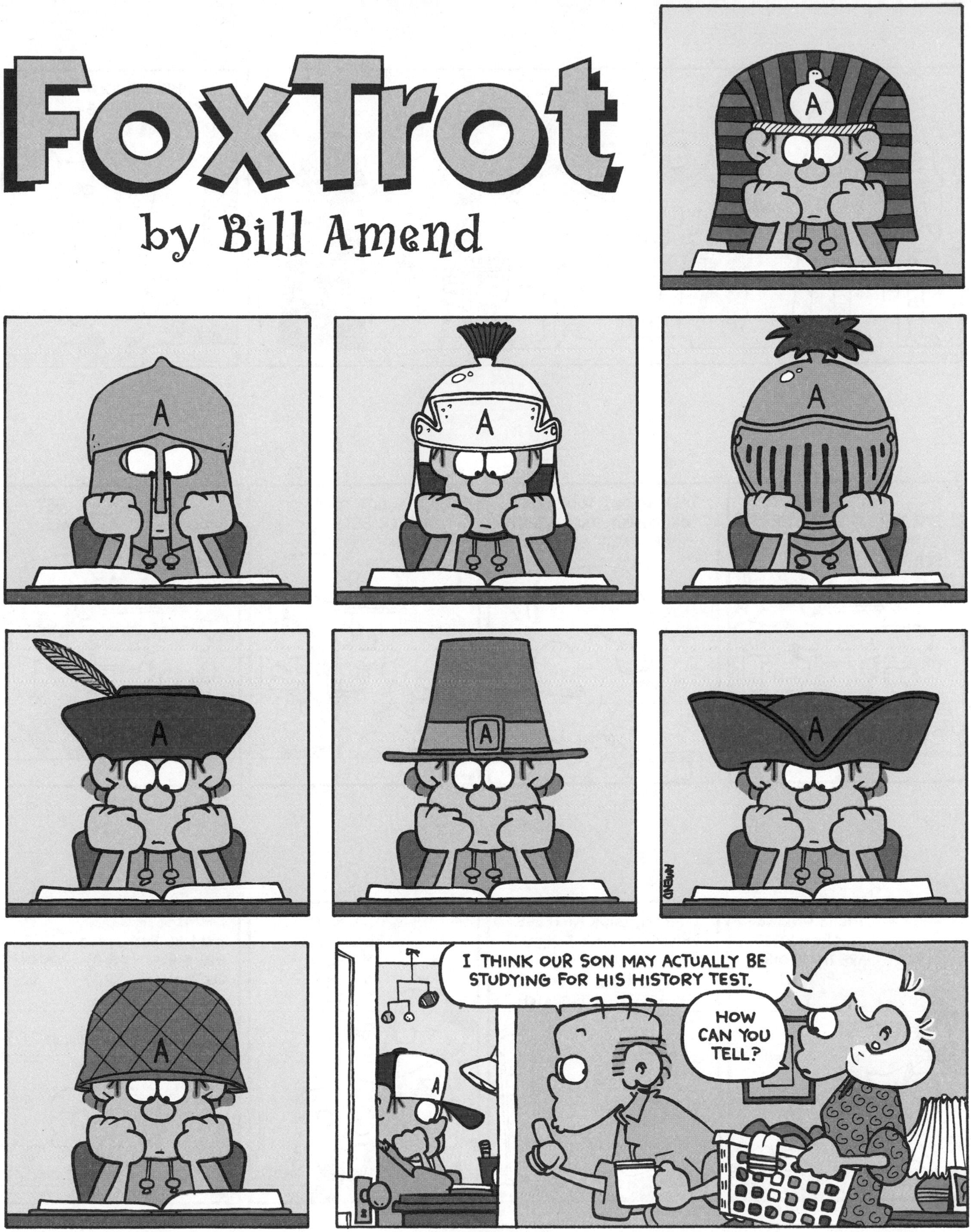
FoxTrot
by Bill Amend
I THINK OUR SON MAY ACTUALLY BE STUDYING FOR HIS HISTORY TEST.
HOW CAN YOU TELL?

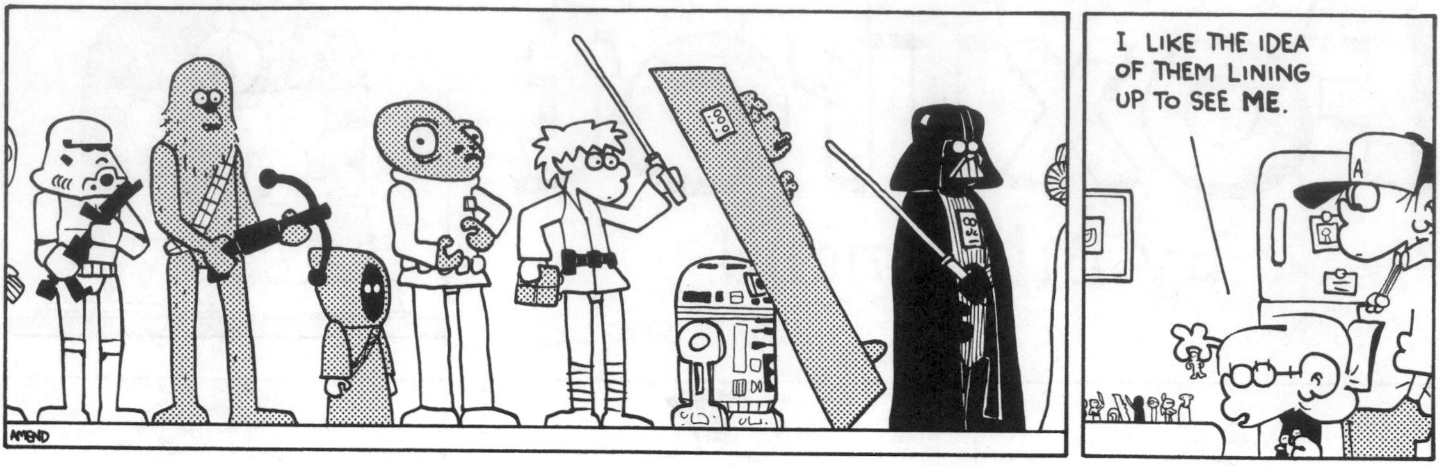
I LIKE THE IDEA OF THEM LINING UP TO SEE **ME**.

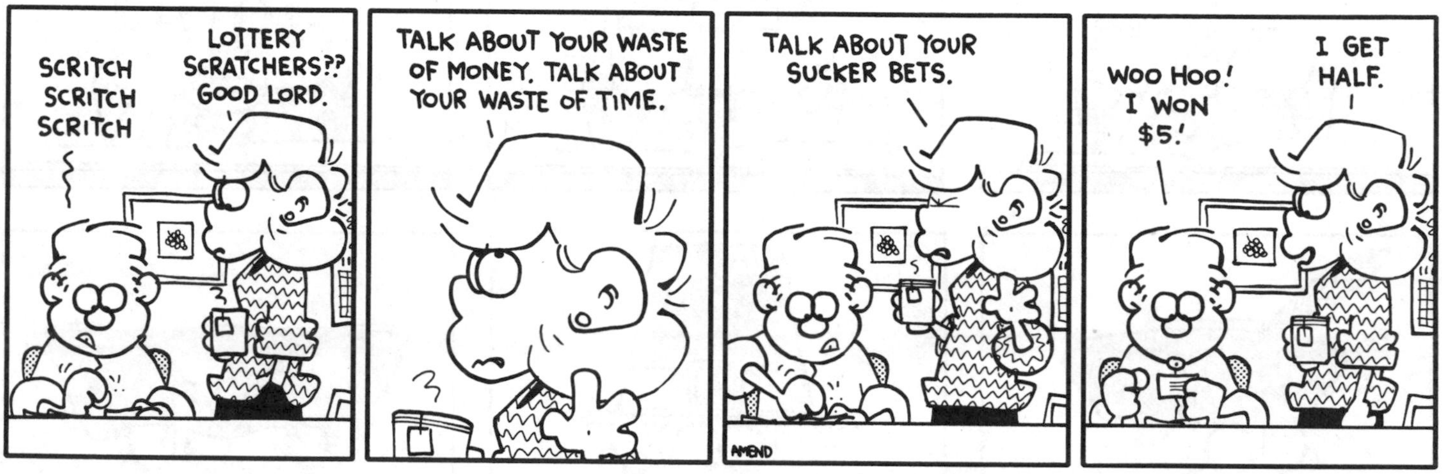
SCRITCH SCRITCH SCRITCH
LOTTERY SCRATCHERS?? GOOD LORD.
TALK ABOUT YOUR WASTE OF MONEY. TALK ABOUT YOUR WASTE OF TIME.
TALK ABOUT YOUR SUCKER BETS.
WOO HOO! I WON $5!
I GET HALF.

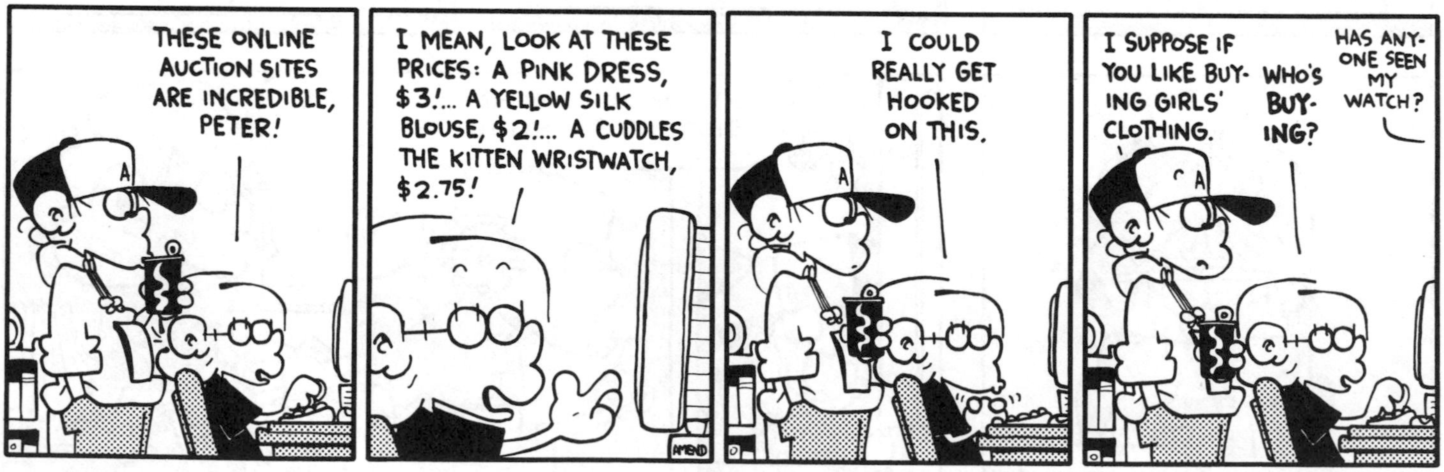
THESE ONLINE AUCTION SITES ARE INCREDIBLE, PETER!
I MEAN, LOOK AT THESE PRICES: A PINK DRESS, $3!... A YELLOW SILK BLOUSE, $2!... A CUDDLES THE KITTEN WRISTWATCH, $2.75!
I COULD REALLY GET HOOKED ON THIS.
I SUPPOSE IF YOU LIKE BUY-ING GIRLS' CLOTHING.
WHO'S **BUY**-ING?
HAS ANY-ONE SEEN MY WATCH?

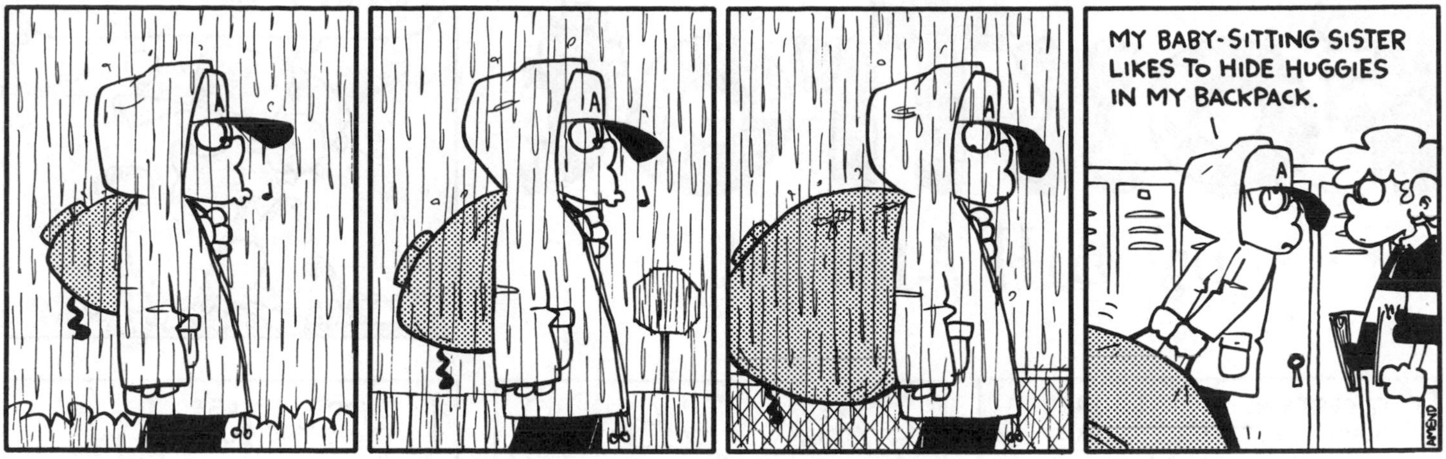
MY BABY-SITTING SISTER LIKES TO HIDE HUGGIES IN MY BACKPACK.
AMEND

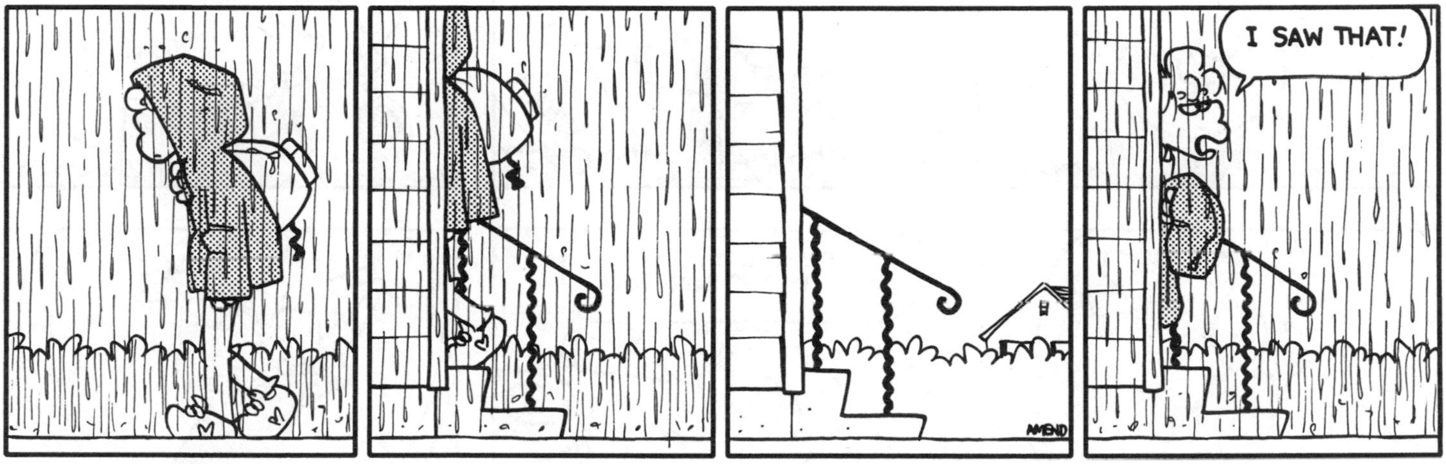
AMEND
I SAW THAT!

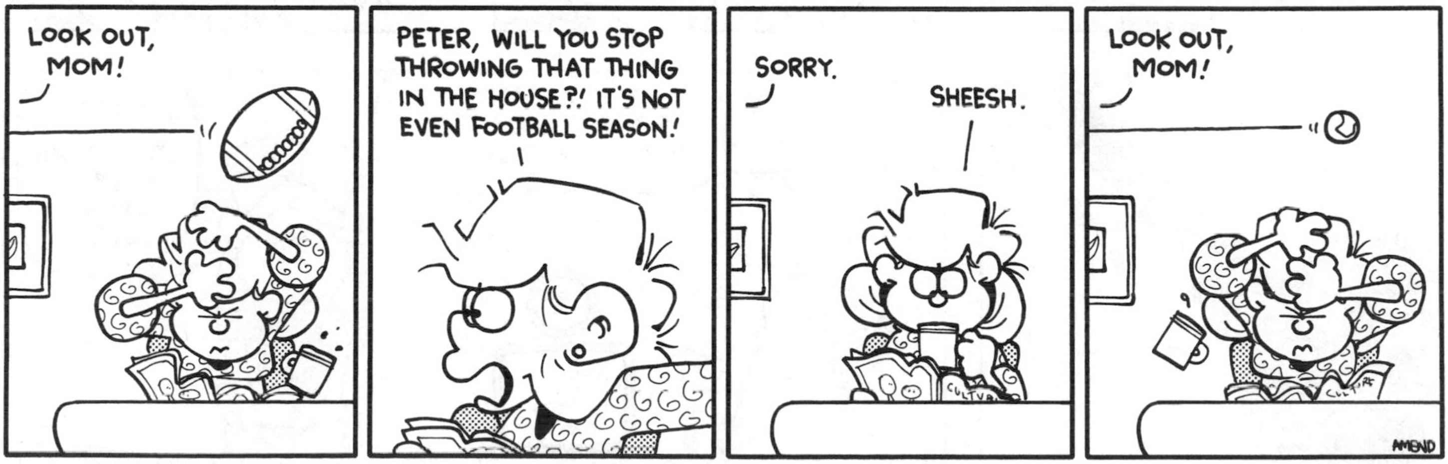
LOOK OUT, MOM!
PETER, WILL YOU STOP THROWING THAT THING IN THE HOUSE?! IT'S NOT EVEN FOOTBALL SEASON!
SORRY.
SHEESH.
LOOK OUT, MOM!
AMEND

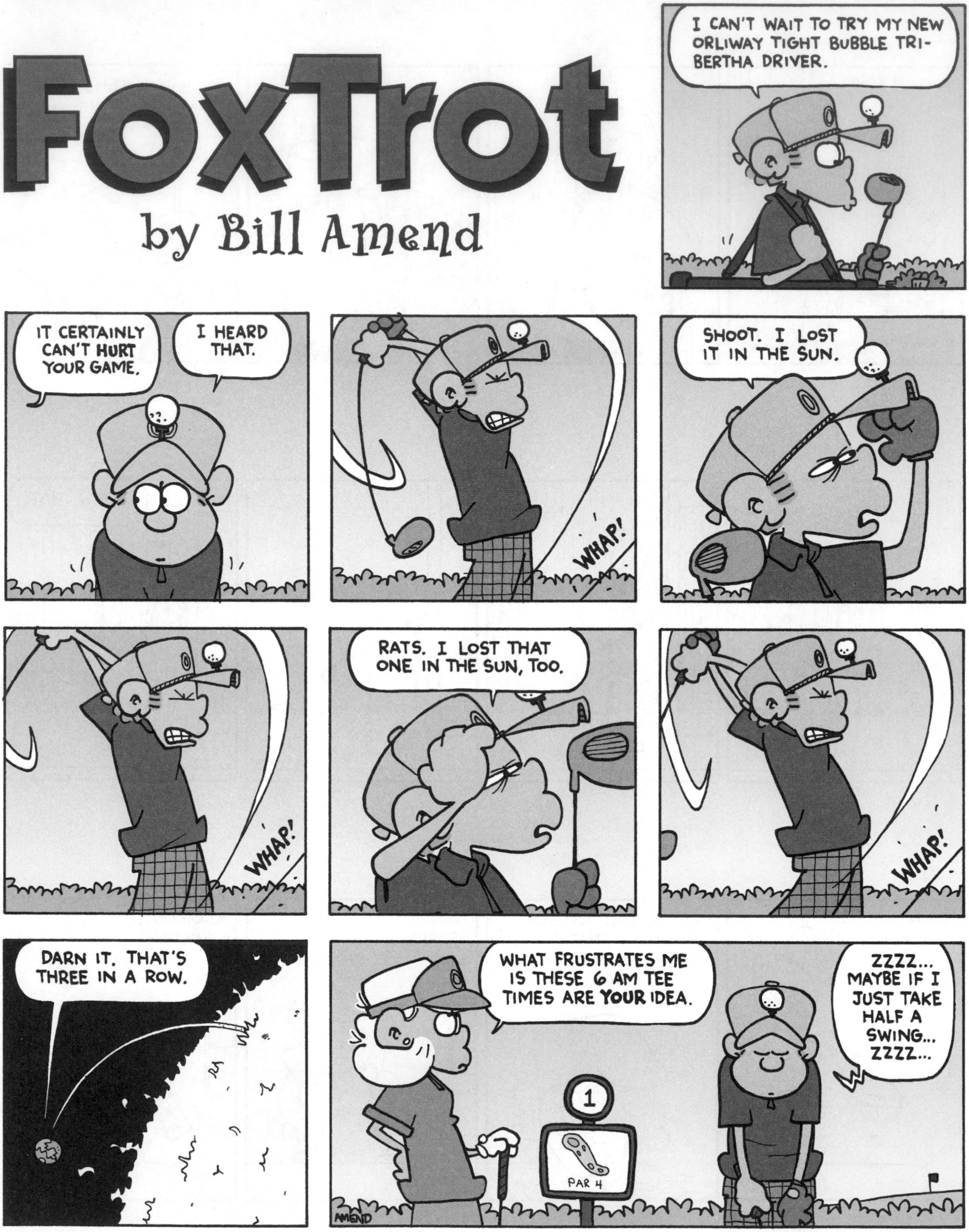
FoxTrot
by Bill Amend
I CAN'T WAIT TO TRY MY NEW ORLIWAY TIGHT BUBBLE TRI-BERTHA DRIVER.
IT CERTAINLY CAN'T HURT YOUR GAME.
I HEARD THAT.
WHAP!
SHOOT. I LOST IT IN THE SUN.
WHAP!
RATS. I LOST THAT ONE IN THE SUN, TOO.
WHAP!
DARN IT. THAT'S THREE IN A ROW.
WHAT FRUSTRATES ME IS THESE 6 AM TEE TIMES ARE YOUR IDEA.
ZZZZ... MAYBE IF I JUST TAKE HALF A SWING... ZZZZ...
1
PAR 4
AMEND

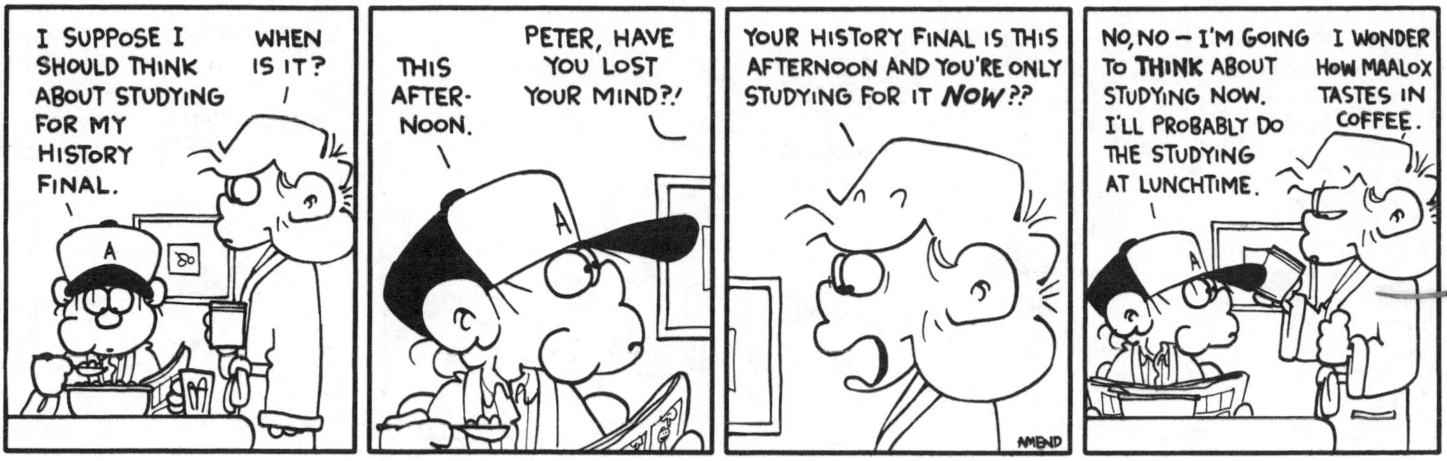
I SUPPOSE I SHOULD THINK ABOUT STUDYING FOR MY HISTORY FINAL.
WHEN IS IT?
THIS AFTER-NOON.
PETER, HAVE YOU LOST YOUR MIND?!
YOUR HISTORY FINAL IS THIS AFTERNOON AND YOU'RE ONLY STUDYING FOR IT NOW??
AMEND
NO, NO — I'M GOING TO THINK ABOUT STUDYING NOW. I'LL PROBABLY DO THE STUDYING AT LUNCHTIME.
I WONDER HOW MAALOX TASTES IN COFFEE.

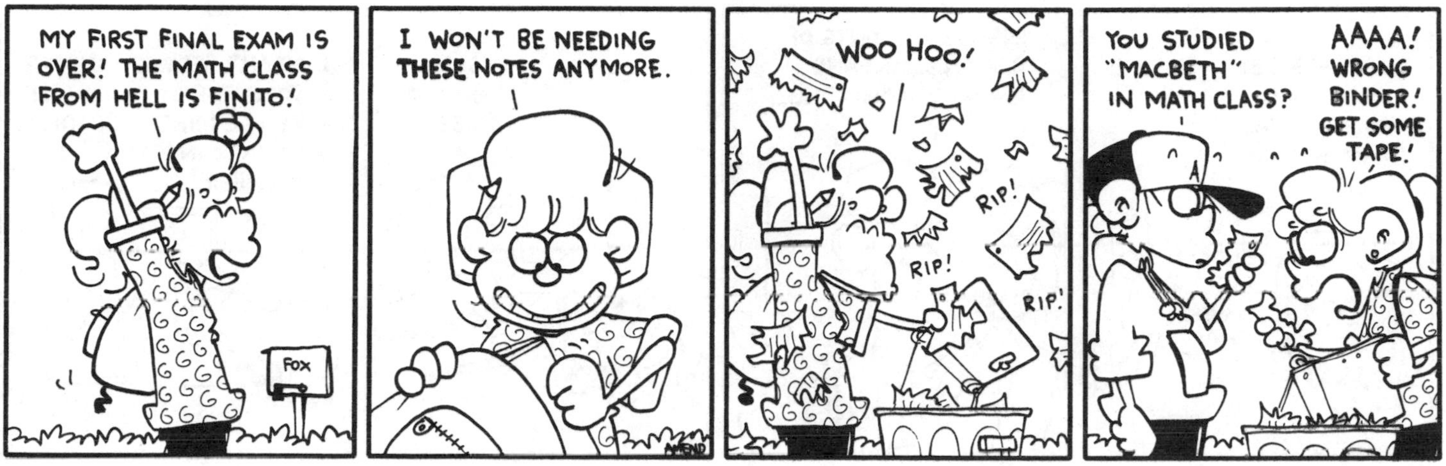
MY FIRST FINAL EXAM IS OVER! THE MATH CLASS FROM HELL IS FINITO!
FOX
I WON'T BE NEEDING THESE NOTES ANYMORE.
AMEND
WOO HOO!
RIP!
RIP!
RIP!
YOU STUDIED "MACBETH" IN MATH CLASS?
AAAA! WRONG BINDER! GET SOME TAPE!

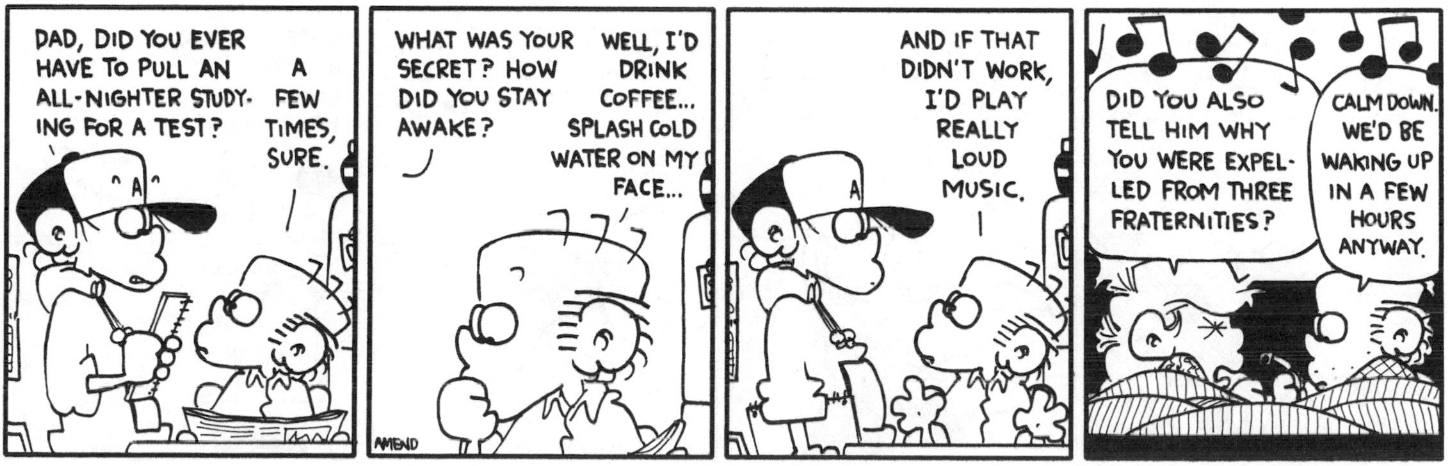
DAD, DID YOU EVER HAVE TO PULL AN ALL-NIGHTER STUDY-ING FOR A TEST?
A FEW TIMES, SURE.
WHAT WAS YOUR SECRET? HOW DID YOU STAY AWAKE?
WELL, I'D DRINK COFFEE... SPLASH COLD WATER ON MY FACE...
AMEND
AND IF THAT DIDN'T WORK, I'D PLAY REALLY LOUD MUSIC.
DID YOU ALSO TELL HIM WHY YOU WERE EXPEL-LED FROM THREE FRATERNITIES?
CALM DOWN. WE'D BE WAKING UP IN A FEW HOURS ANYWAY.

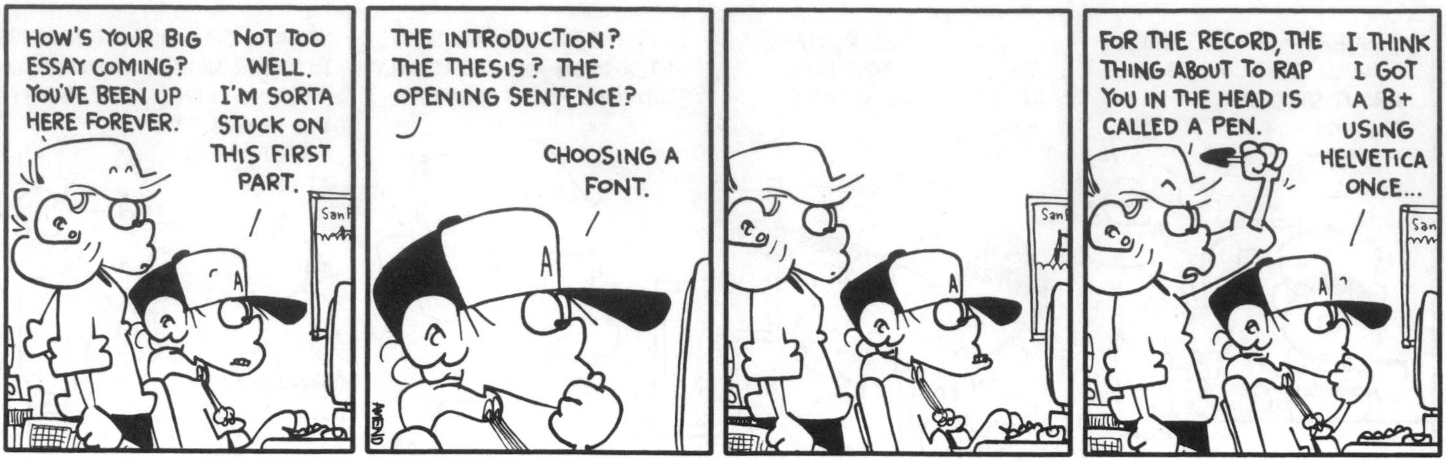
HOW'S YOUR BIG ESSAY COMING? YOU'VE BEEN UP HERE FOREVER.
NOT TOO WELL. I'M SORTA STUCK ON THIS FIRST PART.
THE INTRODUCTION? THE THESIS? THE OPENING SENTENCE?
CHOOSING A FONT.
AMEND
FOR THE RECORD, THE THING ABOUT TO RAP YOU IN THE HEAD IS CALLED A PEN.
I THINK I GOT A B+ USING HELVETICA ONCE...

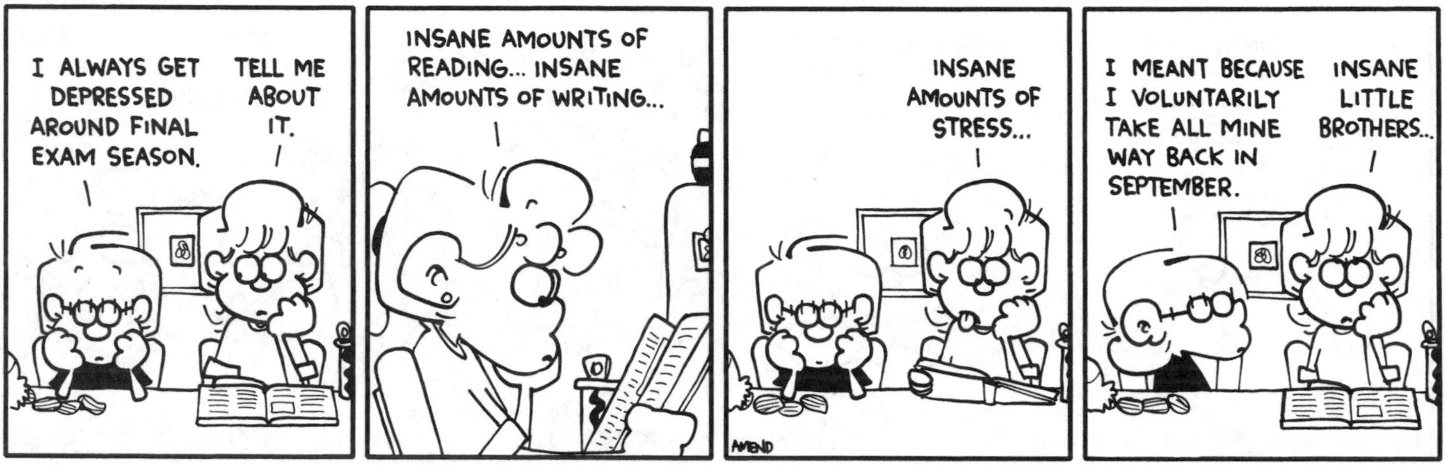
I ALWAYS GET DEPRESSED AROUND FINAL EXAM SEASON.
TELL ME ABOUT IT.
INSANE AMOUNTS OF READING... INSANE AMOUNTS OF WRITING...
INSANE AMOUNTS OF STRESS...
AMEND
I MEANT BECAUSE I VOLUNTARILY TAKE ALL MINE WAY BACK IN SEPTEMBER.
INSANE LITTLE BROTHERS...

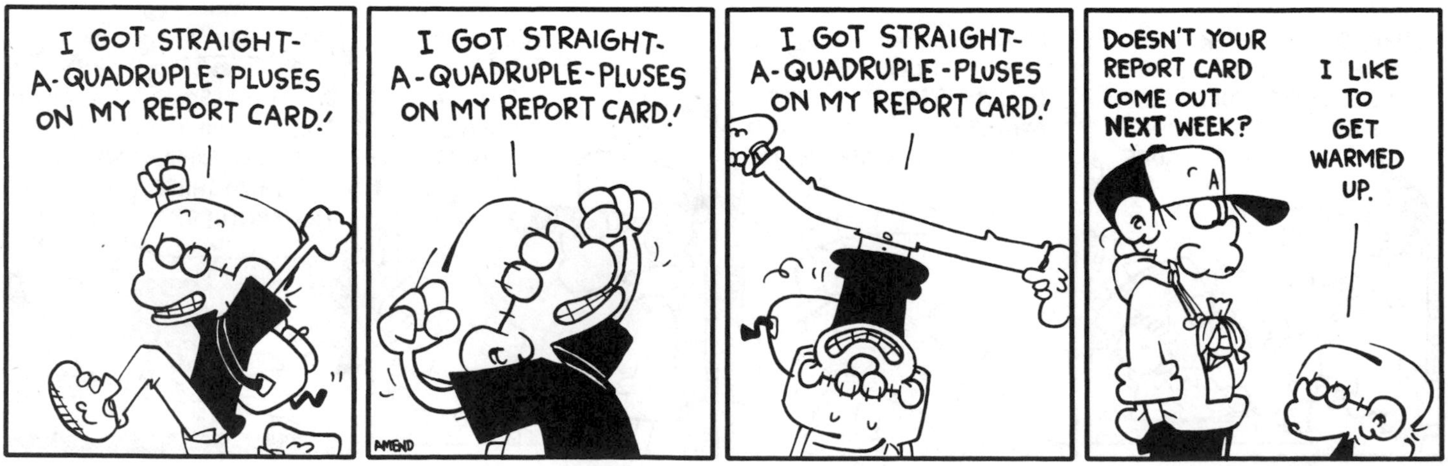
I GOT STRAIGHT-A-QUADRUPLE-PLUSES ON MY REPORT CARD!
I GOT STRAIGHT-A-QUADRUPLE-PLUSES ON MY REPORT CARD!
AMEND
I GOT STRAIGHT-A-QUADRUPLE-PLUSES ON MY REPORT CARD!
DOESN'T YOUR REPORT CARD COME OUT NEXT WEEK?
I LIKE TO GET WARMED UP.

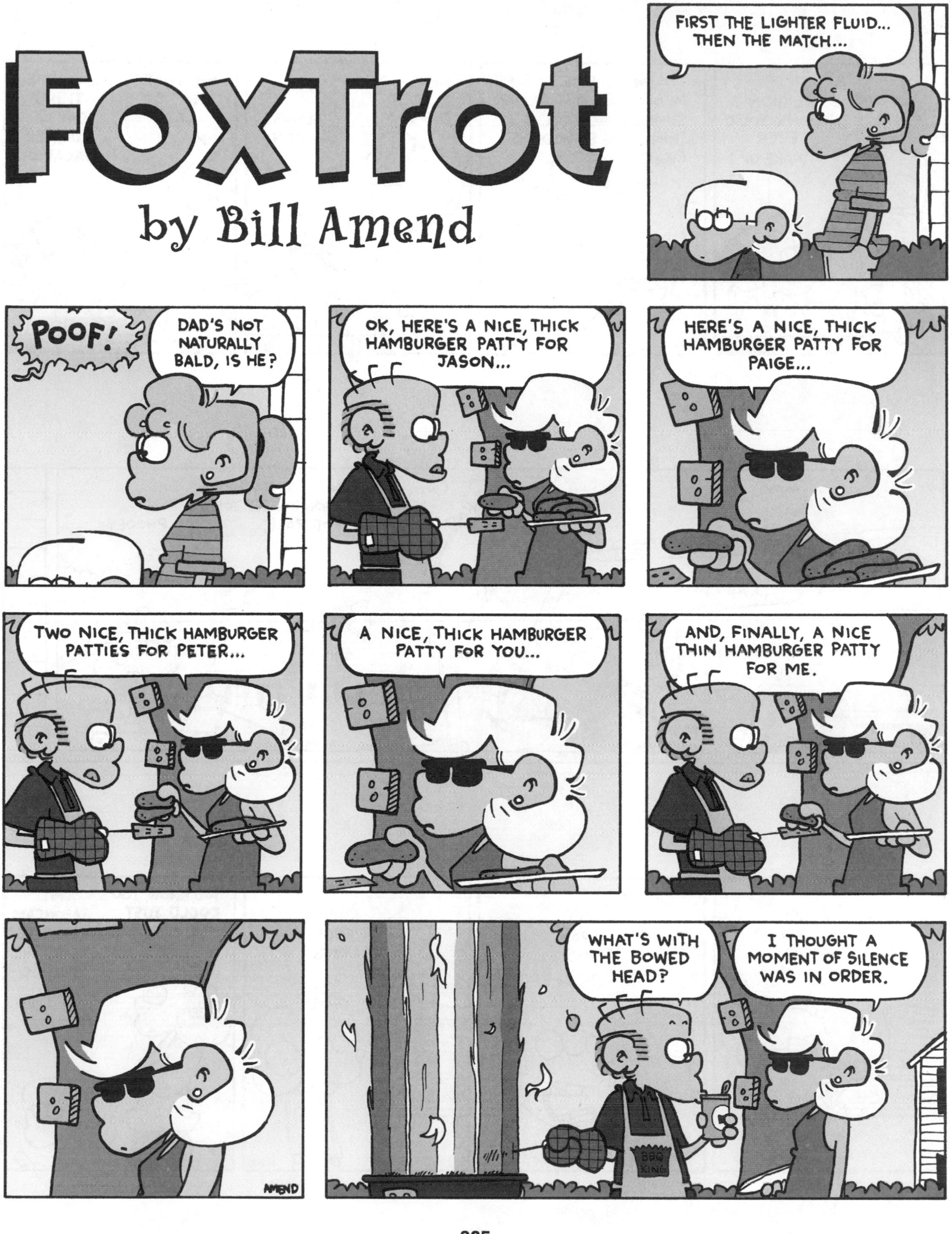
FoxTrot
by Bill Amend
FIRST THE LIGHTER FLUID... THEN THE MATCH...
POOF!
DAD'S NOT NATURALLY BALD, IS HE?
OK, HERE'S A NICE, THICK HAMBURGER PATTY FOR JASON...
HERE'S A NICE, THICK HAMBURGER PATTY FOR PAIGE...
TWO NICE, THICK HAMBURGER PATTIES FOR PETER...
A NICE, THICK HAMBURGER PATTY FOR YOU...
AND, FINALLY, A NICE THIN HAMBURGER PATTY FOR ME.
AMEND
WHAT'S WITH THE BOWED HEAD?
I THOUGHT A MOMENT OF SILENCE WAS IN ORDER.
BBQ KING

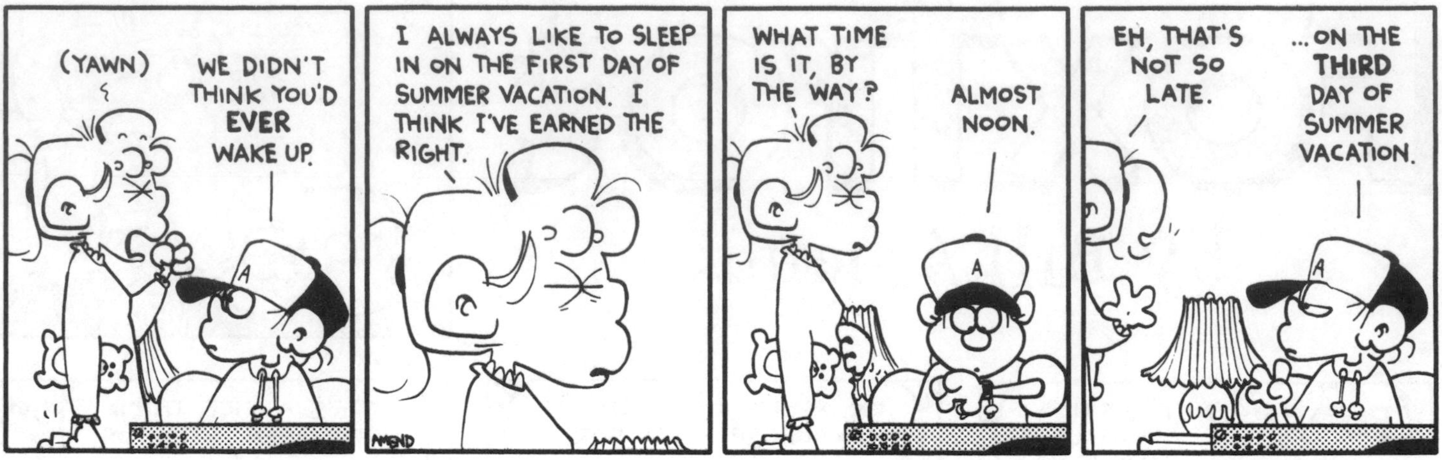
(YAWN)
WE DIDN'T THINK YOU'D **EVER** WAKE UP.
I ALWAYS LIKE TO SLEEP IN ON THE FIRST DAY OF SUMMER VACATION. I THINK I'VE EARNED THE RIGHT.
WHAT TIME IS IT, BY THE WAY?
ALMOST NOON.
EH, THAT'S NOT SO LATE.
...ON THE **THIRD** DAY OF SUMMER VACATION.

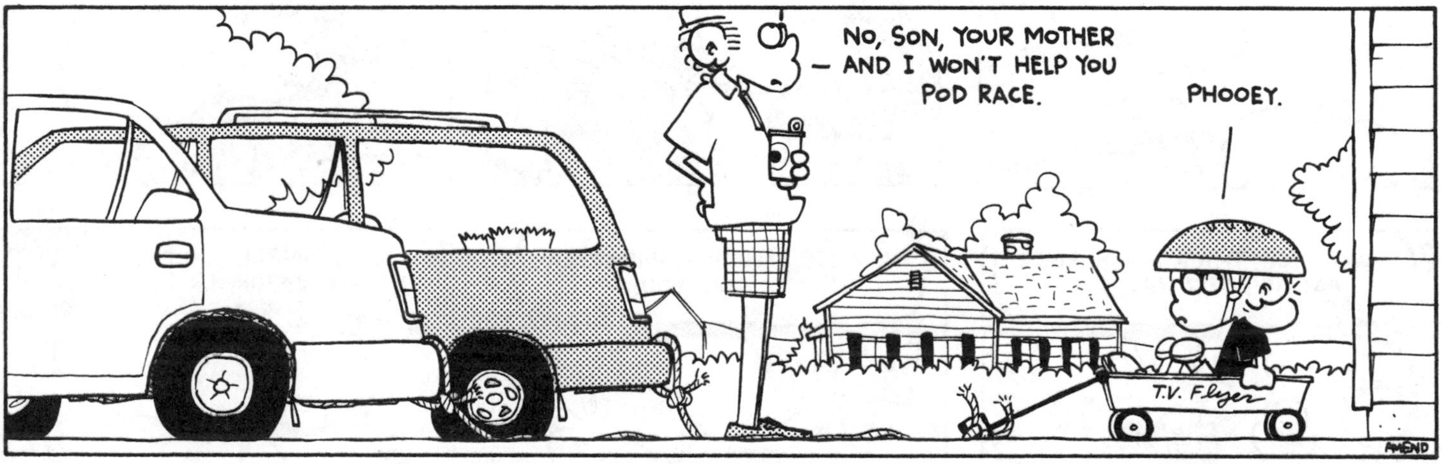
NO, SON, YOUR MOTHER AND I WON'T HELP YOU POD RACE.
PHOOEY.
T.V. Flyer

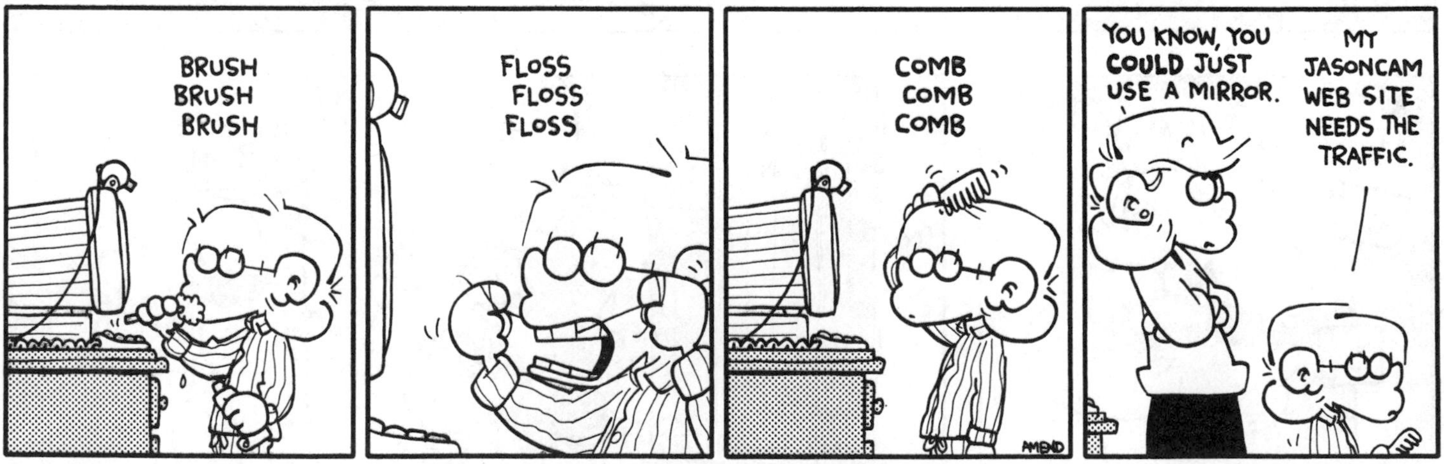
BRUSH BRUSH BRUSH
FLOSS FLOSS FLOSS
COMB COMB COMB
YOU KNOW, YOU **COULD** JUST USE A MIRROR.
MY JASONCAM WEB SITE NEEDS THE TRAFFIC.

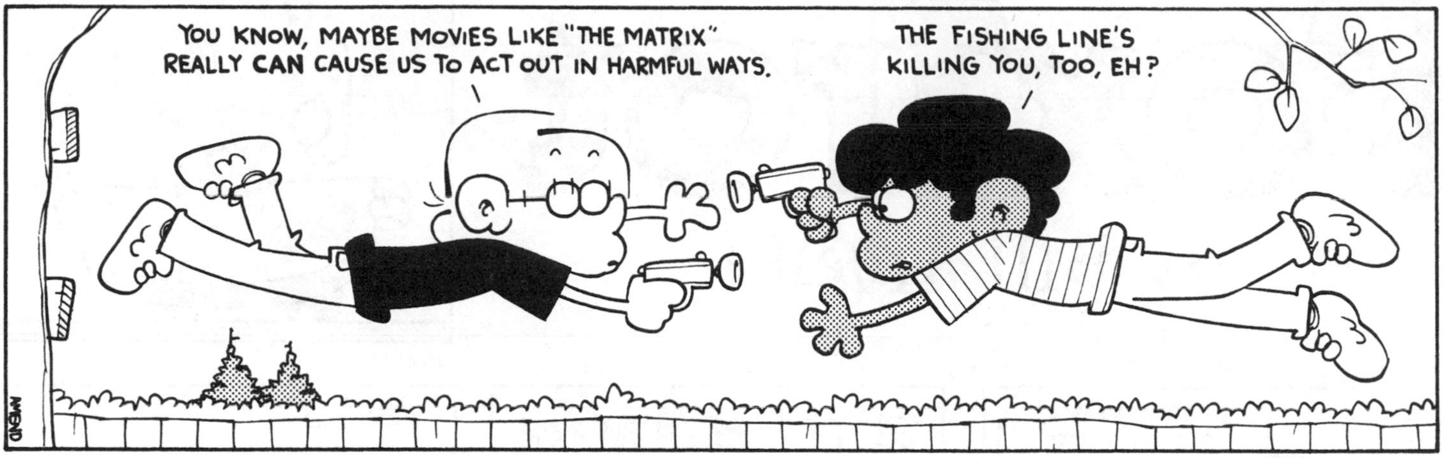
YOU KNOW, MAYBE MOVIES LIKE "THE MATRIX" REALLY CAN CAUSE US TO ACT OUT IN HARMFUL WAYS.
THE FISHING LINE'S KILLING YOU, TOO, EH?
AMEND

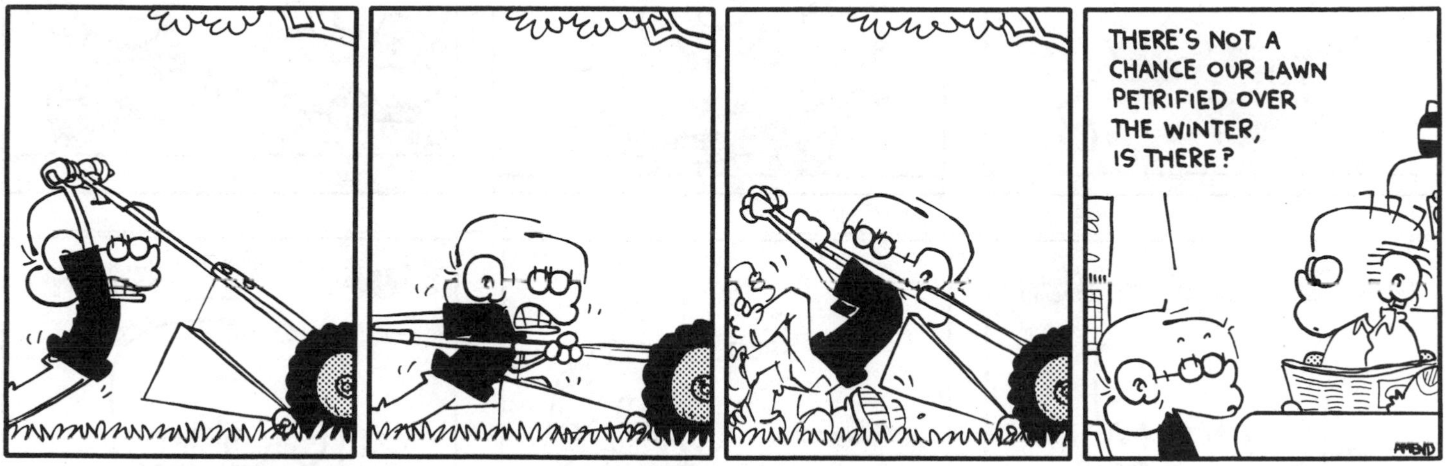
THERE'S NOT A CHANCE OUR LAWN PETRIFIED OVER THE WINTER, IS THERE?
AMEND

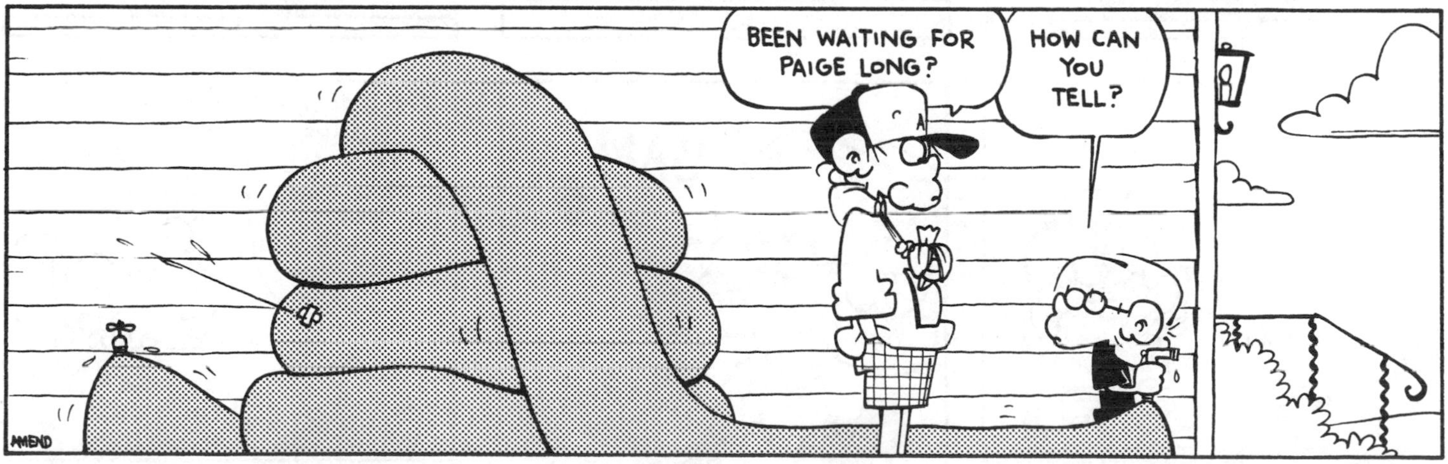
BEEN WAITING FOR PAIGE LONG?
HOW CAN YOU TELL?
AMEND

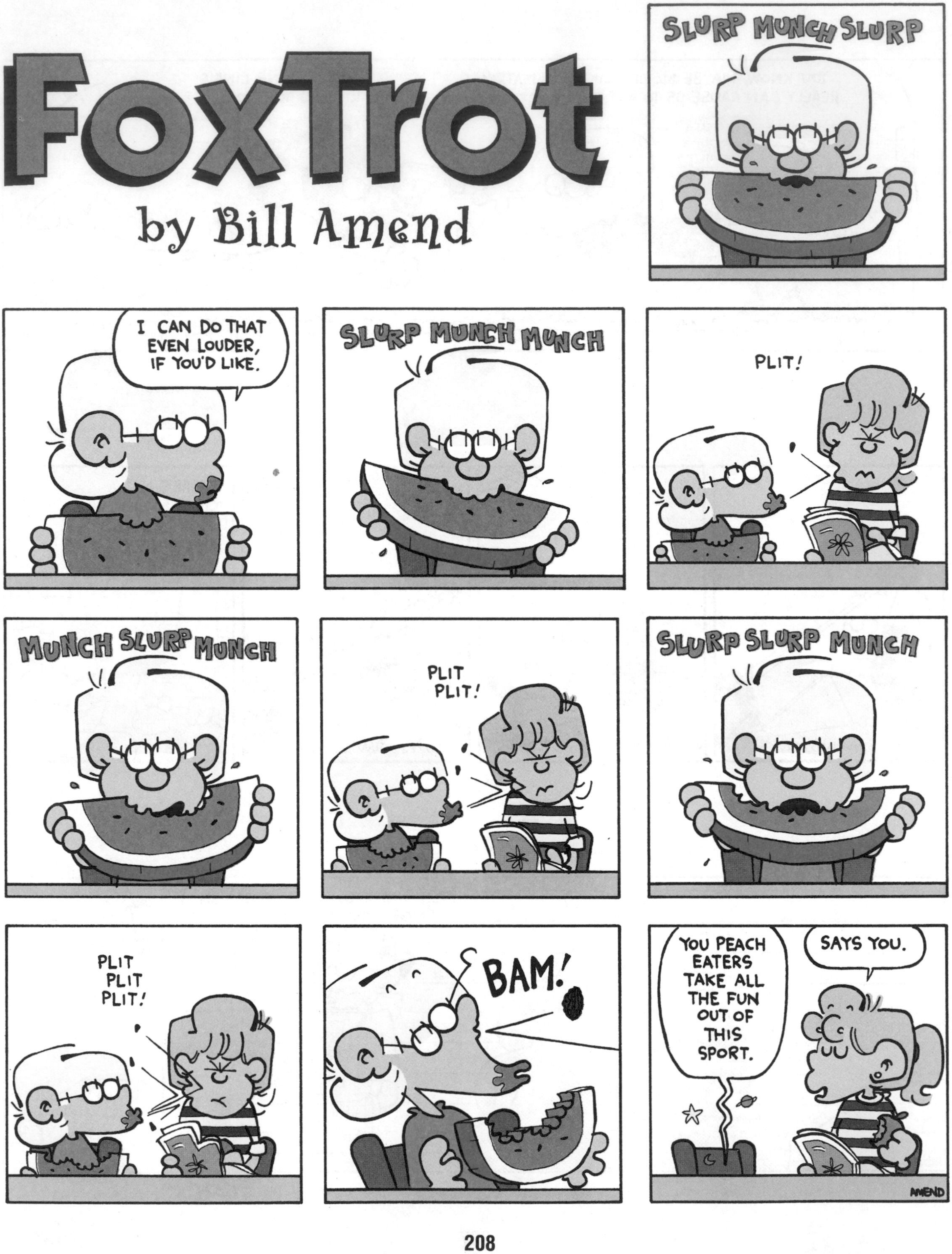
FoxTrot
by Bill Amend
SLURP MUNCH SLURP
I CAN DO THAT EVEN LOUDER, IF YOU'D LIKE.
SLURP MUNCH MUNCH
PLIT!
MUNCH SLURP MUNCH
PLIT PLIT!
SLURP SLURP MUNCH
PLIT PLIT PLIT!
BAM!
YOU PEACH EATERS TAKE ALL THE FUN OUT OF THIS SPORT.
SAYS YOU.
AMEND

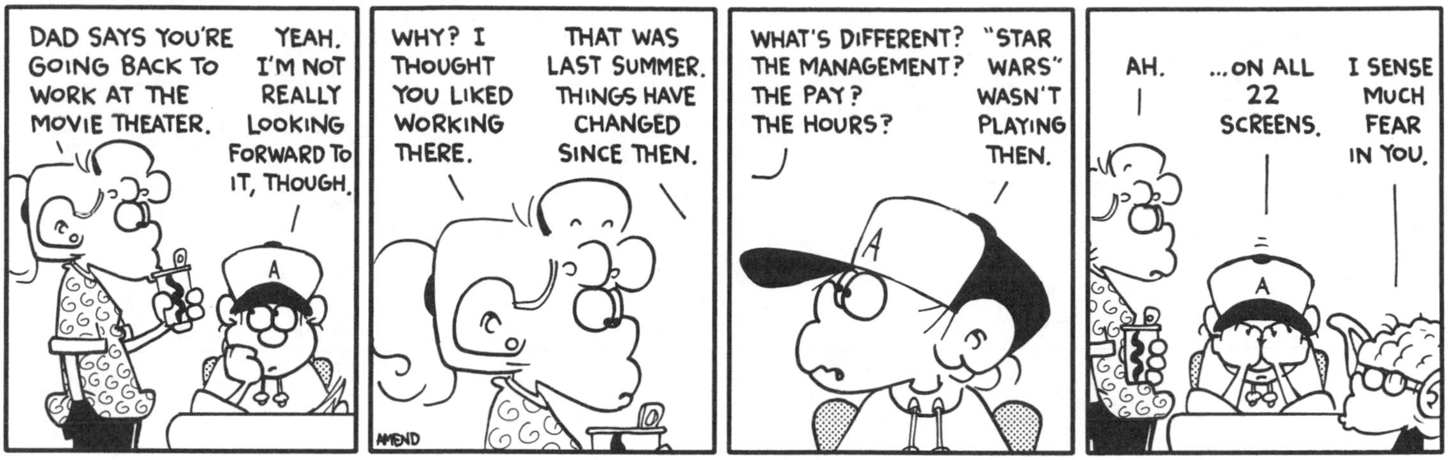
DAD SAYS YOU'RE GOING BACK TO WORK AT THE MOVIE THEATER.
YEAH. I'M NOT REALLY LOOKING FORWARD TO IT, THOUGH.
WHY? I THOUGHT YOU LIKED WORKING THERE.
THAT WAS LAST SUMMER. THINGS HAVE CHANGED SINCE THEN.
WHAT'S DIFFERENT? THE MANAGEMENT? THE PAY? THE HOURS?
"STAR WARS" WASN'T PLAYING THEN.
AH.
...ON ALL 22 SCREENS.
I SENSE MUCH FEAR IN YOU.
AMEND

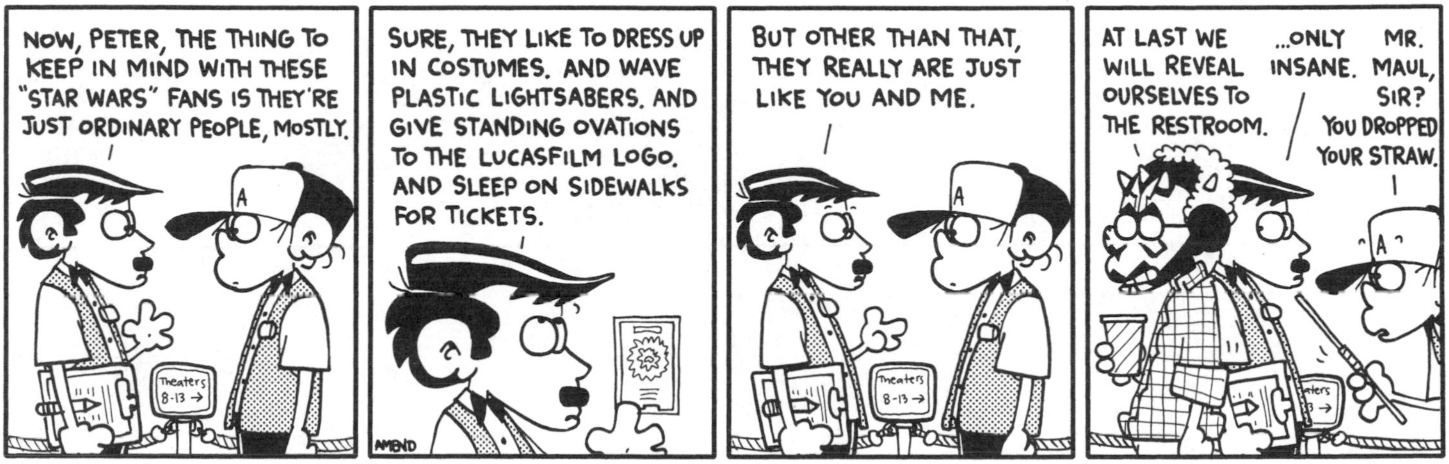
NOW, PETER, THE THING TO KEEP IN MIND WITH THESE "STAR WARS" FANS IS THEY'RE JUST ORDINARY PEOPLE, MOSTLY.
Theaters 8-13 →
SURE, THEY LIKE TO DRESS UP IN COSTUMES. AND WAVE PLASTIC LIGHTSABERS. AND GIVE STANDING OVATIONS TO THE LUCASFILM LOGO. AND SLEEP ON SIDEWALKS FOR TICKETS.
BUT OTHER THAN THAT, THEY REALLY ARE JUST LIKE YOU AND ME.
Theaters 8-13 →
AT LAST WE WILL REVEAL OURSELVES TO THE RESTROOM.
...ONLY INSANE.
MR. MAUL, SIR? YOU DROPPED YOUR STRAW.
AMEND

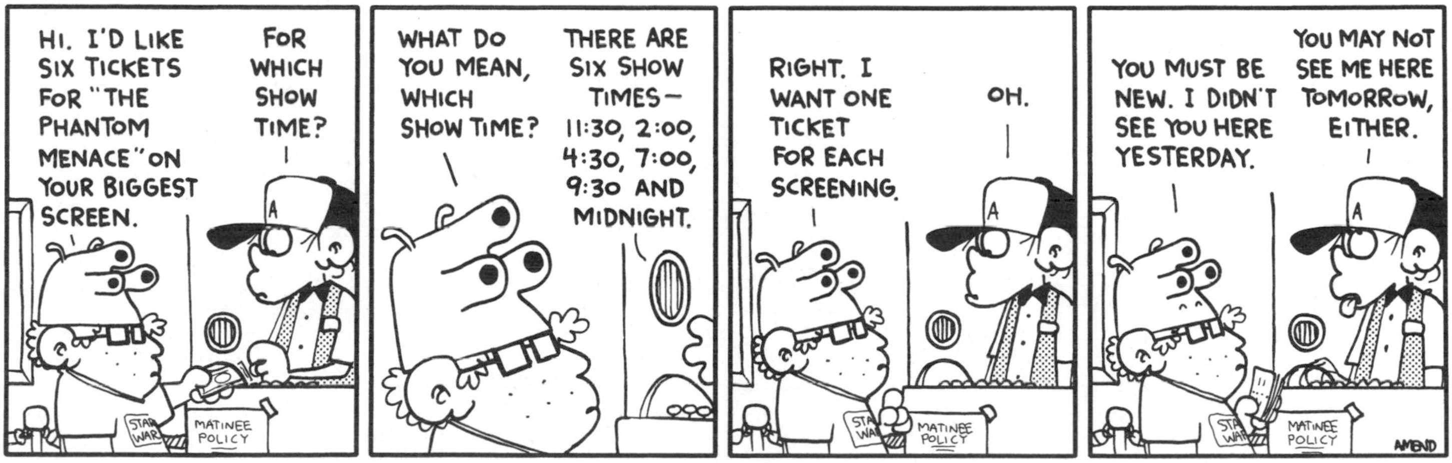
HI. I'D LIKE SIX TICKETS FOR "THE PHANTOM MENACE" ON YOUR BIGGEST SCREEN.
FOR WHICH SHOW TIME?
MATINEE POLICY
WHAT DO YOU MEAN, WHICH SHOW TIME?
THERE ARE SIX SHOW TIMES— 11:30, 2:00, 4:30, 7:00, 9:30 AND MIDNIGHT.
RIGHT. I WANT ONE TICKET FOR EACH SCREENING.
OH.
MATINEE POLICY
YOU MUST BE NEW. I DIDN'T SEE YOU HERE YESTERDAY.
YOU MAY NOT SEE ME HERE TOMORROW, EITHER.
MATINEE POLICY
AMEND

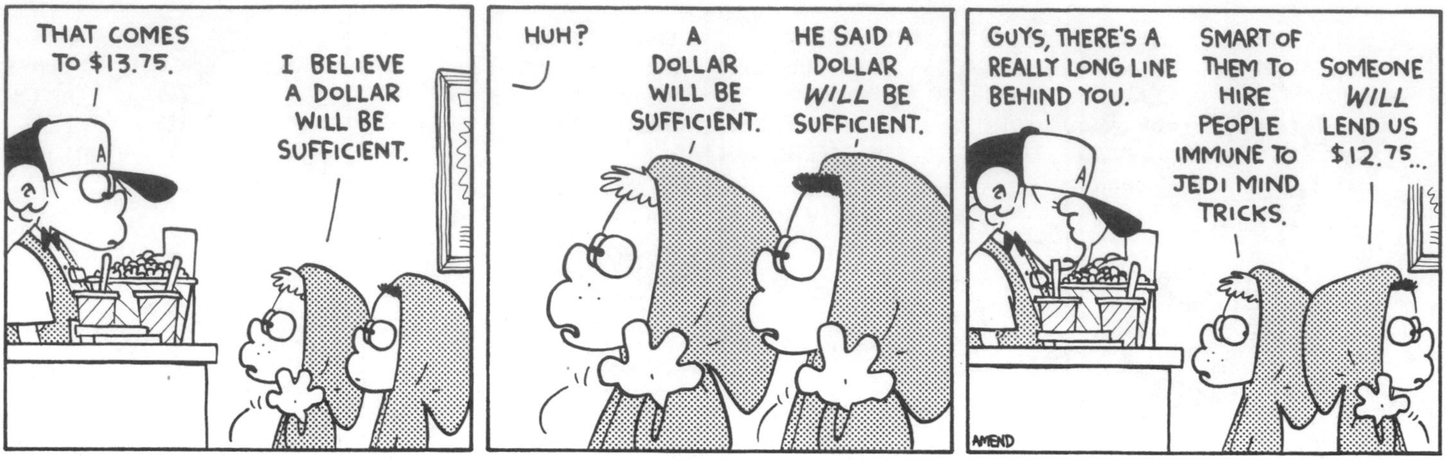
THAT COMES TO $13.75.
I BELIEVE A DOLLAR WILL BE SUFFICIENT.
HUH?
A DOLLAR WILL BE SUFFICIENT.
HE SAID A DOLLAR *WILL* BE SUFFICIENT.
GUYS, THERE'S A REALLY LONG LINE BEHIND YOU.
SMART OF THEM TO HIRE PEOPLE IMMUNE TO JEDI MIND TRICKS.
SOMEONE *WILL* LEND US $12.75...
AMEND

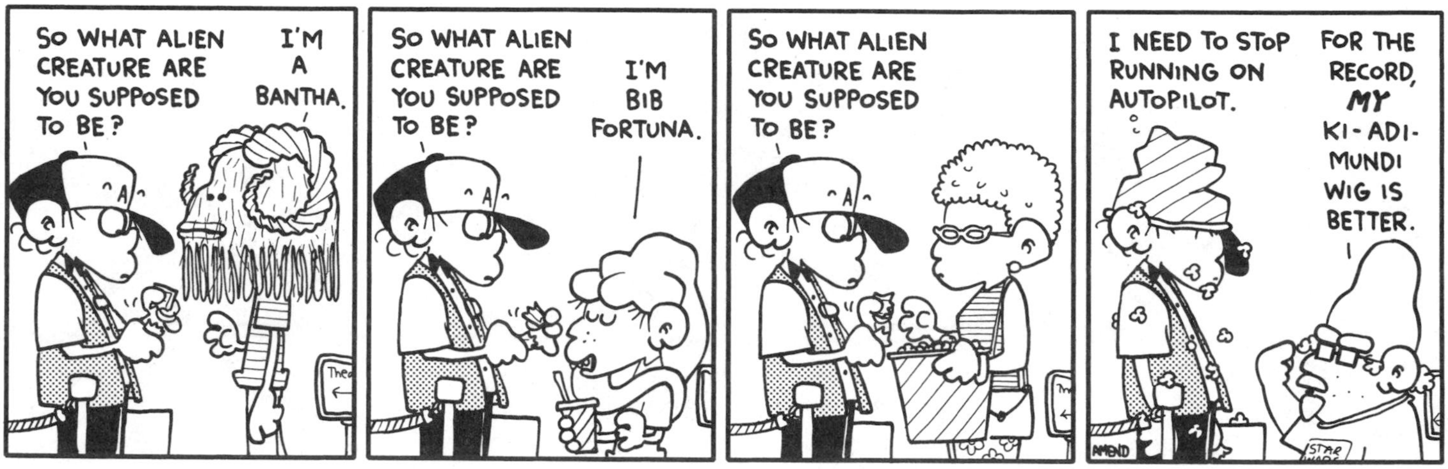
SO WHAT ALIEN CREATURE ARE YOU SUPPOSED TO BE?
I'M A BANTHA.
SO WHAT ALIEN CREATURE ARE YOU SUPPOSED TO BE?
I'M BIB FORTUNA.
SO WHAT ALIEN CREATURE ARE YOU SUPPOSED TO BE?
I NEED TO STOP RUNNING ON AUTOPILOT.
FOR THE RECORD, *MY* KI-ADI-MUNDI WIG IS BETTER.
AMEND

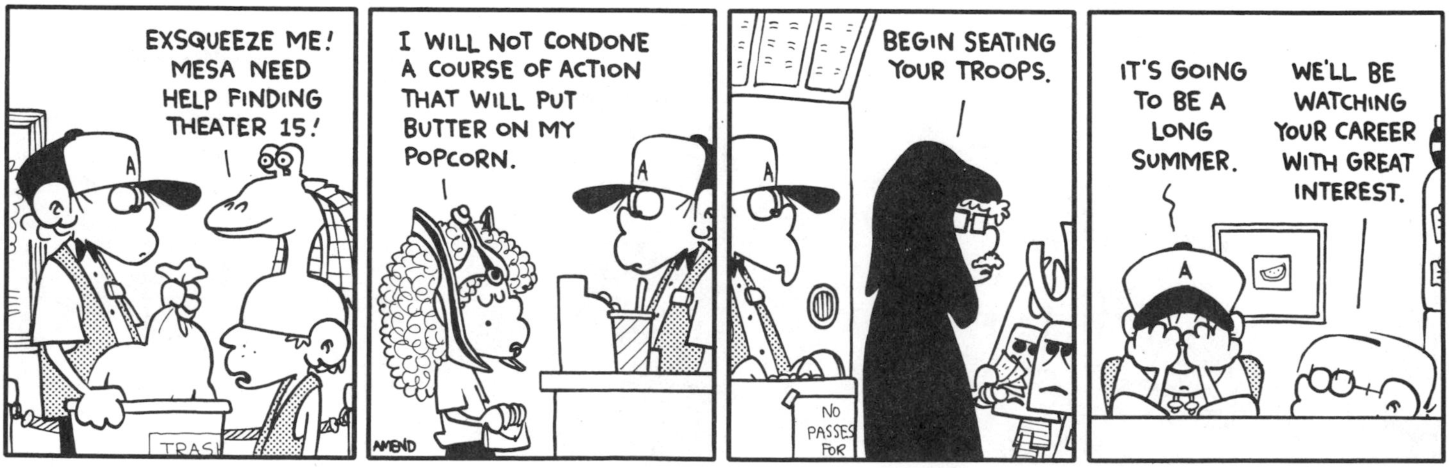
EXSQUEEZE ME! MESA NEED HELP FINDING THEATER 15!
I WILL NOT CONDONE A COURSE OF ACTION THAT WILL PUT BUTTER ON MY POPCORN.
AMEND
BEGIN SEATING YOUR TROOPS.
NO PASSES FOR
IT'S GOING TO BE A LONG SUMMER.
WE'LL BE WATCHING YOUR CAREER WITH GREAT INTEREST.

FoxTrot

by Bill Amend

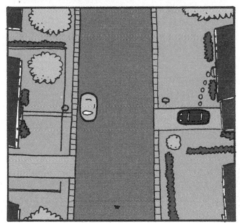

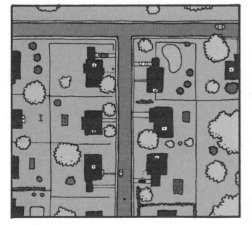

TWO DOZEN SUPERBALLS GLUED TO MY SHOES, AND **NOTHING**.

WHAT DID YOU **THINK** WOULD HAPPEN?

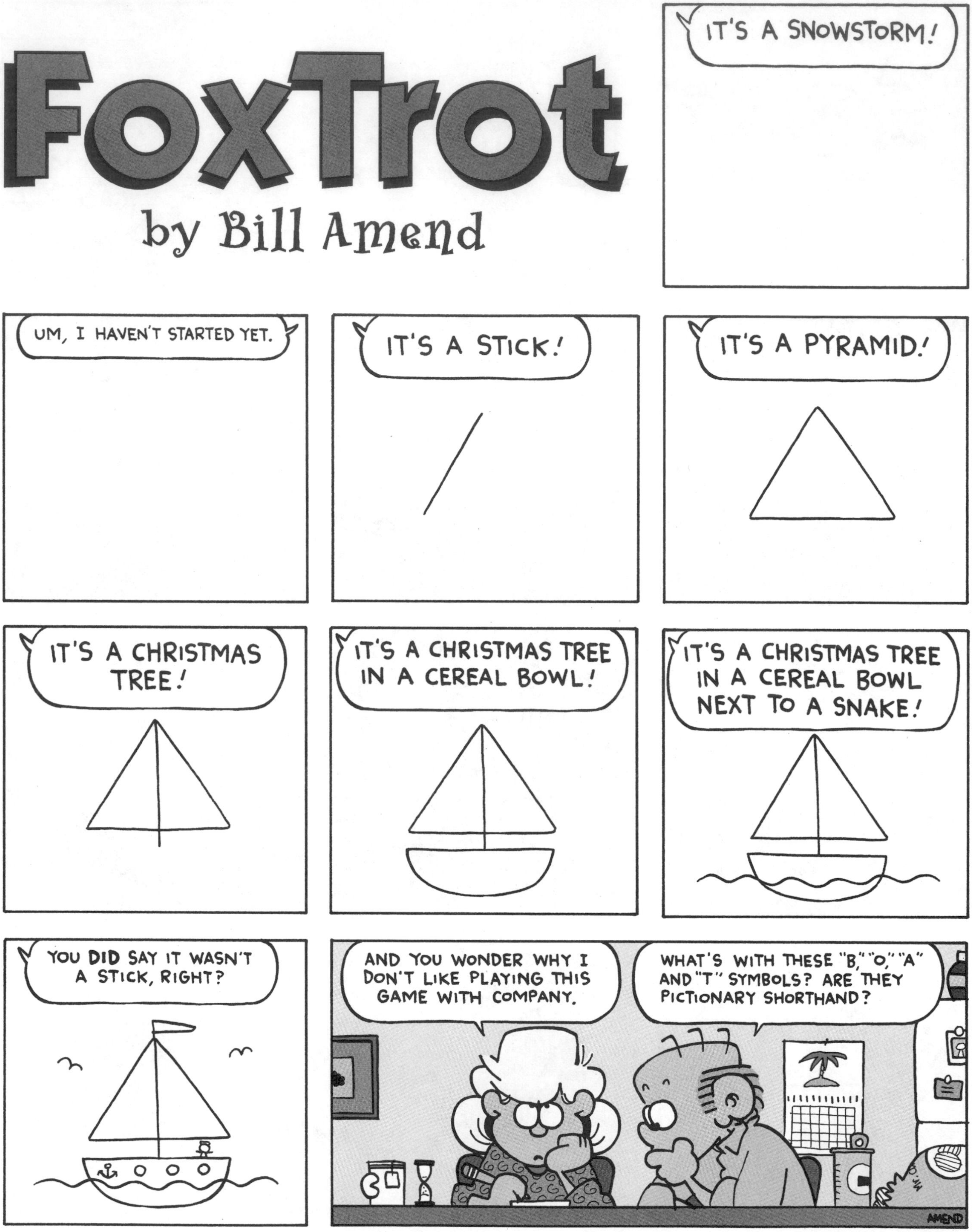
FoxTrot
by Bill Amend
IT'S A SNOWSTORM!
UM, I HAVEN'T STARTED YET.
IT'S A STICK!
IT'S A PYRAMID!
IT'S A CHRISTMAS TREE!
IT'S A CHRISTMAS TREE IN A CEREAL BOWL!
IT'S A CHRISTMAS TREE IN A CEREAL BOWL NEXT TO A SNAKE!
YOU DID SAY IT WASN'T A STICK, RIGHT?
AND YOU WONDER WHY I DON'T LIKE PLAYING THIS GAME WITH COMPANY.
WHAT'S WITH THESE "B," "O," "A" AND "T" SYMBOLS? ARE THEY PICTIONARY SHORTHAND?
AMEND

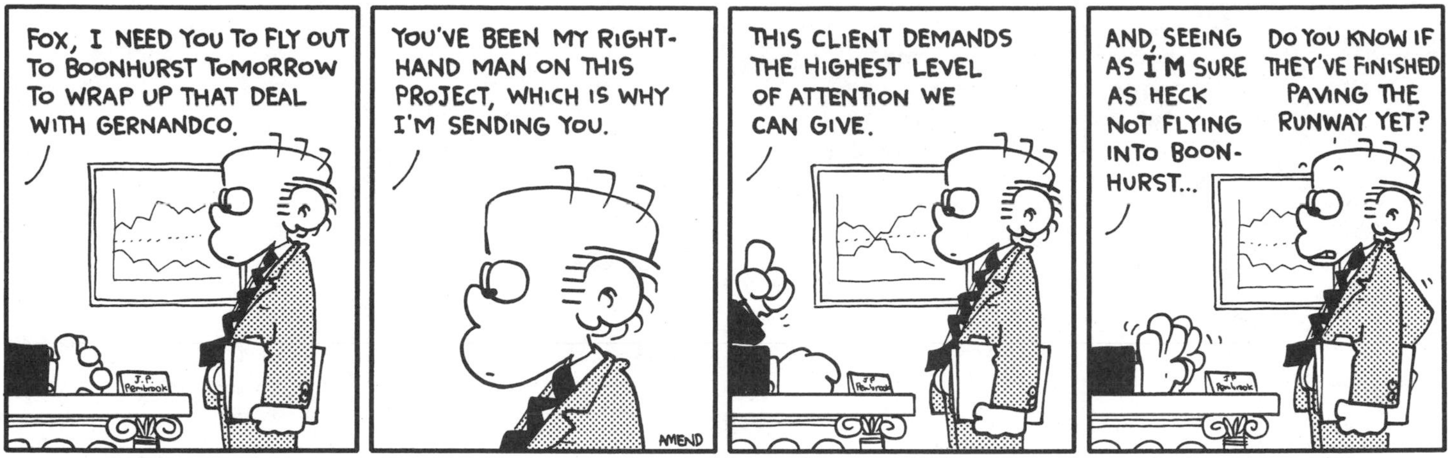
FOX, I NEED YOU TO FLY OUT TO BOONHURST TOMORROW TO WRAP UP THAT DEAL WITH GERNANDCO.
J.P. Pembrook
YOU'VE BEEN MY RIGHT-HAND MAN ON THIS PROJECT, WHICH IS WHY I'M SENDING YOU.
AMEND
THIS CLIENT DEMANDS THE HIGHEST LEVEL OF ATTENTION WE CAN GIVE.
AND, SEEING AS I'M SURE AS HECK NOT FLYING INTO BOONHURST...
DO YOU KNOW IF THEY'VE FINISHED PAVING THE RUNWAY YET?

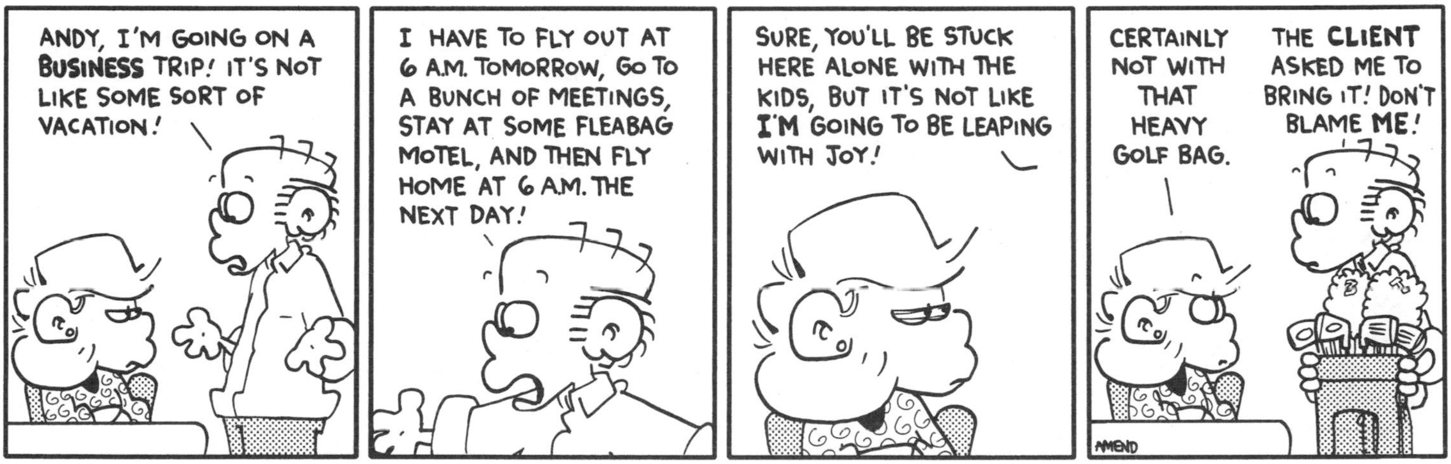
ANDY, I'M GOING ON A BUSINESS TRIP! IT'S NOT LIKE SOME SORT OF VACATION!
I HAVE TO FLY OUT AT 6 A.M. TOMORROW, GO TO A BUNCH OF MEETINGS, STAY AT SOME FLEABAG MOTEL, AND THEN FLY HOME AT 6 A.M. THE NEXT DAY!
SURE, YOU'LL BE STUCK HERE ALONE WITH THE KIDS, BUT IT'S NOT LIKE I'M GOING TO BE LEAPING WITH JOY!
CERTAINLY NOT WITH THAT HEAVY GOLF BAG.
THE CLIENT ASKED ME TO BRING IT! DON'T BLAME ME!
AMEND

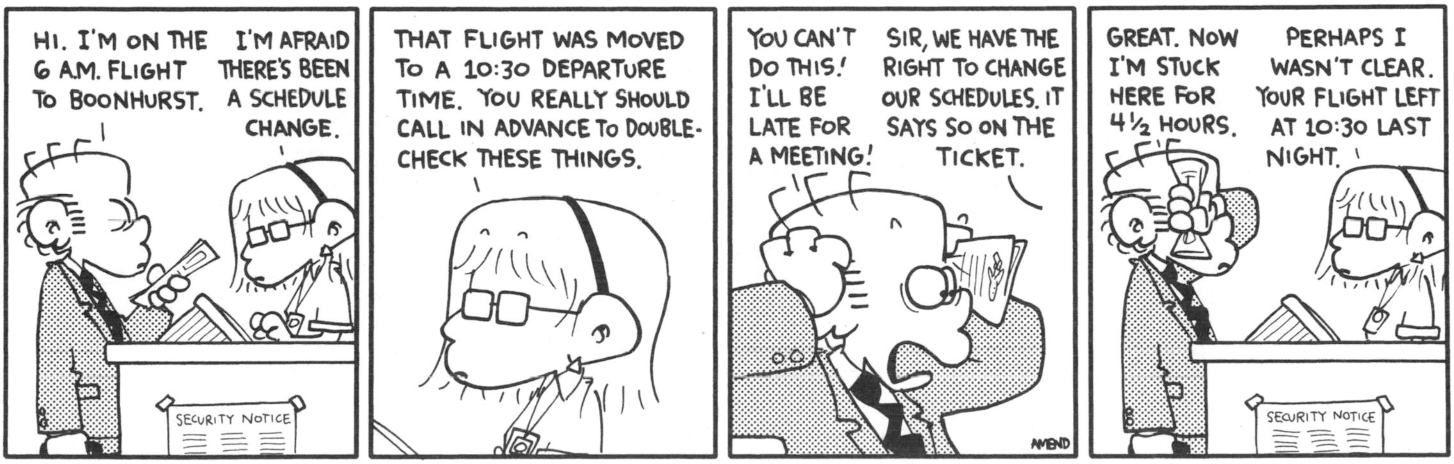
HI. I'M ON THE 6 A.M. FLIGHT TO BOONHURST.
I'M AFRAID THERE'S BEEN A SCHEDULE CHANGE.
SECURITY NOTICE
THAT FLIGHT WAS MOVED TO A 10:30 DEPARTURE TIME. YOU REALLY SHOULD CALL IN ADVANCE TO DOUBLE-CHECK THESE THINGS.
YOU CAN'T DO THIS! I'LL BE LATE FOR A MEETING!
SIR, WE HAVE THE RIGHT TO CHANGE OUR SCHEDULES. IT SAYS SO ON THE TICKET.
AMEND
GREAT. NOW I'M STUCK HERE FOR 4½ HOURS.
PERHAPS I WASN'T CLEAR. YOUR FLIGHT LEFT AT 10:30 LAST NIGHT.
SECURITY NOTICE

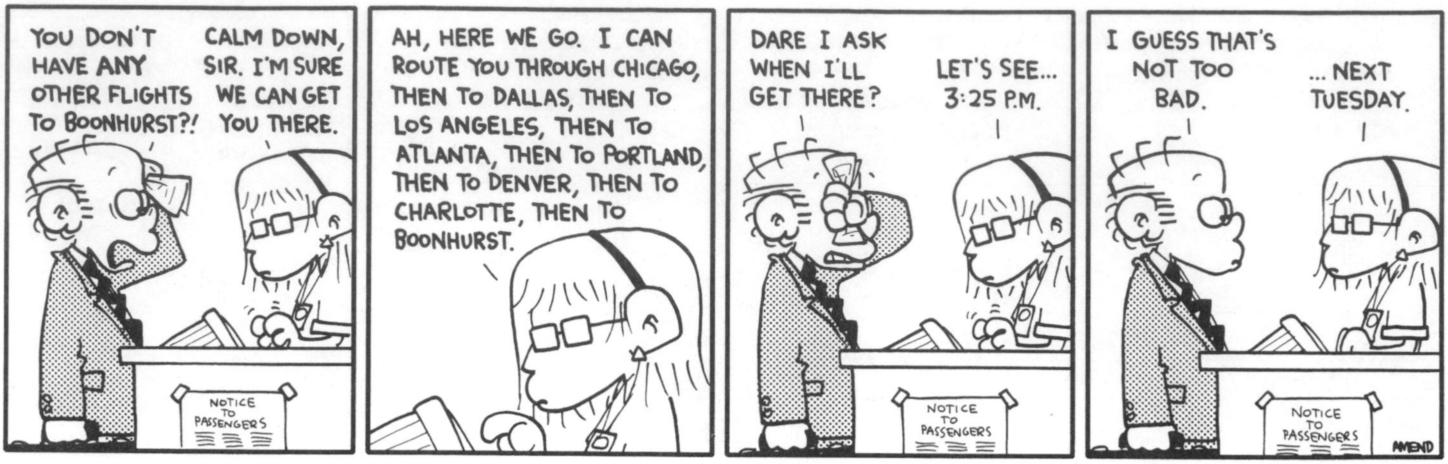
YOU DON'T HAVE ANY OTHER FLIGHTS TO BOONHURST?!
CALM DOWN, SIR. I'M SURE WE CAN GET YOU THERE.
NOTICE TO PASSENGERS
AH, HERE WE GO. I CAN ROUTE YOU THROUGH CHICAGO, THEN TO DALLAS, THEN TO LOS ANGELES, THEN TO ATLANTA, THEN TO PORTLAND, THEN TO DENVER, THEN TO CHARLOTTE, THEN TO BOONHURST.
DARE I ASK WHEN I'LL GET THERE?
LET'S SEE... 3:25 P.M.
NOTICE TO PASSENGERS
I GUESS THAT'S NOT TOO BAD.
... NEXT TUESDAY.
NOTICE TO PASSENGERS
AMEND

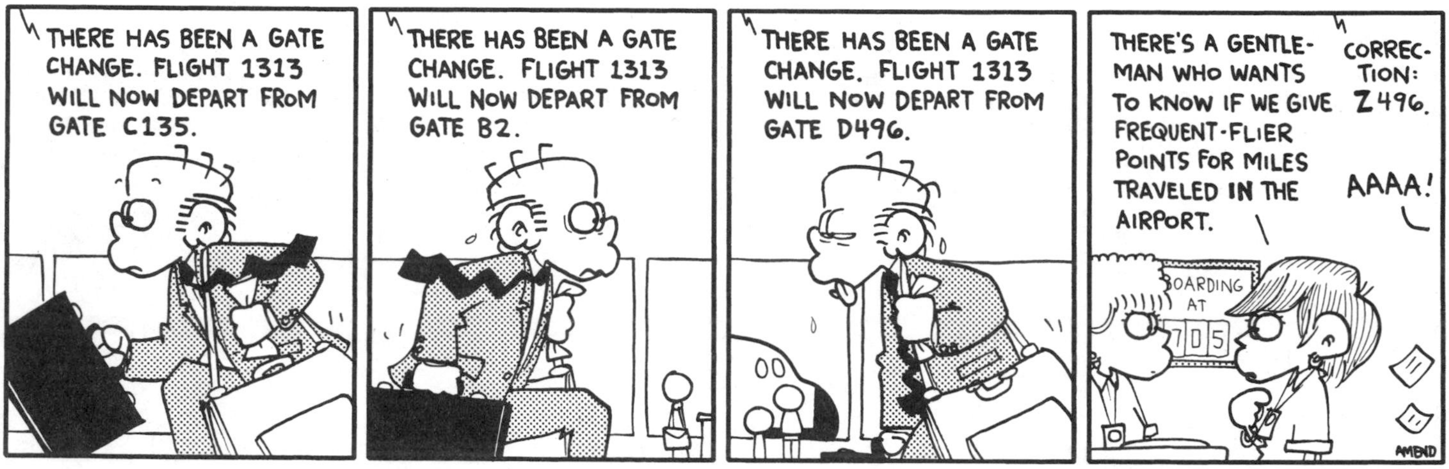
THERE HAS BEEN A GATE CHANGE. FLIGHT 1313 WILL NOW DEPART FROM GATE C135.
THERE HAS BEEN A GATE CHANGE. FLIGHT 1313 WILL NOW DEPART FROM GATE B2.
THERE HAS BEEN A GATE CHANGE. FLIGHT 1313 WILL NOW DEPART FROM GATE D496.
THERE'S A GENTLEMAN WHO WANTS TO KNOW IF WE GIVE FREQUENT-FLIER POINTS FOR MILES TRAVELED IN THE AIRPORT.
CORRECTION: Z496.
AAAA!
BOARDING AT 705
AMEND

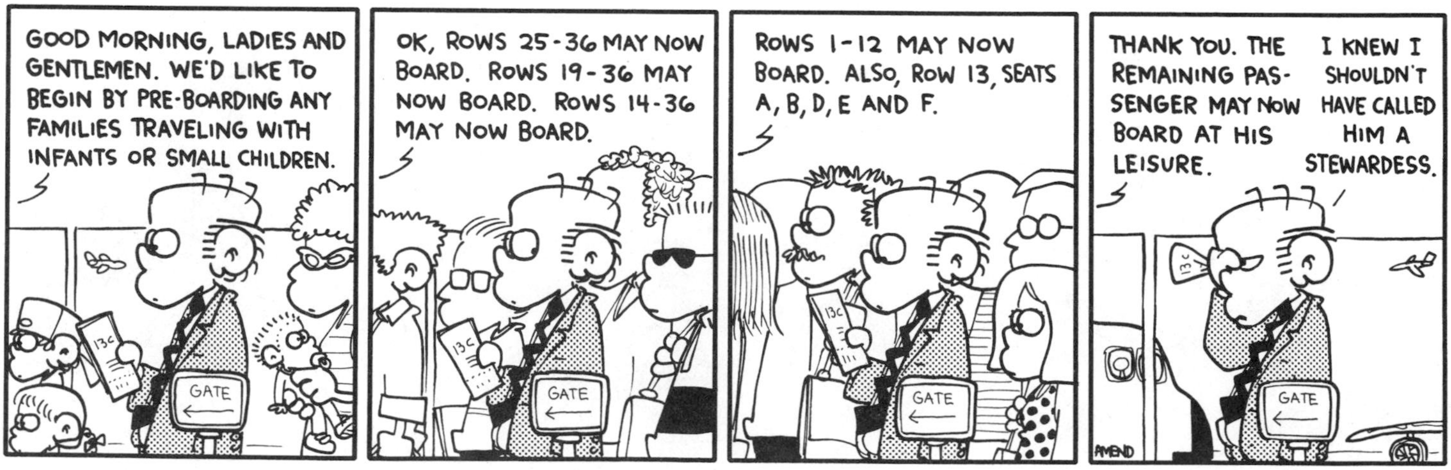
GOOD MORNING, LADIES AND GENTLEMEN. WE'D LIKE TO BEGIN BY PRE-BOARDING ANY FAMILIES TRAVELING WITH INFANTS OR SMALL CHILDREN.
13C
GATE
OK, ROWS 25-36 MAY NOW BOARD. ROWS 19-36 MAY NOW BOARD. ROWS 14-36 MAY NOW BOARD.
13C
GATE
ROWS 1-12 MAY NOW BOARD. ALSO, ROW 13, SEATS A, B, D, E AND F.
13C
GATE
THANK YOU. THE REMAINING PASSENGER MAY NOW BOARD AT HIS LEISURE.
I KNEW I SHOULDN'T HAVE CALLED HIM A STEWARDESS.
13C
GATE
AMEND

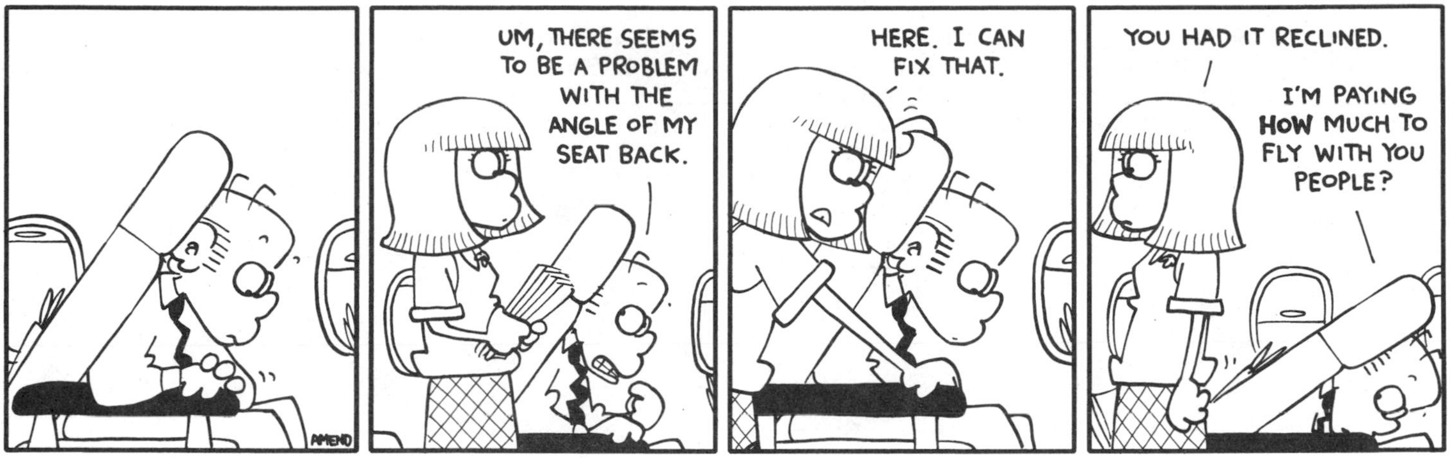
UM, THERE SEEMS TO BE A PROBLEM WITH THE ANGLE OF MY SEAT BACK.
HERE. I CAN FIX THAT.
YOU HAD IT RECLINED.
I'M PAYING **HOW** MUCH TO FLY WITH YOU PEOPLE?

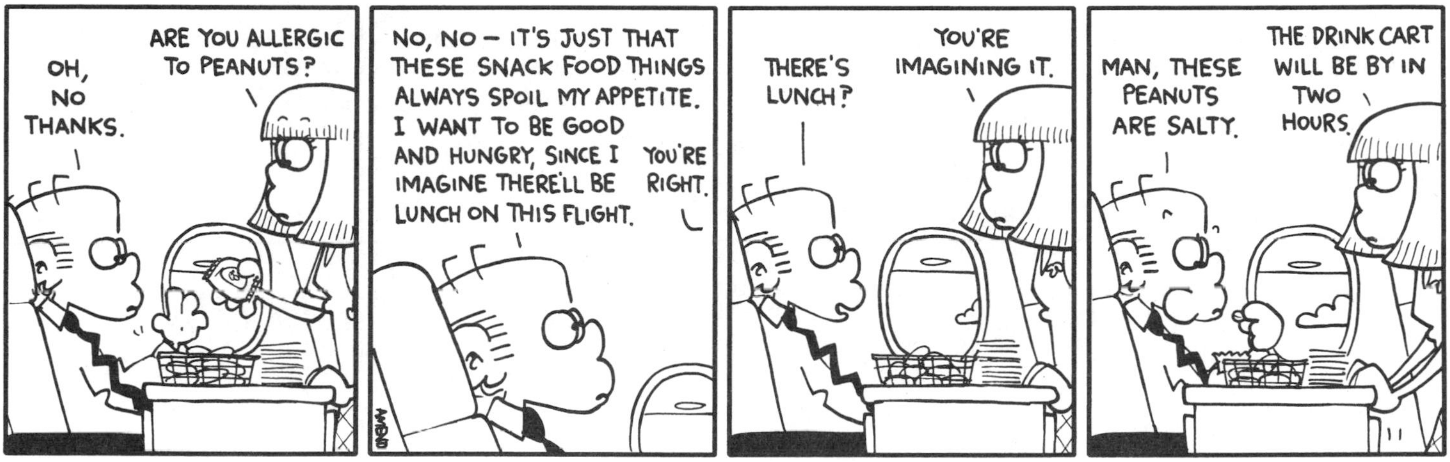
ARE YOU ALLERGIC TO PEANUTS?
OH, NO THANKS.
NO, NO – IT'S JUST THAT THESE SNACK FOOD THINGS ALWAYS SPOIL MY APPETITE. I WANT TO BE GOOD AND HUNGRY, SINCE I IMAGINE THERE'LL BE LUNCH ON THIS FLIGHT.
YOU'RE RIGHT.
THERE'S LUNCH?
YOU'RE IMAGINING IT.
MAN, THESE PEANUTS ARE SALTY.
THE DRINK CART WILL BE BY IN TWO HOURS.

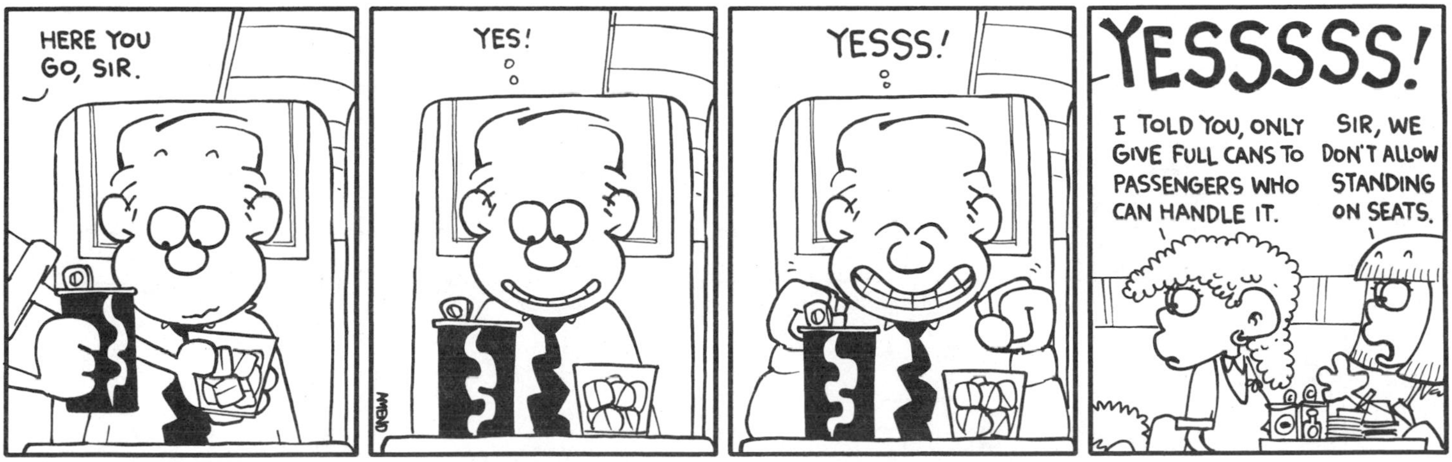
HERE YOU GO, SIR.
YES!
YESSS!
YESSSSS!
I TOLD YOU, ONLY GIVE FULL CANS TO PASSENGERS WHO CAN HANDLE IT.
SIR, WE DON'T ALLOW STANDING ON SEATS.

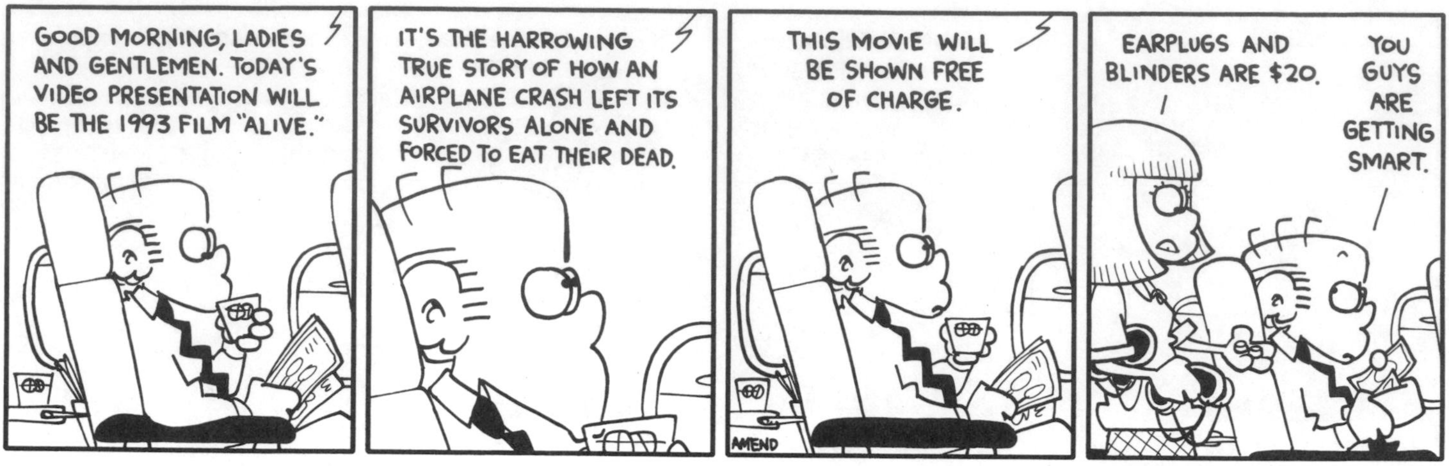
GOOD MORNING, LADIES AND GENTLEMEN. TODAY'S VIDEO PRESENTATION WILL BE THE 1993 FILM "ALIVE."
IT'S THE HARROWING TRUE STORY OF HOW AN AIRPLANE CRASH LEFT ITS SURVIVORS ALONE AND FORCED TO EAT THEIR DEAD.
THIS MOVIE WILL BE SHOWN FREE OF CHARGE.
EARPLUGS AND BLINDERS ARE $20.
YOU GUYS ARE GETTING SMART.

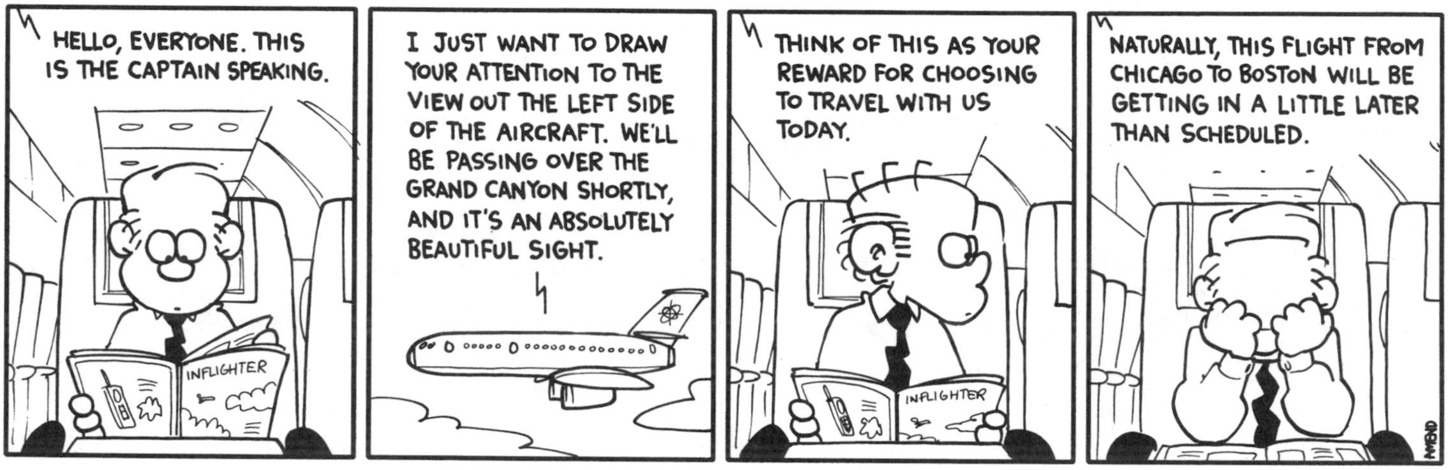
HELLO, EVERYONE. THIS IS THE CAPTAIN SPEAKING.
INFLIGHTER
I JUST WANT TO DRAW YOUR ATTENTION TO THE VIEW OUT THE LEFT SIDE OF THE AIRCRAFT. WE'LL BE PASSING OVER THE GRAND CANYON SHORTLY, AND IT'S AN ABSOLUTELY BEAUTIFUL SIGHT.
THINK OF THIS AS YOUR REWARD FOR CHOOSING TO TRAVEL WITH US TODAY.
INFLIGHTER
NATURALLY, THIS FLIGHT FROM CHICAGO TO BOSTON WILL BE GETTING IN A LITTLE LATER THAN SCHEDULED.

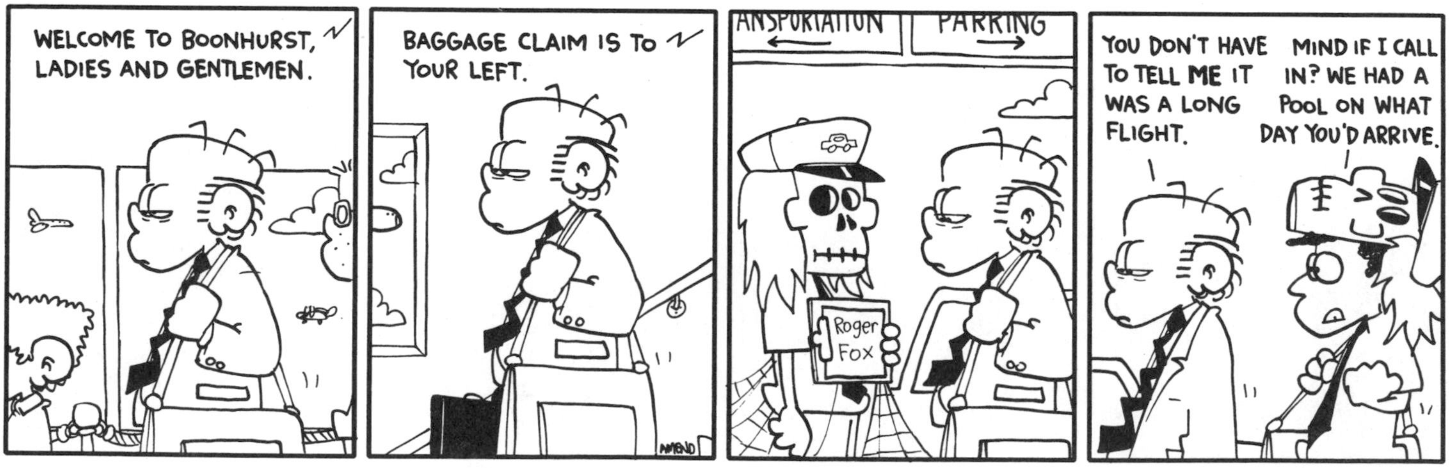
WELCOME TO BOONHURST, LADIES AND GENTLEMEN.
BAGGAGE CLAIM IS TO YOUR LEFT.
PARKING
Roger Fox
YOU DON'T HAVE TO TELL ME IT WAS A LONG FLIGHT.
MIND IF I CALL IN? WE HAD A POOL ON WHAT DAY YOU'D ARRIVE.

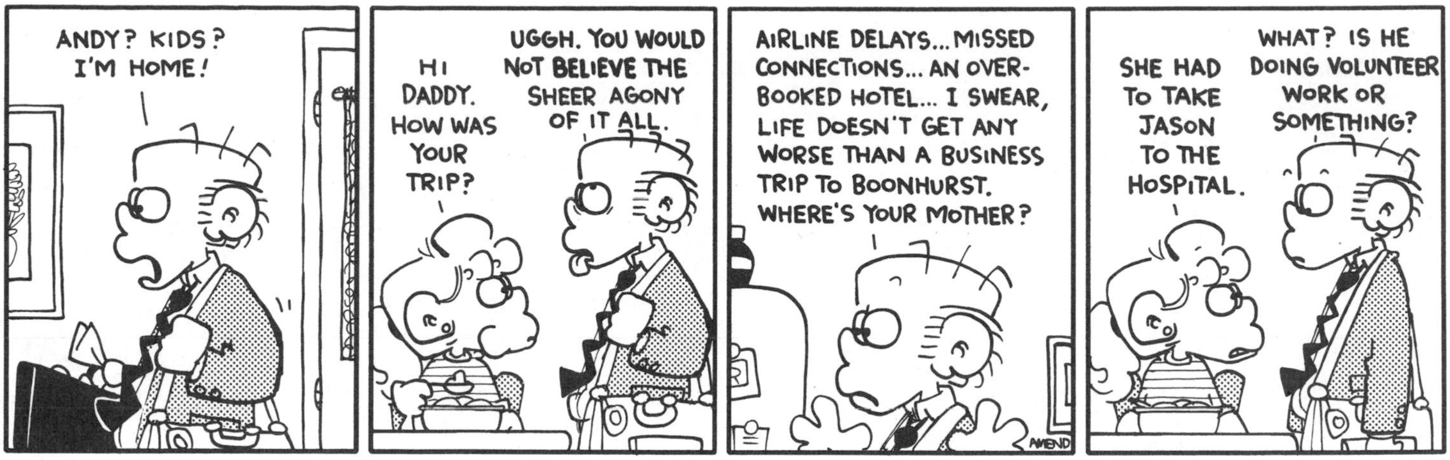
ANDY? KIDS? I'M HOME!
HI DADDY. HOW WAS YOUR TRIP?
UGGH. YOU WOULD NOT BELIEVE THE SHEER AGONY OF IT ALL.
AIRLINE DELAYS... MISSED CONNECTIONS... AN OVER-BOOKED HOTEL... I SWEAR, LIFE DOESN'T GET ANY WORSE THAN A BUSINESS TRIP TO BOONHURST. WHERE'S YOUR MOTHER?
SHE HAD TO TAKE JASON TO THE HOSPITAL.
WHAT? IS HE DOING VOLUNTEER WORK OR SOMETHING?
AMEND

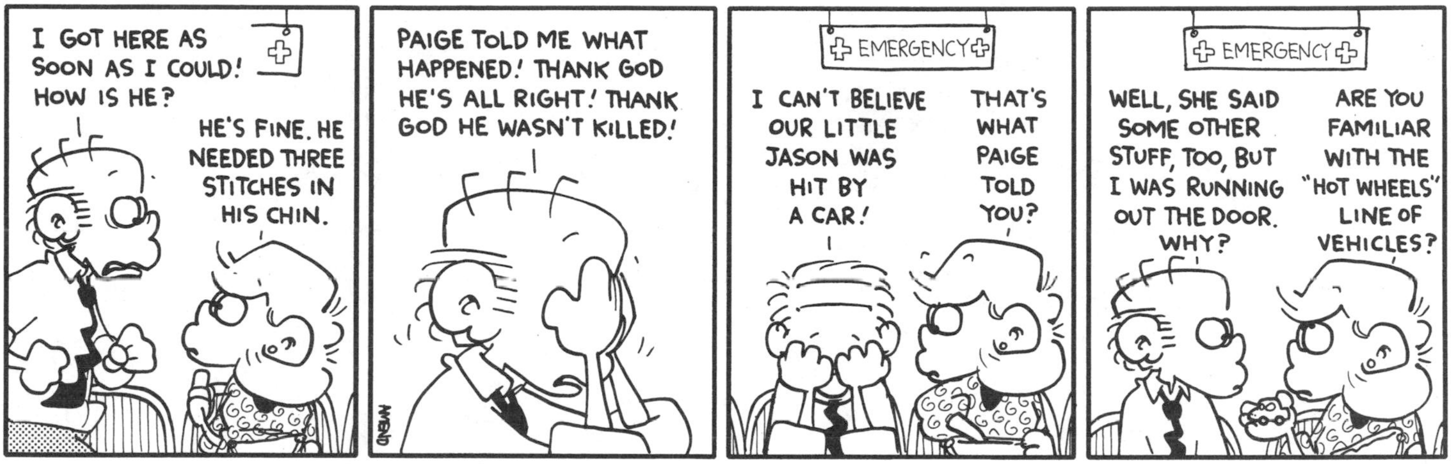
I GOT HERE AS SOON AS I COULD! HOW IS HE?
HE'S FINE. HE NEEDED THREE STITCHES IN HIS CHIN.
PAIGE TOLD ME WHAT HAPPENED! THANK GOD HE'S ALL RIGHT! THANK GOD HE WASN'T KILLED!
AMEND
EMERGENCY
I CAN'T BELIEVE OUR LITTLE JASON WAS HIT BY A CAR!
THAT'S WHAT PAIGE TOLD YOU?
EMERGENCY
WELL, SHE SAID SOME OTHER STUFF, TOO, BUT I WAS RUNNING OUT THE DOOR. WHY?
ARE YOU FAMILIAR WITH THE "HOT WHEELS" LINE OF VEHICLES?

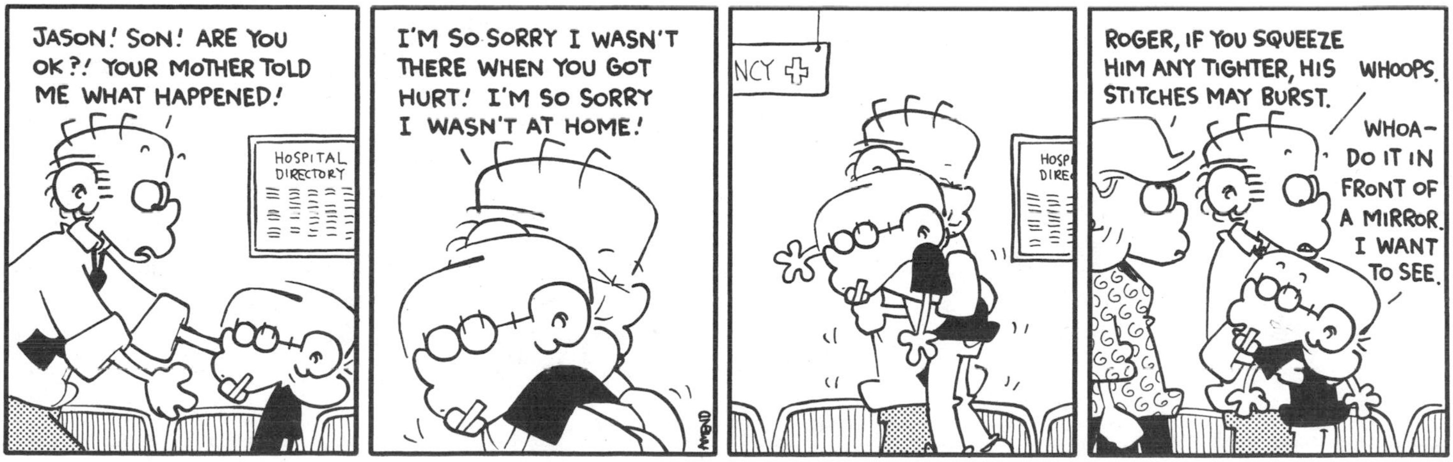
JASON! SON! ARE YOU OK?! YOUR MOTHER TOLD ME WHAT HAPPENED!
HOSPITAL DIRECTORY
I'M SO SORRY I WASN'T THERE WHEN YOU GOT HURT! I'M SO SORRY I WASN'T AT HOME!
AMEND
NCY
ROGER, IF YOU SQUEEZE HIM ANY TIGHTER, HIS STITCHES MAY BURST.
WHOOPS.
WHOA- DO IT IN FRONT OF A MIRROR. I WANT TO SEE.

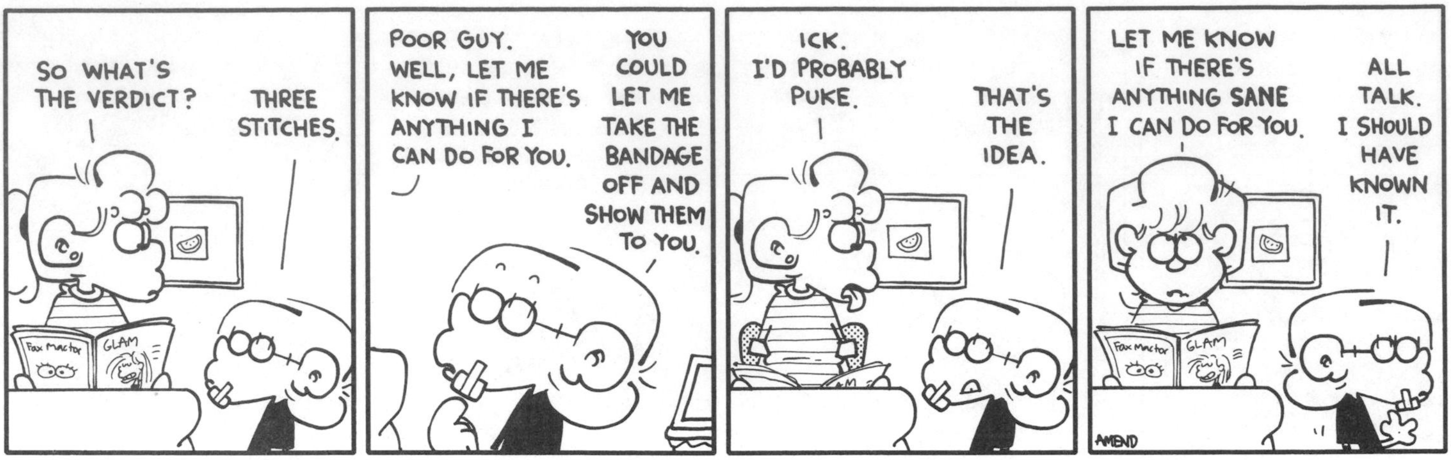
SO WHAT'S THE VERDICT?
THREE STITCHES.
Fax Mactor
GLAM
POOR GUY. WELL, LET ME KNOW IF THERE'S ANYTHING I CAN DO FOR YOU.
YOU COULD LET ME TAKE THE BANDAGE OFF AND SHOW THEM TO YOU.
ICK. I'D PROBABLY PUKE.
THAT'S THE IDEA.
LET ME KNOW IF THERE'S ANYTHING **SANE** I CAN DO FOR YOU.
ALL TALK. I SHOULD HAVE KNOWN IT.
AMEND

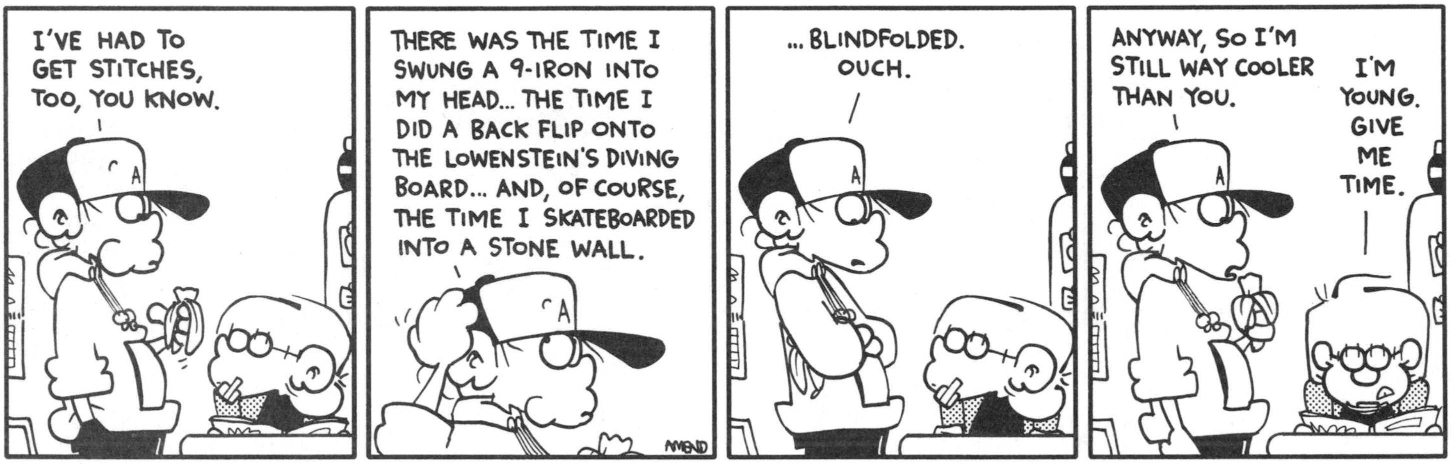
I'VE HAD TO GET STITCHES, TOO, YOU KNOW.
THERE WAS THE TIME I SWUNG A 9-IRON INTO MY HEAD... THE TIME I DID A BACK FLIP ONTO THE LOWENSTEIN'S DIVING BOARD... AND, OF COURSE, THE TIME I SKATEBOARDED INTO A STONE WALL.
AMEND
...BLINDFOLDED. OUCH.
ANYWAY, SO I'M STILL WAY COOLER THAN YOU.
I'M YOUNG. GIVE ME TIME.

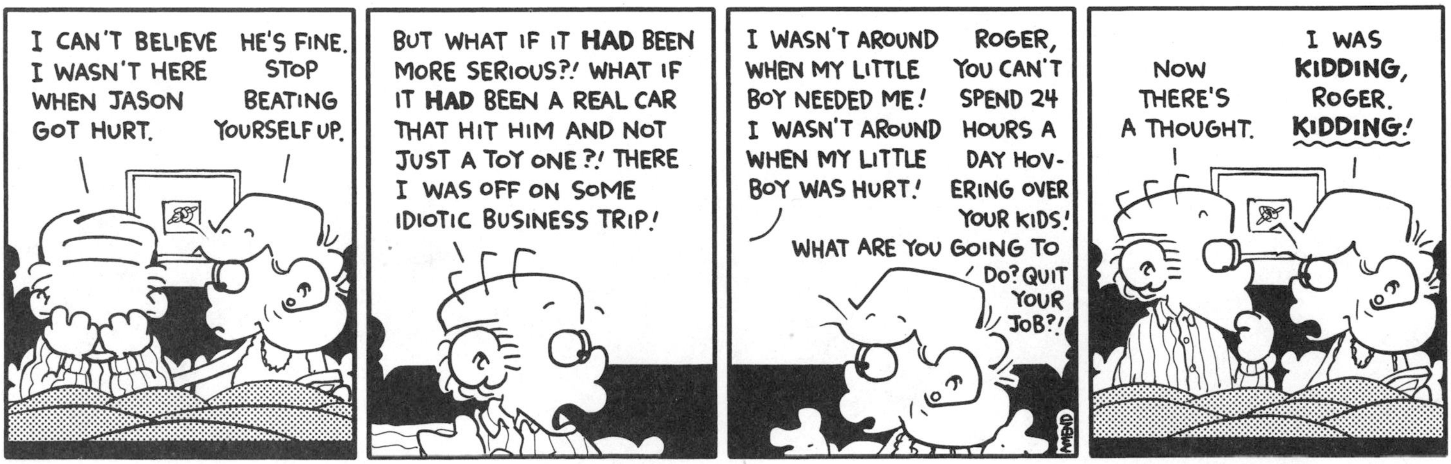
I CAN'T BELIEVE I WASN'T HERE WHEN JASON GOT HURT.
HE'S FINE. STOP BEATING YOURSELF UP.
BUT WHAT IF IT **HAD** BEEN MORE SERIOUS?! WHAT IF IT **HAD** BEEN A REAL CAR THAT HIT HIM AND NOT JUST A TOY ONE?! THERE I WAS OFF ON SOME IDIOTIC BUSINESS TRIP!
I WASN'T AROUND WHEN MY LITTLE BOY NEEDED ME! I WASN'T AROUND WHEN MY LITTLE BOY WAS HURT!
ROGER, YOU CAN'T SPEND 24 HOURS A DAY HOVERING OVER YOUR KIDS!
WHAT ARE YOU GOING TO DO? QUIT YOUR JOB?!
AMEND
NOW THERE'S A THOUGHT.
I WAS **KIDDING**, ROGER. **KIDDING**!

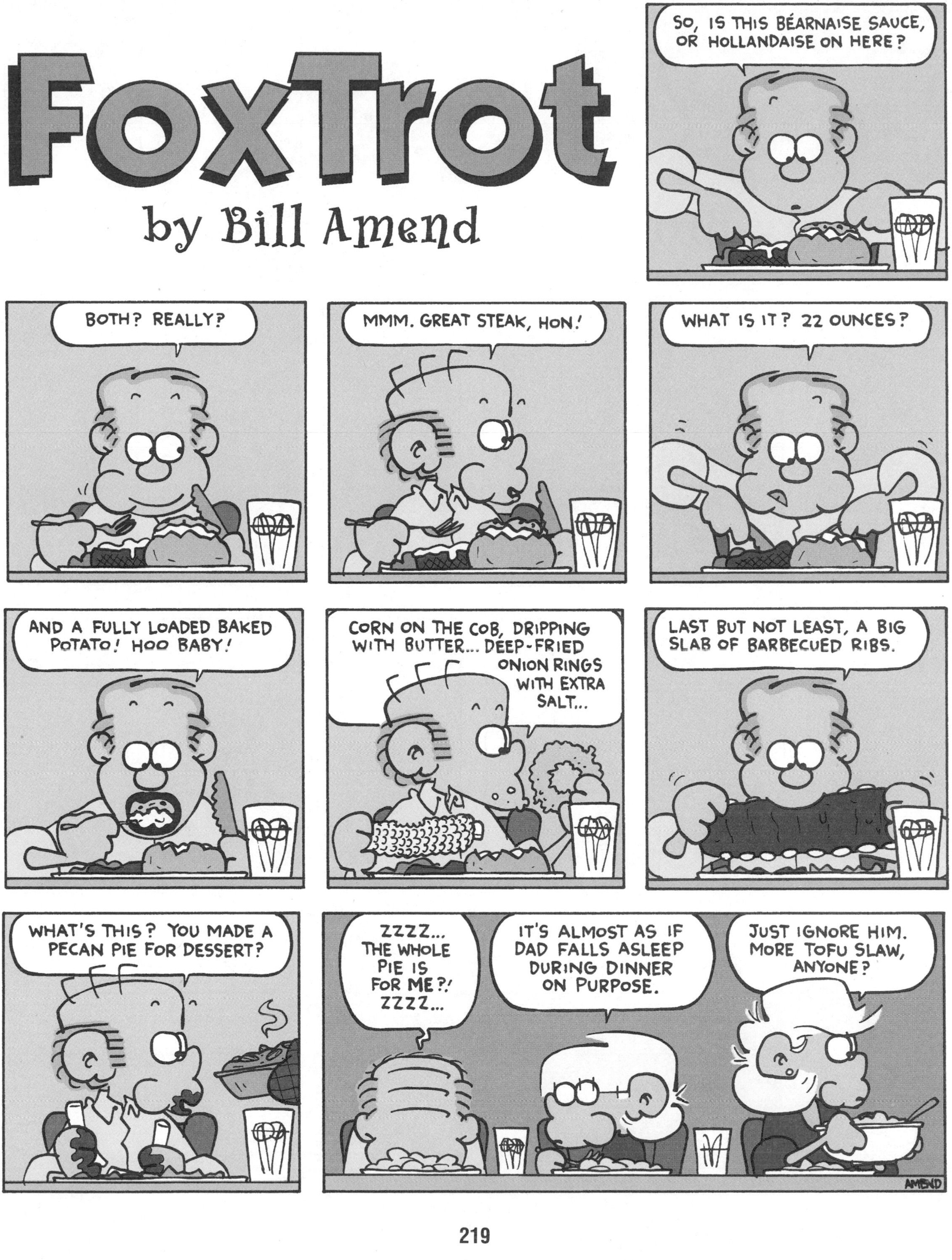
FoxTrot
by Bill Amend
SO, IS THIS BÉARNAISE SAUCE, OR HOLLANDAISE ON HERE?
BOTH? REALLY?
MMM. GREAT STEAK, HON!
WHAT IS IT? 22 OUNCES?
AND A FULLY LOADED BAKED POTATO! HOO BABY!
CORN ON THE COB, DRIPPING WITH BUTTER... DEEP-FRIED ONION RINGS WITH EXTRA SALT...
LAST BUT NOT LEAST, A BIG SLAB OF BARBECUED RIBS.
WHAT'S THIS? YOU MADE A PECAN PIE FOR DESSERT?
ZZZZ... THE WHOLE PIE IS FOR ME?! ZZZZ...
IT'S ALMOST AS IF DAD FALLS ASLEEP DURING DINNER ON PURPOSE.
JUST IGNORE HIM. MORE TOFU SLAW, ANYONE?
AMEND

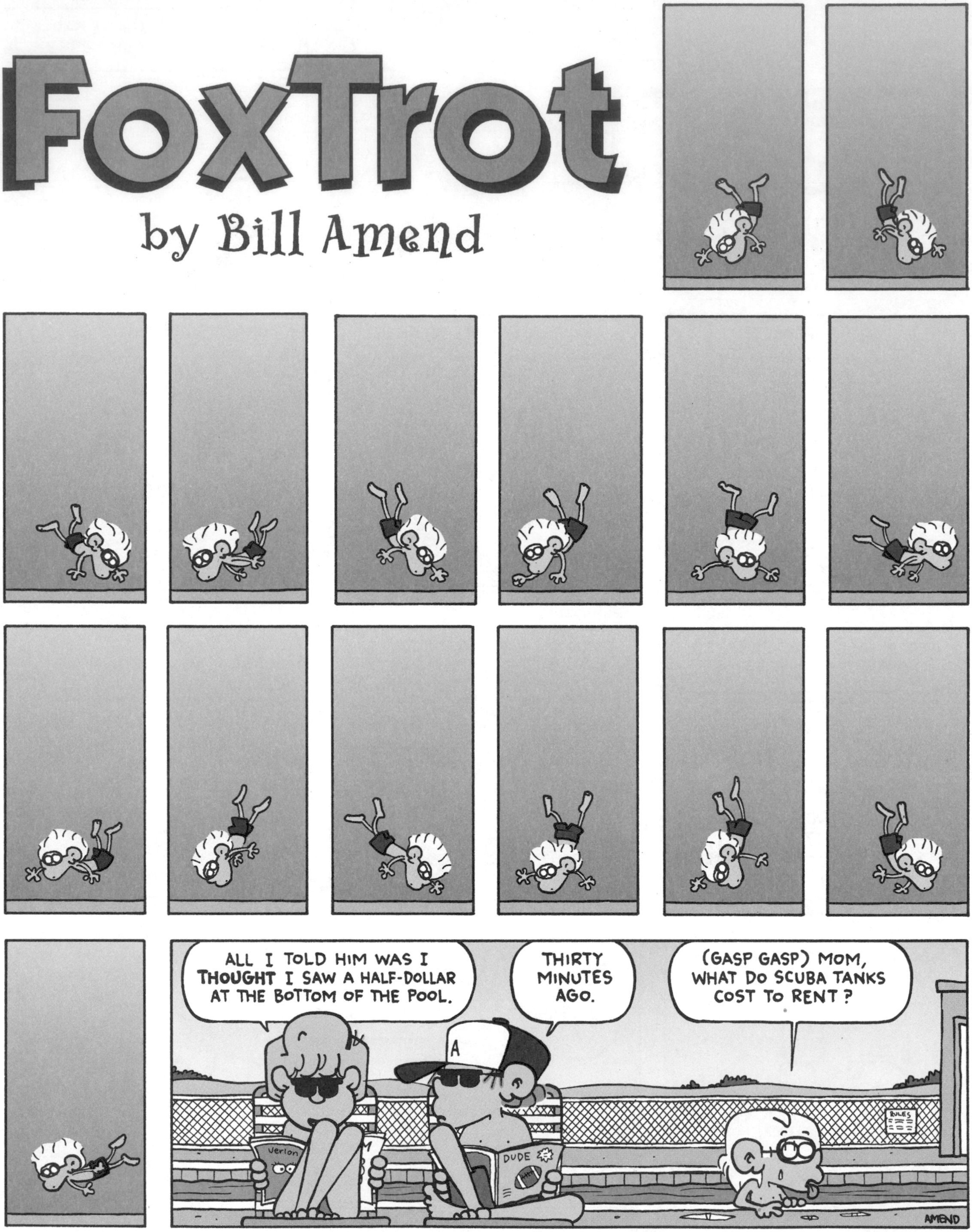
FoxTrot
by Bill Amend
ALL I TOLD HIM WAS I THOUGHT I SAW A HALF-DOLLAR AT THE BOTTOM OF THE POOL.
THIRTY MINUTES AGO.
(GASP GASP) MOM, WHAT DO SCUBA TANKS COST TO RENT?
DUDE
AMEND

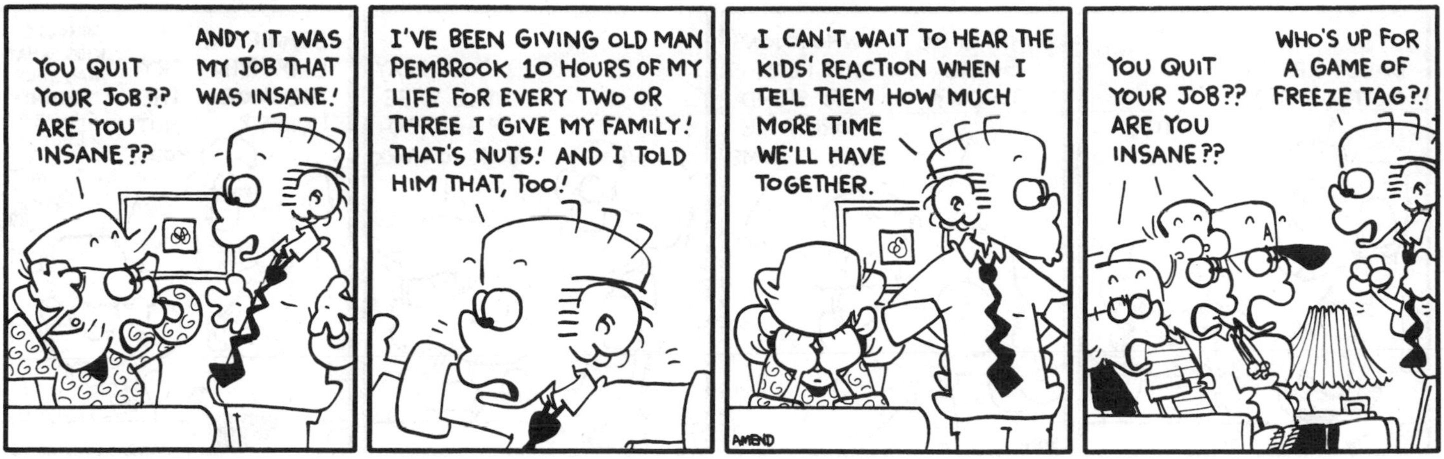
YOU QUIT YOUR JOB?? ARE YOU INSANE??
ANDY, IT WAS MY JOB THAT WAS INSANE!
I'VE BEEN GIVING OLD MAN PEMBROOK 10 HOURS OF MY LIFE FOR EVERY TWO OR THREE I GIVE MY FAMILY! THAT'S NUTS! AND I TOLD HIM THAT, TOO!
I CAN'T WAIT TO HEAR THE KIDS' REACTION WHEN I TELL THEM HOW MUCH MORE TIME WE'LL HAVE TOGETHER.
AMEND
YOU QUIT YOUR JOB?? ARE YOU INSANE??
WHO'S UP FOR A GAME OF FREEZE TAG?!

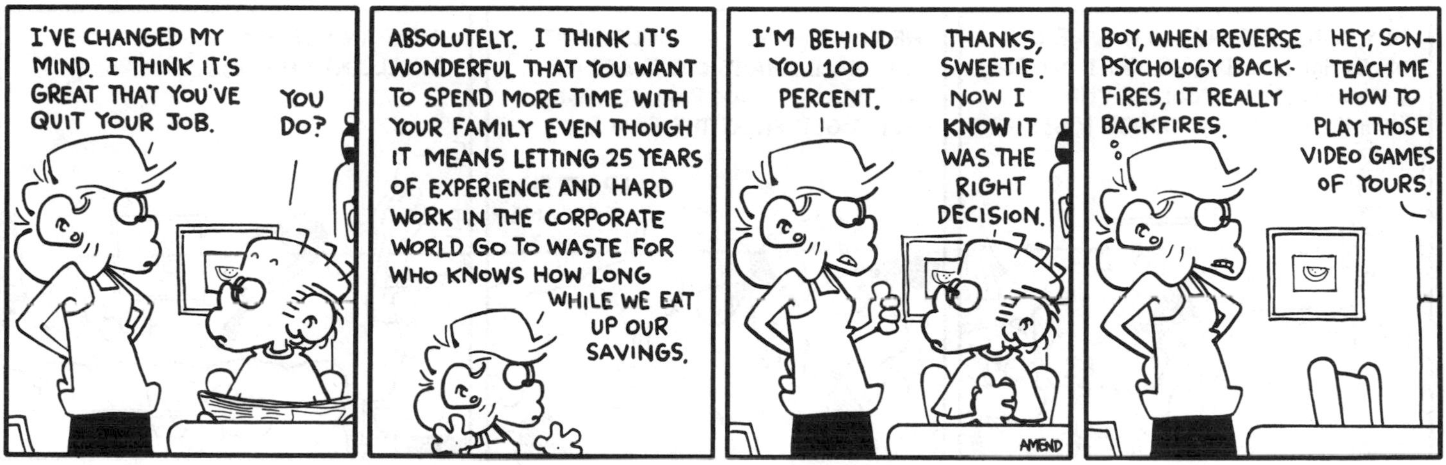
I'VE CHANGED MY MIND. I THINK IT'S GREAT THAT YOU'VE QUIT YOUR JOB.
YOU DO?
ABSOLUTELY. I THINK IT'S WONDERFUL THAT YOU WANT TO SPEND MORE TIME WITH YOUR FAMILY EVEN THOUGH IT MEANS LETTING 25 YEARS OF EXPERIENCE AND HARD WORK IN THE CORPORATE WORLD GO TO WASTE FOR WHO KNOWS HOW LONG WHILE WE EAT UP OUR SAVINGS.
I'M BEHIND YOU 100 PERCENT.
THANKS, SWEETIE. NOW I KNOW IT WAS THE RIGHT DECISION.
AMEND
BOY, WHEN REVERSE PSYCHOLOGY BACKFIRES, IT REALLY BACKFIRES.
HEY, SON–TEACH ME HOW TO PLAY THOSE VIDEO GAMES OF YOURS.

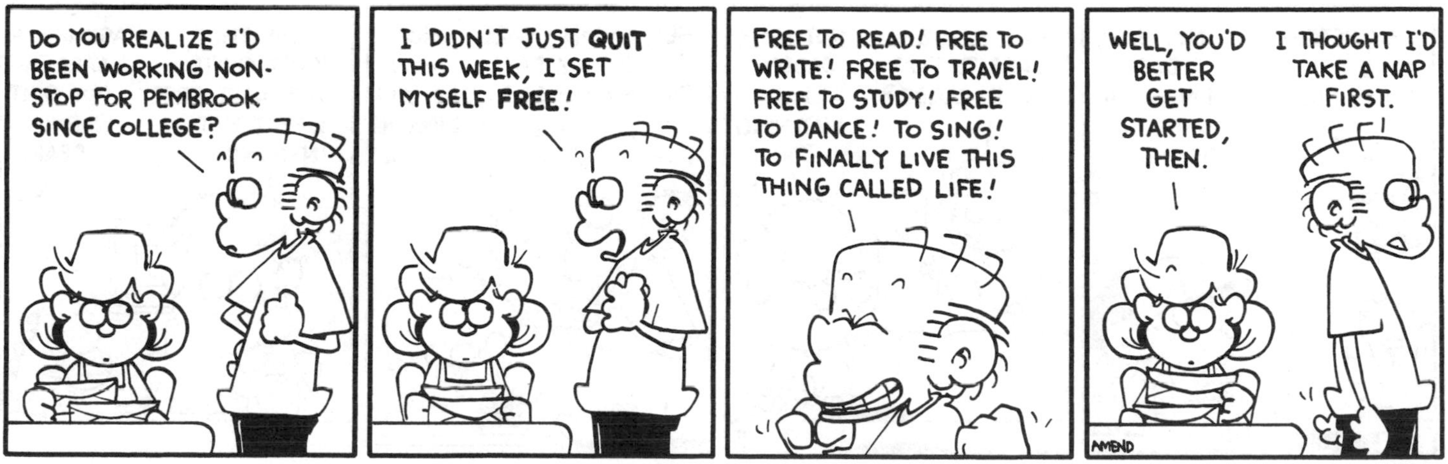
DO YOU REALIZE I'D BEEN WORKING NON-STOP FOR PEMBROOK SINCE COLLEGE?
I DIDN'T JUST QUIT THIS WEEK, I SET MYSELF FREE!
FREE TO READ! FREE TO WRITE! FREE TO TRAVEL! FREE TO STUDY! FREE TO DANCE! TO SING! TO FINALLY LIVE THIS THING CALLED LIFE!
WELL, YOU'D BETTER GET STARTED, THEN.
I THOUGHT I'D TAKE A NAP FIRST.
AMEND

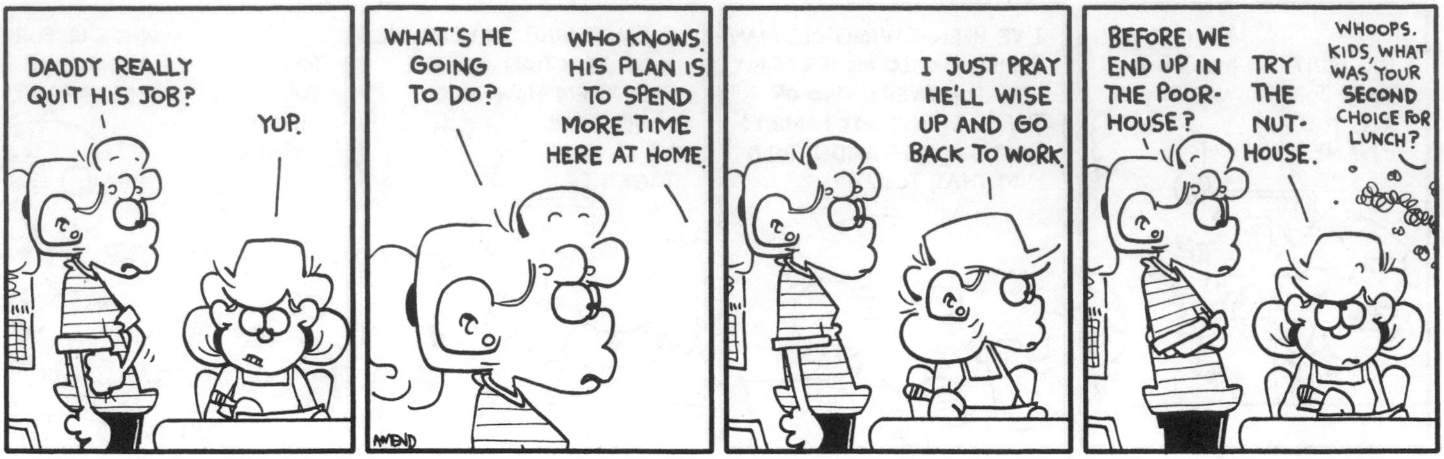
DADDY REALLY QUIT HIS JOB?
YUP.
WHAT'S HE GOING TO DO?
WHO KNOWS. HIS PLAN IS TO SPEND MORE TIME HERE AT HOME.
I JUST PRAY HE'LL WISE UP AND GO BACK TO WORK.
BEFORE WE END UP IN THE POOR-HOUSE?
TRY THE NUT-HOUSE.
WHOOPS. KIDS, WHAT WAS YOUR SECOND CHOICE FOR LUNCH?
AMEND

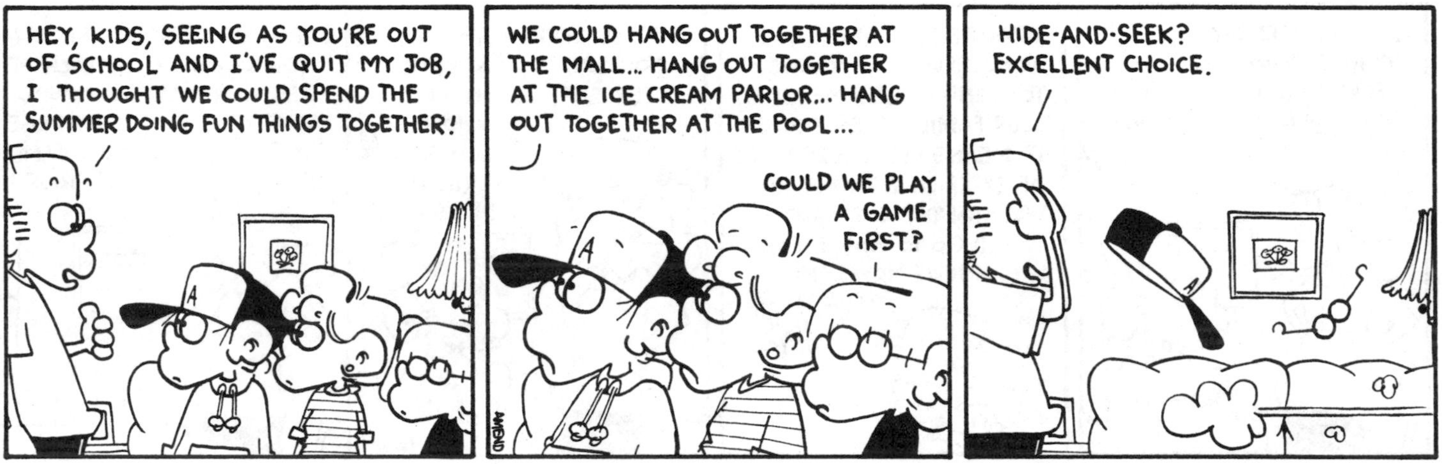
HEY, KIDS, SEEING AS YOU'RE OUT OF SCHOOL AND I'VE QUIT MY JOB, I THOUGHT WE COULD SPEND THE SUMMER DOING FUN THINGS TOGETHER!
WE COULD HANG OUT TOGETHER AT THE MALL... HANG OUT TOGETHER AT THE ICE CREAM PARLOR... HANG OUT TOGETHER AT THE POOL...
COULD WE PLAY A GAME FIRST?
HIDE-AND-SEEK? EXCELLENT CHOICE.

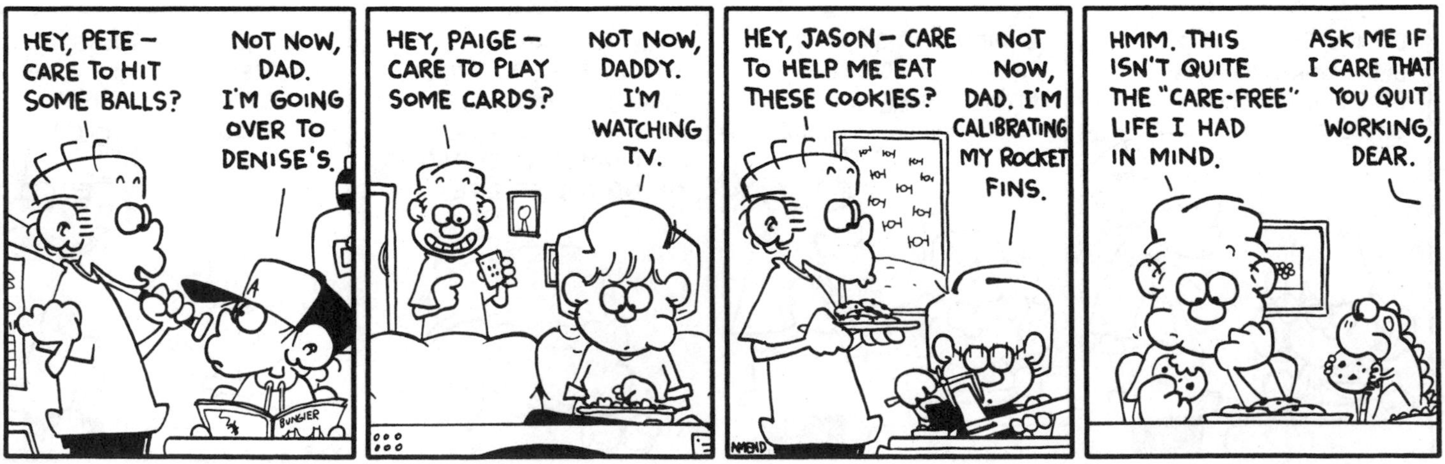
HEY, PETE – CARE TO HIT SOME BALLS?
NOT NOW, DAD. I'M GOING OVER TO DENISE'S.
BUNGIER
HEY, PAIGE – CARE TO PLAY SOME CARDS?
NOT NOW, DADDY. I'M WATCHING TV.
HEY, JASON – CARE TO HELP ME EAT THESE COOKIES?
NOT NOW, DAD. I'M CALIBRATING MY ROCKET FINS.
AMEND
HMM. THIS ISN'T QUITE THE "CARE-FREE" LIFE I HAD IN MIND.
ASK ME IF I CARE THAT YOU QUIT WORKING, DEAR.

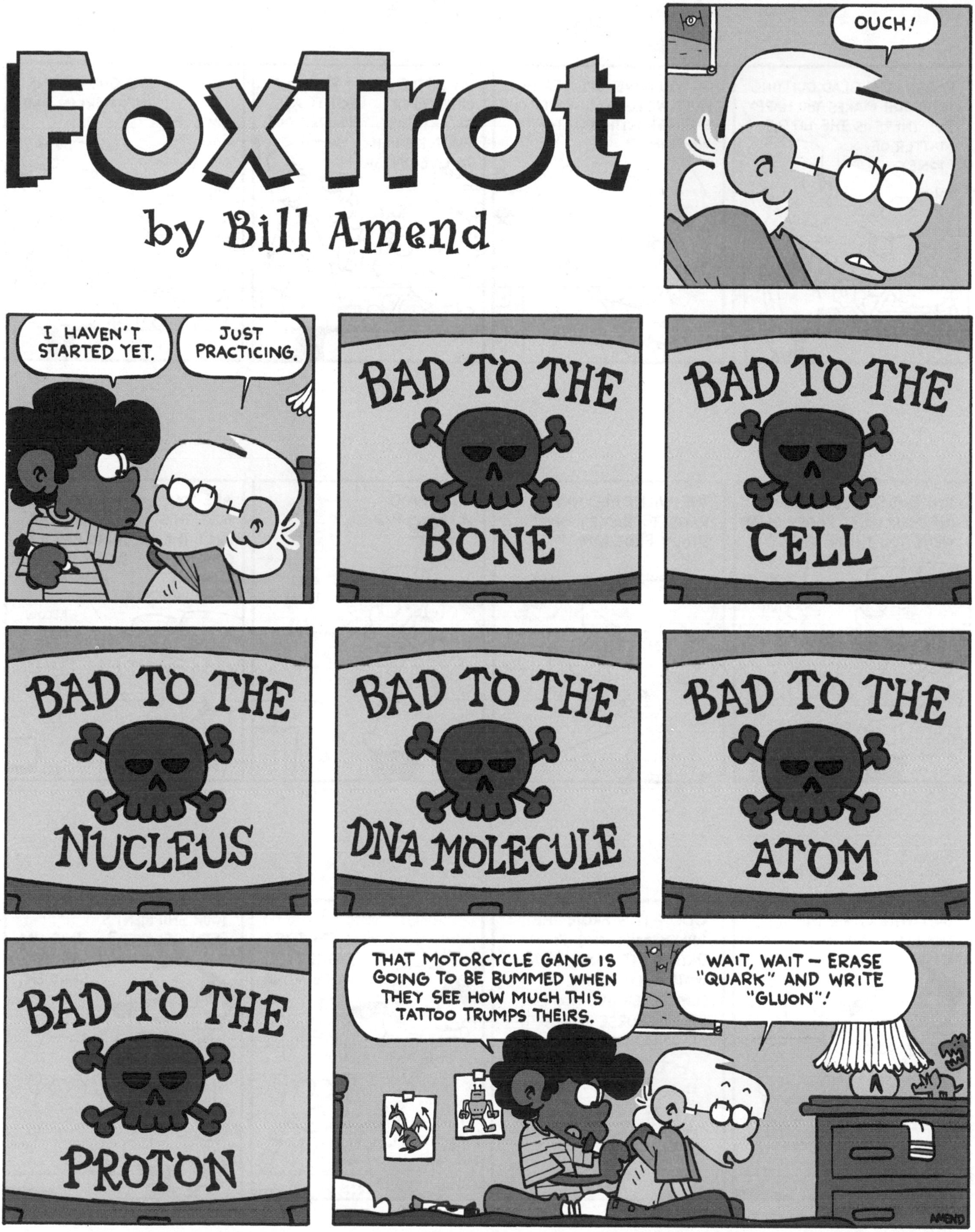
FoxTrot
by Bill Amend
OUCH!
I HAVEN'T STARTED YET.
JUST PRACTICING.
BAD TO THE BONE
BAD TO THE CELL
BAD TO THE NUCLEUS
BAD TO THE DNA MOLECULE
BAD TO THE ATOM
BAD TO THE PROTON
THAT MOTORCYCLE GANG IS GOING TO BE BUMMED WHEN THEY SEE HOW MUCH THIS TATTOO TRUMPS THEIRS.
WAIT, WAIT – ERASE "QUARK" AND WRITE "GLUON"!
AMEND

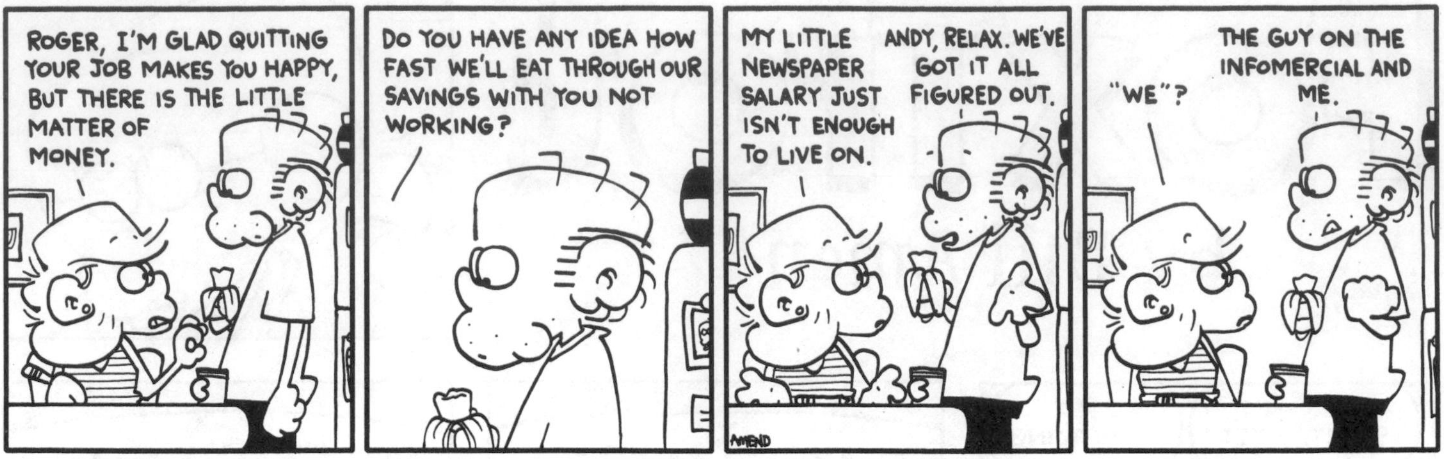
ROGER, I'M GLAD QUITTING YOUR JOB MAKES YOU HAPPY, BUT THERE IS THE LITTLE MATTER OF MONEY.
DO YOU HAVE ANY IDEA HOW FAST WE'LL EAT THROUGH OUR SAVINGS WITH YOU NOT WORKING?
MY LITTLE NEWSPAPER SALARY JUST ISN'T ENOUGH TO LIVE ON.
ANDY, RELAX. WE'VE GOT IT ALL FIGURED OUT.
"WE"?
THE GUY ON THE INFOMERCIAL AND ME.
AMEND

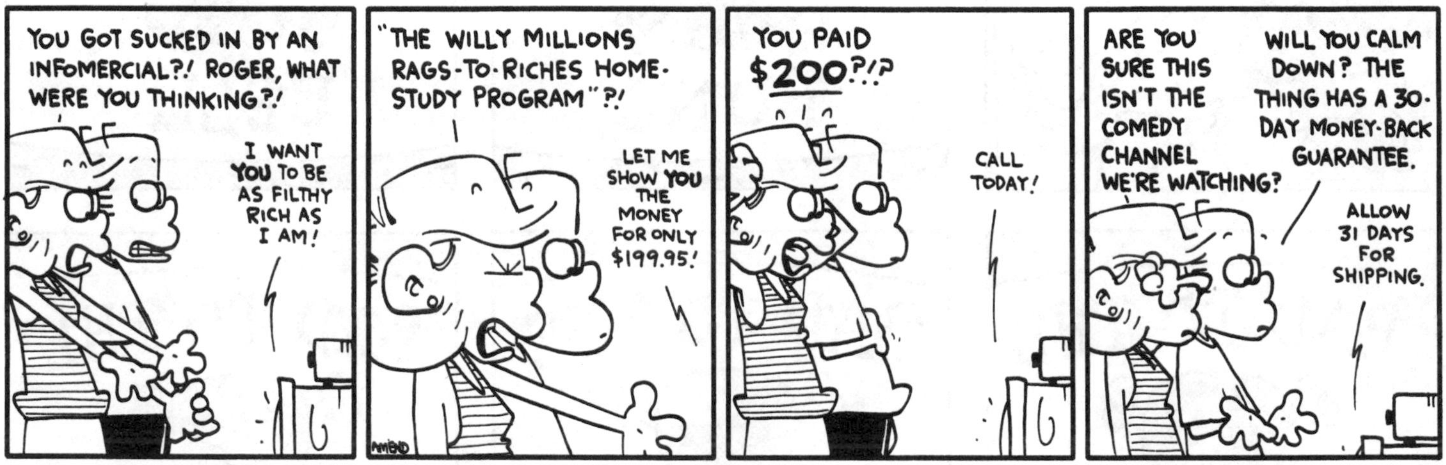
YOU GOT SUCKED IN BY AN INFOMERCIAL?! ROGER, WHAT WERE YOU THINKING?!
I WANT YOU TO BE AS FILTHY RICH AS I AM!
"THE WILLY MILLIONS RAGS-TO-RICHES HOME-STUDY PROGRAM"?!
LET ME SHOW YOU THE MONEY FOR ONLY $199.95!
YOU PAID $200?!?
CALL TODAY!
ARE YOU SURE THIS ISN'T THE COMEDY CHANNEL WE'RE WATCHING?
WILL YOU CALM DOWN? THE THING HAS A 30-DAY MONEY-BACK GUARANTEE.
ALLOW 31 DAYS FOR SHIPPING.
AMEND

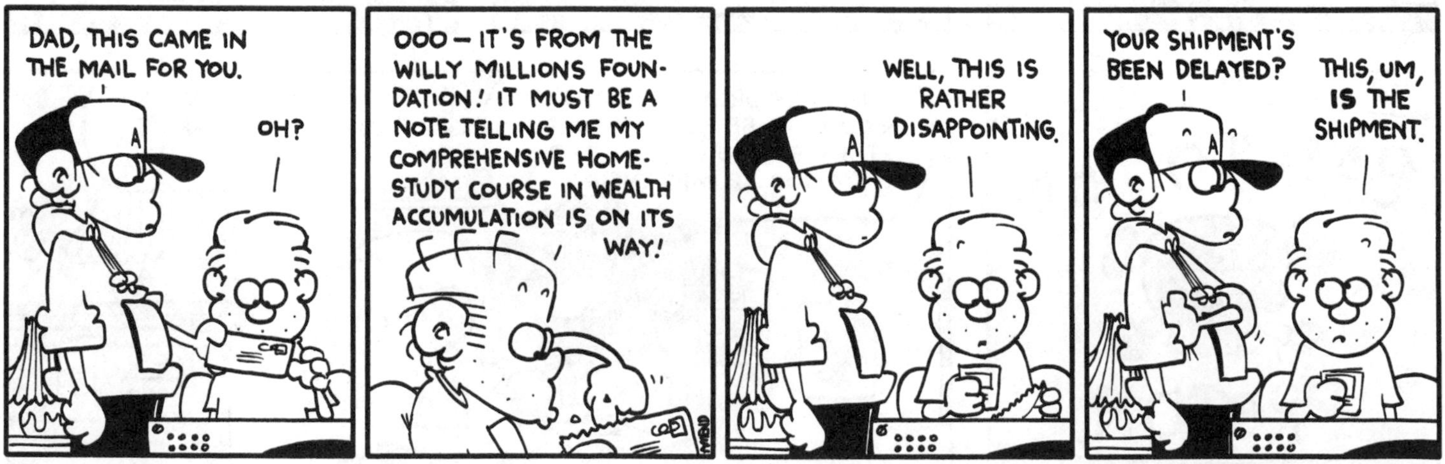
DAD, THIS CAME IN THE MAIL FOR YOU.
OH?
OOO – IT'S FROM THE WILLY MILLIONS FOUNDATION! IT MUST BE A NOTE TELLING ME MY COMPREHENSIVE HOME-STUDY COURSE IN WEALTH ACCUMULATION IS ON ITS WAY!
WELL, THIS IS RATHER DISAPPOINTING.
YOUR SHIPMENT'S BEEN DELAYED?
THIS, UM, IS THE SHIPMENT.
AMEND

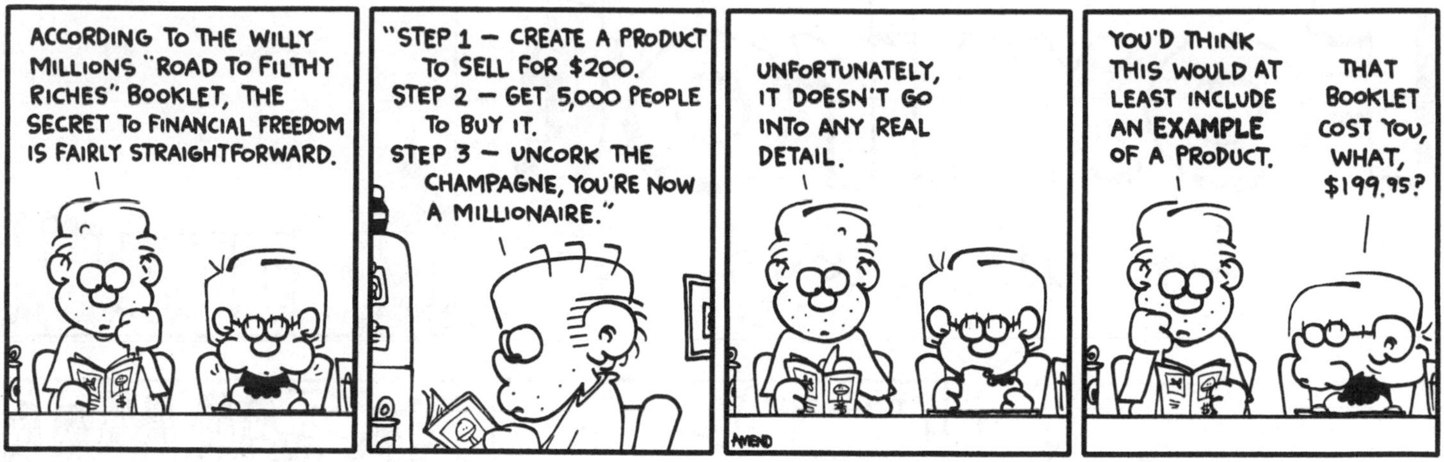
ACCORDING TO THE WILLY MILLIONS "ROAD TO FILTHY RICHES" BOOKLET, THE SECRET TO FINANCIAL FREEDOM IS FAIRLY STRAIGHTFORWARD.
"STEP 1 – CREATE A PRODUCT TO SELL FOR $200. STEP 2 – GET 5,000 PEOPLE TO BUY IT. STEP 3 – UNCORK THE CHAMPAGNE, YOU'RE NOW A MILLIONAIRE."
UNFORTUNATELY, IT DOESN'T GO INTO ANY REAL DETAIL.
YOU'D THINK THIS WOULD AT LEAST INCLUDE AN EXAMPLE OF A PRODUCT.
THAT BOOKLET COST YOU, WHAT, $199.95?
AMEND

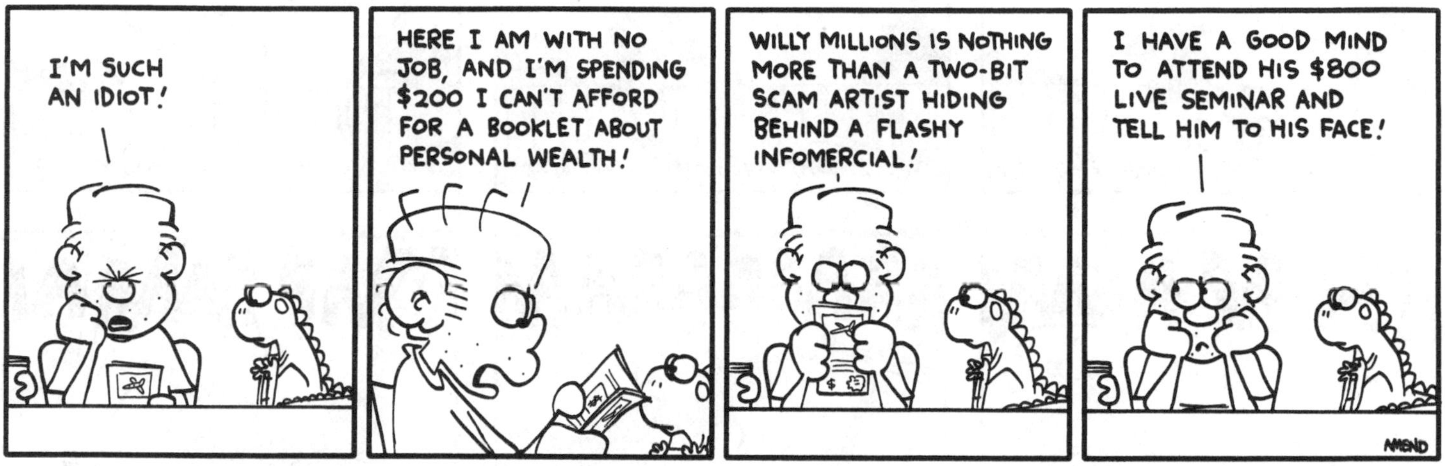
I'M SUCH AN IDIOT!
HERE I AM WITH NO JOB, AND I'M SPENDING $200 I CAN'T AFFORD FOR A BOOKLET ABOUT PERSONAL WEALTH!
WILLY MILLIONS IS NOTHING MORE THAN A TWO-BIT SCAM ARTIST HIDING BEHIND A FLASHY INFOMERCIAL!
I HAVE A GOOD MIND TO ATTEND HIS $800 LIVE SEMINAR AND TELL HIM TO HIS FACE!
AMEND

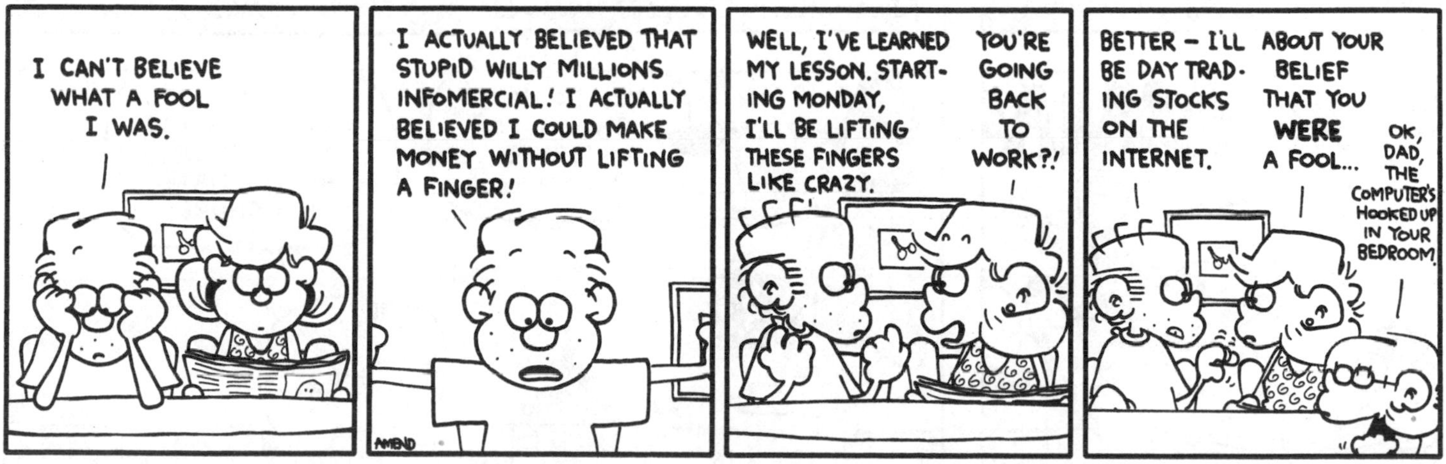
I CAN'T BELIEVE WHAT A FOOL I WAS.
I ACTUALLY BELIEVED THAT STUPID WILLY MILLIONS INFOMERCIAL! I ACTUALLY BELIEVED I COULD MAKE MONEY WITHOUT LIFTING A FINGER!
AMEND
WELL, I'VE LEARNED MY LESSON. STARTING MONDAY, I'LL BE LIFTING THESE FINGERS LIKE CRAZY.
YOU'RE GOING BACK TO WORK?!
BETTER – I'LL BE DAY TRADING STOCKS ON THE INTERNET.
ABOUT YOUR BELIEF THAT YOU WERE A FOOL...
OK, DAD, THE COMPUTER'S HOOKED UP IN YOUR BEDROOM!

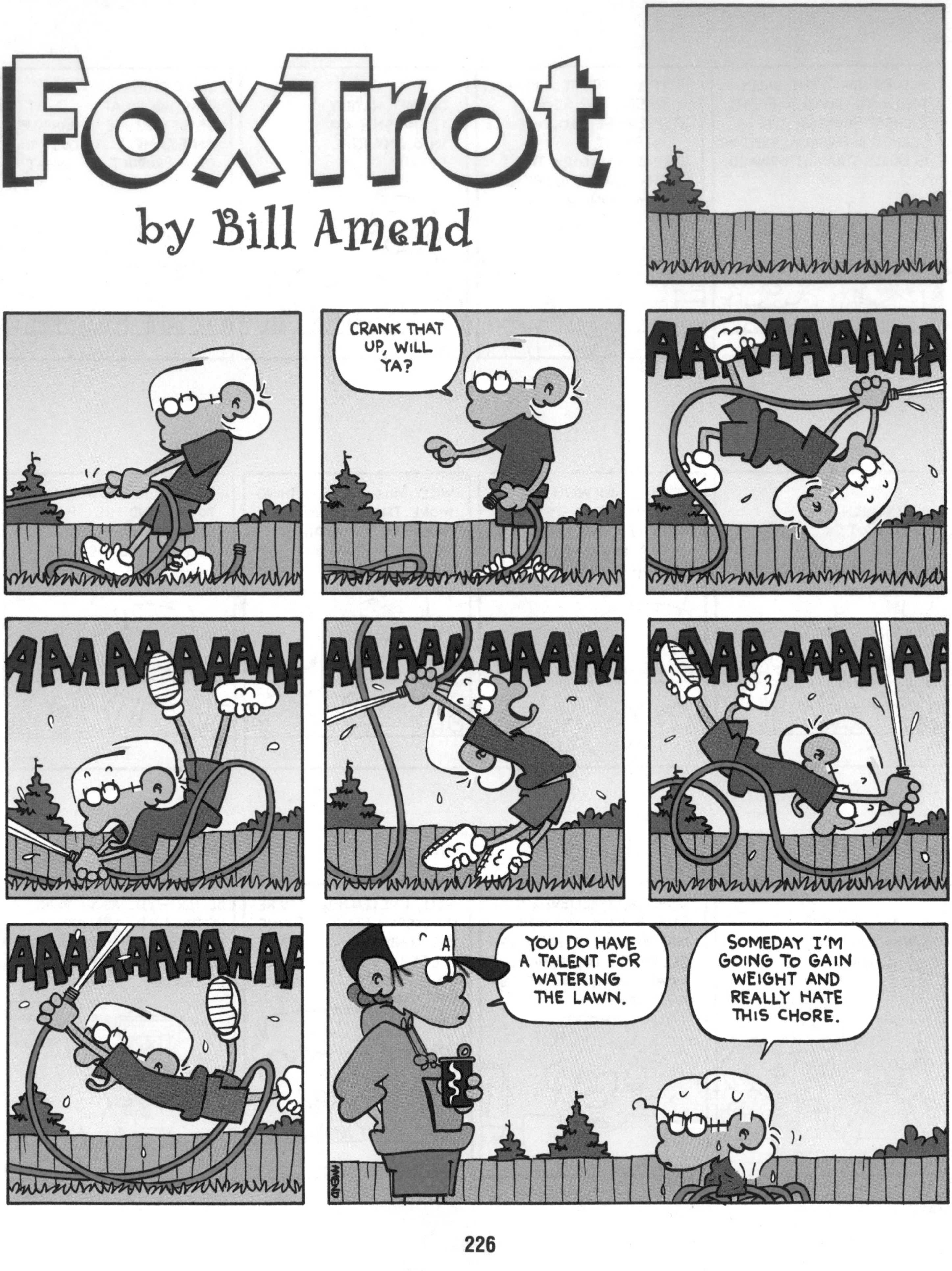
FoxTrot
by Bill Amend
CRANK THAT UP, WILL YA?
YOU DO HAVE A TALENT FOR WATERING THE LAWN.
SOMEDAY I'M GOING TO GAIN WEIGHT AND REALLY HATE THIS CHORE.

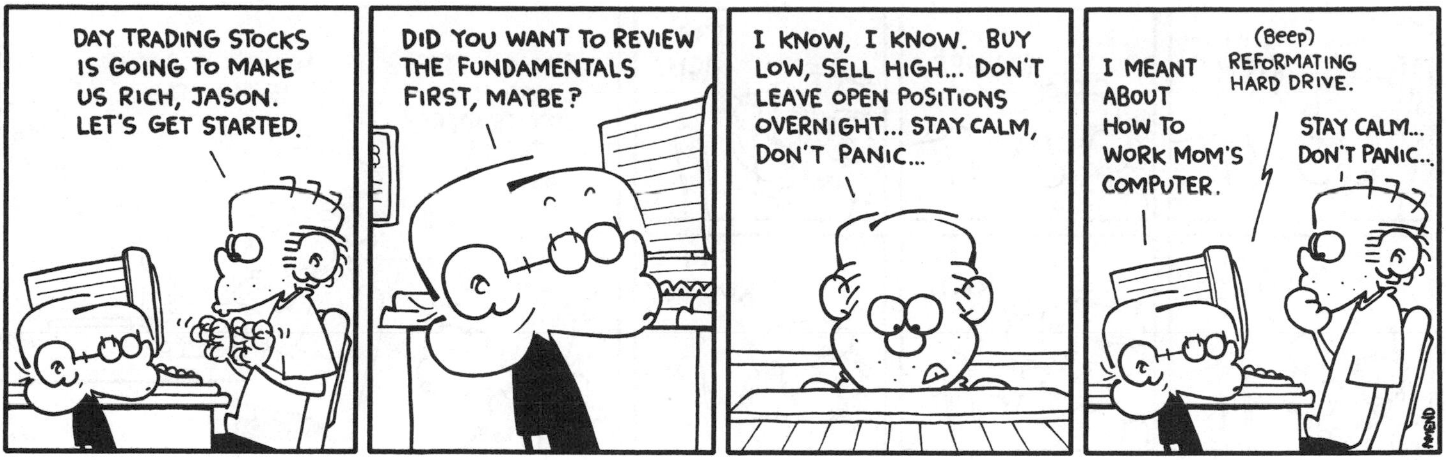
DAY TRADING STOCKS IS GOING TO MAKE US RICH, JASON. LET'S GET STARTED.
DID YOU WANT TO REVIEW THE FUNDAMENTALS FIRST, MAYBE?
I KNOW, I KNOW. BUY LOW, SELL HIGH... DON'T LEAVE OPEN POSITIONS OVERNIGHT... STAY CALM, DON'T PANIC...
I MEANT ABOUT HOW TO WORK MOM'S COMPUTER.
(Beep) REFORMATING HARD DRIVE.
STAY CALM... DON'T PANIC...

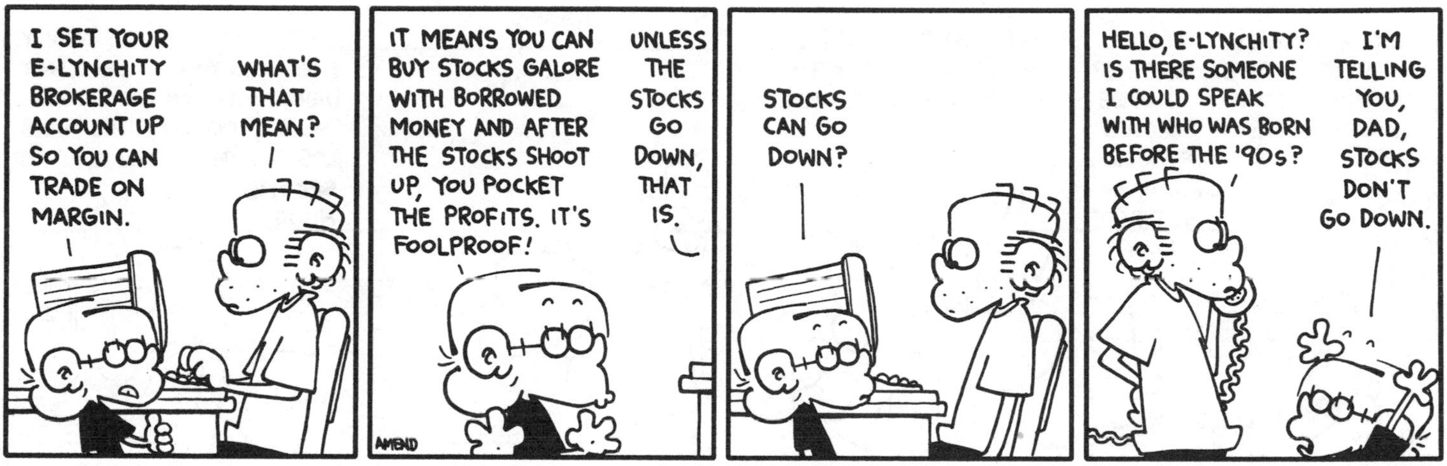
I SET YOUR E-LYNCHITY BROKERAGE ACCOUNT UP SO YOU CAN TRADE ON MARGIN.
WHAT'S THAT MEAN?
IT MEANS YOU CAN BUY STOCKS GALORE WITH BORROWED MONEY AND AFTER THE STOCKS SHOOT UP, YOU POCKET THE PROFITS. IT'S FOOLPROOF!
UNLESS THE STOCKS GO DOWN, THAT IS.
STOCKS CAN GO DOWN?
HELLO, E-LYNCHITY? IS THERE SOMEONE I COULD SPEAK WITH WHO WAS BORN BEFORE THE '90s?
I'M TELLING YOU, DAD, STOCKS DON'T GO DOWN.

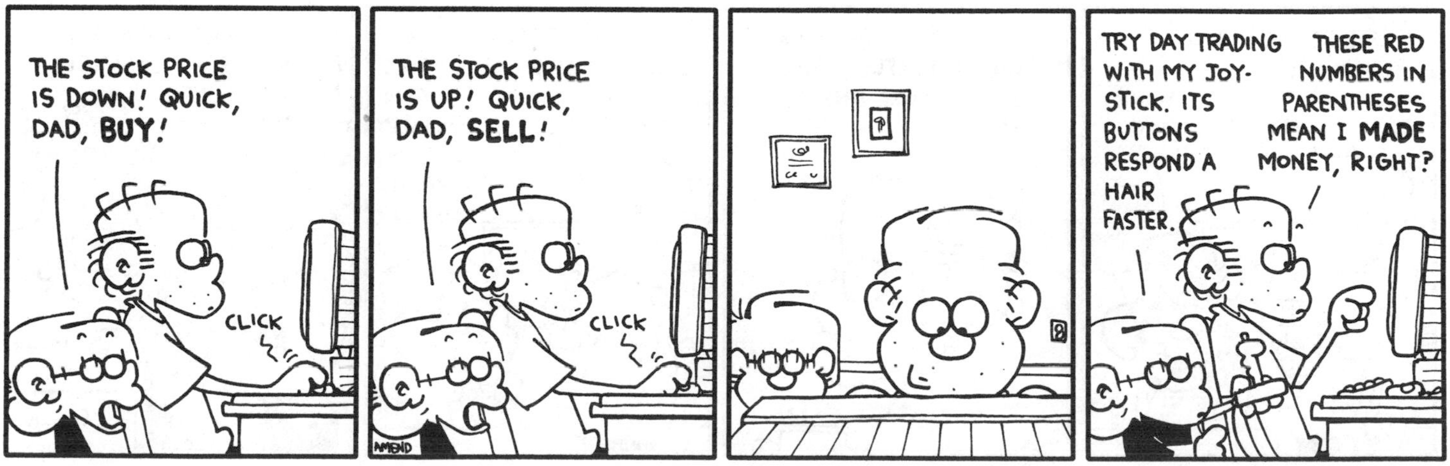
THE STOCK PRICE IS DOWN! QUICK, DAD, BUY!
CLICK
THE STOCK PRICE IS UP! QUICK, DAD, SELL!
CLICK
TRY DAY TRADING WITH MY JOY-STICK. ITS BUTTONS RESPOND A HAIR FASTER.
THESE RED NUMBERS IN PARENTHESES MEAN I MADE MONEY, RIGHT?

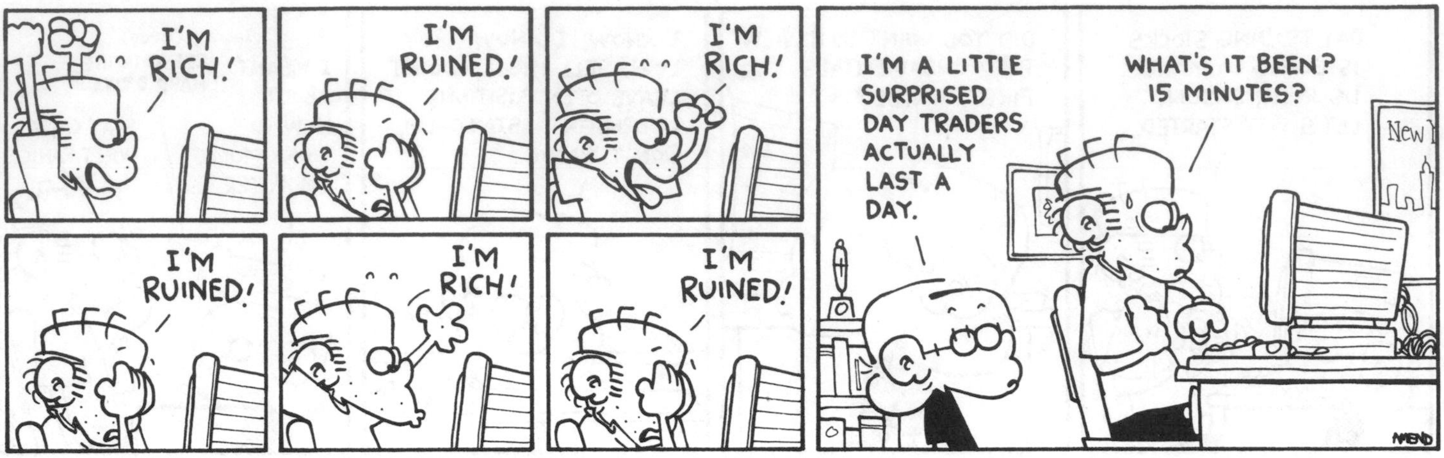
I'M RICH!
I'M RUINED!
I'M RICH!
I'M RUINED!
I'M RICH!
I'M RUINED!
I'M A LITTLE SURPRISED DAY TRADERS ACTUALLY LAST A DAY.
WHAT'S IT BEEN? 15 MINUTES?
AMEND

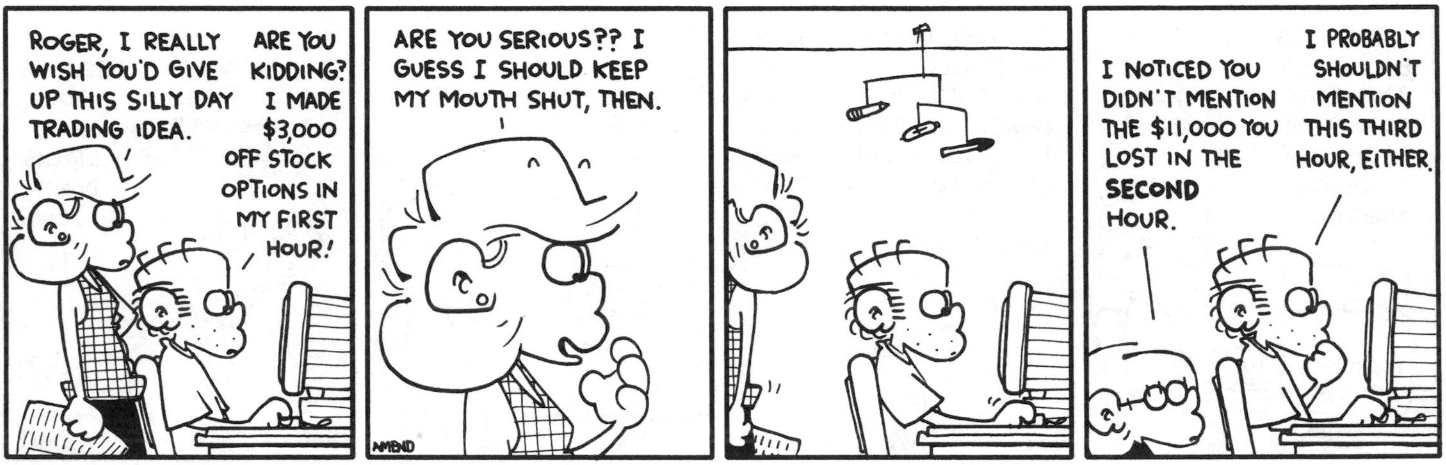
ROGER, I REALLY WISH YOU'D GIVE UP THIS SILLY DAY TRADING IDEA.
ARE YOU KIDDING? I MADE $3,000 OFF STOCK OPTIONS IN MY FIRST HOUR!
ARE YOU SERIOUS?? I GUESS I SHOULD KEEP MY MOUTH SHUT, THEN.
AMEND
I NOTICED YOU DIDN'T MENTION THE $11,000 YOU LOST IN THE SECOND HOUR.
I PROBABLY SHOULDN'T MENTION THIS THIRD HOUR, EITHER.

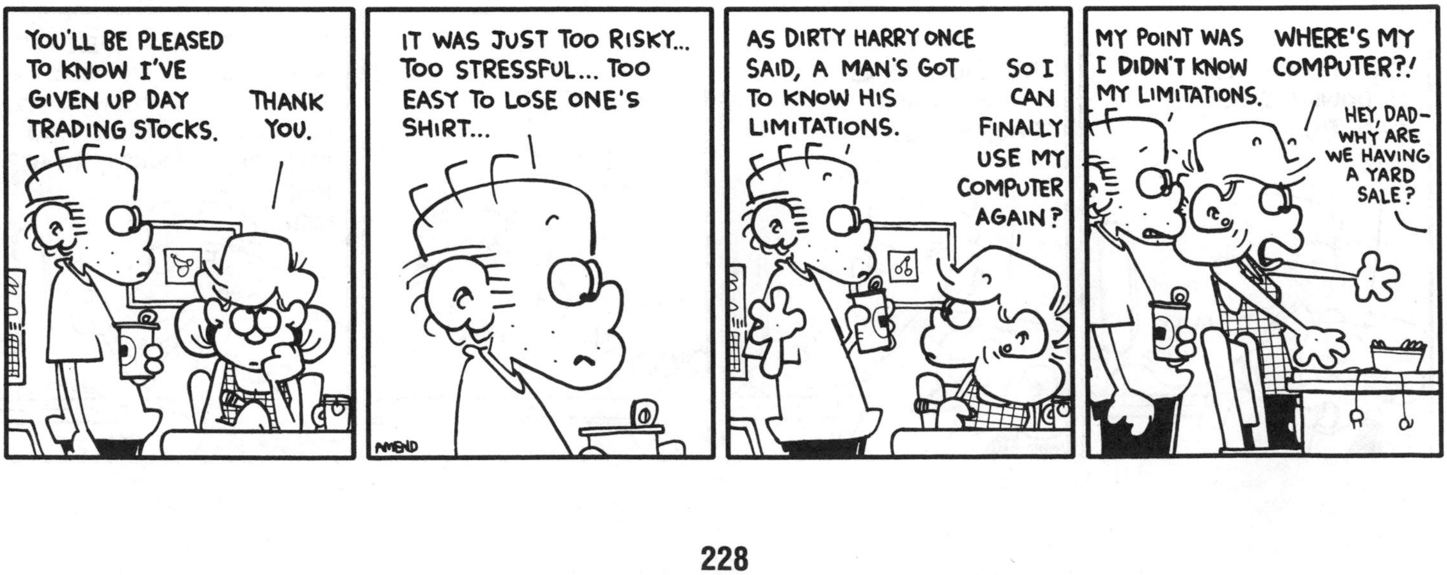
YOU'LL BE PLEASED TO KNOW I'VE GIVEN UP DAY TRADING STOCKS.
THANK YOU.
IT WAS JUST TOO RISKY... TOO STRESSFUL... TOO EASY TO LOSE ONE'S SHIRT...
AMEND
AS DIRTY HARRY ONCE SAID, A MAN'S GOT TO KNOW HIS LIMITATIONS.
SO I CAN FINALLY USE MY COMPUTER AGAIN?
MY POINT WAS I DIDN'T KNOW MY LIMITATIONS.
WHERE'S MY COMPUTER?!
HEY, DAD- WHY ARE WE HAVING A YARD SALE?

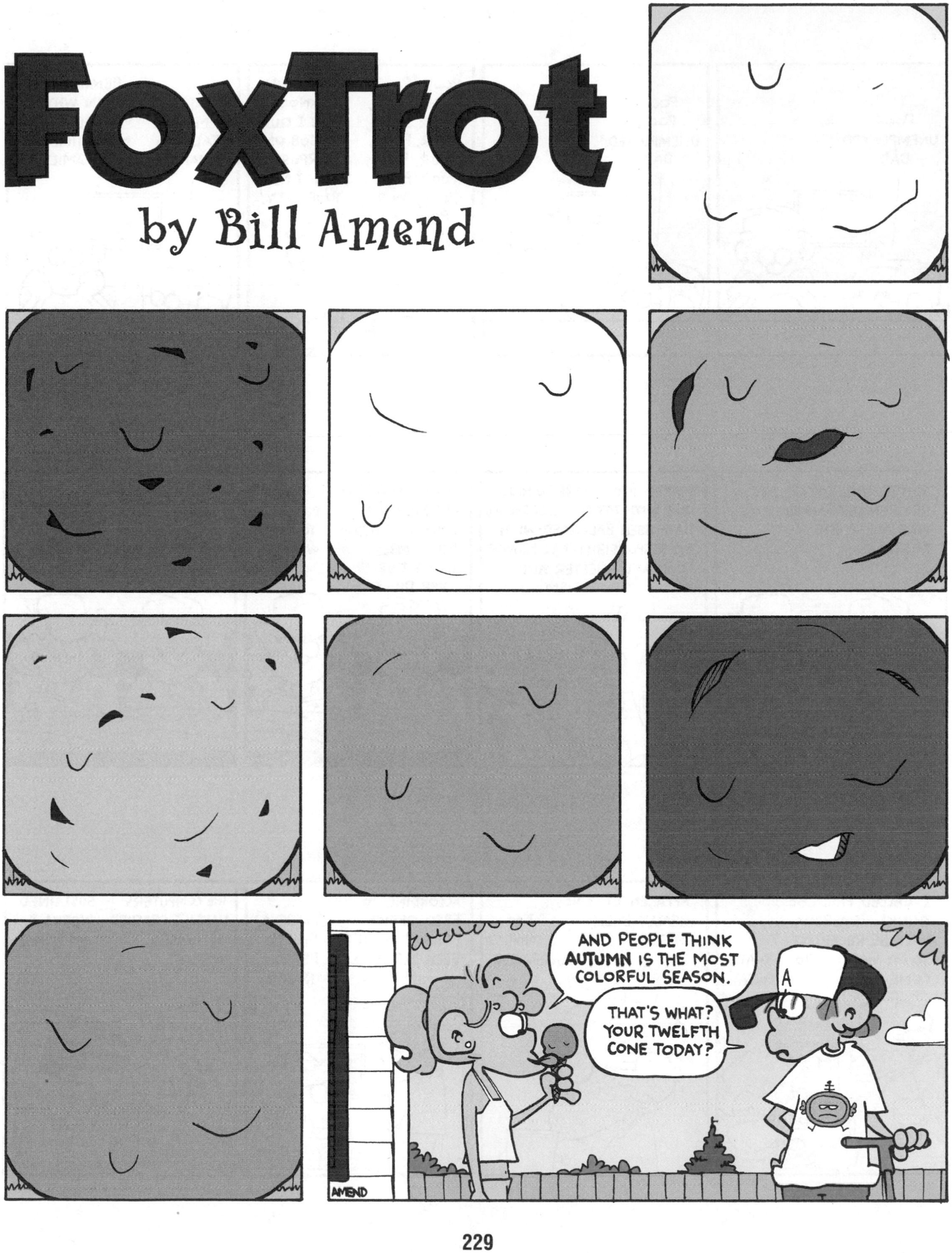
FoxTrot
by Bill Amend
AND PEOPLE THINK AUTUMN IS THE MOST COLORFUL SEASON.
THAT'S WHAT? YOUR TWELFTH CONE TODAY?
AMEND

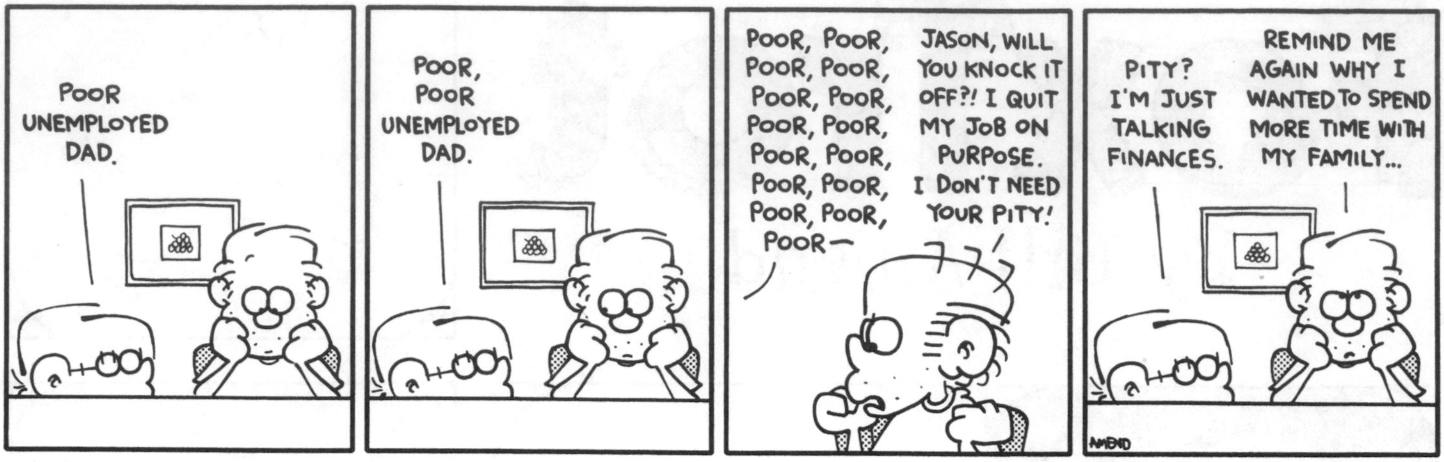
POOR UNEMPLOYED DAD.
POOR, POOR UNEMPLOYED DAD.
POOR, POOR, POOR, POOR, POOR, POOR, POOR, POOR, POOR, POOR, POOR, POOR, POOR, POOR, POOR—
JASON, WILL YOU KNOCK IT OFF?! I QUIT MY JOB ON PURPOSE. I DON'T NEED YOUR PITY!
PITY? I'M JUST TALKING FINANCES.
REMIND ME AGAIN WHY I WANTED TO SPEND MORE TIME WITH MY FAMILY...
AMEND

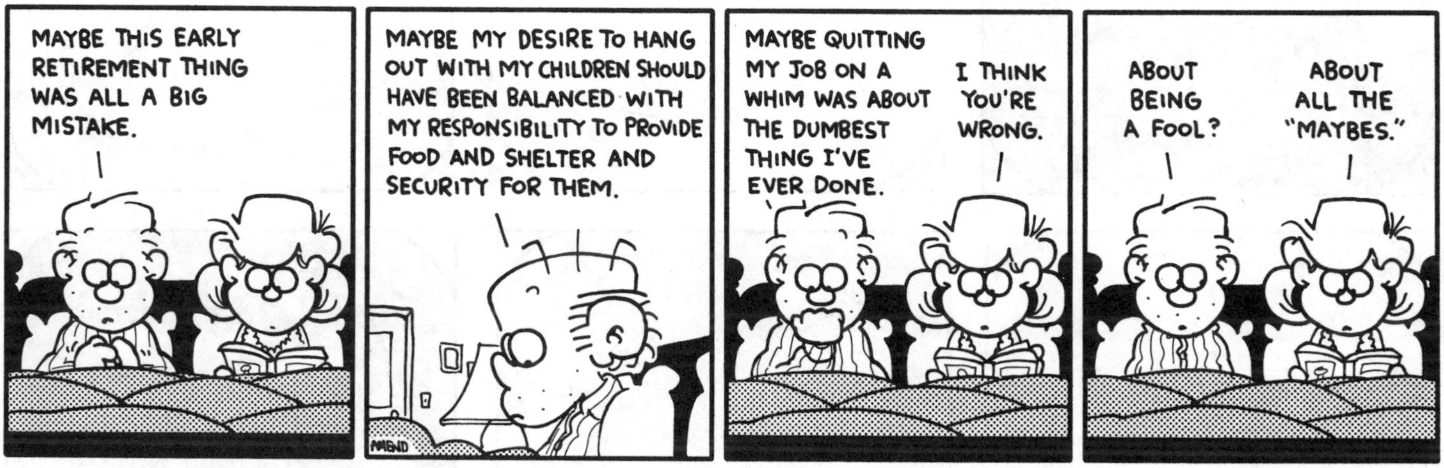
MAYBE THIS EARLY RETIREMENT THING WAS ALL A BIG MISTAKE.
MAYBE MY DESIRE TO HANG OUT WITH MY CHILDREN SHOULD HAVE BEEN BALANCED WITH MY RESPONSIBILITY TO PROVIDE FOOD AND SHELTER AND SECURITY FOR THEM.
AMEND
MAYBE QUITTING MY JOB ON A WHIM WAS ABOUT THE DUMBEST THING I'VE EVER DONE.
I THINK YOU'RE WRONG.
ABOUT BEING A FOOL?
ABOUT ALL THE "MAYBES."

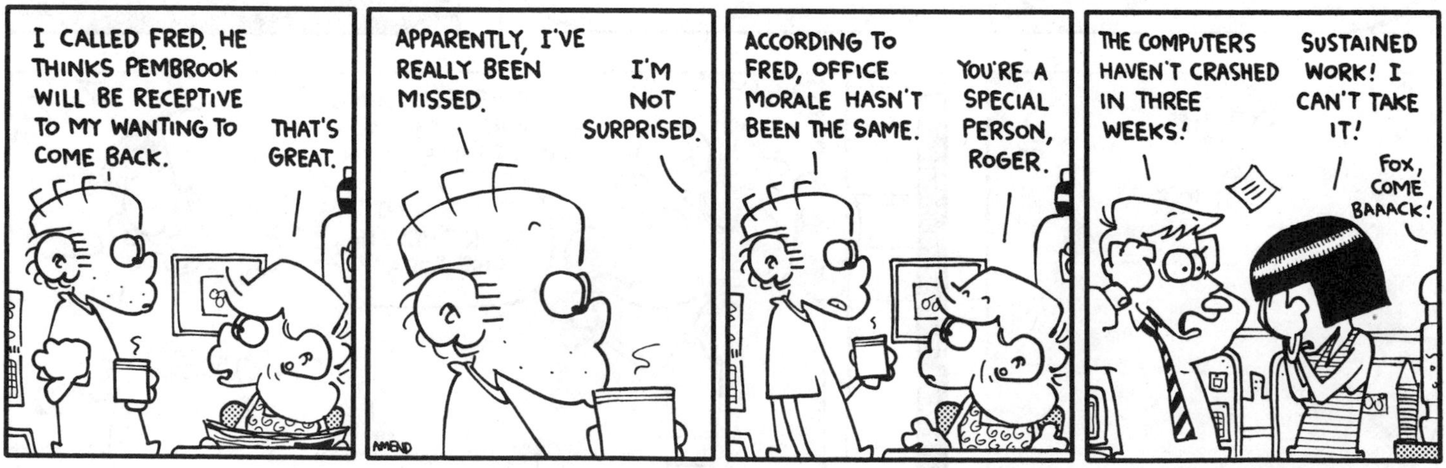
I CALLED FRED. HE THINKS PEMBROOK WILL BE RECEPTIVE TO MY WANTING TO COME BACK.
THAT'S GREAT.
APPARENTLY, I'VE REALLY BEEN MISSED.
I'M NOT SURPRISED.
AMEND
ACCORDING TO FRED, OFFICE MORALE HASN'T BEEN THE SAME.
YOU'RE A SPECIAL PERSON, ROGER.
THE COMPUTERS HAVEN'T CRASHED IN THREE WEEKS!
SUSTAINED WORK! I CAN'T TAKE IT!
FOX, COME BAAACK!

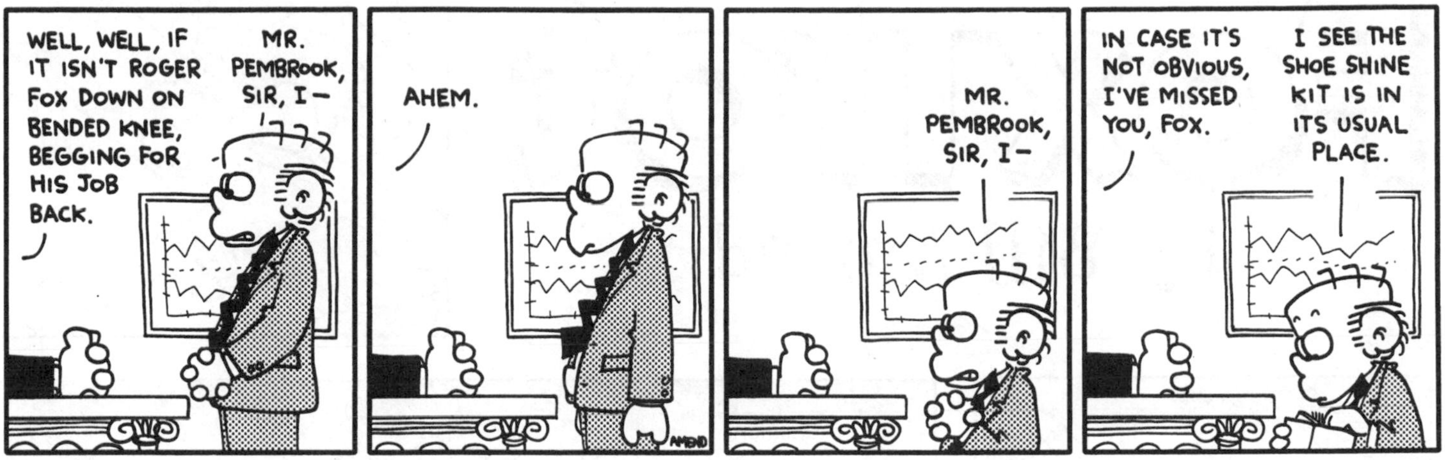
WELL, WELL, IF IT ISN'T ROGER FOX DOWN ON BENDED KNEE, BEGGING FOR HIS JOB BACK.
MR. PEMBROOK, SIR, I—
AHEM.
MR. PEMBROOK, SIR, I—
IN CASE IT'S NOT OBVIOUS, I'VE MISSED YOU, FOX.
I SEE THE SHOE SHINE KIT IS IN ITS USUAL PLACE.
AMEND

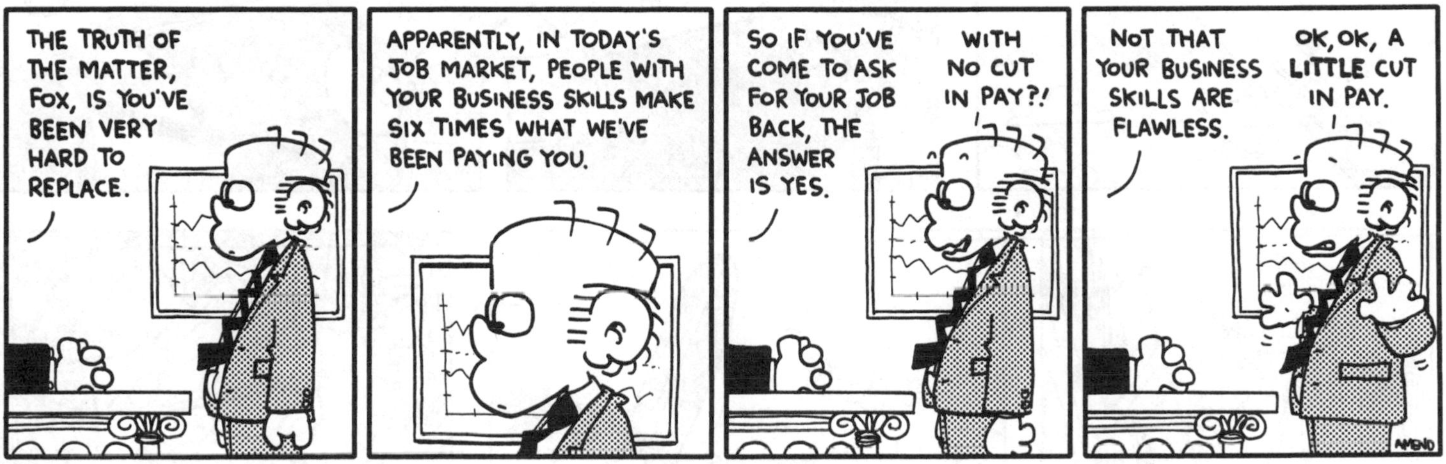
THE TRUTH OF THE MATTER, FOX, IS YOU'VE BEEN VERY HARD TO REPLACE.
APPARENTLY, IN TODAY'S JOB MARKET, PEOPLE WITH YOUR BUSINESS SKILLS MAKE SIX TIMES WHAT WE'VE BEEN PAYING YOU.
SO IF YOU'VE COME TO ASK FOR YOUR JOB BACK, THE ANSWER IS YES.
WITH NO CUT IN PAY?!
NOT THAT YOUR BUSINESS SKILLS ARE FLAWLESS.
OK, OK, A LITTLE CUT IN PAY.
AMEND

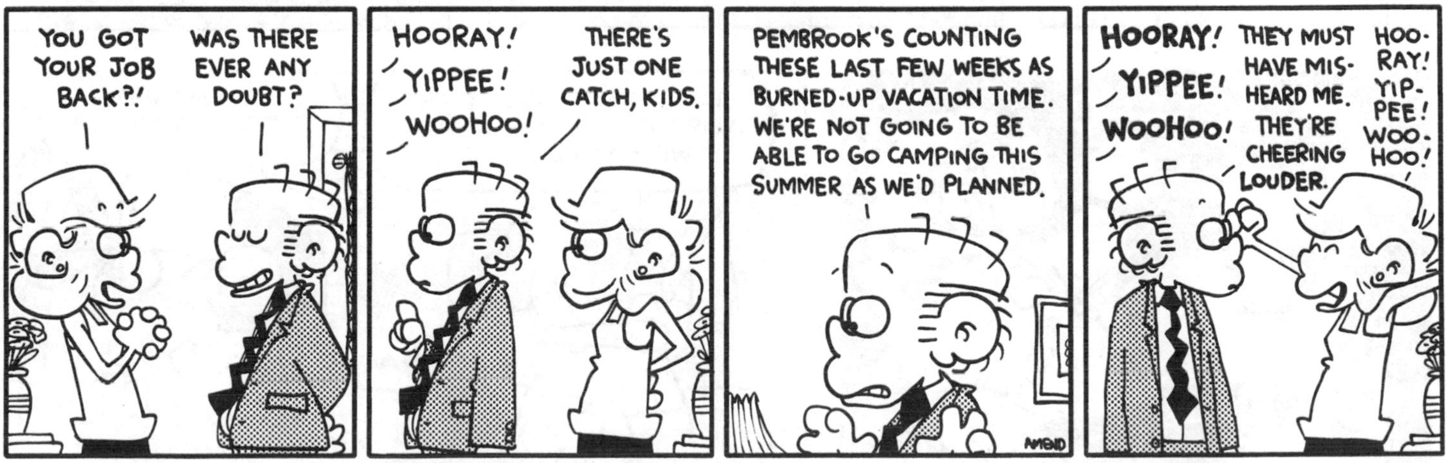
YOU GOT YOUR JOB BACK?!
WAS THERE EVER ANY DOUBT?
HOORAY!
YIPPEE!
WOOHOO!
THERE'S JUST ONE CATCH, KIDS.
PEMBROOK'S COUNTING THESE LAST FEW WEEKS AS BURNED-UP VACATION TIME. WE'RE NOT GOING TO BE ABLE TO GO CAMPING THIS SUMMER AS WE'D PLANNED.
AMEND
HOORAY!
YIPPEE!
WOOHOO!
THEY MUST HAVE MIS-HEARD ME. THEY'RE CHEERING LOUDER.
HOO-RAY! YIP-PEE! WOO-HOO!

FoxTrot
by Bill Amend

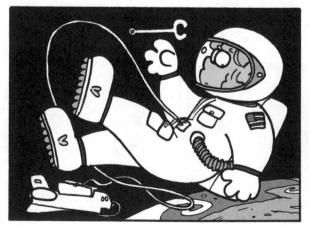

YOU HAVE NO IDEA HOW WEIRD IT IS TO FALL ASLEEP WITH YOU DRIVING.

WHAT WAS WITH THE TARZAN YELL?

232

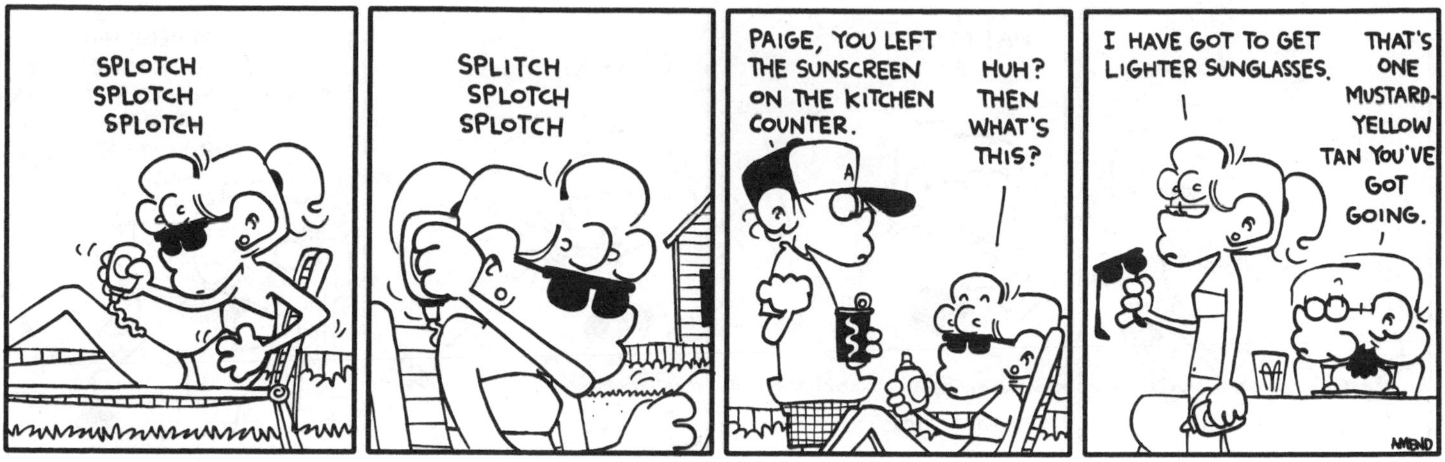
SPLOTCH
SPLOTCH
SPLOTCH
SPLITCH
SPLOTCH
SPLOTCH
PAIGE, YOU LEFT THE SUNSCREEN ON THE KITCHEN COUNTER.
HUH? THEN WHAT'S THIS?
I HAVE GOT TO GET LIGHTER SUNGLASSES.
THAT'S ONE MUSTARD-YELLOW TAN YOU'VE GOT GOING.
AMEND

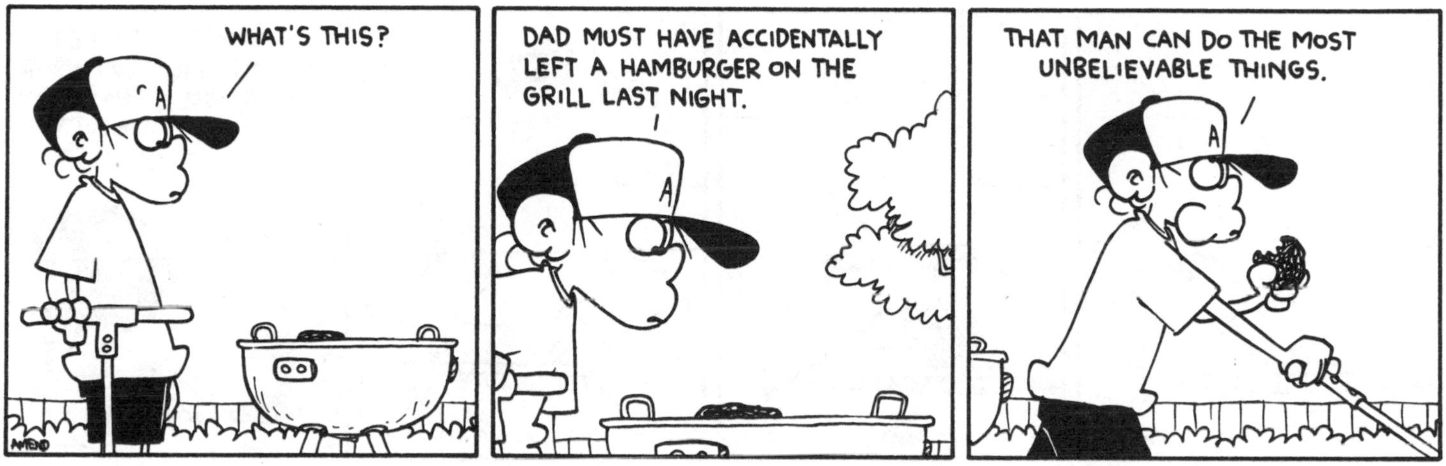
WHAT'S THIS?
AMEND
DAD MUST HAVE ACCIDENTALLY LEFT A HAMBURGER ON THE GRILL LAST NIGHT.
THAT MAN CAN DO THE MOST UNBELIEVABLE THINGS.

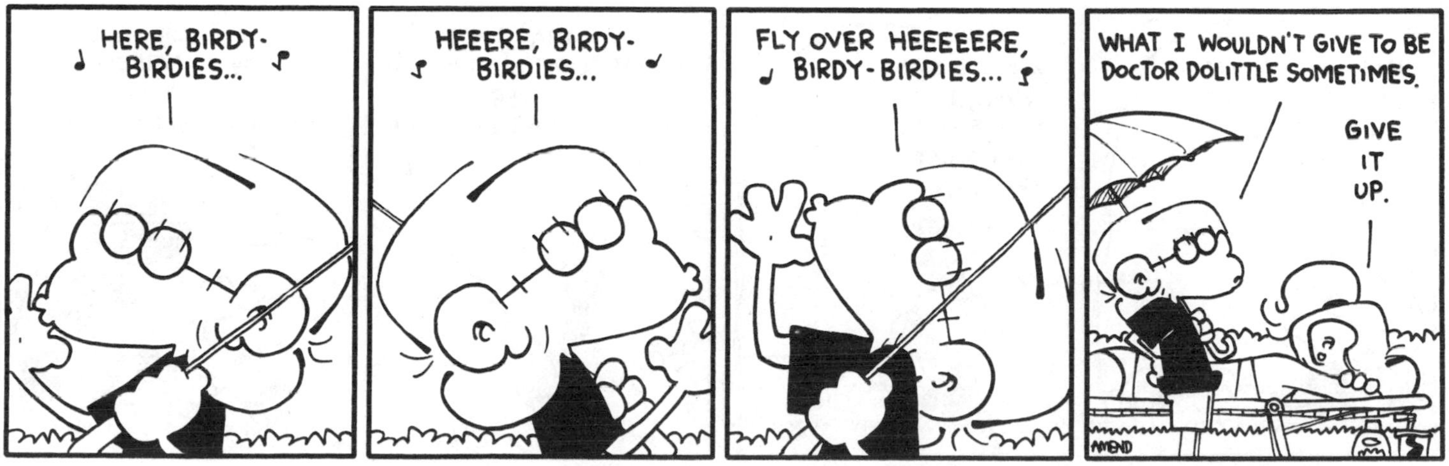
HERE, BIRDY-BIRDIES...
HEEERE, BIRDY-BIRDIES...
FLY OVER HEEEEERE, BIRDY-BIRDIES...
WHAT I WOULDN'T GIVE TO BE DOCTOR DOLITTLE SOMETIMES.
GIVE IT UP.
AMEND

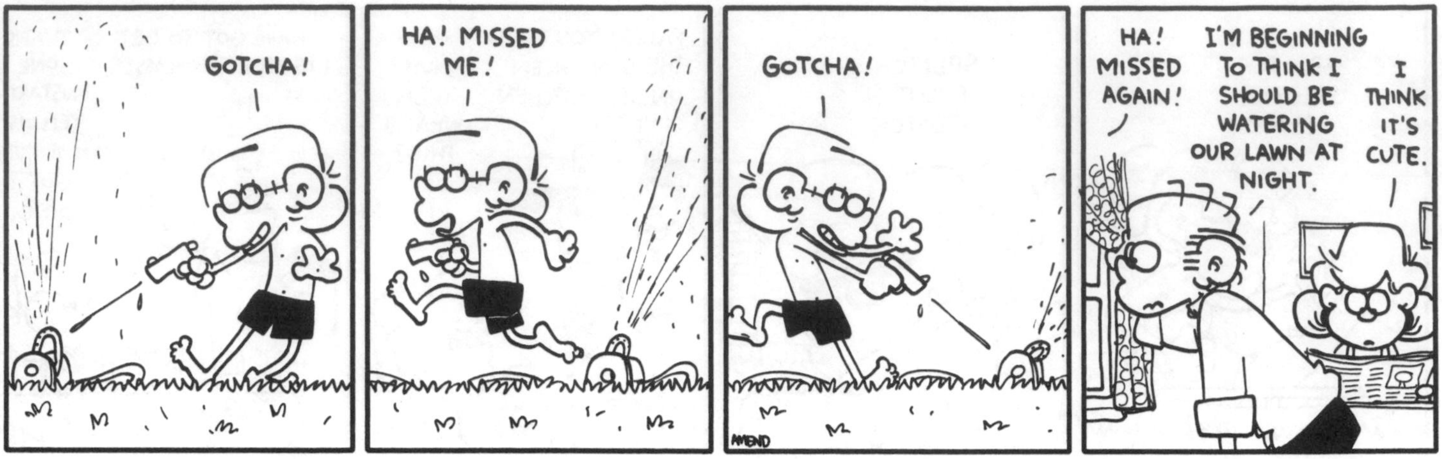
GOTCHA!
HA! MISSED ME!
GOTCHA!
HA! MISSED AGAIN!
I'M BEGINNING TO THINK I SHOULD BE WATERING OUR LAWN AT NIGHT.
I THINK IT'S CUTE.

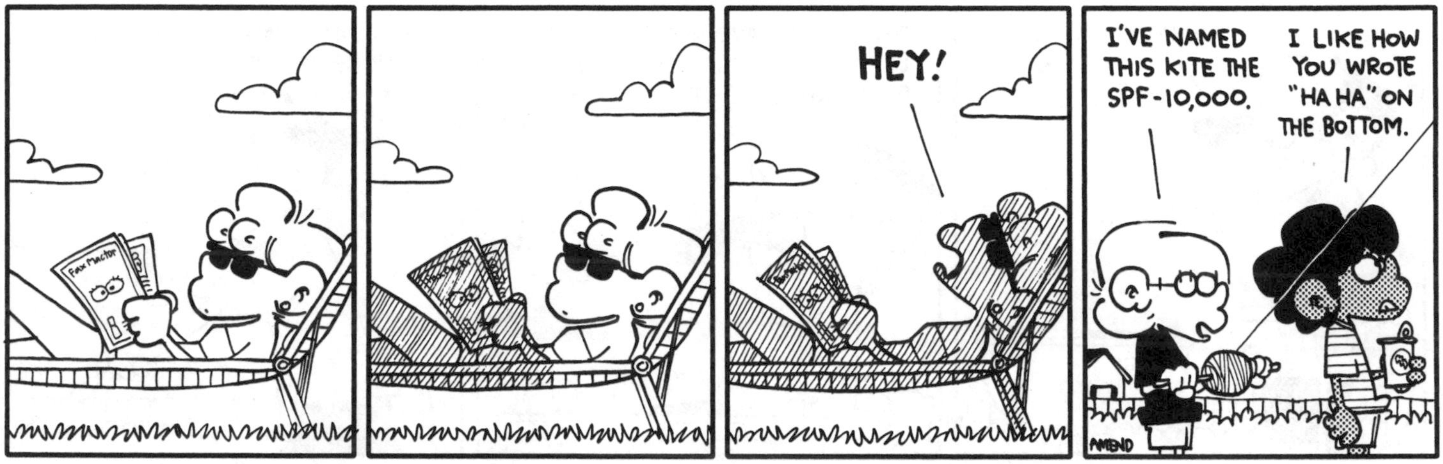
HEY!
I'VE NAMED THIS KITE THE SPF-10,000.
I LIKE HOW YOU WROTE "HA HA" ON THE BOTTOM.

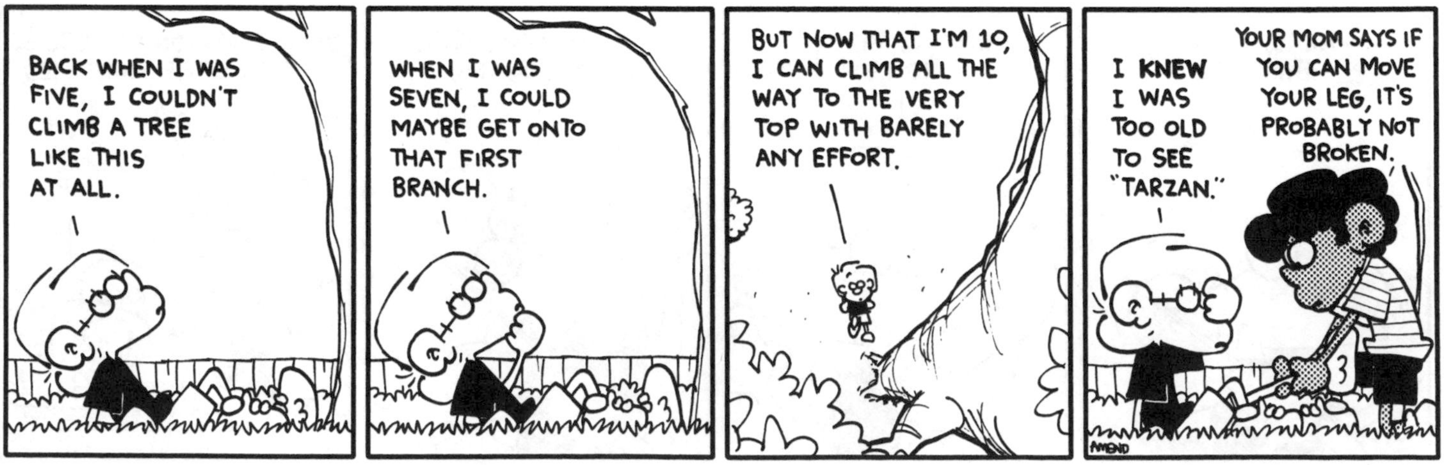
BACK WHEN I WAS FIVE, I COULDN'T CLIMB A TREE LIKE THIS AT ALL.
WHEN I WAS SEVEN, I COULD MAYBE GET ONTO THAT FIRST BRANCH.
BUT NOW THAT I'M 10, I CAN CLIMB ALL THE WAY TO THE VERY TOP WITH BARELY ANY EFFORT.
I KNEW I WAS TOO OLD TO SEE "TARZAN."
YOUR MOM SAYS IF YOU CAN MOVE YOUR LEG, IT'S PROBABLY NOT BROKEN.

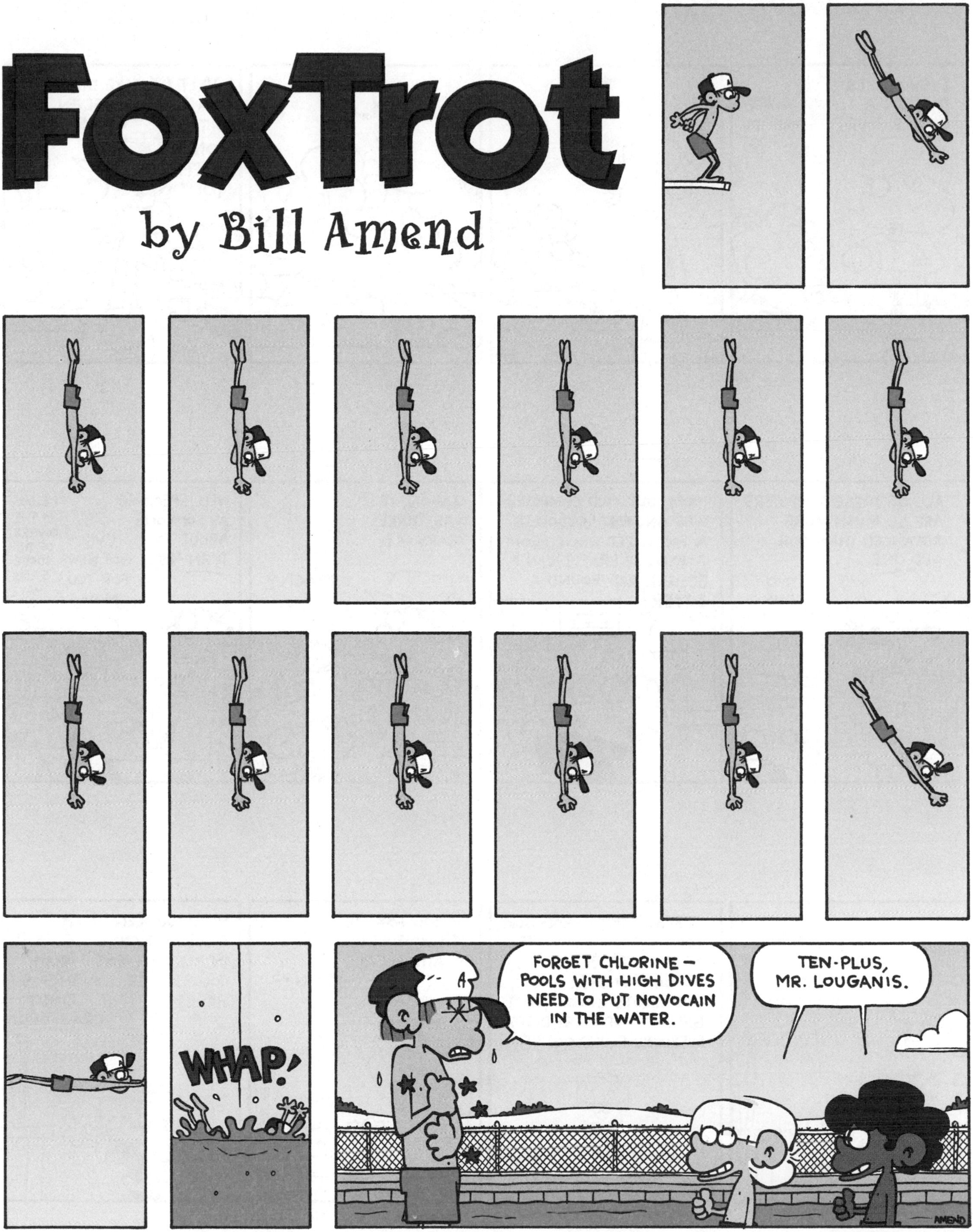
FoxTrot
by Bill Amend
WHAP!
FORGET CHLORINE — POOLS WITH HIGH DIVES NEED TO PUT NOVOCAIN IN THE WATER.
TEN-PLUS, MR. LOUGANIS.
AMEND

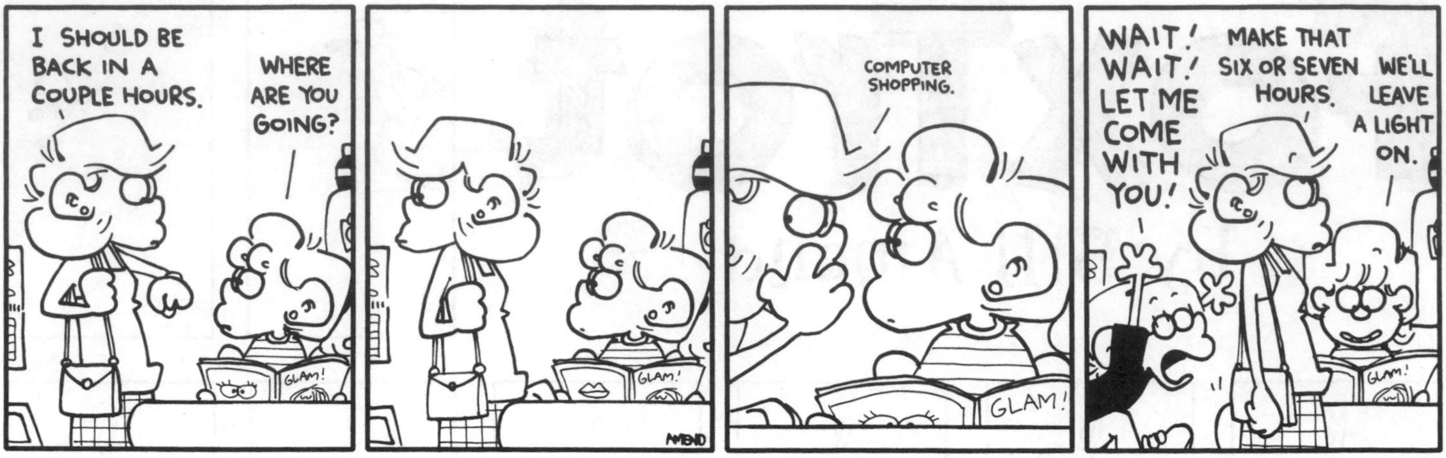
I SHOULD BE BACK IN A COUPLE HOURS.
WHERE ARE YOU GOING?
GLAM!
COMPUTER SHOPPING.
GLAM!
WAIT! WAIT! LET ME COME WITH YOU!
MAKE THAT SIX OR SEVEN HOURS.
WE'LL LEAVE A LIGHT ON.
GLAM!

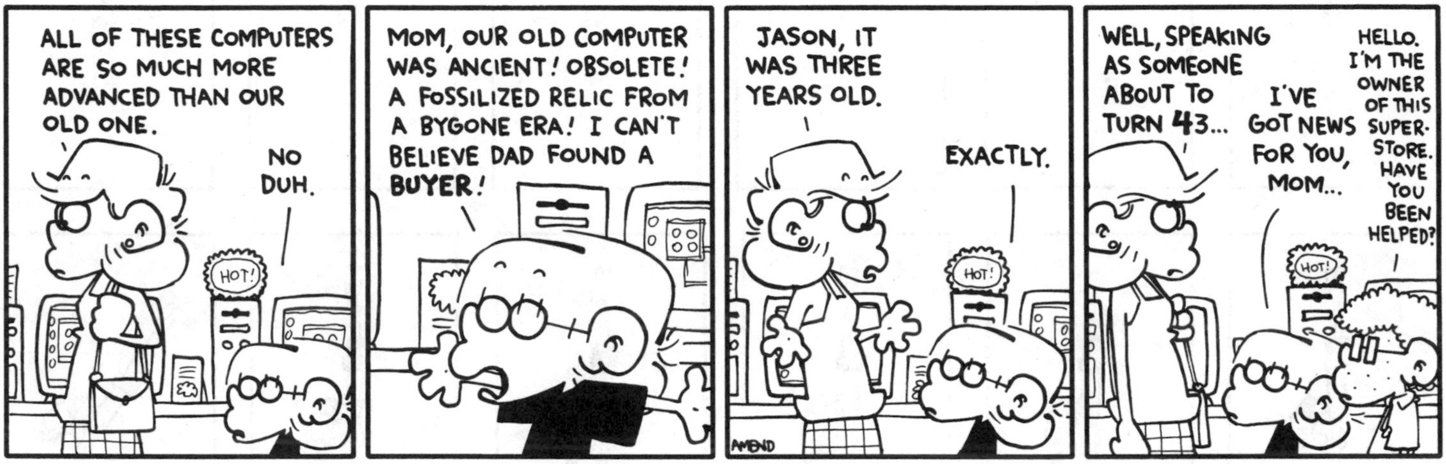
ALL OF THESE COMPUTERS ARE SO MUCH MORE ADVANCED THAN OUR OLD ONE.
NO DUH.
HOT!
MOM, OUR OLD COMPUTER WAS ANCIENT! OBSOLETE! A FOSSILIZED RELIC FROM A BYGONE ERA! I CAN'T BELIEVE DAD FOUND A **BUYER**!
JASON, IT WAS THREE YEARS OLD.
EXACTLY.
HOT!
WELL, SPEAKING AS SOMEONE ABOUT TO TURN 43...
I'VE GOT NEWS FOR YOU, MOM...
HELLO. I'M THE OWNER OF THIS SUPER-STORE. HAVE YOU BEEN HELPED?
HOT!

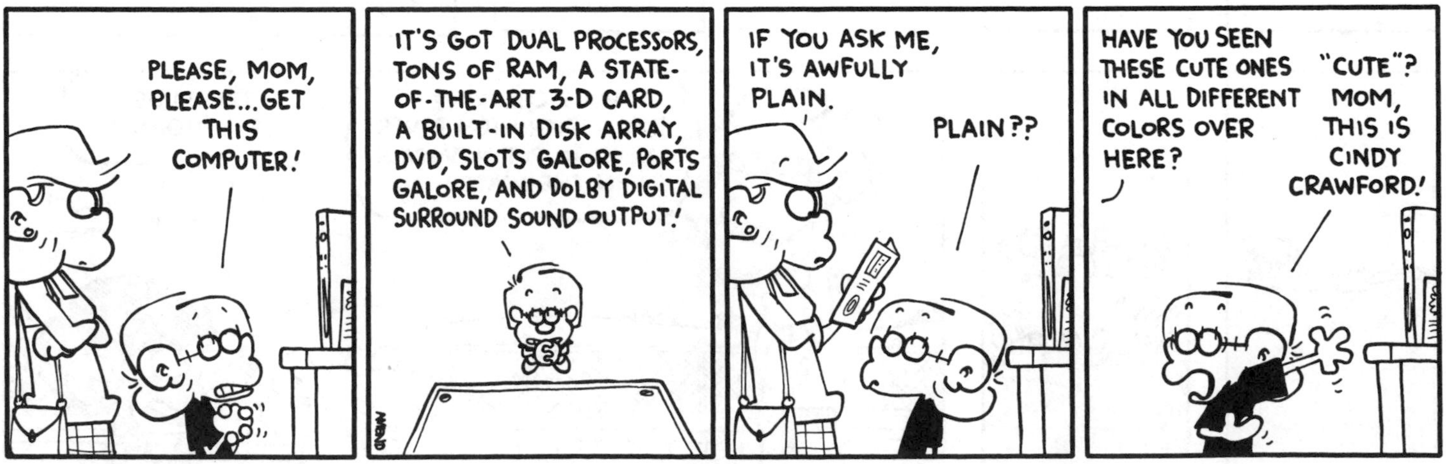
PLEASE, MOM, PLEASE...GET THIS COMPUTER!
IT'S GOT DUAL PROCESSORS, TONS OF RAM, A STATE-OF-THE-ART 3-D CARD, A BUILT-IN DISK ARRAY, DVD, SLOTS GALORE, PORTS GALORE, AND DOLBY DIGITAL SURROUND SOUND OUTPUT!
IF YOU ASK ME, IT'S AWFULLY PLAIN.
PLAIN??
HAVE YOU SEEN THESE CUTE ONES IN ALL DIFFERENT COLORS OVER HERE?
"CUTE"? MOM, THIS IS CINDY CRAWFORD!

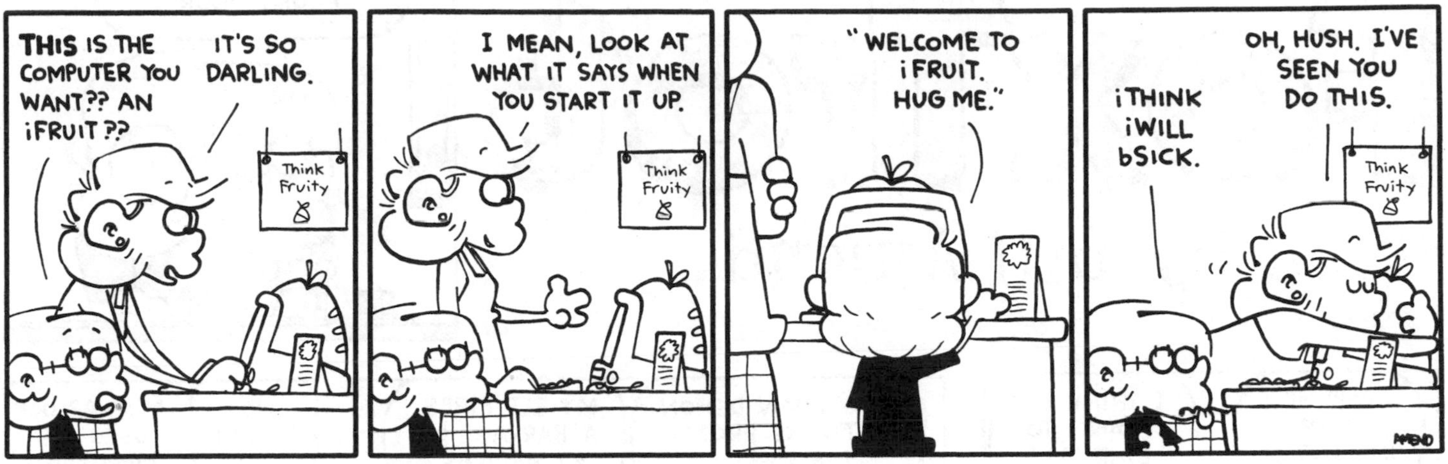
THIS IS THE COMPUTER YOU WANT?? AN iFRUIT??
IT'S SO DARLING.
Think Fruity
I MEAN, LOOK AT WHAT IT SAYS WHEN YOU START IT UP.
Think Fruity
"WELCOME TO iFRUIT. HUG ME."
iTHINK iWILL bSICK.
OH, HUSH. I'VE SEEN YOU DO THIS.
Think Fruity
AMEND

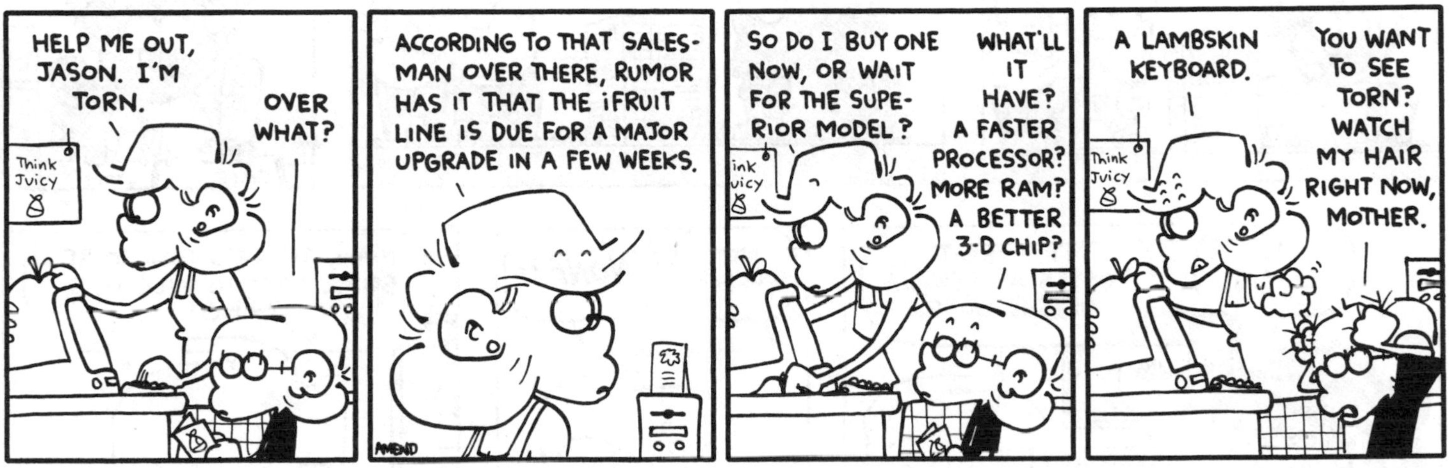
HELP ME OUT, JASON. I'M TORN.
OVER WHAT?
Think Juicy
ACCORDING TO THAT SALES-MAN OVER THERE, RUMOR HAS IT THAT THE iFRUIT LINE IS DUE FOR A MAJOR UPGRADE IN A FEW WEEKS.
AMEND
SO DO I BUY ONE NOW, OR WAIT FOR THE SUPE-RIOR MODEL?
WHAT'LL IT HAVE? A FASTER PROCESSOR? MORE RAM? A BETTER 3-D CHIP?
A LAMBSKIN KEYBOARD.
YOU WANT TO SEE TORN? WATCH MY HAIR RIGHT NOW, MOTHER.
Think Juicy

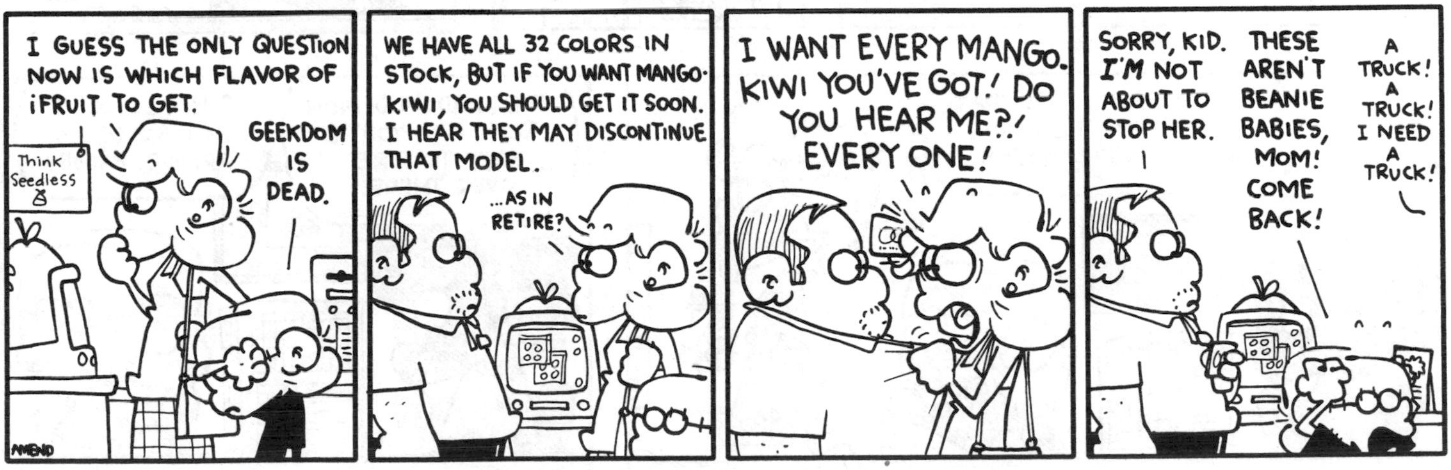
I GUESS THE ONLY QUESTION NOW IS WHICH FLAVOR OF iFRUIT TO GET.
GEEKDOM IS DEAD.
Think Seedless
AMEND
WE HAVE ALL 32 COLORS IN STOCK, BUT IF YOU WANT MANGO-KIWI, YOU SHOULD GET IT SOON. I HEAR THEY MAY DISCONTINUE THAT MODEL.
...AS IN RETIRE?
I WANT EVERY MANGO-KIWI YOU'VE GOT! DO YOU HEAR ME?! EVERY ONE!
SORRY, KID. I'M NOT ABOUT TO STOP HER.
THESE AREN'T BEANIE BABIES, MOM! COME BACK!
A TRUCK! A TRUCK! I NEED A TRUCK!

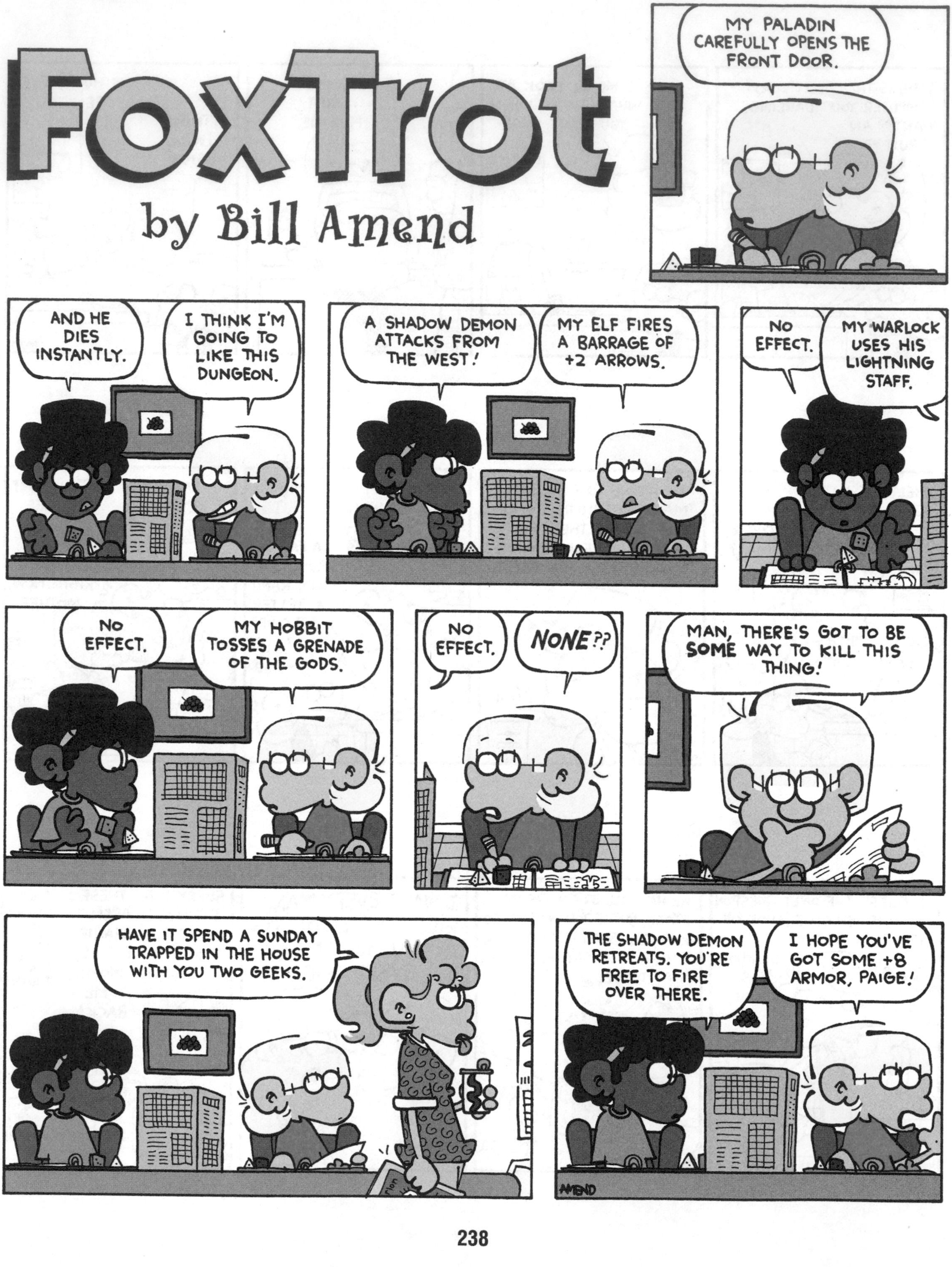
FoxTrot
by Bill Amend
MY PALADIN CAREFULLY OPENS THE FRONT DOOR.
AND HE DIES INSTANTLY.
I THINK I'M GOING TO LIKE THIS DUNGEON.
A SHADOW DEMON ATTACKS FROM THE WEST!
MY ELF FIRES A BARRAGE OF +2 ARROWS.
NO EFFECT.
MY WARLOCK USES HIS LIGHTNING STAFF.
NO EFFECT.
MY HOBBIT TOSSES A GRENADE OF THE GODS.
NO EFFECT.
NONE??
MAN, THERE'S GOT TO BE SOME WAY TO KILL THIS THING!
HAVE IT SPEND A SUNDAY TRAPPED IN THE HOUSE WITH YOU TWO GEEKS.
THE SHADOW DEMON RETREATS. YOU'RE FREE TO FIRE OVER THERE.
I HOPE YOU'VE GOT SOME +8 ARMOR, PAIGE!
AMEND

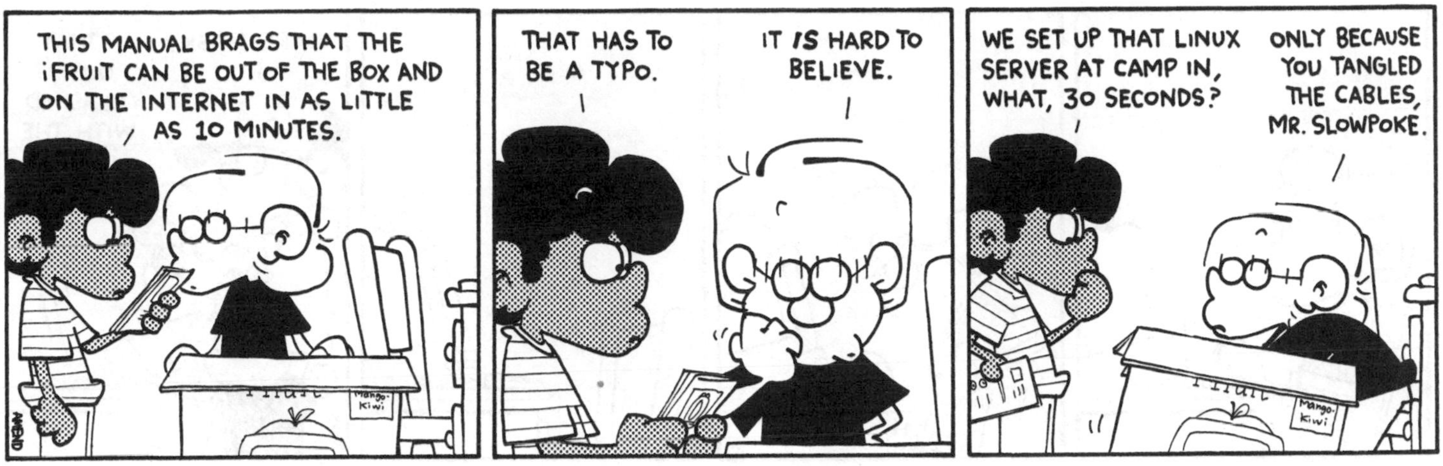
THIS MANUAL BRAGS THAT THE iFRUIT CAN BE OUT OF THE BOX AND ON THE INTERNET IN AS LITTLE AS 10 MINUTES.
THAT HAS TO BE A TYPO.
IT *IS* HARD TO BELIEVE.
WE SET UP THAT LINUX SERVER AT CAMP IN, WHAT, 30 SECONDS?
ONLY BECAUSE YOU TANGLED THE CABLES, MR. SLOWPOKE.

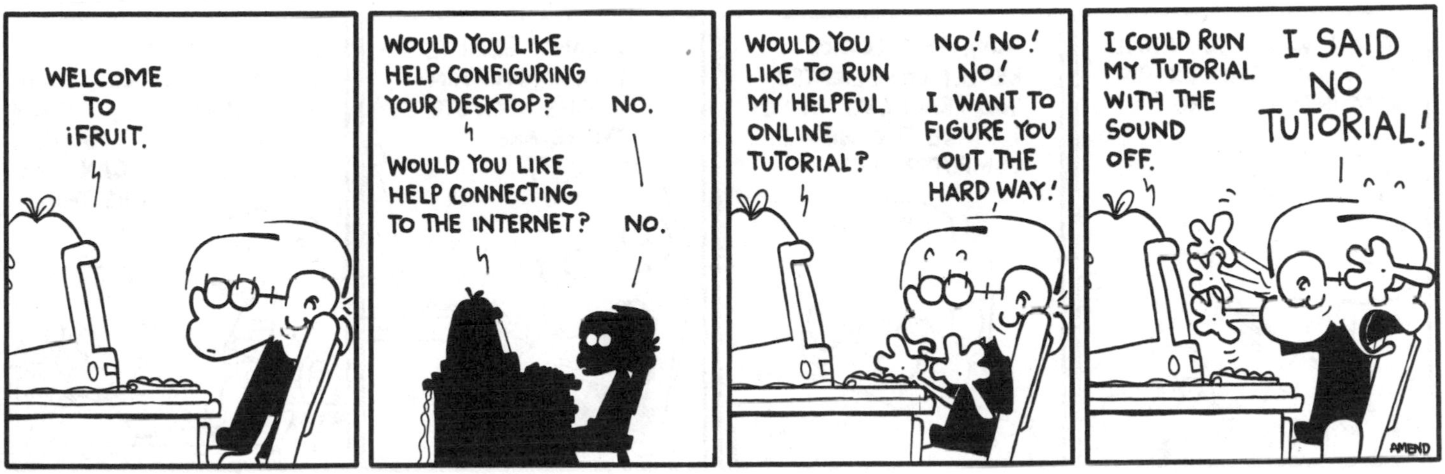
WELCOME TO iFRUIT.
WOULD YOU LIKE HELP CONFIGURING YOUR DESKTOP?
NO.
WOULD YOU LIKE HELP CONNECTING TO THE INTERNET?
NO.
WOULD YOU LIKE TO RUN MY HELPFUL ONLINE TUTORIAL?
NO! NO! NO! I WANT TO FIGURE YOU OUT THE HARD WAY!
I COULD RUN MY TUTORIAL WITH THE SOUND OFF.
I SAID NO TUTORIAL!
AMEND

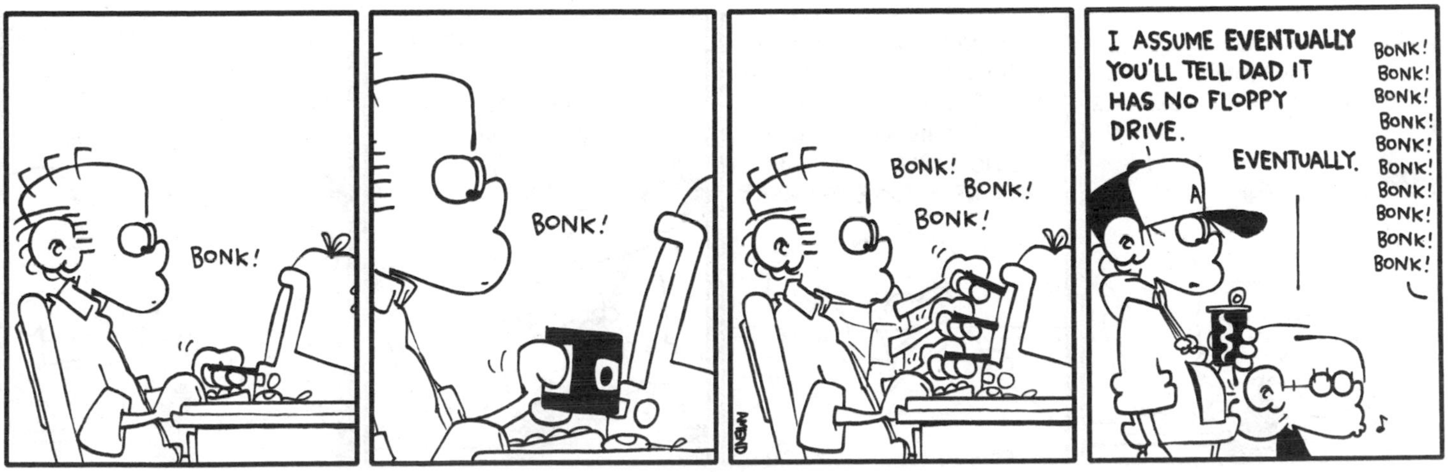
BONK!
BONK!
BONK! BONK! BONK!
I ASSUME **EVENTUALLY** YOU'LL TELL DAD IT HAS NO FLOPPY DRIVE.
EVENTUALLY.
BONK! BONK! BONK! BONK! BONK! BONK! BONK! BONK! BONK! BONK!

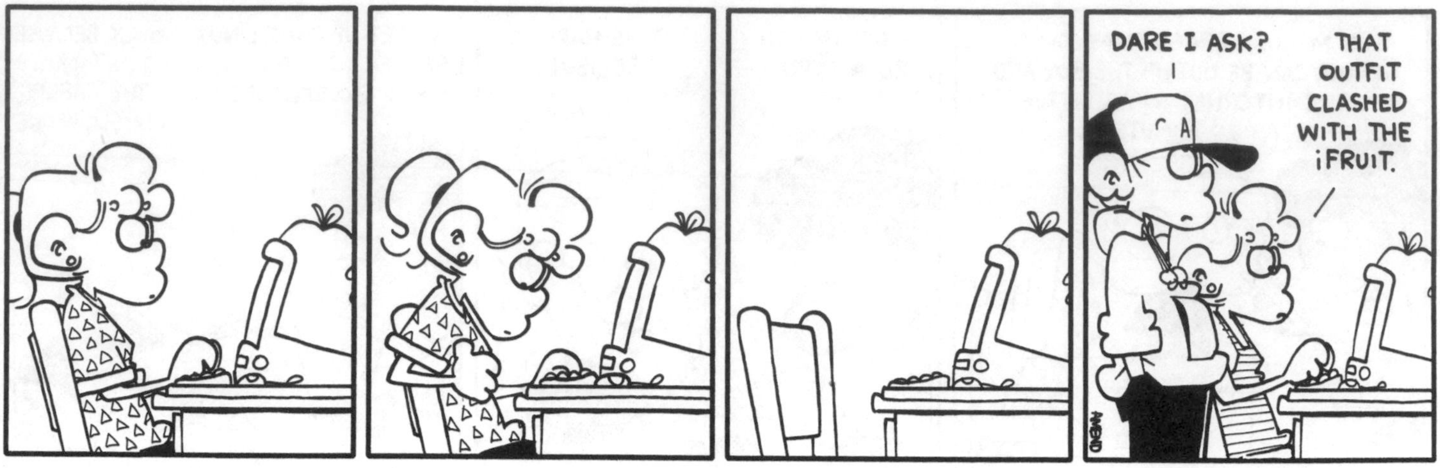
DARE I ASK?
THAT OUTFIT CLASHED WITH THE iFRUIT.

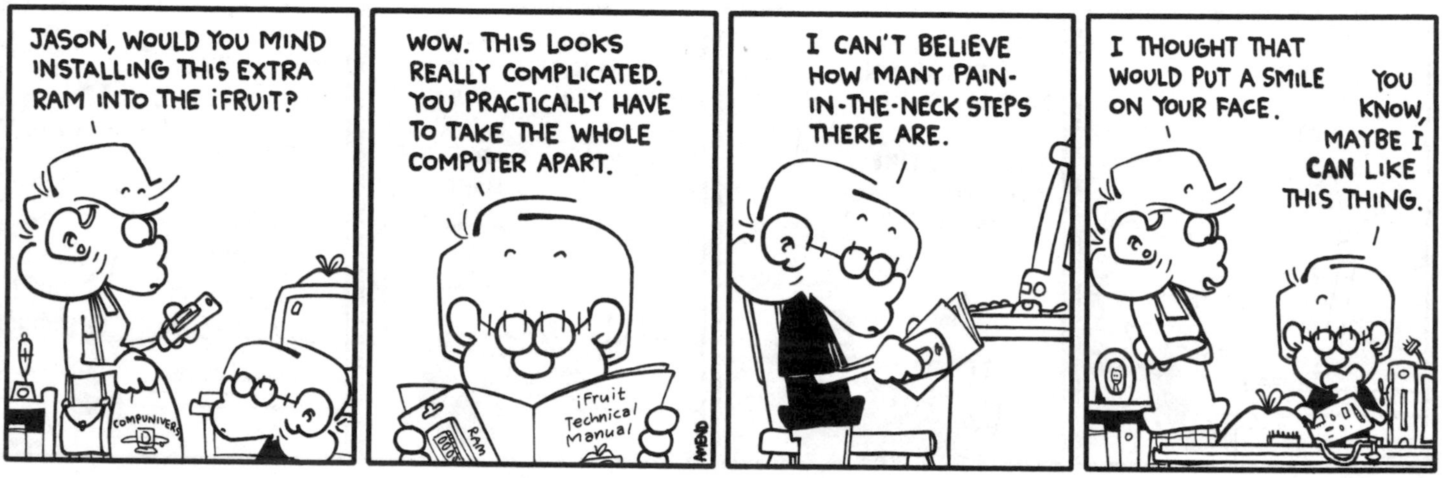
JASON, WOULD YOU MIND INSTALLING THIS EXTRA RAM INTO THE iFRUIT?
WOW. THIS LOOKS REALLY COMPLICATED. YOU PRACTICALLY HAVE TO TAKE THE WHOLE COMPUTER APART.
iFruit Technical Manual
I CAN'T BELIEVE HOW MANY PAIN-IN-THE-NECK STEPS THERE ARE.
I THOUGHT THAT WOULD PUT A SMILE ON YOUR FACE.
YOU KNOW, MAYBE I CAN LIKE THIS THING.

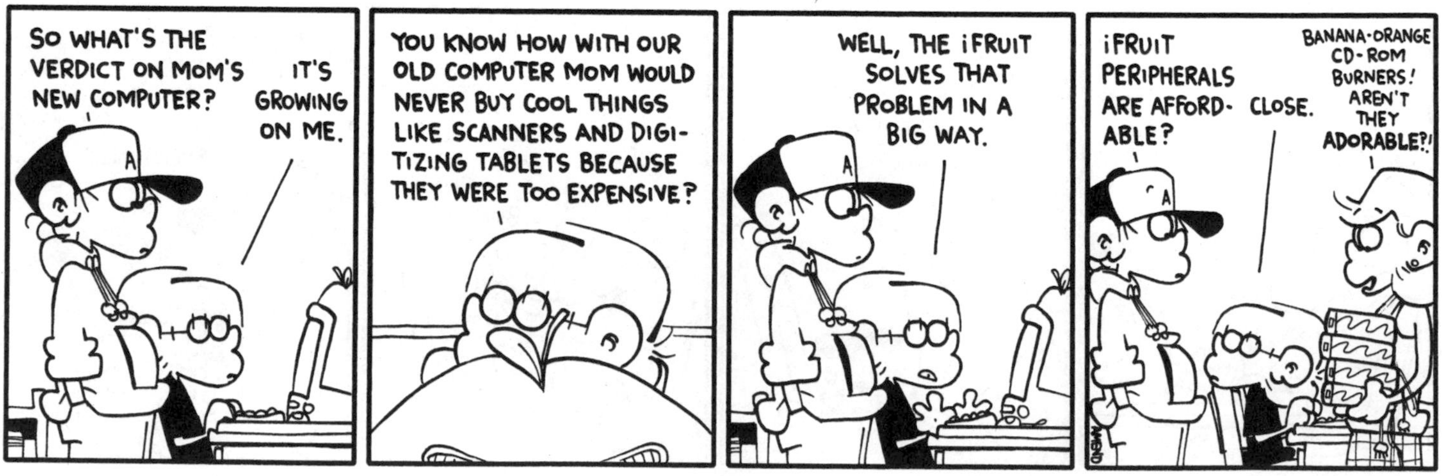
SO WHAT'S THE VERDICT ON MOM'S NEW COMPUTER?
IT'S GROWING ON ME.
YOU KNOW HOW WITH OUR OLD COMPUTER MOM WOULD NEVER BUY COOL THINGS LIKE SCANNERS AND DIGITIZING TABLETS BECAUSE THEY WERE TOO EXPENSIVE?
WELL, THE iFRUIT SOLVES THAT PROBLEM IN A BIG WAY.
iFRUIT PERIPHERALS ARE AFFORDABLE?
CLOSE.
BANANA-ORANGE CD-ROM BURNERS! AREN'T THEY ADORABLE?!

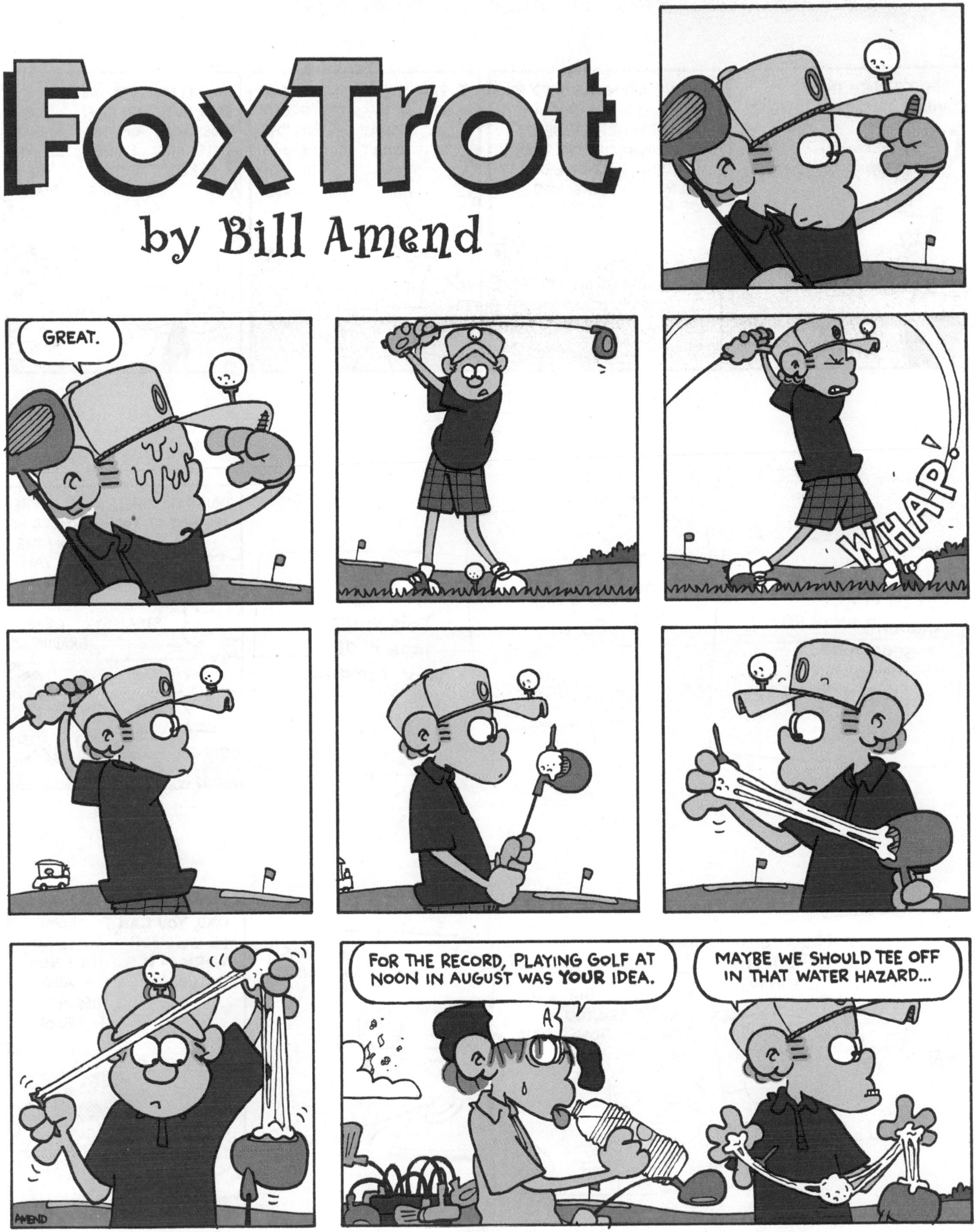
FoxTrot
by Bill Amend
GREAT.
WHAP!
AMEND
FOR THE RECORD, PLAYING GOLF AT NOON IN AUGUST WAS YOUR IDEA.
MAYBE WE SHOULD TEE OFF IN THAT WATER HAZARD...

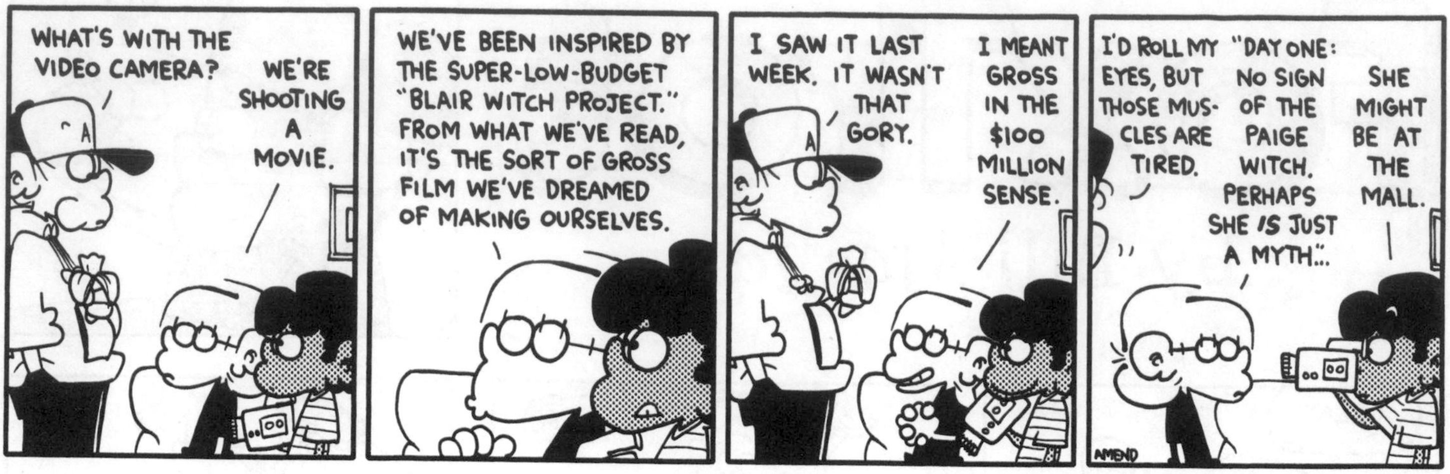
WHAT'S WITH THE VIDEO CAMERA?
WE'RE SHOOTING A MOVIE.
WE'VE BEEN INSPIRED BY THE SUPER-LOW-BUDGET "BLAIR WITCH PROJECT." FROM WHAT WE'VE READ, IT'S THE SORT OF GROSS FILM WE'VE DREAMED OF MAKING OURSELVES.
I SAW IT LAST WEEK. IT WASN'T THAT GORY.
I MEANT GROSS IN THE $100 MILLION SENSE.
I'D ROLL MY EYES, BUT THOSE MUSCLES ARE TIRED.
"DAY ONE: NO SIGN OF THE PAIGE WITCH. PERHAPS SHE *IS* JUST A MYTH"...
SHE MIGHT BE AT THE MALL.
AMEND

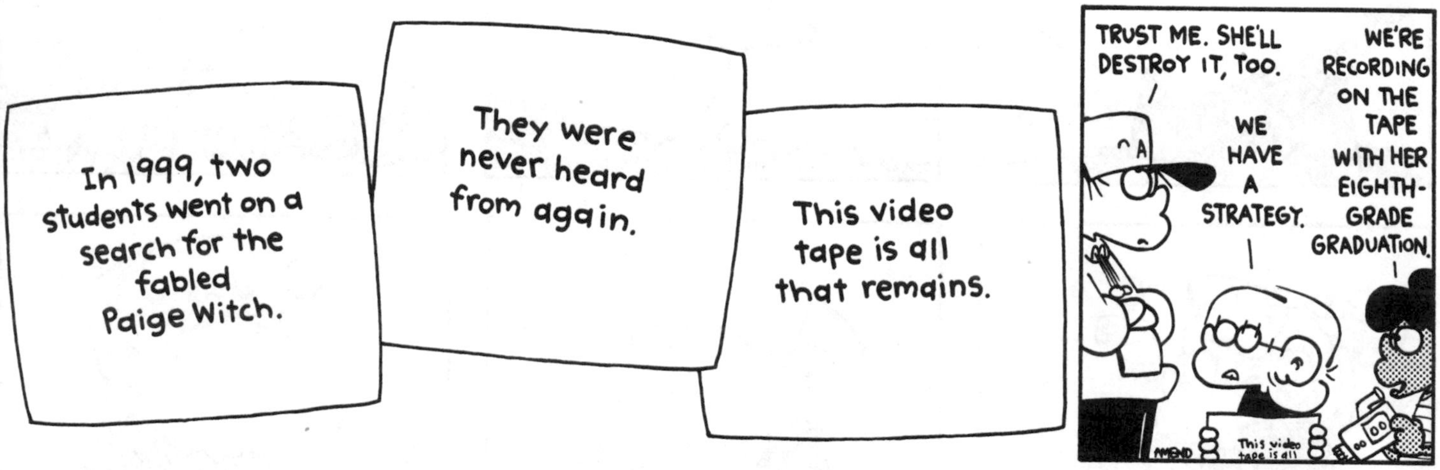
In 1999, two students went on a search for the fabled Paige Witch.
They were never heard from again.
This video tape is all that remains.
TRUST ME. SHE'LL DESTROY IT, TOO.
WE HAVE A STRATEGY.
WE'RE RECORDING ON THE TAPE WITH HER EIGHTH-GRADE GRADUATION.
AMEND

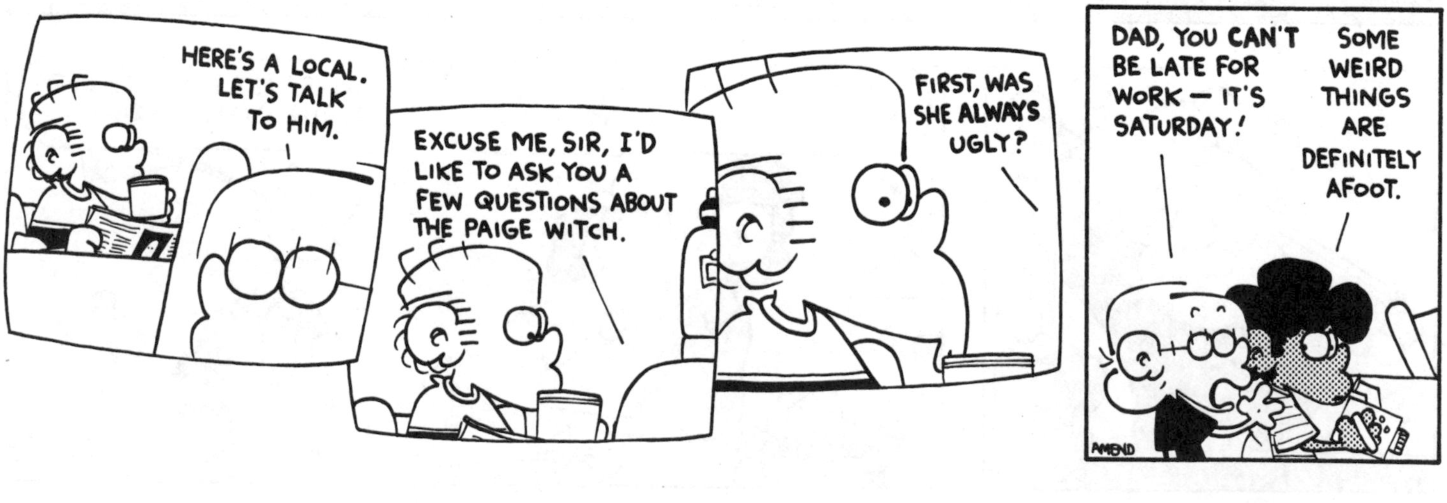
HERE'S A LOCAL. LET'S TALK TO HIM.
EXCUSE ME, SIR, I'D LIKE TO ASK YOU A FEW QUESTIONS ABOUT THE PAIGE WITCH.
FIRST, WAS SHE ALWAYS UGLY?
DAD, YOU CAN'T BE LATE FOR WORK — IT'S SATURDAY!
SOME WEIRD THINGS ARE DEFINITELY AFOOT.
AMEND

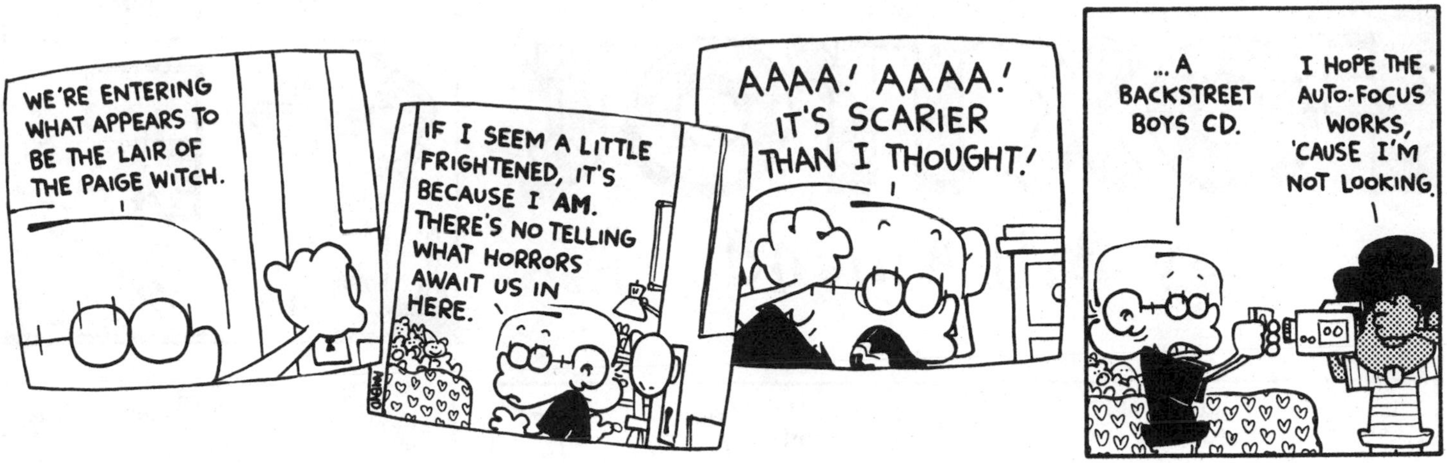
WE'RE ENTERING WHAT APPEARS TO BE THE LAIR OF THE PAIGE WITCH.
IF I SEEM A LITTLE FRIGHTENED, IT'S BECAUSE I AM. THERE'S NO TELLING WHAT HORRORS AWAIT US IN HERE.
AAAA! AAAA! IT'S SCARIER THAN I THOUGHT!
... A BACKSTREET BOYS CD.
I HOPE THE AUTO-FOCUS WORKS, 'CAUSE I'M NOT LOOKING.

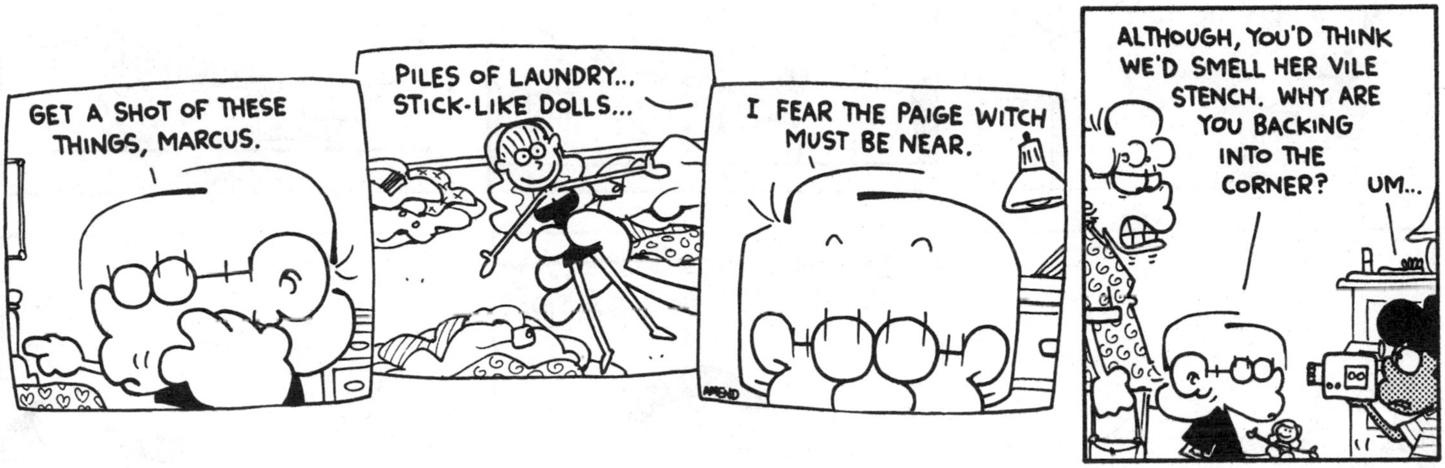
GET A SHOT OF THESE THINGS, MARCUS.
PILES OF LAUNDRY... STICK-LIKE DOLLS...
I FEAR THE PAIGE WITCH MUST BE NEAR.
ALTHOUGH, YOU'D THINK WE'D SMELL HER VILE STENCH. WHY ARE YOU BACKING INTO THE CORNER?
UM...

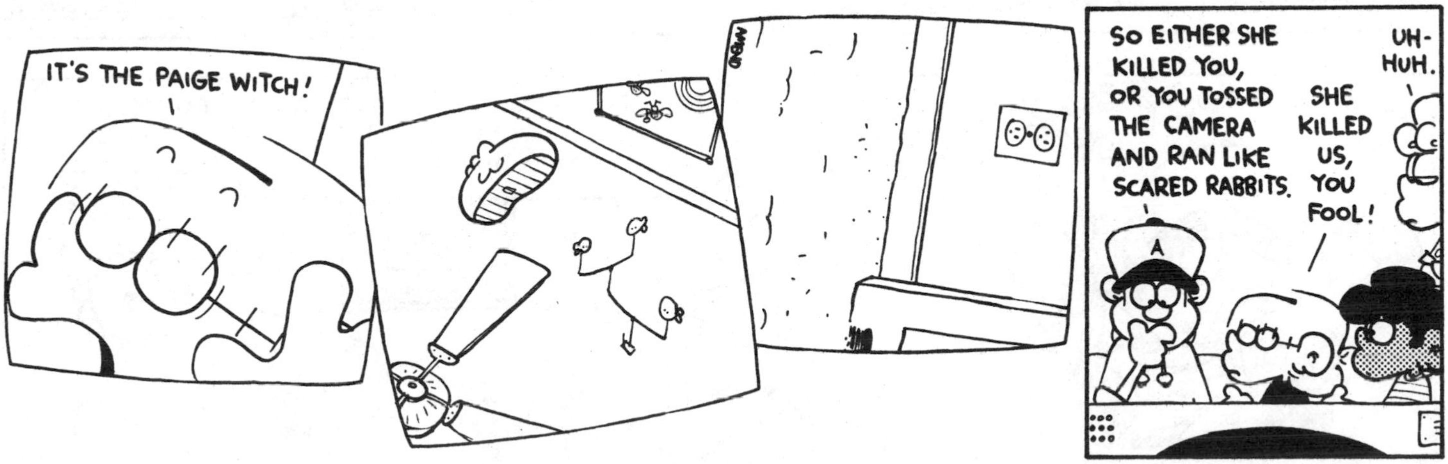
IT'S THE PAIGE WITCH!
SO EITHER SHE KILLED YOU, OR YOU TOSSED THE CAMERA AND RAN LIKE SCARED RABBITS.
UH-HUH.
SHE KILLED US, YOU FOOL!

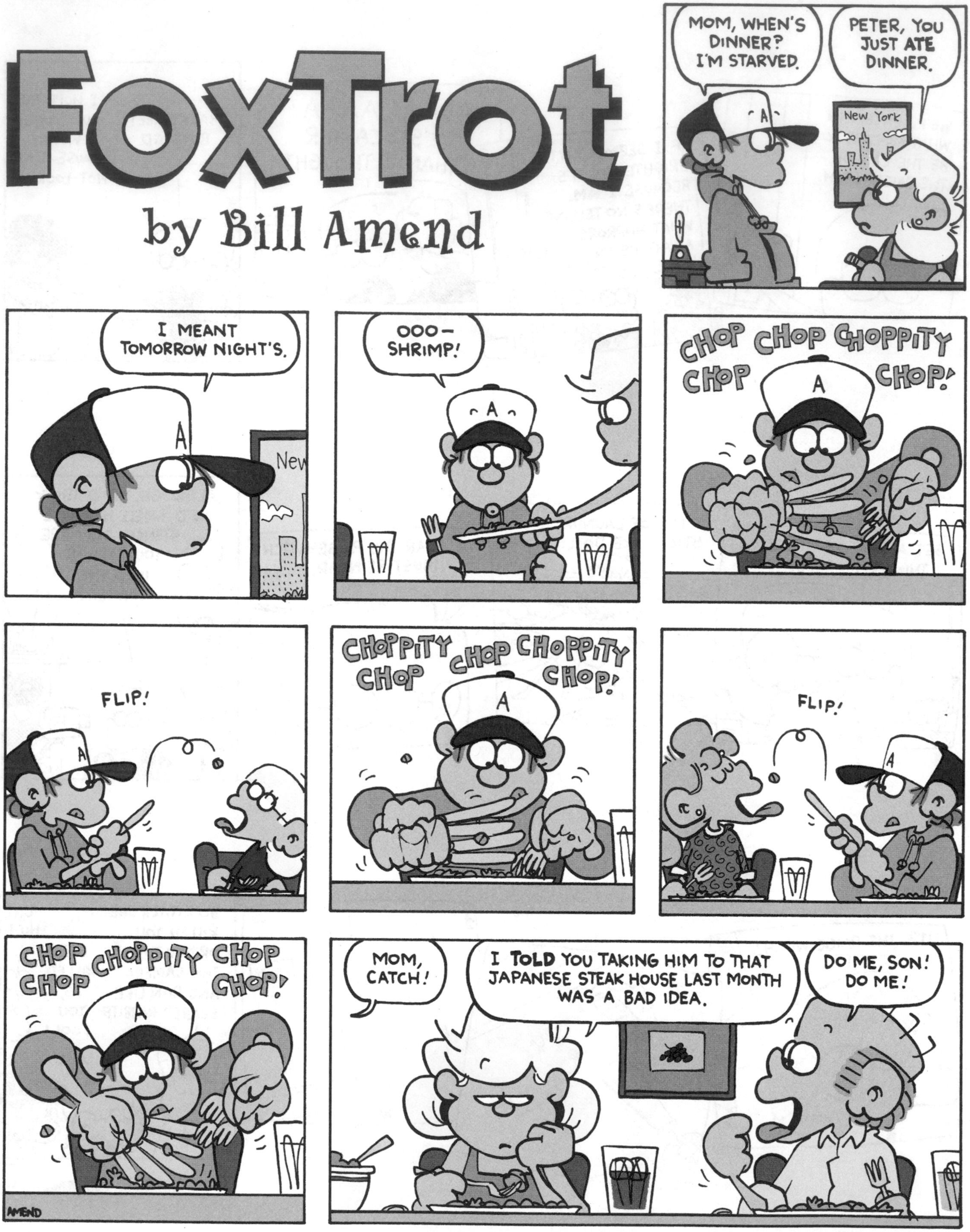
FoxTrot
by Bill Amend
MOM, WHEN'S DINNER? I'M STARVED.
PETER, YOU JUST ATE DINNER.
New York
I MEANT TOMORROW NIGHT'S.
New
OOO— SHRIMP!
CHOP CHOP CHOPPITY CHOP CHOP!
FLIP!
CHOPPITY CHOP CHOP CHOPPITY CHOP!
FLIP!
CHOP CHOP CHOPPITY CHOP CHOP!
AMEND
MOM, CATCH!
I TOLD YOU TAKING HIM TO THAT JAPANESE STEAK HOUSE LAST MONTH WAS A BAD IDEA.
DO ME, SON! DO ME!

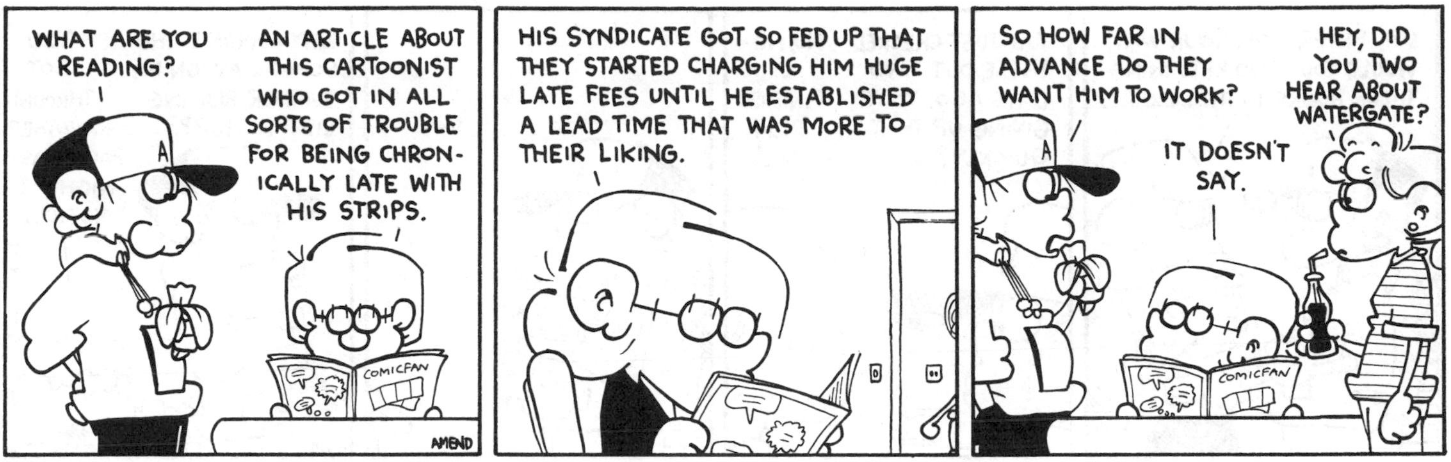
WHAT ARE YOU READING?
AN ARTICLE ABOUT THIS CARTOONIST WHO GOT IN ALL SORTS OF TROUBLE FOR BEING CHRONICALLY LATE WITH HIS STRIPS.
COMICFAN
AMEND
HIS SYNDICATE GOT SO FED UP THAT THEY STARTED CHARGING HIM HUGE LATE FEES UNTIL HE ESTABLISHED A LEAD TIME THAT WAS MORE TO THEIR LIKING.
SO HOW FAR IN ADVANCE DO THEY WANT HIM TO WORK?
IT DOESN'T SAY.
HEY, DID YOU TWO HEAR ABOUT WATERGATE?
COMICFAN

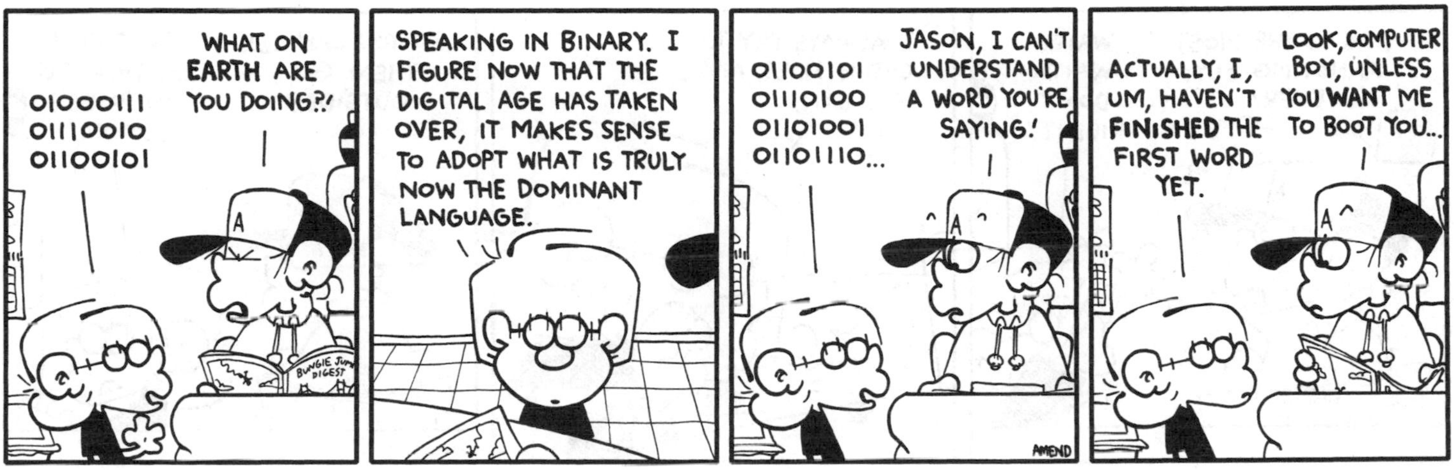
01000111 01110010 01100101
WHAT ON **EARTH** ARE YOU DOING?!
BUNGIE JUMP DIGEST
SPEAKING IN BINARY. I FIGURE NOW THAT THE DIGITAL AGE HAS TAKEN OVER, IT MAKES SENSE TO ADOPT WHAT IS TRULY NOW THE DOMINANT LANGUAGE.
01100101 01110100 01101001 01101110...
JASON, I CAN'T UNDERSTAND A WORD YOU'RE SAYING!
AMEND
ACTUALLY, I, UM, HAVEN'T **FINISHED** THE FIRST WORD YET.
LOOK, COMPUTER BOY, UNLESS YOU **WANT** ME TO BOOT YOU...

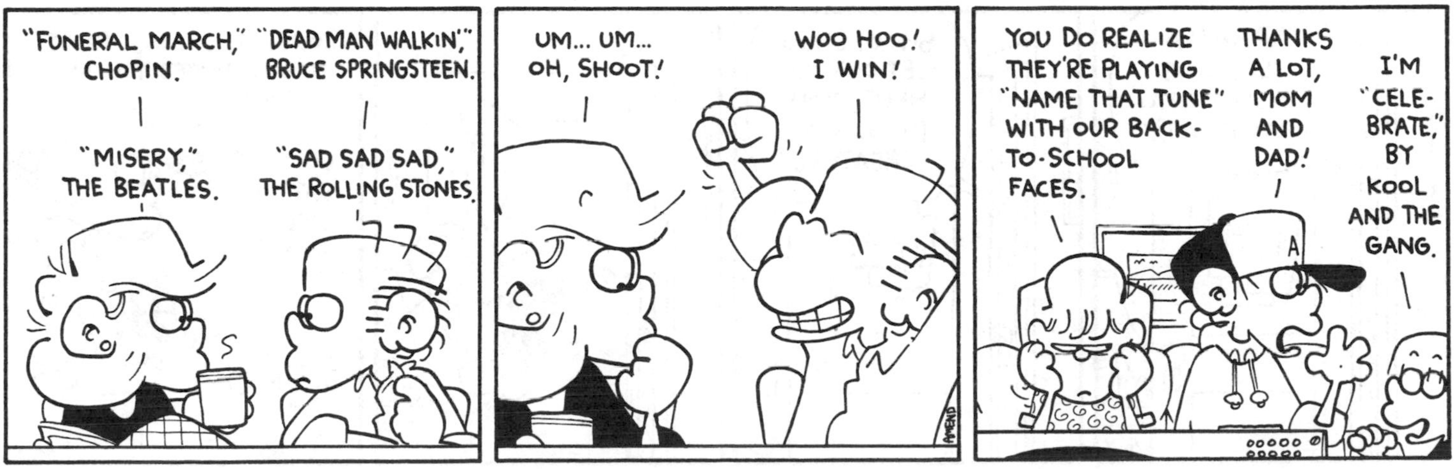
"FUNERAL MARCH," CHOPIN.
"DEAD MAN WALKIN'," BRUCE SPRINGSTEEN.
"MISERY," THE BEATLES.
"SAD SAD SAD," THE ROLLING STONES.
UM... UM... OH, SHOOT!
WOO HOO! I WIN!
AMEND
YOU DO REALIZE THEY'RE PLAYING "NAME THAT TUNE" WITH OUR BACK-TO-SCHOOL FACES.
THANKS A LOT, MOM AND DAD!
I'M "CELEBRATE," BY KOOL AND THE GANG.

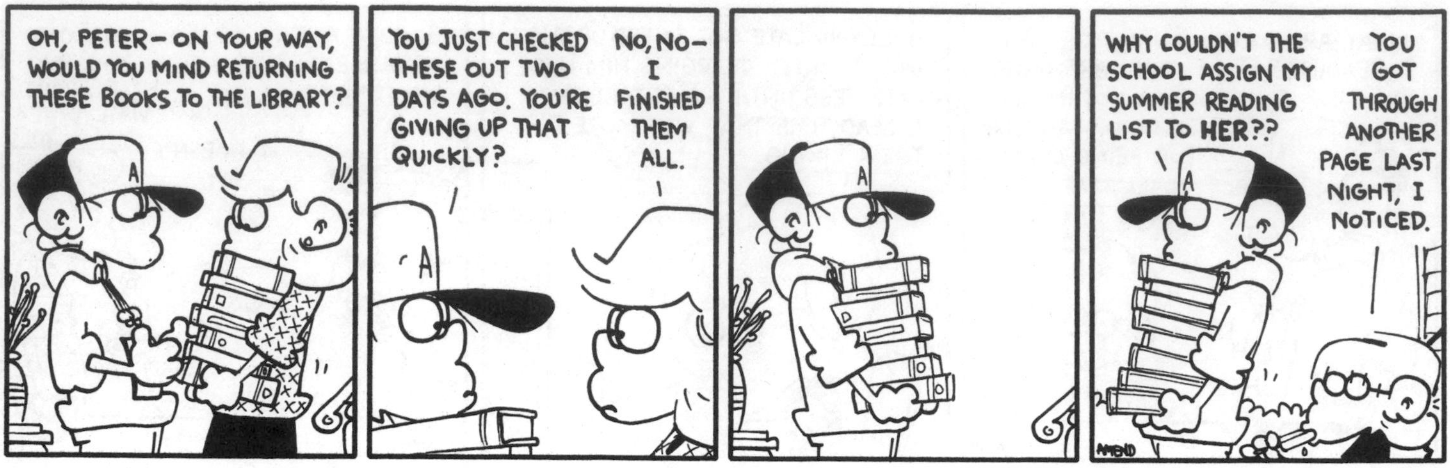
OH, PETER—ON YOUR WAY, WOULD YOU MIND RETURNING THESE BOOKS TO THE LIBRARY?
YOU JUST CHECKED THESE OUT TWO DAYS AGO. YOU'RE GIVING UP THAT QUICKLY?
NO, NO—I FINISHED THEM ALL.
WHY COULDN'T THE SCHOOL ASSIGN MY SUMMER READING LIST TO HER??
YOU GOT THROUGH ANOTHER PAGE LAST NIGHT, I NOTICED.
AMEND

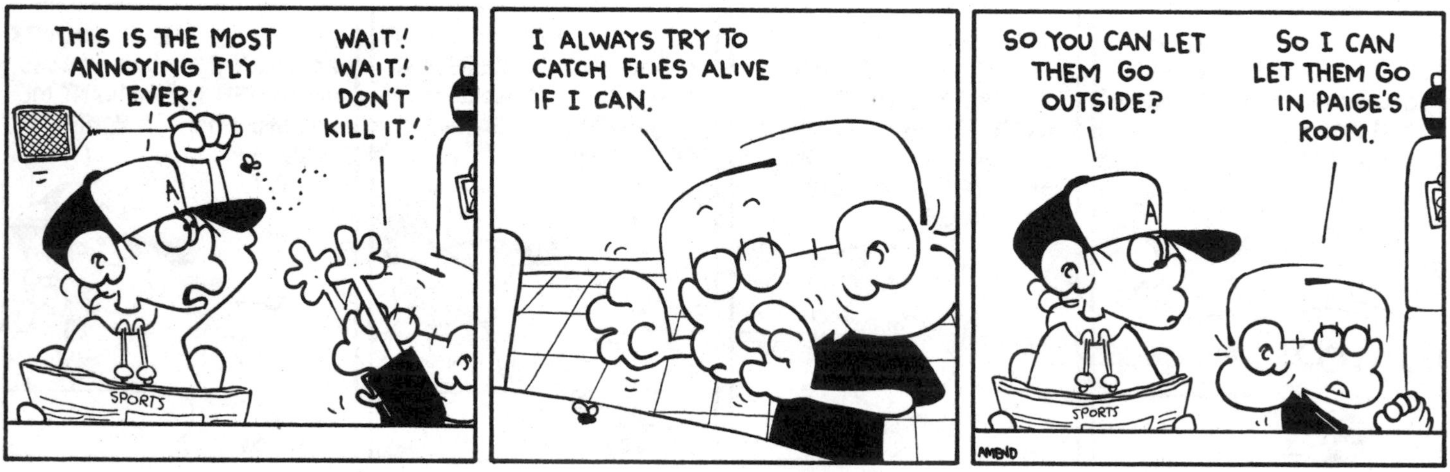
THIS IS THE MOST ANNOYING FLY EVER!
WAIT! WAIT! DON'T KILL IT!
SPORTS
I ALWAYS TRY TO CATCH FLIES ALIVE IF I CAN.
SO YOU CAN LET THEM GO OUTSIDE?
SO I CAN LET THEM GO IN PAIGE'S ROOM.
SPORTS
AMEND

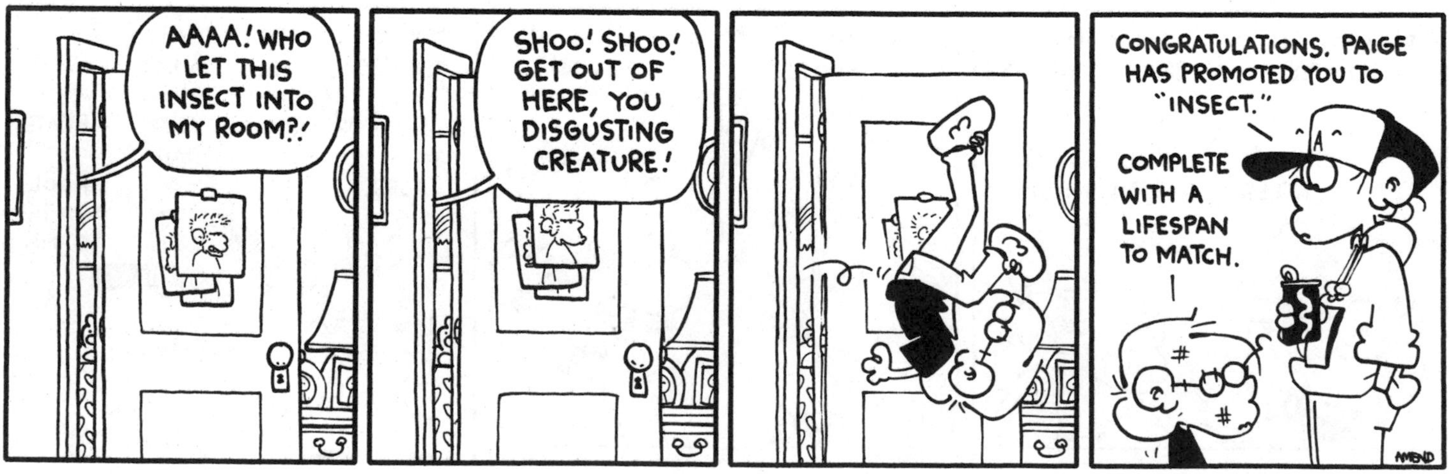
AAAA! WHO LET THIS INSECT INTO MY ROOM?!
SHOO! SHOO! GET OUT OF HERE, YOU DISGUSTING CREATURE!
CONGRATULATIONS. PAIGE HAS PROMOTED YOU TO "INSECT."
COMPLETE WITH A LIFESPAN TO MATCH.
AMEND

FoxTrot

by Bill Amend

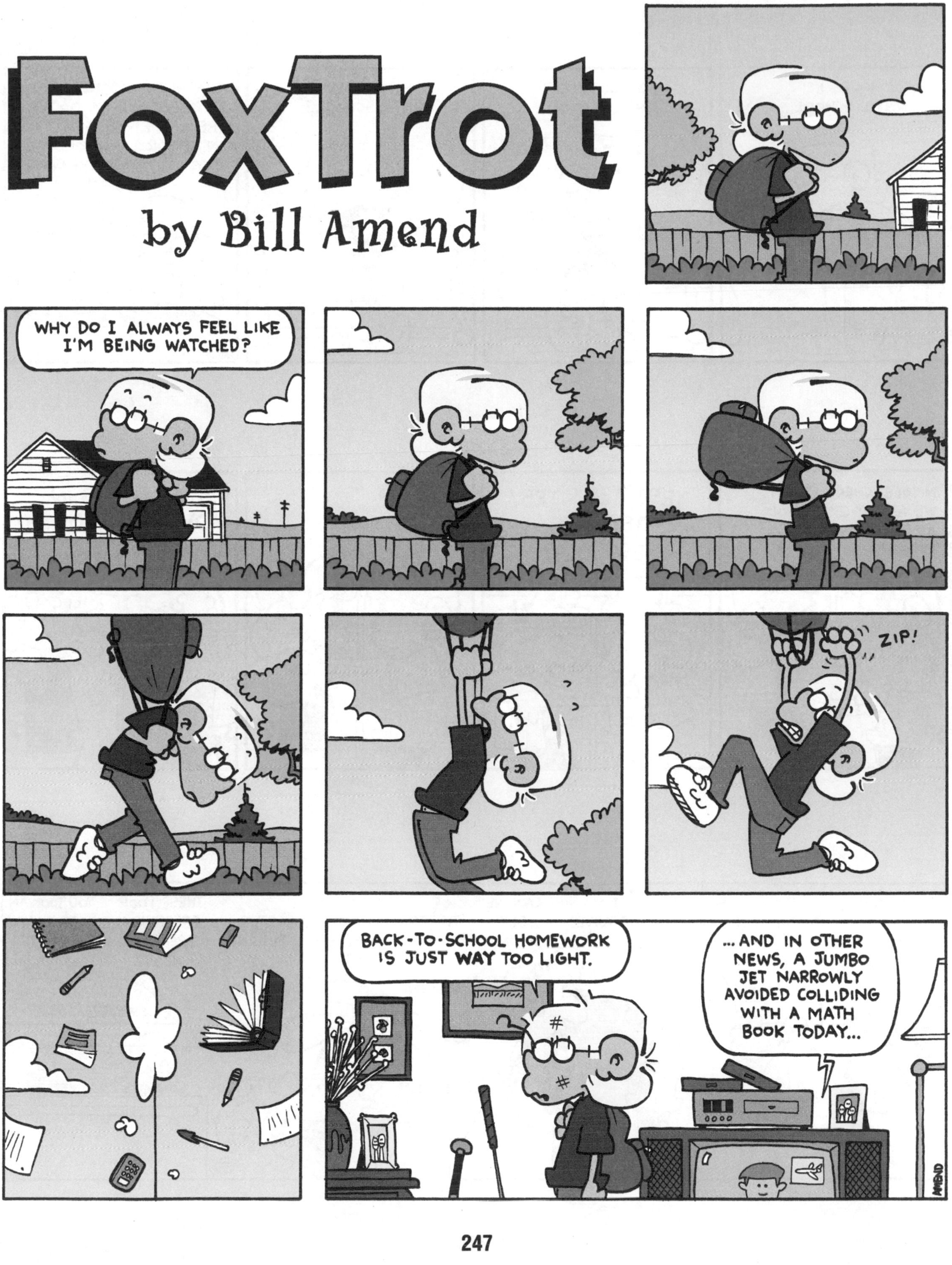
WHY DO I ALWAYS FEEL LIKE I'M BEING WATCHED?
ZIP!
BACK-TO-SCHOOL HOMEWORK IS JUST WAY TOO LIGHT.
...AND IN OTHER NEWS, A JUMBO JET NARROWLY AVOIDED COLLIDING WITH A MATH BOOK TODAY...
AMEND

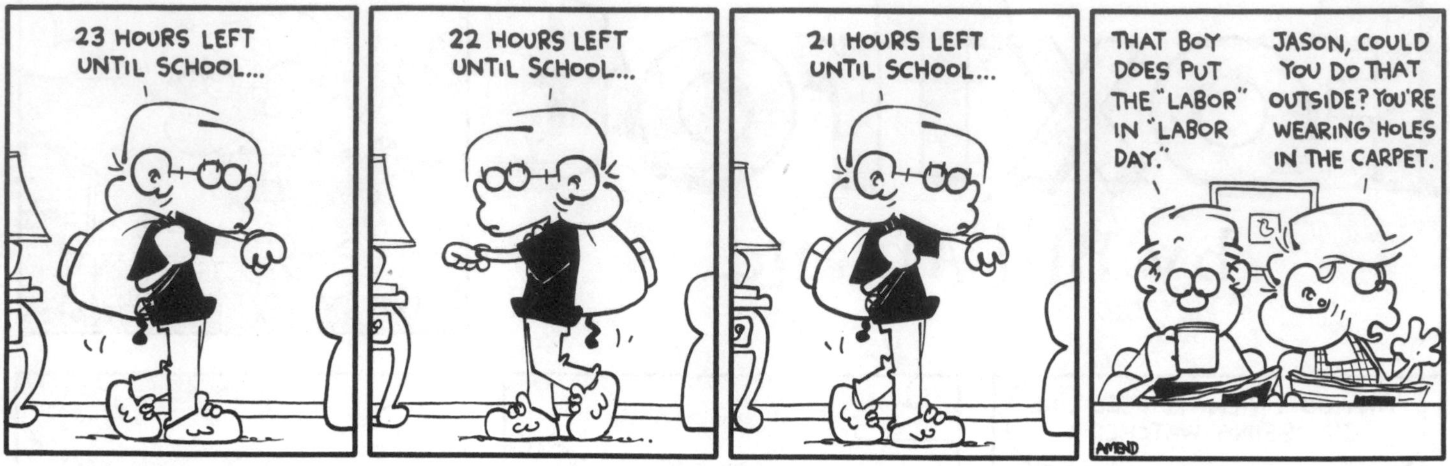
23 HOURS LEFT UNTIL SCHOOL...
22 HOURS LEFT UNTIL SCHOOL...
21 HOURS LEFT UNTIL SCHOOL...
THAT BOY DOES PUT THE "LABOR" IN "LABOR DAY."
JASON, COULD YOU DO THAT OUTSIDE? YOU'RE WEARING HOLES IN THE CARPET.
AMEND

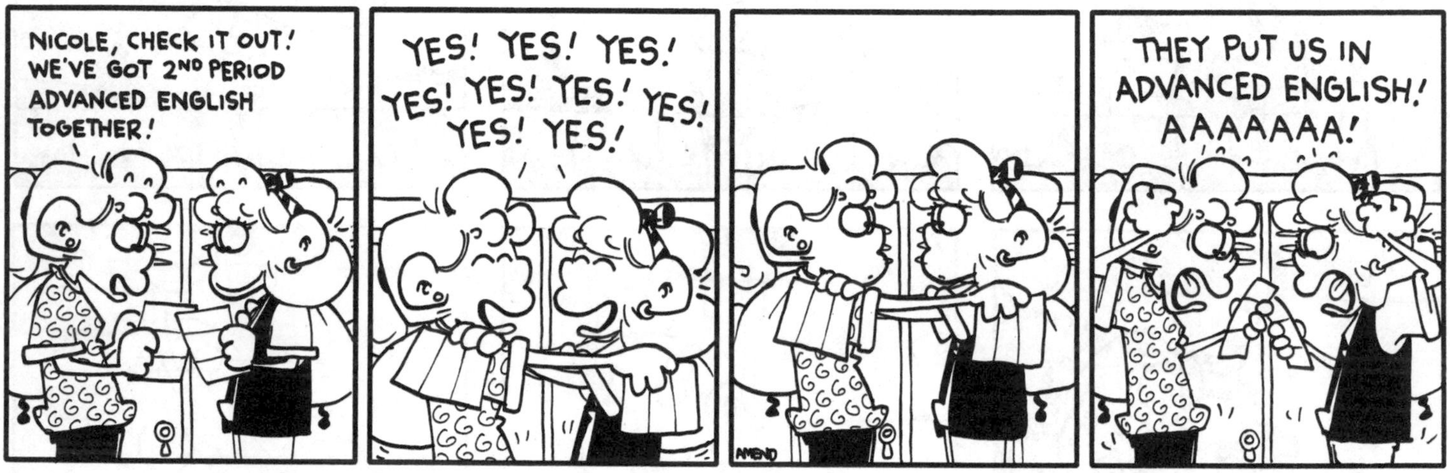
NICOLE, CHECK IT OUT! WE'VE GOT 2ND PERIOD ADVANCED ENGLISH TOGETHER!
YES! YES! YES! YES! YES! YES! YES! YES! YES!
AMEND
THEY PUT US IN ADVANCED ENGLISH! AAAAAAA!

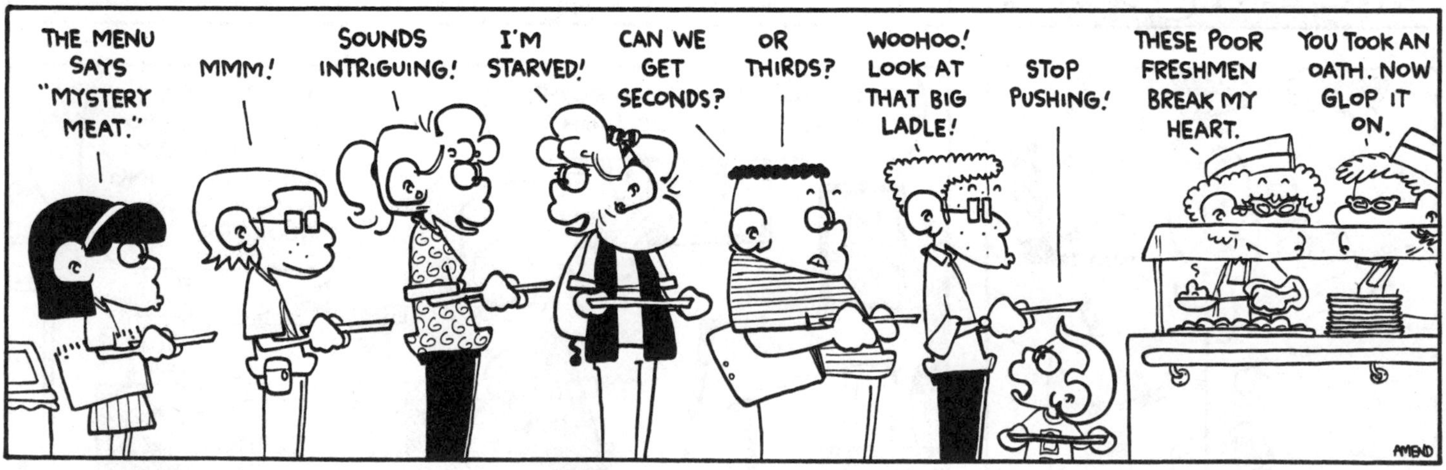
THE MENU SAYS "MYSTERY MEAT."
MMM!
SOUNDS INTRIGUING!
I'M STARVED!
CAN WE GET SECONDS?
OR THIRDS?
WOOHOO! LOOK AT THAT BIG LADLE!
STOP PUSHING!
THESE POOR FRESHMEN BREAK MY HEART.
YOU TOOK AN OATH. NOW GLOP IT ON.
AMEND

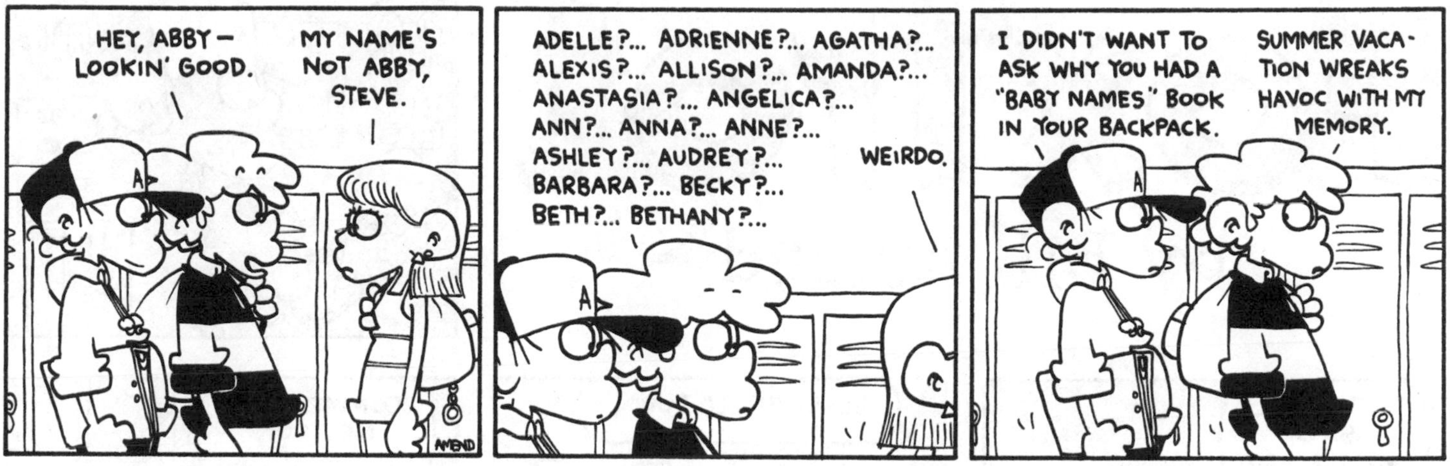
HEY, ABBY— LOOKIN' GOOD.
MY NAME'S NOT ABBY, STEVE.
ADELLE?... ADRIENNE?... AGATHA?... ALEXIS?... ALLISON?... AMANDA?... ANASTASIA?... ANGELICA?... ANN?... ANNA?... ANNE?... ASHLEY?... AUDREY?... BARBARA?... BECKY?... BETH?... BETHANY?...
WEIRDO.
I DIDN'T WANT TO ASK WHY YOU HAD A "BABY NAMES" BOOK IN YOUR BACKPACK.
SUMMER VACATION WREAKS HAVOC WITH MY MEMORY.
AMEND

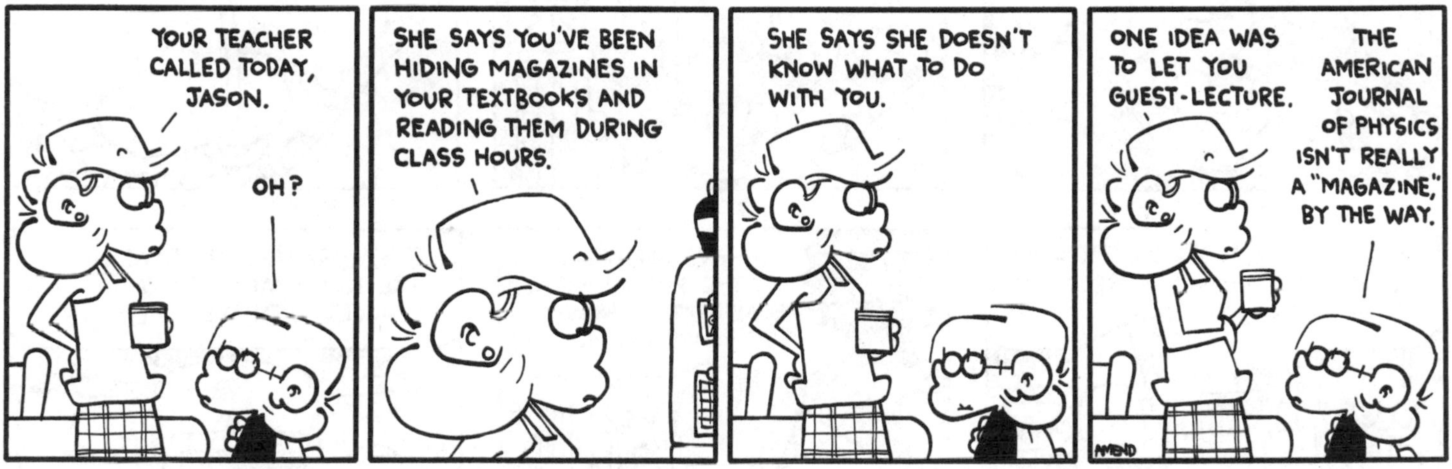
YOUR TEACHER CALLED TODAY, JASON.
OH?
SHE SAYS YOU'VE BEEN HIDING MAGAZINES IN YOUR TEXTBOOKS AND READING THEM DURING CLASS HOURS.
SHE SAYS SHE DOESN'T KNOW WHAT TO DO WITH YOU.
ONE IDEA WAS TO LET YOU GUEST-LECTURE.
THE AMERICAN JOURNAL OF PHYSICS ISN'T REALLY A "MAGAZINE," BY THE WAY.
AMEND

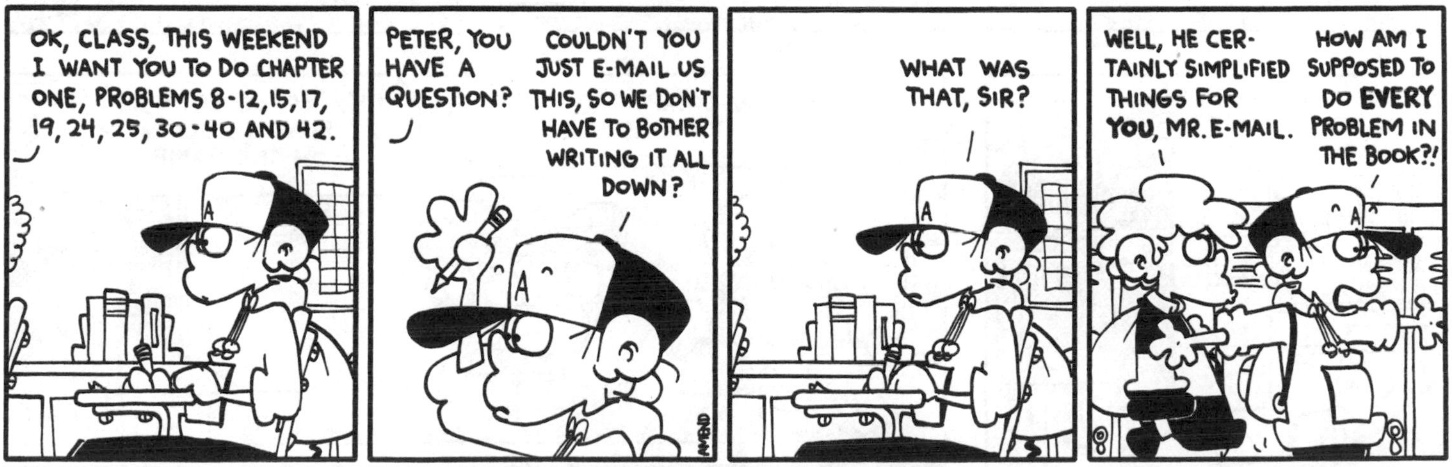
OK, CLASS, THIS WEEKEND I WANT YOU TO DO CHAPTER ONE, PROBLEMS 8-12, 15, 17, 19, 24, 25, 30-40 AND 42.
PETER, YOU HAVE A QUESTION?
COULDN'T YOU JUST E-MAIL US THIS, SO WE DON'T HAVE TO BOTHER WRITING IT ALL DOWN?
AMEND
WHAT WAS THAT, SIR?
WELL, HE CERTAINLY SIMPLIFIED THINGS FOR YOU, MR. E-MAIL.
HOW AM I SUPPOSED TO DO EVERY PROBLEM IN THE BOOK?!

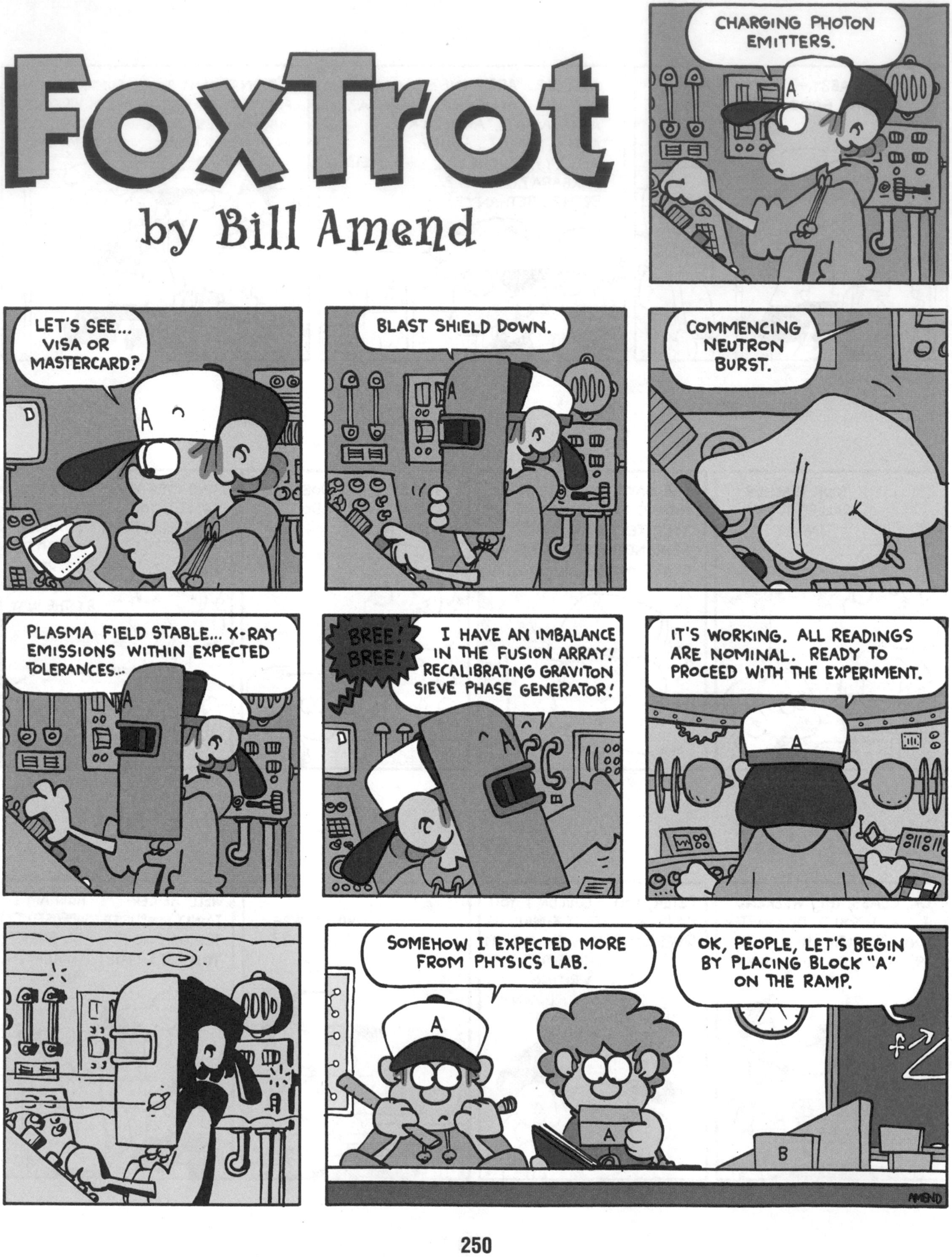
FoxTrot
by Bill Amend
CHARGING PHOTON EMITTERS.
LET'S SEE... VISA OR MASTERCARD?
BLAST SHIELD DOWN.
COMMENCING NEUTRON BURST.
PLASMA FIELD STABLE... X-RAY EMISSIONS WITHIN EXPECTED TOLERANCES...
BREE! BREE!
I HAVE AN IMBALANCE IN THE FUSION ARRAY! RECALIBRATING GRAVITON SIEVE PHASE GENERATOR!
IT'S WORKING. ALL READINGS ARE NOMINAL. READY TO PROCEED WITH THE EXPERIMENT.
SOMEHOW I EXPECTED MORE FROM PHYSICS LAB.
OK, PEOPLE, LET'S BEGIN BY PLACING BLOCK "A" ON THE RAMP.
AMEND